GANGLAND GOTHAM

GANGLAND GOTHAM

NEW YORK'S NOTORIOUS MOB BOSSES

ALLAN R. MAY

GREENWOOD PRESS
An Imprint of ABC-CLIO, LLC

A B C ❖ C L I O

Santa Barbara, California • Denver, Colorado • Oxford, England

Library of Congress Cataloging-in-Publication Data

May, Allan R.
   Gangland Gotham : New York's notorious mob bosses / Allan R. May.
     p. cm.
   Includes bibliographical references and index.
   ISBN 978-0-313-33927-1 (hardcover : alk. paper) — ISBN 978-0-313-08599-4 (ebook)
   1. Organized crime—New York (State)—History—Case studies. 2. Gangsters—New York (State)—Biography.   3. Criminals—New York (State)—Biography.
I. Title.
HV6452.N7M32   2009
364.1092′27471—dc22   2009016191

13   12   11   10   09   1   2   3   4   5

This book is also available on the World Wide Web as an eBook.
Visit www.abc-clio.com for details.

ABC-CLIO, LLC
130 Cremona Drive, P.O. Box 1911
Santa Barbara, California 93116-1911

This book is printed on acid-free paper ∞

Manufactured in the United States of America

Every reasonable effort has been made to trace the owners of copyrighted materials in this book, but in some instances this has proven impossible. The author and publisher will be glad to receive information leading to more complete acknowledgments in subsequent printings of the book and in the meantime extend their apologies for any omissions.

To Connie May

Thank you for your love, support, patience, and perseverance in helping me through this project, only you know how all-consuming it was for me.

CONTENTS

Introduction   *ix*

Acknowledgments   *xiii*

Timeline   *xv*

1   Joe Adonis (Giuseppe Antonio Doto)   1

2   Albert Anastasia (Umberto Anastasio)   37

3   Louis Buchalter   73

4   Frank Costello (Francesco Castiglia)   117

5   Carlo Gambino   155

6   Vito Genovese   183

7   Lucky Luciano (Salvatore Lucania)   213

8   Arnold Rothstein   253

9   Dutch Schultz (Arthur Flegenheimer)   281

10   Abner Zwillman   309

Biographies of Other Prominent Figures Mentioned in the Text   *331*

Appendix   *363*

Bibliography   *405*

Index   *407*

INTRODUCTION

My interest in the history of organized crime goes back to the early 1960s when I saw my first episode of *The Untouchables* television series. Eliot Ness was one of my heroes, and in 1997, I initiated what turned into a memorial service for the famed crime fighter at Lake View Cemetery in Cleveland 40 years after his death.

Over the decades, as my interest grew, I began building a library of books on the subject. Today I believe I have one of the largest libraries in the United States on the subject of organized crime, with nearly 800 titles.

As my interest and my library grew, I noticed many inconsistencies in the telling of stories involving both organized crime figures and the law enforcement figures (police officers, safety directors, prosecutors, mayors, politicians, and judges) who spent their careers putting them away.

In 1998, I was blessed when my organized crime-history writing career began with a short stint working for the dean of organized crime writers, Jerry Capeci, on his *Gang Land News* Web site. Shortly thereafter, I began my association and friendship with fellow Cleveland Heights High School graduate Rick Porrello at his new Web site, *AmericanMafia.com.*

In the stories I wrote for *AmericanMafia.com,* as well in later stories for *Crimemagazine. com* and Court TV's *CrimeLibrary.com,* I tried to focus on the discrepancies that existed in the subjects I wrote about in an effort to clear them up and help the reader understand. I quickly learned that it was not just a matter of trying to point out someone else's mistakes; anyone who has read my early stories knows I've made enough of my own.

The truth is that writing about the history of organized crime from the 1900s is much like writing about the Wild West characters who dominated crime in the 1800s. Readers are simply fascinated with the fantastic tales of these characters and their exploits. The more fantastic they can make the tale, the more popular the characters become. These tales spill over to television and the silver screen, and outlaws like Jesse James and Billy the Kid, as well as the story of the shootout at the OK Corral, become larger than life.

This history repeated itself with outlaws who became famous during the Midwest Crime Wave of 1933–1934. The bank robbers and killers from that era are still household names today—John Dillinger, Bonnie and Clyde, Pretty Boy Floyd, Machinegun Kelly, Baby Face Nelson, and Ma Barker, to name a few. All of these characters have been portrayed—mostly fictionally—in movies starring some of the biggest names in Hollywood.

Their counterparts in the history of organized crime have received the same stardom in Hollywood. Al Capone, Lucky Luciano, Benjamin "Bugsy" Siegel, Meyer Lansky, Legs Diamond, Dutch Schultz, Joseph Bonanno, Abe Reles, Louis Buchalter, Arnold Rothstein, and John Gotti have all been portrayed by marquee names from the entertainment industry. Movies like *The Godfather, Scarface,* and *Goodfellas* were blockbuster hits (*The Godfather* so much so that it spawned two sequels). In addition, one of the most successful television serials of our time was *The Sopranos,* the story of a fictional New Jersey Mafia family.

One has to wonder: With all this fictionalized storytelling, where does the truth begin? One of the explanations I gave the students in the classes I taught was this: "Organized crime history is defined as a chronological chain of events its participants would rather see left unwritten." This fact alone provides for many of the discrepancies involved in the stories we know today.

Another major factor causing these discrepancies is that writers themselves embellish the individuals they are writing about. A perfect example is the story of what was called the Atlantic City Conference. The various biographers of Frank Costello, Lucky Luciano, Meyer Lansky, Johnny Torrio, and Abner Zwillman, all claim their subject was responsible for organizing the conference. How can that be?

One of the biggest discrepancies in organized crime history involves the murder of Dutch Schultz. Both Burton Turkus and Paul Sann in their respective books, *Murder, Inc.* and *Kill the Dutchman,* follow the revelations of Abe Reles during the Murder, Inc. investigations five years after the killings. The stories both men write are implausible when compared against any of the initial eyewitness accounts from the newspaper stories of the day. Neither of the writers took any of this into account when they repeated the mythical tales given to them by Murder, Inc. gunmen Reles and Albert Tannenbaum, both of whom claimed to have received the story second-hand. Still those are the stories that are believed today.

In writing about these numerous discrepancies, I try to define them for the reader by referring to them as the "popular" tale or theory. Even in cases where there are several theories or stories, I try to present each one. In my writing, where there are obvious differences in the reporting over the years, I try my best to stay away from supporting the tale I may personally believe. Instead I try to present each case and let readers choose what they want to believe. In covering the 10 characters in this book, I tried to point out the various discrepancies that have arisen over the years and present the most accurate picture I can for readers so that they can understand the origin of these differences.

The reader may wonder why Meyer Lansky and Benjamin "Bugsy" Siegel have been left out of this assortment of New York/New Jersey underworld leaders. Because of the sheer volume, I decided to eliminate these two because of all the characters, they left the New York/New Jersey area the earliest, having departed for Florida and the West Coast, respectively, in the early to mid-1930s.

Readers of this volume, whether students or anyone else interested in researching or reading about organized crime, will find that *Gangland Gotham* is unique in the following ways:

1. It contains the most comprehensive biographies on Joe Adonis and Albert Anastasia. These are the only two men of the 10 underworld bosses in the book who don't have

individual biographies written about them. It is also the most complete biography of Vito Genovese; the other ends 10 years before his death.

2. It is the first book that clearly dissects the murder of Dutch Schultz, showing that the Dutchman was killed in a cross-fire by his own men (as was believed and reported in some of the newspapers of the day) as opposed to killers sent from Murder, Inc. It also raises questions regarding the motive for his killing.

3. It takes a comprehensive look at the role of Louis "Lepke" Buchalter and follows his trials, which take him from a 14-year federal sentence to the electric chair in Sing Sing prison.

4. The story of Frank Costello sorts out all the legal battles he fought in the 1950s and puts them into a timeline that helps explain all the other underworld activities taking place around them.

5. It produces the most comprehensive review of the Castellammarese War (1930–1931) and debunks many of the myths that have surrounded this event and its key participants—Joe Masseria and Salvatore Maranzano.

6. The Luciano story focuses on the myths of his life, his brutal beating, and his attempt to return to the United States through Cuba following his deportation. It also looks at the fact versus fiction of his dealings with Thomas E. Dewey.

7. *The Last Testament of Lucky Luciano* is comprehensively discussed. Did the infamous mob boss really write it, or was it a complete fraud?

8. The Gambino story takes an in-depth look into his nearly 20-year effort to fool the government by using his heart ailment to thwart deportation attempts.

9. Finally, in a detailed appendix, the book attempts to sort out the fact versus fiction of the Atlantic City Conference, the Havana Meeting, the Apalachin Summit, and other events and personalities.

This work should not be viewed as an authoritative book on the history of organized crime, but rather as a documentation of the vast disparity that has been reported over the years and twisted with the help of many individuals. I hope readers will come to understand that we really don't have a complete understanding of these characters and events. Many people—participants, law enforcement, the media, authors, as well as family members—have their own interpretations and opinions, and there is much inconsistency in what has been reported, talked about, and written.

ACKNOWLEDGMENTS

I wouldn't even think of starting these acknowledgments without first thanking the staff of Pamela Benjamin, head of General Reference, at the Cleveland Public Library. Those people include Tonya Jenkins, Eddie Johnson, Michelle Makkos, Melanie McCarter, Sabrina Miranda, Debbie Nunez, Denise Sanders, and Michelle Skrovan.

A very special thank you to "Fast Eddie" Johnson and Michelle "Red" Makkos, who helped me time and again get newspaper microfilm through interlibrary loans from all over the United States. Without people like this, a project of this nature just cannot be completed. They were always helpful, friendly, and courteous through every wave of new information requested.

I am also grateful to Sabrina, Denise, and Debbie for putting up with me in my quest for the best microfilm machines and the countless times I needed them for paper jams, toner, and just to listen to me gripe.

Another special thank you to Ryan Jaenke, who has now moved on to another position in the library. Ryan was in charge of the newspaper research area for several years and helped me during the early months of this book, as well as on several other projects.

A special thank you to Lynn Duchez Bycko in the Special Collections Department at Cleveland State University. Lynn has served as an advisor, counselor, and therapist for me on this project from the beginning and along the way has become a good friend. She's solely responsible for one of my greatest pleasures in my writing career, my five-by-seven-foot office in the Rhodes Tower on the Cleveland State University campus. While some may see it as a tiny closet, it's my own personal heaven.

Charlotte Michael Versagi has been another counselor and advisor. No one has provided me with greater encouragement in pursuing my writing career. An accomplished writer herself, Charlotte has always been there for me, offering support and advice, and she has been my best friend for years.

A special thank you to Jan Vaughn at the Warren-Trumbull County Public Library, who has supported my career and my book by allowing me to speak there months before it was published.

Next I want to thank the people I turned to for help in both writing the book and for specific details to complete chapters. Those include Charles R. Molino, the most knowledgeable guy I know on the history of organized crime in America, and Riktor "Mad Dog" Mattix. There simply isn't a more knowledgeable person when it comes to the Midwest crime wave and different facets of organized crime history in Chicago; he is the best. Other contributors have been Patrick Downey, a friend and fellow author; Jerry Kovar, my movie expert; and Frank Versagi, whom I call on for technical advice and counsel. I also want to thank Richard Hammer for permission to use some of his personal correspondence.

Then there are my friends and family. I want to thank them for their patience and encouragement while this project has been going on. Although I can't possibly name everyone, I apologize now for leaving anyone out, here goes: Jay Ambler, Tammy Cabot, Carol Carrol, Abby Goldberg, Tom Leahy, Fred Merrick, Jimmy Monastra, John Murray, David Pastor, Rick Porrello, Ron Soeder, Mike Tona, James Trueman, and Fred Wolking.

Another thank you to my editor, John Wagner at Greenwood Press, for having the patience and the belief that I could accomplish this.

And last, but not least, I thank my wife Connie, who has endured so much over these past few years: numerous trips each week to and from Cleveland Public Library and Cleveland State University—many times leaving the house at 6:45 AM and picking me up at 10:00 PM; two years without a vacation, and spending week nights and weekends apart; helping me through the down times when I had doubts that this would ever get done. She stuck with me through thick and thin, always offering encouragement and never allowing me to stay down on myself. For this I am eternally grateful.

TIMELINE

1882	January 17: Arnold Rothstein is born on East 47th Street in Manhattan.
1891	January 26: Frank Costello (Francesco Castiglia) is born in Lauropoli, Calabria, Italy.
1896	August: Costello and his mother arrive in New York City.
1897	February 6: Louis Buchalter is born on Manhattan's Lower East Side.
	November 21: Vito Genovese is born in Resigliano, Italy, outside of Naples.
	November 24: Lucky Luciano (Salvatore Lucania) is born in Lercara Friddi, Sicily.
1900	August 24: Carlo Gambino is born in Palermo, Sicily.
1902	August 6: Dutch Schultz (Arthur Simon Flegenheimer) is born on Manhattan's Lower East Side.
	September 26: Albert Anastasia (Umberto Anastasio) is born in Tropea, Calabria, Italy.
	November 22: Joe Adonis (Giuseppe Doto) is born in Montemarano, Italy.
1904	July 27: Abner "Longy" Zwillman is born in Newark, New Jersey.
1907	Spring: Luciano arrives in New York City with his family.
1909	Adonis arrives with his family in New York City.
	August: Rothstein marries Carolyn Green, a showgirl, in a private ceremony before a justice of the peace in Saratoga Springs.
	November 18: Rothstein plays a legendary marathon billiards game with Jack Conway at McGraw's poolroom.
1912	July 15: Hours after visiting Rothstein, Herman "Beansy" Rosenthal is murdered by four men outside the Metropole Hotel.
	July 29: New York Police Captain Charles Becker is indicted for Rosenthal's murder.

October 5: Big Jack Zelig, a labor racketeer, is murdered on a New York street-car by Red Phil Davidson shortly before he is scheduled to testify at the trial of Rosenthal's killers, whom he hired at the request of Becker. The four killers are convicted and executed in Sing Sing two years later. Becker is later found guilty and executed on July 30, 1915.

1913   May 23: Genovese arrives in the U.S. aboard the *Taormina* at the age of 15.

1914   September 23: Costello marries Loretta "Bobbie" Geigerman.

1916   April: Luciano is arrested for selling opium to an undercover agent.

1917   September 12: Anastasia jumps ship in New York City Harbor and enters the United States illegally.

September 23: October: Rothstein wins $300,000 at the Laurel, Maryland horse racing track betting on Hourless in a special race.

1920   May 16: Anastasia and Giuseppe Florino murder George Terillo at Union and Columbia Streets in Brooklyn.

1921   Tommy Pennochio organizes the "curb exchange" in Lower Manhattan to help bootleggers trade their merchandise with other gangs.

March 17: Anastasia is arrested for the murder of Terillo.

May 25: Anastasia and Florino are sentenced to die in the electric chair at Sing Sing for the murder of Terillo.

July 4: Rothstein wins $850,000 at Aqueduct race track betting on his horse Sidereal.

December 23: Gambino arrives in the United States as a stowaway aboard the S.S. *Vincenzo Floria* at Norfolk, Virginia.

1922   April 16: Murder charges against Anastasia and Florino for the murder of Terillo are dismissed.

August 11: Luciano attends a meeting with "Joe the Boss" Masseria, after which Umberto Valenti is murdered.

1923   August 28: Labor racketeer Nathan "Kid Dropper" Kaplan is murdered by Louis Kushner outside a Manhattan courthouse. Involved in the plot are Jacob "Little Augie" Orgen, Jacob "Gurrah" Shapiro, and Buchalter.

1925   Luciano has Genovese organize the pushcart vendors to help sell numbers in the Italian lottery.

September 10: Costello is sworn in as a U.S. citizen.

December 4: A huge rum-running ring operated by "Big Bill" Dwyer is busted and 43 men are indicted, including Costello and his brother Eddie.

1926   July 26: In first rum-running trial, Dwyer is found guilty and sentenced to two years in the Atlanta penitentiary; the Costello brothers are severed from the case.

1927   January 3: The Costello brothers go on trial in the rum-running indictment. Before the trial is completed, charges against Eddie are dismissed. The jury can't reach a decision on Frank's guilt and he is released; the case is never retried.

October 15: Following a labor dispute, Buchalter and Shapiro ambush and kill "Little Augie" Orgen and wound Legs Diamond on the Lower East Side.

October 23: Buchalter and Shapiro surrender to police for the Orgen murder.

October 25: Buchalter (as Louis Buckhouse) and Shapiro are charged with the homicide of Orgen.

November 4: Charges against Buchalter and Shapiro are dismissed for lack of evidence.

1928 September 8: Rothstein is involved in a marathon card game and loses more than $300,000, after which he feels the game has been rigged. He holds off paying his markers.

October 15: Schultz's bootlegging partner, Joey Noe, is wounded in an ambush outside the Chateau Madrid nightclub.

November 4: George McManus calls Rothstein to come to the Park Central Hotel, where Rothstein is wounded by an unknown gunman.

November 6: Rothstein dies from his wounds.

November 21: Noe dies from his wounds.

1929 The "Big Seven" is established, consisting of the major rumrunners and bootleggers on the Eastern Seaboard.

May 14–16: The Atlantic City Conference is held in New Jersey. Mob leaders of all different ethnic backgrounds and religions attend.

October 17: Luciano is abducted, beaten, and abandoned on Staten Island. Over the years, he will tell several versions of what happened that night and who was responsible.

1930 February 26: The Castellammarese War, pitting "Joe the Boss" Masseria against Salvatore Maranzano, allegedly begins with the murder of Gaetano "Tommy" Reina.

November 5: Steven Ferrigno and Al Mineo are murdered outside a Pelham Parkway apartment.

November 26: Richie "The Boot" Boiardo is ambushed in Newark during a short bootlegging war with Zwillman.

1931 April: The Coll/Schultz War begins.

April 15: The Castellammarese War officially comes to an end with the murder of Masseria in the Nuova Villa Tammaro, a Coney Island restaurant owned by Gerardo Scarpato.

May 31: Peter Coll is murdered by Schultz gunmen.

June 4: Anastasia is granted permanent residence under the Registry Act of 1929.

June 18: Danny Iamascia is killed by police and Schultz is arrested.

July 15: Vincent Coll kidnaps Frenchy DeMange and Owney Madden pays $35,000 ransom.

July 28: Coll's attack on Joey Rao leaves five children wounded; one dies. The press dubs it the "Baby Murder."

August 20: Buchalter marries Betty Wasserman, a 27-year-old widow with one son.

September 10: After the murder of Salvatore Maranzano in his Park Avenue office, on the orders of Luciano, the fictitious "Night of Sicilian Vespers" allegedly occurs.

October 2: Joe Mullen, a Schultz employee, is murdered by ex-Schultz gang members now with Coll.

October 4: Coll is arrested for the "Baby Murder" attack.

December: Coll and Frank Giordano are acquitted in "Baby Murder" trial.

December 18: Legs Diamond is murdered in an Albany rooming house, allegedly by Schultz gunman Bo Weinberg.

1932   February 1: The Coll/Schultz War continues as Schultz gunmen, looking for Coll in a North Bronx home, murder Patsy Del Greco, Fiorio Basile, and Emily Torrizello.

February 9: Vincent Coll is murdered in a drugstore phone booth, allegedly lured there by a call from Owney Madden.

March 16: Genovese orders the murder of Gerard Vernotico so that he can marry his widow. Another man, Antonio Lonzo, a friend of Vernotico, is also murdered by killers Peter Mione and Michael Barrese.

March 28: Genovese marries Anna Vernotico; Tony Bender and his wife serve as witnesses.

April 19: Luciano is arrested and "held for investigation" in Chicago with Meyer Lansky and Capone Mob member Paul Ricca.

June 27: At the Democratic National Convention in Chicago, Luciano rooms with Albert Marinelli, Tammany district leader; Costello rooms with Jimmy Hines.

1933   January 25: Schultz is indicted by the federal government for income tax violations. He becomes a fugitive from justice.

February 19: Buchalter begins a two-week vacation with Zwillman at Hot Springs. The two meet Verne Miller and allegedly convince him to help them in the "Jew War" battle against Irving "Waxey Gordon" Wexler.

March 22: Buchalter and Shapiro's labor racketeering results in Morris Langer, president of the Needle Trades Workers' Industrial Union, being injured by a car bomb in New Jersey.

March 26: Langer dies from his injuries.

April 24: Buchalter and Shapiro thugs, led by Harry "Big Greenie" Greenberg, attack the Needle Trades Workers' Industrial Union headquarters in Manhattan. Two men are killed and several injured.

Spring: Genovese and his wife Anna leave for Italy for a belated honeymoon.

August: Genovese and his wife return to the United States.

November 6: Buchalter and Shapiro, along with 80 others, are named in two massive federal racketeering indictments in the fur trade.

December 31: Fiorella LaGuardia is sworn in to the first of his four terms as mayor of New York City.

1934   May 7: After confiscating Costello's slot machines, LaGuardia receives authority to destroy them and does so, making a public spectacle.

September 13: Associates of Buchalter and Shapiro arrange the shooting of Flour Truckman's Local 138 President William Snyder in a Brooklyn restaurant.

September 15: Samuel Tratner is held on $10,000 bail in the shooting of William Snyder. He soon exposes the brother of a Buchalter associate as the shooter.

September 16: Snyder dies from his wounds.

September 19: Ferdinand Boccia is murdered at Gran Cafe, 533 Metropolitan Ave in Brooklyn, by gunmen sent by Genovese.

September 20: William Gallo is shot five times by Ernest "The Hawk" Rupolo in a related shooting also ordered by Genovese. Gallo survives. Rupolo is arrested for the Gallo shooting, pleads guilty, and is sent to prison until 1943.

November 3: Morris Goldis is arrested and charged with Snyder's murder.

November 28: After nearly two years in hiding, Schultz surrenders in Albany on the tax indictment charges.

1935   April: Costello makes a deal with infamous Louisiana politician Huey Long to install his slot machines in New Orleans.

April 16: Schultz's federal tax trial begins in Syracuse.

April 29: Schultz's trial ends in a hung jury.

July 29: Thomas E. Dewey is named special prosecutor by New York Governor Herbert Lehman.

August 2: In his second tax trial in Malone, New York, Schultz is acquitted.

September 9: Bo Weinberg disappears and is believed to have been killed by Schultz.

October 23: Schultz, Abe Landau, Bernard "Lulu" Rosenkrantz, and Otto "Abbadabba" Berman are ambushed in the Palace Chop House in Newark.

October 24: Schultz dies from his wound, as do his three men.

October 28: Schultz is buried at Gate of Heaven Cemetery.

1936   February 1: Dewey begins crackdown on New York City prostitution.

February 2: Seven men and 80 women are arrested, arraigned, and held on $10,000 bonds as material witnesses.

February 6: Ten ringleaders are indicted—five women and two men are added to material witness list.

February 10: The extraordinary grand jury hears from six vice witnesses.

April 1: Luciano is arrested in Hot Springs, Arkansas, on a New York City bench warrant and is released on bond.

April 2: Luciano is charged in four indictments with 24 counts of compulsory prostitution along with 11 others.

April 3: Luciano's lawyers fight efforts to have him transferred from Hot Springs to Little Rock.

April 4: Luciano is transferred to Little Rock, Pulaski County jail.

April 18: Luciano is brought back to New York City. He arrives at Grand Central Station and is taken to be arraigned. He pleads not guilty.

April 23: A grand jury issues a new indictment with 99 counts against Luciano and 12 co-defendants.

May 11: Jury selection begins in Luciano trial.

May 13: Dewey gives opening statement at Luciano trial.

May 29: Government rests case against Luciano.

June 3: Luciano takes witness stand.

June 6: Dewey gives closing argument for State in Luciano trial.

June 7: Jury finds Luciano and all defendants guilty on all 62 counts.

June 18: Luciano is sentenced to 30 to 50 years and is sent to Sing Sing.

June 30: Luciano is transferred to Dannemora Prison in Clinton County in upstate New York.

September 13: Joe Rosen is murdered in his candy store in Brownsville, Brooklyn, on orders from Buchalter; Louis Capone and Mendy Weiss are involved.

October 26: First federal trial from the November 1933 indictment of Buchalter and Shapiro finally begins. They are charged with violation of Sherman Antitrust Act in the rabbit-skin dressing industry. John Harlan Amen prosecutes the case.

November 8: Buchalter and Shapiro are found guilty.

November 12: Buchalter and Shapiro are sentenced to two years in federal prison and fined $10,000.

November 25: Genovese becomes a naturalized U.S. citizen.

December 3: Federal Appeals Judge Martin Manton allows Buchalter and Shapiro to post bond pending appeal.

1937   March 8: Buchalter's conviction is overturned by Judge Manton, but Shapiro's is affirmed by the circuit court of appeals.

July 6: Buchalter and Shapiro fail to appear for second federal trial on charges violating the Sherman Antitrust Act in the rabbit-skin dressing industry.

July 7: Bench warrants are issued and bail forfeited for Buchalter and Shapiro.

July 9: Newspapers report that Buchalter and Shapiro have been missing for two weeks.

August 9: Buchalter, Shapiro, and 14 others are indicted on state charges for conspiracy to extort clothing manufactures following Dewey investigation.

August 12: LaGuardia recommends large rewards be offered for the arrest of Buchalter and Shapiro.

August 20: Board of Estimate offers $5,000 each for Buchalter and Shapiro.

September 16: Adonis is arrested in Manhattan for truck holdup at Bond Street and Atlantic Avenue in Brooklyn.

September 17: Adonis is taken to Canarsie precinct and questioned about two murders; Adonis is released by Brooklyn judge after complainant in holdup fails to identify him.

September 27: Buchalter associate Max Rubin is questioned by Dewey's extraordinary grand jury.

October 1: Max Rubin is critically wounded by a gunman on East Gunhill Road in the Bronx.

November 30: Buchalter is indicted with 30 other people, including three U.S. Customs agents, for narcotics violations.

Late 1937: Following the Luciano conviction, and with the Buchalter case in limbo, Genovese fears he will be the next underworld figure on Dewey's list. He seeks permission to flee to Italy and asks Steven Franse to watch over Anna.

1938   April 14: Shapiro surrenders at the Federal House of Detention in New York.

June 12: Shapiro's second trial for violation of the Sherman Antitrust Act begins.

June 17: Shapiro is found guilty and sentenced to three years in prison, on top of his earlier sentence.

July 25: Hyman Yuram, indicted with Buchalter, is murdered and his body dumped at Lock Sheldrake in Sullivan County.

October 31: Adonis is named by Thomas Dewey as Brooklyn's Public Enemy No. 1.

1939   January 28: Louis Cohen (the recently released killer of "Kid Dropper" Kaplan) and Danny Fields are murdered on Lewis Street on the Lower East Side on orders from Buchalter.

March 23: Joseph Miller, another man indicted with Buchalter, is shot seven times on West Tremont Avenue, but survives.

April 25: Abraham "Whitey" Friedman, also indicted with Buchalter, is murdered in Brooklyn.

May 10: Abe Reles claims to overhear murder plot involving Morris Diamond with Charles Workman and Mendy Weiss at the home of Anastasia.

May 20: Gambino is convicted in federal court in Philadelphia of tax dodging and is sentenced to 22 months in prison.

May 25: Morris Diamond, Teamsters' Union official, is murdered on orders from Buchalter; Anastasia participates.

July 7: Zwillman marries Mary Degroot Mendels Steinbach.

July 14: Peter Panto, a dissident longshoreman fighting corruption, disappears. He is murdered by Mendy Weiss on orders of Anastasia.

July 25: Irving Penn, an innocent music company executive, is murdered in the Bronx after he is mistaken for Phil Orlovsky, whose death was ordered by Buchalter.

July 27: Bronx district attorney announces that Penn's murder was mistaken identity.

July 28: Dewey announces he will ask the Board of Estimate to offer a $25,000 reward for Buchalter, dead or alive.

July 29: Mayor LaGuardia pledges support for Dewey's reward request for Buchalter.

August 7: Board of Estimate authorizes reward for Lepke increased to $25,000.

August 8: NYPD announces it is printing 1 million wanted posters of Buchalter.

August 14: Zwillman is questioned by a federal grand jury as to Buchalter's whereabouts; five people, including Carl Shapiro, are indicted for harboring Buchalter and Shapiro.

August 21: Zwillman is guilty of contempt for refusing to answer questions of federal grand jury about Buchalter.

August 22: FBI is considering offering $25,000 for Buchalter, making the total reward (including the Board of Estimate reward) $50,000.

August 24: With gossip columnist and radio personality Walter Winchell as an intermediary, Buchalter surrenders to FBI Director J. Edgar Hoover at Fifth Avenue and 28th Street.

August 31: Mendy Weiss is arrested at his Brooklyn home.

September 15: Weiss is indicted by a federal grand jury for narcotics smuggling and is released on bond.

November 22: Harry "Big Greenie" Greenberg is murdered in Los Angeles on orders from Buchalter. Benjamin "Bugsy" Siegel is part of hit team.

November 30: Buchalter goes on trial in U.S. Federal Court on drug smuggling charges.

December 6: Notorious drug smuggler Jacob "Yasha" Katzenberg begins testimony at Buchalter trial.

December 13: Government rests its case in the Buchalter narcotics trial.

December 20: Buchalter is found guilty of conspiring to violate federal narcotics laws.

1940　　January: Gambino tax conviction is overturned because illegal wire taps were used.

January 2: Buchalter is sentenced to 14 years in federal prison for conspiring to violate federal narcotics laws.

January 3: A New York judge orders U.S. marshals to produce Buchalter in General Sessions Court (GSC).

January 4: Buchalter refuses to plead on flour-trucking conspiracy charge and hearings are adjourned.

January 5: Federal judge rules Buchalter has to answer to extortion charges in GSC; attorneys for Buchalter move to have judge's decision reviewed by Circuit Court of Appeals (CCA).

January 6: CCA judge stays Buchalter's transfer to Dewey for prosecution.

January 8: CCA hears arguments about Buchalter's transfer to Dewey and State of New York.

January 9: CCA rules that Buchalter has to answer charges in GSC on bakery and flour-trucking racketeering.

January 16: Dewey hands down a 40-page indictment for extortion in the garment industry, naming nine people.

January 24: Trial of Buchalter, Max Silverman, and his son for racketeering in the bakery and flour-trucking case begins in GSC.

February 1: After jury selection for Buchalter-Silverman trial is completed, judge orders panel sequestered.

February 3: Aaron Held, a former official in the United Flour Trucking Co., testifies for the state in Buchalter-Silverman trial.

February 12: Max Rubin testifies for the state in Buchalter-Silverman trial; Max Silverman collapses during morning session.

February 16: The state rests its case in Buchalter-Silverman trial.

February 26: During defense closing arguments in his trial, Silverman collapses from another heart attack.

March 2: At 1:24 AM, Buchalter and Max and Harold Silverman are found guilty.

March 22: Murder, Inc. case breaks wide open as Abe Reles decides to cooperate with Brooklyn District Attorney William O'Dwyer.

April 5: Buchalter is sentenced to 30 years to life and then is sent to Leavenworth to serve his 14-year federal sentence.

April 13: O'Dwyer links Buchalter to the murder of Joe Rosen in September 1936 with help of Reles.

April 27: Warrant charging Adonis and Sam Gasberg with kidnapping, extortion, and assault of Isidore Wapinsky is issued. Grand jury hands down sealed indictment of Adonis and Gasberg.

May 1: Adonis's White Auto Sales license to deal in used cars is suspended after city license is denied.

May 4: Gasberg is arrested in Los Angeles.

May 6: An eight-state alert is issued for Adonis's arrest.

May 9: Adonis surrenders to Prosecutor Amen in Brooklyn.

May 15: Costello and Phil Kastel are acquitted of income tax evasion in New Orleans.

May 20: Adonis is released on bail.

July 2: Adonis and Gasberg are arraigned on superseding kidnapping indictments in a Brooklyn court.

July 22: Attorneys ask judge to dismiss charges against Adonis and Gasberg.

August 20: Los Angeles County grand jury indicts Buchalter for the murder of Greenburg.

August 29: Judge denies motion for dismissal of charges against Adonis and Gasberg.

August 30: Greenburg murder details are revealed by Reles and Albert Tannenbaum during grand jury testimony.

September 20: O'Dwyer flies to Washington D.C. to request transfer of Buchalter out of federal custody and returned to Brooklyn.

October 24: During Gasberg trial, Isidore Juffe takes stand and accuses Adonis and Gasberg of abduction and beating.

October 25: Juffe testifies he feared being killed so he hid the kidnapping accusation for eight years.

October 30: Gasberg is acquitted of kidnapping; jury is deadlocked on assault charges.

December: O'Dwyer meets with Costello at his Majestic apartment to discuss his chances of running for mayor of New York City.

December 26: Gambino is arrested as an illegal alien.

1941   January 9: O'Dwyer's Murder, Inc investigators begin a search for Panto's body in Lyndhurst, New Jersey.

January 29: A body found encrusted in quicklime is believed to be Panto.

February 6: The body is identified as Panto.

February 7: Tannenbaum statement identifies Anastasia, Weiss, and Jimmy Feracco as the killers of Panto.

April: Mendy Weiss is arrested by federal agents in Kansas City.

April 29: A writ of habeas corpus is signed, directing federal authorities to turn Buchalter over to O'Dwyer for the murder of Rosen.

June 9: As a result of revelations in the Murder, Inc. investigation, Charles Workman pleads no contest to the murder of Dutch Schultz; he is sentenced to life in prison.

June 19: A federal judge upholds that Buchalter be tried for the Rosen murder.

August 4: The trial of Buchalter, Louis Capone, and Mendy Weiss for the murder of Rosen begins with jury selection in Brooklyn.

August 15: Rosen murder trial is postponed because of the number of potential jurors who do not want to serve.

September 15: Jury selection in the murder trial of Rosen resumes.

October 3: Annoyed by slow jury selection process in the Rosen trial, the judge orders night sessions.

October 15: After 19 court sessions, only 10 jurors have been selected in the Rosen murder trial; Capone collapses in the courtroom and is revived by ambulance attendant.

October 17: After five full weeks, a jury of 12 with 2 alternates is seated for the Rosen murder trial.

October 20: Opening arguments are heard in the Rosen murder case.

October 21: The escape of Rosen's slayers is described.

October 22: Rosen's son testifies about a meeting between his father and Buchalter.

October 24: Sholem Bernstein, who drove the getaway car, testifies at the Rosen murder trial.

October 31–November 15: Various witnesses testify for the prosecution in the Rosen murder trial.

November 12: Abe Reles, while under police guard, is found dead at the Half Moon Hotel in Coney Island.

November 17: The state rests its case in the Rosen trial.

November 18: Defense witnesses called in the Rosen trial include Carl Shapiro.

November 19: Jacob Shapiro is brought in from the Atlanta Penitentiary to testify for Buchalter; attorneys decide not to call him.

November 26: In closing arguments, Buchalter's attorney claims his client was framed.

November 29: The jury in the Rosen murder trial receives the case; they deliberate for four-and-a-half hours.

November 30: At 2:45 AM, the jury in the Rosen trial reaches a verdict; all three men are guilty. O'Dwyer announces that President Roosevelt will have to grant a pardon to Buchalter on his federal conviction if the death penalty is imposed.

December 2: All three defendants in the Rosen murder trial are sentenced to die the first week of January 1942.

1942   February 9: The French luxury liner *Normandie,* being converted to a troop carrier, burns and capsizes in New York Harbor. German saboteurs are at first suspected. Naval Intelligence, hoping to curb espionage on the New York City docks, decides to seek assistance from the underworld.

May 4: The "wanted" cards for Anastasia and Anthony Romeo are removed from the district attorney's files on O'Dwyer's orders.

May 12: Convinced that they need Luciano's help, authorities transfer Luciano to Great Meadow Prison in Comstock, New York. Luciano is later visited in Great Meadow by Luciano attorney, Moses Polakoff, and Meyer Lansky.

June 11: With Buchalter sentenced to die, Bronx district attorney dismisses grand jury and hopes of indicting him for the murder of Irving Penn.

June 29: The body of Romeo is found near Wilmington, Delaware; he was rumored to have squealed.

July 30: Anastasia enters the U.S. Army, assigned to Camp Upton, New York; he is later sent to Camp Forrest, Tennessee.

October 1: Anastasia is promoted from private to private first class.

October 21: Anastasia is promoted to technician fifth class.

October 30: New York State Court of Appeals upholds the conviction of Buchalter and the other two men. Court sets week of December 7, 1942, for the executions.

November 5: Sing Sing warden sets night of December 10 for executions of Buchalter and others.

December 6: A stay of execution is granted until January for Buchalter and others.

December 10: Shapiro completes federal sentence and is immediately arrested and taken back to New York.

December 17: Shapiro is arraigned on charges of extortion and conspiracy in the garment industry.

December 30: Counsel for Buchalter asks U.S. Supreme Court to review conviction.

1943   January: Ernest "The Hawk" Rupolo is released from prison.

January 2: A stay of execution is ordered for Buchalter and the other condemned men by U.S. Supreme Court until they can rule on the case.

January 11: Murder of Carlo Tresca takes place on Fifth Avenue near 15th Street. The murder was allegedly ordered by Genovese to curry favor with Italian leader Mussolini. The killer was believed to be Carmine Galante.

March 10: Counsel for Buchalter, Capone, and Weiss ask U.S. Supreme Court to reconsider.

March 15: U.S. Supreme Court agrees to review the Buchalter case.

March 18: While serving in the Army, Anastasia files preliminary application for U.S. citizenship.

April 28: Petition for Anastasia's citizenship is processed and a certificate of arrival issued.

May 7: Counsel for Buchalter presents case to U.S. Supreme Court.

May 14: Anastasia promoted to staff sergeant.

June 1: U.S. Supreme Court upholds the conviction of Buchalter and the others.

June 15: Shapiro's conspiracy and extortion trial begins.

June 16: Anastasia is promoted to technical sergeant.

June 18: New York State Court of Appeals denies reargument, sets July 20 as resentencing date for Buchalter and others.

June 29: Petition is filed for Anastasia's naturalization in the Court of Common Pleas, Lebanon County, Pennsylvania.

July: In the course of the Tresca murder investigation, New York District Attorney Frank Hogan obtains court order to tap Costello's telephone line.

July 8: Department of Justice informs Sing Sing warden that Buchalter will not be released from federal sentence.

July 9: Brooklyn district attorney demands U.S. Attorney General Francis Biddle release Buchalter from federal custody for resentencing; Shapiro pleads guilty to one count of the indictment. Scheduled to be sentenced in September, Shapiro is too ill to appear in court until the next year.

July 20: Buchalter and the other two defendants are scheduled for execution during the week of September 13, 1943. Buchalter execution is dependent on a presidential pardon from his federal sentence.

August 24: Judge Thomas Aurelio is caught on phone tap thanking Costello for his nomination.

August 29: Aurelio phone tap incident reported on front page of *New York Times*.

September 1: Governor Dewey demands that President Roosevelt pardon Buchalter from his federal sentence.

September 2: Executions of Buchalter and others are rescheduled for October 18.

October 14: Costello testifies to grand jury during Aurelio disbarment procedure; executions of Buchalter and others are rescheduled for November 29.

October 15: Anastasia is transferred to Indiantown Gap, Pennsylvania.

November 20: Dewey complains publicly that President Roosevelt is protecting Buchalter from punishment. Dewey postpones the executions until week of January 3.

November 29: U.S. Attorney General Biddle condemns Dewey for his statements regarding Roosevelt.

December 30: Dewey again delays the execution date because of failure of the U.S. Government to surrender Buchalter. New execution date is set for February 10.

1944   Adonis leaves Brooklyn and moves to Fort Lee, New Jersey.

January 17: New York State attorney general accepts Buchalter surrender offer from U.S. Attorney General Biddle.

January 20: Attorney Arthur Garfield Hays seeks new trial for Mendy Weiss.

January 21. Buchalter arrives at Sing Sing death house.

January 25: Governor Dewey sets clemency hearing date of February 2.

January 27: Kings County judge hears new plea by Buchalter defense counsel.

January 28: Judge denies motions for new trial for Buchalter.

February 4: Governor Dewey stays execution of Buchalter until the week of February 28.

February 14: Hays asks court of appeals to consider new evidence if Buchalter reargument is granted.

February 24: Court of appeals refuses to reopen the Buchalter case.

February 26: Executioner is notified to report to Sing Sing on night of March 2 for Buchalter execution.

February 29: New counsel files suit that Buchalter was illegally handed over to the state by the government.

March 1: Federal judge declines to issue a writ that would delay Buchalter's death.

March 2: Governor Dewey gives Buchalter a two-day stay to permit a new appeal and to talk to District Attorney Hogan.

March 4: Buchalter attorney files a writ of certiorari to U.S. Supreme Court in Washington. D.C.; Buchalter, Capone, and Weiss are all put to death in Sing Sing electric chair.

March 5: Buchalter and Weiss are buried at Mount Hebron Cemetery in Flushing, Queens.

March 9: After a big Italian gangland funeral, Capone is buried in Holy Cross Cemetery.

April 17: Rupolo, in a contract murder, shoots a 66-year-old man three times in the face; he survives.

May: U.S. Army Central Intelligence Division Agent Orange C. Dickey begins an investigation of Genovese's black market activities in Italy.

May 5: Shapiro is sentenced to 15 years to life.

June 4: Dickey arrests two Canadian soldiers who stole U.S. Army trucks for Genovese.

June 13: In an effort to avoid a long prison term, Rupolo reveals the details of the Boccia murder to Brooklyn Assistant District Attorney Edward Heffernan.

June 14: Costello leaves $27,200 in a New York City taxicab.

July 5: Peter LaTempa, a participant in the Boccia murder, is sent to the Brooklyn Civil Prison after seeking protective custody.

August 7: Genovese and five others are indicted for the murder of Boccia.

August 9: For the first time, Genovese's role in Boccia murder is made public.

August 27: Dickey arrests Genovese in Nola, Italy.

November 12: Anastasia is honorably discharged from the U.S. Army for being overage.

November 22: Dickey receives FBI files on Genovese.

November 25: *New York Times* announces Genovese has been apprehended in Italy.

December: Warrant is issued for Genovese's arrest for the Boccia murder.

December 6: LaTempa attempts suicide in his cell by trying to hang himself.

1945   January 8: Dickey receives information that Genovese has been indicted in Brooklyn.

January 16: LaTempa is found dead in the Brooklyn Civil Prison.

February 9: LaTempa's death ruled a suicide from an overdose of sedatives.

May 8: Luciano attorney Polakoff swears out petition for a grant of executive clemency for his client, citing his wartime assistance.

May 17: Dickey and Genovese board the ship *James Lykes* at Bari, Italy, to return to New York City.

June 1: Dickey and Genovese arrive in New York and proceed to the Brooklyn district attorney's office.

June 2: Genovese is arraigned in King's County Court for the murder of Boccia.

November 3: New Brooklyn Prosecutor George Beldock promises to pursue Anastasia murder investigation dropped by O'Dwyer.

November 6: William O'Dwyer is elected to the first of two terms as mayor of New York City.

November 16: A grand jury investigating Panto's murder asks about Anastasia's involvement.

December 20: Grand jury hands down presentment on O'Dwyer for his laxity to arrest Anastasia.

1946   January 4: Governor Dewey commutes the sentence of Luciano. After pardon, Luciano is transferred to Sing Sing Prison.

February 2: Luciano is removed from Sing Sing and taken to Ellis Island Prison.

February 9: Luciano is removed from Ellis Island and placed aboard the *Laura Keene* by immigration agents.

February 9: Costello visits Luciano aboard the *Laura Keene*.

February 10: Luciano leaves Brooklyn dock for Italy aboard the *Laura Keene*.

February 28: After a 17-day trip, Luciano arrives in Naples.

June 6: Trial of Genovese for the murder of Boccia begins in a Brooklyn court.

June 7: Genovese's lawyer asks for directed verdict of acquittal.

June 10: Judge dismisses the charges against Genovese because of lack of evidence. The judge scolds Genovese and warns him to leave the state's key witness, Ernest Rupolo, alone.

1947   February 21: After Luciano's presence is reported in Havana, the United States threatens to end the sale of narcotics to Cuba if he is allowed to remain there.

February 22: Luciano is seized by Cuban authorities and placed in an immigration camp.

February 23: Cuban authorities claim Luciano will leave the island in 48 hours.

February 25: Cuban authorities promise to deport Luciano by March 3.

February 27: Cuban president signs deportation order.

February 28: Cuban Supreme Court denies Luciano a writ of habeas corpus.

March 1: Lower court in Havana accepts a petition for a writ of habeas corpus.

March 3: Audienca Court of Appeals orders Luciano to appear to argue for his freedom.

March 13: Luciano will be deported to Genoa aboard the Turkish steamer *Bakir*.

March 19: Luciano placed aboard *Bakir* by Cuban police.

March 20: *Bakir* leaves Havana with Luciano.

April 12: Luciano is removed from *Bakir* in Genoa by local police and is jailed.

May 1: Luciano is taken to Palermo where he will be charged with "illegal emigration."

May 3: Luciano is held in jail in Palermo.

May 14: Luciano is released after a judge warns him to stay out of the public eye.

June 9: Shapiro dies in the prison hospital at Sing Sing. He is buried in Montefiore Cemetery in St. Albans, New York.

June 20: Benjamin "Bugsy" Siegel is murdered at Los Angeles home of his paramour Virginia Hill.

1948   May 22: Luciano is arrested in Palermo and held for questioning about Mafia contacts.

1949   January 24: Costello hosts Salvation Army benefit dinner at Copacabana Club; Genovese is the guest of honor.

June 26: Luciano is linked to Vincent Trupia, who is arrested with $500,000 in cocaine.

July 8: Luciano is held in Rome jail as questioning regarding his drug activity continues.

July 15: Luciano is released from jail but barred from Rome by Italian police.

July 19: Luciano leaves Rome a few hours before police deadline to vacate the city.

1950   March 27: Anna Genovese leaves her husband and moves to New York City with son Philip. Anna begins divorce action but drops it after Genovese begins to pay her $200 a week.

April 25: Adonis is subpoenaed to testify about bookmaking and race track information by Senate subcommittee.

May 17: Adonis is revealed as a 5 percent owner, with others, of the Colonial Inn in Miami.

May 29: District Attorney Hogan subpoenas bank accounts of Adonis, his wife, and son during an investigation of gambler Frank Erickson.

October 22: Walter Lynch, a Democratic Liberal candidate for governor, questions Luciano's pardon and release.

October 24: Fred Moran, New York State parole chief, denies politics were involved with release.

October 25: Lynch insists Dewey was solely responsible for Luciano's commuted sentence.

October 30: Adonis is named in gambling arrest warrant with Salvatore Moretti and three others.

October 31: Adonis surrenders with Moretti in superior court in Hackensack. Kefauver Committee investigators announce they are anxious to question Adonis, who has avoided them.

November 3: Lynch declares Luciano's commutation was done as a favor to Costello.

November 5: With Willie Moretti, Adonis allegedly has meeting at home of Republican State Chairman John Dickerson.

November 9: Adonis is named in a criminal information by a New York County grand jury investigating gambling.

November 10: An interchange of information is announced in the New York/ New Jersey gambling investigations of Adonis.

November 12: Adonis and Salvatore Moretti are requested to appear in Hackensack Supreme Court to be served subpoenas by Kefauver Committee investigators.

November 13: Adonis fails to appear in Hackensack to be served a subpoena.

December 6: Adonis is subpoenaed to testify before the Kefauver Committee in Washington, D.C.

December 10: Adonis tells Kefauver Committee he was born in Passaic, New Jersey, in November 1901.

December 12: Adonis refuses to tell anything to the Kefauver Committee about his business or income.

1951   January 5: Kefauver Committee recommends that Adonis be cited for contempt of Senate.

January 22: Contempt of Senate charges against Adonis are delayed by Nevada Senator Pat McCarren.

January 23: Adonis and seven others are cited for contempt of Senate; Adonis is named in a 15-count gambling indictment handed down by a Bergen County special grand jury.

February 14: Anastasia is questioned by investigators in a closed "secret" hearing before the Kefauver Committee's appearance in New York City.

February 28: Kefauver Committee says a gambling and underworld "axis between New York and Miami" is run by Adonis and Costello.

March 2: Vincent Mangano has been reported missing for the last three weeks.

March 3: Kefauver Committee announces it has been looking for Genovese and Mangano for three weeks.

March 13: Costello begins testimony before Kefauver Committee.

March 15: A doctor's certificate is presented to the committee to keep Costello from testifying because of a throat condition. Costello walks out on committee members.

March 18: Grand jury files from O'Dwyer's investigation of Anastasia in the Panto murder are turned over to Kefauver.

March 19: Anthony Anastasia testifies before the Kefauver Committee that all five brothers jumped ship to enter the United States.

March 20: Albert Anastasia is admitted to St. Mary's Hospital in Passaic, New Jersey, for conjunctivitis.

March 21: The physician for Anastasia wires Kefauver Committee that his patient will be unable to appear; testimony from closed hearing in February revealed during public hearings.

March 26: Zwillman appears before the Kefauver Committee in Washington, D.C.

April 2: Anastasia is cited for contempt of Senate.

April 9: Contempt of Senate citations against Adonis and Costello are made official.

April 19: Body of Vincent Mangano's brother Philip is found on Bergen Beach near Jamaica Bay, Brooklyn.

April 27: Anastasia is questioned about the murder of Phil Mangano.

May 21: Adonis and four others plead no contest to charges of conspiracy to violate New Jersey gambling laws.

May 28: Adonis is sentenced to two to three years and fined $15,000 in Bergen County Superior Court.

May 29: Adonis arrives at New Jersey State Prison in Trenton to begin sentence.

June 27: Bureau of Narcotics agent Charles Siragusa tells Senate Crime Committee (SCC) that Luciano "rules narcotics traffic" from Italy.

June 28: Naples police refute Luciano role in narcotics. Luciano claims he is being persecuted by the United States.

July 17: Dewey political foe, W. Kingsland Macy, says governor should be forced to explain details of Luciano's parole.

July 25: Costello is indicted for contempt of Senate.

July 26: Judge signs writ of habeas corpus so Adonis can appear at Senate contempt arraignment.

July 28: An assistant U.S. attorney says Luciano is the head of a French-Italian heroin smuggling ring.

July 29: SCC says it is "studying" Luciano connection to narcotics ring; Macy asks Kefauver Committee to call Dewey to explain parole.

August 2: After first balking, Adonis agrees to appear for arraignment on the contempt of Senate charge.

August 7: Adonis pleads not guilty to 16 counts of contempt of Senate.

August 12: Zwillman disappears from Newark area to avoid SCC subpoena.

August 16: *Collier's* magazine article declares Zwillman is the "man to see in New Jersey."

August 31: SCC calls Italy "heroin trade center" and Luciano head of the distribution ring.

September 8: Zwillman returns to Newark after four-week sabbatical.

September 11: Former Mayor Frank Hague declares Zwillman is czar of New Jersey Democratic Party.

October 4: Anastasia checks into a hospital for knee x-ray, allegedly to establish an alibi for his whereabouts this day. Costello is visiting Hot Springs. Willie Moretti is murdered in Joe's Elbow Room restaurant in Cliffside Park, New Jersey, allegedly on the orders of Genovese.

October 31: Assassins allegedly track Anastasia to home where one of his men is celebrating a murder acquittal. Anastasia escapes.

November 21: The *New York Times* claims two attempts have been made on Anastasia's life and he has been advised to go to Hot Springs.

1952   January 7: Contempt of Senate trial begins for Costello.

January 15: Jury in Costello trial is hung 11–1 on conviction.

March 14: New Jersey Parole Board announces Adonis is eligible for parole.

March 31: Second trial for contempt of Senate begins against Costello.

April 4: Costello is found guilty of contempt of Senate.

April 8: Costello is sentenced to 18 months in prison and fined $5,000.

May 1: United Nations takes note of Luciano's alleged drug activity.

May 6: Salvatore Moretti suffers a cerebral hemorrhage at New Jersey State Prison in Trenton.

May 7: State Parole Board denies Adonis parole.

June 8: Moretti dies.

July 16: After meeting of the UN Narcotics Commission, Italian police seize Luciano's passport.

June 25: Largest tax lien in New Jersey history is filed against Zwillman.

July 3: Johnny Robilotto is arrested for the Willie Moretti murder. Charges are dropped because of lack of evidence.

August 15: Costello begins jail term for contempt of Senate.

August 22: Costello enters Lewisburg Prison; he is later transferred to Atlanta and then to Milan, Michigan.

September 3: New York State Crime Commission subpoenas the bank record of 300 during its "Pier Inquiry" probe, including the Anastasia brothers and Zwillman.

September 20: Body of Eugenio Giannini is found on West 234th Street; he is allegedly murdered on the orders of Genovese.

September 25: Bureau of Narcotics Director Harry Anslinger tells civic group that Luciano is behind narcotics trade.

October 22: Government moves to strip Costello of citizenship.

November 21: Because Genovese hid his criminal record, his citizenship is revoked by Immigration and Naturalization Service (INS).

November 22: Genovese is not at his Atlantic Highland's home when INS agents try to serve denaturalization papers.

December 5: Anastasia fails to appear for questioning before the New York State Crime Commission's Waterfront investigation.

December 9: Government files denaturalization suit as first step to deport Anastasia.

December 10: Genovese's marital problems become public after Anna files for separate maintenance.

December 19: Testifying before the Waterfront Commission, Anastasia is selective as to what questions he answers.

1953 January 6: Adonis goes on trial charged with 22 counts of contempt of Senate.

February 8: Senator Tobey declares he will break the Anastasia brothers' stranglehold on the waterfront.

February 16: Adonis is found guilty of one count of contempt of Senate by a federal judge. He is sentenced to three months in federal prison.

February 17: Adonis is indicted for perjury by the Bergen County grand jury investigating waterfront racketeering and gambling.

February 20: Department of Justice issues a warrant for the deportation of Adonis for lying about his place of birth.

February 21: Warrant is served on Adonis at New Jersey State Prison.

March 2: In court in Freehold, New Jersey, Anna Genovese makes startling claims about Genovese's income from the rackets.

March 10: Genovese is held in contempt after failing to pay Anna $300 a week by a New Jersey Superior Court judge.

March 12: Costello is indicted for federal income tax evasion; after a builder's lien is filed, Genovese's Atlantic Highlands home is ordered to be sold at sheriff's auction.

April 2: Immigration officials say Adonis's deportation hearing will begin at the prison on April 27.

April 24: Adonis is indicted in Washington, D.C. for making false statements to the Kefauver Committee about his place of birth.

April 27: Adonis deportation case begins in Trenton prison; trial is adjourned until June 1 to allow Adonis's attorney to prepare.

June 1: Two of Adonis's brothers and an uncle testify at the deportation proceedings in Trenton prison.

June 2: Government produces documents to show Adonis was born in Italy in 1902.

June 15: Adonis testifies for seven hours, producing documents in his claim to have been born in Passaic.

June 16: Adonis finishes testifying; INS hearing officer says he'll render decision before the end of July.

June 18: Government charges Zwillman with evading income taxes.

June 19: Steven Franse is found dead in his automobile on East 37th Street, allegedly murdered on orders of Genovese.

July 14: Government drops tax case against Zwillman.

July 16: Adonis is released from Trenton prison; he has to post $5,000 bond for charges of lying to Kefauver Committee.

July 23: In Washington, D.C., Adonis pleads innocent to lying to Kefauver Committee.

August 5: INS official recommends deportation of Adonis; U.S. Attorney General Herbert Brownell orders that Adonis be deported.

August 19: New Jersey Superior Court judge dismisses suits filed by Genovese and Anna.

August 25: New Jersey Superior Court judge allows sheriff's auction of Genovese's Atlantic Highlands home to take place.

September 26: Pretrial examination begins in the denaturalization proceedings of Anastasia; new U.S. attorney in Newark announces push to begin denaturalization hearing of Genovese.

October 29: Costello is released from Milan, Michigan, prison after completion of contempt of Senate sentence.

November 7: IRS announces tax liens totaling $413,964 have been filed against Adonis and his wife.

December 9: Dominick "The Gap" Petrilli is murdered in a bar on East 183rd Street in the Bronx, allegedly on the orders of Genovese.

December 17: Board of Immigration Appeals upholds deportation order of Adonis.

December 29: Government opens civil proceedings to invalidate Anastasia's citizenship.

December 30: Federal judge reserves decision on Anastasia citizenship.

1954   January: Adonis is found guilty of lying to Bergen County grand jury about his place of birth.

January 5: Allegations are made that Luciano once offered to reveal killers of Carlo Tresca to Dewey. Interest is renewed in Luciano pardon.

January 26: List of Luciano visitors while in prison is revealed during New York State House hearings.

January 27: Costello, Lansky, "Socks" Lanza, Willie Moretti, and Mike Miranda are revealed as Great Meadow visitors of Luciano.

January 28: Dewey denounces Democratic effort to make political issue of Luciano's release.

February 2: Adonis is sentenced to two to three years in prison and fined $1,000.

March 10: Anastasia is indicted by federal grand jury in Newark for income tax evasion.

March 22: Royal Canadian Mounted Police official in Vancouver alleges Luciano is the leading supplier of drugs there.

March 25: Adonis is found guilty of lying to Kefauver Committee about his place of birth.

April 1: Federal grand jury in Newark begins hearing testimony against Zwillman for tax evasion.

April 5: Federal income tax evasion case against Costello begins.

April 10: Adonis is sentenced to 18 to 24 months in federal prison.

April 14: Federal judge strips Anastasia of citizenship.

April 26: Judge signs denaturalization order for Anastasia; deportation is postponed pending appeal.

May 13: Jury finds Costello guilty of tax evasion.

May 17: Costello sentenced to five years in prison and fined $30,000.

May 26: Zwillman is charged in a two-count indictment with tax evasion.

September 20: Third Circuit Court of Appeals hears arguments on Anastasia citizenship case.

October 16: Rudolph Halley and 109 other witnesses subpoenaed for Anastasia income tax evasion trial.

October 18: Anastasia income tax evasion trial begins in Newark.

November 19: Italian authorities call Luciano a danger to society and order him to remain indoors at night for two years.

November 20: After a five-week trial, jury begins deliberations in Anastasia tax trial. After the jury fails to reach a verdict, a mistrial is declared.

1955   March 24: U.S. Court of Appeals upholds Adonis conviction for lying to Kefauver Committee.

April 18: U.S. Supreme Court denies Adonis appeal for conviction for lying to Bergen County grand jury.

April 29: While waiting for Anastasia's second income tax trial to begin, Charles Ferri, a government witness, and his wife disappear from their home in Miami, Florida.

May 3: Police search blood-spattered and ransacked home of Ferri.

May 5: Tax evasion trial delayed until May 16, at request of Anastasia's court-appointed counsel.

May 18: Anna Genovese testifies about gambling and kickbacks before the Waterfront Commission.

May 23: Anastasia pleads guilty to two counts of income tax evasion in Camden, New Jersey.

June 3: A federal judge sentences Anastasia to a year in prison and a $20,000 fine.

September 19: U.S. Third Circuit Court of Appeals in Philadelphia rules against federal court on revoking Anastasia's citizenship.

November 14: Adonis agrees to leave United States to avoid prison time; he is placed on five years probation. Adonis must leave country by January 1, 1956, and cannot return during probation period.

November 17: U.S. Third Circuit Court refuses to reconsider ruling; Anastasia retains his citizenship.

December 30: INS announces Adonis will sail to Italy aboard the *Conte Biancamano*.

1956   January 3: Adonis says goodbye to his wife, son, and three daughters and boards *Conte Biancamano* headed for Italy.

January 15: Adonis arrives in Genoa.

February 13: Adonis's attorneys reach agreement with federal government to pay $66,859 in tax settlement.

January 18: Zwillman's federal tax evasion trial begins.

March 1: Jury fails to reach verdict in Zwillman tax trial.

March 5: U.S. Supreme Court upholds Costello's tax evasion conviction.

March 28: Anastasia is released from federal prison in Milan, Michigan.

May 14: Costello begins five-year prison sentence.

November 28: Luciano is one of 11 men who petition President Dwight Eisenhower to readmit them to the United States.

1957   March 11: Costello is released from prison pending appeal of his tax conviction.

May 2: An assassination attempt is made on Costello in the lobby of his Majestic Apartment.

June 3: U.S. Supreme Court upholds five-year tax sentence for Costello.

June 6: Receipts taken from Costello on night of shooting are tied to Tropicana Casino in Las Vegas.

June 17: Anastasia underboss Frank Scalise is murdered in the Bronx.

July 17: Vincent Gigante, Costello's alleged assailant, surrenders to police.

August 16: IRS files a civil suit to collect back taxes from Anastasia totaling $256,543.

October 25: Anastasia is murdered in Grasso's barbershop in the Park Sheraton Hotel.

October 26: Anthony Coppola, Anastasia's bodyguard and chauffeur, is jailed for vagrancy.

October 28: Anastasia is buried in Greenwood Cemetery in South Brooklyn.

November 14: Apalachin Summit, attended by mob leaders across the country, is interrupted by local law enforcement. Genovese allegedly called the meeting; Gambino attended.

December 13: Anna Genovese is subpoenaed to discuss Apalachin meeting by Mercer County, New Jersey, grand jury.

December 14: Anna Genovese is questioned for 75 minutes.

1958   February 11: Meyer Lansky is taken into custody and questioned about the Anastasia murder; he claims he was in Havana at the time.

June 29: Genovese is subpoenaed by McClellan Committee to be questioned about Apalachin Summit.

July 2: Genovese invokes Fifth Amendment more than 150 times before committee.

July 7: Genovese is arrested along with Vincent Gigante for conspiring to import and sell narcotics.

July 8: Genovese is arraigned in federal court and charged with participation in an international drug ring.

July 9: INS says it will await results of narcotics case before pursuing deportation action against Genovese.

September: Armand "Tommy" Rava, another loyalist, disappears.

September 7: Johnny Robilotto, an alleged Anastasia loyalist, is murdered in East Flatbush section of Brooklyn, reportedly on orders of Gambino.

October: Deportation hearings reopened from 1940 for Gambino.

October 17: Costello surrenders and is sent back to complete his five-year tax sentence.

1959   January 12: Narcotics conspiracy trial of Genovese begins in federal court.

February13: Two arrests made for jury tampering during Zwillman's tax trial.

February 20: Costello is stripped of U.S. citizenship.

February 26: A despondent Zwillman commits suicide in his East Orange, New Jersey, mansion.

February 27: Zwillman is buried in B'nai Abraham Memorial Cemetery in Union, New Jersey.

March 17: Government rests its case against Genovese.

April 2: Jury begins deliberations in Genovese trial.

April 3: Genovese is found guilty, along with 14 others, of conspiracy to violate federal narcotics laws.

April 4: Genovese bail raised to $150,000 until scheduled sentencing.

April 17: Genovese is sentenced to 15 years in prison and fined $20,000.

April 30: Government gets court order preventing Genovese from transferring his property.

June 16: Questioned for four hours about his presence at Apalachin, Genovese said it was a party and business meeting.

September 25: Anthony "Little Augie Pisano" Carfano and Janice Drake are found murdered on 94th Street in Jackson Heights, Queens, allegedly on orders from Genovese.

October 23: Two plead guilty to jury tampering charges in Zwillman tax case.

1960   February 12: Bail is revoked and Genovese is taken into custody to await federal prison designation; Genovese Family to be run by triumvirate of Mike Miranda, Thomas Eboli, and Gerry Catena.

April: Thinking the "fix" is in, Joseph Valachi surrenders only to find out otherwise; he is given 15 years, not the 5 he's expecting. Valachi is shipped off to Atlanta to begin his sentence.

May 16: U.S. Supreme Court refuses to hear an appeal to review Genovese's conviction.

1961   March 31: The government starts proceedings to deport Costello.

June 20: Costello is released from Atlanta after completing tax evasion sentence.

December: Valachi is found guilty of heroin trafficking in what he calls a "frame-up."

1962   January 26: Luciano dies of a massive heart attack at Capodicino Airport in Naples at age 65.

January 29: Three hundred people attend funeral service for Luciano at Holy Trinity Church in Naples.

January 31: Lucania family receives permission to bring Luciano's body back to the United States for burial.

February 7: Luciano is buried in family vault at St. John's Cemetery in Middle Village, Queens.

April 8: Anthony "Tony Bender" Strollo, once a top lieutenant of Genovese, disappears.

June 7: Naples officials say Luciano's death was due to heart attack after rumors of poisoning persist.

June 16: After claiming he was given the "kiss of death" by cellmate Genovese, Valachi asks to be placed in the "hole" for his own protection.

June 22: Valachi kills fellow prisoner Joseph Saupp in a case of mistaken identity in Atlanta prison yard.

July 13: U.S. Attorney Robert Morgenthau is notified by an unidentified person that Valachi wants to talk.

July 17: Valachi pleads guilty to second-degree murder charges and is given a life sentence. He is flown to the Westchester County Jail in New York and placed in the hospital wing.

1963   April: Deportation case against Costello is dismissed.

August 4: The *Washington Sunday Star* is the first to release information on Valachi's revelations.

September 9: Valachi is flown by helicopter to Washington, D.C. disguised as an military police officer, to appear before the McClellan Committee.

September 27: Valachi begins his testimony before the McClellan Committee.

October 1: Valachi is back on the witness stand in Washington.

October 2, 8, 9: Valachi testifies before the McClellan Committee.

October 16: Valachi is questioned by a Queens's grand jury about the murder of Anthony Carfano.

October 29: Valachi completes his Senate testimony in secret because of pending court cases.

1964   May 12: Father Salvatore Anastasia claims from Rome that no one ever proved his brother Albert's involvement in any crime.

August 24: The body of Ernest Rupolo, tied to concrete, is found floating in Jamaica Bay.

1965   March 1: U.S. Supreme Court refuses to review decision by court of appeals on Genovese's 1963 defense motion.

1966   November 9: Genovese is transferred from Leavenworth to the Medical Center for Federal Prisoners in Springfield, Missouri.

December 30: Deportation order is issued for Gambino.

1967   February 14: Genovese dies at the Medical Center for Federal Prisoners in Spring-field, Missouri.

February 15: The body of Genovese is flown to Newark and taken to the William S. Anderson Funeral Home in Red Bank.

February 16: A wake is held for Genovese at the Anderson Funeral Home.

February 17: After mass at St. Agnes in Atlantic Highlands, Genovese is buried in St. John's Cemetery in Middle Village, Queens.

April 13: Santo Trafficante is questioned about Anastasia's murder in New York City.

1969   March 24: Twelve witnesses to the Anastasia murder are subpoenaed by District Attorney Frank Hogan.

March 25: Hogan reveals he has "new information" about the Anastasia murder.

1970   March 15: The *New York Times* reports Gambino is the new "boss of bosses."

March 23: Gambino is arrested by the FBI for allegedly being the mastermind of a plot to rob an armored car.

April 30: Joe Colombo leads protest march at the FBI building in Manhattan.

1971   March 16: Thomas E. Dewey dies in Florida.

May 22: Milan police put Adonis in "preventive custody" and request he be exiled to a small village.

June 20: Adonis is exiled to Serra de Conti on the Adriatic coast for four years because of his Mafia connections.

June 28: Joe Colombo is shot and critically wounded in Columbus Circle, alleg-edly on orders from Gambino. His assailant is killed by bodyguards.

July 13: Adonis exile is confirmed; he must observe a 10 PM to 7 AM curfew and avoid use of the telephone.

November 23: Adonis suffers a pulmonary collapse while in exile.

November 26: Adonis dies of heart failure following pulmonary complications in Ancona, Italy.

November 29: An unnamed friend makes arrangements for Adonis's body to be flown back to New Jersey for burial.

December 2: Adonis's body arrives at JFK airport and is taken by hearse to AK Macagna Funeral Home in Cliffside Park.

1972   April 7: Joey Gallo, who was believed to be behind the shooting of Colombo, is murdered outside Umberto's Clam House in Little Italy.

1973   February 7: Costello suffers heart seizure.

February 18: Costello dies.

February 21: Costello is buried in Saint Michaels Cemetery in East Elmhurst, Queens.

1974   January 25: Bomb explodes at Costello mausoleum.

1976   October 15: Gambino dies at his home of heart failure.

October 18: Gambino is buried in Saint John's Cemetery, Middle Village, Queens.

JOE ADONIS (GIUSEPPE ANTONIO DOTO)

AKA "JOEY A."
NOVEMBER 22, 1902–NOVEMBER 26, 1971

The disparity in the activities of Joe Adonis—what was real and what was fiction—makes him one of the most misunderstood underworld leaders in the history of organized crime in America. A young man who came from neither poverty nor the slums, he took to crime and politics and became one of the most recognized names in the underworld.

A handsome gangster with movie star looks, Adonis worked his way up through the Brooklyn underworld. He made his money from bootlegging and gambling with help from the crime connections he made along the way. His foray into politics began with the opening of Joe's Italian Kitchen, a restaurant where he served fine food and the best liquor available to politicians and public office holders. His money, henchmen, and the willingness to use them made him one of the most powerful men in the Borough of Brooklyn, especially after supporting Fiorello LaGuardia for mayor in 1933.

When Adonis switched his support from LaGuardia in 1937, it marked the beginning of his exodus from Brooklyn, across the Hudson River to New Jersey. The move was completed in 1944 when he relocated his family to a $100,000 home in Fort Lee. He established a new head-quarters in Duke's Restaurant, located in Cliffside Park. Throughout the last half of the 1940s, Adonis was a partner in a number of prosperous dice games run in northern New Jersey.

In late 1950, Adonis's criminal activities came to the attention of the Kefauver Committee and a Bergen County, New Jersey, grand jury probing gambling. From December 1950 until January 1956, Adonis was either in prison or under intense scrutiny by law enforcement. Looking at a second stretch in prison for lying about his place of birth, Adonis agreed to be deported to keep his freedom.

BEGINNINGS

Giuseppe Antonio Doto was born on November 22, 1902, in Montemarano, Italy, a small town in the province of Avellino in the Campania region, an agricultural area noted mainly for its vineyards and wineries. He was the third child of Michele and Mary Doto, whose brood consisted of four boys. Giuseppe's three brothers were Antonio (Anthony); the oldest, Ettore (Albert); and Genesio.

The Doto family arrived in the United States by most accounts in 1909. The family was said to have settled in the Gowanus section of Brooklyn. Little is known of Doto's early years. At this time, there are no published biographies on Joe Adonis. Some unfounded stories written about his early life claim that he entered the United States illegally in 1915. Why he would need to do this when his entire family had already settled here is not explained in these tales. Those who have written about him seem to fill in the blanks about his early years with tales of his being a thief, extortionist, armed robber, pimp, and, in some cases, a rapist.[1] In researching Adonis's life, it has been found that most of the misinformation comes from one author and is simply repeated by others.

Unlike many of the underworld figures focused on in this book, Adonis did not grow up in an environment where his family was destitute and he committed crimes to help them out. Michele Doto was a builder and owned property in South Brooklyn. His family would have been considered middle class by the standards of the day. Thus neither a bad environment nor poverty drove Adonis into a life of crime.

One part of Adonis's life now lost to history is how and when he took on the name of Adonis. By the early 1940s, most people didn't know that Adonis was not his real name. When stories about the charitable nature of his mother were published, the newspapers referred to her as Mrs. Adonis. The name was said to have come from his handsome features; however, it is not certain whether he came up with the name himself or if someone else bestowed it on him. In *The Secret Rulers,* former *New York World-Telegram and Sun* reporter Fred J. Cook writes:

> One version has it that a Broadway cutie—Joe A. like all rising young gangsters had a pronounced predilection for the species—took one look at his sturdy handsomeness and gurgled, "That guy looks like a real Adonis." Another version is that a pimply-faced Brooklyn hoodlum, having come across the name of the beautiful youth of Greek mythology somewhere in his travels, misapplied it to young Joseph A. Doto, who thenceforth became the Joe Adonis of American gangdom.[2]

Adonis was said to have a reputation for primping before mirrors and combing his hair incessantly. One popular story claims that Lucky Luciano once witnessed this and asked, "Who do you think you are, Rudolph Valentino?" To which Adonis replied, "For looks, that guy's a bum!"

EARLY CRIMINAL ACTIVITIES

Nearly all the people covered in this book had criminal careers that began in their teenage years; Adonis is one of the few exceptions. His first arrest came on the night of February 26, 1926, when he was 24 years old. An alert Brooklyn police officer, Robert F. Baron, was patrolling the South Brooklyn waterfront after several hijackings had taken place. On this night he was keeping his eye on an automobile with four men inside that had been circling the neighborhood around 39th Street. The automobile came to a stop and one of the men got out and raised the hood as if he were checking on an engine problem.

Officer Baron, who was watching from behind a fence, approached the car with his revolver drawn. He ordered the men out of the vehicle and frisked them. Looking in the automobile, he discovered a sawed-off shotgun, a .45 automatic, and a .38 revolver. He ordered the men back into the car and then got behind the wheel and drove them to the Fourth Avenue Police Station, where they were arrested on weapons charges and stealing an automobile. Two of the men arrested gave their names as Ralph Sprizza, a small-time hood, and James Arosa. The latter name turned out to be an alias used by Joe Adonis.

On March 8, the men were tried for automobile theft in Bay Ridge Magistrate's Court. Among the spectators in the courtroom was Frankie Yale and several of his associates. The brief hearing ended with the charges against the men being dismissed. The next month the same men were acquitted of the gun charges during a hearing in Special Sessions court.

In the meantime, Officer Baron was promoted to detective just six days after making the arrest and handed a gold shield. A few days after his promotion, he arrested Joseph Florino, a subordinate of Frankie Yale and a companion of both Adonis and Albert Anastasia (see Chapter 2). As in the earlier cases, Officer Baron could only watch as the charges against Florino were dismissed.[3]

During the remainder of 1926, Adonis was arrested two more times, first for robbery and later for grand larceny. Charges in both cases were dismissed. In 1927, he was arrested for participating in a street brawl. This time Adonis was convicted and fined $25.

After the murder of Brooklyn underworld kingpin Frankie Yale on July 1, 1928, Anthony "Little Augie Pisano" Carfano became the new power in the borough. The story goes that Adonis was close to Carfano and began to build his own power base in South Brooklyn. By this time in the late 1920s, Adonis was heavily involved in the liquor smuggling business. He opened his own restaurant/speakeasy, which became known as Joe's Italian Kitchen, at the corner of Carroll Street and Fourth Avenue. The place earned a reputation for serving excellent Italian dishes, but, more important, Adonis provided uncut liquor to his customers. It was soon being frequented by politicians, judges, and other borough officials. It was reported that, "None of Adonis's hoodlums were permitted to set foot in it, to remind the politicians who were becoming his friends of his criminal origin."[4]

Other than gaining a reputation as an important lieutenant to both Yale and Carfano, little is known about how Adonis became associated with Lucky Luciano. In the book *The Last Testament of Lucky Luciano* (see Appendix), the crime boss claims he met Adonis for the first time in an ice cream parlor in Little Italy in 1920. He claims Adonis asked him for $10,000 to purchase whiskey from Irving "Waxey Gordon" Wexler in Philadelphia. The problem with this tale, in a book full of questionable tales, is that Adonis was only 18 years old in 1920.

In addition to his first meeting with Luciano, other questionable items about Adonis also arise in *The Last Testament of Lucky Luciano,* one of which states he became a trusted lieutenant of Giuseppe "Joe the Boss" Masseria. How this came about, if it is actually true, is lost to history. Adonis was always listed as one of the attendees of the Atlantic City Conference (see Appendix) in May 1929, but this is more likely due to his association with Carfano, rather than Luciano. Most important, because of *The Last Testament of Lucky Luciano,* the popular belief is that Adonis took part in the murder of Masseria in Scarpato's Villa Nuova Tammaro restaurant in April 1931. There is no evidence tying Adonis to this murder, or to any other underworld murder for that matter.

During the establishment of the five families after the murder of Salvatore Maranzano in September 1931, Adonis reportedly ended up in the Brooklyn family of Vincent Mangano. Although Albert Anastasia was named the underboss of this family, he always seemed to hold a subordinate position to Adonis. In reality, Adonis was the fly in the ointment when it came to the five-family system. Few mobsters of the period wielded as much power and influence as Adonis. Despite an uncertain ranking, he was certainly close to leaders like Luciano, Frank Costello, and Meyer Lansky. Organized crime historians have a hard time dealing with this fact, often trying to pigeon hole the Brooklyn crime boss as a capo in one family or another; however, Adonis seemed to defy placement.

HIJACKER AND BENEFACTOR

Adonis's last arrest during the Prohibition Era came on November 23, 1931, when he was apprehended for smuggling liquor. Arraigned on charges in federal court, the case was eventually dismissed. When Prohibition ended, Adonis decided to enter the legitimate side of liquor distribution. Because of Adonis's reputation, the State Liquor Authority would not consider granting him a license, so he worked through a number of "front men" to finance his wholesale liquor outlets. One of these companies was incorporated with capital stock initially valued at $20,000. By 1936, the stock value had increased to $500,000.

Adonis also became involved in several legitimate business ventures. He had a knack for combining legitimate and illegitimate opportunities and turning them into money-making ventures. Adonis invested in the White Auto Sales Company, whose headquarters was on Carroll Street and Fourth Avenue, across the street from Joe's Italian Kitchen. In July 1934, he established Kings County Cigarette Service, with its headquarters at the rear of White Auto Sales. Two years later, in a building adjacent to White Auto Sales, he founded the Shamrock Cigarette Service.

Between 1934 and 1937, Adonis was allegedly behind the hijacking of cigarettes valued at $6 million off the streets of Brooklyn. During this time, his cigarette vending business prospered, and it was estimated that he placed 10,000 cigarette machines in restaurants and bars around Brooklyn. Any price the stolen cigarettes were sold for was pure profit.

Many of the trucks that transported the cigarettes to retail outlets in Brooklyn and Queens picked up their loads at Bush Terminal, located on the South Brooklyn waterfront. Their passage out of the area took them through the narrow streets of the warehouse district, where they became easy targets for hijackers. Drivers would be bound and blindfolded at gunpoint and their vehicles driven to a rented warehouse where the cigarettes would be unloaded. The truck and driver would then be taken to some outlying area of Brooklyn and left there.

During an investigation of the hijackings, police discovered that one of the warehouses the gang used was the "scene of operations" for Abe Reles and Harry Maione in the East New York section of Brooklyn. As the hijackings continued, authorities realized than an increased police presence on the streets was not a deterrent. Soon detectives were being assigned to accompany the shipments riding inside the truck cabs with the drivers. At the height of the hijacking epidemic, the cigarette companies took extreme and costly measures to protect their shipments. They began using bulletproof truck-cabs, which could be unlocked only from the inside. The vehicles were also being equipped with sirens and had huge numbers painted on their sides to make them easier for police patrols to spot. With the profits he earned, Adonis moved into a $32,500 home in one of the better neighborhoods in the Bay Ridge section of Brooklyn.

There is evidence that after the murder of Frankie Yale in 1928, Adonis also operated independently, although he was a subordinate of Anthony Carfano. At the same time, Adonis worked hard to present an image of a respectable citizen and businessman. His desire to be viewed as a charitable businessman preceded Frank Costello's by a decade. In the mid-1930s, he served as honorary vice-chairman for the United Appeal during a fundraising effort for the Brownsville Hebrew Schools. Notables listed in the program included New York Governor Herbert H. Lehman and attorney Samuel S. Leibowitz.

Along with his three brothers, he became an active member of the Elks, a benevolent fraternity and social organization. Through his mother, Mary, he earned a reputation as a benefactor to the neighborhood's needy. Funded by her son, Mary Doto distributed baskets of food to the poor, helped them with rent payments, purchased coal during the winter, and on occasion loaned money. Many of the people she assisted were aware the money was coming from her son's bootlegging profits. As a result of Adonis's activity in the Elks, Mary Doto became affectionately known as "Mother Elk."

Reflecting back on Adonis years later, Kings County Sheriff James V. Mangano (no relation to brothers Philip and Vincent Mangano) stated, "I knew Joe Adonis down in the neighborhood. I knew him and his family. . .He has a good reputation in the neighborhood. He has helped a lot of poor people down there. I knew his mother well. She did a lot of charitable work down there. Many a family would have gone without food if it hadn't been for her."[5]

When Mary Doto died in July 1934, the *Brooklyn Eagle* reported, "'Mother Elk,' beloved in the neighborhood of 262 Fourth Avenue for her charities and kindnesses, went to her final resting place this morning in Holy Cross Cemetery, attended by 175 coaches. In 50 of these were piled 400 floral pieces, valued at approximately $35,000."[6] The funeral for the 56-year-old, said to be one of the largest ever witnessed in South Brooklyn, was attended by numerous politicians, public office holders, and members of the legal profession.

Whereas Anthony Carfano enjoyed the notoriety of having everyone know he was the mob boss of Brooklyn, Adonis preferred to stay behind the scenes and build a political power base. Within a few years, many began to question who the real leader was in South Brooklyn. The *New York Post* reported, "Smart policemen and politicians, even when Little Augie [Carfano] was the man best known to the public, believed that Adonis was the real leader of the mobs."[7] By 1934, Carfano had faded into the background and was now focusing his attention on Miami Beach, where he became involved in gambling, nightclubs, and horse racing.

PLUNGE INTO POLITICS

By the early 1930s, Adonis had established a name for himself in the Brooklyn underworld. The success of his restaurant/speakeasy earned him an introduction to many of the borough's top politicians. By 1932, Adonis was ready to try his hand at controlling politics in South Brooklyn by backing his own candidate for office.

Control of the Brooklyn Democratic machine was in the hands of Irishman John H. McCooey, known as "Tammany's Uncle John."[8] In 1931, Jerome G. Ambro, who had served in the State Assembly from the 19th Assembly District, was turned down for redesignation by McCooey. Ambro, who was elected for the first time at the age of 24 in 1922, had recently served as counsel to an alibi witness for Jack "Legs" Diamond during a murder trial. When his actions were rebuked by New York State Attorney General John J. Bennett, McCooey took his name off the slate of candidates. Ambro then sought reelection with the backing of Adonis. Ambro won, but the election was marred by street brawls and violence.

The next year, Ambro challenged Henry Hasenflug, a strong McCooey supporter from the 19th District. Again, with Adonis's support, Ambro won. This election did not see the violence that marked the earlier one. Instead, during the Great Depression, Adonis generously spread money around to the district's poor in the name of Ambro. Clothing was sent to thousands of families and 2,500 Christmas baskets were distributed. The same tactics were used during the elections of 1933 and 1934. Soon, McCooey's longtime support began to crumble. This political rebellion, fueled by Adonis's money, caused dissention in the Democratic organization throughout Kings County. During the mayoral campaign of 1933, Adonis declared, "The Democrats haven't recognized the Italians. There is no reason for the Italians to support anybody but LaGuardia."[9]

The election of LaGuardia had a devastating effect on McCooey. The Roosevelt Administration no longer recognized him as the "patronage dispenser" of federal jobs in Kings County, thus reducing his status to titular head of the county Democratic Party. This political setback was believed to be responsible for McCooey's death on January 21, 1934. Francis J. Quayle, the newly elected Kings County sheriff, selected Ambro as his undersheriff. By early 1934, Quayle became the dispenser of political patronage in the county. Because of Adonis's support of Ambro, the hoodlum was now "in a position of major importance in Brooklyn." He now used his restaurant to play host to district leaders and office holders in the borough.

In the wake of McCooey's passing, a triumvirate of Democratic leaders took over— Frank V. Kelly, Thomas F. Wogan, and Francis Sinnott. Despite a Democrat in the White House, after 12 years of Republican leadership, the Democrats in New York City were in disarray. The party was split into two camps—old line Democrats and the recovery forces of Roosevelt's New Deal. Adonis spearheaded a move in Brooklyn to control the local Democratic Party. In the rear of Joe's Italian Kitchen was a "secret room" for important sit-downs. Frequent visitors to this room included Assemblyman Ambro, former Judge David I. Malbin, Sheriff Quayle, future Sheriff James Mangano, and Patrick J. Diamond, warden of the Raymond Street Jail. From here, Adonis worked behind the scenes in many districts and stayed out of the public eye.

The Eighth Assembly District, however, it was a different story. In 1934, former 8th District Assemblyman Michael J. Reilly felt his rival, Patrick J. Diamond, was getting underworld support in his election bid. Reilly went public with his beliefs:

> Who is Joe Adonis?
>   Anyone interested can find out how important he is by going to his restaurant and seeing who sits at the tables. Perhaps I shall reveal their names before this campaign is over.
>   Now I have something else to tell you. And that is that the sheriff of Kings County, himself a district leader, has seen fit to issue orders for the election of Paddy Diamond, the man backed by Joe Adonis.[10]

Both Diamond and Sheriff Quayle denied the allegations and a bloody primary campaign ensued. On the day before the September primary, Reilly filed charges with Governor Lehman demanding that Quayle be removed as sheriff. In the petition, he accused Quayle of "misconduct in the appointment of men attached to his office at the request and sponsorship of a notorious racketeer."[11] The governor dismissed the petition, claiming the accusations came during the heat of a political campaign. With the backing of Adonis, Diamond won the 8th Assembly District. At the close of primary night, candidates supported by Adonis were successful in five other districts. In addition, Frank Kelly, who had a working relationship with Adonis, became the leader of the Kings County Democratic Party.

During the spring primaries of 1935, Jerome Ambro agreed to manage the campaigns of Samuel S. Leibowitz, who was running for district attorney, and Justice Sylvester Sabatino, who was seeking a county judgeship. These men were not supported by the Kelly organization, but Ambro thought he was just powerful enough to buck the system. Kelly was backing incumbent District Attorney William F. X. Geoghan for reelection, and Adonis was committed to supporting him. Adonis met with Ambro and advised him to back down, but he didn't. On June 11, 1935, Sheriff Quayle called Ambro to his office and relieved him of his duties as undersheriff. Quayle told reporters only that Ambro "is no longer a member of my staff," but the motive for his firing became clearer as Ambro stumped for Leibowitz and Sabatino. In the fall primary, Ambro's candidates were roundly defeated. Joseph P. Marcelle then challenged Ambro for his 8th Assembly seat in the next election. Ambro, abandoned by Adonis and deserted by Kelly's machine, was defeated.[12]

Years later, Ambro was subpoenaed to appear before the Kefauver Committee. The committee members questioned him about a connection between Adonis and William O'Dwyer. Ambro stated that O'Dwyer was one of many political and public officials who frequented Joe's Italian Kitchen. Author Fred J. Cook relates that it was there:

> that [Ambro] agreed to give the budding career of William O'Dwyer its first major boost. They were both dining in the Kitchen one day when O'Dwyer approached Ambro. O'Dwyer had been serving under temporary appointment as a city magistrate, and he asked Ambro to say a word on his behalf to Kenneth Sutherland, one of the top Democratic leaders in Brooklyn and a friend of Adonis. Ambro said the word, O'Dwyer became a full-fledged magistrate, and the career that was to lead to City Hall was launched.[13]

By 1935, Adonis began to tire of the frontline political battles. He felt it was no longer necessary for him to stand on the firing line of the Brooklyn political scene. Adonis had attended dozens of dinners, fund raisers, and rallies. He delivered votes and considerable contributions and was now willing to sit back and "reap the fruits of his labor." The *New York Post* reported:

> He was expanding his semi-legitimate and legitimate enterprises, siphoning the profits of rackets and crime into new channels, and greatly increasing his fortune. In this complicated process of becoming a millionaire, he found obscurity a valuable asset.[14]

Adonis would later say that politics was not his business. In October 1935, he closed Joe's Italian Kitchen. His brother Anthony opened a restaurant and bar at 71 Pineapple Street, which he operated for a couple of years. Although patronized by politicians, it never gained the reputation of his brother's restaurant.

During the mid-to-late 1930s, Adonis began spending more time outside the city. He was believed to be involved in the Plantation, a gambling house in Hollywood, Florida, once billed as the biggest casino in the world. He spent his winters in the South. Although he was gone from New York, it was reported that Louis Capone served as caretaker to his illegal activities.

BACKING THE WRONG HORSE

Adonis had openly boasted of his support of Italian candidate Fiorello LaGuardia for mayor in the fall of 1933. There are some reports that he donated $25,000 to the campaign. If this is true, the investment served him well. One historian pointed out, "During this period . . . while LaGuardia was making Costello in Manhattan a whipping boy, and forcing him to move his slot machines down to Louisiana, he acted as if Adonis in Brooklyn did not exist."[15]

The mayor's crusade against his underworld associates changed Adonis's thinking and in 1937, he backed U.S. Senator Royal S. Copeland for mayor. Shortly after Adonis began his support of Copeland, LaGuardia announced that the city was being threatened by "a tin horn gambler." On the eve of the primary, Adonis was arrested as a suspect in a hijacking and questioned regarding the murders of three local ex-cons who were slain following the holdup of a dice game Adonis was associated with. The arrest kept him from being effective on Election Day and Copeland was easily defeated.

In 1932, Adonis became involved in the Automotive Conveying Company at 285 Palisade Avenue in Cliffside Park, New Jersey. This opportunity came about when T.B. Kramer, one of the partners, got into financial trouble. His quest for financial help brought him to the White Auto Sales Company in Brooklyn, where he spoke to John Kerwin, one of the company officials. After listening to Kramer's story, Kerwin told him he had someone in mind who might be able to help. Adonis met Kramer for lunch and drinks across the street at Joe's Italian Kitchen. Kramer would later testify:

> Adonis agreed to put up whatever money we needed to keep the business going. I gave him 49 per cent of the stock as collateral. If I couldn't hold up my end, I was to turn over the business to Joe, but if it worked out he could either stay in or pull out and I was to pay him off at a regular rate of interest.
>
> No papers or agreements in writing ever were made. It was just a gentleman's agreement.[16]

Kramer stated that Adonis insisted his relative, Paul Bonadio, be brought in to oversee financial matters. Kramer ran the sales end of the business and Bonadio handled the books. Four months after the agreement, Kramer said he decided to leave the company. He was emphatic that Adonis did not force him out.

Shortly after Kramer resigned, the Automotive Conveying Company obtained the exclusive contract to haul Ford Motor Company manufactured automobiles, trucks, and parts from the huge assembly plant at Edgewater, New Jersey, to retail Ford dealerships in Connecticut, Delaware, the District of Columbia, Massachusetts, New Jersey, New York, Pennsylvania, Rhode Island, Vermont, and Virginia. By the late 1930s, assets for the Automotive Conveying Company included 27 Ford trucks, 42 truck tractors, 38 semi-trailers, and a large garage at the corner of Palisade Avenue and Wheeler Street in Cliffside Park. The company employed nearly 100 people and its drivers were members of the Teamsters local of the AFL. Half of the 50 shares of common stock were owned by the Adonis family or relatives—11 each for Joe and his wife Jean, 1 for Paul Bonadio, and 2 for Joseph Bonadio.[17] The Adonis shares were held under the Doto name.

Adonis's White Auto Sales once held a contract with Ford to sell automobiles. The contract was canceled by mutual consent in 1937. In April 1940, after a two-week exposé series on Adonis in the *New York Post,* Mayor LaGuardia made another move against the Brooklyn underworld boss. The man Adonis had once rallied Italian voters for in Brooklyn announced that City Hall was denying White Auto Sales a renewal of its secondhand car dealer's license. His reason was that Adonis owned 60 percent of the company's stock and it was under complete control of the underworld boss, this despite denials from company management.

On April 26, the Motor Vehicle Bureau announced it was holding a hearing to determine if the company's dealer's license would be suspended. The bureau charged that White Auto Sales had failed to obtain a used vehicle (or secondhand) license from the city. It also claimed that false statements were made on its state license application. A question on the application asked if "any member of the partnership or officer of the corporation" was convicted of a crime. This part of the application was left blank by Matthew Bourke, the manager and secretary/treasurer of the company. The police immediately began a 24-hour watch on the property, with an officer present to guard the company's office to prevent any business from being transacted.

On May 1, a hearing was held. Adonis was sent a notice but did not appear. Instead, Matthew Bourke was on hand with company counsel to answer questions. Bourke told the deputy commissioner of motor vehicles that Joseph Doto was the president of the company. He said his license to sell used or secondhand automobiles had expired on January 31, 1940. When asked why Adonis had not filed an application to renew his city license, Bourke said it was because Mayor LaGuardia had already announced that he ordered the License Bureau to refuse the renewal request. Questioned about the falsification on the previous application, he responded that he had no knowledge of Adonis ever being convicted of a crime.

At the end of the hearing, the commissioner suspended the company's dealer's license until it could obtain a secondhand license and have the conviction of Adonis investigated. The next day White Auto Sales showroom was empty except for a desk, filing cabinets, and one clerk.[18] The automobiles had been removed and the parts department cleared out.

FUGITIVE

On May 5, 1940, the New York Police Department issued a 48-state alarm for the arrest of Joe Adonis, charging him with assault, extortion, and kidnapping. The bizarre saga began in the early 1930s with Isidore Wapinsky, described as a "fringe operator on the skirts of the underworld in Williamsburg and other sections of Brooklyn."[19] Adonis was actually involved in two incidents. The first occurred when Wapinsky persuaded Adonis to invest in a parcel of Yonkers real estate under the premise that the city was going to purchase the property to build a school.

The land was located on Van Cortlandt Park Avenue, near Knollwood Drive and Selma Avenue. Had Adonis visited the site he would have seen that the land had little chance of being developed. It was described as "extremely hilly and covered with rock ledges and huge boulders which would have made excavation cost prohibitive."[20] In addition, there was already a school nearby that was adequate for the neighborhood. Nevertheless, on June 15, 1931, Adonis purchased the land in the name of his brother Anthony for $10,000 and assumed a $32,400 mortgage from the previous owner.

The *New York Post* reported, "Not a cent of taxes, interest or amortization was paid on the property after it was bought."[21] When there was no purchase offer coming from Yonkers, Adonis realized he had been duped. In June 1932, he received $3,000 from the sale of two lots, but the city of Yonkers soon foreclosed on the property.

The second incident again involved Wapinsky, who borrowed money from Adonis to finance the sale of a "money-manufacturing" machine. The machine was a scam put together by Wapinsky, which allegedly printed "fairly good facsimiles" of currency on chemically treated banknote paper. An investigation showed that a number of "customers" placed prepaid orders for the scam machine after seeing it demonstrated. The purchasers never received delivery. One of the purchasers was a doctor involved in the abortion racket. The physician was being blackmailed by a number of former patients and paid $900 for the machine in hopes of paying the extortionists with counterfeit notes.

Wapinsky's partner in the scam was Isidore Juffe.[22] In late July 1932, the two men had swindled a man out of $10,000 with their "money manufacturing" machine. They soon paid their partners, including Adonis, their cut of the money. The next day, August 2, 1932, Juffe was called by Samuel Gasberg, an aide, bodyguard, and chauffeur for Adonis, and told that Joey A. wanted to see him. Juffe met Gasberg in Brooklyn and from there was driven to a home in Prospect Park.

Once inside the home, Juffe was jumped and tied to a chair. Gasberg demanded $30,000, which is what he claimed Juffe had received from his latest swindle. A rope was tied around Juffe's head and twisted. Juffe would later testify that while this was going on, Wapinsky was being brutalized in another room and that one of his assailants was Albert Anastasia. Juffe claimed he did not see Adonis, but heard him talking to Gasberg. The two men were allowed to call family members for ransom money. Juffe paid $3,000 to obtain his release. Wapinsky's freedom cost him $1,600. These crimes were not reported to the police. Within 30 days, Wapinsky died from the horrific beating he endured. One account claimed he had been stabbed 20 times with an ice pick. Whatever the case, Wapinsky's death certificate listed the cause of death as angina pectoris, a heart disease.

On April 22, 1940, Special Assistant Attorney General John Harlan Amen, who had been investigating Adonis's activities for a year-and-a-half at the urging or Mayor LaGuardia, presented evidence to an extraordinary grand jury about the incident after Isidore Juffe had come forward with the information. That same day, Adonis disappeared from where he was staying in Miami, while Sam Gasberg disappeared from a home in Stockton, California, where he had been residing for several years. Law enforcement officials believed the two men had been secretly informed about the grand jury testimony.

Amen focused his search on Gasberg, who was at one time alleged to be Adonis's "chief strong arm man." Gasberg had served Adonis in various capacities including as a chauffeur to the mob boss and as a bodyguard for his wife Jean. It was reported that Gasberg had a falling out with Adonis and left Brooklyn sometime in 1935 or 1936. He went to California where soon after he deposited $26,000 in a bank in San Francisco. According to rumor, the money came from a deal in which Gasberg had double-crossed Adonis. Although it was reported he had a wife and children in New York, Gasberg moved to Stockton, California, where he took up with a woman named Anna Bloom, a real-estate agent and hotel owner.

Reports from California stated that sometime in 1939, Gasberg was given a vicious beating after Juffe began working as an informant for Special Prosecutor Amen. The beating was said to be a warning to Gasberg that he was not to discuss his previous dealings with Adonis. Amen believed that if Gasberg were apprehended, he might be persuaded to turn on his former boss. Secret indictments for both men were issued by New York Supreme Court Justice John McCrate on April 27, and arrest warrants were issued. Detectives assigned to Amen's office went to Miami to look for Adonis. Once there, one of them quickly left for Stockton.

Together with a West Coast officer, the two did some nifty police work. The *New York Post* reported:

> Gasberg was so badly in need of money that he tried to borrow $20 from an underworld friend and then had offered a Lincoln automobile for sale.
>
> They began watching Miss Bloom's bank account and in a few days a check for $90 came in, made out by Miss Bloom to "Sam Glick." Handwriting experts decided that the endorsement was Gasberg's. The check had been presented at a Los Angeles bank and the detectives found that next door to the bank, at 5509 Wilshire Blvd., a niece of Miss Bloom, Sadie Glick, was living.
>
> "A watch was established at the house and at 10 PM Saturday Gasberg drove up. He was arrested as he stepped out of his car.[23]

After Gasberg's May 4 arrest, the indictments were made public. Both men were charged with kidnapping, extortion, and assault. If it could be proved that Wapinsky died from injuries caused while he was being held, a charge of murder could be added. As the manhunt for Adonis intensified, police prepared 2,000 photographs and 20,000 wanted circulars. Although the FBI claimed it had no interest in Adonis, it stated that if he crossed state lines as a fugitive, he would be subject to arrest by Bureau agents.

On May 7, it was revealed that:

> From a source close to Amen, it was learned that he planned to use the same tactics employed by United States Attorney [John T.] Cahill during his hunt for Louis (Lepke) Buchalter [ten months earlier]. Cahill called all known acquaintances of Lepke before the Federal grand Jury to quiz them about his whereabouts. Amen is considering subpoenaing every politician and racketeer, big and small, who had the slightest contact with Adonis. He hopes that by embarrassing them with summonses, he will make them send out word for Adonis to give himself up.[24]

The next day, Adonis, through a deal set up by his attorney Louis Castellano, surrendered to Amen at his Borough Hall headquarters in Brooklyn. It was reported that "Adonis' decision to come forward and plead to the indictment was the threat attributed to the Amen investigation that, unless he appeared, subpoenas would be issued far and wide for politicians to determine if they knew his whereabouts."[25]

After being informed that Adonis was going to surrender that morning, Amen was meeting with new Brooklyn District Attorney William O'Dwyer to discuss what information they could share on the crime lord. After Adonis appeared, Amen issued the following statement:

> Joseph Doto, alias Joe Adonis, was surrendered by his attorney, Louis J. Castellano, of 32 Court Street, Brooklyn, at the office of Assistant Attorney general John Harlan Amen at 11:15 AM today and is now in custody. He will be arraigned in the course of the afternoon.[26]

Notified of the surrender of Adonis, Mayor LaGuardia stated, "I really believe this is the first breaking up of what I have always referred to as 'one happy family' in Brooklyn. I am sure it is going to have a wholesome effect."[27]

Attorney Castellano, a friend of Adonis since childhood, told reporters that his client arrived at his office earlier that morning and after a long discussion decided he would surrender.

He then called Amen's office to arrange the surrender and make sure his client would be taken "without molestation." The lawyer refused to give any clue as to where Adonis had been since April 22.

From Amen's office, Adonis was taken to the Poplar Street Police station and booked. He was then driven to Manhattan police headquarters where he was photographed and finger-printed. Police took him out a back entrance and returned him to Brooklyn for arraignment. At the courthouse, "Crowds stood in the corridor of the Supreme Court Building to watch Adonis taken into the courtroom, which was already filled to capacity before he walked in. Flashlight bulbs flared and people whispered, 'It's Adonis!' as he walked by."[28]

The day's biggest surprise was yet to come. At the arraignment, Amen revealed the existence of a second indictment involving another kidnapping, that of Isidore Juffe. The *New York Times* reported:

> Mr. Amen explained that both kidnappings occurred at the same time and were related to the same set of facts. He said that Wapinsky and Juffe had acted together in interesting Adonis in several shady ventures and that Adonis became angered when he felt that he was not receiving the proceeds to which his financial investment was entitled, and that he subsequently arranged the dual kidnapping.[29]

During the arraignment, Adonis pleaded not guilty to the two indictments. Amen asked for a $100,000 bail, stating Adonis had not been in the jurisdiction for a number of years. Castellano disputed this claim, saying Adonis had continuously resided in the state. Judge McCrate gave Castellano the opportunity to obtain a lower bail in exchange for revealing where Adonis was during the search for him. Castellano remained silent so McCrate set bail at $75,000, and remanded Adonis to the Brooklyn City Prison, also known as the Raymond Street Jail.

> "When this is all over I'm going to give you fellows a story. I'm going to write it myself. It will be the story of my life. I think it ought to sell for at least a quarter a copy."
> —Joe Adonis, addressing reporters after his arraignment on kidnapping charges on May 9, 1940
> (*Brooklyn Eagle*, May 10, 1940)

Despite the overcrowded conditions at the jail, Adonis was placed in a cell by himself, with the cells on either side left vacant. His lawyer fought to reduce the bail. It was believed that Adonis wanted his bail lowered and chose to go to jail so as not to arouse the suspicions of the IRS by suddenly coming up with $75,000. Meanwhile, in Los Angeles where Gasberg was being held on a $100,000 bail, Adonis's former lieutenant was fighting extradition.

On May 20, Judge McCrate cut Adonis's bail to $50,000. Castellano contacted the Continental Surety Company to arrange the bail, but the company withdrew. Then, two individuals were called on to post the money but were found to be "blacklisted." Finally, after 15 days in the Raymond Street Jail, a cash bail of $32,000 was posted by Jean Adonis and a family friend; the balance was covered by the Doto home and a home of the friend.

At 5:30 PM on May 25, Adonis left the courtroom a free man. He was followed by a crowd of reporters as he moved down the street, who asked for a comment. "Why say anything with the war on?" he responded. "You can't get it in anyhow. If Mr. Amen gave me the OK, I'd say something."[30]

Samuel Gasberg was brought back from Los Angeles and arraigned on May 29. His legal counsel, Joseph Healy, entered a not guilty plea for him. Gasberg was given the reduced bail of $50,000 that Adonis had received. After Healy advised Judge McCrate that his client could only raise $20,000, Gasberg was carted off to the Raymond Street Jail.

Amen filed superseding indictments against Adonis and Gasberg on July 2. This time the indictment charged that both men "were living outside the State under false names on occasions between August 1, 1932, and April 27, 1940." This wording would help prevent the men from claiming the statute of limitations had expired on the charges.

On July 22, counsel for Adonis and Gasberg filed a motion for the dismissal of the indictments. The lawyers claimed that Amen's directive for his inquiry was to look solely into official corruption in Brooklyn, which this case had nothing to do with. After reviewing the minutes of the secret grand jury, Judge McCrate denied the motion on August 29.

Counsel for Adonis asked for and received permission for separate trials. In late October, the trial for Gasberg began in Brooklyn Supreme Court before Judge McCrate. Isidore Juffe was the state's key witness. He took the stand on October 24. When asked why it took eight years to come forward, Juffe replied: "I would have been bumped off." Juffe told a fantastic tale of scams and kangaroo courts to a mystified jury.

On October 30, after 11 hours of deliberations, which continued overnight, the jury rendered a verdict at 7:30 AM. They found Gasberg not guilty of kidnapping Juffe, but were deadlocked on the charges of assault and extorting $4,600 from him and Wapinsky. McCrate sent Gasberg back to jail on the unresolved charges. Gasberg's second trial, for extortion (the assault charge having been dismissed), began four months later, with Juffe again the prosecution's key witness. On February 18, 1941, Gasberg was acquitted of the extortion charge. In summing up the case, Judge McCrate cited Juffe's past as a reason for the verdict. He declared, "It is almost impossible for any prosecuting official, no matter how honest he is, to get a conviction where he has to deal with a type like Juffe."[31]

The charges against Adonis were dismissed after the failure to get a conviction against Gasberg, but the damage to Adonis had been done. The exposure he received through the media was overwhelming and would lead to his decision to abandon Brooklyn for New Jersey.

MOVING ON IN THE 1940s

By the mid-1940s, Adonis had tired of Brooklyn. He had been spending his winters in Florida and most of his business—legal and illegal—was being conducted across the Hudson River in New Jersey. In 1944, he decided to move his family across the river to Fort Lee, New Jersey. The family took up residence in a new home valued at $100,000.

In his new residence, Adonis was not far from Duke's Restaurant, a place he had been using as early as 1941 to conduct underworld business.[32] Located in Cliffside Park, across the street from the Palisades Amusement Park, the eatery was described as "the nerve center of organized crime in the Metropolitan area." The place was away from New York City, where Mayor LaGuardia and Special Prosecutor Thomas E. Dewey had been putting tremendous pressure on the underworld element since the mid-1930s.

This is not to say that New York City Prosecutor Frank S. Hogan turned his back on the hoodlums once they crossed the river and were out of the city. A special watch was set up in a number of places in New Jersey. New York City detectives keeping an eye on Duke's were surprised at the "clockwork regularity" in which the subjects of their surveillance showed up at the restaurant. Those frequently seen there were Adonis, Vincent Alo, Albert Anastasia, Jerry Catena, Thomas Eboli, Thomas Lucchese, Anthony "Tony Bender" Strollo, and Salvatore and Willie Moretti.

Whereas most of these hoodlums, including Costello, showed up on Tuesdays for what seemed to be a scheduled weekly meeting, Adonis and the Morettis used Duke's as their headquarters. The restaurant, in addition to serving excellent food that drew a local crowd, had two rooms that the mobsters used for their private meetings. Duke's remained the principal meeting place for the New York/New Jersey mobsters until 1947.[33]

During the late 1930s and early 1940s, the Adonis gambling empire continued to grow. In the New York/New Jersey area, Adonis, Costello, and Frank Erickson had built a formidable axis. According to Costello biographer George Walsh:

> In 1942, Adonis was a principal partner with the prime minister in Piping Rock Casino in Saratoga, New York, a posh gambling establishment that had been operating illegally for almost a decade. Inside the casino, where Saratoga police were forbidden by their superiors to enter, Joey A—as he was known—would sit at a private table, watching the croupiers, dealers and dicemen. With his low voice, gentlemanly manner, and conservative tailoring, he might have been a banker.[34]

In March 1945, Adonis, Frank Costello, and Frank Erickson were named in a college basketball gambling inquiry after five Brooklyn College teammates admitted to accepting $1,000 to throw a game in Boston. New York Police Commissioner Lewis J. Valentine called the three "leading figures in the gambling ring" in the city. As the probe widened, police were unable to locate several of the key witnesses they wanted to speak to; among them were Adonis, Erickson, and James Rutkin, an associate of Abner Zwillman.

During a hearing before Kings County Judge Samuel S. Leibowitz, Valentine testified that Madison Square Garden acting president, Ned S. Irish, had told him that gambling was rampant during all athletic events at the sports Mecca. He also stated that Irish had provided him with a list of gamblers who frequented the Garden, conducting business in the lobby and in the aisles during basketball and hockey games, as well as boxing matches. Valentine said Irish had repeatedly told him he was afraid that a scandal would break out over conditions at the arena. When Irish had testified earlier, however, he claimed he knew of no real gambling at the Garden and that the list of alleged gamblers had been prepared by an employee, not him. During his testimony, Valentine admitted he had no information that linked Adonis, Costello, or Erickson to gambling activities at the Garden.

During the 1930s and 1940s, it was common practice in New York for candidates to claim that their opponents were backed by underworld figures, or people with links to underworld figures. The fall of 1945 was no exception. William O'Dwyer was swept into office, even though he was "specifically linked" to Frank Costello, Irving Sherman, and Joe Adonis. Judge Jonah J. Goldstein, who opposed O'Dwyer in that election, told listeners the following over radio station WABC on the night of October 17:

> Another one of the key underworld figures who supports O'Dwyer's candidacy is Joe Adonis. He is the underworld ruler of Brooklyn and its real behind-the-scenes political

power. Don't take my word for this statement. Ask anyone who knows anything about the political background of Brooklyn who the real power is in the borough. They will answer, "Joe Adonis."

Adonis' power is so strong that he was able to tell the Brooklyn Democratic leadership that they had to nominate O'Dwyer, even though the decent Democratic leadership did not want O'Dwyer as their nominee. Adonis also told the leaders some other things and when he tells certain people things, they do what he suggests or else. Adonis said it was to be O'Dwyer, just as Costello and Sherman had said it was to be O'Dwyer.

This trio—Costello, Sherman and Adonis—are part of the upper crust of the underworld. Joe Adonis, the invisible ruler of Brooklyn, is more commonly referred to by his henchman in hushed tones as "Joey A."

Now, Mr. O'Dwyer, I ask you some specific questions about Joe Adonis, alias "Joey A."

Do you personally know Joe Adonis?

Is it not a fact that Joe Adonis is supporting your campaign and furnishing financial aid in cash?

When were you last in the company of Joe Adonis?

Were either Frank Costello or Irving Sherman, or both of them in your company at the same time with Joe Adonis?

Remember, Mr. O'Dwyer, the citizens of New York expect specific answers. No reply from your managers or paid publicity man will be accepted.[35]

Ten days later, Goldstein told another audience that Adonis was running Brooklyn "by remote control from Bergen County, New Jersey," where he operated one of the biggest gambling houses in the county. On October 29, Goldstein was invited to appear before a Bergen County grand jury that was investigating gambling in the area. The mayoral candidate was challenged by Bergen County Prosecutor Walter G. Winne, who asked Goldstein to appear himself or send some representatives "to give evidence to the grand jury of the truth of your remarks."

Apparently annoyed by the challenge, Goldstein replied that his appearance would serve "no useful purpose." He declared, "Those charged with law enforcement in your county know or should know that Joe Adonis, who lives in your county, operated a gambling establishment there. Transportation was even provided to the 'establishment' for those living in New York. I am informed that Joe Adonis is now operating a gambling establishment in a near-by county."[36]

Four years later, during the mayoral election of 1949, it was Republican candidate Edward Corsi leveling accusations. He claimed that Ferdinand Pecora, the Democratic-Liberal candidate, was backed by Adonis, Costello, and Vito Genovese.

KEFAUVER COMMITTEE

In 1950, before the Kefauver Committee began its 14-city tour, Adonis was subpoenaed to appear before another Senate subcommittee. On April 25, the Senate Interstate & Foreign Commerce subcommittee issued subpoenas to Adonis and Frank Erickson for questioning as to how bookmaking and track information were disseminated to bookmakers. The chairman of the subcommittee, Arizona Senator Ernest W. McFarland, said his group would conduct an investigation into the activities of Adonis and Erickson. At the time their subpoenas were issued, Adonis was visiting Hot Springs, Arkansas, where a physician declared he was too ill to travel to Washington, D.C. to testify.

On May 2, New York District Attorney Frank Hogan's men conducted a raid at the Park Avenue office of Frank Erickson. Among other things, they found documents regarding the partnership of the Colonial Inn in Hallendale, Florida. In addition to Adonis, the documents listed Meyer and Jake Lansky, Vincent Alo, and two Detroit mobsters as shareholders of the gambling den.[37] The records, exposed during a seizure hearing before a general sessions judge on May 17, showed that between November 1945 and October 1946, Adonis received a 5 percent share of the profits totaling $34,276 and an unexplained "charities share" for $2,038. Before May was over, Hogan obtained a show cause order from the Bergen County Superior Court in Hackensack for banks in Fort Lee and Edgewater, New Jersey, to produce the account information of Joseph A. Doto, Sr., Joseph A. Doto, Jr., and Jean Doto.

By this time, the Kefauver Committee had already conducted its first public hearings in Miami, Florida. Committee members were anxious to aid Hogan with information they had gathered about the Colonial Inn and another gambling establishment called the Green Acres. As the Kefauver Hearings moved on throughout the summer of 1950, Adonis dodged being served with a subpoena.

Adonis, however, could not dodge what was happening in Bergen County. Embarrassed over the revelations of District Attorney Hogan in New York City about gamblers operating freely in the Garden State, New Jersey officials called on Nelson F. Stamler, a member of the attorney general's staff, to "clean out" the state. He launched his war against the gamblers, telling the media, "I've been told to clean up this mess and pull no punches." Stamler, as special deputy attorney general, conducted hundreds of raids in northeastern counties of the state, resulting in the indictments of more than 100 people.

On Halloween Eve 1950, Nelson F. Stamler announced the arrest warrants for five local gamblers—Adonis, Salvatore Moretti, James P. "Pinkie" Lynch, Arthur Longano, and Anthony Guarini. When police went to make the arrests, four of the men couldn't be located at their homes. The fifth one, Guarini, was serving a sentence on a bookmaking conviction in the New Jersey State Prison at Trenton. The next day, Adonis and Moretti appeared in Superior Court in Hackensack to surrender to Judge J. Wallace Leyden. With John E. Selser, a former Bergen County prosecutor representing them, the men waived the reading of the complaint and pleaded not guilty. Stamler asked the judge to set bail at $25,000, "because these men have all too successfully dodged subpoenas in the past and I want them within easy reach for this investigation." Judge Leyden set bail at $15,000.

With the surrender of Adonis in Hackensack, Kefauver Committee investigators revealed they had been trying to locate the gambler to serve him with a subpoena. The chief investigator for the committee announced that he was confident that agents would make contact with Adonis to question him. When Adonis and Salvatore Moretti were called by Stamler on November 13 to appear at the Supreme Court in Hackensack, however, they were no shows. Instead, attorney Selser appeared alone and stated that his clients bail terms did not require them to honor any requests of the deputy attorney general.

On November 27, after being arraigned in New York City on a two-count criminal information, Adonis and Moretti were finally handed subpoenas by a Kefauver Committee representative. The call to testify before the committee came on December 6. The committee announced that a portion of its latest hearings would cover gambling and racketeering in northern New Jersey. In announcing Adonis's appearance, Kefauver stated that the gambler had a long association with members of the underworld that "involves some of the top names in the American calendar of crime," and that although he had a long record of arrests, he "has never been sentenced to a prison term."[38] The hearings, to be held in Washington D.C., were scheduled to last two days. Before heading to the nation's capital, Adonis had to obtain permission from Judge Leyden to leave the state while under bail.

On December 12, Adonis sat before the Kefauver Committee to answer the questions put to him by Chief Counsel Rudolph Halley. Before being questioned, Adonis announced to the committee that he would refuse to answer most of the committee's questions on the legal ground that the answers might incriminate him. He stated he had criminal charges pending against him in both New Jersey and New York, and that his income tax returns were being reviewed by the IRS. Adonis said he doubted a statement in the subpoena that the Senate committee wanted his testimony to help formulate legislation in interstate crime. He claimed the committee hoped to use his testimony for the purpose of trapping him into "admissions" that prosecutors could later use against him. Adonis said, "For these reasons, I respectfully claim the right not to aid the Government directly or indirectly in prosecuting me."[39]

Adonis explained to the committee that the statement he made had been written by him with help from his legal counsel, Harold H. Corbin. The attorney, unlike other counsel who sat beside their clients, was seated in the back of the courtroom. Kefauver invited him to sit with his client. Corbin responded, "I have no objection to coming up, but I think he is able to take care of himself."[40]

When the questioning began, Adonis admitted to using a number of aliases during what he termed were "minor conflicts" with the law. Among these aliases were Joe and James Arosa and Joe DeMio. Adonis said he was born in Brooklyn and lived there until 1944. He then moved to New Jersey, explaining to the committee that he liked the climate better because his residence there was 300 feet above sea level. From this point on his testimony was "a matter of tedious repetition." The *New York Times* wrote:

> "I decline to answer on the grounds that it might tend to incriminate me," the witness would reply.
>
> "You are directed to answer," Senator Kefauver would say, to complete the record.
>
> "I decline to answer on the grounds that it might tend to incriminate me," Adonis would Intone again.
>
> At one point, Mr. Halley asked him if he was afraid to answer the committee's questions, and the witness lost his temper for the only time during his appearance.
>
> "I am not afraid of anything," he shouted back, glaring at the committee with its lawyers and investigators.[41]

After this exchange, Halley read into the record a letter from Ford Motor Company Vice President John S. Bugas, after Adonis refused to answer any questions about his legitimate business activities. The letter stated that the automobile company was in the process of trying to contract with another carrier, but that Adonis was willing "to sell out his interest" in order to prevent this.[42]

During the course of questioning, Adonis refused to answer questions about "bookmaking, slot machines, numbers racket, narcotics or organized prostitution and if he had ever made payments to any law enforcement officials."[43] He also refused to discuss any ownership participation in the Piping Rock Casino or the Arrowhead Inn in Saratoga Springs, New York, as well as the Colonial Inn, Club Boheme, and Green Acres Club in southern Florida.

As with all witnesses, he was asked a litany of names and his relationship with them. Adonis pled the Fifth Amendment on most, but acknowledged knowing Lucky Luciano for 20 years. He claimed he had not seen him in the past two years. When asked if he had seen Luciano in Havana, Adonis refused to answer.

Another person he refused to acknowledge was Virginia Hill. Adonis reportedly met Hill while she lived briefly in New York City. The two were rumored to be lovers during her short time there. When she went to Hollywood to study acting, Adonis allegedly made frequent trips to visit her. While in Los Angeles, she quickly gave up her acting ambitions and became a party girl and attracted the attention of Benjamin Siegel. Hill soon became his paramour. It has been reported that Adonis and Siegel became bitter enemies over Hill. These stories carried over into the movies as witnessed in the 1991 movie *Bugsy,* where Warren Beatty's Benjamin Siegel character delivers a vicious beating to Adonis while the two were aboard the *Laura Keene* for Luciano's farewell party. The truth of the matter is, with Adonis's low key extramarital relationships, he was probably glad to have such a high-profile mistress as Virginia Hill out of his well-coiffed hair.

At one point during the questioning, Halley inquired about the Mafia. Adonis answered, "He had seen the name in the newspapers, that he knew many Sicilians, but none of them had ever told him they belonged to it, and that 'I don't believe there's any such thing.'"[44] His response was the same when asked about the *Unione Siciliana.*

It was clear to Halley and the senators that attorney Corbin was right about Adonis's ability to take care of himself. The *New York Times* concluded:

> After extracting nothing from Adonis in an hour and a half of questioning, the committee members agreed with the attorney's judgment. Adonis was a cool, collected and well prepared witness.[45]

At the end of Adonis's testimony, Senator Kefauver informed him that the committee would probably recommend that he be cited for contempt of the Senate.[46] In late 1951, *Crime in America* by Estes Kefauver was published, which covered the committee hearings from May 1950 to May 1951. In the book, the Tennessee senator offered the following comments about the committee's questioning of Adonis:

> As for Joe Adonis . . . the committee found him one of the toughest, most determinedly contemptuous, and in some way the most sinister of all the racketeers we questioned.
>
> To me, Adonis—that very name which he adopted for himself symbolizes his ego—was the evil personification of modern criminality. This man with bloodstained hands for years has set himself up as bigger than the law and unfortunately was able to get away with it. . .
>
> Joe Adonis is slick, smooth; an expensively tailored figure with iron-gray hair pomaded into a Hollywood-style hair-do. His eyes are little and weak, and all during the hearing "Adonis," too vain apparently to wear glasses before the public, squinted at us—enmity and contempt plainly showing in his glance—as we questioned him.[47]

Meanwhile, on January 5, 1951, the Kefauver Committee voted to recommend to the Senate that Adonis be cited. Kefauver presented a resolution on January 22 to cite Adonis for his refusal to answer the committee's questions. The crusading senator received an unexpected delay in the vote when Nevada Senator Pat McCarran requested that the resolution go before the Senate Judiciary Committee, of which he was chairman, "for a week's study."

> "When we were through questioning Joseph Doto-Adonis there was no doubt in the minds of the committee members that this gangster had achieved pre-eminence in all three fields that have become an unholy trinity in areas of the United States—crime, politics and business."
>
> —Senator Estes Kefauver (Kefauver, *Crime in America*, 1951, p. 293)

An angry Kefauver declared that if the Senate didn't back the committee's resolution, it would be "manifestly impossible" to carry on its work. The next day, McCarran addressed the Senate in support of his stand. The senator was looking specifically at the case of Adonis, who had pleaded his Fifth Amendment privileges. McCarran pointed out that just a month earlier, the United States Supreme Court upheld the rights of a witness to refuse to answer questions under the rights furnished by the amendment. "A grave legal question is involved," he stated. McCarran felt his judiciary committee was the place that the matter should be studied and an action recommended to the Senate.

Kefauver addressed the Senate. He informed the members that the committee was hoping to finish its work in the next four weeks with important hearings to be held in New York City. He pointed out that reluctant witnesses would be encouraged not to answer questions because of the delay.

Committee member Charles W. Tobey was a little more colorful in his plea to the Senate to move ahead with the citations. He had seen firsthand the contemptuous attitude of some of the witnesses. Claiming that delaying the vote citing these individuals would be tantamount to "giving aid and comfort to public enemies," the New Hampshire senator urged members to "stand up and be counted," to "show this scum of the earth" they cannot trifle with the United States Senate.[48]

The Senate voted 59 to 12 not to send the citation resolution to McCarran's Judiciary Committee. From there, it took only voice votes to issue eight contempt of Senate citations. In addition to Adonis and fellow Bergen County defendants—Moretti, Longano, and Lynch—the Senate cited Anthony J. Accardo of Chicago and Jack Dragna of Los Angeles. If convicted of the contempt charges, Adonis would be looking at a $1,000 fine, one year in prison, or both, for each of the 16 counts in the contempt citation. At the moment, however, Adonis was facing more daunting charges back in New Jersey.

BERGEN COUNTY GAMBLING

The combined efforts of New Jersey/New York law enforcement to tumble Joe Adonis began in earnest during the fall of 1950. After the November 27 arraignment in New York Special Sessions court, officials from both states waited patiently while Adonis took his turn with the Kefauver Committee. Now they would press their case against a gambling "empire" they said was controlled by Adonis and his henchmen, which they described as "the biggest of its kind east of the Mississippi."[49]

Frank Hogan was willing to hand over the initial prosecution to New Jersey because their state laws provided for a greater criminal penalty. Adonis, if convicted, could face a term of five or more years in prison on each count. In New York, he could only be convicted of misdemeanor charges. Although yet to be indicted in either jurisdiction, Adonis was free on a $15,000 bail in New Jersey and a $20,000 bail in New York.

Hogan's criminal information counts claimed that the five men "conspired to violate the New York State Penal Law between April 1947 and February 1950 in that they 'persuaded' others to gamble."[50] In 1947, the gamblers contracted with Chatham Cadillac Rental Service LTD to dispatch chauffeur-driven limousines to pick up gamblers at their homes, places of business, and night spots and transport them to New Jersey. The *New York Times* described the operation as follows:

> On reaching his destination, a bettor was ushered into a luxuriously appointed dining room, which was a feature of the so-called "carpet" gambling house that catered to both men and women. However, Mr. Hogan said, before entering the dining room, where the finest of food and choice liquors were available free of charge, the bettor was "politely frisked."
>
> Adjoining the dining room, supervised by a veteran maitre d'hotel, was the gaming room, in which seventy to eighty persons on weekdays and as many as 150 on Saturday nights crowded about two dice tables, a roulette wheel and a chemin-de-fer game.[51]

The "carpet" gambling house Hogan was describing was a place in Lodi, New Jersey,[52] known locally as "Costa's Barn" or simply "the Barn," on Route 6 in that borough. A two-story cinderblock building, it was said to be "one of the largest gambling games in the East." George Walsh provides the following description of the gambling den:

> Costa's Barn, the name given a Quonset hut located behind a gas station in the rural atmosphere of Lodi, New Jersey, was typical of the gambling dens. From the outside, it appeared drab and nondescript. But inside, Costa's was a lavish nightspot: the waitresses and cigarette girls were enticing, the dining room offered fine food and wines on the house, the games were run by suave croupiers and dealers. Once Adonis felt the pressure from the Hogan investigation, he quickly converted Costa's to a "sawdust" operation—presumably to give himself more flexibility in shutting it down in case of a raid. A snack bar replaced the dining room, the gambling was largely restricted to dice tables. No matter. Fleets of Cadillacs continued to ferry countless New Yorkers to and from Lodi all night long.[53]

On January 23, 1951, the same day Adonis was cited by the U.S. Senate for contempt, a Bergen County grand jury indicted seven people for gambling. Adonis, Moretti, Longano, Lynch, and Guarini were charged with operating three gambling houses between January 1949 and January 1950. In addition, the county also indicted Giovanni Garrantano, alias John Hayes, a former Lodi police officer, and Leonard Costa, owner of the gambling barn, who was a fugitive hiding in Florida. The houses were known as The Studio, 1010 Palisade Avenue, Fort Lee; Costa's Barn, on Route 6, Lodi; and Haye's Garage, 224 Union Street, Lodi.[54]

Three day later Adonis, Moretti, Longano, and Lynch were arraigned before Judge Leyden. They pleaded not guilty to the charges contained in the 15 indictments. The trial was scheduled to begin on Monday, May 21. On the Friday before, New York General Sessions Judge Harold A. Stevens issued an order on 12 "substantial business and professional men" in New York City to show cause as to why they should not appear as prosecution witnesses and testify against Adonis.

Court convened at 10:00 AM Monday morning in Hackensack to a sparse crowd of mainly newspaper reporters and photographers. Although there seemed to be a national interest in the trial, the citizens of Hackensack did not share the same curiosity, and there were few spectators. Instead, a panel of 125 potential jurors waited to be questioned. For the first 90 minutes, attorney John Selser traveled back and forth between the clerk's room, where his clients waited, and an ante-room, where New Jersey Attorney General Theodore D. Parsons and Nelson Stamler conferred. At 11:30, all parties entered the courtroom with Judge Leyden.

In a surprise move, Selser announced that he was entering a plea of *non vult* (no contest) for the five defendants.[55] A stunned Stamler asked defense counsel for an explanation. Judge Leyden stated, "I cannot see the difference between a plea of non vult and guilty."

"It is the same thing," Selser responded. "The offer has resulted after tremendous negotiation. Two of the defendants say they were not the principals, but that they are willing to throw themselves at the mercy of the court. That is the reason for the plea of non vult instead of guilty."[56]

Following Selser's explanation, Judge Leyden told the prosecutors that with the *non vult* plea, Adonis and the others avoided civil suits because they did not plead to criminal guilt. Parsons nodded his agreement as acceptance of the plea. While the newspapers heralded the conviction and, pending prison sentence, claimed it was a victory that the New York authorities had not achieved in 25 years, one has to wonder how much influence the never-identified "substantial business and professional men" had in forcing the defendant's decision. Just minutes after the *non vult* plea was made, General Sessions Judge Stevens vacated the show-cause order issued to the 12 men.

On May 28, Adonis and his four co-defendants faced Judge Leyden for sentencing in Bergen County Superior Court. Attorney Selser spoke first, asking clemency for Adonis and Moretti, denying the two men had any interest in the gambling rooms, and that the other three defendants were the actual operators.

Selser then claimed, "There never was a persecution like that which has appeared in the newspapers about Adonis. I think it is a vicious, rotten persecution that is not justified by fact. He pleaded guilty because he knows the country has to have its pound of flesh."[57] In declaring the innocence of Adonis and Moretti, Selser characterized the men as "the white lilies in the field."

Attorney General Parsons did not quite see this virtue in any of the defendants. Although the maximum sentences could have come to 18 years, Parsons recommended terms of just 18 months. By now, Adonis and the others had been on their feet for a half-hour listening to their attorney's plea and the recommendation of Parsons. Judge Leyden then ignored the attorney general's recommendation, as well a 1940 amendment to New Jersey's penal code, which he personally considered unconstitutional, and handed down stiffer sentences in the sentencing decree:

> Judge J. Wallace Leyden fixed concurrent two-to-three-year terms for conspiracy and on two counts for operating two floating dice games in Lodi. He imposed a four-to-five-year sentence for operating the Fort Lee game, suspended sentence and directed that the five were to be on five years' probation for this count at the expiration of their jail terms. He ordered them to pay a $5,000 fine for each dice room conviction.[58]

Adonis's face turned red as the sentence was read. It was apparent that a two-to-three-year stretch and a $15,000 fine was not what he was expecting. When Selser questioned whether Adonis could apply for parole after 10 months, Parsons reminded him that this option was not available to a prisoner with a previous conviction. He would have to serve a full two years before he would be considered for parole. After the sentences were announced, the five men were handcuffed to one another and led across the street to the county jail. As Adonis passed a group of photographers, he uttered a simple, "So long."

The next day, Adonis arrived at the New Jersey State Prison in Trenton. Warden William H. McCarty told inquiring reporters, "They are not big names to us here. They are just another number to us, and they start from scratch." Each man was given a physical and a prison haircut, and then assigned to quarantine for 15 days. After the quarantine the men would be under observation for three months "to determine their aptitudes" for prison jobs.[59]

PRISON TIME

Adonis's time in prison was marked by numerous trials and courtroom appearances. Since the conviction of the five men, authorities had been able to find and arraign Leonard Costa, the alleged operator of Costa's Barn in Lodi. When his case came to trial in November 1951, all five prisoners were brought back to Hackensack to testify. In describing the courtroom session, the *New York Times* reported:

> Profound loss of memory afflicted a majority of the state's fifteen witnesses headed by Joe Adonis when they were called here today to tell what they knew about gambling in Costa's Barn on Route 6 near Lodi between January and March 1949.
>
> The witnesses had two things in common. First they all swore to tell "the truth, the whole truth and nothing but the truth." Second they could just not remember back to the first quarter of 1949.[60]

Typical of the testimony was an answer given by Salvatore Moretti, whose brother Willie was murdered in a Cliffside Park restaurant less than six weeks earlier. When asked if he pleaded no contest to a gambling indictment involving Costa's Barn, he responded, "I don't know. I pleaded guilty to a number of indictments. What they were pertaining to and what they were not pertaining to I cannot truthfully say, because I do not know." After a three-day trial, at which Costa was represented by John Selser, the jury deliberated an hour and 20 minutes before coming back with a guilty verdict.[61]

On January 14, 1952, Adonis's counsel asked the New Jersey State Supreme Court to relieve him of his $15,000 fine and five-year probation term, claiming them to be unconstitutional under the 1940 change in state laws. Two months later, while this motion was still under review, Adonis's name was on a list of state prisoners for parole consideration. Parole, however, was denied.

Meanwhile, Adonis and Moretti were called to testify at the misconduct-in-office trial of Michael Orecchio, the former chief of detectives for Bergen County. Orecchio was charged with laxity in investigating gambling complaints. One of the early witnesses in the trial, held in March 1952, was Adonis attorney John Selser. As the former first assistant prosecutor of Bergen County in the late 1940s, Selser had personally investigated Costa's Barn and the Aristocrat Baby Carriage Factory, where dice games were held. The results of his investigation were relayed to Orecchio and Bergen County Prosecutor Walter G. Winne.

On March 18, Winne was called to the stand. Winne, who was also under indictment for laxity in office, was superseded in office in December 1950, when the massive gambling investigation was in full swing. During Winne's testimony, prosecutors showed a letter to him from New York City Police Department's Chief Inspector Martin J. Browne. The note, dated December 10, 1947, stated that Adonis, Frank Costello, and the Moretti brothers were operating dice games in Bergen County. The letter also listed the operations at Aristocrat Baby Carriage Factory, the Automotive Conveying Company, and the Club Bali. Winne denied any knowledge of the letter.

The Orecchio trial dragged on for five weeks during which a succession of minor witnesses were called who gave testimony of a technical nature. Both jurors and spectators had trouble focusing on the trial. That all changed at 12:40 PM on April 8 when Adonis was called to the stand. Unlike his testimony during the trial of Leonard Costa five months earlier, Adonis was more open with his answers. He admitted to having been involved in the gambling operations in Bergen County between 1947 and 1950, and that he was acquainted with both Costello and Erickson. He stopped, however, at discussing his earnings from gambling, claiming that anything he said might cause him trouble with the IRS.

When the questioning got around to Orecchio, Adonis claimed that he had never been contacted by the Bergen County Prosecutor's office, that he had never paid protection money to Orecchio, and that he had never even spoken to him. During his 50-minute appearance, Adonis talked about being a partner in floating crap games in Lodi and Fort Lee. He also explained one of the differences between "sawdust" and "carpet" joints. Adonis stated that the "carpet" joints (also known as "rug" joints) were patronized by both men and women, but the "sawdust" joints catered only to men.

The time Adonis had spent in jail had noticeably changed him. The *New York Times* reported, Adonis "looked like a chastened man. He spoke quietly, looked tired and his complexion was sallow. There were bags under his eyes and his face twitched frequently."[62]

On April 30, after the longest criminal trial to date of a single defendant in New Jersey history, Orecchio was found guilty of 3 of the 25 counts in the indictment. The counts he was found guilty of dealt specifically with his failure to put an end to the dice games being run by Adonis and Moretti at Costa's Barn and The Studio.[63]

On May 6, shortly before Salvatore Moretti was to have his first parole hearing, he suffered a cerebral hemorrhage in his cell. He was taken to the prison hospital in critical condition in a coma. On June 8, Moretti's condition took a turn for the worse and he died in the early afternoon at the age of 46.

On the same day Moretti was to have his parole hearing, Adonis had his hearing. The State Parole Board, although its practice was only to announce decisions when they were favorable to the inmates, reported that Adonis's application was denied. The board chairman said the announcement was made simply because of "widespread interest in the case."[64]

In September 1952, after failure in the lower court to be relieved of the five-year probation period, Adonis appealed to the New Jersey Supreme Court. On September 22, the court denied Adonis's motion without writing an opinion. The newspapers reported:

> Under the probation, Adonis would be required to report at least once a month to a county probation officer, obtain employment approved by the officer, permit the officer to visit him at his home and refrain from leaving the state without permission. The requirements also forbid association with persons or places of dubious reputations. Violation of any of these rules could require Adonis to serve the four-to-five-year term.[65]

On January 6, 1953, more than two years after his testimony before the Kefauver Committee, the contempt of Senate trial of Joe Adonis finally went to court. Arguments were heard before Federal Judge John F. X. McGohey with no jury. The government's case, argued before "twenty drowsy spectators," focused on Adonis's refusal to answer questions put to him about his interests in the Automotive Conveyance Company in Bergen County. Assistant U.S. Attorney Robert Morton declared, "Adonis had no reasonable basis for asserting a claim of constitutional privilege on these questions because the automotive company was not an illegal enterprise, and that nothing he could say about it could possibly have incriminated him."[66]

Adonis was represented by attorneys Harold Corbin and Edward J. Bennett, who claimed that their client had legitimate concerns because his income tax returns were being audited by the IRS and that was a "perfect legal basis" for exercising his Fifth Amendment rights. Corbin maintained that the government was out to "get" his client, that "they tried to wrench from him, out of his own mouth, admissions or confessions of crime." To make his point, Corbin quoted from one of the Kefauver Committee's interim reports:

> There is no doubt in the minds of the members of this Committee that there exists at least two major crime syndicates . . . one with an axis between Miami and the Capone syndicate . . . another with an axis between New York and Miami headed by Frank Costello and Joe Adonis.[67]

After listening to arguments, Judge McGohey set January 19 as the final date for submission of memoranda, and January 21 as the date for final arguments. The odds were in favor of Adonis. There had been 22 previous contempt of Senate cases for refusing to answer questions of the Kefauver Committee. All of the cases were either dismissed at trial in federal court, or reversed on appeal. Frank Costello was sentenced to an 18-month term, but that was for walking out on the committee, not for refusing to answer questions.

On February 16, Judge McGohey found Adonis guilty of one of the 16 counts against him. He was not guilty of refusing to answer questions about his income, investments, or relationships with other underworld figures. Instead, he was found guilty of refusing to answer to the question: "Did you ever make a political contribution to any campaign, state, local or national?" The judge contended, "It is not a crime generally to make a campaign contribution."

Judge McGohey sentenced Adonis to three months in a federal facility and refused to allow the sentence to run concurrent with his New Jersey prison term. The judge issued a warrant for Adonis's detention on completion of his gambling sentence. On June 23, 1953, Adonis's conviction for contempt of Senate was reversed by the Circuit Court of Appeals in New York.

NEW JERSEY CORRUPTION

While Adonis was doing his time in the New Jersey State Prison, the corruption trials initiated in 1950 by Nelson Stamler continued. In many of the trials Adonis's name frequently came up in testimony. Stamler's aggressive actions caused him to make a number of enemies. In late January 1953, Stamler was suddenly on the outside looking in as Attorney General Theodore Parsons dismissed him for "impeding justice by making false statements."

Stamler's investigation was massive, but by mid-1952 he was backlogged and six months later he was fired. Stamler responded to Parson's accusations by declaring, "Until the people who permitted gambling are punished, my job is not finished, and that will reach some pretty high levels of government."[68]

The investigation into gambling in Bergen County, which brought down Adonis and his cohorts, was also supposed to focus on who the gamblers were paying for protection. One of those suspected of receiving money was Harold J. Adonis (no relation to the underworld boss), the former executive clerk to New Jersey Governor Alfred E. Driscoll. Willie Moretti had once told a public official that Driscoll had received $190,000 in bribes, all funneled through his executive clerk. Harold Adonis was alleged to have accepted $228,000 from gamblers to help cripple Stamler's 1950 gambling probe. Harold Adonis was indicted on November 9, 1952; however, he had already fled to Caracas, Venezuela, in South America and then to Europe, where he ended up in The Hague. While authorities in the Netherlands held him, two New Jersey state troopers were sent abroad on December 12, 1952 to bring Harold Adonis back. Two months later they returned empty handed, as authorities there refused to extradite Adonis because bribery was not an extraditable offense.

When the New Jersey Joint Legislative Committee met to investigate the Stamler dismissal and the Driscoll bribe allegations, Parsons was the first witness. He told the committee that he was informed by John Dickerson, the Republican state chairman, that he was paid a visit one night by Willie and Salvatore Moretti and Joe Adonis. According to Parsons, Willie Moretti told Dickerson that Harold Adonis was paid $12,000 a month for 19 months by gamblers operating in Bergen County, and that he gave $10,000 to Governor Driscoll. Moretti also allegedly told him that Stamler had received $14,000 for "protecting" gamblers in Passaic County.

In April 1953, Stamler was called before the committee. He responded to the accusations from Dickerson by accusing the Republican leader of routinely accepting "gifts" from underworld figures. When Dickerson took the stand in late April, he related sordid tales of bribery and corruption including a $25,000 payment to the Driscoll campaign in 1949 by Passaic businessman Joseph Bozza. On May 9, the *New York Times* reported:

> A picture of appalling conditions in a county prosecutor's office, widespread gambling and an apathetic public that resented any interference in either was presented here today to the legislative committee investigating the dismissal in January of Deputy Attorney General Nelson F. Stamler.[69]

Helping to paint this picture was attorney John Selser. One of the things Selser testified about was the sentences handed down to Joe Adonis and his four co-defendants. Selser said he had met with Parsons about the case and after several weeks they agreed to a plea deal. Parsons would recommend an 18- to 24-month sentence for each defendant and a $5,000 fine. Part of the agreement was that Selser was not to discuss the deal with Stamler. The attorney said Parsons reneged on the deal and when the men pled out, they received a substantially longer sentence and higher fines.

On August 5, 1953, Harold Adonis finally agreed to leave The Hague and return to the United States. In March 1954, a jury found him guilty of tax evasion and he was sentenced to a five-year prison term. On January 13, 1960, more than eight years after he was indicted, a jury acquitted Harold Adonis of charges that he conspired to protect Bergen County gamblers. After an eight-day trial, jurors took just 1 hour and 35 minutes to find him not guilty.

In April 1954, Joe Adonis and the three remaining gamblers imprisoned with him testified at the trial of Walter Winne. During the committee hearings, the name of the former New Jersey attorney general and one-time U.S. attorney came up frequently. He had already been removed as attorney general and was indicted for nonfeasance in office. Winne was charged in a 16-count indictment with failure to close 15 known gambling operations. A key witness was Vincent A. G. O'Connor, a former member of New York District Attorney Frank Hogan's staff. He testified that, on several occasions, he had provided information about Adonis's gambling operations to Winne, who failed to act on them. At the trial, Adonis and his fellow inmates were questioned about local gambling operations and admitted to participating in dice games at Costa's Barn, as well as other locations between 1946 and 1950. Adonis said "The Barn" was the main operation.

The trial of Walter Winne surpassed the Orecchio trial as the longest single-defendant criminal case in the state's history. At the end of the 53-day trial, a jury deliberated five-and-a-half hours before finding the former Bergen County prosecutor not guilty. The decision suddenly placed in peril the remaining 100 pending grand jury indictments against law enforcement officers and city and county officials of Bergen County.

DEPORTATION INITIATIVE

In the midst of the investigations and trials, attorneys in the Justice Department reviewing Joe Adonis's trials and testimony came across an interesting discrepancy. In his appearances before the Bergen County grand jury, Adonis acknowledged he had been born in two different places—Italy and Passaic, New Jersey.

At a parole hearing in January 1953, Adonis responded to board members' questions with answers they deemed "unrealistic." Homer Zink, chairman of the New Jersey State Parole Board, said afterward, "We determined that he should serve his maximum sentence with time off only for good behavior and work performed during his incarceration." This left Adonis looking at a projected release date of August 6.

The week of February 16, 1953, would not go down as a banner week in the life of Joe Adonis. Tucked safely away in the New Jersey State Prison, what could go wrong? On Tuesday, February 17, Adonis was convicted of the contempt of Senate charge and sentenced to three months in a federal penitentiary. On Wednesday, he was indicted for perjury by a Bergen County grand jury investigating waterfront racketeering and gambling. The indictment claimed he lied about his age and place of birth. Finally, on Friday, the Department of Justice issued a warrant for his deportation. On Saturday, the deportation warrant was served to Adonis in the Trenton prison.

The Immigration & Naturalization Service (INS) charged that Adonis fraudulently obtained a birth certificate, which stated he was born on November 5, 1901 in Passaic, New Jersey. Their investigation uncovered that he was actually born in Italy in 1902 and brought to this country by his mother in 1909. The warrant charged that after a trip to Cuba in 1946, Adonis returned through Miami, which was illegal because he did not possess required immigration documents. The government contended that this was a violation of the McCarran Act, making Adonis eligible for deportation.[70]

The government was not interested in waiting for Adonis to complete his prison term on August 6. They announced that they were prepared to begin their hearing on April 27 at the prison. Parole Board Chairman Homer Zink had no objection to the hearing, but insisted that the government would have to obtain permission from the board if Adonis lost the case and they wanted to deport him before the end of his term. At the time, New Jersey authorities said Adonis was a key witness in the pending bribery trial of Harold J. Adonis, and it might insist on keeping Adonis in the state until the case was resolved.

On April 24, the federal government indicted Adonis on two counts of perjury for uttering false statements to the Kefauver Committee. The first charge was for falsely stating that
he was born in Passaic, New Jersey. The second charge was for lying about being a citizen
of the United States. If convicted, Adonis was looking at a sentence of up to 10 years and a
fine of $10,000.

Three days later, the INS hearing took place in the reception room of the Trenton prison
facility. Attending the session was a "special inquiry officer" of the INS, a government attorney, defense counsel Samuel Paige, three newspaper reporters, a prison guard, and Joe
Adonis. The government attorney read aloud the charges to the group. The newspaper
reported:

> They accused Adonis of being an alien and of having entered the country from Havana on
> Jan. 1, 1948 without having first obtained the required visa.[71] The Government further con-
> tends that Adonis, upon his arrival at Miami by plane, failed to furnish Immigration au-
> thorities with pertinent information required by law. In addition, the Government holds,
> he has been convicted of crimes involving moral turpitude within five years of his entry.[72]

When the attorney was finished, he asked Adonis if he understood the charges against
him. The prisoner smiled and replied, "I don't know. There are so many of them." After
some bickering over procedures, the hour-long session was adjourned until June 1 to allow
attorney Paige time to prepare his case.

The parties met again on June 1. This time Adonis's uncle and two brothers were on hand
for the seven-hour hearing. The uncle, Ferdinand DeVito, gave his version of the Doto family
history, in which he stated that Joe and his three brothers were all born in Montemarano,
Italy, the sons of Michele and Mary Doto. When the brothers testified, they recalled little of
their past. Antonio, the oldest, said he was born in Montemarano in 1898 and arrived in the
United States in 1909, but could not remember if he traveled here with anybody. Alberto
(Ettore), who also claimed to be born in Montemarano, couldn't recall where he went to
school in Brooklyn, but remembered he was enrolled up until the eighth grade. Both brothers testified that their parents told them that Joe was born in America. The next day, Alberto
was questioned again. Now he claimed he couldn't remember anything that happened in his
life before turning 17. He said he couldn't even remember where his brother Joe lived before
entering prison.

The government called nine witnesses, but the most damaging evidence was an official document, which they claimed was a copy of the birth certificate of Giuseppe Antonio
Doto. The certificate showed his date of birth as November 22, 1902, and his birthplace,
Montemarano, Italy. His parents were listed as Michele and Maria Doto. In addition to this
birth certificate, the government also produced copies of the birth certificates for his parents
and three brothers, as well as the manifest from the ship on which they arrived in America.[73]
The government also put on a New York City detective, who claimed he had arrested Adonis
in 1922 for felonious assault, at which time he had given Italy as his place of birth.[74]

On June 4, Adonis's aunt, Orlanda Gallo, testified that she had been told by both of
Adonis's parents that Joe had been born in America. The hearing was then adjourned until
June 15. On that date, Adonis testified for nearly seven hours in an effort to convince government officials that he was a citizen of the United States. "He offered in evidence to support
his contention, his marriage license and certificate, his Selective Service papers, his father's
death certificate and the birth certificates of his four children."[75]

The government attorney pointed out that the Doto marriage certificate from 1932 listed his place of birth as Brooklyn, but his Selective Service papers stated he was born in Passaic. Adonis explained that his father told him he was born in Passaic, and at his request was able to produce a birth certificate two weeks later from that city. At the end of the hearing, the INS special inquiry officer announced he would render a decision before the end of July.

On July 3, the New Jersey State Prison announced that Adonis would be released on July 16. The government's hope of deporting Adonis before his prison sentence was complete failed when the special inquiry officer delayed his decision to allow additional time for the defense counsel to present more evidence. Prison officials said Adonis was being released earlier than the August 6 date because of good behavior, having been a model inmate and having worked satisfactorily as a "night iceman." His five-year probation period would now go into effect, during which he could not leave Bergen County without permission.

On his release, federal marshals were waiting with a bench warrant charging Adonis with perjury. They met him at the prison gate and drove him to the Federal Building in Trenton, where he posted a $5,000 bail for appearance on July 23 in Washington D.C. for a hearing on perjury charges for lying to the Kefauver Committee members about his age and place of birth. From the Federal Building, a state police car took him to Hackensack for an appearance before Judge Leyden. Adonis was wanted as a material witness in the investigation into bribery charges of state officials involving Harold J. Adonis, who was still in the Netherlands. The judge freed Adonis after he posted a $1,000 bail. In addition to the $6,000 he had just posted, Adonis was still under a $10,000 bail pending the INS action to deport him. Before leaving the Bergen County seat, he was warned by a county probation officer that he could not consort with his old associates for the next five years. Then Joe Adonis headed home to sleep in his own bed for the first time in 26 months.

Adonis traveled to Washington D.C. on July 23, where he appeared in U.S. District Court before Federal Judge Edward A. Tamm. Represented by defense counsel Harold Corbin and William Collins, he pleaded not guilty to charges of lying to the Kefauver Committee members about his age and birthplace. Judge Tamm allowed him to remain free on the $5,000 bail, pending a trial date that was yet to be set.

On August 5, 1953, the special inquiry officer of the INS recommended that Adonis be deported. His decision was based on the fact that Adonis "lacked a valid passport" when he last entered this country after a visit to Cuba seven years ago. The INS also contended that Adonis "failed to register as an alien and to keep it advised of his address under alien registration laws."[76] Following this recommendation, U.S. Attorney General Herbert Brownell, Jr. ordered that Adonis be deported. The *New York Times* reported:

> Immigration authorities in Philadelphia disclosed last night that the Government would move swiftly to effect the deportation of the notorious racketeer. They said that plans had been drawn up to dispose of appeals quickly and that Adonis "should be deported with little delay."[77]

The government's deportation schedule was overly optimistic. Adonis was given 10 days to appeal the decision to the Immigration Board of Appeals. It was not until December 17, 1953 that the board upheld the deportation order. While this legal battle was being fought, Adonis was facing a new government attack. On November 7, the IRS filed tax liens against Adonis and his wife Jean. The liens covered the period 1945 through 1951.[78]

In January 1954, Adonis was convicted of lying to a Bergen County grand jury about his place of birth. The judge sentenced Adonis to two to three years in prison on February 2, 1954, but suspended the sentence pending Adonis's appeal of his deportation order. On November 8, the New Jersey Supreme Court upheld the lower court's decision that Adonis had lied. He appealed next to the U.S. Supreme Court, but his petition was rejected on April 18, 1955.

In March 1954, Adonis's trial for perjury before the Kefauver Committee took place. The trial was held before Federal Judge Walter M. Bastian in Washington D.C. Bastian acquitted Adonis on the charge of swearing falsely that he was born in Passaic, New Jersey, but found him guilty of telling committee members that he was a U.S. citizen. When Adonis was sentenced on April 9, the judge gave him 18 to 24 months in prison. Adonis was allowed to remain free on his $10,000 bail while he appealed the decision. It took a year for the U.S. Court of Appeals to render a decision on the case. On March 24, 1955, the appeals court upheld the federal court's ruling. In October, the U.S. Supreme Court rejected Adonis's final appeal.

By the fall of 1955, Adonis was facing 18 to 24 months in federal prison, two to three years in state prison, and deportation by the INS. At this point he decided to call it quits. Preferring the freedom of Italy to a prison cell, Adonis offered to leave the United States. Federal Judge Walter Bastian, who had been elevated to the Federal Court of Appeals, returned to the District Court on November 14, 1955, to hear the agreement between Adonis's counsel and officials from the INS and the Department of Justice.

Bastian suspended the prison sentence and placed Adonis on five year's probation.[79] During this period, Adonis could not return to the United States and the judge stipulated that his presence in Canada, Mexico, or any "near-by island," such as Cuba, would not be in compliance with the agreement. Adonis's counsel, William Collins, assured the court his client would go to Italy.

The judge set a date of January 1, 1956, for Adonis to depart. Collins told Bastian it would be "an extraordinary hardship" for Adonis to leave his family during the holidays and asked for more time for him to arrange his financial affairs; however, the judge was adamant that January 1 was the date.

Adonis received a slight break on the date, perhaps since the boat on which he booked passage was not sailing until January 3. On that morning, Adonis arose early at his Fort Lee home and said goodbye to his wife Jean, his son Joseph, Jr., and his three daughters—Maria Dolores, Ann Marie, and Elizabeth. He was then driven to Pier 84 on the Hudson River, near West 44th Street. Adonis received permission to embark an hour earlier than the regular time to avoid the media circus.

Just before 8:00 AM, Adonis boarded the *Conte Biancamano* and entered his cabin. Described as one of the most expensive suites on the boat, Adonis paid $740 for a bedroom, sitting room, and private bath. The Italian liner, headed for Genoa, was scheduled to set sail at noon. As Adonis waited in his cabin, a throng of newspaper reporters and photographers gathered outside. Adonis refused to meet with them until just before noon when he granted a brief interview with one reporter.

Adonis told the reporter that he didn't want to leave, but, "It's a must." He said his wife and children would not be joining him in Italy. Perhaps his reputation as a womanizer had long before destroyed his marriage. As far as any plans to return to the United States, Adonis replied, "I have no plans whatever at this time." The departing mob boss was then asked if he was going to "look up" his former associate, Lucky Luciano. Adonis emphatically replied, "I'm not going to look him up and I hope that he doesn't look me up."[80]

LIFE IN EXILE

Adonis arrived in Genoa, Italy on January 15, 1956, after 12 days on the ocean. He first traveled to Naples, where he stayed briefly with relatives in the area. He then tried to settle in Rome, but police there branded him a "socially undesirable element" and ordered him to leave the city. An article discussing his activities just after his arrival stated, "For months he moved around Italy trying to avoid publicity and at one point took up farming. But his reputation trailed him and three months after his arrival, a priest refused him as a godfather at a baptism."[81] He soon settled in Milan, where he lived alone in the downtown area, residing on the seventh-floor of a luxury apartment.

Unlike Lucky Luciano, whose legend continued to grow in exile, Adonis, from most reports, simply settled down and lived off his illegal earnings. In *The Last Testament of Lucky Luciano,* the deported mob boss talked about Meyer Lansky banking money in a Zurich, Switzerland bank. Lansky suggested that Luciano should start putting some money away there. Luciano claimed that Joe Adonis was making a trip to bring him some money and that they agreed to meet in Zurich.

Luciano commented about all of Adonis's pending problems—the Kefauver Committee, the New Jersey/New York indictment, and his deportation case. When Adonis arrived in Zurich, he handed Luciano an envelope containing $100,000. Adonis then proceeded to deposit $3 million into an account he had established there. When confronted by Luciano about the large deposit, Adonis explained that it was money he had "socked away" over the years, and he was hiding it in case he "had to leave the States."

Luciano had what can best be described as a "hissy fit," as he told Adonis he should split his $3 million with him, claiming he was nothing before Luciano met him, referring to his ice cream parlor tale back in 1920:

> Luciano: Your memory stinks, Joe. Don't you know I made you?
> Adonis: Maybe you did, Charlie, but you can't break me.

Luciano declared, "Thirty years of friendship went right down the crapper, then and there. I never trusted the son of a bitch again." Luciano said he then wrote to Lansky about the incident. "He said that what Joe A. told me at the Zurich airport was right. For a couple of years [Adonis] had been worried that he was gonna get deported, so he'd been savin' every nickel and bankin' it all for the rainy day."[82]

Luciano set the timing for this incident in 1951, which makes it improbable that this could have taken place owing to Adonis's legal problems. Adonis was arraigned in Hackensack and placed on a $15,000 bail on October 31, 1950. Since mid-November 1950, he had been avoiding a Kefauver Committee subpoena, and on November 27 he was arraigned in New York City and placed on a $20,000 bail. In December he needed permission from Judge Leyden to leave the jurisdiction for an appearance before the Kefauver Committee in Washington D.C. In January he was formally indicted in Hackensack and was under a $35,000 bail until pleading guilty when his trial began in May; he then went straight to prison.

It seems unlikely that Adonis would have boarded an airplane and gone to Switzerland, with law enforcement looking for an excuse to put him behind bars. In addition, the first inkling Adonis received of any deportation action against him did not come to light until February 1953. Deportation cases against underworld figures became a popular government tool, but not until after the Kefauver Hearings ended in March 1951. That Adonis could have worried about it "for a couple of years" in early 1951 seems implausible.

In the book, Luciano doesn't have anything good to say about Adonis again. When they met after Adonis's arrival, Luciano claims there was "little warmth" between them. At one point he declares that Adonis was taking Genovese's side against him.[83]

After Luciano's death in January 1962, the authors of *The Last Testament of Lucky Luciano* claim Adonis received permission from Italian government officials to attend the funeral. "He arrived with a mournful expression, tears in his eyes and a final tribute to his old friend—a massive floral wreath with a black band on which, in gold letters, was inscribed the ancient gangland farewell: 'So Long, Pal.'"[84]

Through the remainder of the 1960s there was hardly a mention of Joe Adonis or his activities. In the book, *Men of Respect,* the author writes that after Adonis got settled, "From then until the early seventies an organized smuggling network, with connections in all the European nations, revolved around him."[85] In the brief passage on Adonis, the author doesn't mention what it was the "network" was smuggling.

The beginning of the end for the once powerful Brooklyn mob boss came on May 22, 1971, when he was jailed in Milan on a "preventive custody" warrant. Adonis's arrest was part of huge roundup of suspected Mafia members following the May 5 murder of Pietro Scaglione, the chief prosecutor of Palermo, and his driver. In what was described as the largest postwar crackdown on the Mafia, 114 suspected members were arrested. Before a magistrate, Adonis claimed he was suffering from a heart condition and was not fit for jail; however, a physician ruled against him and he was placed in Milan's San Vittore Jail. The local police chief demanded his immediate removal from the city. Exile was a common practice in the country. Mafia members were routinely sent to remote areas—islands along the coast or small villages—to keep them out of mainstream activities.

On June 20, a Milan tribunal banished Adonis to the small village of Serra de' Conti, located 40 miles west of the Adriatic coastal city of Ancona. The four-year sentence to this municipality of 3,000-plus people was simply because of Adonis's "suspected" underworld connections. He pleaded with the magistrate, "I'm a sick man. If you send me to exile, it'll kill me." After appeals were exhausted, Adonis was sent away in July. While in exile, Adonis was forbidden to use a telephone and was placed on a 10:00 PM to 7:00 AM curfew.

On November 23, one day after his 69th birthday, Adonis suffered a pulmonary collapse and was rushed to the Regional General Hospital in Ancona in critical condition. Word of his condition was sent to his family in the United States. Jean Doto and two of her children arrived shortly before his death on the afternoon of November 26.[86] Doctors said that heart failure resulting from pulmonary complications was the cause of death.

A friend of Adonis, who refused to reveal his name, arrived in Ancona from America and made arrangements to have his body returned to the United States. The body arrived at Kennedy International Airport on December 2, in a solid bronze coffin. On the coffin was a large silver crucifix and a plaque inscribed with the name Giuseppe Antonio Doto. Adonis's daughter and her husband accompanied the body, which was driven by hearse to the

A. K. Macagna Funeral Home in Cliffside Park, New Jersey. After a private funeral, Adonis was laid to rest at Madonna Cemetery and Mausoleum in Fort Lee.

NOTES

1. Like nearly all the underworld leaders featured in this book, Adonis was believed to have been involved in the narcotics trade. By 1940, the Federal Narcotics Bureau had a file on Adonis an inch thick. Despite this suspicion, Adonis was never arrested or charged with any crimes connected to the trafficking of narcotics.

2. Fred J. Cook, *The Secret Rulers* (New York: Duell, Sloan and Pearce, 1966), p. 107.

3. Fourteen years after these arrests, Officer Robert F. Baron was interviewed by reporters from the *New York Post* who were preparing an expose on Joe Adonis. Baron said he remained a detective for Brooklyn South for another nine years. During the fall elections of 1934, Adonis-backed candidates in Brooklyn obtained a significant foothold in the borough. The next year Baron said he was "broken" down to patrolman after being framed by a woman during a domestic dispute in which she said he allowed her husband to beat her. Baron was adamant that the loss of his detective's shield was due to his reputation of being "unpopular" with Brooklyn gangsters.—*New York Post*, April 17, 1940, "What Happens to a Cop Who Annoys Joe Adonis?"

4. *New York Post*, April 17, 1940, "What Happens to a Cop Who Annoys Joe Adonis?"

5. *New York Post*, April 19, 1940, "Joe Adonis Lawbreaker by Choice, Not Chance."

6. *Brooklyn Eagle*, July 24, 1934, "$35,000 in Floral Tributes At Funeral of 'Mother Elk.'" In the article, Joe Adonis's mother is referred to as "Mary Adonis, the wife of Michael Adonis, retired builder." Apparently his parents didn't mind having his chosen nickname imposed on them, or it's entirely possible that the family's real name, Doto, was unknown to outsiders.

7. *New York Post*, April 19, 1940, "Joe Adonis Lawbreaker by Choice, Not Chance."

8. John Henry McCooey was born in New York on June 18, 1864. A shipyard worker as a young man, McCooey became involved in Democratic politics in Brooklyn. In 1909, he was a candidate for borough president. The following year he became chairman of the Kings County Democratic Party, a position he would hold until his death 24 year later. McCooey was a delegate to the Democratic National Convention from New York in every election from 1912 to 1932. McCooey spent 42 years as a public servant, but none in an elected position. He died of myocarditis, a heart condition, on January 21, 1934 and was buried in Holy Cross Cemetery.—www.politicalgraveyard.com

9. *New York Post*, April 25, 1940, "Mayor Acts on Joe Adonis; Blocks Auto Firm Permit."

10. *New York Post*, April 26, 1940, "Joe Adonis and the Machine."

11. Ibid.

12. Jerome G. Ambro's political career was far from over. Ambro served a total of nine terms as a Democratic assemblyman from Brooklyn. In addition, he served as Democratic district leader and chairman of the Kings County Federation of Italian-American Democratic Clubs. Ambro died on March 17, 1979.

13. Cook, *The Secret Rulers*, pp. 111–112.

14. *New York Post*, April 26, 1940, "Adonis 'Retired' at His Peak."

15. George Walsh, *Public Enemies: The Mayor, the Mob, and the Crime That Was* (New York: W. W. Norton & Company, 1980), p. 15.

16. *New York Post*, April 29, 1940, "Adonis Firm Gets 3 Million to Haul Autos for Ford."

17. On September 21, 1962, Paul Bonadio was involved in a sensational automobile accident near Times Square, which took the lives of several people. Bonadio and his half-brother were leaving a garage on West 43rd Street. Suddenly, the car lurched forward and made a U-turn, crashing

into Rosoff's Restaurant, where an estimated 200 people were dining during this early Friday afternoon. The car smashed through the front wall and into an alcove in the bar section, killing two people instantly, while a third died on the way to the hospital. Six other people were injured, including one man whose leg had to be amputated and another man who was a staff reporter for the *New York Times*.

Bonadio, who was not injured, was arrested and charged with vehicular homicide. During his arraignment the next day, Bonadio blamed the accident on the power brakes and power steering. He claimed, "I came out of the garage and the brakes and steering failed. I didn't turn the wheel, it went by itself." Members of the Police Department Accident Investigation Squad reported, "The vehicle was mechanically free of any defects and was in good working order at the time of the accident."

The newspapers reported that he was a cousin of Joe Adonis. But Bonadio denied that he was related to the now deported mob boss, even though he lived in the same town, Fort Lee, New Jersey.

On September 28 the widow of one of the victims filed a $750,000 damage suit claiming Bonadio was negligent and careless. Bonadio was not insured, as New Jersey did not require mandatory automobile insurance at the time. The case was heard in criminal court on October 23, at which time Bonadio was cleared of vehicular homicide charges.

18. The notoriety of Joe Adonis was so widespread by now that the White Motor Company of Cleveland, Ohio, at the time one of the oldest manufacturers of trucks in the United States, felt compelled to issue a statement that they were in no way connected to the hoodlum's White Auto Sales, Inc. of Brooklyn.

19. *New York Times,* May 6, 1940, "Adonis Is Indicted on Kidnap Charge: Aide Under Arrest."

20. *New York Post,* May 7, 1940, "Adonis Hunt Concentrated in 2 Cities."

21. Ibid.

22. Isidore Juffe was a small-time swindler and con man with a long record of arrests and short record of convictions. He claimed once that he had "bribed and fixed" his way through 28 arrests in 25 years and that it had cost him plenty. After this claim, many of the newspapers referred to him as Isidore "I Paid Plenty" Juffe. On trial in 1938, he testified that he had paid Brooklyn Assistant District Attorney Alexander R. Baldwin $800 to avoid being indicted in a fur racket case. This payment had two ramifications. First, Governor Herbert Lehman assigned John Harlan Amen to the position of special prosecutor to investigate political corruption in Brooklyn. Later, it led Kings County Judge William O'Dwyer to run against William F.X. Geoghan as the Democratic candidate for Brooklyn district attorney.

Juffe ended up serving as an informant to Special Prosecutor Amen in a number of cases. When he was through, he opened a small restaurant in Brooklyn, which he ran under the name of Isaac Juffe. In December 1941, he suffered a heart attack and was rushed to Kings County Hospital where he died. His true identity was revealed after his death.

23. *New York Post,* May 6, 1940, "Kidnap Charge May Be Widened if Gasberg Talks."

24. *New York Daily News,* May 7, 1940, "Hint Murder Charge for Adonis if Found."

25. *Brooklyn Eagle,* May 9, 1940, "Adonis Surrenders, Ends Wide Amen Hunt."

26. *New York Sun,* May 9, 1940, "Joe Adonis Gives Up to Prosecutor Amen."

27. *New York World-Telegram,* May 9, 1940, "Adonis Surrenders to Amen Amid Secrecy in Brooklyn."

28. *New York Post,* May 9, 1940, "Joe Adonis Surrenders in Brooklyn."

29. *New York Times,* May 10, 1940, "Adonis Surrenders in Two Kidnappings."

30. *Brooklyn Eagle,* May 25, 1940, "Joe Adonis at Liberty in Bail of $50,000."

31. *New York Times,* February 19, 1941, "Gasberg Is Acquitted."

32. The name of Duke's Restaurant, which was owned by John "Duke" DeNoia, by some accounts a New Jersey mobster once connected with Lucky Luciano, was also listed as Duke's Place and Duke's Bar & Grill.

33. Some historians say Duke's Restaurant remained a viable meeting place for the mob until after the Kefauver Hearings in 1951, when it received much negative publicity.

34. Walsh, *Public Enemies: The Mayor, the Mob, and the Crime That Was*, p. 11.

35. From an address by Judge Jonah J. Goldstein, Republican-Liberal-Fusion candidate for Mayor, broadcast over WABC radio on the night of October 17, 1945.

36. *New York Times*, October 30, 1945, "Goldstein Called Sale Aid in Strike."

37. Robert Lacey, *Little Man: Meyer Lansky and the Gangster Life* (Toronto: Little, Brown and Company, 1991), p. 142.

38. *New York Times*, December 7, 1950, "Crime Inquiring Call Goes to Joe Adonis."

39. *New York Times*, December 13, 1950, "Joe Adonis Defies Senate Crime Unit."

40. Ibid.

41. Ibid.

42. Ibid. On July 27, 1951, the Ford Motor Company announced, through a telegram to Committee Senator Herbert R. O'Conor, that Joe Adonis had sold all his interests in the Automotive Conveying Company.

43. Ibid.

44. Ibid.

45. Ibid.

46. This charge was also referred to as "contempt of Congress."

47. Estes Kefauver, *Crime in America* (Garden City, New York: Doubleday & Company, 1951), p. 292.

48. *New York Times*, January 24, 1951, "Senate Cites Eight, Including Adonis."

49. *New York Times*, November 10, 1950, "Adonis Is Cited by Jury Here in Move to Aid Jersey Case."

50. Ibid.

51. Ibid.

52. Lodi is a borough in Bergen County, New Jersey. It is the home of the "Satin Dolls," a go-go bar that was used as the fictitious strip club "Bada Bing" from the acclaimed HBO television series, "The Sopranos." Other locations in Lodi were also used for filming during the series including Lodi High School, Lodi Pizza, a local trash collecting business, and several private residences.

53. Walsh, *Public Enemies: The Mayor, the Mob, and the Crime That Was*, pp. 154–155.

54. The Studio on Palisade Avenue in Fort Lee was owned by Cinema Studios of New York City. On December 12, 1951, Bergen County Judge Herman Vanderwart fined the company $3,500 for permitting the premises to be used for gambling "by the Joe Adonis syndicate."

55. *Non vult* is a legal term and is used synonymously with *nolo contendere*, both meaning "no defense" or "no contest." In practical terms, it means the defendant is not contesting the conviction, but is not admitting guilt.

56. *New York Times*, May 22, 1951, "Adonis Faces Jail; Pleads No Defense in Jersey Gaming."

57. *New York Times*, May 29, 1951, "Adonis, 3 Aides Get Terms of 2 to 3 Years."

58. Ibid. The *New York Times* wrote, "In imposing prison terms and fines for the same crimes, Judge Leyden ignored a 1940 amendment to the state's criminal statute that prohibits the double penalty. He said he considered the amendment unconstitutional. The double penalty was permitted under the previous law, passed in 1898."

59. *New York Times*, May 30, 1951, "Adonis Is Inmate of Jersey Prison."

60. *New York Times*, November 14, 1951, "Gamblers Fogged at January Inquiry."

61. After the conviction of Leonard Costa on November 15, 1951, the judge set November 30 as the sentencing date. When the prosecutor reminded the judge that Costa had once fled to Miami, the judge doubled the bond for him and said he would have to post the additional amount to remain free. Costa, a father of four, was sentenced to a year-and-a-half to two years in the New Jersey State Prison in Trenton and fined $3,500. Costa appealed the conviction. On May 29, 1952, the Appellate Division of the New Jersey State Superior Court reversed the conviction.

62. *New York Times,* April 9, 1952, "Adonis Ill at Ease as State Witness."

63. Michael Orecchio was sentenced to a prison term of two to three years. The former Bergen County chief of detectives appealed the case and on September 28, 1953 the Appellate Division of the New Jersey State Superior Court reversed the conviction. The next year, on June 28, 1954, the New Jersey Supreme Court set aside the conviction and ordered a new trial.

64. *New York Times,* May 8, 1952, "Adonis Denied Parole."

65. *New York Times,* September, 16, 1952, "Adonis Sues to Avoid Five-Year Probation."

66. *New York Times,* January 7, 1953, "Convict Joe Adonis Natty at His Trial."

67. Kefauver Committee Interim Report, February 28, 1951.

68. *New York Times,* April 12, 1972, "Judge Nelson Stamler, 62 Dead, Jersey Racket Buster in 1950s."

69. *New York Times,* May 9, 1953, "Public Is Blamed in Bergen Gaming." After the seven-month investigation, Nelson Stamler failed to regain his office. He blamed this on his investigations getting "too close" to certain politicians. Stamler's public career did not end here. Many considered him a courageous "racket buster." In 1959, he was elected to the New Jersey State Assembly and three years later to the state Senate. In 1967, after two terms in the state Senate, he was appointed to the Union County bench, a position he held when he died of an undisclosed illness in Montego Bay, Jamaica, on April 13, 1972. Stamler was 62 years old.

70. The Internal Security Act of 1950, more popularly known as the McCarran Act or the "anticommunist law," was enacted with a focus to keep the United States safe from subversives. The wording of the act, which in later years would be reversed by the courts, allowed the government to use it against Joe Adonis in his innocuous return from a trip to Cuba.

71. The date of January 1, 1948 changed in various newspaper accounts. Sometimes it was listed as January 1947, after a trip to Havana in late December 1946. This latter date seems to make sense if you consider that this was the time when Lucky Luciano had settled in Cuba. It is not unreasonable to believe, however, that Adonis would have made subsequent visits to Havana, as it had become an underworld gambling Mecca.

72. *New York Times,* April 28, 1953, "Joe Adonis Goes on Trial in Jail."

73. I have been unable to locate on the Ellis Island Web site any information showing that the family arrived in America together under the name Doto.

74. This testimony is questionable, as nearly all sources claim that Joe Adonis's first arrest did not occur until February 1926.

75. *New York Times,* June 16, 1953, "Joe Adonis Asserts He Was Born in U.S."

76. *New York Times*, August 6, 1953, "U.S. Orders Adonis Deported to Italy."

77. Ibid.

78. On February 13, 1956, a month after Joe Adonis arrived in Italy, his tax attorney, Joseph P. Lefkowitz, presented Federal Judge Arnold Raum with a settlement agreement approved by the IRS. Adonis would pay the government $66,859 in settlement of the tax lien. The settlement did not include interest.

79. *New York Times* reported, "Although the order said nothing about what might happen at the end of five years, authorities generally agreed that Adonis would not be permitted re-entry at the expiration of the probationary period."—*New York Times,* November 15, 1955, "Adonis, Perjurer, To Leave Country."

80. *New York Times,* January 4, 1956, "Joe Adonis Quits U.S. Voluntarily."

81. *New York Times,* May 23, 1971, "Joe Adonis Is Jailed in Milan While Court Decides on Exile."

82. Martin Gosch and Richard Hammer, *The Last Testament of Lucky Luciano* (Boston: Little, Brown and Company, 1974), pp. 369–370.

83. Ibid., pp. 419–420.

84. Ibid., p. 449.

85. Raimondo Catanzaro, *Men of Respect* (English translation) (New York: The Free Press, a division of Macmillan, Inc., 1992), p. 194.

86. One of the fictional tales that came after the death of Joe Adonis appeared in the *World Encyclopedia of Organized Crime,* by Jay Robert Nash. The author claims that Adonis's arrest consisted of him being "dragged" from his home in Milan and taken "to a remote hillside location for questioning. It was reported that he died of a heart attack during this unorthodox if not unjustifiable interrogation." This story, like many of the fictional tidbits produced by Nash, is all too often repeated as fact.

BIBLIOGRAPHY

Catanzaro, Raimondo. *Men of Respect.* English trans. New York: The Free Press, a division of Macmillan, 1992.

Cook, Fred J. *The Secret Rulers.* New York: Duell, Sloan and Pearce, 1966.

Gosch, Martin, and Richard Hammer. *The Last Testament of Lucky Luciano.* Boston: Little, Brown and Company, 1974.

Katz, Leonard. *Uncle Frank.* New York: Drake Publishers, 1973.

Kefauver, Estes. *Crime in America.* Garden City, NY: Doubleday & Company, 1951.

Lacey, Robert. *Little Man: Meyer Lansky and the Gangster Life.* Toronto: Little, Brown and Company, 1991.

Walsh, George. *Public Enemies: The Mayor, the Mob, and the Crime That Was.* New York: W. W. Norton & Company, 1980.

2

ALBERT ANASTASIA (UMBERTO ANASTASIO)

AKA "THE MAD HATTER"
SEPTEMBER 26, 1902–OCTOBER 25, 1957

Albert Anastasia was one of the most vicious and feared mob bosses in the history of the New York City underworld. A confidante of mob leaders Joe Adonis, Louis Buchalter, Frank Costello, and Lucky Luciano, Anastasia murdered his way to the top of one of the five New York crime families in 1951.

Anastasia earned his early reputation on the New York docks after jumping ship to enter the United States illegally at the age of 15. He became a leader in controlling the rackets, strike breaking, and strong-arm activities along the waterfront. This reputation led to his involvement with a group of local killers who would become infamous as Murder, Inc. (see Appendix). Within this more-fable-than-fact gang of assassins, Anastasia was rumored to have "put the finger" on at least 63 victims, while participating in 30 murders himself.

While a crime boss in the 1950s, Anastasia abused his power time and again. His most heinous crime was ordering the brazen daytime murder of an innocent young man who had the temerity, at least in Albert's mind, to turn in fugitive bank robber Willie Sutton after recognizing him on a New York City subway train.

Anastasia was able to dodge an indictment during the Murder, Inc. trials of the early 1940s, but he could not evade Senator Estes Kefauver's crime committee. Although he refused to answer most questions, the result was continued government harassment involving citizenship, taxes, and waterfront activities throughout the 1950s.

Along with longtime associate Frank Scalise, Anastasia was involved in the selling of Mafia memberships for as much as $50,000. When the scam was uncovered, Scalise became the fall guy and was murdered in memorable fashion.

Anastasia proved to be a roadblock in the path of Vito Genovese on his way to becoming the Boss of All Bosses. This led to the murder of Anastasia as he sat in a barber's chair in a Manhattan hotel barbershop in October 1957.

EARLY YEARS

Umberto Anastasio was born on September 26, 1902, in the fishing village of Tropea, in the Vibo Valentia province of the Calabria Region of Italy. Umberto was one of 12 siblings—nine brothers and three sisters—three of whom died in infancy. Some sources claim Umberto was the oldest of the children. If this was the case, Mama Anastasio must have been a busy woman pushing out children at the rate of one per year between 1902 and 1914 when her husband died. What may be more accurate is that Umberto was the oldest of the sons who migrated to America, of which there were six.

Anastasia's father supported his burgeoning family as a railroad worker. After his death, his sons went to work at an early age to help support the family. They found work on fishing boats, freighters, and farms; at least one followed his father's footsteps and worked for the railroad. Umberto and his brothers Joseph (Giuseppe) and Anthony (Antonio) worked as deck hands on tramp steamers. Not yet teenagers, they worked in some of the toughest ports in the world. One of the Anastasio boys eventually relocated to Australia, and two others remained in Italy, but the remaining brothers would eventually find their way to America.

> "He talked infrequently, and then in a hoarse voice. His Italian was hardly better than his English, since his schooling had ended at the age of 11."
>
> —*New York Times*, October 26, 1957,
> "Anastasia Rose in Stormy Ranks," 12:7

September 12, 1917, is the date given to Umberto's illegal entry into the United States by jumping ship in New York harbor. He was only 15, but his hard work had added muscle to his five-foot, seven-inch frame, which made him an imposing figure. He found work on the docks in the Red Hook section of Brooklyn, but soon fell in with a criminal element. During one run-in with the law, Umberto used the name Alberto. The name was shortened to Albert, a name he was known by for the rest of his life. He also began using the last name Anastasia. It was later claimed that he did so as not to embarrass other family members—although they hardly led lives of stellar law-abiding citizens.[1]

One of Albert's early companions was Giuseppe "Joseph" Florino, a Brooklyn tough, seven years Anastasia's senior. On May 16, 1920, the two got into an argument with George Terillo after he accused them of stealing from his friend.[2] The argument ended with Terillo being shot dead at the corner of Union and Columbia Streets in Brooklyn. Florino and Anastasia fled. On March 6, 1921, Florino was arrested for the murder and Anastasia was apprehended 11 days later.

The murder trial began two months later before New York Supreme Court Justice James C. Van Siclen. On May 10, Mrs. Margaret Farrara Vicce, described as a "fiery young Venetian," appeared as the state's star witness. During her testimony, Vicce said she witnessed the murder after walking out of a movie theater on Columbia Street. She testified that she heard Terillo demand the return of the "loot" Anastasia and Florino had taken, before the two men shot him. She claimed she had known Florino for two years because he had once entered her apartment on lower President Street and stole $50 from her husband.

When she screamed, he choked her. Florino jumped from his chair and called her a liar, after which a deputy sheriff, "plumped him back into his seat with considerable suddenness and force." The *Brooklyn Daily Eagle* reported:

> At one point in her testimony Margaret protested to Justice Van Siclen that Anastasio was "looking at her" and both were accused of "making signs." Many observers in the courtroom saw both prisoners frequently hold two fingers against their temples while Margaret testified. This is believed by some to be a vendetta sign commanding silence.[3]

The two men were represented by four attorneys at the trial. During cross-examination, defense counsel questioned Vicce at length about "her past." After her testimony, a special detail of detectives escorted her to the train station where she boarded a train for Providence, Rhode Island, where she had moved from Brooklyn after the murder.

That same night the jury began deliberations. The newspapers reported that as a result of the defendants' actions, "unusual precautions to prevent riot and a possible rescue" were in place. When the jury arrived at a verdict around 11:00 PM, "A great throng of Calabrians, fellow countrymen of the prisoners, who had filled the courtroom and overflowed into the corridors of the courthouse, were driven back to the street and the courthouse gates were locked."[4] The jury then announced it had found Anastasia and Florino guilty of first-degree murder.

Deputies removed the men to a cell beneath the courthouse. Florino "tore his hair" after being led back. Both men "paced the tiny enclosure like tigers newly caged." Deputies then "smuggled out" the jury through a secret entrance, out of the sight of the Calabrian crowd. Moments later, Anastasia and Florino were taken out the same way, placed in a police wagon, and rushed to the Raymond Street Jail. The angry crowd waited outside for more than an hour before being made aware of what transpired. When they began to protest, police dispersed them.

An investigation was made into the "fitness" of the testimony of Margaret Farrara Vicce, which delayed the sentencing for two days. Then on May 25, Anastasia and Florino were brought back before Judge Van Siclen. Asked if they had anything to say before sentence was passed, Anastasia remained silent. Florino, however, spoke for nearly an hour. He told the judge that he had been involved romantically with Vicce and that she has asked him to leave his wife and children for her. Claiming Vicce to be a jealous woman whose love he had spurned, Florino said she had threatened to have him jailed and "has at last succeeded in putting me in the electric chair."[5]

After hearing Florino's plea and denying defense counsel's motion for a new trail, Judge Van Siclen ordered both men to be put to death during the week of July 3, 1921. Taken to the death house at Sing Sing prison, the men waited as defense counsel worked to save their lives. After months on death row, Anastasia and Florino were granted a retrial; however, four witnesses failed to appear. Rumors abounded. Some sources claim that all four disappeared; others claimed they were all murdered. One source stated a witness was scared into going back to Italy. Whatever the circumstances, the state no longer had a case and the two men were acquitted and released from prison.

The near-brush with legal extermination did nothing to set either man straight. Just months after their acquittal on August 16, 1922, Anastasia and Florino were accused of murdering a Red Hook grocer. The charges were dismissed in Magistrate's Court six days later.

On April 6, 1923, Anastasia was arrested in Brooklyn for felonious assault; the charges were dropped later that month. Exactly two months later on June 6, Anastasia was arrested in Brooklyn for carrying a revolver. On July 13 he began a two-year prison term on Blackwell's Island.

While Albert was serving time for carrying a gun, his brothers were arrested for using one. In 1924, Anthony and Joseph, following their brother's lead, jumped ship in New York City. On October 11, 1925, the two brothers, along with two other men, were arrested for the murder of Antonio Auteri. The 24-year-old Auteri had been found with a bullet in his heart at the corner of Walcott and Richards Streets in Brooklyn. He was rushed to Methodist Episcopal Hospital, where he lived long enough to name his assailants. Auteri and the four men arrested, all lived at the same address, 273 Van Brunt Street, a block from the Brooklyn docks. The brothers were held in jail for 10 days before a magistrate dismissed the charges but ordered both brothers deported, as neither had a passport.

In 1929, Anthony returned to New York after jumping ship in San Francisco. On April 13, 1931, another brother, Gerardo (also known as Jerry), jumped ship in New Orleans. Concerned about his own illegal presence in this country, on June 4, 1931, Albert was granted permanent residence with a "certificate of arrival" under the Registry Act of 1929.[6]

WATERFRONT BOSS

During the second half of the 1920s, Anastasia worked on the docks of the Brooklyn waterfront. By now he had gained a reputation as a ruthless thug and murderer. In *Hoodlums—New York,* the authors described the scene:

> The Brooklyn waterfront is one of the busiest shipping centers in the world, and racketeers always have found the pickings correspondingly rich. By the mid-20s, the boy from Tropea had become a pier superintendent—a strategic spot for running the assorted shakedowns and extortions, the loan-sharking, the bookmaking and crap games, the cargo thefts and robberies and the smuggling of everything from aliens to dope. Longshoreman were forced to kick back anywhere from $10 a week to 40% or 50% of their pay. In addition, without ever holding a union office, Anastasia got control of six locals of the International Longshoreman's Association and looted their treasuries of $400 to $500 a month apiece.[7]

Anastasia's activities brought him into contact with such rising underworld luminaries as Joe Adonis, Anthony "Little Augie Pisano" Carfano, Vito Genovese, and Willie Moretti. These relationships would soon result in introductions to Frank Costello, Lucky Luciano, Lepke Buchalter, Jacob "Gurrah" Shapiro, and the Mangano brothers—Phil and Vincent.

According to mob lore, Anastasia developed a fierce loyalty to Lucky Luciano.[8] He was an attendee of the Atlantic City Conference (see Appendix) in May 1929. Although Anastasia' only involvement in the Castellammarese War (see Appendix) was his alleged presence at Scarpato's Villa Tammaro restaurant on Coney Island on April 15, 1931, it was certainly significant. It was there that he was part of the alleged hit squad that murdered Giuseppe "Joe the Boss" Masseria while Luciano relieved himself in the men's room.

After the murder, during a banquet where Salvatore Maranzano announced the reporting structure of the five families, Anastasia was designated as the underboss of the Mangano Family. Although confirmed by Joseph Valachi (see Appendix), Joseph Bonanno, and in the book *The Last Testament of Lucky Luciano* (see Appendix), the role of Anastasia in this family certainly raises questions. Who actually ran this family? Was it Vincent or Phil, or did the brothers run it in tandem? What was Joe Adonis's role? Some sources described him as the actual underboss; some say he was a co-underboss with Anastasia. Still others claim Adonis emerged from Anthony Carfano's shadow to become the sole boss of the Brooklyn underworld. Perhaps most perplexing: if Anastasia was working for the Manganos, how did he become such a close confidante of Lucky Luciano, Frank Costello, and Lepke Buchalter in the years that followed? If he was truly a second fiddle in the Mangano Family, Anastasia seemed content to remain in that capacity for the next 20 years before finally striking out on his own.

Even as the alleged underboss, Anastasia apparently continued to keep an active hand in murder, something most higher-ups in the underworld would consider beneath them. In 1932, he was arrested for the August 7 murder of John Bazzano. The Pittsburgh mobster was found "stabbed and strangled and cut into pieces of assorted size, and stuffed into a burlap bag"[9] before being deposited in the middle of Center Street in the Red Hook section of Brooklyn. Bazzano was believed to be behind the murders of the three Volpe brothers—Arthur, James, and John—on July 29, in a Pittsburgh coffee shop that he owned. Bazzano was allegedly "called" to New York to explain his actions. His body was discovered 10 days after the triple murder in Pittsburgh.

On August 17, police arrested 19 people during a series of raids. Some of the arrested were registered in Manhattan hotels; others were apprehended in nightclubs and speakeasies. Police claimed that a celebration was to take place and that the four alleged killers of Bazzano were to be rewarded. Several of the people apprehended were released, including two women. Among those arraigned were Anastasia (whose first name was given as Robert), John "Johnny Bath Beach" Oddo, Anthony "The Chief" Bonasero and Joseph Traina from New York, Sam DiCarlo, brother of Buffalo mob boss Joe "The Wolf" DiCarlo, Paul Palmieri from Niagara Falls, and six men from Pittsburgh. All of the prisoners were represented by Samuel S. Leibowitz. On August 19, a Brooklyn judge released all the men because of insufficient evidence.

In 1933, Anastasia was again represented by Leibowitz when he was arrested for the August 2 murder of Joseph Santora, the father of 12 children, who worked as a union laundry man. Upset about having to kick back $20 a week to hoodlums, Santora became a little too vocal when he went to the police and ended up in the morgue. At the time Anastasia was still a relatively minor underworld character in the eyes of the police, but his appearance at police headquarters began to change all that. The *New York Herald Tribune* reported that, "His appearance won him the unanimous vote of the detectives as the best dressed prisoner who had ever appeared before them." Dressed in an expensive gray suit, Anastasia twirled a homburg arrogantly as he walked past detectives at the station. Anastasia was indicted for the murder along with Anthony "Tony Spring" Romeo. Before the trial began, charges against Romeo were dismissed because of lack of evidence. Anastasia was tried for the murder of Santora, but he was acquitted by a directed verdict when it was discovered that the state's star witness had committed perjury.

ON THE WATERFRONT

During the late 1920s and through the 1930s, the center of criminal activities on the Brooklyn docks was the City Democratic Club, located at Clinton and Degraw Streets in a building owned by Vincent Mangano. The club was organized to represent the political interests of Americans of Italian descent and naturalized Italians. But over the years, the City Democratic Club became a headquarters and meeting place for members of the Brooklyn underworld.

There were frequent meetings at the club between Anastasia and the Mangano brothers. Albert served as a member of different committees and functions. Other regular visitors to the club were Joe Adonis, Anthony Romeo, "Dandy Jack" Parisi, Giuseppe Florino, and Louis Capone, as well as Anastasias brothers.

During the late 1920s, John "Johnny Silk Stockings" Giustra muscled his way into the leadership of six chapters of the International Longshoremen's Association (ILA) (Locals 327, 328, 346, 903, 938, and 1199). After Giustra was murdered, during the summer of 1931, it was alleged that Vincent Mangano took over with Anthony Romeo acting as the figure-head.[10] With the locals now run by Mangano's people, they began their own "shape up" racket. The "shape up" was the process of deciding which men were going to be employed. The decision, made by the "shape up boss," was based on who was willing to kick back a percentage of their wages.

The men hired were also required to make certain "contributions." One of these was to sign a contract to have their hair cut at a certain barbershop on the pier. Payments were always taken in advance, and workers who actually showed up to use this service soon found themselves out of work. Another "contribution" took place in the fall each year when workers were required to purchase grapes for their wine making, a popular Italian pastime. The men were charged an exorbitant price for the grapes. In addition, workers were required to purchase tickets to social events held at the City Democratic Club. It was reported that sometimes 8,000 to 10,000 tickets were sold for a function where only 400 or 500 could attend. All told, some workers were turning more than 40 to 50 percent of their wages to the underworld.

The ILA locals eventually came under the control of Emil Camarda, whose family, "a clan of union officials," was involved with them for years. They became known as the "Camarda locals"; however, the real power behind them was the Anastasia family, with Albert and Anthony, "Tough Tony," calling the shots. In 1939, a young man by the name of Peter Panto, disgusted and tired of the kickbacks and racketeer activity taking place on the docks, decided to do something. He began by organizing a number of small, private meetings. When he was satisfied that he had solid support, a public meeting was held at which a reported 1,250 members attended on July 8. A couple of days after the meeting, Panto met with Emil Camarda and was advised to "cease his agitation." Panto defied him, declaring that his efforts would continue until "the situation was all cleaned up."

Panto quickly paid a visit to Marcy Protter, a Brooklyn attorney hired by his group to represent the rank and file committee. After relating Camarda's conversation to counsel, Protter advised him that his life was in danger and "under no circumstances go about alone." If he was called to a meeting, he was to travel with others because there was safety in numbers.

On the night of July 14, the 28-year-old Panto was with his fiancée, a young lady with the unlikely name of Alice Maffia. Marcy Protter related the following chain of events while testifying before the New York State Crime Commission in its investigation of the waterfront rackets in 1952:

He had been shaving when someone came in to tell him there was a telephone call for him down at the corner—either the candy store or drug store—and there was with him at the time a brother of the girl to who he was then engaged to be married. He went to answer the telephone call and when he came back he spoke to this young lad, and said there was something funny about that telephone call. He said, "I don't think it is entirely on the square." He had to meet two men, and he didn't know what was going to happen, but he told his intended brother-in-law, this young boy, that if he didn't show up by 10 o'clock the next morning that he should notify the police.[11]

Why Panto decided to go out alone is a question that has never been answered. The young man had a certain level of bravado and had once told Protter that the men he was up against could not frighten him. What is more likely, simply because this is the way the underworld works, is that Panto was lured out alone by someone he knew and trusted, even if he felt the request was not "on the square."

There are several versions of what happened next. One has him leaving in a car with Emil Camarda,[12] Anthony Romeo, and Gus Scannavino. Another, provided by Abe Reles, who got the story second hand, claims that Panto was met by two brothers who were paid $175 to deliver Panto into the hands of Anastasia's men, who were to kill him.

These men were alleged to be James Feracco, Joseph Florino, Anthony Romeo, and Mendy Weiss. Burton Turkus relates the story by Reles, who claims he was told by Weiss that he strangled Panto. During the murder, the younger and lighter Panto put up a terrific fight and at one point managed to get one of Weiss's fingers in his mouth and nearly chewed it off, forcing Weiss to later see a doctor. Reles claimed, "Mendy strangled him as a favor for Albert." Relating the conversation with Weiss later, Reles recalled the killer saying, "Gee, I hated to take that kid. But I had to do it for Albert, because Albert has been good to me."

In December 1952, during the New York State Crime Commission's waterfront probe, a report on the killing suddenly surfaced that was said to have been buried by O'Dwyer. It was from an interview between Assistant Brooklyn District Attorney Edward Heffernan and Murder, Inc. turncoat, Albert "Allie Tick-Tock" Tannenbaum on February 7, 1941. Tannenbaum met with Emmanuel "Mendy" Weiss shortly after Panto's disappearance and noticed several scratches on the hood's hands and questioned him about them:

> He said, "We had a close one the other night." I said, "Yeah?" So he goes on to tell me that [Jimmy] Feracco and [Albert] Anastasia and himself were in a house waiting for somebody to bring some wop out there that they were supposed to kill and bury.
>
> He said, "The guy just stepped into the door and must have realized what it was about and he tried to get out. He almost got out." He said, "It's a lucky thing I was there. If I wasn't there, he would have gotten away. I grabbed him and mugged him . . . and he started to fight and he tried to break the mug, and that's when he scratched me. But he didn't get away."
>
> I said, "What was it about?" He said, "It's Panto, some guy Albert had a lot of trouble with down on the waterfront, and he was threatening to get Albert into a lot of trouble. He was threatening to expose the whole thing, and the only thing Albert could do was to get rid of him. He tried all sorts of different ways to win him over and quiet him down, but he couldn't do anything with him. He had to kill him."[13]

The dumping of Panto's body in the gutter would cause a public outcry, not to mention upheaval by his followers in the union. Instead, his body was taken to a "chicken yard" near a relative of James Feracco in Lyndhurst, New Jersey, and buried.

"KID TWIST" SPEAKS

According to Burton Turkus, it was through Anastasia's waterfront activities that he first became associated with the group of criminals who would become infamous as the Murder, Inc. Turkus simply claims, "Albert became their boss, their commander."[14] As the gang's leader, all "contracts" were forwarded to Anastasia and he in turn distributed the work to Louis Capone, Harry "Happy" Maione, Abe Reles, and Harry "Pittsburgh Phil" Strauss to see that they were carried out. William O'Dwyer declared that no underworld murder "was committed in Brooklyn without Anastasia's permission and approval." Reles claimed that Anastasia played a role in at least 20 murders.

> "In Brooklyn, we all are together with the mob on the docks—
> and it takes in from two to five blocks in from the water, too . . .
> Albert A., who is our boss, is the head guy on the docks. He is
> the Law."
> —Abe Reles discussing role of Albert Anastasia during
> testimony. (Raymond, *Waterfront Priest*, 1955, p. 27)

One of the mysteries about Anastasia is how he came to be so close to Louis Buchalter while Lepke was a fugitive from June 1937 to August 1939. During the two years he was on the lam, Anastasia personally took charge of placing Lepke in various safe houses around the city and then seeing to his needs. Chief among those needs was the murder or intimidation of witnesses who Buchalter felt could hurt him by talking to Special Prosecutor Thomas E. Dewey. More than a dozen of the murders Lepke ordered took place during the first half of 1939, when the manhunt for him intensified. One of the misconceptions about Murder, Inc. was that Buchalter was in charge; instead, Lepke was its biggest customer.

In early 1939, the Dewey crime steamroller was investigating the trucking rackets. Morris "Moishe" Diamond, a Polish immigrant, was the business agent for Local 138, International Brotherhood of Teamsters and Chauffeurs, a position once held by William Snyder, who was murdered in 1934 (see Chapter 3). The *New York Times* reported that Dewey's office denied that Diamond had ever been a witness, but Turkus declared that Diamond "went to Dewey's office to tell of the manipulations, and the mob found out."[15]

Turkus claimed that Buchalter ordered Diamond's assassination. Reles, who said he was not involved in any part of the murder plot, happened to be at Anastasia's home on May 10 on "bookmaking business" when the murder was being discussed between Albert, Mendy Weiss, and Charles "Charlie the Bug" Workman. Apparently, Buchalter was upset that it had yet to be carried out and Anastasia was pressing Weiss to get Diamond's address. It was reported that this was one of the few murders that Anastasia organized in which Reles was not involved; thus it would allow "Kid Twist" to provide corroborating testimony as a nonaccomplice.

The murder took place just after 6 o'clock on the morning of May 25. "Dandy Jack" Parisi shot Diamond at the corner of 18th Avenue and 68th Street in the Borough Park section of Brooklyn. Parisi then escaped in an automobile driven by Julie Catalano, while Anastasia was parked a block away, perhaps serving as a "crash car" if needed. Diamond was taken to Israel

Zion Hospital where he died from five bullet wounds within the hour. The murder investigation was headed up by Brooklyn Detective Captain Frank Bals.

The next victim on the hit list was Phil Orlovsky, a former business agent and manager of Cutters Local, No.4. Instead of killing Orlovsky, Martin "Buggsy" Goldstein stepped out onto the running board of a car driven by Seymour "Blue Jaw" Magoon and fatally shot Irving Penn, a music publishing company executive who lived in the same Bronx apartment building as Orlovsky and was mistaken for the former Buchalter underling. The ensuing public backlash put enough heat on Frank Costello and other mob leaders so that they advised Buchalter it was time to surrender. Anastasia was against this advice and told Buchalter. Nevertheless, when Buchalter made the decision to turn himself in to J. Edgar Hoover, through intermediary Walter Winchell, Anastasia drove him there.

As soon as the rumors leaked that Abe Reles was talking, in March 1940, Anastasia fled his home and went into hiding, as did Anthony Romeo, James Feracco, Joseph Florino, "Dandy Jack" Parisi, and other associates, as the newspapers quickly tied the men to the Panto murder. When Reles revealed Anastasia's role in the murder of Morris Diamond, his brother Anthony was arrested and held as a material witness on a $100,000 bond. He was incarcerated for a week before the bail was cut in half.

By May 1940, O'Dwyer opened an investigation into the Brooklyn waterfront rackets. At the same time another investigation was being conducted by John Harlan Amen. The documents and grand jury testimony from the Amen inquiry were turned over to O'Dwyer at his request, but just as quickly he closed down the probe and no prosecutions were ever pursued.

The next month O'Dwyer invited ILA President Joe Ryan and Emil Camarda to a meeting in his office, where he disclosed some facts learned in his investigation. After leaving the meeting, Ryan announced that major reforms would be carried out on the Brooklyn docks, including having the charters of the "Camarda locals" revoked. Ryan followed through, "but new charters with different numbers were issued to the very same mobsters who controlled the old ones."[16]

News articles claimed that Reles would name the "boss" of Murder, Inc., the "Mr. Big," but so far O'Dwyer was refusing to release that detail. The mystery seemed solved when "other sources" claimed that "the prosecutor is more anxious to capture Albert Anastasia . . . than any other fugitive."[17] On April 2, the *New York World-Telegram* reported, "Whether Anastasia was the president of Murder, Inc., or merely one of the senior vice presidents the prosecutor doesn't know, but he is said to be convinced that if there are higher executives he can reach them only through Anastasia."[18]

In addition to Anastasia, the prosecutor was also looking for Joseph Florino, his longtime associate. The prosecutor's office was worried that with Anastasia, Florino, and Vito "Chicken Head" Gurino on the loose, none of his witnesses would be safe. O'Dwyer announced that the witnesses not already being held in police custody would be protected by detectives. At the time, it was reported that Florino was suffering from a lung ailment and had fled to Arizona, with Vito Gurino serving as his bodyguard. It was suspected that Anastasia had fled to Italy.

On May 13, 1940, O'Dwyer began a search for Peter Panto's body. With assistance from the Bergen County, New Jersey, prosecutor's office, digging began in the back yard of Jerry Coronato at 747 Riverside Avenue in Lyndhurst. Coronato was serving time in the New Jersey State Prison at Trenton for rape. His sister, Rose, was married to James "Dirt Neck

Jimmy" Feracco, who lived across the street from Coronato. Feracco was questioned by authorities in early April, before leaving Rose and his child behind. Rose was later taken into custody. Two weeks of excavating had not uncovered anything or anyone and the work was halted.

Then in January 1941, steam shovels rolled again in Lyndhurst, New Jersey. After three weeks of careful digging, a body was discovered on January 29 in a shallow grave, encrusted in a block of frozen earth and quicklime. Workers were careful in removing the entire chunk of earth. At one point a piece of the frozen quicklime fell off, exposing part of a skeleton and pieces of clothing. The block of earth was first taken to a Lyndhurst morgue. Assistant Kings County Prosecutor Thomas Craddock Hughes, concerned that evidence might fall in the hands of the killing syndicate, ordered the block taken to the Kings County Morgue in Brooklyn. Placed on an open truck, the block was driven to the morgue under heavy police guard. O'Dwyer, who was in Los Angeles conferring with the district attorney on the Benjamin Siegel murder trial, said that if the body turned out to be Panto's, he was ready to prosecute the killers—"that he knew their identities."

On the evening of February 6, O'Dwyer's office announced that the body they discovered was that of Panto. The body had been identified by Peter Massie, Panto's successor in the antigangster union movement within the ILA. Although the identity of the body was not revealed, identification was said to be based on two broken teeth.

The newspapers reminded O'Dwyer of his promise to prosecute, even naming Anastasia, Weiss, and Feracco, all currently in hiding, as the men responsible for Panto's death; however, no indictment was ever made against Anastasia. When Reles fell to his death on November 12, 1941, O'Dwyer simply claimed that his "perfect murder case" against Anastasia had gone out the window with "Kid Twist." Interestingly, he never specified which was the "perfect murder case," The Panto murder or the killing of Morris Diamond. O'Dwyer would claim later that he couldn't prosecute the Panto case, because the body was found outside his jurisdiction.

During this time Anastasia and Romeo remained in hiding.[19] On May 4, 1942, acting on the orders of James J. Moran, the chief clerk in the District Attorney's office and a longtime O'Dwyer confidant, the "wanted" cards on Albert Anastasia and Anthony Romeo were removed from the files. After more than two years in hiding, both men soon reappeared; Anastasia had been residing in Utica, New York.

On May 12, a police lieutenant arrested Romeo, not knowing that he was no longer a wanted suspect. Romeo, while being held, was never questioned by O'Dwyer's office. On May 19, Romeo was arrested for vagrancy on Columbia Street. He told the police that he had been told to get out of Brooklyn, "because the gang did not want him to testify about its activities."[20] Romeo said he planned to leave the next day, but when he was released from the vagrancy charge, he decided to stay.

On June 9, Romeo left his home on Quentin Road to go to the race track. Eight days later, a knotted bundle of clothes was found along the bank of the Brandywine River, near Wilmington, Delaware. In one of the pockets was a card "indicating" that the clothes belonged to Romeo. On June 30, Romeo's body was discovered in a wooded knoll, not far from where his clothes were found. He had been given a vicious beating before being shot to death. Police surmised he had been killed because he refused to leave Brooklyn. Another rumor stated that he was a suspected squealer. Josephine Romeo, his wife, was taken to Wilmington to make a positive identification of the body. In less-than-grieving-widow tones, she told

Wilmington detectives, "I guess he got what was coming to him. I'm glad it's over. I've been slipping in and out of morgues for two years now, always expecting to find his body when police called me."[21]

After 26 months of hiding and being away from his family, Anastasia went away again, this time it was into the U.S. Army to help in the war effort. The *New York Times* detailed Anastasia's entire military career from his enlistment in Utica, where he had hid out a good portion of the time he was gone:

> The Army enlisted Anastasia on July 30, 1942, as "Umberto Anastasio." On Oct. 1, he was promoted from private to private first class, twenty days later to technician fifth class. On May 11, 1943, Anastasia became a sergeant; then on May 14, a staff sergeant.
>
> By June 16, he was a technical sergeant. He was released from service on Nov. 12, 1944.
>
> Anastasia was assigned to Camp Union, N.Y., when he entered the Army. Then he was transferred to Company O, 319th Infantry Regiment, at Camp Forrest, Tenn., where he remained until Oct. 14, 1942.[22]
>
> From Camp Forrest, Anastasia was moved to Indiantown Gap, Pa., on Oct. 15, 1942, serving there until his discharge—a period that covered his three-day rise from sergeant to staff sergeant.[23]

While enlisted, Anastasia reportedly trained GIs how to be longshoremen so they could help service ports on overseas duty. Before he left the army, he had some business to take care of. In March 1943, he applied for a preliminary application to become a U.S. citizen. As a soldier in defense of the United States, he came "under a special dispensation extended to foreign-born GIs by a grateful Uncle Sam."[24] On June 29, while stationed at Indiantown Gap, he was granted U.S. citizenship. Staff Sergeant Umberto Anastasio was honorably discharged from the U.S. Army for being overage, 42, on November 12, 1944.

O'DWYER GETS THE BLAME—AND THE MAYOR'S OFFICE

Hoping to capitalize on his popularity after prosecuting the Murder, Inc. gang, William O'Dwyer ran for mayor in the fall of 1941. He lost to incumbent Fiorello LaGuardia, who was seeking his third term. On June 1, 1942, he entered the Army Air Force with the rank of major. He was assigned to the procurement department and sent to Wright Field in Dayton, Ohio. While stationed there, he made his infamous visit to the Central Park West apartment of Frank Costello (see Chapter 4).

The popular belief is that O'Dwyer had curried favor with the underworld and Costello by not prosecuting Anastasia. To this day, many believe that Frank Bals, the man O'Dwyer placed in charge of protecting Abe Reles, and who rode O'Dwyer's coattails to higher office, was responsible for seeing that "Kid Twist" went out the window at the Half Moon Hotel.

While serving at Wright Field, O'Dwyer won the praise of his superiors. In 1944, Under Secretary of War Robert Patterson commented, "O'Dwyer has done more than anyone else to prevent fraud and scandal in the army air force. His work is of the utmost importance, and I deem him the best-qualified man for it."[25] O'Dwyer was soon headed to Italy, having been appointed by President Roosevelt to oversee the economic section of the Allied Control Commission.

Once in Rome, O'Dwyer earned further accolades for his work. One biographer noted, "He supervised both financial aid and food shipments to the newly-emerging Italian government, and performed his duties so diligently he was credited with saving thousands of civilian lives."[26] His effort was rewarded with a promotion to brigadier general.

Once back to civilian life in New York, O'Dwyer obtained the Democratic nomination for mayor. With LaGuardia declining to run for a fourth term, it was a cinch that O'Dwyer would be voted in as the new mayor; however, it proved to be a daunting task. O'Dwyer was attacked by Judge Jonah T. Goldstein, his Republican opponent. Goldstein claimed that O'Dwyer's nomination was engineered by Joe Adonis, Frank Costello, and Irving Sherman, the last known as an intimate friend of Benjamin Siegel. Sherman was reputedly the front man for Costello, serving as an intermediary between the underworld and O'Dwyer.

The next attack on O'Dwyer came from his old office, the Kings County District Attorney. When O'Dwyer resigned as prosecutor to run for mayor, his position was filled by George J. Beldock, a Republican appointed by Governor Thomas Dewey. On October 29, eight days before the election, a special Kings County grand jury handed down a 29-page presentment, charging O'Dwyer, Joseph Hanley, Edward Heffernan, and James Moran with "gross laxity, inefficiency and maladministration" in office. The presentment stated: "We have found an abandonment of the waterfront rackets investigation and a complete failure to prosecute the perpetrators of serious crimes, although the evidence was admittedly sufficient to require prosecution."[27]

The next evening, O'Dwyer and Beldock made radio addresses during competing broadcasts. Responding to his critics regarding his reputed ties to organized crime leaders, O'Dwyer declared:

> I am today in exactly the same state of mind toward gangsters and the underworld that I was in 1940. Lest the underworld might take too much comfort from what has happened in Brooklyn within the last few weeks, I want to give them a message now—if they are here they had better pack up and get out fast, because when I go in as Mayor of the City of New York it will be just as hot for them in 1946 as it was in Brooklyn in 1940. They will travel the same trail that led others to the electric chair.[28]

In his statement, Beldock focused on Anastasia, the waterfront rackets, and the murder of Peter Panto.

The Peter Panto murder would continue to dog O'Dwyer even into his reelection in 1949. In early 1951, he was called before the Kefauver Committee and grilled as to why no indictment was ever requested against Anastasia. As for Anastasia, by now he had earned the nickname "The Lord High Executioner" and would forever be linked to the murder ring. Until the day he died, and well past that, his name seldom appeared in the newspapers without the words, "former head of the Brooklyn gang known as Murder, Inc."

RETURN TO NEW YORK

After his discharge from the army, Anastasia returned to New York City and his activities on the waterfront. By this time his brother Anthony had begun his ascent to the top of the Brooklyn labor unions on the docks. While Albert was training longshoremen in the service, former associates of his were at work. Benedetto "Benny" Macri, described as a "young protégé" of Anastasia, helped organize the Sancor Marine Corporation, a shipyard operation, and served as the treasurer. Benny and his brother Vincent Macri served in a number of capacities for Anastasia, from bodyguards to businessmen. Both were very loyal.

Sancor was able to obtain a number of government contracts for its ship work, but the quality of their work was questionable. Interviewed years later about their productivity, an official from the U.S. Maritime Commission commented, "It was a hell of a strange yard. They did as much damage to our ships as they repaired. There seemed to be evidence of culpable negligence."[29] The company was operating at some level of success and within a few years relocated from Brooklyn to North Bergen, New Jersey.

In the mid-1940s, Anastasia moved his family into a newly built yellow stucco, Spanish-style home at 75 Pine Bluff Road, Palisades, New Jersey, a suburb of Fort Lee. The house, built between 1945 and 1947, and overlooking the Hudson River, was just a few blocks away from the home of his close friend Joe Adonis. The house was listed under the names of Elsa and Albert Barghesi, the maiden name of Anastasia's wife. Anastasia was certainly concerned with security at his new home. The property was inaccessible on the eastside because of the steep cliffs of the Palisades, which had a 200-foot drop to the waterfront. Located at the foot of Pine Bluff Road, it was on the very edge of a cliff. The rest of the house was surrounded by a 7-foot wire fence, topped with barbed wire. Inside the grounds, Doberman pinschers roamed freely.

According to various reports, the house cost anywhere from $50,000 to $100,000 to build. With postwar building materials hard to obtain, Anastasia allegedly used materials from the shipyard. It was reported that Benny Macri supplied workmen from Sancor to assist in the building of the palatial home. Some of the workers later claimed they had worked for weeks on the home while on the Sancor payroll. At its peak, Sancor employed nearly 400 men. On June 6, 1947, the company filed for bankruptcy in Brooklyn Federal Court. The company was in the red nearly $485,000, with a government claim of $500,000 for back taxes and damage claims.

In addition to bleeding Sancor dry, Anastasia had taken on the role of "enforcer" in strike-breaking activities, according to the New Jersey attorney general's office. In 1946, Anastasia and his brother Anthony were involved in a lengthy strike at the Phelps-Dodge copper plant in Elizabeth, New Jersey. During the eight-month strike, Anthony was reported to have provided strikebreakers at the cost of $1,000 a day. The men were supplied by the AA Stevedoring Company, owned by the Anastasias. Anthony was seen leading a group of "thugs and goons" to break a picket line and send several men to the hospital. During the strike one man was shot to death.

No one questioned Albert's overall position and power on the waterfront, but his presence on the docks was "rarely seen" after moving into his Fort Lee home. In 1948, Albert diversified his activities and became a part-owner of the Madison Dress Company,[30] located in Hazelton, Pennsylvania.

1951

As with many of the mobsters chronicled in this book, 1951 was a watershed year. This proved even more so for Anastasia, who reached the pinnacle of his career. In mid-February, Anastasia and his brother Anthony were questioned in a closed "secret" hearing by Senator Estes Kefauver before scheduled public hearings that were to take place in New York the next month. When the committee had finished for the day, Kefauver claimed that Albert Anastasia had invoked his Fifth Amendment rights to so many questions that he was going to be cited for contempt of Senate, unless of course he provided answers the committee would accept on their return on March 19.

Among the few questions Anastasia answered was that he was retired from the docks and was a partner in the Madison Dress Company. He told the investigators that after his discharge from the army, he returned to Brooklyn and worked for his brother Anthony for about four to six months. "I was a stevedore superintendent, and hired people to work. A superintendent is above the hire foreman. The hire foreman designates the men in the gangs and the superintendent walks around the pier and sees that they do their work."[31] But he wouldn't discuss his personal finances, he refused to name the contractor who built his Fort Lee home, and he would not answer questions about Macri supplying labor to build the home.

On March 2, the *New York Times* reported that Vincent Mangano and Vito Genovese, both being sought by Kefauver Committee investigators for questioning, had been missing for three weeks. Genovese had simply gone into hiding to avoid having to appear before the committee. Mangano, on the other hand, the reputed head of the family since 1931, disappeared forever. He was never heard from again and his body was never found.

The New York City hearings of the Kefauver Committee began on Monday, March 19, with the first session lasting well into the evening hours. Anthony Anastasio was the last witness called. He told the committee that he and his brothers had all entered the country by "jumping ship," but they had legalized their entry by reentering through Canada on regular visas. Senator Herbert O'Conor responded by stating he would ask immigration officials in Washington D.C. to check the naturalization applications of the brothers and, if they proved to be fraudulent, have them deported."[32]

Albert was not around to testify. A physician wired the Senate Committee to inform them that Anastasia was admitted to St. Mary's Hospital in Passaic on the night of March 20, suffering from conjunctivitis. In his absence, his testimony from the "secret" hearing back on February 14 was read into the record. On April 2, Kefauver announced that a contempt charge against Albert Anastasia would be forthcoming.

The threat of a Senate contempt charge did not deter Anastasia from his plans to take over the Mangano gang. At around 10:00 on the morning of April 19, the wife of a fishing boat operator discovered the body of a man among the tall grass in marshland near Jamaica Bay in the Bergen Beach section of Brooklyn. The body was face down in the dirt, dressed, but missing pants, shoes, and an overcoat.

There was no identification on the body, which was removed to the Medical Examiner's office, where it was fingerprinted. The body had three bullet wounds—one in each cheek and a third in the back of the neck—all fired at close range. It was determined that the man had been dead between 10 and 24 hours. By 4:30 that afternoon, police fingerprint records confirmed the body to be that of Philip Mangano.

It would be another 12 years before Joseph Valachi would first inform the world of the Mangano brothers' position in the underworld hierarchy. So it is no surprise that the *New York Times* reported the murder on page 18 under the headline "Aide of Joe Adonis" found murdered. Two days later, after the questioning of 75 people, police said they had failed to locate a single lead.

On April 27, following the questioning of Frank Costello regarding the murder, the *New York Times* reported, "In assorted publications, some official, Mangano, Costello, Adonis and Albert Anastasia, the gangster, have been connected with the crime syndicate known as the Mafia." The article described Mangano as "an important member of the Adonis gang." Interestingly, none of the *New York Times* articles reporting Philip Mangano's death ever mentioned his missing brother Vincent.

That same day, both Anastasia and Adonis were questioned by New Jersey authorities. Both men admitted to knowing Mangano for more than 20 years, but neither claimed to have seen him in the past six months. After the questioning of Philip's son Vincent, Assistant Kings County District Attorney Samuel Gitlin stated that Mangano was an alleged Mafia leader. Vincent claimed that his family had urged Philip to leave New York after exposure from the Kefauver Committee hearings. He claimed his father had visited Virginia twice, where he was looking into purchasing a contracting business.[33]

In Joseph Bonanno's *A Man of Honor,* he speaks in fond terms of his relationship with Vincent Mangano, but fails to mention Philip once in the book. He comments:

> After Mangano's death, his family recognized Anastasia as the new father, and Albert took his place on the Commission. No one seemed to resent Albert's elevation more that [Willie] Moretti. Anastasia now was head of his own Family and closer to Costello than ever. Up to then, it had been Moretti who was the closest to Costello. Moretti had prided himself on being the "iron" behind Costello's influence.[34]

Bonanno goes on to say that when Anastasia appeared before the Commission, following Mangano's disappearance, he didn't acknowledge any responsibility, claiming only that he had proof Mangano was plotting to kill him. Costello vouched for Anastasia, which assured him of a position on the Commission. Bonanno claimed that Moretti was upset with Costello for corroborating Anastasia's story and felt betrayed, having never been made aware of their plans. In Bonanno's recounting, he does not seem to consider how sick Moretti was by this point.

On the morning of October 4, 1951, Anastasia left his Fort Lee home and went to St. Mary's Hospital to have his knee x-rayed. Later that morning, four men greeted Moretti when he arrived at Joe's restaurant in Cliffside Park, across from the Palisades Amusement Park. When a waitress went to get menus for the men, she heard several gunshots. When she returned to the dining room, she found it empty, except for the lifeless body of Moretti sprawled on the tile floor.

By most accounts, Anastasia was aware of the pending assassination of the 57-year-old mob leader, perhaps even being part of the approval process. He had checked himself into the hospital simply to establish an alibi for himself; however, there were also reports that Anastasia was on the hit list himself. One story claimed he was supposed to be with Moretti that morning but had been warned as to what was going to happen. He then checked into the hospital to stay out of harm's way.

It was also reported that on the night of October 30, Anastasia attended a celebration after the acquittal of Benny Macri for the murder of William Lurye.[35] While he was there, two armed gunmen arrived uninvited. According to the *New York Times,* the New York City Anti Crime Committee reported that Anastasia "fled out the back door as his enemies burst in the front, pistols in hand." This information, released by the committee three weeks after the incident occurred, also stated that Anastasia "has not left his home in Fort Lee, N.J., in six weeks unless accompanied by Benedict (sic) or [Vincent] Macri or members of his immediate family."[36]

After the Lurye murder trial, neither brother was mentioned in the newspapers until the spring of 1954. By that time Benny was reported to have been on the run since the previous year, having gone into hiding after attempting to sell a stolen government bond worth $100,000. On April 25, the body of Vincent Macri was found by a resident of Wickham Avenue in the Bronx. The man noticed that a 1953 green and cream-colored convertible had been left unattended for a couple days. He discovered the car keys on the floor when he went to investigate. After opening the trunk he found a body jammed inside. Identification was made through a driver's license in the glove compartment. Macri was shot twice at close range in the right temple. Police theorized his body had been dragged to his car before being deposited in the trunk.

At the time, Vincent was under investigation by both the Federal Bureau of Narcotics and the Treasury Department. He was rumored to be a close associate of Bergen County, New Jersey gambling figures and a regular visitor to Joe's Restaurant in Cliffside Park, where Willie Moretti met his demise.

Detectives went to Vincent Macri's home in the Bronx to question his wife Betty. She said she had last seen her husband when he arrived home on Friday evening, April 23, around 6:30 PM. When she asked him about taking one of their three children to a school function, he said he had to go out and see someone, but would return in five minutes. Despite being gone for more than 36 hours, Betty Macri did not notify anyone until Sunday afternoon when she called Vincent's brother Nicholas.

On May 1, police in Harrison, New Jersey, found an abandoned, blood-stained automobile near the Passaic River. On hearing of its discovery, Edward Cohen, Benny Macri's business partner, called police and told them the car was his, but he had lent it to Benny three weeks earlier. Three days later, after confirmation that the blood found in the abandoned automobile matched Benny Macri's type, police began dragging the Passaic River for his body. It was never found.

THE WATERFRONT HEARINGS

In Virgil W. Peterson's *The Mob: 200 Years of Organized Crime in New York,* the author gives us the following description of the New York docks during the mid-twentieth century:

> The Port of New York, the greatest in the world, has been described as an outlaw frontier. For many years, pier facilities representing an investment of almost a billion dollars were under the control of gangsters, many of whom were ex-convicts and murderers. At the time of the hearings, the waterfront of the port had over seven hundred miles of shoreline. Of some three hundred deep-sea piers, the city of New York owned 159. The port area included piers in the Hudson River, the East River, in Brooklyn, Staten Island, and New Jersey. In 1948, 19.3 percent in tonnage of all exports and imports of the United States passed through the Port of New York and represented a value of over seven billion dollars.[37]

The New York State Crime Commission was established in the wake of the Kefauver Committee during the winter of 1951. It began after a conference between Governors Thomas E. Dewey of New York and Alfred E. Driscoll of New Jersey. Joseph M. Proskauer, a former New York Supreme Court justice, was selected to oversee the commission. The chief target of the commission was the New York/New Jersey waterfront.

On September 3, 1952, the commission subpoenaed the bank records of 300 individuals including public officials, politicians, underworld figures, and union executives. The *New York Times* reported that the bank subpoenas, seeking transactions back to January 1, 1946, "demanded that the banks provide all records on both open and closed accounts, including cancelled checks, information on safe deposit boxes and whether the persons listed had obtained mortgage loans."[38]

Upsetting to the commission members was the leak to the newspapers of the secret subpoenas, as well as the list of names. Included on that list, for several persons, were the names of wives and relatives in case some individuals had tried to camouflage transactions under their names. Underworld names easily recognized included the four Anastasio brothers, Vincent Alo, Anthony Carfano, Vito Genovese, Anthony Giustra, Meyer Lansky, Thomas Lucchese, John Oddo, Joseph Profaci, Constantino Scannavino, and Abner Zwillman. Also included was Vincent Mangano, even though he had been missing for 18 months.

The hearings were scheduled to be held in early December, well after the fall elections. During the first week, Albert and Gerardo were scheduled to appear on December 5. Albert was to meet privately with commission members at an office on Broadway, but failed to appear. His attorney notified the commission counsel that his client was at home in bed recovering from a recent automobile accident. The attorney assured the commission that Anastasia "will be available. There is nothing he has to fear. He severed all connections with waterfront operations fourteen years ago."[39]

Gerardo appeared at the commission's public hearing at the New York County Courthouse but refused to answer questions asked by Special Counsel Theodore Kiendl. Gerardo's counsel declared his client wished "to challenge the constitutionality of the commission." He was sharply rebuked by the presiding commissioner and told he was "out of order that he had no privilege of challenge at a public hearing."

On December 19, Albert took the stand and gave a defiant performance, which the *New York Times* called "the most dramatic incident of the hearings to date." Anastasia was sworn in using his birth name. After a brief statement by his lawyer, questioning began. Anastasia discussed his employment as a longshoreman soon after his arrival in America, but said he could not remember the name or number of the local he was a member of, or if he paid dues. In an appearance that lasted an hour, Anastasia refused to answer 97 questions put to him by the commission.

The public hearings by the New York State Crime Commission continued until March 1953, at which time a subcommittee of the U.S. Senate Interstate & Foreign Commerce Committee began hearings on the New Jersey/New York Waterfront. When the New York State Crime Commission released their report in May, many of the recommendations it made were provided by Reverend John Michael Corridan, known as the "Waterfront Priest," who had spent six years studying the plight of the longshoreman.

A Waterfront Commission Act and Compact was established. Among the recommendations adopted was the creation of a commission requiring the licensing of stevedoring businesses, hiring agents, pier superintendents, and port watchmen. Longshoremen were required to register, and those with long criminal records or ties to the underworld were turned away. Most important, the decade's old "shape up" system was eliminated.

DENATURALIZATION BATTLE

In the wake of the Kefauver Hearings, the government initiated efforts to deport 100 underworld figures. Big names in the New York/New Jersey area included Frank Costello, Thomas Lucchese, Vito Genovese, and Albert Anastasia.

The effort to deport Anastasia did not begin soon enough to help one man. On February 18, 1952, Arnold L. Schuster, a 24-year-old clothing salesman who worked at his father's tailor store, was on a subway when he recognized wanted bank robber Willie Sutton sitting across from him. They both got off at the same stop and Schuster followed him to a filling station. While Sutton was there, Schuster went looking for a police officer to inform him of his find.

Later that day, Schuster heard of the capture and arrest of Sutton, but what he did not hear was his role in the apprehension. Hearing a rumor that there was a $70,000 reward for the bank robber, Schuster notified the police the next day and on February 20, he was officially recognized for his role in the capture. Schuster was on the front page of the newspapers and on the evening news. The reward turned out to be $500, but even more unfortunate for Schuster, his "15 minutes of fame" was seen on TV by Albert Anastasia. According to Joseph Valachi, Anastasia became enraged, and even though he did not know Sutton, he exploded, "I can't stand squealers. Hit that guy!"[40]

On the night of March 8, Schuster was walking home from work and was 10 houses away from his home on Forty-Fifth Street in Brooklyn. A man walking toward him suddenly pulled a gun and began firing. It was a brutal killing. Schuster was shot once in each eye and twice in the groin and left lying on the sidewalk.[41] According to Valachi, Frederick J. Tenuto, was the killer. With all the publicity of the brazen killing, to cover himself, Anastasia ordered Tenuto killed and his body was never found.[42] When this story was revealed by Valachi in October 1963, the New York Police Department called the story a "stale rumor" from a "small, publicity-loving bum." Still, it proved the viciousness of Anastasia and showed that the title of the "Lord High Executioner" was deserved.

In the midst of the New York Waterfront Crime Commission hearings, the U.S. government made its first move to deport Anastasia by filing suit in Newark to denaturalize him. The basis for the suit was "statements under oath that he had never used any name but his true one, Umberto Anastasio; that he had never been arrested; and that he had been lawfully admitted to the United States in 1917."[43]

The suit claimed that Anastasia had obtained naturalization papers "illegally and fraudulently" by means of false statements made to deceive officials and prevent them from conducting a proper investigation into his citizenship application. His application stated that he "had never been arrested, summoned in court as a defendant, convicted, fined, imprisoned, or placed on probation for an act involving a felony, misdemeanor or breach of any ordinance." He was also accused of using fraud to obtain a "certificate of arrival" in 1931 from the Immigration & Naturalization Service.

On December 9, 1952, deputy marshals went to the Fort Lee residence of Anastasia to serve the summons and complaint. They were detained at the padlocked front gate by two Doberman pinschers and had to wait until Anastasia's son, 22-year-old Umberto, Jr., came out of the house. The young man warned the deputies and the reporters that tagged along with them, "Don't put your foot in here, the dogs will bite it off."[44] He claimed his father was still in bed, recovering from injuries suffered in a recent automobile accident, the same injuries that Anastasia's lawyer said prevented him from appearing before the Waterfront Commission.

The government's denaturalization efforts lay dormant for the next nine months as the country switched from 20 years of Democratic leadership to the Republican administration of Dwight D. Eisenhower. These changes at the top level of government normally meant a turnover in the U.S. attorney's offices. As the new regime of William F. Tompkins began in Newark, he announced that one of his top priorities was to expedite the denaturalization efforts for Anastasia and Genovese, as well as to "scrutinize the activities" of Abner "Longy" Zwillman.

Despite the desire to expedite the proceeding, the case did not come before the court until December 29, 1953. A civil proceeding, regarded as a preliminary action before actual deportation could be pursued, was held before Federal Judge William F. Smith in Newark. The government presented its evidence that Anastasia had made false application in 1943 by concealing a record of nine arrests between March 1921 and October 1936. The proceeding lasted two days, during which Anastasia did not take the stand. Afterward, Judge Smith reserved the decision. On April 14, 1954, Judge Smith announced the cancellation of Anastasia's citizenship. In his opinion, the judge stated:

> The statements made by the defendant, both in his application and his oral examination, were knowingly false. The defendant had been arrested on [nine] occasions; thrice on a charge of homicide, once on a charge of felonious assault; and once on a charge of unlawful possession of a revolver.
>
> The defendant willfully and deliberately concealed his criminal record and thereby perpetrated a fraud upon the Immigrant Inspector and upon the Commissioner General of Immigration.[45]

The order to denaturalize Anastasia was signed by Judge Smith in federal court on April 26. An assistant U.S. attorney told the judge that deportation proceedings would be put on hold to allow time for an appeal by Anastasia's counsel. Nearly a year-and-a-half passed before the U.S. Court of Appeals for the Third Circuit in Philadelphia heard arguments. On September 19, 1955, the higher court overturned Judge Smith's ruling in a 2 to 1 decision. The majority opinion held that when Anastasia was examined in 1943, the experienced naturalization examiner "must have realized the petitioner had fraudulently concealed his criminal record in 1931." Since the investigation was completed and approval for the application for citizenship recommended, the jurists questioned, "in light of these circumstances, how can it be said that the Government was the victim of any fraud on the part of the defendant when he received his naturalization in 1943?"[46]

On November 17, the same court refused to reconsider its decision to restore Anastasia's citizenship. Finally, on May 14, 1956, the matter was settled for good when the U.S. Supreme Court refused to review the lower court's decision.

FEDERAL INCOME TAX CASE

In addition to the deportation cases, another result of the Kefauver Hearings was the launching of a number of federal income tax evasion cases against underworld figures, especially the subpoenaed witnesses who adamantly refused to discuss their finances with the committee. On March 10, 1954, while the denaturalization decision by Judge Smith was still pending, a federal grand jury in Newark indicted Anastasia on two counts of income tax evasion totaling $11,742 for the years 1947 and 1948. If found guilty, Anastasia was looking at a prison sentence of up to five years on each count. An hour after the indictment was announced by Federal Judge Alfred E. Modarelli, Anastasia appeared in court to plead not guilty.

U.S. Attorney William Tompkins asked for a bail of $25,000, which was opposed by Anastasia's counsel Anthony J. Calandra. The attorney claimed his client had known for two years that his returns were being audited by the IRS and "he has made no effort to liquidate his assets or flee jurisdiction." Judge Modarelli set bond at $10,000, claiming the defendant did not need to have this additional burden placed upon him "because he is Umberto Anastasio, who has received a lot of publicity."[47]

In October 1954, the government subpoenaed 110 witnesses to testify at Anastasia's tax trial, including Rudolph Halley, the former chief counsel for the Kefauver Committee. The case would be presented on a "net worth and expenditure" method, which meant the government would show how Anastasia "spent money far in excess of his reported income, which was not derived from loans, gifts or inheritance."[48]

The focus of the government's case was the costs associated with the construction, furnishing, and decorating of Anastasia's Fort Lee home. During his "secret" session with the Kefauver Committee investigators, Anastasia claimed the cost of the home was $50,000. During the trail, witness testimony showed that expenditures had exceeded $75,000. One of the key witnesses was Charles Ferri, the former owner of a heating and plumbing business in Fort Lee. He testified that Anastasia had paid him $8,700 for four bathrooms and a heating system.

The trial began on Monday, October 18 and lasted five weeks. The jury, consisting of seven men and five women, was given the case after the noon hour on Friday, November 19. Anastasia did not take the stand. His counsel claimed that Albert's wife, Elsa, "defrayed the bulk of the costs from adequate cash reserves."[49]

The panel deliberated 13 hours, until 1:30 AM Saturday morning before telling Judge Modarelli they were deadlocked. The judge, reluctant to dismiss the panel after the expense of a five-week trial, put them in a hotel for the night. They returned to their deliberations at 10:30 AM, but at 2:00 PM they reported there was no prospect of breaking the deadlock. Judge Modarelli declared a mistrial and dismissed the panel. The government attorney claimed they would retry the case at the earliest possible date.

Six days later the government announced that the earliest possible date was February 15, 1955. Delays pushed that date back to May 10. Before that date arrived, however, the government suddenly found itself short one key witness. Charles Ferri had retired from his Fort Lee plumbing and heating business 18 months earlier and had moved with his wife to a "richly furnished" suburban home northeast of Miami. On April 29, the 68-year-old Ferri was served with a subpoena to appear as a witness for Anastasia's second income tax trial. That evening he and his wife visited their daughter. It was the last time they were seen alive. Two days passed and when the daughter couldn't contact her parents she and her husband went to their home. On the lawn were Ferri's blood-stained shoes. When they entered the house they found a blood-spattered scene. Police surmised the couple was killed, their bodies wrapped in a drape, which had been torn from a living room window, and taken to a place to be disposed.

After a few more postponements, the second trial was scheduled to begin on May 31. The new trial was slated to be held in Camden, New Jersey, after Anastasia asked for and received a change of venue. On May 23, however, Anastasia, along with his attorney Anthony Calandra and a priest, appeared at the federal courthouse in Camden, where Judge Thomas M. Madden interrupted a jury trial to hear an unexpected plea.

Anastasia pleaded guilty to tax evasion as a surprised U.S. Attorney Raymond Del Tufo listened and offered no objection. Judge Madden warned Anastasia before his plea that he could be sent to jail and, after hearing the plea, set June 3 for the sentencing date. Anastasia was looking at the possibility of a 10-year sentence in a federal penitentiary.

On June 3, claiming his client had had a clean record since 1935, attorney Calandra asked Judge Madden for a suspended sentence and a fine. He told the judge that he had heard from a reliable source that the jury in the first trial had voted nine to three for acquittal before being dismissed. Prosecutor Del Tufo recommended that the judge use the same sentencing structure that was applied to Frank Costello's conviction a year earlier—a recommendation that Madden followed. The judge sentenced Anastasia to one year in prison and a fine of $10,000 on each count. The prison terms were to be served concurrently, but the total fine of $20,000 carried a proviso that it had to be paid in full before Anastasia would be set free.

With the government's key witness, Charles Ferri, presumed dead, Del Tufo admitted that his absence would have presented a "formidable" obstacle during a second trial. This, coupled with the fact that the first jury was hung at nine to three for acquittal, raised the question: "Why was Anastasia so willing to risk a 10-year stretch in the penitentiary."

On sentencing day, instead of 10 years, Anastasia received 10 months in the federal penitentiary in Milan, Michigan, and was released on March 28, 1956. His tax woes were not over yet. On August 16, 1957, the federal government filed a civil suit to recover more than $250,000 in back taxes and penalties for the years 1946 through 1952. Attorneys for Anastasia claimed harassment and that the government estimates were exaggerated. The case would never go to trial.

STORMS CLOUDS OF 1957

In May 1956, Anastasia agreed to testify behind closed doors before members of the Senate Permanent Investigations Subcommittee. He was questioned about racketeer-controlled companies that held contracts to produce and ship military uniforms. Next up was the Senate Select Committee on Improper Activities in the Labor or Management Field, known as both the "Rackets Committee" and the "McClellan Committee." The committee had plans to subpoena Anastasia for questioning in early 1957. The subpoena was never served, as counsel for Anastasia said his client would appear voluntarily.

While both Anastasia and Frank Costello were embroiled with constant legal battles, Vito Genovese was plotting his move to take control of the crime family he had relinquished 20 years earlier. He had already eliminated Willie Moretti, the New Jersey ally of the two, in October 1951. Another ally, Joe Adonis, had allowed himself to be deported to Italy in January 1956.

Then on May 2, 1957, Genovese made his boldest move of all by trying to assassinate Costello in his apartment lobby on Central Park West. The murder attempt failed, but for all intents and purposes Costello was ready to capitulate.

The New York underworld sat back and waited to see who was going to make the next move. That move came on June 17, 1957, with the murder of Frank Scalise. Anastasia's reputed underboss was shot down at a Bronx produce stand by two gunmen. It was never confirmed who was behind the killing. Some believe it was part of Vito Genovese's plan to take over the New York underworld. Another theory was that Anastasia had Scalise killed because he was "commercializing" the Mafia by selling memberships.

On Friday, October 25, 1957, Anastasia left his Fort Lee sanctuary about 7:00 AM and headed toward the George Washington Bridge, making his way into Manhattan. He was driving a 1957 Oldsmobile that belonged to Anthony Coppola, who served in various capacities for Anastasia, including bodyguard, chauffeur, and messenger.

His movements before 10:00 AM are a mystery to this day, but around 10:10 he walked into the barbershop of Arthur Grasso, located in the Park Sheraton Hotel at Seventh Avenue and West 55th Street. This was the same hotel, known then as the Park Central, in which Arnold Rothstein received his fatal wound on November 4, 1928. On duty this day were five barbers, two bootblacks, a manicurist, and a valet.

After hanging up his topcoat and suit jacket, Anastasia took a seat and waited patiently for 63-year-old Joseph Bocchino to finish with a customer. At 10:20 he took his place in Chair No. 4, which he must have considered to be in a strategic position. In the 10-chair barbershop, it was the only chair that provided a full view of the shop, by way of mirrored walls, and gave him a window view out to West 55th Street.

Anastasia sat facing the mirror as Bocchino put the barber sheet over him and draped a cloth around his neck. He seemed completely at ease as the barber began working with the electric shears on the curls at the back of his head. Within a minute or so, two men entered the shop through the hotel entrance in the corridor, which was to Anastasia's right rear. Both held scarves across the lower halves of their faces and had hats pulled low on their foreheads. Once across the threshold, they drew revolvers. Encountering Grasso at the cashier's booth in the right corner as they walked in, one gunman spoke through his scarf, "Keep your mouth shut if you don't want your head blown off."[50]

The two gunmen then stepped quickly toward Chair No. 4, ignoring the other two customers in the shop. In Anastasia's relaxed state, he must have had his eyes closed or he would have clearly seen the two assassins advancing on him in the mirror. Some later stories claimed hot towels covered his face, but this wasn't verified by the newspaper stories of the day. Both gunmen then took up positions behind Anastasia. The *New York Times* describes what happened next:

Both men seemed to open fire at once. The shots came in short spurts. One gun roared, and stopped. The other gun roared and stopped. The sound had a weird cadence.

Anastasia leaped forward with the first report. His heavy feet kicked at the foot rest and tore it away. He landed on his feet, weaving. He did not turn around to face the killers. He lunged further forward, still facing the mirror. The second spurt of bullets threw him against the glass shelving in front of the mirror. He grabbed for the shelving and brought a glass of bay rum to the tiles with a shattering crash. He took two further shots. Then the last shot—so the police figure it—took him back of the head.

The heavy body turned. Anastasia fell to the floor two chairs away. He fell on his left side. One pudgy hand was outstretched. The fluorescent lights kicked fire from the diamonds in his fat finger ring. He lay still.[51]

The shooting was hardly the work of the legendary Mafia hit man. Ten bullets were fired at Anastasia from point-blank range. Two hit him in the left hand and wrist, a third entered his back, and a fourth grazed his hip. The fifth bullet proved to be the death shot, hitting Anastasia in the back of the head, it penetrated the left side of his brain.

The gunmen did not speak as they "strode" to the door they had entered moments earlier. Bystanders in the hotel corridor either dropped to the floor or fled in panic at the sound of the gunfire. No one seemed to notice which way the gunmen turned once they left the barbershop. Near a glass-enclosed vestibule leading out to West 55th Street, one of the men dropped a .38 Colt revolver with five of its six shells spent. The second weapon, a .32 Smith & Wesson revolver, was found in a trash can in the subway, the entrance of which was about 40 feet from the vestibule and hotel entrance on West 55th.

Dr. Robert Cestari, from nearby St. Clare's Hospital, entered the barbershop and knelt next to Anastasia. He rolled him over on his back and opened his shirt, thus resolving the mystery of why Anastasia was photographed bare-chested lying on the barbershop floor. Applying a stethoscope to his chest, Cestari checked for a heartbeat, which was not there. "He's dead," the doctor announced.

> "Albert Anastasia's grisly and dramatic demise in the Midtown Manhattan barbershop was to lift him immediately into American gangsterdom's hall of fame. Erratic and psychopathic, Anastasia was a Bugsy Siegel without the charm. He had hurt and threatened so many people that, once it happened, his violent end could be seen to have had a certain inevitability—even a certain justice—about it."
>
> —Lacey, *Little Man: Meyer Lansky and the Gangster Life*, 1991, p. 239

By now the hotel corridor, the barbershop, and West 55th Street was teeming with New York City policemen and detectives. Newspaper reporters, photographers, and cameramen rushed to the scene. One newspaper office contacted one of its reporters at Brooklyn Police Headquarters. He telephoned Anthony Anastasia at his ILA office on Court Street and broke the news to him. Anthony, accompanied by some of his union men, raced out of the office and sped into Manhattan by car. Anthony rushed into the barbershop, where a detective pulled aside a sheet covering his brother. The union leader sobbed openly as he was led back to his car. Anastasia was driven a short distance to the West 54th Street Station, where he was briefly questioned by detectives before they allowed him to leave.

Anastasia's remains were hauled out of Grasso's barbershop in a body bag and placed in a waiting police wagon while the newsreel cameras captured the scene. At the Bellevue Hospital morgue, Umberto Anastasio, Jr. appeared to officially identify his father's body a few hours later, after the autopsy was completed. In addition to his wife and son, Anastasia left behind three younger children: Richard 14, Gloriana 8, and Joyanna 8 months old.

The body of Anastasia was taken to the funeral chapel of Andrew Torregrossa & Sons on 79th Street in Brooklyn on Friday evening. He was laid out in a maroon-colored steel coffin, dressed in a dark-blue suit, white shirt, and blue tie. Wrapped around his right hand were red rosary beads, which held his left wrist, covering the area where the two bullets struck. The next day more than a hundred visitors viewed the body. Detectives wrote down the license plate numbers of the automobiles as they dropped off the mourners. Those who had parked some distance away were followed back to their cars by police so that their license numbers could be obtained.

On the cold morning of October 28, about 50 people entered the funeral chapel to pay their last respects. Because of Anastasia's notorious past, he was not allowed the last rites of the Catholic Church and, although the Anastasios had a family plot in Holy Cross Cemetery in Brooklyn, Albert was refused burial in consecrated ground. Father Salvatore Anastasio had not even bothered to check with the Brooklyn or New Jersey Catholic diocese for permission. At the funeral chapel a simple prayer was said by the director. In one description of the funeral, a reporter wrote: "Anastasia's funeral was lacking in the opulence that have characterized gangster funerals in the past. He reposed in an inexpensive steel coffin, and no long retinue of flower-bedecked mourners' cars accompanied the hearse to the cemetery"[52]

At Greenwood Cemetery earlier that morning, Father Anastasio visited and blessed the grave that would contain his older brother. He did not attend the graveside service. There were 12 mourners in attendance, including Anastasia's wife and son (the three youngest children remained at home), as well as brothers Anthony, Frank, and Gerardo. The burial took place not far from a fence where the morbid-fascinated gathered. A number of large floral pieces blocked their view. For any outsider who dared venture near, a dozen detectives were present to ward them off. The brief graveside ceremony was over in seven minutes.

AFTERMATH

The first person detectives wanted to question was Anthony Coppola. The 49-year-old bodyguard surrendered to police early Friday evening. He was questioned until 5:00 o'clock Saturday morning and released. At 2:00 that afternoon, he was picked up and questioned throughout the afternoon and night. He was finally booked at 1:10 on Sunday morning for vagrancy, this a result of his "unproductive" answers.

Another man police wanted to question was Anthony Strollo, who had disappeared after the shooting. By the end of the day Saturday, police had questioned more than 160 people, including Frank Costello at his Central Park West apartment. Chief of Detectives James B. Leggett, when pressed for a comment on how the investigation was going answered, "No motive. No progress." The chief later claimed there were "150 angles to the case." Two popular theories of motive for the murder were Anastasia's involvement in gambling or narcotics, the latter of which never panned out.

Police were able to track the purchase of one of the murder weapons to a Gary, Indiana, company, which bought the gun in Evanston, Illinois, in 1934. The discovery supported a theory that the killers had been imported from the Midwest.

On October 28, Coppola was acquitted of vagrancy in Manhattan Arrest Court. He was quickly rearrested, taken to District Attorney Frank Hogan's office, and held as a material witness under a $50,000 bail.

Manhattan West detectives formed a "special squad" of 100 detectives and worked out of the West 54th Street Station investigating the murder. Police believed the killing was connected to the wounding of Costello, theorizing that Anastasia had been in on the attempt to murder the "prime minister." In support of this theory, Coppola had been questioned as a suspect following the Costello shooting. Because police had Costello under guard or constant surveillance after the assassination attempt, this theory was soon discounted.

Meanwhile, Arthur Grasso, the proprietor of the barbershop where Anastasia was murdered, was having problems with hotel management that was trying to evict him. The general manager of the hotel filed an affidavit that stated the following:

> We submit that the incident in his shop was avoidable and was the result of his failure to heed the terms of the lease. We suggest that the plaintiff knew Mr. Anastasia and that he suffered him to come into the premises of the shop several times a week for at least a period of two years.[53]

Grasso's lease had another six years to run. He filed a suit asking for $500,000 in damages, which is what he claimed he would lose if he lost his shop. When the case ended up in court on November 4, a New York Supreme Court justice refused to stop the hotel management's efforts to evict Grasso. Attorneys for the barber then went to a municipal court judge, who ruled that the hotel had "taken the law into its own hands," by closing the shop. The hotel was then ordered to return the keys. Exactly one month after the highly publicized murder, the barbershop reopened.

The investigation was still going strong when New York State Police Sergeant Edgar Croswell broke up what came to be known as the Apalachin Summit (see Appendix) on November 14. Speculation for years to come was that one of the agenda items that day was to be Genovese's explanation for the shooting of Costello and the murder of Anastasia, as well as the announcement of the promotion of Carlo Gambino to lead the former Anastasia gang.

Shortly after the murder, Anastasia's wife and son left the Fort Lee home forever. In late November an auction was held for the home's furnishings. Originally valued at $25,000 to $30,000, the furnishings were purchased by a local auctioneer for $4,300. The auction was held on November 23 in a vacant automobile showroom in Teaneck, New Jersey. Items for sale included mirrors, mirrored crystals, a steam bath, rowing machine, leather sofas, custom-made bedroom furniture, crystal dressing tables, a grand piano, and several paintings—one of which depicted a Roman gladiator beheading a man.

The night before the auction, IRS officials tried to get an injunction because of a pending civil suit filed in August. Auction gallery officials and the IRS reached an agreement that all proceeds would be put into escrow, pending the outcome of the government's case. The next day the auctioneer was able to sell only a few items before a boisterous overflow crowd of 1,000 people caused the police to close the public sale as a fire hazard. The auction company continued the sale two days later at its headquarters. At the end of the bidding, the gallery had collected a mere $6,000 for the items.

Elsa Anastasia left the United States for Canada, settling in Toronto. She never became a naturalized citizen. During the preceding year, she had filed an application for citizenship papers, but when it came time for her to appear in federal court in Newark on March 11,

1958, to finalize the process, she failed to show. Her chance for citizenship was forfeited when the judge dismissed her application.

As for the Fort Lee home, the house stood vacant for months, at times being the target of vandals, perhaps because of rumors that Anastasia had hidden money in the house. During the summer of 1958, a claim for $63,215 was placed on the property by Benjamin Yanow, a New York accountant who held a first mortgage. A sheriff's sale was scheduled for August 25 at the Bergen County Sheriff's Department in Hackensack.

On the day of the auction, Yanow made the only serious bid on the house through his lawyer. His bid of $64,000 covered the mortgage and a Borough of Fort Lee tax lien. In the process, it was agreed that if the government exercised its right of redemption in its civil suit and seized the house, Yanow would be reimbursed. Despite Yanow's claim that he was going to occupy the house, the home was sold just four days later to comedian Buddy Hackett for an undisclosed amount.

In the months and years after the murder of Anastasia, the police never seemed to give up hope of discovering who the murderers were. The Apalachin debacle brought a whole new round of questioning for many of the New York/New Jersey attendees. Police also wanted to question Meyer Lansky, who had been in Havana the whole time. They got their chance when Lansky arrived at New York International Airport (Idlewild Airport) from Miami on February 11, 1958. He was questioned and released. Later that month Liz Renay, a girlfriend of West Coast gangster Mickey Cohen, was questioned. It was rumored that she was also an intimate of Anthony Coppola.

As for Coppola, he had remained in jail for months as a material witness. At one point his counsel petitioned New York Governor William Averill Harriman, to get his automobile, which Anastasia had driven the day of his murder, out of the police impound lot. The following month, Coppola was freed after posting a reduced $25,000 bail.

Another person police wanted to question was Vincent J. Squillante, an official in a private waste carting business. Detectives working the case said they had received "confidential information" that Squillante knew something about the murder. It was later rumored that Squillante was one of the two customers in Grasso's barbershop that morning, seated in Chair No. 5, which was in the corner to Anastasia's left, facing a different mirror and on the other side of the West 55th Street window. After the shooting, Squillante allegedly jumped out of the chair and said, "Let me out of here," and fled. At the time detectives got the tip, however, Squillante was in the federal penitentiary at Lewisburg, Pennsylvania, serving out a sentence for a probation violation on an income tax conviction.[54]

On the night of September 29, 1958, less than 48 hours after being released from Lewisburg, police picked up Squillante in the Bronx for questioning. When several hours of interrogation produced only a chorus of, "I take the Fifth Amendment" too many times, Squillante was charged with vagrancy and placed in a cell. The next day he was arraigned in the Bronx Magistrate's Court, where he was released after posting a $5,000 bail. Before he could get out of the courthouse, he was subpoenaed to appear the next day for questioning about the murder.

In May 1964, Father Salvatore Anastasio made some interesting revelations in Rome, Italy. The priest, who had been ordained in Italy in 1948 after Albert paid for his schooling, had spent the past six years "interviewing dozens of persons and collecting documents" to clear his brother's name. Salvatore said he had returned to Rome to seek a publisher for the results of his work. Among the items he discussed with reporters were the following:

- The work was done to refute charges that his brother had headed Murder, Inc., and that accusations of his involvement had never been proved.

- As a young man Albert had been beaten and robbed on the New York docks shortly after jumping ship in 1917. Because of this he began to carry a gun, was turned in, and paid his debt to society.

- After his release from the Sing Sing death house, all of Anastasia's troubles were a "result of malicious gossip by the press, business rivals, and Brooklyn's District Attorney William O'Dwyer."

- The newspaper stories caused Salvatore to have a nervous breakdown and be hospitalized.

Salvatore recalled a confrontation he had with Albert as a young priest:

> I begged him to tell me the whole truth, as in the confessional. I told him that I had need of it like medicine for getting well. I wanted all the truth, however good or bad.
>
> He answered me: "Toruzzo"—he called me that—"you're bad for me. You're torturing yourself with the suspicion that your brother is an assassin. You scare me, not the Kefauver Commission. I have done nothing—maybe a little tax evasion. Forget what they say. Have faith in me."[55]

FALL OF THE HOUSE OF ANASTASIO

Between May 1956 and March 1963, five members of the Anastasio family died, including four of the five brothers involved in waterfront activities. The first to go was Giuseppe "Joseph" Anastasio. After Joseph entered the United States illegally for the second time, he returned to New York City. With his brother's help, he was soon made the hiring boss of Pier 14, North River. It was soon reported that cargo was being stolen "by the ton." Joseph was held responsible and fired, but the union soon forced his reinstatement.

Anthony Anastasia once described his brother Joseph as a conservative person, "a man who never drank or gambled, who lived quietly in his modest Brooklyn home with his wife and two children." In 1944, he was arrested for bookmaking and the next year he was involved in a second fatal shooting (the first was in 1925). The charges for both crimes were dismissed.

Because of Anthony's testimony before the Kefauver Committee, Joseph was arrested and held for deportation. According to a *New York Times* article, in January 1951, "he wrangled a 'good conduct' certificate from the Police Department and reentered the country legally from Canada, applying for citizenship."

Joseph died in Long Island College Hospital in Brooklyn on May 13, 1956, of an undisclosed illness at the age of 51. He was followed in death by Albert on October 25, 1957.

Gerardo "Jerry" Anastasia was a regular fixture on the Brooklyn docks and at one time rose to the position of business agent of Local 338-1. After being convicted of lying to a special grand jury investigating waterfront activities, he was sentenced to one year in federal prison in January 1957. Less than two months after his incarceration, he was released because of a throat ailment. Gerardo suffered from throat cancer for a number of years. On December 2, 1958, he died of a "malignancy" in Long Island College Hospital. On July 25, 1959, Gerardo's 16-year-old son, Albert Anastasio, died in a drowning accident in Lake St. Dominic near Monticello, New York.

In the years after his brother's murder, Anthony "Tough Tony" Anastasia lost much of his prestige within the underworld but was still a power on the Brooklyn docks. On March 1, 1963, at the age of 57, he succumbed to a heart attack at the same hospital where his brothers died. At the time, Anthony was vice president of the ILA's Local 1814, which boasted 15,000 members.

The Brooklyn waterfront closed down as a tribute to "Tough Tony" when he died. Less than two weeks after his death, the executive council of the ILA elected Anthony's son-in-law, Anthony Scotto, to succeed him. In November 1963, Anthony Anastasia was honored by having a $5,000 annual scholarship for a son or daughter of a Local 1814 member established in his name.

A "WHO DONE IT"

Manhattan District Attorney Frank Hogan never gave up the search for the killers of Albert Anastasia. Joseph Valachi's revelations in the fall of 1963 of Anastasia being killed on the orders of Vito Genovese has stood as the benchmark motive for the murder. Valachi claimed that after the attempted murder of Frank Costello, the "prime minister" accepted his "forced" retirement, but Anastasia "began to talk loud" about reinstating him. Valachi said that Vito Genovese discovered that Costello and Anastasia were holding "secret meetings." He contacted Albert's lieutenant, Carlo Gambino, and convinced him they could both benefit by getting the "Mad Hatter" out of the way.

There was no official declaration of motive from the police, only that they felt the assassination of Anastasia and the attempt to kill Costello were related. Some felt that a younger element in the underworld was trying to supplant an older regime.

As far as the actual murder suspects in the Anastasia killing are concerned, it has been a long-held belief that members of the Gallo brothers' gang were the shooters. This myth was perpetuated by Joe "Crazy Joe" Gallo. Sidney Slater was an associate of the Gallos, who ran a "B-Girl" bar for them on East 56th Street in Manhattan. About a week after the murder, Joey Gallo walked in with members of his gang. Gallo biographer Harvey Aronson writes:

> This particular evening, Joey showed up with Joe Jelly and three other gang members— Punchy Illiano, Ralph Mafrici and Sonny Cammerone. Before long Joey motioned to Slater and three of the bar girls to join his table. They had a few drinks, and the Anastasia killing cropped up in the conversation. Joey grinned and ripped off a one-liner that can best be described as Gallo's humor. "From now on, Sidney," he said, "you can just call the five of us the barbershop quintet."[56]

If Carlo Gambino was truly behind the murder of Anastasia, it is unlikely he would have used killers outside the crime family. He would have used people he had complete faith in and not a hoodlum like Joey Gallo who already had the reputation of being a loose cannon.

Another popular theory as to why Anastasia was murdered involved a rumor that he was trying to establish a foothold in gambling in Havana, Cuba. Meyer Lansky and Costello, as well as Tampa, Florida, mob boss Santo Trafficante, Jr., had a large piece of the multimillion-dollar gambling industry in the city—all of which was legal.

In *The Mafia in Havana*, the author claims that Anastasia had spent five or six days in Havana sometime in 1957 and was impressed with all he saw. Hilton Hotels International was making plans to open a new $24 million hotel/casino and would be leasing the casino for $1 million a year. A Hilton executive claimed to have gone to great lengths to hire competent people—a former FBI chief from Chicago and an attorney who was a former investigator for the Kefauver Committee—to review applications of those wanting to lease the casino. The *New York Times* reported:

> The Hilton chain executive reported that thirteen groups had sought to lease the casino in its Havana hotel and that all but one had been turned down because they either had underworld connections or had refused to subject themselves to "rigid investigation."[57]

Santo Trafficante had scheduled a trip to New York City a week before the Anastasia murder, with four Cubans including Roberto "Chiri" Mendoza, a Cuban contractor and sugar plantation owner, whose syndicate received the rights to lease the casino. Members of his syndicate included a former lieutenant governor of Nevada, as well as a Nevada state senator. Anastasia met with the Cubans in a room that he kept at the Warwick Hotel during this period. The key to the room was in his pocket and found by detectives searching his body after the murder.

Trafficante was staying at the Warwick Hotel and left the morning of the killing, flying back to Tampa. Three weeks later, Trafficante attended the Apalachin Summit, where he used the name Louis Santo when he was nabbed by Sergeant Edgar Croswell's welcome wagon.

In early January 1958, Frank Hogan spoke to Hilton Hotel's International executives. At a press conference after the meeting, a ranking Hilton official surmised that Hogan believed Anastasia's murder was tied to his desire to get involved with Havana gambling operations. On January 7, Hogan issued a nationwide alarm for Santo Trafficante and Joseph Silesi, one of the rejected Hilton applicants. Informed that both men were in Havana, Hogan stated, "They know we want them as witnesses. If they are in Cuba, they are outside our jurisdiction and not subject to our processes."[58]

In Havana, Trafficante was made aware of Hogan's nationwide alarm. He told reporters, "I travel back and forth [between Cuba and the United States] on business all the time. The next time I'm in New York I'll be glad to call on Hogan. I don't know what this is all about. I'm not hiding from anyone."[59] Trafficante also responded to allegations of Anastasia's muscling attempts by claiming he had no knowledge of any efforts on the "Mad Hatter's" part to become involved in gambling in the Cuban capital. Meyer Lansky biographer Robert Lacey wrote:

> As the New York police pieced together the curious chain of events that had brought Albert Anastasia and Chiri Mendoza together in the Warwick Hotel, they could discern no role for Meyer Lansky in the barbershop murder. Cuban gambling, they decided, was not the issue after all—and their New York inquiries were revealing an abundance of evidence as to the trouble which Albert Anastasia had been stirring up closer to home.[60]

A bizarre affidavit reported on in the *New York Times* on May 20 claimed that Anastasia and Trafficante attended a meeting at the home of Joseph Barbara in 1956, after the shooting of Costello, to discuss "a reorganization of underworld interests" in redistributing Costello's illegal enterprises among Mafia members. There are credible reports that a meeting did take place in 1956; however, Costello was in jail and was not wounded until May 1957.[61]

In September 1959, William Roderick Solomon, a resident of an Indian reservation in Ontario, Canada, told Port Huron, Michigan, police he was paid $5,000 to act as a lookout at the Park Sheraton Hotel. He said he met the men who hired him at the Harlem Valley State Hospital, a facility for the mentally ill, in Wingdale, New York. At the time of his revelations, Solomon was being held by the Port Huron police for public drunkenness.

In August 1965, word came from Palermo that police officials there claimed Anastasia had been murdered by hired assassins from the Sicilian capital. This disclosure followed the roundup of 10 Sicilian Mafia bosses, including Giuseppe Genco Russo, Santo Sorge, and Gaetano Russo. The Italians news agency Ansa reported, "the sentence of death was pronounced on Anastasia at a meeting here during a power struggle for control of an American crime syndicate."[62]

In early 1968, "new information" came to Hogan's attention. It took nearly a year before word of it became public. On March 24, 1969, 12 witnesses, 11 of whom were in Grasso's barbershop at the time of the shooting, were subpoenaed by Hogan's office. A spokesperson for the office would only say, "We want to re-evaluate their testimony in light of our new information."[63] The year's delay had resulted because the district attorney felt the information had to be "adequately investigated." The next day, after "some" of the witnesses were questioned, the spokesperson stated: "The case is by no means solved. All we are trying to do is determine if we have enough information to go to a grand jury."[64]

On March 27, The *New York Daily News* reported that the prime suspect in the murder of Anastasia had applied to the New York State Parole Board for permission to leave the country and join his family in Italy. The suspect, who was never named in the article, had been paroled from an assault and robbery conviction in 1968, after serving seven years in Greenhaven Prison. An interoffice memo to the special agent in charge of the New York FBI office from the "Director, FBI" ordered: "Through appropriate discreet contact of the New York State Parole Board determine the identity of the alleged suspect and advise the Bureau."

Finally, organized crime authority Jerry Capeci, in his weekly on-line column, *This Week In Gang Land,* revealed the following new version of the killers in an October 18, 2001, article titled, "The Men Who Hit Albert Anastasia."

> According to knowledgeable sources on both sides of the law, the killing was carried out by a three-man hit team selected by then-capo Joseph (Joe the Blonde) Biondo, who became Gambino's underboss and remained in the post until shortly before he died in 1966.

Capeci stated that the two shooters were Stephen "Stevie Coogan" Grammauta and Arnold "Witty" Wittenberg and that Stephen Armone was the "leader of the crew." All three men were involved in the drug trade.

NOTES

1. There has been some confusion regarding Anthony Anastasia's last name. Some sources claim that both Albert and Anthony changed the spelling, using an "a" as the last vowel, whereas others claim that Anthony kept to the original spelling. The newspaper sources used for this book (most notably the *New York Times*—at least up until the time of Albert's death) nearly always used the Anastasia name when referring to Anthony and the name Anastasio for Giuseppe (Joseph) and Gerardo.

An interesting footnote about Albert, when the Terillo murder trial began in 1921, the *Brooklyn Daily Eagle* used the name Alberto Anastasio, but the *New York Times* had him listed as Albert Anastasia.

2. George Terillo's name has also appeared as Terrillo and Turello.

3. *Brooklyn Daily Eagle,* May 10, 1921, "Vendetta Signals Fail to Seal Lips of Woman on Stand."

4. *Brooklyn Daily Eagle,* May 11, 1921, "Convict Florino and Anastasia of 1st Degree Murder." Note: This is the only time Albert was referred to as Anastasia. The newspaper had referred to him throughout the trial as Alberto Anastasio, even in the body of this article. As late as April 1940, the *Brooklyn Eagle* referred to Albert as Anastasio.

5. *Brooklyn Daily Eagle,* May 25, 1921, "3 Get Death Chair; Florino Denounces Woman's Testimony."

6. The Registry Act of March 2, 1929, "Amended existing immigration law authorizing the establishment of a record of lawful admission for certain aliens not ineligible for citizenship when no record of admission for permanent residence could be found and the alien could prove entrance to the United States before July 1, 1924 (subsequently amended to June 3, 1921 by the Act of August 7, 1939–1953 Statutes-at-Large 1243). Later incorporated into the Alien Registration Act of 1940."—U.S. Citizenship and Immigration Services, Legislation from 1901–1940.

7. Ted Prager and Leeds Moberley, *Hoodlums—New York* (New York: Retail Distributors, 1959), p. 15.

8. When Lucky Luciano was deported in February 1946, Anastasia provided the muscle on the docks to keep the newspaper reporters and photographers away while the farewell celebration took place (see Chapter 7).

9. Burton Turkus and Sid Feder, *Murder, Inc.* (New York: Farrar, Straus and Young, 1951), p. 462.

10. On April 21, 1940, in the period after Abe Reles began "singing" to the Brooklyn district attorney's office, the *Brooklyn Eagle* published an article that discussed the leadership of the Brooklyn underworld and its activities along the Brooklyn docks. "Extensive research and independent investigation by the Brooklyn Eagle has made it possible to make public for the first time 'Directory of Directors' of the Crime-Beside-the-Harbor Corporation."

It described the "corporation" as being headed by Joe Adonis and as its "top directors": Vincent Mangano, chairman of the board; Albert Anastasio (sic), first vice chairman; Joseph Florino, second vice president; Anthony Romeo; Gerolimo Mangano, Philip Mangano, Anthony Anastasio, and Jack Parisi.

Under Vincent Mangano, it gave the following information: "Vincent Mangano, the chairman of the board, is a shrewd, intelligent leader who profited from his apprenticeship in earlier gangs. Under "Little Augie" he had advanced himself to a place where he had charge of all the waterfront rackets in the area between the Brooklyn Bridge and 52nd St., Bay Ridge. He ruled with an iron hand. He never permitted a crusading faction among the suckers to make any headway against the crime lords' domination.

> Mangano has issued most of his orders in the corporation through subordinates. He has had little contact with the minor mobsters and is now a wealthy man. Several reports have him hiding in Italy. (*Brooklyn Eagle,* April 21, 1940, "Dock Crime Corporation 'Directors' Are Listed")

11. *New York Times,* December 19, 1952, "Excerpts from Testimony Given Yesterday at the Crime Commission Hearing."

12. Emil Camarda was a longtime member of the International Longshoremen's Association. His father had organized Local 338 in Brooklyn before World War I. Emil became a member in

1916 and a vice president two years later. He was appointed general vice president for the Atlantic Coast in 1931.

On October 2, 1941, Emil Camarda was gunned down in the office of Salvatore Sabatino, vice president of Sabatino & Company on Broadway. Camarda and Sabatino had been boyhood chums. According to the initial reporting, Camarda met Sabatino at a bar on Broadway in the afternoon. The two got into a heated argument and were ordered out of the establishment. The argument resumed in Sabatino's office, where Camarda was killed by two gunshots. According to the police report, Sabatino was upset with Camarda when he asked him to get a job for a friend of his who was Irish. Sabatino fumed that Camarda was more interested in "getting jobs for the Irish."

Sabatino, whose brother was Sylvester Sabatino, a Brooklyn City Court judge, fled the building. The next day he surrendered at District Attorney Thomas E. Dewey's office. He was charged with murder. His lawyers would say only that reports published about the murder were untrue and that the truth would come out at trial.

At his arraignment, Sabatino was represented by a trio of high-powered attorneys of the day—Caesar B. F. Barra, Frank Barrera, and Leo J. Healy. He pleaded not guilty and was denied bail. Two days later the funeral for Camarda was held. The service was attended by 600 mourners. There were 200 honorary pallbearers who formed an honor guard to escort the coffin into the church. Twenty flower cars and 50 automobiles containing mourners followed the hearse to Holy Cross Cemetery in Flatbush.

On October 9, Sabatino was indicted for first-degree murder. On December 1, the trial began in general sessions court. The defense team now consisted of Barra and James D. C. Murray. Before jury selection could take place, Barra and Murray asked Judge John A. Mullen for a conference in chambers. When they returned, Sabatino was allowed to plead guilty to a reduced charge of first-degree manslaughter. Brooklyn Assistant District Attorney Jacob Grumet went along after deciding that, because the men had been lifelong friends, it would be difficult to prove motive in the killing.

At the sentencing on December 10, businessmen, Catholic clergyman, and several New York Supreme Court Justices testified for Sabatino. A son said his father had taken to alcohol recently because of the long illness of another son. Mullen sentenced Sabatino to Sing Sing for 5 to 10 years.

13. *Time,* December 29, 1952, "Nine Hundred & Forty Thieves."

14. Turkus and Feder, *Murder, Inc.* p. 463.

15. Ibid., p. 464.

16. Raymond, Allen, *Waterfront Priest* (New York: Henry Holt and Company, 1955), p. 166

17. *New York World-Telegram,* April 2, 1940, '"Top Man' Named in Murder, Inc."

18. Ibid.

19. If the book *The Last Testament of Lucky Luciano* is to be believed, Albert Anastasia was responsible for the sabotage and sinking of the former French liner *Normandie* in New York harbor on February 9, 1942. The liner had been renamed the *U.S.S. Lafayette* and was being converted into a troop carrier when sparks from welding torches set a stack of life preservers on fire. An official inquiry declared the fire accidental. According to Luciano's version, this was the bargaining chip he needed with the government to initiate his plan to get out of a long prison sentence. Although it would not necessarily be important for Anastasia to be in New York, it should be noted that he had been in hiding, most likely in Utica, during the time Luciano claims to have been communicating with him about this incident.

20. *Brooklyn Eagle,* July 2, 1942, "Romeo Slain for Gang Defi, Police Declare."

21. Ibid.

22. Other sources claim Anastasia was first assigned to the 88th Division at Camp Forrest, Tennessee. He was kept back when his division went overseas because of his age.

23. *New York Times,* November 1, 1957, "Rapid Army Rise Detailed."

24. Prager and Moberley, *Hoodlums—New York* p. 23.

25. George Walsh, *Public Enemies: The Mayor, the Mob, and the Crime That Was* (New York: W. W. Norton & Company, 1980), p. 112.

26. Ibid.

27. *New York Times,* October 30, 1945, "O'Dwyer Accused by a Grand Jury of Laxity in Office."

28. *New York Times,* October 31, 1945, "O'Dwyer Hits Jury Action; Cites Record."

29. Prager and Moberley, *Hoodlums—New York,* p. 25.

30. Some articles and books have the business listed as the Modern Dress Company.

31. Virgil W. Peterson, *The Mob: 200 Years of Organized Crime in New York* (Ottawa, IL: Green Hill Publishers, 1983), p. 279.

32. Anthony Anastasio's revelations before the Kefauver Committee created immediate problems for Gerardo and Giuseppe. Gerardo was being sworn in as a U.S. citizen on the morning of March 20, 1951 in Brooklyn Federal Court. Less than an hour after the ceremony, an official from the immigration service arrived and requested that Gerardo's name be scratched from the list until a thorough check of his record could be made. Federal Judge Robert Inch refused the request, stating that each applicant had already been thoroughly screened. He agreed to hold up the formal signing of the order and issuing the citizenship certificate until a hearing could be held on March 22.

At the brief hearing, after immigration officials testified, Judge Inch ordered a further hearing be held on April 24, at which time Gerardo's citizenship sponsors were to be present.

On March 27, Giuseppe (Joseph) Anastasio was arrested at his home at 3:00 AM. A check on his citizenship status revealed he was still an alien. Giuseppe had only one charge on his record, the murder charge from 1925, which was dismissed, after which he was deported. He reentered the country illegally in 1929 by jumping ship in San Francisco. Giuseppe was taken to the Fort Hamilton Station, charged with violating the Immigration Law of 1924, and then ferried out to Ellis Island to await disposition on bail.

On April 3, a writ of habeas corpus was signed claiming that because his name is Anastasio, Giuseppe was being held because he was a victim of "newspaper notoriety." Two days later he was released on a $2,000 bond.

Gerardo's hearing was held in Brooklyn Federal Court on April 24. The government claimed that although Gerardo had not been accused of breaking any laws for three years before his petitioning for citizenship, both of his sponsors had police records. Gerardo's attorney stated that Gerardo was a hard-working longshoremen's union delegate and was responsible for raising three children alone after his wife's death. He claimed that Gerardo was not aware of the criminal records of his sponsors and that he had seen little of his more infamous brothers in recent year. After hearing testimony from both sides, Judge Inch granted Gerardo U.S. citizenship.

33. Vincent Mangano was declared legally dead in 1961.

34. Joseph Bonanno with Sergio Lalli, *A Man of Honor* (New York: Simon and Schuster, 1983), p. 170.

35. Benedetto "Benny" Macri was one of the participants in the highly publicized murder of William Lurye, a special organizer for the International Ladies Garment Workers Union on May 9, 1949. Macri and Anthony Giustra stabbed Lurye to death in a telephone booth in the lobby of an office building on West 35th Street.

Macri was a fugitive for two years, and Giustra was never seen again. On the night of June 18, 1951, through a deal arranged by Anastasia, Macri was escorted by gossip columnist and radio personality Walter Winchell into the West 20th Police Station, where he surrendered. Macri's murder trial began on October 11. With the help of some perjured testimony, purchased with Anastasia's help, Macri was acquitted on October 29.

36. *New York Times,* November 21, 1951, "2 Attempts to Kill Anastasia Reported."

37. Peterson, *The Mob: 200 Years of Organized Crime in New York,* p. 280.

38. *New York Times,* September 4, 1952, "Pier Inquiry Asks Bank Files of 300; Politicians on List."

39. *New York Times,* December 9, 1952, "Ship Man Calls Pier Reform Senseless Unless Law Aids."

40. Peter Maas, *The Valachi Papers* (New York: G. P. Putnam's Sons, 1968), p. 206.

41. After the death of Arnold L. Schuster, his father Max filed a negligence suit against the City of New York for $1,025,000, claiming the police department failed to protect his son. On the eve of the one-year anniversary of the murder, the suit was dismissed by a Brooklyn judge. In the meantime, the police, after initially considering Frederick J. Tenuto a prime suspect, were focusing on John "Chappie" Mazziotta for the killing. A massive manhunt was on for him, and there were reports that he had been killed and his body dumped in an Ozone Park swamp.

In April 1954, two men who had been held as material witnesses for two years received "limited freedom." Throughout this ordeal, Max Schuster and his wife received numerous death threats and were provided with a constant police guard. In May 1956, a 72-year-old tailor that Schuster employed was beaten over the head in the tailor shop.

By 1957, Mazziotta had been believed dead for a number of years. In August that year, a rumor spread that Tommy "The Bull" Pennochio was freed after a parole violation based on the promise that he would try to find Mazziotta.

Max Schuster never gave up his battle to sue the city and on March 6, 1961, just two days before the ninth anniversary of his son's murder, the case came before a jury. During the trial, the Schusters told of the many threats they received, while the police countered that their offers of protection were spurned. Bank robber Willie Sutton was called to testify from prison, where he was serving a 30-year-to-life sentence.

On March 28, after a three-week trial, a jury deliberated seven hours before returning with a decision that a cash award of $30,000 be given to the Schuster family, a far cry from the $1,050,000 they had filed suit for in this second trial.

42. Maas, *The Valachi Papers,* p. 206.

43. *New York Times,* December 10, 1952, "U.S. Files Suit as First Step to Deport Albert Anastasia."

44. Ibid.

45. *New York Times,* April 15, 1954, "Albert Anastasia Loses Citizenship."

46. *New York Herald Tribune,* September 20, 1955, "Anastasia Citizenship Plea Upheld."

47. *New York Times,* March 11, 1954, "Albert Anastasia Indicted on Taxes."

48. *New York Times,* October 17, 1954, "U.S. Subpoenas Halley."

49. *New York Times,* November 21, 1954, "Anastasia Tax Case Ends in a Mistrial."

50. Some accounts claim that Arthur Grasso was standing next to Anastasia at the time, chatting with him.

51. *New York Times,* October 26, 1957, "Anastasia Slain in a Hotel Here; Led Murder, Inc."

52. *New York Times,* October 29, 1957, "Anastasia Buried with Stark Rites."

53. *New York Times,* November 5, 1957, "Anastasia's Barber Loses Eviction Plea."

54. Vincent J. "Jimmy Jerome" Squillante was a pint-sized (5-foot, 1-inch) racketeer in the New York garbage industry, who gained a monopoly on the waste removal from New York City hotels, restaurants, and nightclubs, many times by claiming his godfather was Albert Anastasia.

In 1953, he pled guilty to having filed false income tax returns for 1948 and 1949. He was placed on probation for three years and ordered to pay the government $14,500. This probation period was extended another two years. On November 27, 1957, Federal Judge Irving R. Kaufman ruled that Squillante had violated the terms of his probation by consorting with known criminals and lying to his probation officer. In asking the judge to revoke the probation, Chief Assistant U.S. Attorney Arthur H. Christy stated Squillante "is a man who for some time has traded on the false label that he was the godson of Albert Anastasia." Christy proved this with more than just lip service. He brought in the church record to show that Squillante's claim was "utterly phony." Kaufman revoked the probation and sentenced him to a year in federal prison.

In December 1958, Squillante, his brother Nunzio, and another man were found guilty of three counts of extortion in the waste disposal business. On February 18, 1959, Squillante stood before a Nassau County court judge and "wept like a baby" as the jurist pronounced sentence. Squillante was handed a 7½- to 15-year term. Sent to Sing Sing, he spent 19 days there before being released on a writ of habeas corpus pending an appeal. On December 14, 1959, an appeals court reversed the conviction.

Unfortunately for Squillante and his brother, they had been indicted a month earlier on charges of conspiracy to rig bids for government contracts. On the day the trial was scheduled to begin on October 20, 1960, Squillante was reported missing. A month later, the FBI joined the search. The popular theory is that Squillante was murdered and his body placed in an automobile and taken to a salvage yard where it was crushed into a metal block by a hydraulic press.

55. *New York Times,* May 5, 1964, "Anastasia Name Is Held Maligned."

56. Harvey Aronson, *The Killing of Joey Gallo* (New York: G. P. Putnam's Sons, 1973), p. 55.

57. *New York Times,* January 9, 1958, "Gambling in Cuba Tied to U.S. Gangs."

58. Ibid.

59. Ibid.

60. Robert Lacey, *Little Man: Meyer Lansky and the Gangster Life* (London: Little, Brown and Company, 1991), p. 245.

61. *New York Times,* May 20, 1967, "Affidavit Tells if Secret Mafia Parley on Costello."

62. *New York Times,* August 5, 1965, "Anastasia Death Tied to Mafia, Which May Have Sent Sicilians."

63. *New York Times,* March 25, 1969, "12 Get Subpoenas in Anastasia Case."

64. *New York Times,* March 26, 1969, "New Data Reported in Anastasia Case."

BIBLIOGRAPHY

Aronson, Harvey. *The Killing of Joey Gallo.* New York: G. P. Putnam's Sons, 1973.

Bonanno, Joseph, with Sergio Lalli. *A Man of Honor.* New York: Simon and Schuster, 1983.

Cirules, Enrique. *The Mafia in Havana.* New York: Ocean Press, 2004.

Gosch, Martin, and Richard Hammer. *The Last Testament of Lucky Luciano.* Boston: Little, Brown and Company, 1974.

Lacey, Robert. *Little Man: Meyer Lansky and the Gangster Life.* London: Little, Brown and Company, 1991.

Maas, Peter. *The Valachi Papers.* New York: G. P. Putnam's Sons, 1968.

Peterson, Virgil W. *The Mob: 200 Years of Organized Crime in New York.* Ottawa, IL: Green Hill Publishers, 1983.

Prager, Ted, and Leeds Moberley. *Hoodlums—New York.* New York: Retail Distributors, 1959.

Raymond, Allen. *Waterfront Priest.* New York: Henry Holt & Company, 1955.

Turkus, Burton, and Sid Feder. *Murder, Inc.* New York: Farrar, Straus and Young, 1951.

Walsh, George. *Public Enemies: The Mayor, the Mob, and the Crime That Was.* New York: W. W. Norton & Company, 1980.

3

LOUIS BUCHALTER

AKA "LEPKE"
FEBRUARY 2, 1897–MARCH 4, 1944

Most of the underworld figures discussed in this book made their money through bootlegging, gambling, or a combination of both. Some, like Lucky Luciano, became involved in prostitution. Many, including the police, prosecutors, and judges, saw these criminals as providing goods and services that had been outlawed by society, and their deeds as victimless crimes.

In the case of Louis "Lepke" Buchalter, the crimes were different. In the crimes of the most notorious labor racketeer of all time, there definitely was a victim—the working man and his family. It was the ugly side of organized crime in which the innocent were forced to share their wages, their businesses, and their livelihoods with a brutal band of heartless hoodlums who used any method possible to bring their victims in line. The results of Buchalter's crimes affected everyone in New York City as well as nationally through increased costs for food, clothing, and other daily necessities.

With his right-hand man, Jacob "Gurrah" Shapiro, Buchalter terrorized the garment district of New York City and brought it under his control through connivance, bribery, and violence. The band of thugs Buchalter hired to keep order in his underworld kingdom became known as Murder, Inc. (see Appendix), whose roster of hit men contained some of the most sadistic killers in the city. And if that were not enough, Lepke used the money from his crimes to invest in the narcotics business, which brought illicit drugs to the United States to feed the habits of thousands of addicts . . . and create new ones.

In the late-1930s, the name Lepke struck fear in the hearts of those who knew his ruthless methods, but in the end Lepke Buchalter received his just reward. To this day he remains the only mob boss in the history of this country's underworld to be put to death by capital punishment.

"Where other criminals tore their plunder from the gambler, the alcoholic, and the dope addict, this unimpressive-looking crime king preyed on the ordinary needs of the ordinary citizen. He cut in on the clothes people wore, the bread they ate . . .In fact, on the very work they did. The pay envelopes they earned."

—Burton B. Turkus (Turkus and Feder, *Murder, Inc.*, 1951, p. 332)

BEGINNINGS

Like many members of this country's underworld, there was nothing in Louis Buchalter's early life that would lead anyone to believe he was headed for a life of crime. His mother was from Russia, where she married a fellow countryman—Solomon Kauver. Said to be a lumber salesman, Kauver sought desperately to leave Russia because of the pogroms.[1] Before they left, Rose bore him four children, two boys and two girls. One son, who later moved to Denver where he earned a Ph.D., was a rabbi and served as a professor at Denver University; the other was a businessman in New York City. One daughter became a New York City school teacher and managed a summer camp for young ladies in Pittsfield, Massachusetts; the other was a housewife. But in 1892, the Kauver family was just one of thousands who sought to leave oppressive conditions in Russia to begin a new life in America.

Sometime after their arrival, Solomon Kauver died. Rose soon wedded Barnett Buchalter. It was the second marriage for both. Buchalter had children from his previous marriage. Through this union Rose gave birth to three more sons.[2] The last was Louis, born on February 6, 1897.[3] The youngest of Rose's brood was nicknamed "Lepkeleh," defined as a Yiddish diminutive meaning "Little Louis." The name was shortened to "Lepke," a nickname Louis Buchalter would be known by his entire life.[4]

The Buchalters faced the same struggles most immigrant families encountered while trying to survive on Manhattan's teeming Lower East Side. Barnett operated a hardware store on Essex Street, earning a meager income to raise his family. Lepke started his elementary education at Public School #75. He later transferred to Public School #62 where he completed the sixth grade. During this time he helped his father by working part-time at the hardware store.

In 1909, tragedy came Rose's way again when Barnett died.[5] Lepke and his mother moved to the Williamsburg section of Brooklyn, living with Rose's daughter. In June 1912, Buchalter finished classes at Public School #94. It would be his last year of education—at least in a traditional school system. With his father out of the picture and his closest family now scattered, Lepke spent much of his time back on the streets of the Lower East Side, where trouble could easily be found.

There is some evidence that as a young man, Lepke tried to help his family financially. His FBI report reveals: "He was first employed after leaving school, as a salesman for a concern engaged in selling theatrical goods, such as spangles, tights and costumes and also handling imported Austrian chandeliers, which were then in fashion." Other sources say he was a delivery boy, turning over his wages to his mother, who was said to be doing such menial work as selling herring door to door and serving kosher food to the elderly. In late 1912, Rose left Brooklyn for Denver, where she moved in with a son from her first marriage. Although the plans were for Lepke to stay with a relative, he was now on his own.

By looking at Buchalter's police record, it is hard to tell if he was a successful criminal. Rap sheets simply show arrests and convictions, not what crimes were successfully committed. In Lepke's case, between September 1915 and November 1931, he was arrested 12 times, mostly for botched burglaries and robberies; in all but three cases the charges were dismissed.

His first arrest in September 1915 was for assault after stealing a package off a delivery wagon on the East Side in hopes of selling the contents to a fence. The charges were dismissed. On February 29, 1916, Buchalter was arrested in Bridgeport, Connecticut. He was charged with theft after he and "accomplices" stole two suitcases containing jewelry samples that a salesman had left outside the doorway of a customer.[6] Lepke told the police that his name was Louis Kauver, using the name of his mother's first husband. He was sentenced to an intermediate term at the Connecticut Reformatory located in Cheshire, which at the time was an "unwalled" institution.

Information gathered by the medical director of the reformatory shows that Buchalter was 5-feet, 6-inches tall and weighed 156 pounds. Although it is unclear if Buchalter was completely forthcoming with all the information he related, the director concluded his report with the following:

> Inmate is a clean cut intelligent Hebrew, who led a normal life in spite of little supervision until August, 1916. Then worked for an uncle . . . who reduced his wages to $8 a week. This he didn't like and went to New York, got in with a bad crowd doing petty jobs. His delinquency was probably result of mental conflict coupled with companions. *Outlook is excellent.*

The most startling conclusion from the report was the director's comment regarding Buchalter's intelligence. He declared it was "above average." Lepke would later state he served less than two months before being placed on parole; however, records show he wasn't released on parole until July 12, 1917. Eleven days later he broke parole by fleeing the state. A parole violator warrant was issued for him, but never executed. It was not dismissed until December 1931. Meanwhile, Lepke headed back to New York City to resume his petty criminal career.

It is not known when Lepke first met Jacob "Gurrah" Shapiro. Legend has it that they met while both were stealing from the same pushcart vendor on the Lower East Side and decided to combine forces. One story claims:

> Together they would cross the Williamsburg Bridge and torment the pushcart peddlers in the Brownsville section of Brooklyn. That's where Shapiro got his nickname, Gurrah. The immigrant pushcart peddlers would plead with him, "Gurrahere Jake," meaning "Get out of here, Jake." Whereupon Jake would smash one of them in the face, turn over his cart and give his place to another peddler from whom Lepke had received tribute.[7]

Buchalter returned to New York City after absconding from Connecticut. Two months later, on September 28, 1917, he was arrested in Brooklyn for grand larceny. On January 11, 1918, he was handed an 18-month stretch in Sing Sing. During this term he was transferred to Auburn Prison, where he remained until his release on January 27, 1919. One year later he was arrested for another burglary and received a stiffer sentence—30 months in Sing Sing. Buchalter served 21 months of this sentence before he was released from Great Meadow Prison in March 1922. This would be the last prison stretch Lepke would serve until the late 1930s.

A NEW LINE OF CRIME

There are few verifiable facts concerning Buchalter's activities between his release from prison in March 1922 and the murder of Jacob Orgen in October 1927. By most accounts, after Buchalter's release from prison, he returned to New York City and reestablished his friendship with Gurrah Shapiro, who by this time was a member of Orgen's gang The two, working as labor sluggers, carried out the orders of Orgen, who by the mid-1920s, had become New York City's top labor racketeer.

New York City has a colorful heritage when it comes to labor racketeers, beginning with Edward "Monk Eastman" Osterman, who, as early as 1897, was helping to solve labor disputes by use of violence, that is, brutalizing men who were trying to organize a union in the garment industry. Carted off to jail in 1904, he was replaced by Maxwell "Kid Twist" Zwiebach.[8] The "Kid" reigned until he insulted an associate of Paulo "Paul Kelly" Vaccarelli in 1908, resulting in Zwiebach and a companion "Cyclone Louie" being slaughtered on a New York City street.

Out of the haze of gun smoke came William "Big Jack Zelig" Alberts, who became associated with infamous New York City Police Captain Charles Becker. Zelig allegedly lined up the four killers of Becker's nemesis Herman "Beansy" Rosenthal. Zelig was called to testify at the Becker trial, but he was gunned down on a streetcar two days before he was to appear. Becker and four others eventually paid for the crime with their lives.

Zelig was replaced by Benjamin "Dopey Benny" Fein, who took the art of labor slugging to new heights by establishing a rate chart for mayhem. Fein would rent his "goon squads" to anyone willing to pay, whether company owner or union organizers. Despite his poor education and "moronic" looks, Fein survived the labor wars and walked away in the mid-1910s. With Fein out of the business, a war soon erupted between Nathan "Kid Dropper" Kaplan and John "Johnny Spanish" Weiler. The war ended outside a Second Avenue restaurant in Manhattan on the night of July 29, 1919, when Kaplan and two associates shot Weiler to death.

Kaplan would remain the key figure in the labor rackets for the next four years, but his leadership would be challenged by a former Benjamin Fein lieutenant named Jacob Orgen. Known as "Little Augie," Orgen became a formidable foe of Kaplan and during the summer of 1923 was ready to wrest control. The first step came during a shootout near Essex and Delancey Streets on the night of August 1. Shapiro, working for Orgen, was wounded in the affray and was dropped off by companions at Post Graduate Hospital where he was arrested. Shapiro, defying underworld rules, allegedly named Kaplan as participating in the gunplay.

On August 28, Kaplan and several others appeared at the Essex Market Court to be arraigned on criminal charges. During the hearing, Shapiro claimed he had been mistaken in his identification. Charges against Kaplan were dismissed, but he was about to be escorted to the West Side Court, where he was to be arraigned on violation of the Sullivan Law. Surrounded by police officers, and in the personal custody of Detective Captain Cornelius

Willemse, Kaplan was placed in a taxicab to be transported to the next court appearance (Willemse would claim he was leaving town). Despite the police presence, a young man darted from the crowd and came up to the back of the cab. From there he pulled a pistol and blasted away at Kaplan through the cab's rear window, mortally wounding him in the lungs. The gunman, 22-year-old Louis Cohen, a wet wash laundry worker, claimed Kaplan had threatened to kill him. He told police:

> The Kid came to me and told me if I wanted to live I had to pay him $500. I had no $500 and I had a wife and several children. So I went down there today determined to kill him. I hung around outside for about an hour. I knew before I went down that his political influence would get him out of this jam. So I decided I would kill him before he got me. That's the way it was. I got him before he got me.[9]

At trial in December, represented by State Senator James J. "Jimmy" Walker, the flamboyant future mayor, Cohen was found guilty of second-degree murder and given a 20-year sentence. He was released on parole in February 1937.

During these years of the mid-1920s, Buchalter and Shapiro certainly did not become wealthy performing goon activities for Orgen. Both men supplemented their income by continuing to commit petty crimes. In September and October 1925, Buchalter was arrested for robbery. The last one, which involved Shapiro, was a stick-up at the Fish Market. In both cases the charges were dismissed.

One of Buchalter and Shapiro's closest associates during this period was Hyman "Curly" Holtz. Described as a "monstrously cruel roughneck," Holtz became a top lieutenant of the pair and would remain so in the years to come. It was during this time that Orgen allegedly began taking orders from Arnold Rothstein. At the time, one of Rothstein's bodyguard's was Jack "Legs" Diamond, a fearless but reckless hoodlum who became one of the era's most colorful gangsters. In 1926, the International Ladies' Garment Workers' Union went out on strike. The disastrous work stoppage, which began in the summer, lasted 26 weeks and affected 50,000 workers. The strike was marked by massive violence.

In the early stages, management hired the services of "Legs" Diamond, and the union's gorillas were led by "Little Augie." Many found it peculiar that two of Rothstein's protégés were on opposite sides of the issue. But with the work stoppage and violence costing the industry and its workers millions of dollars, it was no surprise when Rothstein was called on to negotiate a settlement. There are no reports regarding Buchalter and Shapiro's participation in the lengthy strike.

Both men were rising stars in the Orgen gang, so at some point, Buchalter must have come to the attention of Arnold Rothstein. The relationship between the two, if indeed there ever was one, has been embellished by writers over the years.

In the months after the strike's settlement, Diamond and Orgen began working closer together. Eddie Diamond, "Legs's" brother, served as a bodyguard for "Little Augie." By many accounts, "Legs" was also a bodyguard, although there is some belief that Diamond's status was more of a partner. Orgen was also reportedly moving into the bootleg business, targeting the nightclubs along Broadway and feeling that the best days of the labor-slugging business were over. In fact, Orgen had left the battlegrounds of the Lower East Side and moved his wife and infant daughter to "the opulence of an up-town apartment" on West 106th Street.

Orgen, Diamond, Buchalter, and Shapiro seemed from the outside to be working together under the Rothstein umbrella, but personality clashes and differences in philosophies reached a peak early in 1927. Buchalter and Shapiro rented out their strong-arm men during a painters' strike in Brooklyn. The two wanted to drag out the matter in hopes of collecting as much money as possible by supplying goons; however, management went to Orgen with a $50,000 offer in hopes of avoiding a prolonged strike. Orgen brought "Legs" Diamond in on the plan to threaten the lives of the union leaders if they didn't end the work stoppage, completely sidestepping Buchalter and Shapiro and bringing the strike to an end.

On October 15, 1927, "Little Augie" Orgen's criminal career came to an end. Shortly after 8:00 that evening, Orgen was walking with "Legs" Diamond on Delancey Street near Norfolk Street. There are many versions of what happened near that corner teeming with pedestrian traffic, but the result was that "Little Augie" took a single bullet to the right temple and died instantly.[10] Diamond was wounded twice.[11] Despite the crowds along the sidewalks, neither the police nor the newspapers could get an accurate account of the shooting. The newspapers reported anywhere from three to five men being involved, some on foot, others in a slow-moving getaway car.

Tales of the legendary murder today have Buchalter driving the automobile and pulling it to the curb to allow Shapiro to jump out and start blasting, while Lepke blazed away from behind the wheel. Many accounts claim that Curley Holtz was a member of the hit team.

Eight days after the shooting, on October 23, Buchalter and Shapiro, accompanied by their lawyer, a former assistant district attorney, surrendered themselves at the Clinton Avenue Police Station. Fearing a repeat of the murder of Nathan Kaplan, this time by associates loyal to the late Jacob Orgen, a large police presence was on hand outside the station when the prisoners were to be brought out. Police outside the station told the crowd which door the men would come through, while police inside quickly escorted them out a different one without incident. Despite the two men being charged formally with homicide two days later, there was never any evidence to prove that either one participated in the murder; no witness could or would identify them as being the shooters or being inside the stolen getaway car. The two were held in custody until November 4, when the charges were dismissed.

> "So gunmen came and gunmen went—no one too powerful and too feared to become the target of an assassin's bullets—and we came into the era of Louis "Lepke" Buchalter, the kingpin of them all, the head of Murder, Inc., the most ruthless and diabolical operator in the history of gangdom."
> —Lewis J. Valentine, *Night Stick: The Autobiography of Lewis J. Valentine*, 1947, p. 131

If Buchalter developed any meaningful relationship with Rothstein, it could only have taken place in the 12 months between Orgen's murder and the slaying of Rothstein. Even the casual observer would have to consider the fact that both Orgen and Diamond were working for Rothstein, and the men responsible for ending this relationship were Buchalter and Shapiro. Would there be any attempt at revenge? Or could the murder of Orgen have been committed with Rothstein's blessing?

Before the month of November was out, there was an attempt on Holtz's life during a drive-by shooting in the Bronx. Suspected of being behind the murder attempt was Louis "Louis the Wop" Fabrizio, an alleged lieutenant of "sinister reputation" for the late Jacob Orgen. On May 21, 1928, after puncturing Fabrizio's tire, gunmen shot him down as he attended to the vehicle in the middle of Second Street.

Two years after Jacob Orgen's murder, the stock market crashed and the country plunged into the depths of the Great Depression, leaving millions unemployed. Any man lucky enough to keep his job was satisfied and not looking to strike or cause any problems that could cost him his livelihood. The need for racketeers to supply strikebreakers and thugs suddenly came to an end.

Buchalter and Shapiro began to consider new fields, and by 1931 they were looking for others ways to extort money. The New York needle trades were their new target, and after a slow start, their names became synonymous with the words "labor racketeering." John Hutchinson in the book, *The Imperfect Union,* stated:

> Buchalter and Shapiro were among the leaders of their kind; there would be few like them again in the brazenness, if not the scale, of their extortions. But they owed less to their adventurousness and ability than to an unfortunate set of social circumstances. Their chief success was in the New York needle trades—the history of that industry illustrating as well as any the entrée that a proper combination of circumstances will give to the professional criminal.[12]

Hutchinson concluded that while these conditions still existed after the demise of the duo, "Buchalter and Shapiro had no true successors."

The labor-racketeering efforts by Buchalter and Shapiro were first directed at New York City's expansive men's garments industry. In 1891, the United Garment Workers of America was founded. The first of the modern needle trade unions, it was also the most dominant until 1914. That year the Amalgamated Clothing Workers of America was founded under Sidney Hillman. Throughout the 1920s, manufacturers who were struck by the Amalgamated hired thugs, usually supplied by Arnold Rothstein, to drive the strikers away from the picket lines. Soon, the Amalgamated hired its own thugs, said to be used solely for self-defense. Hillman, as we shall see, was accused of much more. Years later an Amalgamated president claimed:

> The simple truth is that neither Hillman nor the Amalgamated Clothing Workers of America ever trafficked or dealt with any underworld figures. Hillman and his associates, at considerable personal risk, moved vigorously and effectively to eliminate them. They remain eliminated to this very day. The charges against Hillman are still in dispute. There is more substantial evidence, however, of links between the underworld and some secondary leaders in the union.[13]

Buchalter and Shapiro thugs were hired to work the picket line and beat back the strikebreaking hoods when they appeared. The two reputedly offered additional services such as arson, disabling elevators, pouring acid on clothing stocks, and hijacking trucks, as well as beatings and an occasional murder.

Hoping to gain a strategic foothold in the Amalgamated, Buchalter forged an alliance with Philip Orlovsky, a Hillman opponent and head of Local 4 of the union. Buchalter took control of Local 4 and quickly moved to take charge of others in the Amalgamated by threatening the top officials. Hillman did not remain idle. He ordered an inspection of Local 4's records and quickly uncovered "huge irregularities." Hillman called a meeting of the union's executive board and declared he would "fight the underworld to the finish."

During the summer of 1931, Hillman lobbied corrupt New York City Mayor "Jimmy" Walker for support and, with the protection of officers from the New York Police Department's homicide squad, called a general strike focusing on the racket-protected shops.

On August 24, the General Executive Board of the Amalgamated filed charges against the leaders of Local 4, revealing that nearly $150,000 had disappeared. Affidavits were submitted charging Phil Orlovsky with stealing the local's books and threatening members. Five days later, Amalgamated officials successfully presented a motion for trusteeship at the offices of Local 4. After a brief skirmish, the leaders of Local 4 were arrested. Buchalter and Shapiro's attempt to gain a foothold in the union had failed.

MORE YEARS OF MYSTERY

Another mystery about Buchalter and Shapiro was their relationship with other top gang leaders in New York City's underworld. How had they come to know and become the equals of Joe Adonis, Albert Anastasia, Frank Costello, Meyer Lansky, Lucky Luciano, Benjamin Seigel, as well as Longy Zwillman in New Jersey? By at least one account, the team of Buchalter/Shapiro held membership in the "Group of 7" (see Appendix), the gaggle of gangs that ran the underworld on the Eastern Seaboard beginning in the late 1920s.

In May 1929, both Buchalter and Shapiro attended the Atlantic City Conference (see Appendix) in which gang leaders of different religions and nationalities from around the country allegedly met to discuss intergang cooperation and what the future held in the anticipated post-Prohibition period. The presence of Lepke and Gurrah would indicate that they had risen to an appreciable level within the underworld.

Despite their apparent status, other sources have claimed they held subservient roles. In *The Last Testament of Lucky Luciano* (see Appendix), the mob boss recalled that Meyer Lansky introduced him to Buchalter. He described Lepke as "mostly strong-arm and very little brain," a description that most historians would disagree with. Of course in this narrative, Luciano takes credit for organizing and taking over the unions. Lansky's biographers, in *Mogul of the Mob,* claimed Lansky made Buchalter a "respectable" criminal and warned him not to become involved in narcotics, claiming in the end that Lepke had become an "embarrassment" to Lansky and a "menace" to organized crime. The only gang leader who seemed to stay loyal to Lepke to the bitter end was Albert Anastasia.

Whatever their position in the hierarchy, it didn't keep Buchalter and Shapiro from getting arrested. On July 17, 1929, they along with three other men broke into a dress factory on Broadway, where the owner had refused to play ball when it came to operating as a closed shop at his establishment. The men went to work with acid, crowbars, and stench bombs, destroying machinery and inventory valued at $25,000. The pair was later arrested at the Harrester Restaurant and charged with burglary and malicious mischief. Despite an array of eyewitnesses who saw the men enter the building, when it came time to testify, their recollections had failed and the next month the case was dismissed. The incident was said to mark Buchalter's last involvement in hands-on criminal activity.

On November 11, 1931, Buchalter and Shapiro were involved in an incident that produced a classic gangland group mug shot, but little else. Acting on an anonymous tip, police raided the Hotel Franconia at Broadway and 72nd Street in Manhattan. In addition to Lepke and Gurrah, the police arrested seven other Jewish underworld figures: Benjamin "Bugsy" Siegel, Joseph "Doc" Stacher, Harry "Big Greenie" Greenberg, Harry Teitelbaum, Louis Kravitz, Hyman "Curley" Holtz, Philip "Little Farvel" Kavolick, and Joseph Rosen.[14] They were charged with consorting with known criminals—each other. In the famous mug shot, taken of the entire group in a lineup, Buchalter is wearing a black patch over his left eye. His explanation for the gathering was that he was moving out of his suite at the Franconia Hotel. As for the patch, he said he was "suffering from a peashot in his eye." The men were taken into custody and grilled by detectives before being released; charges were finally dismissed on Christmas Eve.[15]

The same day Buchalter was arrested for consorting, he was also arrested in the Bronx for extortion. That case would take until June 15, 1932, before being discharged with the consent of the district attorney. One year later, on June 12, 1933, Buchalter was again arrested for "consorting." This time it took place in his penthouse apartment on East 68th Street. In the middle of the afternoon, Buchalter and "Trigger Mike" Coppola were lounging around in silk pajamas and robes when four officers arrived. They entered the residence and arrested the two for vagrancy and associating with known criminals. A cursory search of the apartment revealed, in addition to a wide array of expensive clothes, a half-dozen golf bags with clubs. As in the previous consorting case, these charges were dropped.

On August 30, 1931, Buchalter married 26-year-old Beatrice "Betty" Wasserman, a widow with one child. One of the witnesses to sign the marriage license was Morris "Moey Dimples" Wolensky. Born Beatrice Arbeiter in London in 1904, Wasserman moved with her family to the United States four years later. Betty was educated in the New York school system and in 1920, at the age of 16, married Jacob Wasserman, a veteran of the World War. In December 1928, after an operation for appendicitis, Wasserman died from complications. The union produced one child, a son named Harold, whom Buchalter legally adopted in 1934.

After Wasserman's death Betty went back to New York where she found work as a night club hostess for Ben Marden. She was employed at several of New York City's hottest nightclubs as a hostess. A note on her in Buchalter's FBI file stated, "She frequents night clubs considerably, keeps late hours, plays cards and the horses to a considerable extent."

FUR TRADE UNIONS

After their battle with Sidney Hillman in the Garment Workers' Union, Buchalter and Shapiro turned their attention to the fur industry. According to author John Hutchinson:

> The industry was vulnerable to the predatory and the corrupt. Fur manufacturing was a skilled trade, performed largely by hand and resistant to mechanization. Thus entry into the business was easy, the capital equipment for a small business costing less than $100. Most shops were small: one-quarter had only one or two employees; one-half employed four workers, or less. The industry was highly susceptible to changes in fashion, season and economic conditions, unstable in prices, prodigious in business failures, and desperate in its ethics.[16]

In an industry hit hardest by the Great Depression, the damage was amplified by the fact that as a result of the seasonal demand for fur garments, the average worker found employment only four months of the year. One of the last of the needle trade crafts to organize a union, the International Fur Workers Union was established in 1912. The employees of the industry worked with the "skins of fox, raccoon, beaver, badger, seal, ermine, opossum, otter, ocelot, mole, muskrat, squirrel, weasel, sable fitch and mink."

The process flow was that the skins "are purchased from hunters by persons known as 'collectors.' The collectors sell and deliver to dealers, who in turn ship the skins to dressers, who transform the raw hides into skins of commercial value. The dressers then ship the treated hides back to the dealers, who have the hides dyed. The hides then are sold to manufacturers."[17]

During early strikes, employers hired gangsters who made no exceptions in who was brutalized on the picket lines, which included a work force of women and young girls. The union itself had its own internal strife, highlighted by disputes between the radical Communist membership and the conservatives in leadership. After a 30-week strike in 1920, the Communist faction in the union took control.

By January 1931, competition had become sharp in the industry. This led to the organizing of the Protective Fur Dressers' Corporation by owners of a number of fur dressing concerns, who entered into an illegal alliance to prevent any dealer outside of their group, "from shipping, selling and delivering skins in New York City."[18] The purpose of the protective was to force rabbit skin dressers to join, while compelling the dealers to do business only with members of the protective, resulting in the elimination of any unorganized competition. According to John Hutchinson, Buchalter and Shapiro's introduction into the fur trade unions came in April 1932, when they were approached by Abraham Beckerman, the general manager of the Fur Dressers Factor Corporation. By now the two had earned a reputation in the labor industry and were known as the "Gorilla Boys." One of their first acts was to install their own man, Samuel Mittelman, as president of the protective.

Beckerman would later testify at Shapiro's trial that the duo was hired "to keep the members in line; if any individual broke prices, he should be compelled to stay in line." When asked by the judge what happened when people got out of line, Beckerman responded, "Somebody got hurt or threatened, or whatever had to be done. Bombs were used in a couple of places—threats and violence."[19]

To help enforce the protective's directives, Buchalter and Shapiro gained control of the Needle Trades Workers' Industrial Union, which was responsible for providing 85 percent of the workers to all fur dressing shops. This union was also considered a Communist-backed operation and was known as the Left Wing Union. The remaining 15 percent was controlled by the Right Wing Union of the Lamb & Rabbit Workers' Union, which Buchalter and Shapiro also controlled.

The hoods working for Buchalter and Shapiro used violence to force the rabbit skin dressing concerns to work only with the union shop. Oscar Yeager, who ran one concern that refused to adhere to Buchalter's rule, was stabbed in the back and nearly had his hand severed, after which he spent 21 days in the hospital. In August 1932, the Waverly Fur Dressing Company of Newark, New Jersey, was bombed. The owner, who refused to join the protective, had acid thrown in his face the following February, while standing on a Manhattan street corner. Max Ruthberg, owner of M. Ruthberg and Company, was beaten over the head and had his face burned with acid.

The early spring of 1933 produced a number of violent incidents in which Buchalter and Shapiro, or some of the union associates, had a direct role. On March 22, a bomb was placed under the hood of a car operated by Morris Langer, president of the Needle Trade Workers, near his home in New Jersey. Critically injured, Langer died four days later. A parade by fellow union members was held in his honor in Newark.

Shortly after Langer's death, Buchalter sent Samuel Mittelman to meet with Samuel Burt and Irving Potash, the New York secretary of the Left Wing Union. In trying to persuade the two to "play ball," Mittelman boasted that his protective was backed by Buchalter and Shapiro. He also mentioned several times the "unfortunate accident" that had befallen Mr. Langer. By the end of the meeting, it was clear that Potash and Burt, although intimidated, were not going along.

In response to the offer being declined by the Left Wing Union, George Gottesman, a Buchalter lieutenant who went by the name of Harry "Big Greenie" Greenberg, organized a group of thugs to attack the unionists. On the morning of April 24, the group organized at the Arlington Hotel. Around 10:00 AM, armed with gas pipes, they entered a building at 131 West 28th Street. They climbed a staircase to the second floor where the Needle Trade Workers Industrial Union was headquartered. At the receptionist's desk they demanded to know the whereabouts of Ben Gold, the national secretary of the union, and Potash, the New York secretary. When she refused to tell them, one of the goons cut the telephone cords to the switchboard. The receptionist screamed and a free-for-all began.

The thugs used their pipes to club office workers and union members over the head and smash the glass partitions in the headquarters. If the invaders thought they would just beat a docile workforce into submission, they were sorely mistaken. Several of the union members grabbed razor-edged furrier's knives, tools of the trade, and began fighting back. At least two workers were armed with revolvers and opened fire.

With such heavy resistance, the invaders began to flee, running headlong into officers who were quickly summoned from the local precinct house. Some of the goons escaped by jumping out windows. By the time police got things under control, one man was dead, three had bullet wounds (one of which proved fatal), two had fractured skulls, and several were cut badly. It seemed as though most of the injured were the thugs who started the invasion. Nine people were arrested on charges of assault and homicide. Gold, who was in another part of the building, was unharmed, and Potash was away from the office that morning.

During the summer of 1933, Samuel Nissenbaum, the proprietor of Acme Fur Tanning Company, a fur dressing plant in Gloversville, New York, received an anonymous telephone call warning him to "lay off and not take any more work out of New York." When Nissenbaum refused, his operation was bombed. One of his customers, Irving Schild, had been warned not to give business to the Gloversville plant. When he balked several stench bombs were thrown into his store.

On November 6, 1933, after three months of intensive investigation by John Harlan Amen, a special assistant to U.S. Attorney General Homer S. Cummings, a federal grand jury handed up three indictments naming 80 individuals, 68 corporations, and five labor organizations in one of the largest antitrust actions ever taken. Buchalter and Shapiro were both named and bench warrants were issued for their arrest. On November 21, Buchalter was arrested for violation of the Sherman Antitrust Act. Arraigned the following day, he pleaded not guilty and was released after posting a $7,500 bail.

BAKERY AND FLOUR-TRUCKING INDUSTRY

Buchalter and Shapiro came into prominence in the bakery and flour-trucking industry in 1929, when they took control of Local 138, known then as the Flour, Furniture, Grocery & Bakers' Supply Drivers Union. The pair began to force independent truck drivers to join their Flour Truckmen's Association, where they were made to pay membership fees and

monthly dues. At the same time the duo was also gaining control of the employer's association, known as the Brooklyn and New York Flour Truckmen's Association. Buchalter's
dominance was said to have come from his control over William Snyder, president of Local
138, while his "front" in the employer's association was Daniel Richter.

Over the next few years, Buchalter and Shapiro made money through siphoning membership fees and extortion by threats of work stoppages and strikes. During this time, Buchalter
was defied by two brothers, Aaron and Isidore Held, who refused to pay tribute in any form.
When the Held brothers resigned from the employer association, their drivers were ordered
by Local 138 to go on strike. The brothers were told that the only way the strike would end
was for them to rejoin the association and pay the required fees. Aaron Held agreed to these
conditions, but he later filed a lawsuit charging Buchalter, Richter, and Snyder with extortion. Buchalter pulled a disappearing act, while Richter and Snyder were tried in the Bronx
County Court and acquitted. Afterwards, Buchalter turned himself in to the Bronx authorities, only to have the charges dismissed.

By 1934, activities returned to normal with some changes at the top. Max Silverman
replaced Richter as the president of the renamed Flour Truckmen's Association. William
Goldis and Samuel Schorr had also joined the management team. With the employer's association under control, in September of that year a leadership change was about to take place
in the union of Local 138.

William Snyder, the 42-year-old president of the local, gradually began to grow independent and refused to take orders. On the night of September 13, a meeting was scheduled in
a private room in Garfein's Restaurant on Avenue A. In the room were 14 officials crowded
around several tables shoved together. Snyder, said to be the last one to arrive, was seated
with his back to the door. Around 10:00 PM, William Goldis got up from his chair, walked
out the front door, and opened a "casement window" from the street. Shortly thereafter,
Morris Goldis, the younger brother of William, walked into the meeting room behind Snyder and shot him in the back. Snyder jumped to his feet, turned to face his attacker, and was
shot twice more.

Snyder, still alive, was driven to People's Hospital by Max Silverman, where he died from
his wounds two days later. Police questioned the people seated around the tables. The story
from each was the same. At the sound of gunfire, they had ducked under the table and had
not seen the triggerman.

The police did not go away empty-handed. A witness had retained the license plate number of the car in which Goldis had escaped. Police found that it had been rented by a young
man named Samuel Tratner. When questioned, Tratner admitted he had rented the car for
Morris Goldis, who had given him the money. Police showed a mug shot of Goldis to two
witnesses who had been eating in the dining room of Garfein's; both recognized him as the
man who had walked out of the meeting room after the shooting, gun in hand. By the time
police arrived at the Goldis home, Morris had vanished.

Tratner was arrested. Although he and his family were penniless, he hired as legal counsel Charles A. Schneider, described as "a powerful politician of the Eighth Assembly District of New York County." The same lawyer appeared as counsel of record for Morris
Goldis and surrendered him to the district attorney seven weeks after the murder. Soon
afterward, the two restaurant witnesses refused to identify Goldis in homicide court and
Tratner changed his story, now denying he had rented the car for Morris Goldis, who was
released.

William Goldis was elected president of Local 138 and quickly placed his brother on the payroll. To ensure that things ran smoothly, Buchalter sent over one of his associates. Max Rubin was a former school teacher who had become involved in union activities in 1918. An educated man, he was a rare quantity in the Buchalter and Shapiro thug-filled ranks. His purpose at Local 138 was to "hang around" and help straighten out any problems that arose between the leadership of Silverman, Goldis, and Schorr. In short, he served as a mediator for Buchalter between union members and the employer association. Some sources claim he acted as Lepke's "spy."

FEDERAL FUR RACKET TRIAL

Despite the massive and well-publicized indictment by the federal government in November 1933, the case would not come to trial for nearly three years. In August 1935, after several trial delays, Buchalter and Shapiro were not present when their names were called at another preliminary hearing. Buchalter's counsel, J. Arthur Adler, told a federal judge that his client was "weary" from all the postponements and had gone to Carlsbad (a world-renown spa town in Bohemia in the Czech Republic) to "take the cure."[20] The unsympathetic judge declared the men's bonds forfeited, but would void this action if the men were in court by September 3. Both complied. Still the case dragged on.

Thomas E. Dewey, who had been named special prosecutor by Governor Herbert Lehman on July 29, began adding labor racketeering activities to his list of underworld crimes to investigate. By the end of August, he had taken over the prosecution of five members of the joint council of the Fur Workers Union, which was managed by Ben Gold. One of Dewey's first moves against the operations of Buchalter and Shapiro came on October 20 when detectives assigned to the district attorney's staff raided the Perfection Coat Front Manufacturing Company on West 19th Street in Manhattan. This same month, a key Buchalter associate, Max Silverman, became a fugitive.

Dewey's men kept up the pressure. In April, Oscar Saffer, a Broadway clothing merchant, was arraigned and charged with filing false tax returns for 1933. Dewey staff member, Murray I. Gurfein, told Justice Philip J. McCook that Saffer was a "pay-off man" for Buchalter and Shapiro and that $150,000 had passed through the books of his business on its way to the pair.

On July 7, after an extensive investigation by Special Prosecutor Dewey and Justice Philip McCook, Governor Lehman announced the impaneling of two special, or extraordinary, grand juries to continue the investigation work of the two men. McCook would preside over one of the grand juries, and New York State Supreme Court Justice Ferdinand Pecora conducted the other. While Dewey and McCook were meeting with the governor, the special prosecutor's staff raided the Loma Dress Company on Seventh Avenue, seizing business records. The raiders, directed by Gurfein, were watched by a curious lunch-hour crowd as they loaded the documents into three taxicabs and carted them to Dewey's headquarters in the Woolworth Building. As for Buchalter and Shapiro, the newspapers claimed the pair had been missing from the city for the past two weeks.

The goal of Dewey's staff was to gather evidence and find witnesses to testify before the grand juries and for the state at trial. Many of the people interviewed were in fear for their lives about having to talk about Buchalter and Shapiro. Most of these people had already been terrorized and extorted by the duo's army of thugs. It didn't help matters when on

September 13, 1936, a former truck driver, forced to dissolve his business because of Buchalter, was found brutally murdered in his Brooklyn candy store. Just before 7:00 that Sunday morning, four men entered the store and shot him to death.

The newspapers immediately reported that Joseph Rosen had been questioned by Dewey. This claim was vehemently denied by the special prosecutor. "This is the second time that a murdered man has been falsely stated to have been a witness before my office. It is a vicious practice, and I propose to stop it."[21] Dewey was in fact infuriated because he thought talk of this nature would only serve to hamper his investigation by creating "unwarranted fear" in some witnesses. His office had promised witnesses full protection from reprisals if they cooperated.

The next month Dewey's investigation of Buchalter and Shapiro began to broaden after a raid on the Pechter Baking Corporation on Cherry Street. Described as one of the largest baking concerns in the city, its records were seized and two officers were subpoenaed after several months of investigation. The *New York Times* reported, "Between 300 and 400 witnesses have been examined before the two extraordinary grand juries . . . in connection with the baking racket."[22] Max Silverman, still a fugitive, was said to be the "active operating head" of the bakery racket, fronting for Buchalter and Shapiro.

By now Buchalter and Shapiro had other problems to deal with. The trial for the first federal indictment for racketeering in the Fur Industries' rabbit-skin trade finally got underway. During the nearly three-year period since the indictments, there had been 23 pleas of guilty, 4 cases severed, and the rest had been dismissed; only two defendants were left to be tried, Buchalter and Shapiro.

On October 26, 1936, after a two-hour jury selection, the government's opening statement was made by John Harlan Amen. The prosecutor claimed that in 1932 and 1933, the Protective Fur Dressers' Corporation achieved a complete monopoly of the rabbit-dressing industry through violence, which consisted of "assault on dealers, dressers and manufacturers, their families and employees, destruction of their property, forcible detention and hijacking of trucks conveying rabbit skins, destruction of skins, placing 'stink bombs' and explosive bombs in the places of business of dealers, dressers and manufacturers, and throwing acid upon dealers and rabbit skins."[23]

The *New York Herald Tribune* reported:

> In presenting the case against Buchalter and Shapiro, [Amen] said he would have to rely to a large extent on circumstantial evidence. He could not, he said, show that the defendants on trial were the men who actually "cut people's eyes out" in the reign of terror which was carried on in furtherance of the monopoly. To do that, he said, "you would have to go to the dens of Chicago and Detroit to find the actual men who committed the violence."[24]

Amen promised the panel: "We will show that they were directly or indirectly responsible for every bit of violence in this case and that they were the men behind the guns."

Beginning on October 27, a parade of fur dealers and fur dressers marched to the stand to testify. The early witnesses were called solely to lay the groundwork in the government's case to show that "violence and coercion" were practiced in establishing the monopoly. At this point neither of the defendants was linked to the activities. Then, one by one the victims took the stand to be questioned as to how they were coerced into carrying out the protective's orders.

Frank Brickner told about being stabbed in the back and nearly losing his hand; Julius Litwace talked about having acid thrown in his face; Max Rothberg revealed how he had been beaten over the head; and Joseph E. Joseph related how his face had been burned with acid.

The following day's witnesses included Samuel Nissenbaum, the Gloversville plant owner whose operation was bombed during the summer of 1933; Irving Schild, into whose store stench bombs were thrown; Harry Liebmann, who was hit in the head with a bottle; and Charles Vandeweghe, the Paterson, New Jersey, dresser who was driven out of business. Several of the witnesses developed memory lapses or became evasive during their testimony. In the case of Liebmann, he at first denied that he had been knocked unconscious with a bottle, but after some prodding replied, "I was bleeding, but it was all right." Each time a witness hesitated, Amen read back their grand jury testimony or were urged by Judge Knox to remember.

On October 29, testimony from Irving Potash finally linked Buchalter and Shapiro to the activities through his conversations with Samuel Mittleman, Ben Gold, and his introduction to "Gurrah." Also this day, Julius Bernfeld told the harrowing story of being attacked while with his daughter and losing his eye in a succeeding attack. As the trail came to the end of its first week, Samuel Burt took the stand and related his conversations with Mittleman, in which the threat of ending up like Morris Langer, the New Jersey car-bomb victim, was implied.

On November 2, the government presented evidence to link Buchalter and Shapiro to Harry Greenberg and the April 1933 assault on the Needle Trades Workers' Industrial Union headquarters. Prosecutor Amen showed that the room the raiders used to organize in at the Arlington Hotel was registered under the "Solomon account," the same name used by Shapiro when he stayed at the hotel on another occasion two months before the attack.

After seven days of testimony, the government rested its case on November 4. Defense counsel Adler then entered a motion to have the charges against Buchalter dismissed because of lack of evidence. Judge Knox told prosecutors that if he didn't hear more evidence against Lepke, he would be "obliged" to grant the motion. The next day, after telling Judge Knox that none of the more than 30 witnesses who took the stand "connected either of the defendants with a single act of violence testified to," chief defense attorney Maxwell Mattuck rested, without calling any witnesses. In his closing statement, Mattuck claimed his clients were innocent victims of a Communist union plot to divert responsibility for violence perpetrated on a rival right-wing union. Despite his hint of dismissal, Judge Knox denied motions to drop the charges against Buchalter.

Prosecutor Amen faced a daunting task during his summation. He had to defend a weak case in which government witnesses had failed to connect Buchalter and Shapiro with the violence that was described in testimony. Amen repeated the threatening words that Potash had testified were uttered by Sam Mittleman. He then told the jury that, "Defendants of this character never commit acts of violence personally, seldom are seen and never talk."

The jury was handed the case at 3:55 on Friday afternoon, November 6. When a decision could not be reached by 11:00 PM, they were taken to a hotel for the night. Saturday morning deliberations began again. By mid-afternoon the jury sent Knox a note saying they were unable to agree. The judge called the jurors to the courtroom and stated, "You have been out for less than an hour since I read a considerable part of the evidence and instructed you. I'm going to send you back. This is a case where a verdict should be reached one way or another.

As a matter of fact, I was surprised that you didn't reach a verdict last night. I don't want to coerce any member of the jury but you must not be stubborn."[25]

The jurors went back to the jury room determined to come to a unanimous decision. At 12:30 AM Sunday morning they announced they had one. By the time Knox reached the courtroom from his home it was nearly 1:20 AM. After 33 hours the jury declared that both men were guilty of violating the Sherman Antitrust law.

Amen asked the court for immediate sentencing, which Knox denied. Attorney Adler asked that the men be released on an increased bond: "These men have been convicted on atmosphere, not evidence, and the sentence will not stand up on appeal." To this Knox agreed.

On November 12, Buchalter and Shapiro were sentenced to two years in prison and fined $10,000 apiece. In delivering the sentences, Knox declared that "the penalty provided by the act is a mere slap on the wrist and quite inadequate to deal with the conditions shown in this trial." Clearly disgusted at what he saw as an inadequate sentence, Knox refused to grant the men's release on bond pending appeal, and they were received at the Federal Detention Center in Manhattan.

On November 16, Adler filed an appeal with the U.S. Circuit Court of Appeals. Buchalter and Shapiro remained incarcerated until a hearing before Federal Appeals Judge Martin T. Manton, senior member of the Circuit Court on December 3. According to Burton Turkus, at that time the judge "mysteriously and remarkably opened the doors—permitting them to post bail and walk out."[26]

On March 8, 1937, claiming that there had not been enough evidence linking Buchalter to crimes he was convicted of, the U.S. Circuit Court of Appeals, with Judge Manton leading the way, set aside Lepke's conviction. At the same time, it affirmed Shapiro's conviction. On June 1, the U.S. Supreme Court refused to review the lower court's ruling on Shapiro. When Gurrah failed to surrender himself, three weeks later on June 21, his bail of $10,000 was forfeited.

On July 6, the second of the 1933 indictments was scheduled to go to trial in the courtroom of Federal Judge Sidney C. Mize. This case involved members of the Fur Dressers Factor Corp. On trial were 89 corporate and individual co-defendants. It was billed as the largest antitrust indictment, in terms of number of defendants, ever returned. The trial's star attractions, Lepke and Gurrah, however, were nowhere to be found, and six other defendants had also failed to appear. The next day bench warrants were sworn out for the arrest of Buchalter and Shapiro, and the two men were officially named fugitives from justice.

GARMENT INDUSTRY EXTORTION

On August 9, 1937, after the completion of an 18-month investigation, one of the special grand juries, the one presided over by Justice Pecora, handed down an indictment charging 16 men with conspiring to extort money in the garment industry. Dewey, Gurfein, and two assistants presented the evidence obtained to the grand jury. Of the 16 men named, only five were arrested. The others, including Buchalter and Shapiro, were fugitives.

According to the indictment, "The tribute collectors . . . simply walked in, demanded money and, if it was not produced, threatened to wreck the establishment or drench it with stench bombs." Bail for the five defendants, which included Joseph Miller, was set at $35,000 each. Miller, according to Gurfein, was responsible for bringing Buchalter and Shapiro into the garment industry.

With the key figures in the case on the lam, Dewey sent a letter to New York City Mayor Fiorella LaGuardia requesting that he petition the Board of Estimate to offer rewards for the men's capture. In Dewey's request for the rewards was the comment the "individuals were remaining out of jurisdiction of the city courts in the hope that obstacles would develop in their prosecution." In Buchalter's case, instead of obstacles developing, people began dying. On August 20, the board posted $5,000 rewards for each man.

On September 24, Max Silverman, who had disappeared 21 months earlier, was arrested in Los Angeles. Accused of being a leader of the bakery and flour-trucking racket, Silverman allegedly was involved with Lucky Luciano and Dutch Schultz, as well as Buchalter and Shapiro. A California judge set his bail at $250,000. Just days after his arrest, another special grand jury under Judge Pecora returned an indictment naming Silverman, Buchalter, and Shapiro, along with four unnamed defendants, for extortion in the bakery industry during 1934 and 1935. The *New York Times* reported: "During the two-year investigation by Mr. Dewey's staff, more than 2,000 witnesses have been questioned and the books of several hundred baking firms examined. The indictment charged that money was extorted from various baking concerns by threats of sluggings and stench bombings."

While Silverman was being flown back to New York from Los Angeles, accompanied by Assistant District Attorney Frank Hogan and two detectives, Buchalter lashed out at another potential witness. Max Rubin was critically wounded in the Bronx. After months of being told by Buchalter to stay out of town to avoid being questioned by Dewey, Rubin had come home and then picked up by Dewey's investigators and questioned before the special grand jury . His cooperation before the special grand jury on September 27 provided valuable information on the activities of Max Silverman, as well as Buchalter and Shapiro. At the conclusion of his testimony, Rubin twice declined the offer of bodyguards from Dewey. On October 1, while Rubin was walking home on East Gunhill Road in the middle of the afternoon, a gunman ran up from behind and fired a single bullet into the base of his skull.

ON THE LAM

Buchalter would be on the run from July 1937 until August 1939. During that time it is estimated he spent little if any time in hiding with Shapiro. In fact, with their split after the Fur Trade Trial, the men were never again together as partners. Buchalter moved between safe houses during these 26 months on the lam, aided by Albert Anastasia and Abe Reles, who served as his official contact.

By early 1939, Buchalter was tired of being a fugitive and began to prepare for the day when he would surrender. Part of this preparation was to soften the blow of any trial, and the best approach to this was to get rid of witnesses. Buchalter had initially ordered a number of men to leave town because he believed Tom Dewey would question them about his activities. Some of the people responded, but others returned and were questioned by the special prosecutor. This is when, according to Reles, Buchalter began ordering the murder of people he thought could connect him to the crimes he had been indicted for. The killings had actually begun two-and-a-half years earlier. One of the first to go was Irv Askenas, a taxi driver murdered in late summer 1936, who had been questioned by Dewey. Next was Joe Rosen, the trucker Buchalter had run out of business and who had refused to heed Lepke's advice. Rosen was murdered in his candy store on September 13, 1936. In May 1937, the victim was George "Whitey" Rudnick, who was seen talking in an automobile with one of Dewey's assistants.

Of the 15 men indicted with Buchalter for conspiracy to extort money in the garment industry on August 9, 1937, several became targets. In 1938, Buchalter ordered two of those co-defendants murdered—Hyman Yuram, on July 25, and Leon Scharf in November. But it was in 1939 that Buchalter really got busy ordering the following murders:

- **January 28, 1939**—Irving "Danny Fields" Friedman, a collector and fellow co-defendant, who was rumored to be turning state's evidence; and Louis Cohen, the killer of Nathan Kaplan.

- **March 23, 1939**—Joseph Miller, another co-defendant, a retired dress maker who was muscled out of the Perfection Coat Front Company, was shot seven times and survived, but not before beating one of the assailants senseless.

- **April 25, 1939**—Abraham "Whitey" Friedman, another co-defendant, who allegedly supplied Buchalter with goons during strikes.

- **May 25, 1939**—Morris "Moishe" Diamond, a partner of Buchalter in the trucking racket.

- **July 25, 1939**—Irving Penn, a music company executive, who was mistaken for Philip Orlovsky.

- **November 23, 1939**—Harry Gottesman, known as Harry "Big Greenie" Greenberg, was murdered in Hollywood, California, where he was hiding out under the alias of George Schacter. Greenberg had demanded money from Buchalter in return for not talking to Dewey. Part of the hit team was Benjamin "Bugsy" Siegel.

Buchalter's scheme to murder all those who could testify against him came to a bloody end on the morning of July 25. A hit team consisting of Martin "Buggsy" Goldstein, Seymour "Blue Jaw" Magoon, and Abe "Pretty" Levine, waiting outside the apartment of Phil Orlovsky at 250 East 178th Street in the Bronx, put five bullets into the wrong man. Irving Penn, a 42-year-old music company executive, had the misfortune to have a similar build as Orlovsky. The dying man was left lying on the sidewalk as the gunmen sped off in a stolen car, with stolen license plates. The vehicle was abandoned several blocks away on the same street. A few hours later, after telling police he did not have an enemy in the world, Penn, a devoted husband and father of two daughters, died in Fordham Hospital.

Bronx District Attorney Samuel E. Foley believed that because of Penn's unusual size, 260 pounds, he would have been hard to mistake for someone else. Because two other men who had connections to Dewey's investigation of Buchalter had been gunned down in the Bronx in recent months, Foley considered that Penn may have been another witness. Numerous calls to Dewey's office that day to inquire about this possibility were not returned.

Orlovsky, who normally departed his home around 8:15, had left at 7:00 that morning to take care of some office matters, because he had a scheduled meeting at Dewey's office that afternoon. Seven hours after the shooting, Dewey's office requested a police guard for Orlovsky, tipping Bronx investigators to the motive for the mistaken identity murder of Penn. Foley was incensed by the actions of the New York County prosecutor's office (Dewey was vacationing at the time). Calling Orlovsky a "Dewey informant" who should have had protection, Foley blasted Dewey in the newspapers.

Dewey was himself incensed over the murder of an innocent man and cut his vacation short to return to New York and press the hunt for Buchalter. Denying that Orlovsky was an informant, Dewey issued a five-page statement declaring, "I want to say now that if Mr. Orlovsky, who is one of the toughest men in New York, would talk, the underworld would be cracked wide open."[27] Dewey revealed that Buchalter was conducting a "war of extermination" and that even more victims than Foley had cited had been murdered or vanished. Dewey told reporters that the effort to capture Lepke would be "re-doubled" and that he would ask the Board of Estimate to increase the reward to $25,000. Dewey revealed that he was holding "tri-weekly" conferences with J. Edgar Hoover and Police Commissioner Valentine in an effort to capture Buchalter. It was reported that the search for Lepke was costing taxpayers $200,000 a year.

On July 31, it was announced that Dewey had subpoenaed the accounting records of 50 companies that Buchalter was known to be involved with in the garment industry. The purpose was to find Lepke's source of revenue and cut it off. In addition, Dewey began holding Buchalter associates as material witnesses with high bails, also in an effort to deplete Lepke's financial resources.

On August 3, federal officials announced that "Narcotic King" Jacob "Yasha" Katzenberg had provided the FBI with a "mass" of information regarding Buchalter's participation in an international drug smuggling ring. A day after the announcement about Katzenberg, The *New York World-Telegram*, which seemed to take the lead in the renewed effort to capture Buchalter, announced that police had put a day and night watch on Shapiro's wife and daughter after rumors abounded that Gurrah was ready to turn informer.

When the overall reward for Buchalter's capture increased to $35,000, more than 300 letters poured in alleging "the exact whereabouts" of the labor racketeer. On August 9, one day after the New York Police Department announced the printing of 1 million wanted posters of Buchalter, Dewey canceled a trip to see his mother in Owosso, Michigan. During the trip, Dewey was to be feted at the county fair. A nationwide list of public enemies published a few days later listed Buchalter as Number 4, behind two bank robbers and an escaped bank robber. Of course with all the publicity and the high rewards for Lepke, law enforcement was inundated with sightings of the racketeer all over the country, just like they had been five years earlier when John Dillinger headed the most wanted list.

The federal government was stepping up its efforts by subpoenaing underworld figures across the country and forcing them to appear before grand juries. An FBI report revealed, "In the parlance of the underworld, 'The heat was on.' They faced the Grand Jury with the realization that the FBI Agents knew in detail their activities and were confronted with one of two possibilities, either telling the truth or refusing to answer questions."

In New Jersey, a special federal grand jury called Ben Marden and Abner Zwillman. Questioned about his relationship with Buchalter, Zwillman did not deny a friendship, but claimed he hadn't seen him for three or four years. He was asked if he knew the whereabouts of Buchalter. Zwillman replied in what many considered a veiled message: "No, of course not. I wish I did. I would tell him that the sensible thing to do would be to give himself up."[28] In Philadelphia, authorities grabbed Harry "Nig" Stromberg and placed him before a grand jury for questioning.

On August 13, Buchalter lieutenant Joseph "Strawberry Joe" Amorusa was arrested in New Paltz in the Catskills following some crack police work by a detective who was vacationing there. Amorusa had been a fugitive for about two years and had settled in as a "gentlemen farmer" in this rural community. He was living with a 29-year-old woman from the Bronx, although he had a wife and two children back in Brooklyn. A search of the house revealed canceled checks that showed he was "extremely well furnished" with money.

The next day, a special federal grand jury indicted five people and two corporations on charges of harboring Buchalter and Shapiro. The men included Shapiro's brother and brother-in-law.

While news about Buchalter was on the front pages practically every day during August 1939, Dewey decided it was time to visit his mother. He began a week's stay on August 21. The day after Dewey began his vacation, the FBI announced that the government was increasing its reward for Buchalter to $25,000, putting a $50,000 price tag on Lepke's head. An FBI report stated:

> Following the accidental killing of Isadore Penn, who resided in the same building with Philip Orslovsky [sic], considerable pressure was brought to bear in New York City and innumerable statements appeared in the press to the effect that Buchalter was gradually seeking to exterminate all witnesses who could appear against him. It can now be revealed that the Federal Bureau of Investigation, fearing this, had affidavits taken from some of the witnesses, in the presence of a Federal District Judge, and their statements recorded by sound movies.[29]

On Sunday evening, August 20, radio personality and *New York Daily Mirror* columnist Walter Winchell, a friend of J. Edgar Hoover, was authorized by the director, "to publicly state that Buchalter's civil rights would be respected and maintained should he surrender." Within a few days, an ultimatum was issued that no further consideration would be given unless Buchalter surrendered by 4:00 PM on August 24.

According to Burton Turkus in *Murder, Inc.* Anastasia had moved Buchalter into a new safe house on August 1, where he was "more secure than ever." After the government increased the reward, however, Turkus stated:

> The FBI felt it had to beat state authorities to Lepke to "save face," after two years of futility. So, J. Edgar Hoover sent a flat fiat to Joey Adonis and Frank Costello, the ranking "brass" of Unione Siciliano: Unless Lepke came out of his hole and gave up *to the* FBI, every Italian mobster in the country would be picked up. Mr. A. and Frank C. could not afford to let this happen. They sent an ultimatum to their old pal, "Sorry, chum—surrender to the Feds or we'll have to deliver you personally."

The popular tale is that Morris "Moey Dimples" Wolensky, a trusted friend of Buchalter, delivered the ultimatum, but that a deal had been worked out that by surrendering to the FBI, Lepke would be tried solely on the narcotics charges and do his time in a federal prison.[30] Dewey had already announced that he had enough evidence to put Buchalter away for 500 years on state charges, so Lepke took the bait and despite Anastasia's advice not to, Buchalter surrendered.

On the night of August 24, 1939, while Dewey was enjoying a Michigan vacation at his mother's, Albert Anastasia drove Buchalter to what was the beginning of his end. Lepke sat in the back seat with Louis Capone's sister and a borrowed child, a disguise in case they ran across a nosey patrolman on their way to their destiny. Walter Winchell was to act as the intermediary. According to an FBI report:

Then came another phone call, instructing that the intermediary, Walter Winchell, "drive up to Proctor's Theatre in Yonkers." Before reaching the theatre a car loaded with strangers drew alongside the automobile driven by Walter Winchell. One of the men got out, holding a handkerchief over his face, and instructed Winchell to go to the drugstore on the corner of 19th Street and 8th Avenue; to enter one of the phone booths and about nine o'clock someone would come up to him and tell him where to notify the G-Men to meet him. Promptly at nine o'clock an individual approached and stated, "go back in there and tell Hoover to be at 28th Street and 5th Avenue between 10:10 and 10:20."

In accordance with the representations which had been made, the Director, unaccompanied, kept the rendezvous. At 10:17 the search ended when "Lepke," wearing dark glasses, disguised with a mustache, kept his word.

At the designated location, 28th Street and Fifth Avenue, Anastasia pulled behind an automobile containing J. Edgar Hoover. Lepke got out and was joined by Walter Winchell, who introduced one of the most wanted men in America to the Director of the FBI:

Winchell: Mr. Hoover, this is Lepke.
Hoover: How do you do?
Buchalter: Glad to meet you.

Buchalter later told a friend that, from his conversation with Hoover, he realized there had been no deal. "Dimples" had double-crossed him.[31]

From the beginning, the government made it known they were not going to share their famous prisoner with Dewey. While Dewey was out of the state, his assistants tried in vain to get custody of Buchalter, but they were refused permission to even speak with him. U.S. Attorney Cahill stated he would give up Lepke to state prosecutors only if they had an "ironbound" murder case.

FEDERAL NARCOTICS TRIAL

As with many of Buchalter's criminal activities, it's hard to tell just exactly when he first got involved with narcotics. The popular theory is that after the death of Arnold Rothstein in November 1928, Buchalter and Lucky Luciano took over his narcotics network. Just what that meant for Buchalter no one knows; there's certainly no documentation of his participation in any drug activities until 1931.

As Buchalter was in the hands of federal authorities, they would have their way with him first. The day after his surrender to Hoover, Buchalter was arraigned in federal court on 10 charges of violation of the narcotics laws.

The indictments were issued on November 30, 1937, 21 months before Buchalter surrendered. At the time, 30 people were arrested, including three U.S. Customs officials and a number of women. Lepke was listed as one of "five principals" in the drug ring. One of the others was "Yasha" Katzenberg, a key member of the operation, who, while serving his sentence, let the government know he was ready to testify against Lepke, once he was apprehended, in return for some "consideration."

On August 28, 1939, U.S. Attorney John T. Cahill was anxious to go to trial. Buchalter seemed to be taking his time in finding counsel. The only thing he had accomplished since his arrest was to shave off the small mustache he had grown while on the lam. The next afternoon, Lepke appeared in court with counsel William W. Kleinman, a former assistant district attorney from Brooklyn, who was given one day to confer with his client. When Kleinman appeared alone in court the next day, where Cahill was prepared to set a trial date, the defense lawyer asked for and received a 10-day adjournment to be able to familiarize himself with the case and to file any motions he deemed necessary. When this period was concluded, a tentative trial date of October 16 was set.

Buchalter was moved out of a cell in the "high tower" of the Federal Courthouse, where he had been placed because he was said to "be in danger," and placed in the Federal Detention Center on September 15. Apparently, the danger he was supposed to have been in had subsided, or so the FBI decided. District Attorney Dewey used this opportunity to renew his request to interrogate the prisoner.

There were a number of postponements before the trial began at the end of November, which proved to be a busy month. A harboring trial, charging Shapiro's brother Carl and four defendants, got underway. All would be found guilty, but the conviction would be reversed on appeal. Max Silverman, his son Harold, and Samuel Schorr were arraigned in general sessions court for extortion in the bakery and flour-trucking industry. The first-degree murder trial of William and Morris Goldis for the slaying of William Snyder was scheduled to begin. And finally, one-time Buchalter and Shapiro lieutenant Harry Greenberg was murdered in Hollywood, allegedly on orders from Lepke.

By the time the narcotics trial began on November 30, only four defendants remained: Buchalter, Max Schmukler, Morris Sweder, and David Kardonick. The others had either made a plea or were fugitives. In opening statements before Federal Judge Knox, Assistant U.S. Attorney Joseph P. Martin told the jurors that the defendants conspired to take $188,000 abroad and import $10 million in narcotics into this country. Lepke, after first not wanting to get involved, decided to participate for 60 percent of the profits, later settling for a mere 50 percent. Buchalter showed a keen interest in the opening, as did his wife Beatrice, who was seated in the second row.

During his two-hour opening statement Martin explained how the ring worked, with the assistance of the bribed customs agents, and how the couriers traveled to China, Denmark, France, Italy, Japan, and Mexico to retrieve the drugs. Defense counsel William Kleinman countered that any testimony against his client would come from "self-confessed smugglers and peddlers of drugs, men who were willing to lie to protect themselves" and receive reduced prison terms. Attorneys for Kardonick and Sweder pointed out that their client's problems developed because they had gotten dragged in by relatives.

On December 1, Nate Gross took the stand as the first government witness. He immediately brought Buchalter into his testimony by claiming he went to see him to complain that a relative, David Dishbach, was being cheated out of his share of the profits. The *New York Times* reported: "He was on the stand two and a half hours, during which some of the closest questioning was done by Judge John C. Knox, who left his seat and stood over the witness at one time in an effort to get him to clarify his halting and often inaudible testimony."

At the next session, it was "suggested" that the first two government witnesses, who included Nate Gross, were being intimidated. After answering a question on redirect by Martin, the judge grilled him:

Knox: Why didn't you say that the other day?
Gross: I may have got mixed up.

Knox: You didn't get mixed up. Are you trying to protect Lepke or anyone else?

Gross: I'm not trying to protect anyone.

The next witness was Emma Dishbach, whose husband was an indicted conspirator, but a fugitive in Mexico. She talked about a gefilte fish dinner at which Lepke, Katzenberg, and Jake Lvovsky were guests at her home to discuss the narcotics business with her husband David. Before Lepke entered the house he sent in two guards who searched the entire house, including under the beds. She said that during dinner a piece of fish got stuck in Katzenberg's throat and he "almost died."

On December 5, a Russian-speaking pickpocket, who was brought in from Dannemora Prison, took the stand. Solomon Stein talked of meeting Buchalter in Paris in 1931. When Stein was told to identify Lepke, he "shuffled from the stand, hands in pocket" to the defense table to point him out.

Yasha Katzenberg, the government's key witness, took the stand on December 6. Serving a 10-year sentence, Katzenberg was once referred to by the League of Nations as an "international menace." During his first day of testimony, he described the operation, but gave little information that tied it to Buchalter.

The next day, Katzenberg's testimony revealed that Buchalter had demanded 50 percent of the profits of the business through Louis Kravitz, described as a "business manager" for Lepke. Katzenberg then spoke directly with Lepke and got him to come down in his percentage for a while.

On December 13, the government completed its case after calling 23 witnesses. The next morning defense counsel asked for a directed verdict of acquittal. Knox took the motion seriously against only one man, Morris Sweder, whose print shop was alleged to be a front for the operation. The next day, Sweder and his son-in-law took the stand, and after questioning by both sides, Cahill recommended the dismissal. Knox allowed him to walk out of the courtroom a free man.

On December 14, Max Schmukler took the stand. The defendant claimed he was "guiltless" of the crime . . . and any other crime for that matter. Cahill, however, began a relentless cross-examination of the man and in the end got him to admit that he had been using aliases and had a criminal record going back to 1896.

Buchalter's counsel obtained a writ to bring back Jake Lvovsky, who pleaded guilty and was serving his sentence at Leavenworth, to testify for the defense. On December 18, Lvovsky testified, denying that Buchalter had ever been his partner in the narcotics business. He proved to be a hostile witness both to the prosecution and the defense. At one point, Lvovsky turned to Judge Knox and whined, "I said that man had nothing to do with me, what else do you want from me?"

William Kleinman had refused to put Buchalter on the stand. On December 19, he gave his closing argument. In presenting it, he tried to get the jurors to forget about "Lepke" and reach a verdict on Buchalter, the defendant:

I know what is in your minds. Because there isn't a person who lives in the City of New York who hasn't heard stories about Lepke, hasn't read them, hasn't discussed them.

You can't tell me that there hasn't been some moment at which you have thought, "Oh well, this is a prosecution against Lepke; what difference does it make—the end justifies the means."

You must give him the same kind of square deal and a fair trial that each of you would expect in his place. I'm not making any comparisons—but there is only one brand of justice and he is entitled to that, nothing less, nothing more.[32]

On Wednesday night, December 20, the jury of four men and eight women reached a verdict after less than five hours of deliberation. Judge Knox, attending a black-tie dinner party, was notified and returned to take the bench still wearing a tuxedo. At 10:47 PM, the jury announced the conviction of Buchalter and Max Schmukler. The third defendant, David Kardonick, was acquitted.

Judge Knox declared that the jury had reached a "righteous verdict" and set January 2 as the sentencing date, and the time for Buchalter's defense counsel to announce their decision on whether or not to go to trial on the remaining charges in the narcotics indictment. Lepke was looking at a two-year prison term and a $10,000 fine. If convicted of the remaining nine counts, however, he could face the maximum of 162 additional years and fines totaling $180,000.

On January 2, after reaching an agreement with U.S. Attorney John T. Cahill, Buchalter pled guilty to the nine remaining narcotics charges, as well as the two remaining indictments issued in 1933 for the federal rabbit-fur racketeering case. In return for the plea, Buchalter was sentenced to just 14 years in prison, a 10-year probation period and a mere $2,500 fine.[33] Judge Knox, who had complained that the previous sentence was "a slap on the wrist," reluctantly agreed to Cahill's recommendation, citing that "government doctors" felt that because of Lepke's health problems, this would be commensurate to a life sentence.

Whether or not this would prove to be a life sentence, only time would tell. Buchalter's main concern, however, wasn't his sentence, or even his own health issues. It was what U.S. Attorney General Frank Murphy did after the sentencing hearing. With the custody question of Lepke now in his hands, he opened the door for Buchalter to be turned over to Dewey to be tried on state charges. In his instructions to Cahill, to deliver Buchalter for trial to New York County's Court of General Sessions, Murphy's communication stipulated, "that in event of conviction in State court any sentence imposed is to be served only after service of federal sentences heretofore imposed."

BAKERY AND FLOUR-TRUCKING RACKETEERING TRIAL

Dewey's staff wasted no time in announcing they wanted to try Buchalter immediately on extortion charges in the bakery and flour-trucking rackets. The indictment consisted of 23 counts—21 counts of extortion from 14 companies and 2 counts of attempted extortion. Lepke's legal counsel moved just as fast to block their efforts. General Sessions Judge John J. Freschi issued a writ of habeas corpus to have Buchalter present in court on January 4 to plead to the charges. Kleinman's contention was that as a result of Buchalter's highly publicized two years as a fugitive, he could not receive a fair trial in state court.

After some legal wrangling, the trial was scheduled to begin on January 24. A week before the trial, Dewey's office announced another indictment. This represented the work of the last 10 successive grand juries, which had been going on for four years, investigating racketeering in the garment industry by Buchalter and Shapiro. The 40-page indictment named nine gangsters in the extortion of $515,000 involving 36 businesses. In announcing the charges,

Dewey let it be known that no action would take place until the pending trial for Buchalter was completed.

On trial with Buchalter would be William Goldis, Samuel Schorr, Max Silverman, and his son Harold. The trial began with a bang when Goldis entered a plea of guilty before the first juror was selected. Buchalter, seated at the defense table, looked at Goldis and said, "You are a dirty rat!"

After a weeklong jury selection, the panel was sworn in on February 1. Judge Freschi then surprised the jurors by announcing they would be sequestered for the duration of the trial. Throughout the trial Buchalter remained in the custody of U.S. marshals and, when not in court, was kept at the Federal House of Detention.

The next day the state called its first witness, Aaron Held, who described the extortion ordeal he endured from 1930 until he dissolved his company in late 1936. Held spent more than four full days on the stand, mostly being cross-examined by defense counsel. The second day was highlighted by Max Silverman collapsing at the defense table, a near daily occurrence that continued throughout the trial.

On February 7, Abraham Lubetkin was questioned about his confrontation with Goldis and Schorr regarding a demand for unionization at his company. Lubetkin said he agreed to pay the pair so much per employee, plus an additional $2,500. After Lubetkin's morning testimony, Samuel Schorr suddenly entered a plea of guilty. Like Goldis, he agreed to testify against his former co-defendants; however, neither man was called by the government.

The next day Abraham Schornstein and Fred Gerhardt testified to the payments they were forced to make to Buchalter's men. For the first time, testimony tied Harold Silverman to the crimes. A parade of witnesses followed, each with his own tale of horror. Joseph Zwacker testified that after the appointment of Dewey as special prosecutor in 1935, Goldis approached him and threatened that if he ever mentioned a word of his activities to Dewey he "would die with his shoes on."[34]

On February 12, the state's star witness, Max Rubin, took the stand. Providing details of Buchalter's and Max and Harold Silverman's activities dating back to the early 1930s, Rubin, the ex-school teacher, proved to be an excellent witness. On his first day of testimony, he also told of his own ordeal of being ordered out of the city by Lepke and what transpired when he didn't obey orders.

One of the highlights of Rubin's testimony was the implication of William Solomon, the Tammany Leader of the 17th Assembly District. Rubin claimed he attended a meeting with Buchalter and Solomon, where details were worked out for a $15,000 extortion of the Gottfried Baking Company to call off a "shake down strike." Rubin collected $10,000 at Solomon's insurance office, where the Tammany leader received 10 percent. Solomon, who was under indictment in a bribery case involving a state contract, denied the accusation, claiming he had never met Buchalter.

Rubin brought up murders attributed to Buchalter's men, but each time his statements were stricken from the record. At one point, however, Buchalter's attorney asked him if he recalled the murder of Joseph Rosen. Rubin replied, "Very, very well—and how well!"

On February 15, Samuel Miller, a lawyer and officer for the Gottfried Baking Company, testified that in 1935 he paid Buchalter's $20,000 demand to settle a labor issue. When cross-examined, Miller was asked if he knew he was committing a crime when paying the demand. Miller responded that he had no recourse and that he had complained about Buchalter's activities to the U.S. attorney general, the National Labor Relations Board, the FBI, and the

New York State Attorney General's office. Miller also corroborated Rubin's testimony regarding the payoff to William Solomon.

After 10 days of testimony from 17 witnesses, the state rested its case on Friday, February 16. Judge Freschi gave defense counsel until Monday afternoon to begin its case. Meanwhile, the jurors were sequestered for the weekend under guard at the Vanderbilt Hotel.

On Monday, prosecutors Jacob Grumet and Frank Hogan asked Judge Knox to quash five counts in the indictment, to which he consented. Knox then listened to nearly 150 defense motions to remove pieces of testimony. The judge would need until Wednesday to review the numerous motions, most of which were denied. With approval of the prosecution, two more counts were quashed on request of defense counsel.

During this period, there were rumors that Buchalter and his fellow defendants were trying to negotiate deals through their lawyers. Max Silverman was trying to plead guilty in a deal that would give him seven-and-a-half years in prison, but would also eliminate him from a first-degree murder indictment he was still facing in the death of William Snyder. Prosecutors rejected whatever proposals defense counsel presented.

Over the next few days the defense called a number of witnesses. Some were called as character witnesses for Max and Harold Silverman, others to refute the testimony of government witnesses. One of the men called was Moe Sedway, who admitted that the owners of the Gottfried Baking Company were his cousins.

On February 26, while defense attorneys were giving their closing statements, Max Silverman collapsed again. In the reporting by the *New York Times,* Silverman's maladies began as problems from diabetes. Later in the trial they were said to be caused by nephritis, a kidney ailment. On this day the newspaper reported, "Silverman suffered another heart attack." By the end of the trial, his health episodes in the courtroom totaled more than two days of trial time.

After Silverman's recovery, Buchalter's attorney William Kleinman gave his closing statement. Avoiding mention of Lepke's recent conviction, Kleinman asked the jurors to disregard during their deliberations "this myth, this bogy man, who is charged with everything, all the time and under all circumstances."[35]

The judge's instructions to the jury took eight hours before the case was handed to the panel. Deliberations lasted 13 hours and 39 minutes. At 1:24 AM on March 2, the jurors announced they had found Buchalter guilty of all 15 counts remaining on the indictment. Max Silverman was found guilty of the same counts, and his son Harold was convicted on seven.

The jury's decision was most pleasing to Dewey. Praising the work of Grumet and Hogan, the district attorney stated, "The conviction of Lepke Buchalter assures the public of permanent protection against one of the most powerful and dangerous racket leaders this country has ever known."[36]

After a few postponements, the three men came before Judge Freschi on April 5 for sentencing. The 2-hour 20-minute sentence hearing began with Freschi telling the trio, "The people of this community are entitled to the enjoyment of liberty and peace and not to be terrorized by criminals of your type."[37] He then sentenced Buchalter as a fourth offender, giving him 30 years to life. Freschi stipulated that the sentence would not begin until Lepke completed his 14-year sentence in federal prison. It was reported that Buchalter "smirked" for most of the reading.[38]

JOE ROSEN MURDER TRIAL

Buchalter was soon shipped off to Leavenworth Prison to begin the federal portion of his long sentence. He was gone only a few days before more trouble arose. The investigation by Brooklyn District Attorney William O'Dwyer following the disclosures made by Abe Reles was just heating up. On April 13, a week after Buchalter's sentence was announced, it was revealed that Reles had implicated Lepke in the September 1936 murder of Joseph Rosen. At the same time, Louis Capone, who was being held as a material witness, was brought from his jail cell to be questioned by O'Dwyer's investigators.

> "For me, this was the big one. It meant cutting into the very heart of this evil ring we had uncovered, after chopping away at its tentacles. It meant getting Lepke, a king of the rackets. It would be the end, if convicted, of a ranking commander—a chief of staff for the Syndicate. It would show, for the first time, that the men who pulled the strings on lawlessness were no longer 'sacred.'"
>
> —Burton B. Turkus (Turkus and Feder, *Murder, Inc.*, 1951, p. 370.)

In the revelations made by Reles, and corroborated by Allie Tannenbaum, Buchalter and Albert Anastasia emerged as the leaders behind what would gain sensational headlines as Murder, Inc. Lepke would be portrayed as a boss of this notorious syndicate of killers, which included the likes of Frank "The Dasher" Abbandando, Martin "Buggsy" Goldstein, Harry "Happy" Maione, and Harry "Pittsburgh Phil" Strauss.

Buchalter's first indictment, however, came not from Brooklyn District Attorney O'Dwyer, but from authorities on the opposite coast in Los Angeles. On August 20, 1940, after Reles and Tannenbaum testified before a Los Angeles County grand jury, Lepke was indicted for ordering the murder of Harry Greenberg. Named in the indictment were Benjamin "Bugsy" Siegel, Emmanuel "Mendy" Weiss, Harry "Champ" Segal, and Frankie Carbo.

During Dewey's investigations into Buchalter's rackets, Mendy Weiss had been arrested and held as a material witness. After posting a $10,000 bail, he fled New York. Indicted for the Greenberg murder and a suspect in the murder of Benjamin Tannenbaum in February 1941, Weiss knew that the authorities were hot after him. In addition to the Greenberg murder, Weiss was a suspect in the murders of Dutch Schultz and three associates and longshoreman Peter Panto, and he had been indicted in Kings County for the murder of Joe Rosen. All of this came after Reles began talking. On April 8, 1941, Weiss was arrested by FBI agents in Kansas City, Missouri, on narcotics charges. Returned to Brooklyn, on April 11, he was arraigned in the Kings County Courthouse for the Rosen murder and pled not guilty. At the same time Assistant District Attorney Burton B. Turkus announced that O'Dwyer was talking with federal authorities about bringing Buchalter in from Leavenworth to be tried for the same murder.

As a new battle to bring Buchalter back to face murder charges began, federal prosecutors were still trying to get even with the people who had helped harbor Lepke during his two years as a fugitive. On April 18, 14 people were named in a federal harboring indictment. Among the men were Albert Anastasia, Louis Capone, Philip Cohen, Mendy Weiss, and Charles Workman. Another of the men named, Sidney Salles, was shot in the head and killed as he walked along First Avenue just hours after the indictment was released.

On April 29, Kings County Judge Franklin Taylor signed a writ of habeas corpus requesting that federal authorities produce Buchalter in Brooklyn for arraignment on May 9 to answer to the murder charges of Joe Rosen. On the day of the arraignment, Judge George W. Martin walked into his courtroom and was confronted by 40 law enforcement officers from various agencies lining the walls and taking up the entire spectator gallery. "This is ridiculous. Why don't you send for a company of marines?" Martin asked sarcastically.

Buchalter was led into the courtroom while handcuffed to a deputy marshal. In a low voice he told the judge, "I have never been notified what all this is about; I would like to see my people and arrange for counsel." The *New York Times* reported that Buchalter was "visibly nervous and with a tremor in his throat," and that "he appeared almost frightened at times." The newspaper also claimed that, "There have been frequent rumors that Lepke might be induced to 'talk' when faced with a murder trial."

Judge Martin allowed Buchalter to meet briefly with his wife and brother, Joseph. When he returned, Buchalter asked for a week to arrange for counsel, which the judge granted. On May 29, after Buchalter's attorneys told Martin that they were contesting the jurisdiction of the Brooklyn court to try their client while he was in federal custody, the judge entered a plea of not guilty for Lepke. The scene then switched to federal court on June 19, where Buchalter's defense counsel argued in vane that Lepke "had a right to finish out the federal sentence before going on trial again." Federal Judge Edward A. Conger didn't agree and ruled that Buchalter must stand trial.

On August 4, the last trial of Louis Buchalter got off to a slow start before Kings County Court Judge Franklin Taylor. A total of 250 potential jurors were called to appear. The judge announced that when the jury process was completed, the jurors would be sequestered for the duration of the trial, which was expected to last four weeks. Taylor spent the entire first day listening to excuses from people who did not want to serve as jurors. Most of the excuses involved people having plans to go on vacation; others had just returned from vacations and claimed they were needed back at work. At the end of the first day's session, only one juror had been seated. The selection process got worse on the second day as people complained about having to sit through a prolonged trial in the oppressive August heat. At this point, Judge Taylor postponed the trial until after Labor Day.

When trial resumed on Monday, September 15, the first order of business was granting separation to defendant Philip "Little Farvel" Cohen. Trying to seat a jury, however, proved no easier than it had 42 days earlier. At the end of the day, not a single juror had been selected. By the end of the week, only one juror had been seated. Now, in addition to the weekend, jury selection would have to wait because of a Jewish holiday.

The main reason for the delay was the candidacy of William O'Dwyer for mayor of New York City. Defense attorneys led by Hyman Barshay wanted to postpone the trial until after the November election, but they were turned down. They also failed in their fight to obtain a change of venue. Now they were taking their time to ensure that any potential juror who supported O'Dwyer for mayor was not going to make it onto the jury. Defense attorneys were taking as much as two or three hours questioning potential jurors before getting them to admit something that could be used as grounds for dismissal.

A week into October only three jurors had been selected. The judge ordered night sessions to help speed up the seating process. Because Buchalter and Weiss were federal prisoners, they were kept in the Federal House of Detention each night, while Capone was housed in the Tombs. On Tuesday, October 7, federal marshals watching the two allowed them to have dinner at Joe's Restaurant, a popular diner near the courthouse, which was a favorite spot of Brooklyn politicians, public officials, and judges. Judge Taylor had arrived for dinner that night and had to choose another restaurant because of the presence of the two defendants. When court reconvened that night, Judge Taylor forbade any more outings for the pair, stating they could have their meals sent to the prisoner's pen in the courthouse.

After jury selection continued that night, Capone, like Max Silverman in the earlier Buchalter trial, collapsed in the courtroom. The next day, Judge Taylor was informed that the medication Capone had on his person at all times was enough to "commit suicide at will." He ordered that Capone be allowed to carry only enough to maintain his daily needs.

On October 10, after the selection of 10 jurors, Judge Taylor ordered an additional 100 talisman be brought to the court. On October 16, Louis Capone collapsed again in the courtroom because of "mild hypertension and elevated blood pressure." After a heated exchange between Judge Taylor and Sydney Rosenthal, counsel for Capone, the judge allowed the defendant to carry the medicine with him.

On Friday, October 17, after five weeks of the selection process, a jury was finally impaneled. During the process nearly 335 potential jurors had been questioned. On Monday, October 20, after opening statements, the first witness for the state was called. Estelle Rosen, widow of the murdered candy store operator, told of a man who had come into the store the night before the murder, wandered around in a "studied manner," then bought a cigarette for a penny before leaving. When asked if that man was in the courtroom, she pointed to Mendy Weiss and stated, "Yes, that one with the glasses. Only he didn't have on glasses then."

The next day Harold Rosen, the son of the murder victim, took the stand. The son recalled an argument resulting in a face-to-face encounter his father had with Buchalter in the Broadway Central Hotel during the early part of 1933, six months before his father's trucking business collapsed. Rosen's daughter Sylvia was also called as a witness. She testified that her father was at a meeting where Shapiro told him which firms he could do business with. Gurrah was said to have read the names of the companies from a set of books while Buchalter watched over his shoulder.

On October 27, Sholem Bernstein was the first of the informants to testify against the three defendants. He told the court about stealing the black Chevrolet automobile that was used to transport the killers Weiss, "Pittsburgh Phil" Strauss, and James "Dirty Face Jimmy" Feracco to the candy store that Sunday morning. Weiss and Strauss went in and did the shooting, while Feracco stood watch out front and Bernstein stayed behind the wheel. Under cross-examination, Bernstein was forced to admit all the crimes he had committed, including murders, and the fact that he had lied during another trial. At one point he shouted at Alfred Talley, Weiss's counsel, "I'm a stool pigeon! In other words, a rat! Does that satisfy you?"

Bernstein next told of Capone's role in the murder. He had helped plan the killing, laid out the escape route, and drove one of the getaway cars. It was reported that Bernstein took some particular joy in testifying against Capone. The reason offered was that Bernstein considered himself an accomplished burglar, but when he got connected with the Brooklyn murder ring, Capone was the boss and Bernstein was scared of him. His role was to steal automobiles, which he considered beneath him. Yet, over the years he was ordered to steal 75 to 100 automobiles for the gang.

Bernstein spent five days on the witness stand, mostly being grilled in cross-examination by different members of defense counsel. At times he seemed unable to hold his tongue, and he loved the verbal exchanges with the lawyers. He talked about baseball games between the Murder, Inc. informants and their guards on Long Island. He once blurted out the name of a killer from an unsolved murder, and Judge Taylor ordered it stricken from the record. A couple of times he pointed out lies told at different trials by Abe Reles, which could not have helped the prosecution, as "Kid Twist" was scheduled to testify later at the trial.

On Halloween day, fireworks went off in the courtroom on the first day of Max Rubin's testimony. Turkus was having Rubin tell about his early days in the Amalgamated Clothing Workers Union and some of the activities of Buchalter and Shapiro. Holding two fingers together, Turkus turned to the jury and said "It has been established that Lepke and the Amalgamated were just like that." It was here that counsel for Buchalter took exception:

"I came here to defend a man who is charged with a crime," Barshay shouted.

"Well do it." Judge Taylor snapped.

"I will to the best of my ability," Barshay responded. "I regret that I must say this, but the district attorney has gone far afield. The activities of the Amalgamated union in the year 1932 have nothing to do with the issue in this trial and I charge that the district attorney has only one purpose in adducing this testimony.

"This case is being used by the District Attorney as a political sounding board in a political campaign and the District Attorney has carefully calculated so that this testimony would be brought out on this very day because of the political campaign and I repeat that this political campaign has nothing whatever to do with this trial.

"I regret to say this, but it isn't fair on the part of the District Attorney. I warned Mr. Turkus I would have to make this statement, but he has disregarded my warning."

"Your objection has been very fervent." Judge Taylor said dryly, "but let us proceed with the trial."[39]

Rubin continued with his testimony about Buchalter's activities, only to be interrupted by Barshay again, who now demanded a mistrial. This time Rubin jumped up in the witness box and shouted, "You had better be careful! I know you! I've heard of Hyman Barshay! Don't you try to bulldoze me!"

The cross-examination for Rubin went on for several days. On November 5, Barshay asked Rubin if he had told a garment center friend, "If it's the last thing I do, I'll burn Lepke, and when he goes to the chair I'll feel that I have lived my life."

"I never said that!" Rubin shouted. Then turning toward Buchalter and smiling broadly he added, "But I certainly would have been justified in saying it."

After the Rosen killing, Rubin felt he was in trouble. Barshay asked him about this:

Rubin: I was in tremendous trouble. I thought the world would cave in on me.
Barshay: Was your conscience bothering you?
Rubin: Was your conscience bothering you?
Barshay: I won't roll in the gutter with you.
Rubin: [shaking with rage and rising from his seat] I rolled in the gutter with a bullet in my head.

On November 7, Paul Berger took the stand. Described as a "professional finger man" for Buchalter, Berger testified about the Rosen killing. On Friday, September 11, 1936, Lepke told Berger, "I want you to point out Joe Rosen." He then took Berger to meet Mendy Weiss. Berger said Weiss drove him to Rosen's candy store and got out and walked by several times while Rosen fixed newspapers on a stand. Weiss then told him, "I'll know him now." Two days later, Berger said he read about Rosen's murder.

Berger finished his testimony on Monday, November 10. The next day was Armistice Day and the courts were closed for the holiday. On Wednesday morning Allie Tannenbaum was scheduled to testify. One of the top informants from the Brooklyn murder gang, Tannenbaum was being kept at the Half Moon Hotel in Coney Island with Abe Reles. Sometime around 6:45 AM, Reles went out the window of the hotel, dropping 42 feet to his death.

Lepke and his fellow defendants were advised of Reles's death later that morning. Any thoughts they had were kept to themselves. That afternoon Tannenbaum took the stand and, although pale and shaken, delivered damaging testimony. Tannenbaum, on direct examination, testified to taking part in six murders for the gang, including being one of the getaway drivers after the murder of Harry Greenberg in Hollywood. The next day, when questioned about the Rosen murder, he said he heard Buchalter compliment Weiss for "doing a nice clean job."

Perhaps the most poignant moment of the trial occurred on Friday, November 14. Max Rubin was again on the witness stand for further cross-examination. Barshay got Rubin to admit that "every vital point of his testimony against Lepke in this trial was contradicted by a statement he made to William McCarthy," a Brooklyn assistant district attorney working under then District Attorney William F. X. Geoghan, in December 1937.

Turkus then asked Rubin why he lied, but before he could answer, Barshay insisted that the jury be removed from the courtroom. The *New York World Telegram* picked up the story from there:

And when the jury was gone Rubin exploded, springing from his chair, pounding the railing with a frantic fist, shouting:

"I had just been shot! I was shot in the head! Just after I had gone into the (Dewey) grand jury where nobody was supposed to know I had gone! And nobody was supposed to know what I had said!"

His face was blood-red, swollen. His eyes were streaming tears of hate, of rage. He was shaking as he pointed an accusing finger at the immobile Lepke, as he cried:

"But he found out where I had been! He found out what I had said! And then was I going to give a statement to this man McCarthy? The hell I was! Like hell I would! I had been shot. My wife, my family—they were all in danger!"

He gasped for breath, and now the tears were gushing from his eyes and he pounded the rail in fury.

"If I were to give a statement to that man McCarthy," he yelled, "it would be like giving it to that man there!"

And he jabbed his trembling finger at Lepke again and again.

"He knew what went on in the grand jury! And he knew what was going on over here! He had an in! I know he had an in! He told it to me"

His voice broke off, and he sank back in the chair, wearily, breathing heavily, and now his voice was dull and beaten.[40]

Judge Taylor could only tell the witness that another outburst would not be tolerated. He then turned to Turkus and instructed the prosecutor to ask questions that could be answered only by a yes or a no. Turkus protested to the judge declaring, "Even if Mr. McCarthy could have offered [Rubin] immunity from prosecution he could not have offered immunity from Lepke, who was on the loose. If Mr. Geoghan did not have some assistants who betrayed him he might not be in this position."

Now it was Barshay's turn to explode. A former assistant himself to Geoghan, Barshay shouted, "All the people in District Attorney O'Dwyer's office rolled into one could not come up to Mr. Geoghan's shoes." Alfred Talley then spoke out, defending Geoghan. He called Rubin a "vile and polluted source."

Rubin responded by screaming, "You filthy swine! I never committed murder! I'm 52 years old and I was decent until I met this man!" (pointing at Buchalter).

After a recess to allow all parties to settle down, the jury reentered the courtroom. At that point the jury would only hear Rubin answer "yes" to a question by Turkus as to whether he lied to McCarthy because of "fear of Lepke, due to the fact that you had been shot following your testimony before the Dewey grand jury."[41]

On Saturday, November 15, Seymour "Bluejaw" Magoon took the stand. His only bit of testimony seemed to be that Capone told him he had taken part in the Rosen murder. On Monday, the federal narcotics agents from Kansas City who had arrested Mendy Weiss testified. After having called 33 witnesses (Reles would have been the 34th), the state rested its case.

The defense built its case around Rosen's trucking business, bringing on witnesses to state that it was failing and in bankruptcy, so why would Buchalter want anything to do with it? Rubin and Tannenbaum had testified that they were in Lepke's office on September 11, 1936, and they overheard him make threatening remarks about Rosen. The defense called Carl Shapiro, Gurrah's brother, who testified that he had been in the office that day and that neither Rubin nor Tannenbaum was present.

Jacob Shapiro had been brought to New York from the Atlanta Penitentiary and lodged in the Federal House of Detention. Defense lawyers were debating on whether to call him as a witness to deny the testimony of Rosen's daughter Sylvia who said Gurrah read the names of companies her father wasn't to do business with. The defense claimed Shapiro could neither read nor write. The newspapers reported that the transfer of Shapiro was made with the provision that he and Buchalter would be separated at all times and not be permitted to talk to one another.

Several of the last defense witnesses were called by Weiss's attorney, Alfred Talley. One was William Kleinman, who served as defense counsel for Lepke during his federal narcotics trial. Kleinman, now a major in the U.S. Army, was called in from Camp Wheeler, Georgia. Talley, through a barrage of objections from Turkus, was able to state that Weiss had been seen with Kleinman in a restaurant with Police Commissioner Valentine in April 1940. This proved, according to Talley, that police had nothing on Weiss until he was "framed" by informers. Talley claimed that when Weiss was picked up in 1940, Estelle Rosen was unable to identify him in the district attorney's office.

Also called was Weiss's brother Sidney, who testified that Mendy was "giving a birthday party for his younger brother to patch up a family quarrel," during the time of the murder. The defense also called Blanche Weiss, Mendy's wife, who corroborated the story, claiming that she and family members were with him the night before the murder and didn't get home until 5:00 AM. They then slept until noon. The prosecution had put on witnesses that claimed Weiss spent the night at the home of "Little Farvel" Cohen with other members of the murder crew.[42] Mendy's mother took the stand and told the same tale about patching up a family quarrel. "I said to Mendy, 'a party would be nice,' and Mendy says, 'All right, mom, we'll have a party. Everything will be nice.'"

On November 25, attorney Talley wanted Estelle Rosen called back to the stand to explain why she couldn't identify Weiss the first time she saw him in the district attorney's office. Turkus, who thought the attorney had a good point, told Judge Taylor, "I want to be fair. I ask the court to charge the jury not to consider Mrs. Rosen's identification of Weiss as the man who was in the store the night of September 12, 1936. That will take it out of the case entirely."[43] With that, both sides rested their case.

On Wednesday, November 26, Barshay gave his closing argument. He claimed Buchalter was the victim of a frame-up perpetrated by Rubin, Berger, and Tannenbaum. He claimed Rubin was "motivated by revenge and hatred. He wanted to get even for the shooting, which he blamed on Lepke." Barshay told the jury he didn't call Buchalter or Shapiro as witnesses because "nobody would believe them." Because of Judge Taylor's illness, the final arguments for Capone and Weiss were not delivered until Friday.

Turkus's closing and Judge Taylor's jury instruction took all day Saturday to deliver. The jury was finally handed the case at 10:15 Saturday night. After four-and-a-half hours of deliberations, the jury returned to the courtroom at 2:45 AM Sunday. Before the verdict could be read, all family members were ordered out of the courtroom. It was then announced that all three defendants were found guilty.

As soon as the verdict was read, the convicted men were returned to their cells. Buchalter and Weiss, both federal prisoners, were taken back to the Federal Detention Center in an eight-car caravan of heavily armed guards. Capone was taken back to the Tombs. As Prosecutor Turkus left the courthouse he was jeered at, abused, and threatened by members of the Weiss family.

Buchalter's conviction, as well as that of Capone and Weiss, carried with it a mandatory death sentence. The conviction also carried with it an automatic appeal. Even before sentence was passed, the newspapers declared Lepke's fate would be in the hands of President Franklin D. Roosevelt. District Attorney O'Dwyer told reporters, "If the verdict is sustained, I think it will be necessary to have the President pardon him [from his Federal narcotics sentence] and turn him over to the custody of the State."[44]

On December 2, the three men were returned to the courthouse and stood before Judge Taylor to hear their sentences. The courtroom was crowded with detectives and deputy marshals, but family members of the trio were refused admittance. Buchalter was the first to be sentenced. Grabbing the railing of the clerk's bench to brace himself, Lepke declined the clerk's offer to make a statement before sentence was passed. One by one, each man was sentenced to die in the electric chair during the week of January 4, 1942. Capone and Weiss arrived at Sing Sing the next day, where they were lodged in the death house. Buchalter was still in federal custody, and would continue to be held at the Federal House of Detention in Manhattan.[45]

THE LONG ROAD TO THE HOT SEAT

There would be a long, drawn out appeals process before Buchalter would join his former co-defendants. In a surprisingly close 4 to 3 decision, the court of appeals affirmed the convictions of the three men on October 30, 1942. Barshays, Lepke's attorney, immediately announced he would appeal his client's case to the U.S. Supreme Court. The court set a new date for the executions, the week of December 7. A few days later Sing Sing Warden Robert Kirby set December 10 as the night of the executions. Plans were then made to have Buchalter transferred from the Federal House of Detention to Sing Sing.

Less than a week before the scheduled executions, U.S. Supreme Court Justice Owen J. Roberts granted a stay after a five-hour meeting with the condemned men's legal counsel. The stay was allowed to give attorneys time to appeal to the Supreme Court. They were given until January 4, 1943.

The stay order let Acting New York Governor Charles Poletti off the hook from having to make a decision about the men. Poletti had conducted a clemency hearing for the trio a day earlier. After Justice Robert's ruling, Poletti announced, "in view of this order, I shall not take any further executive action in these three cases." By the time executive action would be needed, Poletti would be out of the governor's office, replaced by newly elected Governor Thomas E. Dewey.

In his petition to the Supreme Court, Buchalter claimed his trial was used as a "political football by the newspapers, the court and the district attorney," and that he was denied due process of law because his request for a change of venue was denied. On January 2, after the filing of a writ of certiorari, Justice Roberts extended the stays of execution until the Supreme Court could decide the matter.[46]

On February 15, the U.S. Supreme Court rejected the petition to review the convictions of the three men. The state was then faced with having to make the proper applications to set a new date for the execution. Once the date was set, defense counsel could then ask Governor Dewey for a new clemency hearing. If Dewey denied this request, the State would then have to petition President Roosevelt for a pardon for Buchalter from his federal conviction to move forward with his execution.

The Kings County prosecutor's office quickly put together the paperwork for a new execution date. Defense counsel, now led by Bertram Wegman and Arthur Garfield Hays, responded with a renewed impassioned plea to the U.S. Supreme Court. In this petition the attorneys used the fact that the justices of the New York State Court of Appeals were closely split on the conviction, with three of the seven judges holding that the men were deprived of a "fair chance to defend their lives." This time the tactic worked and the Supreme Court reversed its ruling and agreed to review the convictions.

A team of five attorneys descended on Washington D.C. on May 7 to present oral arguments before the highest court in the land. They contended that "the verdict was predetermined by the wave of hysteria which engulfed the jury, the trial judge and the prosecutor." Kings County Assistant District Attorney Solomon Klein argued that the defendants "were represented by able and experienced counsel, who were given ample opportunity to prepare for trial. Wide latitude was given the defense in the cross-examination of the people's witnesses and in summations to the jury. And upon appeal to the Court of Appeals petitions were given a full and conscientious hearing."

On June 1, seven Supreme Court justices ruled unanimously that the trio had received a fair trial. In an unusual move, the Supreme Court sent its mandate to vacate the stays of execution to the lower court just one week after its decision. The normal time was 25 days. There was no explanation for this speedy delivery.

Before the ink was dry on the mandate, attorneys for the men notified the Brooklyn district attorney's office that they were filing a motion for reargument before the New York

State Court of Appeals. On June 18 the motion was denied and a date of July 20 was set for resentencing.[47]

The state now encountered a new problem. Instead of a legal battle with the attorneys fighting for Buchalter's life, the federal government was refusing to turn over the prisoner. During his murder trial, Buchalter allegedly told his federal guards "that no matter what the outcome he would never die in the electric chair." This feeling of immunity was also confirmed by a few associates who claimed that if Lepke "talked," it would prove to be an embarrassment to several high-profile figures.

Thomas C. Hughes, who became the acting Kings County district attorney while William O'Dwyer served in the military, requested that U.S. Attorney General Francis Biddle release Buchalter from federal custody and have him appear in Albany for the resentencing and execution of sentence. In a response from the Department of Justice, Hughes was told that the government was "not persuaded" to make recommendation to Biddle to release Buchalter from his 14-year term before the expiration of sentence. To get Lepke to the death house door would require a pardon from his federal sentence by the president.

The government allowed Buchalter to appear for the resentencing on July 20. Under heavy federal guard, Lepke was brought to the court of appeals to be sentenced to death, along with Capone and Weiss, during the week of September 13. At the end of the hearing, Buchalter was returned to the Federal Detention Center.

Shortly after the resentencing, attorneys for Capone and Weiss requested a hearing before Governor Dewey, seeking executive clemency for their clients. On September 1, two weeks before the scheduled executions, Buchalter was still in federal custody, and Dewey was demanding that President Roosevelt pardon him and release Lepke to the State of New York. Dewey refused to set a date for the clemency hearing, saying he would not do so until Buchalter was surrendered. He then issued a respite, delaying the execution date until the week of October 18.

As the new execution date approached, there was no reaction on the part of Roosevelt to pardon Buchalter. On October 16, the governor granted another respite until the week of November 29. Dewey was adamant that the two "lesser figures" in the crime were not going to be executed while the mastermind took refuge in federal custody.

The fight over Buchalter had now reached the stage of a political stalemate. Dewey, a Republican who would challenge Roosevelt, a Democrat, in the next presidential election, claimed that Buchalter was being "protected from punishment by the failure of the President of the United States to grant the customary conditional pardon." On November 20, Dewey postponed the execution for the third time, pushing it back until the week of January 3, 1944.

Attorney General Biddle responded to the attack by issuing a statement prevailing on Dewey to hold his clemency hearing and make a decision first. Biddle stated, "The Attorney General will not recommend release of Buchalter from his Federal sentence as long as any possibility exists that his state sentence might also be commuted."

During the next few days the battle of words continued. Biddle criticized Dewey for communicating through the media instead of directly with the Department of Justice. The attorney general claimed Dewey had never made a formal request for the president to grant a commutation. Biddle stated that if a state clemency hearing were held, the federal government would produce Buchalter. The government's stand was clear; it wanted to be assured of Lepke's execution before releasing him to the state.

New York State Attorney General Nathan L. Goldstein responded to Biddle's attack. More than once questioning Biddle's knowledge of the law, Goldstein wrote:

> The Governor cannot grant a clemency hearing to Buchalter until he is in the custody of the State, and he will not indulge in the mockery of permitting two minor figures in a murder to go to the electric chair while the major figure is safely protected from the execution by the Federal Government.
>   As a lawyer you know the Governor cannot commit himself, in advance of a hearing, on the exercise of the highest power vested in an executive, that of life or death.[48]

Goldstein also pointed out that the prisoner did not attend the hearing. To the lay person the question that immediately comes to mind is: "If Buchalter need not be present for the clemency hearing, why not go ahead and hold it?" Attorney General Biddle made it perfectly clear that if Buchalter was to be executed, he would be turned over. A cryptic message in Goldstein's response, however, raised other questions. Claiming that Dewey was not interested in giving assurance to "interested parties" that Lepke would indeed be executed if surrendered, the state attorney general wrote, "the State of New York is not interested in protecting Buchalter or any of the persons with whom he has had dealings."

Just who were the "persons" Goldstein was referring to? Who was he suggesting that the federal government or the president was interested in protecting? Was Buchalter holding an ace up his sleeve hoping to play it to keep himself out of the chair? Pundits of the day were sure there was something "political" in the wind. Swirling in the political rumor mill were concerns that Buchalter would release statements about labor racketeering that would implicate people close to Roosevelt.

On December 30, Governor Dewey issued his fourth respite for the executions of Capone and Weiss, still claiming he would not allow the two to go to their deaths without their leader, and blaming the federal government for failing to surrender Buchalter. Two weeks later, on January 14, Biddle sent a letter to Goldstein that the government was ready to release Buchalter to the state. While the contents of the letter were not revealed, the *New York Times* reported that Biddle "was turning Lepke over to the State for custody, presumably revocable at any time, but with the understanding that it was not to be revoked if Lepke was to go to the electric chair." In his response to Biddle, Goldstein confirmed, "I take it that the surrender of the custody of the prisoner is unconditional in the event of execution."

Before the transfer of Buchalter took place, Arthur Garfield Hays, representing Weiss, filed paperwork for a new trial based on the discovery of new evidence. The brother and sister of Harry "Happy" Maione, one of the killers from the Murder, Inc. gang, had signed an affidavit that Maione had confessed to them before his execution on February 19, 1942, that he had participated in the murder of Joe Rosen and that Capone and Weiss were not involved.

On the morning of January 21, Buchalter was removed from the Federal House of Detention and driven to Ossining, New York, where he was officially transferred to the State of New York. Although most accounts claim Lepke was placed with his former co-defendants, a few days later it was reported he was not confined in the same section with Capone and Weiss and was not permitted to see them. A new execution date of February 10 was scheduled.

Attorneys for Buchalter and Capone filed motions seeking a new trial on January 25. They had an affidavit from a man held as a material witness at the Bronx County jail, who claimed he had been told by Murder, Inc. informants, that "Pittsburgh Phil" Strauss and Martin "Buggsy' Goldstein had murdered Rosen.

The attorneys for the trio were determined to avoid having to give their arguments for a new trial before Judge Franklin Taylor. When Taylor heard about the motion for a new trial, he cut short a Florida vacation to come home and review the application. On January 26, the lawyers appeared before Kings County Judge Samuel S. Leibowitz, asking him to hear their arguments claiming that Taylor had been prejudiced.

Leibowitz declined to hear the arguments and the next day Judge Taylor held court. While reserving his decision on the merits of the actual arguments, in quick succession he shot down three motions. He denied the motion by Wegman to refer the arguments to Leibowitz; he denied Rosenthal's request to refer them to any other judge; and he refused a cabled request from Hays, who was vacationing in Cuba, for a postponement until his return.

The attorneys then presented their affidavits stating that the alleged killers of Rosen were Maione, Strauss and Goldstein—all of whom were conveniently dead, having been executed for their crimes. Solomon Klein, appearing for the state, told the court that the arguments were a "last desperate effort by associates and former associates" to save the men. He claimed the affidavits were not "worth the paper they are written on." The next day Judge Taylor, without preparation of a memorandum, simply wrote "denied" on the court papers and had them sent to the clerk of court's office. Defense counsel was left to petition the court of appeals for a review.

The long-discussed clemency hearing for the three men was held on February 2 in Albany. The attorneys for the three appeared, as well as the condemned men's wives. During the two-and-a-half-hour public hearing, there were two bombshells. First, Arthur Garfield Hays told Governor Dewey that he had a conversation with Colonel William O'Dwyer during the fall of 1943 and claimed the district attorney said he was prepared to request clemency, "if Mr. Dewey will ask me about it." Dewey was taken by surprise by the comment, as were assistant district attorneys Burton Turkus and Solomon Klein, who refused to "accept Mr. Hays' concept of the conversation."[49]

The second bombshell was delivered by Turkus. Addressing the hearing room audience Turkus revealed:

> Not alone did Lepke and the other gangsters execute other mobsters, not alone did they kill witnesses, not alone did they kill an innocent man by mistake, but Lepke and the other mob bosses sat down at a table and deliberated the execution of a high public official who at that time was investigating vigorously and successfully the racketeering activities of Lepke and his associates. The life of this high public official was spared only because Lepke feared that the wrath of the entire country would come down upon them and they would be driven out of the country.

For some never explained reason, Turkus never stated that the "high public official" was Dewey. It seemed crystal clear to nearly everyone present, with the exception of Dewey himself, that he was the intended victim. That he was the target of a Murder, Inc. plot had so totally escaped him that years later he would claim he was not made aware of the scheme until the publication of Turkus's book *Murder, Inc.* in 1951.

On February 4, Governor Dewey granted a fifth reprieve after being notified that defense counsel had obtained permission to seek a reargument before the court of appeals. The execution date was pushed back until the week of February 28.

The lawyers appeared in Albany on February 14 to ask for a reargument of the appeal for a new trial based on three points:

1. The new evidence in the form of affidavits from Maione's family, in which they claimed Harry Maione confessed that he murdered Joe Rosen; an affidavit from a former Sing Sing death house guard, who claimed he overheard Maione tell another condemned man, Frank "The Dasher" Abbandando, that Capone and Weiss were innocent because he committed the murder.
2. That Judge Franklin Taylor was prejudiced.
3. The close split of the court of appeals in their 4 to 3 vote.

Ten days after the hearing the court of appeals ruled on the motion by simply rubber-stamping the request: "Motion for reargument denied."

Buchalter remained confidant that something would happen to keep him from his appointment with destiny. On the day that the state's executioner was ordered to report to the Sing Sing death house, Lepke was quoted as saying, "A lot can happen in the time that is left." On March 1, with the execution scheduled for the next evening, Bertram Wegman filed a petition of habeas corpus in federal court, claiming Lepke's transfer by the federal government was illegal—Buchalter had been transferred by federal authorities without a commutation of his sentence. Wegman claimed that Lepke was "deprived" of his right to a hearing before President Roosevelt.

Contrary to what had been reported in the newspapers regarding a presidential commutation being necessary, Federal Judge Clarence Galston rejected Wegman's petition. The judge made his ruling from the bench without taking any additional time to review Wegman's argument. Galston declared that Buchalter had no right to decide on which sentence he would serve before the other. Wegman would now have to appear before the United States Circuit Court of Appeals if Buchalter's life were to be saved.

THE LAST DAYS OF LEPKE

On Thursday, March 2, 1944, time was running out in Sing Sing prison for Buchalter and his two murder companions. From the preexecution chamber that the underworld called the "Dance Hall," Lepke seemed confident that Wegman's legal maneuverings would pay off; after all, his execution date had already been changed five times. Weiss and Capone were optimistic that if reprieve came for the boss, then they would ride his coattails to safety from the hot seat.

During the day the condemned men shaved, showered, and dressed in the traditional death-night garb of white socks, carpet slippers, and black trousers with a slit in one leg to allow an electrode connected to the chair to be attached to the bare skin. From the preexecution chamber the men were just 25 feet from the chair. Laid out in partitions, the prisoners could not see one another, but they could communicate. Given the traditional choice of selecting their last meals, Buchalter requested steak, French fries, salad, and pie for lunch and roast chicken, shoestring potatoes, and salad for dinner. Weiss and Capone, as always following the boss's lead, ordered the same.

"Something can happen yet," Buchalter called out to his death-cell mates. "I can feel it."

Something did happen. Late on the afternoon of March 2, Manhattan District Attorney Frank Hogan received a message from Warden William E. Snyder stating that Lepke wanted to talk to him. That Lepke was convicted in Brooklyn and Hogan was from Manhattan was not lost on the newspapers. Hogan and two assistants drove to Sing Sing where they spoke to Lepke in his cell for 90 minutes. Hogan returned to the city and telephoned Dewey. Whatever Lepke said to the district attorney, Hogan never revealed publicly.

Just 70 minutes before Buchalter, Capone, and Weiss were to meet their fate, Governor Dewey granted the trio a two-day extension to allow Wegman an opportunity to appeal to the U.S. Supreme Court. Warden Snyder sent Reverend Bernard Martin to deliver the news to the men.

A spokesperson for the governor insisted the delay was granted only to give Wegman the opportunity to apply for Buchalter's appeal to the Supreme Court; however rumors were running rampant that Lepke was ready and willing to talk. With Dewey already a candidate for the presidency, the information Buchalter was rumored to have disclosed was so sensitive that it could "propel" Dewey into the White House.

Since Buchalter was imprisoned in 1939, stories persisted about what he might be willing to reveal regarding "men in high places." Lepke once claimed, "If I would talk, a lot of big people would get hurt. When I say big, I mean big. The names would surprise you."

During the two-day reprieve, the New York newspapers ran wild with speculation as to what Buchalter revealed to Hogan. Chief among the rumors was that the mob boss could provide information on Sidney Hillman, the president of the Amalgamated Clothing Workers of America. Hillman was a member of President Roosevelt's wartime administration, as well as his inner circle. With Hillman's connections to organized labor, Dewey, it was believed, could link him to Buchalter and parlay this information into a corruption scandal to hang over the Democrats in the November 1944 elections.

Despite all the speculation and rumors, just before 1:00 PM Saturday, March 4, the U.S. Supreme Court rejected, without comment, Wegman's plea that Buchalter was wrongly released from federal prison. Lepke's fate, along with Weiss and Capone's, was sealed.

Shortly after the rejection, a hasty meeting was called at the Depot Square Hotel located in Ossining, a mile from the prison. There, in a crowded combination bar and restaurant, appeared Betty Buchalter. Wearing sunglasses, she pulled a yellow piece of notebook paper from her purse and stated, "My husband just dictated this statement in his death cell. I wrote it down, word for word."

I am anxious to have it clearly understood that I did not offer to talk and give information in exchange for any promise of commutation of my death sentence. I did not ask for that! (The exclamation point was Lepke's.)

The one and only thing I have asked for is to have a commission appointed to examine the facts. If that examination does not show that I am not guilty, I am willing to go to the chair, regardless of what information I have given or can give.

In *Murder, Inc.,* Burton Turkus claims the following:

By releasing the statement through his wife, Lepke also was, I am convinced, giving an unmistakable signal to the mob. He was broadcasting to his Syndicate associates that he had not and would not talk of them or of the national cartel. About politicians and political connections and the like—yes: the crime magnates would seek no reprisal for that. But not about the top bosses of crime. It was pure and simple life insurance. No member of his family would be safe if the crime chiefs believed he had opened up on the organization itself.

The final attempt to delay the execution came from an unlikely source. Rabbi Jacob Katz was the Jewish chaplain at the prison and served as Lepke and Weiss's spiritual advisor. Executions at the prison traditionally took place on Thursday nights at 11:00 PM. These electrocutions would be the first death sentences performed on a Saturday night since 1917. Katz telephoned the governor that morning and asked him not to conduct the executions that evening because it was the Jewish Sabbath. Because of Sabbath services, Katz said he could not leave his responsibilities in the Bronx until sundown, which would give him only "a scant three hours" with his two charges.

Katz stated, "It has been the custom for the chaplain to be with the condemned the whole day long on the last day of his life. It creates a very human feeling between the condemned and the chaplain and society, and with his God. So much so that whatever nervousness, whatever tension has been created is reduced to a state of resignation and submission to one's fate on the part of the condemned." The warden, who no doubt reasoned that this consideration was never extended to any of the condemned victims Buchalter ordered dispatched, denied the request.

Having had their last meals for the second time in three days, the trio realized when no word from the governor's mansion was received by 10:45 that all hope was lost. With the witness room packed with 36 onlookers, Capone was the first to take his turn in the hot seat. They figured that with his health problems, it was better that he go first. Flanked by two guards, and following Reverend Martin, Capone was strapped in at 11:02 PM and pronounced dead three minutes later.

Weiss came next. Walking behind Rabbi Katz, he was the only one to speak. "Can I say something?" he asked meekly. "I'm here," he slowly stated, "on a framed-up case." Chewing hard on a piece of gum he seemed to lose his train of thought for the moment, but then concluded with, "And Governor Dewey knows it." He finished with, "Give my love to my family . . . and everything." At 11:10 PM Weiss was declared dead.

Buchalter quickly walked in with Rabbi Katz. His step was described as brisk and defiant. Resignation reigned supreme as Lepke almost threw himself into the chair. Frank Coniff, a reporter for the *New York Journal American,* who was one of the 36 witnesses, described the execution. He wrote, "You look at the face . . . you cannot tear your eyes away. Sweat beads his forehead. Saliva drools from the corner of his lips. The face is discolored. It is not a pretty sight." At 11:16, Louis "Lepke" Buchalter was declared dead.

The next day, in accordance with the Orthodox Jewish ritual, funeral rites were held for Buchalter and Weiss. Services for Lepke were held at the Park West Memorial Chapel, where only family members were permitted. His body was then taken to Mount Hebron Cemetery in Flushing, Queens, where he was laid to rest in a plain oaken casket in a plot near his mother Rose, who had died two years earlier. Less than 30 minutes later the hearse bearing Weiss's body arrived.

On March 9, the funeral for Louis Capone was held in Coney Island. Unlike the services for Capone's death house companions, his farewell was "flamboyant." In describing the event one newspaper stated, "It was a funeral in the prohibition-era gangland tradition. There were five open cars carrying gaudy floral tributes and forty automobiles packed with mourners, friends and former associates." Nearly 400 people attended the mass in Our Lady of Solace Roman Catholic Church, and another 250 lined the street outside. Afterward, the cortege made its way to Holy Cross Cemetery for burial services.

A fitting requiem to Buchalter was delivered by Burton Turkus in 1951 when he wrote:

A kingpin of national crime was gone, a czar of the rackets. The Syndicate that rules the underworld and has connections in the highest political places had lost its first major figure to the Law. Ironically, for all his power and his killings, it was the murder of a little man that caught up with Lepke, and ended him. Justice proved she plays no favorites; she works for the man who pulls the strings as well as the one who pulls the trigger. Before then, no executive of organized crime ever sat in the chair. Since Lepke, there has been no other.[50]

NOTES

1. Defined as organized and officially encouraged slaughters or persecutions of minority groups, pogroms are mostly associated with the Jews. The most noted pogroms took place in Russia and Eastern and Central Europe between 1850 and the Russian Civil War of 1917.

2. Emanuel Buchalter became a dentist, with offices in Manhattan and Brooklyn. Isidore Buchalter was a registered pharmacist.

3. Some sources list the date of birth as February 12, the same day as Abraham Lincoln.

4. The following explanation of the nickname "Lepke" comes from a story in the *New York World-Telegram* on August 8, 1939:

> The nickname, Lepke . . . is a misspelled variation of the Jewish word for Louis-Label. As a youngster, his parents called him Labkeleh, meaning little Louie. But as he grew older, they called him Labke. When a newspaperman first used the latter name he made it Lepke, and Lepke it has been ever since.

5. Some sources list the year of death as 1910. It is unclear at this point how many, if any, of Rose's children from her first marriage were still living at home. An FBI report states that, "Following his father's death, the family moved to Brooklyn, New York, where they were supported largely by Buchalter's half sister."

6. Even the official reports are a little unclear as to what exactly happened. One report claims Lepke took a valise from an automobile and later explained he did so because he "was out of funds." In any case, Buchalter refused to give any information on his accomplices.

7. *New York World-Telegram,* August 8, 1939, "Million Dollar Fugitive." This story was just one of several similar tales explaining where the nickname of "Gurrah" came about for Jacob Shapiro.

8. Sometimes spelled Zwerbach.

9. There are many colorful accounts of this sensational shooting including one in the book *Behind the Green Lights* written by Cornelius Willemse, who barely escaped death as one of Cohen's shots ripped through his straw boater. Some historians would later claim that Cohen, whose name was also listed as Kushner, was an impressionable member of the Orgen gang and had been talked into the assassination by gang members, including Buchalter and Shapiro, on the promise of having to serve only five years.

10. An interesting footnote to the burial of Jacob "Little Augie" Orgen. On his coffin was a silver plate that read: Jacob Orgen, Age 25 Years. "Little Augie" was 33 when he died. His father had the plate created that way to indicate that his son was dead to him eight years earlier when he decided to lead a life of crime. The distraught father was the last to leave his son's gravesite after a short, rain-drenched service at Mount Judah Cemetery in Brooklyn on October 17, 1927.

11. The wounding of "Legs" Diamond during the murder of Jacob Orgen provides one of the many glimpses into the bizarre world of reporting organized crime events. The *New York Times* reported: Diamond, "was shot twice under the heart, and when removed to Bellevue Hospital was reported to be dying." The *New York Herald Tribune* wrote that "Johnny (Legs) Diamond" had

taken two bullets in the abdomen and "was in ward M2 at Bellevue Hospital last night, the 'serious ward.' Physicians held little hope for recovery."

Compare this to the description of the shooting in two later biographies about Arnold Rothstein. In the book *Rothstein*, David Pietrusza stated, "Diamond took bullets in the leg and arm." Finally in Leo Katcher's *The Big Bank Roll*, the author simply stated, "Diamond was not touched." The seriousness of his wounds lay somewhere in between. Diamond left the hospital two weeks after the shooting.

12. John Hutchinson, *The Imperfect Union* (New York: E. P. Dutton, 1970), p. 73.

13. Ibid., p. 75.

14. This is not the same Joseph Rosen that was murdered in September 1936, whose killing Buchalter would be accused of ordering and eventually cost him his life.

This is also the last known picture taken of Curley Holtz alive. It was alleged that later in 1931, he was sent by Buchalter to Europe with a "large sum" to make a narcotics purchase. While there, Holtz purchased a small amount and kept the balance of what Buchalter had given him. On arriving back in the United States, he passed along word to the authority that narcotics were hidden aboard the ship. This way when they were seized, they would cover up for the amount Holtz had helped himself to. But when Buchalter heard about the amount of the seizure, he knew it didn't add up to the amount of money he had given Holtz. According to one account, "A gun . . . was thrust down Curley's throat. Now Curley, it is believed, lies in a cement block under the murky waters of the East River."

15. The *New York World-Telegram* series on Buchalter, "Million Dollar Fugitive," in the fourth segment, "Max Rubin Has the Goods on Lepke," reporter Jack Foster gave a reason for the raid. He claimed Sidney Hillman had gone to New York City Mayor James J. "Jimmy" Walker and "demanded that steps be taken to block the attempts of Lepke, Gurrah and their mob to terrorize Amalgamated members." Foster reported that Mayor Walker turned the matter over to his police force, who in turn made the raid on Franconia and arrested the men to harass them. Foster wrote, "Police held them in the suite for several hours—questioning them, trying to drag some scraps of evidence out of them—because they knew that as soon as they reached headquarters they would be bailed out."

16. Hutchinson, *The Imperfect Union*, p. 78.

17. *New York Times*, November 7, 1933, "80 Indicted Here in Huge Fur 'Trust.'"

18. Ibid.

19. *New York Times*, June 17, 1938, "Testifies He Paid $20,000 to Gurrah."

20. Louis Buchalter was said to have suffered from a kidney ailment most of his adult life.

21. *New York Herald Tribune*, September 14, 1936, "4 Gunmen Slay Racket Foe in Brooklyn Store."

22. *New York Times*, October 22, 1936, "New Dewey Drive Revealed by Raid in Bakery Racket."

23. *New York Herald Tribune*, October 27, 1936, "Lepke, Gurrah Go on Trial as Fur Racketeers."

24. Ibid.

25. *New York Times*, November 8, 1936, "Two Convicted as Fur Racket Terrorists After Federal Jury Deliberates 33 Hours."

26. Burton B. Turkus and Sid Feder, *Murder, Inc.*, pp. 348–349.

27. *New York World-Telegram*, July 28, 1939, "'Penn's Double' Is Key to Racket, Says Dewey."

28. *New York World-Telegram*, August 11, 1939, "Chapman No.1 Public Enemy; Lepke No. 4." Abner Zwillman would be called again later in the month for questioning about Buchalter. This time he refused to answer the questions of the special federal grand jury and was cited for contempt and sentenced to six months in prison by Federal Judge Johnson J. Hayes. The next day Hayes set

bail at $10,000 and gave Zwillman a few days to "purge" himself of the contempt charges by appearing before the grand jury and answering their questions.

29. FBI files on Louis Buchalter, Freedom of Information Act files.

30. According to *The Last Testament of Lucky Luciano,* the authors claim Luciano was responsible for creating the story that a deal had been worked out with J. Edgar Hoover to get Buchalter to surrender. This decision came after a meeting with Tommy Lucchese in Dannemora Prison, where Lucchese had visited with Luciano to complain about Buchalter attempting to increase his control of the garment industry rackets. Luciano's plan was to convince Lepke that a plan had been consummated, and it had to be delivered by someone he trusted. He then claimed he sent Lansky a letter outlining his plan and for Meyer to select the delivery boy. Lansky chose Moe "Dimples" Wolensky, who may not have been aware of the trap he was placing Lepke in by delivering the message. The authors claim Luciano told Costello to make sure Dewey knew Luciano was responsible for this, as it was part of his master plan to get out of prison.

31. In 1943, a person never identified by any name other than "a friend" visited Buchalter in prison and told him that Morris Wolensky had been murdered in a midtown Manhattan restaurant. The story that emanated from this tale was that the "friend," in repeating the story stated, "You know, when Louis heard that Dimples got it . . . I never saw him look happier. I always thought Dimples was his pal."

In *The Rise and Fall of the Jewish Gangster in America,* author Albert Fried weighs in on Wolensky's assumed treachery. "Years later, presumably at Lepke's request, Anastasia avenged the wrong by murdering Moey Dimples; gangsterdom recognizes no unwitting acts of treason. Did Lepke and Anastasia ever find out who had put Moey Dimples up to it? Probably not. And if they did find out what could they have done about it? How could they, or Anastasia alone, have gone after Lansky and Luciano—that is, the entire gang/syndicate leadership? Lepke had been sacrificed and that was that."

32. *New York Times,* December 20, 1939, ' "Myth' About Lepke Assailed at Trial."

33. According to the *New York Times,* "He [Knox] fixed a two-year sentence and $2,500 fine on the narcotics conspiracy conviction. Two more years were added as punishment in the fur racket cases, and another term of ten years was set for a narcotics smuggling indictment. The ten years' suspended sentences were apportioned among the remaining indictments." *New York Times,* January 3, 1940, "Lepke Sentenced to 14-Year Term."

34. *New York Times,* February 11, 1940, "Death Threat Bared in Trail of Lepke."

35. *New York Times,* February 28, 1940, "Sums Up Lepke Defense."

36. *New York Times,* March 3, 1940, "Lepke Conviction Gratifies Dewey."

37. *New York Times,* April 6, 1940, "Lepke Sentenced to 30 Years to Life."

38. Max Silverman was given a sentence of 20 to 30 years; his son Harold, received three to six years. On November 12, 1940, Samuel Schorr, who pleaded guilty to all counts, received a three- to six-year term. On February 4, 1941, after reaching a plea deal in the murder of William Snyder, William Goldis was sentenced for that crime and for the bakery and flour-trucking extortion case. At the sentencing, Assistant District Attorney Jacob Grumet told Judge Freschi that the "Goldis brothers had been the principal means of getting the inside story of the Lepke-Gurrah reign of terror." Freschi imposed a sentence of 1 year to 18 months in Sing Sing. On June 30, 1941, Morris Goldis was sentenced to a mere five to eight years in a reduced charge of first-degree manslaughter.

39. *New York World-Telegram,* October 31, 1941, "Barshay Charges O'Dwyer Plays Politics with Lepke."

40. *New York World-Telegram,* November 14, 1941, "Rubin Tells How He Was Shot After Testifying in Rackets Investigation."

41. Ibid.

42. On September 16, 1949 Philip "Little Farvel' Cohen was found dead on the road in Valley Stream, Long Island. He had been shot four times in the head and neck.

43. *New York World-Telegram,* November 25, 1941, "Both Sides Rest in the Lepke Murder Trial."

44. *New York Times,* December 1, 1941, "Lepke's Fate Put Up to President by Death Verdict."

45. Weiss had been in federal custody since his arrest on narcotics charges in Kansas City, but because he was never tried in federal court, his captors were only too happy to turn him over to the State of New York for execution.

46. *Writ of certiorari,* informally called "Cert Petition," is a document that a losing party files with the Supreme Court asking the Supreme Court to review the decision of a lower court. It includes a list of the parties, a statement of the facts of the case, the legal questions presented for review, and arguments as to why the Court should grant the writ. "Review on writ of certiorari is not a matter of right, but a judicial discretion. A petition for writ of certiorari will be granted only for compelling reasons." Rule 10, Rules of the U.S. Supreme Court.—www.techlawjournal

47. New York State law required that the resentencing be made by the judge of the New York State Court of Appeals instead of the trial judge.

48. *New York Times,* December 1, 1943, "State Bars Pledge to Execute Lepke."

49. The *New York World Telegraph* reported that later that night Acting District Attorney Thomas C. Hughes spoke by telephone with Colonel O'Dwyer, who denied making any such promise.

50. Turkus and Feder, *Murder, Inc.,* pp. 415–416.

BIBLIOGRAPHY

Biography of Buchalter

Kavieff, Paul R. *The Life and Times of Lepke Buchalter.* Fort Lee, NJ: Barricade Books, 2006.

Other Publications

Dewey, Thomas E. *Twenty Against The Underworld.* Garden City, NY: Doubleday & Company, 1974.

Fried, Albert. *The Rise and Fall of the Jewish Gangster in America.* New York: Holt, Rinehart and Winston, 1980.

Hutchinson, John. *The Imperfect Union.* New York: E. P. Dutton & Co., 1970.

Turkus, Burton B., and Sid Feder. *Murder, Inc.* New York: Farrar, Straus and Young, 1951.

Willemse, Cornelius W. *Behind the Green Lights.* Garden City, NY: Garden City Publishing, Inc., 1931.

4

FRANK COSTELLO (FRANCESCO CASTIGLIA)

AKA "PRIME MINISTER OF THE UNDERWORLD"
JANUARY 26, 1891–FEBRUARY 18, 1973

Although he was the subject of no less than seven biographies, Frank Costello remains an enigma. How he rose to become the top underworld figure in New York City, if not the entire country, is a puzzle to this day. A *Collier's Magazine* article about Costello in April 1947 emphasized this unsolved question. The title of the article was "America's Number One Mystery Man."

Unlike other mob bosses, Costello was known as a man of peace. He would rather pay a man off than bump him off. There was always room to negotiate; there was always time to reason. His management methods earned him the sobriquet: the "Prime Minister of the Underworld." Despite rumors, there is no evidence that Costello ever killed a man or ordered his death.

One of the more amazing facts about Costello was that, as leader of the New York underworld for an unprecedented 20 years, he never employed the services of a bodyguard or chauffeur, even though he kept the same daily routines. A half-century before the introduction of Tony Soprano into the American pop culture, Costello had become the first mob leader to seek the services of a psychiatrist in hopes of treating bouts of depression and insomnia.

With the power-hungry Vito Genovese stopping at nothing to reclaim the position he had relinquished to the "Prime Minister" in the mid-1930s, Costello survived an assassination attempt and wrote his own ticket out of the underworld. In the end, he died peacefully in bed.

EARLY YEARS

Frank Costello entered the world as Francesco Castiglia on January 26, 1891, in Lauropoli, Italy, in the southern-most province of Calabria. Francesco was the sixth and last child of Luigi Castiglia and Maria Saveria Aloise. He was preceded by four sisters and a brother, Eduardo, who was 10 years older.

Luigi, an Italian war veteran who fought with Garibaldi's Legion in the mid-1860s during the short-lived Austro-Prussian War, tended the family farm and tried to provide for his family. Maria helped out by serving as a midwife in time of need. The impoverished conditions the Castiglia family endured were part of a common struggle in southern Italy during the latter part of the nineteenth century. The promise of better opportunities in the New World was calling Luigi, as well as tens of thousands of others.

When Luigi sailed for America in 1893, he could only afford to take half of his family—two daughters and Eduardo. He figured with the riches he would soon be making, it wouldn't be long before he could send for Maria and the others; however, it would be two years before the family was reunited. In the meantime, Maria had to work that much harder to provide for her children.

In 1895, when the tickets finally arrived from America, there were only two of them. Since Francesco was young enough to travel for free, this meant that one daughter would have to stay behind with relatives. When Francesco got older, he would talk about his voyage across the Atlantic as follows:

> It was just the three of us: my mother, my sister, and me. All we took with us from the old country was this huge iron pot my mother liked to cook in. They just fixed up the pot like a bed by lining it with a blanket, and that's where I slept for the entire crossing.[1]

The reunited Castiglia family moved into a three-story tenement building on East 108th Street in the East Harlem section of Manhattan. Despite the new surroundings and a new profession—grocery store proprietor—Luigi ran into the same problem he did in Lauropoli, an inability to provide for his family.

Francesco also had trouble adjusting. He was slow to learn the new language and did not begin school until he was nine years old. By the time he was in fifth grade, now 13 years old, Francesco left school for good and began to roam the streets of East Harlem with other teenagers.

TEENAGE HOODLUM

Francesco's first arrest came on April 25, 1908, when he was 17 years old. He and two other youths followed a coal dealer into the basement of his business and demanded money. The man refused and a fight ensued. After Francesco hit him in the head with a hammer, the three fled with $17.50. Francesco was arrested and charged with robbery and assault, but a general sessions court judge dropped the charges on May 8.

On October 16, 1912, Francesco, again in the company of two companions, assaulted and robbed a young housewife at the corner of Third Avenue and East 108th Street. This time the trio got away with $1,635 in cash and $200 worth of jewelry. When arrested, Francesco gave his name as Castello, perhaps hoping the police would not be able to connect him with the earlier crime. Again, he walked away when the charges were inexplicably dismissed.

During this time Francesco and his brother Eduardo, who now went by Edward or Eddie, began working together. The two met some of the other teenage hoods in the neighborhood and began forming friendships. Included were Owney Madden and Willie Moretti. One of the scams Francesco pulled was pretending to be a stevedore recruiter. Men seeking work on the West Side docks would pay the brothers on the premise that they would get hired.

In 1914, Costello was introduced to Loretta "Bobbie" Geigerman, the younger sister of one of Francesco's companions. When the two decided to get married on September 23, the marriage license gave her age as 19, even though a later investigation showed she was only 15. On the license for the first time Francesco used the name Frank Costello. Geigerman was Jewish and Costello was Catholic. Somehow they decided on an Episcopalian minister to perform the rite, which was conducted at the home of a friend.[2] The couple, who never had children, was married for nearly 60 years.

Costello's marriage did not turn into a reform movement. His next arrest would prove to be the most significant for him. On March 12, 1915, for reasons that never came to light, Costello was carrying a revolver as two policemen watched him bolt out of a barbershop and race down a series of back alleys. As police closed in on him, they saw the winded teenager throw the revolver into a vacant lot. They arrested Costello and recovered the weapon.

When booked, Costello used the name Saverio, an adaptation of his mother's maiden name. At arraignment, he was charged with carrying a concealed weapon, a felony. For the third time Costello pleaded not guilty, but his luck had run out—this time there would be no dismissal of the charges and he was held in the Tombs on a high bond.

With Costello looking at seven years in prison, his lawyer met with the prosecutor's office to make a deal. The charge would be reduced if Costello agreed to plead guilty. It was now up to General Sessions Judge Edward Swann to determine whether Costello got a year in prison, received probation, or was given something in between.

On May 15, Costello faced Swann. The judge read through the probation report, which consisted of a plethora of lies orchestrated by his lawyer. Judge Swann saw through them, however, and sentenced Costello to a year in the City Penitentiary on Blackwell's Island.[3] The lesson was not lost on Costello. He never carried a gun again.

Costello spent 11 months in prison. When he returned home in the spring of 1916, the country was on the brink of war with Germany. The next year Costello's number came up in the draft. He tried to claim exemption because he was an alien, but his claim was refused.[4] He was never called, but his draft record stated he was self-employed as a fruit dealer, giving his business address as the location of his father's grocery store, and his home address as West 116th Street. Whatever business Costello was in, it must have paid well. Acquaintances in the neighborhood recalled that he was always well dressed and that everyone seemed to look up to him.

In May 1919, Costello was involved in another "trio robbery." This time he and his companions confronted a man in a Queens's park and took $100 from him. One of his companions was Vincent Rao. A charge of grand larceny was placed against Costello, but, as in the first two robberies, the charges were dropped.

In August of that year, Costello met Harry Horowitz and they established the Harry Horowitz Novelty Company. The venture cashed in on the punchboard craze that was sweeping the country. After an initial investment of $3,000, the company reported sales of $100,000 during the first year. But just as quickly the craze, with its Kewpie doll prizes, blew over and the company declared bankruptcy, pocketing the profits and never paying the expenses.

THE NEW CRAZE—PROHIBITION

By late 1920, Costello was putting his profits from the Kewpie doll scam into bootlegging. His first partner in the new venture was his brother Eddie. Costello biographer Leonard Katz gave the following comparison of the brothers in his book *Uncle Frank:*

> Eddie was heavier and more powerfully built than Frank, but he had the same generous Castiglia nose, and when you saw them together the family resemblance was obvious. The resemblance ended there, though. Eddie was a crude, ignorant thug who police say was a hit man for the mob in the late twenties. Frank supplied the brains and Eddie the brawn. Although Frank was every bit as tough as his brother and millions of brain cells smarter, he watched his step because he feared going back to prison.[5]

Most biographies claim that the Costello brother's operation was financed by the "Big Bankroll" himself, Arnold Rothstein (A.R.). They suggest that as early as 1921, Costello began his association with the famed gambler. Although Rothstein was involved in financing a number of bootleg operations, however, there is no evidence that Frank Costello and A.R. ever transacted business together until years later when a loan was revealed after Rothstein's death in 1928.[6]

In the early years of Prohibition, the Costello brothers began to cultivate business relationships with the other top bootleggers in the city by appearing almost daily at what was called the "Curb Exchange." Located in Manhattan's Little Italy, the exchange was held to swap liquor that was hijacked or drawn out of government bonded warehouses with counterfeit permits. The bootleggers could barter the illegal alcohol according to the needs of their customers. That the exchange area practically encircled police headquarters did little to halt the trade, nor did it deter the occasional gun battles that took place there over territorial encroachments.

It was here that Frank Costello was said to have been introduced to Giuseppe "Joe the Boss" Masseria, described as the top Mafia boss of New York, Salvatore "Lucky Luciano" Lucania, Meyer Lansky, and Benjamin "Bugsy" Siegel.[7] When the government put the clamps on the accessibility of the bonded alcohol, bootleggers began to look outside the country to obtain the best liquor available for their thirsty clientele. Soon liquor began pouring in from Canada, the Bahamas, and Cuba, as well as Europe.

As early as July 1921, the newspapers were reporting a "Rum Row" off the northeastern Atlantic coast running from Boston to Washington D.C., according to what source was describing its parameters. The liquor-laden ships anchored three miles off the coast and serviced their customers, usually in the form of fast speedboats, from the safety of international waters. The first effort by the government to combat the smugglers was to increase the international limit to 12 miles.

Once the liquor was on dry land, it was taken to warehouses where it would be "cut." The cutting process consisted of diluting the product with water, malt, alcohol, and artificial coloring, so that each bottle of the real stuff was turned into three, thus tripling the profits. To accomplish this, additional bottles that resembled the originals had to be purchased and counterfeit labels produced. The raiding of places that produced these materials was commonplace during the Prohibition years.

Sometimes getting the liquor to the warehouses and cutting plants was just as perilous as getting it ashore. Hijackers were always ready to steal a load and gun down anyone who tried to stop them. The bootleggers countered these attempts by hiring armed escorts to protect their trucks, not only from the hijackers but also from local police officials and Prohibition agents if the latter two couldn't be bought off. Benjamin Siegel and Meyer Lansky were said to have made money by providing the protection for these trucks from their "Bug & Meyer" gang.

One of the oft-repeated stories of Costello's bootlegging days was that he was in business with Joseph Kennedy. Costello once talked about this to John Miller, a friend and columnist from the *National Enquirer:*

> "The way he talked about him," Miller said, "you had the sense that they were close during prohibition and then something happened. Frank said that he helped Kennedy become wealthy. What happened between them I don't know. But the way Frank talked you had the feeling that in later years he had tried to reach Joe Kennedy for something and that he was completely ignored. Frank didn't mind if someone said no to him. He could understand that. But nothing made him angrier than to be just ignored, as if he didn't exist."[8]

According to Costello, Kennedy had approached him for help with smuggling liquor into the country. A deal was allegedly worked out whereby Kennedy would have the liquor brought to Rum Row, and Costello would handle it from there. Shortly before he died, Costello told this story to author Peter Maas. The story made it into the *New York Times* and caused "quite a flap."

Stephen Smith, a Kennedy relative acting as family spokesperson, denied that any such business relationship existed between the two men. Then he also denied that Joe Kennedy was ever involved with bootlegging.[9]

"BIG BILL" DWYER

During the early years of Prohibition, Frank Costello became involved in the huge rum-running operation of William Vincent Dwyer. Costello's role in the operation is not entirely known. Some people claim he was Dwyer's partner; others give the credit to Costello for the success of the operation. Newspaper accounts and courtroom testimony, however, depict Costello in a lesser role.

Costello used the profits he earned from the operation to invest in legitimate businesses—a realty company that constructed houses in the Bronx and an automobile agency. He also reconnected with Harry Horwitz in a company called Daintes Products, which made "chocolate-covered ice cream pops." In 1925, Costello and his wife could afford to move out of Harlem to a Bayside home in a middle-class Queens neighborhood.

The rum-running operation came to an end on December 3, 1925. The arrests of ring members were ordered from Washington D.C. by General Lincoln C. Andrews, the assistant director of the U.S. Treasury, who oversaw the enforcement wing of the Prohibition Bureau. The initial warrants called for the arrest of 43 men, including Dwyer and the Costello brothers. As the arrests were being conducted, a telegram was dispatched to Andrews in Washington: "Beg to report capture of Dwyer and his principal assistants. Forty-three warrants out and biggest round-up in history of prohibition enforcement still in progress."[10]

U.S. Attorney Emory R. Buckner announced that "the ring's business was as highly organized as that of any efficient manufacturer or merchant, and included a purchasing department, corruption department, intelligence and distribution departments."[11] Edward

Costello, said to be the "purchasing agent for the group," must have been in the "purchasing department," with Frank a member of the "corruption department," as he was accused of paying off members of the Coast Guard. During Dwyer's arraignment, an assistant U.S. attorney told Federal Judge Henry Goddard:

> For more than two years Coast Guard boats have been in the pay of this defendant; so much so that in the Sea Grill Restaurant, at 141 West Forty-fifth Street, which he owns, and which recently was padlocked, Government employes (sic) were paid off by his representatives. There Government men, low-salaried employes, were feasted and entertained with wine, women and song.[12]

The incident remained front-page news for several days as more stories about the gang's activities poured out, and additional arrests were made. A special federal grand jury began to investigate the ring. On January 26, 1926, three sealed indictments were released naming 61 persons.[13] The first two indictments charged conspiracy to violate the Prohibition law and conspiracy to bribe members of the Coast Guard. The third indictment charged Dwyer and one other man with having sent out a vessel, the *William J. Mahoney,* which was not seaworthy. The Costello brothers were named only in the first indictment.

By July 7, when the first case came to trial, the Costello brothers and 16 others had been severed from the case. Many of the indicted, especially the Coast Guard members, made plea deals with the government in exchange for their testimony. The trial began with 11 defendants. By the time a verdict was reached on July 26, only eight defendants remained. Dwyer and one other man were found guilty; the remaining six were acquitted. Dwyer was sentenced to two years in the federal penitentiary in Atlanta and fined $10,000. Appeals kept Dwyer out of prison until July 1927. With all his legal efforts exhausted, he purchased his own train ticket to Atlanta.

The second rum ring trial, involving the Costello brothers, began on January 3, 1927. The government prosecutors portrayed Frank as a "payoff man," but little information regarding his activities within the ring were reported in the newspapers during the trial. Six former Coast Guard members, who had taken a plea and agreed to testify, stated that Costello had bribed them. Defense lawyers turned the tables on the government, making its witnesses out to be the criminals in the case. Before the trial was over, charges against Edward Costello were dropped. During closing arguments one of the prosecutors told of Costello investing $100,000 of his illegal gains in legitimate businesses. In the end, the jury didn't believe the testimony of the government's witnesses and acquitted eight of the defendants. They were unable to reach a verdict on Frank Costello and five others.

Despite the mistrial, the case against Costello was never retried. The charges against him were dropped in 1933, but the case was not officially dismissed until 1942 when a U.S. attorney admitted the file had disappeared.[14] Costello had a dual purpose for wanting to avoid conviction. He had filed a declaration of intent for citizenship on March 26, 1923. He listed his home address as 234 East 108th Street and his occupation as a real estate broker. In his final petition, he gave his address as 2450 Broadway and his business as real estate. According to the citizenship laws of the day, the only crimes he would have had to list were convictions for moral turpitude. On September 10, 1925, he became a U.S. citizen, less than three months before his arrest on rum-running charges. In addition to facing jail time, if convicted, he could have faced deportation because the government could claim he lied when he applied for citizenship by stating he was a real estate broker. Both of his sponsors for citizenship had been indicted in the same rum-running case.

NEW FIELDS

The exposure from the trial changed the direction of the Costello brothers. Edward virtually disappeared from the New York underworld. He is never mentioned from this point on in any of the biographies of his famous brother. For Frank, it meant a career change. His new profession was slot machine baron.

In 1928, Costello negotiated with the Mills Novelty Company of Chicago, the largest manufacturer of slot machines in the United States, for the exclusive right to place the devices in New York City. After "greasing" the right palms, Costello began placing the first of what would later be estimated at more than 5,100 slot machines throughout the city. The slot machines appeared in clubs, restaurants, speakeasies, and stores. The machines were an instant hit and everyone played them. Unfortunately, many of the machines that ended up in candy stores and five-and-dimes were accessible to children who would drop their lunch money or newspaper earnings into the one-arm bandits. Small steps were sometimes provided so that even the smallest children could reach the handles.

In 1930, when Costello began to face pressure because of antigambling laws, he came up with a novel way around the law. Biographer Leonard Katz explained:

> Each slot machine was fixed so that it would throw out a small packet of candy mints every time a nickel was dropped in the slot and the handle pulled. If a player came up with three cherries, for instance, then in addition to the mints, the machine would throw out slugs which could be used for replays or redeemed for cash with the storekeeper in whose business the machine was placed. It was a stroke of genius and lucrative enough to eventually rival the profits reaped from bootlegging.[15]

It was estimated that Costello's slots were reaping $50,000 a day. In the business operation, Costello employed salesmen, service technicians, collectors, accountants, and a little "muscle" every now and then if any of the machines were stolen. Patrolmen and police officials were said to have been paid not to disrupt the operation by confiscating the machines.

After the death of Arnold Rothstein in November 1928, Costello became the prime player in gambling and bookmaking in New York City. Just how this division of power was agreed on is unclear, but Costello began working with a pair of former Rothstein associates: "Dandy Phil" Kastel, in the slot machine operations, and Frank Erickson, who became Costello's "gambling coordinator."

In the years after Rothstein's death, three events occurred that would solidify Costello's importance to the New York underworld. The first was the Atlantic City Conference (see Appendix) in May 1929. Most mob historians agree that Costello was one of the prime movers and shakers behind this get-together at the Atlantic Coast pleasure resort.

The second was the Castellammarese War (see Appendix). Of all the up-and-coming gangsters associated with this conflict, no one seemed to keep a lower profile than Costello. His scant participation seems to be in arranging the surrender of "Joe the Boss" Masseria to the Bronx Police Department for questioning after his attempted assassination on November 5, 1930, during which Alfred Mineo and Steven Ferrigno were murdered. One of the great mysteries after the war was why Costello wasn't made the underboss to Luciano when the Five Family system was inaugurated; however, Costello seemed content with the status quo and continued to build his gambling business. Not even the murder of Salvatore Maranzano in September 1931 changed the situation.

The third event was the Democratic National Convention in Chicago during 1932. Despite the new power structure of the New York underworld, in which many considered Luciano to be first among equals, Costello remained a power in his own right, especially in the political field, a position he had inexplicably inherited from Rothstein.

An indication of how far he had come in just four short years, Costello shared a room at the Drake Hotel in Chicago during the convention with Tammany Boss James "Jimmy" Hines. Joining him was Luciano, who roomed with Albert Marinelli, the second district assembly leader from Tammany. The reason given by most historians for their presence there was to spread money around in the hopes of solidifying political protection back in New York City. What they achieved, if anything, is unknown, but while Costello and Luciano hoped to build their criminal empire through their work in Chicago, back home, legal authorities were waiting to destroy them and their underworld associates. These enemies included Samuel Seabury, Fiorella La Guardia, and Thomas E. Dewey.[16]

"SLOT MACHINE KING"

By 1932, Costello had become known as the "slot machine king" of New York City, but changes in the political climate were about to bring his kingdom crashing down. They began with the Seabury Investigations, which resulted in the forced resignation of corrupt Democratic New York City Mayor James "Jimmy" Walker.

A reform movement was now in motion and, in the fall of 1933, popular Italian politician Fiorella LaGuardia, a Republican, was elected mayor. With LaGuardia in office for the next 12 years, the Republicans held much of the political patronage jobs. In the past, many of the lower court magistrates were appointed by corrupt Tammany officials. These magistrates had the ability to fix cases for members of the underworld who were willing to meet their price. Now with less to offer, Tammany officials were more willing to accept the graft offered by the gangsters.

When LaGuardia was sworn into office at midnight on December 31, his first order of business was to crack down on the gamblers. "Let's drive the bums out of town," he told supporters. The new mayor ordered Luciano thrown into jail. He then he took on Costello's slot machines, ordering his police to seize the devices. The mayor made a spectacle of smashing the machines with a fire axe, while allowing photographers and newsreel cameras to capture the event. Costello's attorneys convinced New York State Supreme Court Judge Selah B. Strong that the machines were merely dispensers of mints, and an injunction was issued to prevent any more seizures. LaGuardia ignored the injunction and continued to have the slot machines impounded, forcing Costello to retrieve the rest and place them in storage.

At this point, Costello seemed to take a hiatus from his underworld activities. He became a member of the exclusive Lakeville Country Club in Great Neck, Long Island, where he let people know that he was a retired bootlegger. It was here that Costello began his association with the legitimate world and worked hard to clean up his image.

In an interview with Edward T. Folliard, an award-winning journalist with the *Washington Post,* Costello once shared one of his personal characteristics, "All I know I stole. If I saw you hold a cigarette in a certain way, and I liked it, I would steal it from you." This applied to his style of dress, mannerisms and speech. As the years passed and Costello found himself in the presence of businessmen and politicians, he worked hard to improve his grammar.

During this period, Costello, a heavy smoker, began to have throat problems resulting in a raspy voice that plagued him for the rest of his life; his voice never rose above a loud whisper. Two explanations were offered for this problem. One was that he had a malignancy that was treated with radiation, and the second was that he had polyps burned off his vocal chords by a doctor who botched the procedure.

The Costellos moved back to Manhattan, this time to a suite in the Majestic Apartment building on Central Park West. After the conviction of Al Capone for income tax evasion, Costello made sure to clear up his own tax situation. He had not paid income taxes from 1919 to 1932. His settlement with New York State alone cost him $305,000.

Costello's slot machines lay dormant until the spring of 1935, when he moved them to Louisiana at the invitation of U.S. Senator Huey P. Long. Known as "The Kingfish," the southern politician had a colorful history and was considered a dictator of Louisiana politics, having served as governor of the state before becoming senator.

There are numerous stories as to how the deal was consummated, but that spring 1,000 slot machines were on their way to the Pelican State, where they would be under the watchful eye of Phil Kastel and the four Geigerman brothers. The Pelican Novelty Company was formed with Meyer Lansky's brother Jake as one of the officers. Carlos Marcello, the local Mafia boss, became one of the partners; he would become a longtime friend and supporter of Costello. On September 8, 1935, Huey Long was mortally wounded while walking through the corridor of the Louisiana House of Representatives in Baton Rouge. After his assassination, it became necessary to involve more people in the payoffs to keep the slot machines out of the law's way. Over the years, the slot machines endured the ebb and flow of local acceptance and political and civic attacks. The machines continued to make money under the management of Kastel.

On October 9, 1939, a federal grand jury in New Orleans returned a nine-count indictment charging the evasion of nearly $530,000 in taxes since 1935 by six individuals including Costello, Kastel, and two of the Geigerman brothers. In New York City, Costello avoided arrest until he was lured to the federal courthouse under the pretext that he was going to be called to testify before U.S. Attorney John T. Cahill's grand jury investigating national crime. There he was arrested and held on a $75,000 bond. When the case finally came to trial, Federal Judge Wayne G. Boran decided that the government had not provided sufficient evidence and directed a verdict of acquittal.

The Costello/Kastel slot machine operations in Louisiana continued to make money for the men into the mid-1940s. At that time, Costello and Meyer Lansky invested in the Beverly Hills Club, a plush nightclub and gambling casino that brought in some of the top entertainers in the country.

MOVING UP

Costello's brief retirement in the New York underworld came to an end in 1937. After Luciano's imprisonment on compulsory prostitution charges and Genovese's flight to Italy to avoid Thomas E. Dewey and a murder warrant, Costello was selected to serve as acting boss of the Luciano gang.

With Irving "Waxey Gordon" Wexler, Dutch Schultz, and Lucky Luciano in prison or in the ground, Lepke Buchalter was the next hoodlum on Dewey's radar screen. In 1937, Lepke went on the lam and a nationwide manhunt began. In early 1939, Lepke had potential witnesses against him exterminated by members of Murder, Inc. (see Appendix). But the slaying of Irving Penn, a music publisher mistaken for one of Buchalter's targets in late July 1939, raised the ire of the public, as well as that of J. Edgar Hoover.

Hoover's FBI, which began harassing hoodlums all over the country, had sent word to Costello through syndicated columnist Walter Winchell that unless Lepke gave himself up, the harassment would continue. Costello sent word to Buchalter that for the good of the organization, he needed to surrender, which Lepke soon did. The decision would eventually cost him his life and he went to the electric chair cursing Costello's name (see Chapter 3).[17]

Through the late 1930s, Costello, while head of the crime family, built a formidable political base that he cultivated daily. Many weekday mornings were spent having breakfast at his Majestic Apartment home with Tammany leaders. Costello, unlike others of his ilk, preferred to begin his days early. Next, he would hold court at the Waldorf-Astoria, followed by lunch at the Madison Hotel. In *Uncle Frank,* Leonard Katz described a typical scene at the Madison Hotel:

> Sometimes you'd see two tables of men waiting patiently to see him at the Madison. Costello would be sitting at a third table, and when the person he was talking to was through, someone from one of the other tables would take his place.[18]

By late afternoon, Costello could be found at the Copacabana nightclub, with drink in hand, surrounded by friends. Costello didn't just build friendships with Tammany Democrats, he courted Republicans as well. Costello's move to rule Tammany received help from an unlikely source. A LaGuardia biographer revealed that the mayor's Tammany bashing had virtually stripped the society of its ability to graft. "To avert Tammany's disappearance, the club delivered itself over to the underworld, and ironically paid with its Irish identity. In its heyday Tammany had sold organized crime protection, but by the 1940s the gangster Frank Costello called the shots, and before he was through Tammany spoke with an Italian accent."[19]

"Costello was extremely acceptable to the politicians because he neither looked nor acted like a hood. Most of the Italian mobsters; on the other hand, appeared menacing to outsiders, were suspicious of anyone who wasn't Italian, sought only the company of each other, and were a source of embarrassment to the politicians who lived by the façade of their respectability. Costello was the first member of the Italian mobs to come uptown and mix with relatively polite society."—Leonard Katz describing how Frank Costello moved so freely between the political world and the underworld

—Katz, *Uncle Frank,* 1973, p. 116

In 1942, the leadership of Tammany Hall came open. It was here that Costello pulled off his biggest political coup. He was able to break a stalemate in the selection process and Congressman Michael Kennedy, a West Side district leader, took the reins. Kennedy had campaigned for the position and let Costello know that he would be grateful to receive it. Costello, who was actually backing another former Congressman before the stalemate, threw his support to Kennedy.

The selection of Michael Kennedy as the new leader of Tammany Hall thrust Costello into the position of one of the most powerful Democratic power brokers in the city, as Leonard Katz described:

> Kennedy was the puppet and Costello the puppeteer. Every judge the Democrats put on the bench, every assistant district attorney job that came their way through patronage, every sensitive post that Tammany was able to fill, and every policy position arrived at by Tammany's executive committee now had to meet with his approval.[20]

Costello's mastering of this political power showed his true genius, as he never abused it and handled it with complete restraint. Decisions and appointments were made through compromise and consensus, but in the end Costello's word was absolute.

THE 1940s

The decade of the 1940s proved to be the highlight of Costello's years as the underworld boss of New York City. It began on a bright note with his take over of Tammany Hall politics. Then, after a roller coaster ride of events, it ended with ominous storm clouds on the horizon heading into the 1950s.

A New Tammany Mayor

In 1941, Tammany and Costello's first concern was to put a Democrat back in the mayor's seat. The man they were supporting for the position, William O'Dwyer was an odd choice.

In 1941, after coming off his highly publicized prosecutions of the Murder, Inc. gang, Brooklyn District Attorney William O'Dwyer decided to run for higher office. That November, he lost to Incumbent Fiorella LaGuardia who began his third term. The next year, Major O'Dwyer, now serving in the Army Air Force, was stationed at Wright Field in Dayton, Ohio (he would later serve with the Allied Military Government (AMG) in the occupation of Italy with the rank of brigadier general). He still had aspirations of becoming mayor. Elements in Tammany Hall, however, had other ideas, and O'Dwyer's chances of getting the Democratic nod were beginning to fade.

Hoping to shore up his chances, O'Dwyer arranged to meet with Costello at his Majestic Apartment suite. Shortly after this meeting, opposition to O'Dwyer at Tammany Hall disappeared . In the fall of 1945, O'Dwyer was elected mayor, ending the 12-year rule of the Republicans and LaGuardia.

When O'Dwyer ran for reelection in 1949, his Republican opponent, Newbold Morris, accused him of being Costello's front man. Costello countered by accusing Morris of seeking his financial aid and influence in the Italian community. Morris denied the accusations, but lost to O'Dwyer that November. In a prearranged deal, however, O'Dwyer was named ambassador to Mexico by President Harry Truman the next year and Vincent Impellitteri became the new mayor. Impellitteri was said to be "wholly owned" by Vito Marcantonio and Tommy Lucchese, underboss of the family that would soon bear his name.

The Thomas Aurelio Affair

In August 1943, Thomas A. Aurelio stood at the threshold of a dream. After 9 years as an assistant prosecutor and 12 as a judge in New York City, he was about to be elected to a seat on the Supreme Court for the State of New York. As the nominee of both the Democratic and the Republican parties, the election appeared to be a formality.

Aurelio's career had the sense of manifest destiny to it. He was a native New Yorker who grew up on the city's East Side. Educated in the public school system, he went to college at New York University where he also earned a law degree. During World War I, he served in Company F of the 51st Infantry Regiment. After the armistice, he taught American soldiers commercial law in a military school in Germany.

Returning home, Aurelio was admitted to the bar. In 1922, he was appointed assistant district attorney at the age of 27. Mayor Jimmy Walker appointed him judge in 1931, and four years later he was reappointed by Mayor Fiorella LaGuardia. During a glowing swearing-in ceremony, LaGuardia stated, "I have re-appointed you because I know of your record, and have known you as a boy and a law student. You are the kind of career man I want on the bench." A review of Aurelio's record as a judge showed his strong support of the police when their efforts brought them into conflict with big-name criminals.

As impeccable as Aurelio's career had been, a seemingly unrelated event—the murder in January 1943 of Italian-language newspaper editor Carlo Tresca (see Chapter 6)—would inadvertently snare Aurelio and derail his cakewalk to the New York Supreme Court. After Tresca's murder, Manhattan District Attorney Frank S. Hogan received permission to tap Costello's telephone at his Central Park West apartment. "We really didn't think Costello had anything to do with the murder of Tresca, but we thought we might pick up some information as to the identity of the killer," Hogan stated.

On the night of August 23, the Democratic Party nominated Aurelio for justice of the Supreme Court. At 8:35 the next morning, Aurelio telephoned Costello:

Aurelio: Good morning, Francesco. How are you, and thanks for everything.
Costello: Congratulations. It went over perfect. When I tell you something's in the bag, you can rest assured. Well, we will have to get together, you, your Mrs. and myself, and have dinner some night soon.
Aurelio: That would be fine, but right now I want to assure you of my loyalty for all you have done. It's undying.[21]

The entire conversation was picked up by the telephone tap and appeared, verbatim, five days later in the Sunday edition of the *New York Times*. The revelations forced both political parties to try to remove Aurelio from the ballot, but it was too late. The next option was to select another candidate and run him as an independent with the support of both parties. The third alternative was for both parties to throw their support to the candidate from the American Labor Party. The problem with the first choice was that the filing deadline for an independent candidate was due to expire at midnight in less than 48 hours and 5,000 signatures were needed.

Despite intense pressure to step down, Aurelio refused to withdraw his name from the ballot. Although he acknowledged making the phone call, he denied that he knew about Costello's past. He stated, "During my brief acquaintance with Mr. Costello of approximately six months standing, I knew him to be a businessman of good repute, and I definitely disavow any knowledge of his criminal background."

On October 25, a disbarment hearing for Aurelio began. Costello was the first witness called and was on the stand for the entire day. Quite candid in his testimony, Costello told Referee Charles B. Sears that not only had he helped Aurelio win the Democratic nomination, he boasted that he had put Michael Kennedy into the leadership of Tammany Hall.

Under questioning from District Attorney Frank Hogan, Costello told the court that before Aurelio's selection, he had been informed that Michael Kennedy had begun "to cool" on the magistrate. When the rumor came up a second time, Costello said he confronted his Tammany bigwig. Trying to badger Kennedy into committing for Aurelio, Costello chided, "Now you've got to be either a man or a mouse. Come out with it. Declare yourself. You're the leader of Tammany Hall. Are you going to be the boss or aren't you?"

During Aurelio's turn on the witness stand he was grilled relentlessly by Hogan. He denied that he had ever sought Costello's help or knew of his criminal past. He shed tears as he vehemently denied any wrongdoing.

After referee Sears brought the disbarment hearing to a close on October 28, he met with reporters in his chambers. He told them he had no idea how long it would be before he filed his report and rendered a decision. When pressed to state if it would be before the election, which was just five days away, he replied, "I can't say."

Two days later, on a Saturday, Sears filed his verdict with the appellate division. In it, he declared that charges against Aurelio were "not proven." On Monday, the four justices sitting in the appellate division voted unanimously to uphold Sears's decision. The next day Aurelio was elected to the New York State Supreme Court by a margin of 50,000 votes over the closest opponent, taking the seventh and last seat on the bench. On June 15, 1944, a New York County grand jury, which had been carrying on its investigation of Costello's "influence peddling" since the previous September, was discharged after a motion by Frank Hogan, after no criminal wrong-doing could be proved.

Years later, when a reporter asked him about the incident and if the two men were still friends, Costello scoffed and declared, "I can't even get a parking ticket fixed with him."[22]

The $27,000 Mistake

On June 14, 1944, New York City taxi driver Edward Waters dropped off a passenger at the Sherry-Netherland Hotel at 59th Street and Fifth Avenue. No sooner had the passenger alighted than Waters saw that he had left behind two envelopes. Waters called to the man, who disappeared down 59th Street. When the cabbie opened the envelopes, he found them stuffed with $100 bills. Waters drove to the East 67th Street Precinct House, where he turned the money over to the desk sergeant. The officer counted out 271 $100 bills and two $50 bills, totaling $27,200.

Six months earlier, Mayor LaGuardia signed into law a new ordinance declaring that a claimant to lost money or property, "must not only prove that he lost it, but that he had a lawful title or property right" to possession. This law was to prevent someone from claiming the money or property if it had been obtained illegally.

Two days after the discovery of the money was reported in the newspapers, Costello, his lawyer George Wolf, the cab driver Waters, and Frederick Chapey, the man who hailed the cab for Costello that night, appeared at the police property room to claim the money from property clerk Maurice Simmons. The clerk refused to return the money after police officials and Mayor LaGuardia declared it "outlaw money," acquired by Costello by illegal means. LaGuardia declared, "What I am interested in, is where did the bum (his favorite nickname for Costello) get it and where was he taking it?" (Attorney Wolf years later revealed Costello had received the money from "Dandy Phil" Kastel, who had arrived in New York to give Frank his share of the New Orleans operations).

So began a three-year legal battle by Costello to collect the funds he so carelessly left behind in the taxicab. On June 19, Costello served a summons on the property clerk Simmons to recover the money. The next day, the IRS filed two tax liens, claiming Costello and his wife owed back taxes. Costello acknowledged the tax debt, but claimed he had reached an agreement with the government to pay it off in $1,000 monthly installments.

Before the week was out, Chapey, who was head of security at the Hotel New Yorker at Eighth Avenue and 34th Street, from where the cab was hailed, resigned after 13 years on the job. Although no reason was given for the resignation, Chapey was quoted as saying, "I guess it's a crime to tell the truth."

Costello claimed that $15,000 of the money was to go toward the closing of a real estate deal and that the balance was borrowed by him from someone, whose name he did not wish to disclose. Within days, the newspapers reported Costello had been the recent purchaser of three Wall Street buildings valued at $512,000. The buildings were obtained by the 79 Wall Street Corporation, of which Costello was president. On June 26, U.S. marshals filed a levy to have the money turned over to them at the request of the Eastern District of Louisiana to satisfy two tax liens filed by the IRS.

On July 12, Costello made good on a promise to the honest cab driver. On the stage of the Beacon Theatre in Port Washington, Edward Waters was presented with $3,500 in War Bonds purchased from the local War Finance Committee. The reward was presented to Waters by the theater's manager. When asked by reporters what he was going to do with the reward money, Waters bluntly replied that it was "nobody's business."

The first hearing on the matter took place on September 8. New York Supreme Court Justice Ferdinand Pecora denied Costello's application for judgment on the grounds that the federal government would have to answer the complaint because of the tax liens it had filed. By this time, Costello was so enraged with the police department for holding the funds that he promised he would turn the money over to the IRS to satisfy the tax lien. In court with him to substantiate the claim was U.S. Attorney John B. Creegan.

At the next court session on October 27, New York State Supreme Court Judge, Carroll Walters ordered property clerk Simmons to hand over the money to the federal government, declaring:

> I cannot tolerate the idea that the Police Department may keep a citizen's property for no better reason than its own innuendo that perhaps the citizen acquired the property in a gambling transaction.[23]

With that, the New York Supreme Court ruled in Costello's favor, but the police department would appeal. More than seven months passed and the police were still sitting on the money. On May 29, 1945, George Wolf and Government Attorney Creegan appeared before the Appellate Division to get the money released. Appellate Judge Joseph Callahan asked Creegan if the government would "levy on the proceeds of crime," to which the government attorney replied in the affirmative.

"Apparently the United States Government has no scruples as to where this tax money comes from," scoffed Callahan.

"That's right, sir," Creegan replied.

The following month, a year since Costello had left the money in Edward Water's cab, the appellate division ruled 4 to 1 to reverse the New York State Supreme Court's decision and determined that the plaintiff would have to go to trial if he was going to recover his money. On February 26, 1946, the New York State Court of Appeals in Albany heard arguments from both sides. It may have been the only time in history where the federal government stood with a Mafia boss to help him win a case. Despite this unique legal team, the court ruled against Costello and affirmed the appellate court's decision to let the police department keep the money.

The only way Costello could get his money now was to go to trial against the city. In doing so, he would have to testify at the Police Property Room concerning the money, something he dreaded. After receiving a subpoena to testify, he went to the court to have it voided. When the judge denied his request, he was forced to submit to several interview sessions by New York City Assistant Corporate Counsel Frank Horan. Held at the property clerk's office, the sessions began on December 21, 1946, and were completed on January 11 of the next year.

The trial, heard in the New York Supreme Court, got underway on January 29, 1947. A jury of 11 men and 1 woman was seated. On the second day Costello took the stand and was bombarded with questions from Frank Horan about his bootlegging days and his association with underworld bosses from the time of Prohibition.

Under examination from George Wolf, Costello told the jury that one of the envelopes contained $15,450 and had been given to him by Philip Kastel, his vending machine partner in Louisiana; the remaining $11,750 had been a loan from Dudley Geigerman, his brother-in-law. Costello claimed, "He had been negotiating to purchase tax liens on real estate in Water Street, adjoining property he owned in Wall Street, and that he had intended to turn the money over to his attorney, Mr. Wolf, who was to buy the owner's equity in the property and then purchase the tax liens form the city."[24]

During his closing statement, Wolf addressed Horan's claim that Costello obtained the money through illegal bookmaking operations. "Every act of Frank Costello is under surveillance every minute of the day. The eyes of the city have been on him at all times. If Costello were a bookmaker they would have had a line of police officers here to testify,"[25] the attorney stated.

After more than 30 months of waiting, a jury took just 60 minutes to decide that Costello was the rightful owner of the money. On February 20, George Wolf went to the property clerk's office to collect the proceeds. After the IRS took its cut, plus interest, and the city was reimbursed for litigation costs, Wolf walked off with $121.65. All Costello received from the ordeal was a bill from his lawyer and a lot of unwanted publicity from the media.

Goings and Comings

The year 1946 turned out to be a watershed year for Frank Costello. While battling the police department for the return of his money, changes were taking place in the underworld landscape. In February 1946, as a result of Lucky Luciano's "wartime role" in helping the allies, now Governor Thomas Dewey pardoned the imprisoned mob boss in a deal that called for his deportation to Sicily (see Chapter 7). Costello biographers claim that Frank was responsible for digging up dirt on Dewey and providing it to Luciano for his use to obtain the pardon.

Luciano's cruise to Italy was followed a few months later by the return trip of Vito Genovese (see Chapter 6). Don Vitone was being brought back to stand trial for the murder of Ferdinand Boccia in September 1934. Genovese would remain in jail for more than a year before the trial was held. When the charges against him were dropped, he would begin pursuit of the position he vacated to Costello when he fled a decade earlier.

In December 1946, Garland H. Williams, supervisor of the Federal Bureau of Narcotics' New York City office, accused Costello publicly of being the "mastermind" of a Mafia-backed, multimillion dollar drug ring operating in East Harlem. On December 20, the day before he was to be questioned by Frank Horan at the Police Property Room, Costello's lawyer George Wolf called a press conference at his office so that Costello could refute the accusations. Members of the press were given a prepared statement by Costello, in which he denied any connection with the Mafia and the narcotics racket, which he referred to as "low and filthy—trading on human misery."[26]

The calling of a press conference by an underworld boss was an unprecedented event in the city. To make his statement credible, Costello also had to answer questions from the reporters in attendance. Many of these questions centered on his slot machine business in Louisiana and his associations at Tammany Hall.

One reporter asked about the accusations that he was "the power behind Tammany Hall."

"Well, they call me everything. That's ridiculous," he answered. Costello claimed he knew many Tammany leaders "because I was born in New York (which was not true) and I'm a friendly fellow."

Next came a question about his relationship with Lucky Luciano. "Were you associated with Charley (Lucky) Lucania and did you see him off?" referring to the mob boss's bon voyage party before leaving for Italy aboard the *Laura Keene*.

Costello paused, and then stated, "I was never associated with him."

"But did you see him off?" the persistent reporter asked.

"Well, I wouldn't care to answer that question," Costello replied.[27]

It was around this time that Luciano claimed in his book that what came to be known as the "Havana Conference" was held in Cuba. If the book *The Last Testament of Lucky Luciano* (see Appendix) can be believed, Costello was in Havana two days after the news conference. There is some corroboration of the information in the book that the dates of Costello's presence there are correct. The newspapers reported that Costello had been questioned by Horan on December 21. Luciano claimed his guests arrived on December 22. A *New York Times* article claimed Costello was to be questioned about the $27,200 again on January 4, but the inquiry was adjourned until January 11 because Costello couldn't obtain an airline reservation in time to return to the city from Florida.[28]

Big Gambling Buildup

Costello's relationships with Joe Adonis, Meyer Lansky, and Benjamin Siegel continued well past the post-Prohibition period; and gambling houses and casinos continued to thrive for the group in New Orleans, Miami, Bergen County (New Jersey), Saratoga (New York), Havana, and a new hot spot—Las Vegas.

Most of these operations were financed by Costello. No one knows how much money he personally pumped into the Flamingo or how much he got back after the murder of Benjamin Siegel in June 1947.

SHRINKS AND CHARITY

Nearly 50 years before television gangster icon Tony Soprano debuted in a psychiatrist's office, Frank Costello, suffering from bouts of depression and insomnia (no doubt brought on by the sudden return of Vito Genovese), made his own foray onto the psychiatrist's couch. During the mid-to-late 1940s, Costello began seeing Dr. Richard H. Hoffman, described as "a well-known shrink with a Park Avenue clientele." One story had the two men meeting while Costello was taking a walk through Central Park.

While being treated over a two-year period, Costello allegedly discussed with Hoffman his hatred toward his father, an inferiority complex as a result of his Italian heritage, his negative image as portrayed by the media, and his rationalization for involvement in bootlegging and gambling because everyone else was doing it. Hoffman suggested to Costello that he initiate changes in his life by making new friends and using his organizational talents in other areas such as charitable causes.

When the newspapers found out about the relationship, they questioned Hoffman, who admitted that Costello was a patient. One of the things the doctor revealed was that he suggested that Costello associate with a "better class" of people. Embarrassed by the breach of confidence made by the psychiatrist, Costello broke off the sessions and declared that during their relationship he had introduced Hoffman to a "better class" of people than the doctor had ever introduced to him. Costello also claimed the doctor often sought his advice about his other patients and found his suggestions useful.

One of the suggestions Costello used from Hoffman was to take his organizing abilities and use them for charity. Costello soon became a member and/or contributor to the Salvation Army, the Legal Aid Society, and the Irvington House, a convalescent home for young rheumatic fever patients. During 1948, Costello was a substantial donator to the Salvation Army's fundraising campaign. At the beginning of 1949, the organization asked its top 200 contributors to serve as vice-chairmen of the new drive. Salvation Army officials later claimed they did not recognize Costello as the well-publicized slot machine baron or the man behind much of the political gossip in the city.

Costello organized a "Dinner and Entertainment" outing for the night of January 24, 1949. The event was held at the Copacabana Club and cost $100 per person, the proceeds going to the Salvation Army Association. A few weeks before the dinner, more than $10,000 had been turned over to the association. On the night of the dinner, Tammany leader and Manhattan Borough President Hugo E. Rogers and five New York State Supreme Court justices, including Thomas Aurelio, were in attendance. In addition, Dr. Hoffman was there, and seated at the head table with Costello was Vito Genovese.[29]

Despite the charitable nature of the evening, the press found out about Costello's sponsorship of the event and had a field day. The next day, through his attorney George Wolf, Costello resigned as vice-chairman "fearful that any further publicity in connection with his participation in the 1949 campaign may adversely affect it."[30]

On February 1, City Councilman Edward Rager introduced a resolution to begin an investigation of Hugo's office. Calling Costello's dinner, "a time-honored device of gangsters to appear reputable," the Republican councilman went on to say, "honest government must perish when public officials charged with administering the affairs of a community are dominated by underworld overlords, specializing in vice and corruption."

UNDER THE KEFAUVER MICROSCOPE

The 1950s opened with a bang for Costello. On Valentine's Day, Robert Montgomery, a "screen and radio personality," filed an affidavit as a private citizen at the federal courthouse charging Costello with obtaining his American citizenship by fraud. The radio commentator said Costello lied on his application for citizenship in 1925, when he claimed he was a person of "good moral character."

The U.S. Attorney's office announced it would review the claim with the Department of Justice, but it was unlikely any action would be taken. Costello had entered the country legally and under the immigration laws of the time, the only deportable crimes were ones involving moral turpitude. The incident quickly blew over, but on the horizon Costello was facing much more serious issues.

On May 10, 1950, U.S. Vice President Alben W. Barkley appointed the five U.S. Senators who made up the Kefauver Committee. On the day of his appointment, Republican Senator Charles W. Tobey of New Hampshire immediately urged that Frank Costello and Frank Erickson be called. The fiery politician heard the two men testify the previous month before a Senate Commerce subcommittee, of which he was a member, and had accused them of "contradictory and evasive testimony." A statement Tobey released said, "If perjury is the only crime on which such characters can be nailed, let us start with that." The first city investigated by the committee was Miami, where Costello was linked to the gambling profits, mostly as a result of material that had been seized at Erickson's office in Manhattan.

That fall, however, all the talk about Costello involved the New York City mayoral election. Acting Mayor Democrat Vincent Impellitteri, who had replaced William O'Dwyer when he was named ambassador to Mexico, was up against Democratic-Liberal candidate Ferdinand Pecora, an ex-New York Supreme Court justice, and Edward Corsi, the Republican candidate. The mayor claimed Pecora was Costello's man and during a radio speech on October 23 stated, "I am not questioning Judge Pecora's character. But I do say that he is nothing more than a respectable front for the lowest, vilest elements this town ever saw."[31]

Corsi, on the other hand, while agreeing that Pecora was backed by Costello, as well as Joe Adonis and Vito Genovese, claimed that Impellitteri was the puppet of Thomas Lucchese. After a bitter and ugly campaign, Impellitteri emerged the victor.

On February 13, 1951, Kefauver Committee members and investigators were in New York City to conduct interviews in executive session (these meant private or sometimes called "secret" hearings) with a number of witnesses who they were considering calling before the public hearings, which were scheduled for the following month. These private hearings were held on the 28th floor of the U.S. Courthouse in Foley Square. Rudolph Halley, chief counsel for the committee, scheduled 45 witnesses for the two-day hearings.

Costello appeared twice before the committee, both times with attorney George Wolf. Because reporters were not allowed to observe the proceedings, much of what was reported was pure speculation. The most discussed part of Costello's questioning seemed to focus on his meeting with William O'Dwyer back in 1942. After the hearings, it was announced that both men (O'Dwyer at his own request) would be called to testify during the public hearings.

On Monday, March 12, the Kefauver "road show" was back on the 28th floor of the courthouse in Foley Square, this time with the television and newsreel cameras rolling, while being broadcast live on radio. New York City would be the crown jewel for the committee, and Frank Costello was the highest ranking underworld witness to be called.

The first witness called was attorney George Morton Levy, who served as president of the Nassau County Trotting Association, Inc., which operated the Roosevelt Raceway in Westbury, Long Island. Levy told the committee that he had known Costello for a number of years, and at one time he had done some legal work for him. In addition, he was a constant golfing companion of Costello in a foursome, that normally included Frank Erickson and Joseph Schoenbaum, a former employee of the IRS. He claimed, however, that he had never talked business with Costello and had no idea what he did other than he had an "influence" with gamblers.

Levy then told a fantastic tale of paying Costello $60,000 over four years to keep bookmakers away from the track after management had been warned its license would be revoked if the bookmaking continued. Levy said the bookmakers stopped; he had no idea what Costello did, but "the mere hiring of the fellow was invaluable."

Other witnesses that first day were Joe Adonis and Frank Erickson, both of whom invoked their Fifth Amendment right not to answer questions on more occasions than not. Both men were eventually cited for contempt of Senate. Because of the limited space on the 28th floor, a judge on the third floor allowed them access to his courtroom for the following day's session.

Having seen his associates, Adonis and Erickson, during their televised testimony the day before, Costello did not wish to fall under the same scrutiny. His attorney George Wolf addressed the matter with committee members. When asked for the basis of his objection to the television cameras, Wolf replied, "On the ground that Mr. Costello doesn't care to submit himself as a spectacle. And on the further ground that it will prevent proper conference with his attorney in receiving proper advice during the course of the testimony."[32] The committee agreed to the request and the television cameras photographed Costello from the neck down, focusing mainly on his hands, which told their own story.

As in most cases during the Kefauver Hearings, the underworld figure's attorney would ask to read a statement before the committee's questioning. This was done in an attempt to preexonerate the client and to make it seem like the client was trying to do the right thing, but was being persecuted by the government. In Costello's statement, he said that he was upset because when he had appeared before the committee on February 13, he had been told that his testimony had been forthright; yet when the committee's interim report was released, he was "branded as an arch criminal." Costello declared that, "You have prejudged me without a bit of respectable proof to support your judgement." He completed his statement with, "I am not only asking that you respect fundamental rights and principles—I am begging you to treat me as a human being."

The comments were directed to Senator O'Conor, who was acting as chairman during the day's hearing. Kefauver chose to answer, claiming that the interim report, even though it came out after Costello was questioned, had been written earlier than February 13. He also pointed out that "you mistake forthrightness with proof of innocence or no wrongdoing."

Halley began with questions about Costello's youth and early criminal activity and then turned quickly to his naturalization, which took place in 1925. Halley and Senator Tobey began a dialogue to show that the witnesses to Costello's naturalization were members of the rum-running ring and had been indicted with Costello. They concluded that Costello and the witnesses, Frank Goss and Harry Sausser, conspired together "to obtain a naturalization by fraud."

Costello claimed he wasn't involved in the rum running ring until "around '27, '28, '29," even though he was indicted in December 1926. The following exchange then took place:

Halley: Now, Mr. Costello, bearing in mind that you are under oath, will you state whether or not prior to having been naturalized as a citizen of the United States you were engaged in the illicit liquor business in the United States?

Costello: I was not.

Halley: You were admitted to citizenship, were you not, on September 10, 1925? Prior to the month of September, 1925, did you or did you not engage in the business of selling, purchasing, transporting or possessing alcoholic beverages within the United States?

Costello: No.

Costello then stated that the Sausser that served as his naturalization witness was in real estate in Huntington, Long Island, at the time and not the man indicted with him. When asked how many Harry Saussers did he know, Costello replied, "I don't know. I might have known two or three."

An incredulous Halley then asked "Do you expect this committee to believe that story?" Costello angrily replied, "I am not expecting you to believe anything. I know you weren't going to believe anything when I first come here. I have been prejudged."

Costello was then questioned about his slot machine business (in both New York and Louisiana) and his partners in that business. He discussed his business arrangement with Huey Long and said that his slot machine business ended when the New Orleans Police Department seized 600 of his machines. He said he was retired from the slot machine business in Louisiana, but was involved in ownership of the Beverly Country Club in New Orleans with Phil Kastel and Carlos Marcello.

When Costello refused to divulge his net worth, there began a slow tedious process of going through all the income he had earned over the years. When the subject turned to his business arrangement with George Levy, Costello was asked what he did to earn $60,000. "Practically nothing," he answered.

Before ending the day's session, Acting Chairman Senator O'Conor reminded Costello and his counsel that there was still one question he had refused to answer. He advised him to think about it overnight and that if it remained unanswered, it would be necessary to cite him for contempt.

In his book about his years as legal counsel to Costello, attorney George Wolf related the following insight to the first day of Costello's testimony declaring, "I can say for the record that few attorneys ever had a more difficult client to represent at a hearing." Wolf wrote:

As we took the witness stand together, I noticed the actor Robert Montgomery sitting behind us. He had wangled a job as a radio reporter doing the commentary on the hearings, and it is amusing to me that his reports said that I constantly whispered all the answers to Costello before he made them. Actually time and again I would hear my client blurt out an amazing untruth—just to show the senators who's boss, or thinking he would evade the issue. I would kick him sharply in the shins every time he made false and perjurious response. In many instances the truth would have proved harmless. After one session we were in a taxi and I remember Frank pulling up his trouser leg and showing me black and blue marks, saying, "Dammit, you're killing me in there, George! Take it easy."[33]

Costello's headless figure on national television garnered a lot of media attention. The *New York Times* reported:

When the questions got rough, Costello crumpled a handkerchief in his hands. Or he rubbed his palms together. Or he interlaced his fingers. Or he grasped a half-filled glass of water. Or he beat a silent tattoo on the table top. Or he rolled a little ball of paper between his thumb and index finger. Or he stroked the sidepieces of his glasses lying on the table. His was video's first ballet of the hands.[34]

The "hand ballet" was the image most Americans who watched the testimony recall. Although the television cameramen were ordered to steer clear of the witness's face, the newsreel cameramen were not. Some of the evening newscasts used the newsreel footage that night for their audiences. A *New York Times* reporter ridiculed Costello's personal traits, comparing him to a "straw boss stevedore," and calling his appearance before the committee a "flop."

On Wednesday morning, Costello was grilled about his participation in the Louisiana slot machine business with Phil Kastel. The questioning then moved to his role in a liquor distributorship involving the brands King's Ransom and House of Lords scotch. Committee members were irritated by many of the responses in which Costello displayed a faulty memory.

During Costello's testimony, which ended at noon, he was asked if he had paid a telephone company employee named James McLaughlin to check his telephone lines back in 1943 after his tapped telephone conversation with Thomas Aurelio became public. Costello was adamant that he had never asked anyone to check them. In the afternoon session, McLaughlin testified that Costello had paid him to check his line for wiretaps.

At the end of the day, Kefauver announced, "The testimony given by Frank Costello will be referred to the Department of Justice because of inconsistencies in his statements and those of the former telephone worker. So on the face of it, someone has committed perjury. I say so now so that, when Mr. Costello returns to the stand tomorrow morning, he may have a chance to reconsider his testimony."

Costello was called to appear again on Thursday afternoon. Counsel Halley was ready to grill the mob boss about the testimony of James McLaughlin, but he didn't get a chance, as Costello pulled off one of the more memorable moments of the hearings.

Attorney Wolf claimed his client was ill and could not "reply properly" to questions asked by the committee because of the "Klieg lights, heat, and frequent interruptions." Wolf asked for a postponement until Costello was physically and mentally prepared to continue. He claimed his client felt he was being treated as a defendant instead of a witness for which he had been subpoenaed. At one point the attorney produced a note from a doctor stating Costello "should remain in bed and have complete voice rest for several days."

Kefauver overruled Wolf's motion for a postponement and ordered Halley to begin questioning. But it was Costello who was asking the questions:

Costello: Mr. Halley, am I a defendant in this courtroom?
Halley: No.
Costello: Am I under arrest?
Halley: No.
Costello: Then I am walking out.

At this point Kefauver and Halley defined what the consequences of Costello's action could bring. Costello replied, "Mr. Halley, with all due respect to the senators, I have an awful lot of respect for them, I am not going to answer another question. You said I am not under arrest, and I am going to walk out." Moments later Costello left the courthouse with his lawyer, telling reporters, "I am going right home and going to bed."

The next morning the doctor who prescribed bed rest for Costello was the first witness questioned by the committee. He told about his examination of Costello and then was asked whether Costello, in his present condition, could answer questions for about an hour. The doctor replied that he could. Costello was ordered back for the afternoon session. He appeared with a new doctor's note, but again was ordered to testify by Kefauver. Costello again refused. Wolf told the members of the committee they should name a physician to examine his client. Costello then walked out again without answering questions.

On Monday afternoon, March 19, Costello was the committee's final witness of the day after having been approved to answer questions "for an hour or two," by a physician selected by the committee. The first question put to him was about the testimony of James McLaughlin. Costello said he stood by his previous answer.

The committee then wanted to hear about his relationship with William O'Dwyer. Costello admitted that O'Dwyer had been to his home in 1942, but he insisted that the visit was in regard to a war frauds incident and was not political in nature.[35]

Halley asked the witness to describe his political influence. Costello insisted that it came from the fact that he had "been living all my life, in Manhattan Island," and had grown to know the people he supported. He freely admitted to helping Thomas Aurelio during his bid for the Supreme Court nomination and supporting Michael Kennedy for leader of Tammany Hall. Costello downplayed his political "influence," thus being able to deny politicians were indebted to him, and confessed that he had never voted in his life. On Tuesday, Costello was again grilled about his political influence. The mob leader claimed that since the Aurelio incident in 1943, where he "burned his fingers," he didn't discuss politics with his political friends.

Wednesday, the last day of the New York hearings, Costello was questioned extensively about his finances and investments. He claimed he did not own any real estate and that his Sands Point, Long Island home, purchased in May 1944, was paid for and in the name of his wife. Costello admitted to having about $90,000 in his bank account and $43,000 in a strongbox at his Majestic apartment. Halley then asked if he had cash in excess of $10,000 anywhere else. Costello would not answer, stating that this would involve talking about his net worth, a question he had previously refused to answer.

After Costello's final appearance before the committee, the first response to his testimony, ironically, came from a trio of thugs in search of the $43,000 the mob boss had testified he kept in his home. Around 4:30 on the morning of Saturday, March 24, three men, one of them brandishing a revolver, entered the Majestic Apartment building and ordered two

> "You are looking back over the years, now, to that time when you became a citizen . . . you must have in your mind some things you have done that you can speak of to your credit as an American citizen. If so, what are they?"
> "Paid my tax."
> —Frank Costello responding to a question by Senator Charles W. Tobey during the Kefauver Committee hearings on March 21, 1951.

elevator operators to take them to the penthouse apartment of the Costellos, located on the 18th floor. The Costellos were away at the time, perhaps at their Sands Point home for the weekend, and the would-be robbers could not gain entrance.

THE LEGAL NIGHTMARE

The years after the Kefauver Hearings turned into a never-ending legal battle for Costello. The government came at him on three legal fronts. First they charged him with contempt of the United States Senate, then the Internal Revenue Service charged him with tax evasion, and finally the government tried to deport him.

Contempt of United States Senate

On July 25, 1951, Costello, along with Joe Adonis and Frank Erickson, were indicted by a federal grand jury for contempt of the United States Senate. Costello went on trial in federal court on January 7, 1952, for 11 counts of contempt, four for refusing to answer questions regarding his net worth, four for refusing to answer questions about his political acquaintances, and three for walking out on the committee. His lawyers argued that many of the questions Costello refused to answer initially, he answered at a later date. Federal Judge Sylvester Ryan ruled that a witness before the committee "may not select the time when he will answer a question; he must answer when it is asked of him." The government's case consisted of four witnesses—a subpoena server, two throat specialists, and Rudolph Halley, who had recently been elected president of New York City Council.

The defense, led by George Wolf, contended that as a result of Costello's throat condition and the circus-like atmosphere brought on by the media coverage, especially the television cameras and lights, his client's mental condition was impaired. Meyer Berger, covering the trial for the *New York Times* reported:

> The jury's sole problem, in effect, will be to decide whether Costello was physically and mentally able to answer the committee's questions under the conditions and in the surroundings that confronted him at the public hearings.[36]

Costello did not take the stand in his own defense and Wolf called no defense witnesses. The case was given to the jury on January 14. The jurors returned the next day and announced they were deadlocked. Information that came from the deliberation room revealed that on eight of the counts, the panel was evenly split, or close to it. On the remaining four counts, which included "willful default," the charge of Costello walking out, there had been only one holdout for conviction. Judge Ryan was forced to discharge the panel.

The second trial had a completely different flavor. Originally scheduled to begin February 25, the trial did not begin until March 31 because of legal wrangling and George Wolf's illness. New counsel, Kenneth M. Spence, a former assistant U.S. attorney, contended that only questions of law were involved and chose to waive a jury trial. Federal Judge Ryan decided that there were questions of fact for a jury to decide.

Maintaining his stand that only questions of law needed to be decided, Spence stipulated that Costello was well enough to have answered the questions put to him. The attorney called no witnesses and surprised the courtroom when he declined to present closing argument. On the morning the government was to give its summation, the day began with Judge Ryan dismissing two jurors. One was the jury foreperson, because it came to light she had been active in the campaign to elect Rudolph Halley. Before the panel received the case, the judge dismissed one of the counts. After six hours of deliberations, the jury came back at 10:00 on the night of April 4 with a guilty verdict on the remaining 10 counts.

On April 8, Costello stood before Judge Ryan and was sentenced to 18 months in prison and a fine of $5,000. Ryan then ordered his bail revoked. Four hours later, Costello walked out a free man after a three-judge appeals court panel ordered his bail continued. The U.S. Court of Appeals heard arguments on May 12. On July 3, the court dismissed seven of the counts against Costello, reducing the fine to $2,000, but keeping the prison term intact.

By August 15, 1952, all of Costello's appeals and requests to remain free on bail until the U.S. Supreme Court made a decision to review his case were exhausted. He surrendered at the federal courthouse in Foley Square. Placed in a holding cell in the courthouse basement, Costello told a deputy U.S. marshal, "Tell the boys I've come in to do my bit. Tell them I don't want no favors from nobody. Tell them I expect to be treated like anybody else without no special requests."[37]

Costello was off to the Federal House of Detention to await assignment by the Bureau of Prisons. On August 22, he was assigned to the federal penitentiary in Lewisburg, Pennsylvania. In early October, citing security reasons, the Department of Justice transferred Costello to the federal penitentiary in Atlanta. The next month, on November 10, the U.S. Supreme Court refused to review the mobster's conviction. An appeal for a second review was denied on December 8.

On December 12, Costello's attorneys filed a writ of habeas corpus claiming that, according to federal law, persons convicted of misdemeanor contempt of Senate charges were to serve their sentences in a "common jail." Ten days later, Costello found himself on a bus headed for the Milan Federal Correctional Institution in Michigan. His only time outside the correctional facility came in late April when he was taken back to New York City to respond to charges in his federal tax case. On April 23, 1953, Costello, described as "gaunt" and looking 30 pounds lighter, pleaded not guilty to evading income taxes.

The new federal indictment ruined any chance Costello had for an early parole. He served his full sentence, getting time off for good behavior. On October 29, 1953, after 14 months behind bars, he walked out of the Milan prison and was met by Loretta. Surrounded by reporters, Costello begged, "Will you fellows please quit chasing me? Do you want me to get killed dodging these cars?" He and his wife traveled back to New York City by train. The terms of his bond for the tax evasion charges required that he be confined to the Southern District of New York immediately upon release.

Denaturalization Proceedings

Less than a month after Costello was sent away to prison, the Department of Justice announced on September 9, 1952, that it was instituting denaturalization proceedings against the jailed underworld leader. If the government succeeded in its attempts to have him denaturalized, then it would be up to the Immigration and Naturalization Service to deport him. The government's case consisted of the following charges:

- That in his 1923 petition he fraudulently misrepresented his occupation to be real-estate.
- That his witnesses, Frank Goss and Harry Sausser, misrepresented their occupations.
- That his only alias was Frank Castiglia, when he had used others.
- That he had no prior arrests.
- That he had no prior convictions.

On October 22, the Department of Justice filed a petition to cancel Costello's naturalization based on the fact that he had "not been of good moral character" for the five years preceding his application for citizenship. The government, which was already being criticized for waiting 27 years to take action, readily admitted that the civil court's calendar showed it was two years behind in trying cases.

On November 5, 1954, Costello refused to answer questions about his activities before 1925, when he became a citizen. He invoked his Fifth Amendment right against self-incrimination. Government attorneys called for his immediate denaturalization. One month later, Federal Judge John F. X. McGohey denied the government's motion and instead fined Costello $500 for disobeying the court's order to answer questions.

More than a year later, on December 27, 1955, Costello finally agreed to answer questions about his activities before 1925. Costello was still concerned about self-incrimination until the judge advised him that charges were unlikely because of the statute of limitations. Costello's concerns were certainly legitimate. The Immigration and Naturalization Service announced that Joe Adonis was on his way back to Italy, choosing deportation over imprisonment.

The government's case was stymied when Costello was sent away to prison on a tax evasion sentence. With government prosecutors pushing the case, Costello hired Washington attorney Edward Bennett Williams, fresh from representing Senator Joseph R. McCarthy in Senate contempt proceedings, as his legal counsel. In August 1956, Costello was transferred from the Atlanta Penitentiary to the Federal House of Detention in New York to prepare for his case, which was scheduled for September 4. Two weeks before the trial, Costello filed for a one-month adjournment claiming he was having heart problems.

Attorney Williams's defense was that the suit had been based on illegal wiretapping at Costello's offices on Lexington Avenue in 1925. At the time, wiretap evidence was inadmissible in federal court. The case finally came to trial in late September. Costello took the stand and told Federal Judge Edmund L. Palmieri, "I am still very ill and have terrible pains. I am taking the stand because I cherish my citizenship. My prison sentence is equivalent to a life sentence, but I still want to retain my citizenship."[38]

On September 28, 1956, Judge Palmieri dismissed the charges against Costello claiming that the illegal wiretaps tainted the evidence. In a gambler's jargon, Costello responded, "By the law of averages, I was bound to win this one." The decision, made without prejudice, would allow the government to renew the charges at a later time, which it did.

Federal Income Tax Case

On January 16, 1953, the IRS filed income tax liens totaling $486,722 against Frank and Loretta Costello for unpaid income taxes from 1941 to 1945. The tax liens would prevent them from selling any of their assets. Three weeks later, the government moved to foreclose on Costello property in Florida, Kansas, Louisiana, and Texas, claiming they were worth more than $200,000. The government foreclosure allowed the newspapers to list all the financial holdings of the Costellos. A federal judge denied a request by the government to appoint a receiver for the property.

On March 12, Costello was indicted for income tax evasion after a yearlong investigation involving four agents from the Treasury Department's intelligence unit racket squad. He was charged with evading $73,000 in tax payments for the years 1946 through 1949.

Costello's tax trial began on Monday, April 5, 1954, before Federal Judge John McGohey. Costello was represented by Joseph L. Delaney. The government built its case around trying to prove to the jury that Costello had outspent his income for the years 1946 through 1949. Costello's tax returns for the four years showed a net income of just over $75,000. Records at one of the banks the Costellos used showed deposits of nearly $270,000 during the same period.

The government called 150 witnesses and placed 350 exhibits into evidence. Among the witnesses called were Costello's barber and his wife's florist. The detailed investigation by the Treasury agents showed purchases from underwear and pajamas, to a granite mausoleum in St. Michael's Cemetery in Queens. After a six-week trial, the jury returned in just a little over eight hours with a verdict. At 9:35 PM on May 13, the panel announced they had found Costello guilty of three of the four counts.

On May 17, Judge McGohey sentenced Costello to five years in prison and fined him $30,000. He was denied bail and immediately taken to the Federal House of Detention. Three days later, Costello was ordered back to court to answer questions about his assets and property. Costello offered to pay the $30,000 fine from the assets the government held liens on, but he refused to answer questions about his assets. For this he was held in contempt and fined $500.

Despite the efforts of government attorneys to keep Costello in jail, on June 18 a U.S. Supreme Court justice ordered that bail be set at $50,000. The next day Costello was released. The verdict was still going through a slow appeals process. On April 5, 1955, the U.S. Court of Appeals, while reversing one count and reducing the fine to $20,000, unanimously upheld the verdict.

In October 1955, the U.S. Supreme Court agreed to review the conviction. While this was taking place, the State of New York filed three tax warrants against Costello and his wife for back state taxes. These warrants charged that the Costellos owed more than $96,000 with interest and penalties.

After a nearly two-year battle, on March 5, 1956, U.S. Supreme Court Justice Hugo Black announced a 7–0 decision upholding Costello's conviction. Not even a late appeal from the American Civil Liberties Union claiming that Costello had been convicted on "hearsay evidence" could help the aging mob boss. On April 23, the Supreme Court refused to reconsider its decision.

The next day Costello made an amazing offer. Following the lead of Joe Adonis, he agreed to go into voluntary exile if the government agreed to suspend the five-year prison sentence. The offer had been relayed by attorney Joseph Delaney. U.S. Attorney Paul W. Williams refused the offer. Costello's next move was to ask the government to suspend the prison sentence because of health reasons. He claimed the sentence would be "tantamount to life imprisonment" as a result of "my advanced age, my present state of health" Judge McGohey denied his plea and ordered him to surrender.

On May 14, just weeks before his denaturalization trial was to begin, Costello surrendered and was taken back to the Federal House of Detention on West Main Street to await assignment. The next day, Delaney filed a motion that the sentence imposed on Costello was longer than the maximum allowed by law, claiming the crime was a misdemeanor with a sentence that should not exceed one year.

Costello was off to serve his tax sentence at the federal penitentiary in Atlanta. In December, Edward Bennett Williams, who had been representing Costello in his denaturalization case, was successful in getting evidence thrown out because it had been obtained through illegal wiretaps. He now filed a motion to set aside the tax evasion conviction, claiming that evidence was received in the same manner.

The next month, the U.S. Supreme Court agreed to hear arguments as to whether the sentence handed down on Costello's conviction was excessive. Costello was transferred back to the Federal House of Detention. Williams contended that his client should have been sentenced under a section of the Internal Revenue Code that called for a misdemeanor, which would have sentenced Costello to one year in prison and a fine of $1,000. When Costello applied for bail in February, the court of appeals turned him down.

Williams then went before the U.S. Supreme Court to argue bail. He claimed that if his contention was correct, Costello had already served his full sentence under the law. The Supreme Court agreed to a bail of $25,000. At the same time, the court allowed bond for Benny Binion of Texas, who was in a similar situation as Costello. Both men would be waiting for the Supreme Court decision involving a convicted automobile dealer from Chicago, whose case was scheduled to be heard on April 29.

The decision gave Costello a reprieve after being in prison for 10 months; however, it nearly cost him his life.

"THIS IS FOR YOU, FRANK"

After being released on bail in March, Costello went back to his old routine. This called for rising early for breakfast, holding court at the Waldorf, getting a shave and a haircut, going to the Biltmore Hotel in the afternoon where he enjoyed a steam bath, and then dining out with friends in the evening.

Costello followed this routine on Thursday, May 2. At the Waldorf, an associate handed him a slip of paper that contained some financial results from the Tropicana Night Club in Las Vegas. Costello slipped the scrap of paper in his jacket pocket and forgot about it. After leaving the Biltmore around 5:00 PM, he took a cab to Chandler's restaurant on East 46th Street, where he met with Anthony "Tony Bender" Strollo, a chief lieutenant of Vito Genovese and Vincent Mauro. Strollo soon left, but Mauro stayed and chatted with Costello.

In recent weeks, the two men seemed to have spent a lot of time together and Costello was beginning to enjoy his company. They were soon joined by Phil Kennedy. A close friend of Costello, Kennedy was once a minor league baseball player in the Philadelphia Phillies organization and a former model who now owned a modeling agency. Mauro turned down an invitation by Costello to join him and friends for dinner. Stating he would keep in touch during the evening and maybe meet him later, Mauro went his separate way.

Costello left Chandler's with Kennedy about 6:00 PM and went to L'Aiglon, a French restaurant on East 55th Street, where they met Costello's wife Loretta; Generoso Pope, Jr., publisher of the *National Enquirer;* John Miller, a columnist for the *Enquirer* and his wife Cindy, who was in her ninth month of pregnancy; and another couple. During the dinner, which lasted until nearly 10:00 PM, several telephone calls of importance were exchanged. Costello was waiting for results from the federal trial that would determine if he had been sentenced properly. If the decision favored the defendant, it would have a positive effect on his appeal. When the call came, Costello was informed that the government had won its case. Costello went back to the table, his face never betraying his legal setback.

Another set of calls were being exchanged by John Miller and Vincent Mauro, who were close friends. Mauro had called the restaurant twice to speak to Miller, apologizing each time for not being able to meet them.

After dinner, Loretta wanted to go to the Copacabana nightclub to see the show. Her husband, anticipating a phone call from attorney Williams, suggested they go to the Monsignor, which was also on East 55th Street. Just before leaving the L'Aiglon, Miller received a third telephone call from Mauro. This time he asked Miller to call him at another nightclub if Costello left the Monsignor before Mauro arrived, stating he didn't want to travel there if Frank had already left.

At 10:45, Costello announced he was heading home to receive the important telephone call from Williams. Loretta, who was having a good time, decided to stay and would leave later with the Millers. Costello was joined in the cab ride home by Phil Kennedy, who lived just a few blocks from the Majestic.

Ten minutes, later the cab dropped Costello off in front of the Majestic and he walked in past the doorman, Norval Keith. As soon as Costello entered the lobby a heavyset man rushed past Keith after him. The man, within 10 feet of Costello, called out "This is for you, Frank." At the sound of his name, Costello turned and was looking down the barrel of a gun just as it went off.

Unlike most mob hits, where the killer puts multiple bullets in the head of his victim to make sure the job is done, the gunman incredibly fired just a single shot. The bullet pierced the band on the hat Costello was wearing, hitting him behind the right ear, slicing his scalp without penetrating his skull. The bullet followed a path to the back of his head and exited near the nape of his neck, before bouncing off a few of the walls in the lobby.

The gunman fled as fast as he had entered. He jumped into an awaiting black limousine that had been double-parked for sometime outside the Majestic, waiting for the "Prime Minister's" return. Phil Kennedy, whose cab had been waiting at a red light not far from the apartment, heard the gunshot and jumped out of the cab and headed toward the apartment entrance. The bullet had not even knocked Costello down. He was sitting on a bench in the lobby, holding his head when Kennedy entered. Kennedy quickly haled another cab, which took Costello to the emergency room of Roosevelt Hospital. The hospital was soon overflowing with police.

After being released from the hospital a short while later, Costello was taken to the West Fifty-Fourth Street Station House to be questioned. Costello claimed he did not see his attacker and didn't know who would try to kill him because he didn't have an enemy in the world. Police didn't believe his story, simply because the angle of the bullet wound indicated Costello was facing his would-be assassin.

After realizing that he had suffered little more than a flesh wound, Costello was more upset that he had even allowed himself to be taken to the hospital, knowing all the publicity it had caused. Even more upsetting, the police had used the opportunity to search him and had found the gambling results from the Tropicana on the scrap of paper he had tucked away that morning. Costello called the search illegal and said he wouldn't answer any questions without his lawyer.

By the next day it was announced that 66 detectives had been placed on the investigation, but without help from the victim their efforts were fruitless. Police were sure Costello was lying and that he knew his attacker. They were so upset they even considered jailing Costello as a material witness. By Monday, the police had questioned more than 200 people; still all they had was the description of the gunman provided by the doorman Keith. The newspapers, meanwhile, speculated on a number of theories, but none of them mentioned the name of Genovese.

Costello was ordered to appear before the grand jury on Tuesday afternoon. He invoked his Fifth Amendment privilege and refused to answer questions about the scrap of paper in his pocket. When an order to do so by a judge was ignored, he was sentenced to 30 days for contempt of court and taken to the Tombs prison. Despite protests from the American Civil Liberties Union, regarding the search and removal of papers from his pockets, Costello was transferred to Riker's Island two days later.

Meanwhile, authorities in Nevada, who were in charge of keeping the "hoodlum element" out of the state's gambling casinos, were interested in finding out if Costello had some hidden interests. They were pursuing their own investigation.

On the afternoon of May 22, a judge released Costello from Riker's Island on a $1,000 bond so that he could appeal his 30-day sentence, even though it was half served. When Costello stepped off the ferry from Riker's Island, among the group greeting him were 18 youngsters who cheered for him and crowded around him hoping to shake his hand. Since the shooting, police had ordered round-the-clock protection for Costello and, for the first time in his life, the mob boss had bodyguards. Even when Costello traveled to Sands Point for the Memorial Day weekend, the guards went with him.

"So, I'm walking, and way down at the end I see a little figure walking toward me. He's getting closer, and suddenly I realize it's Harry Truman! He starts to say, 'Hello Frank,' and just as he's about to say it, I say, 'Keep your mouth shut, you dumb bastard. They're watching us. Don't louse us both up.'"

—Frank Costello relating an incident in Sands Point, Long Island, while taking a walk one morning under the watchful eye of the FBI. (Katz, *Uncle Frank*, 1973, p. 13)

On June 11, District Attorney Frank Hogan's office announced it had used a handwriting expert to track down the writer of the note obtained the night of the shooting. It belonged to Michael Tanico, an employee of the Tropicana Hotel, who had previously worked as a cashier at the Beverly Country Club in New Orleans.[39] The figures on the note represented the hotel casino's activity for a 24-day period ending on April 26, 1957.

The Tropicana, which opened on April 3, had 24 owners of record, but Costello was not among them. Nevada gaming laws prevented anyone with a criminal record from having an interest in any of the casinos. Phil Kastel was said to be the "moving spirit" in organizing the Tropicana, but he was forced out after the Nevada Gaming Control Board became aware of his criminal record in February 1957.

On July 16, the New York Police Department announced it was looking for Vincent Gigante for questioning in the shooting of Costello. Gigante, an ex-boxer known as "The Chin," because of his large protruding chin, surrendered to police on August 19. The next day the 29-year-old father of four pled not guilty. When the prosecutor asked that bond to be set at $150,000, Gigante's lawyer claimed his client was only being charged with "attempted assault" and that they were prepared for an immediate hearing. He told the court his client would rather have no bail than the $150,000 the prosecutor was asking; the judge obliged him. On August 22, a grand jury indicted Gigante for attempted murder in the first degree.

The trial for Vincent Gigante did not begin until May 1958. The defendant was represented by Maurice Edelbaum. The key witness for the prosecution was the doorman Norval Keith. On May 15, he testified that Gigante was the man he saw shoot Costello and then run to a waiting black limousine. During cross-examination, however, it was revealed that Keith was blind in one eye and the other eye was impaired. A detective, familiar with Gigante, testified the ex-boxer had lost 30 to 40 pounds between the time of the shooting and his arrest. Costello took the stand on May 20, sticking to the story he had told police for a year, that he had not seen the gunman who shot him.

On May 27, an all-male jury deliberated six hours before returning with a verdict just before midnight. The panel decided that Gigante was not guilty of the shooting of Costello. In *Uncle Frank,* Leonard Katz related:

> A week before Costello was shot, according to Joe Valachi (see Appendix), Vito Genovese, Tony Bender, and Vinnie Mauro held a strategy meeting. Genovese said he had received some interesting information; Frank Costello had turned informer for the Government. That was why Costello had been released. The story of him getting out while his tax case was being appealed was just a clever cover. Costello had turned into a stool pigeon because he was old and sick and couldn't take it anymore. He ordered Mauro to have Costello hit.[40]

Valachi would later claim that the contract to kill Costello was given to Gigante, Thomas "Tommy Ryan" Eboli, and Dominick DeQuatro. The attempted murder of Costello was the first part of a two-part process by Vito Genovese to make himself boss-of-bosses of the New York underworld. The second part occurred on the morning of October 25, 1957, when two gunmen shot and killed Albert Anastasia in a barber's chair at the Park-Sheraton Hotel, the same hotel in which Arnold Rothstein had received his fatal wound. The next step for Vito would be the Apalachin Summit (see Chapter 6 and Appendix).

THE LEGAL BATTLES CONTINUE

Federal Income Tax Case

On June 3, while the search for Costello's shooter was still in progress, the U.S. Supreme Court upheld the sentence of the ailing mob boss for federal income tax evasion. Ten days later, Costello's attorney, Edward Bennett Williams, was in court arguing that the wiretaps on Costello's telephone, in use from 1943 to 1954, were illegal. Information from those taps was used in the tax evasion case. Costello caught a break when the Department of Justice decided to delay the trial until early fall. Williams needed to return to Washington D.C., where he was representing Teamster's big-wig James R. "Jimmy" Hoffa, who was on trial for attempted bribery and obstruction of justice.

On October 8, 1957, during a motion hearing to set aside Costello's conviction, a special agent of the IRS testified that he screened the tax returns of prospective jurors before the mob boss's 1954 tax trial. Williams told McGohey that his client was deprived of a fair trial because the panel did not reflect a true cross section of the community. McGohey allowed Williams to amend his petition to include this information in his request that Costello's conviction be set aside.

When the new hearing began, Williams told the court that because of evidence obtained from an illegal wiretap, a mail watch by U.S. postal authorities, and the jury pool screening, that his client's rights were violated. After the hearing, which lasted several days, McGohey said he would reserve decision. While the judge was considering the case, the U.S. Supreme Court voted unanimously on December 9 that wiretapping by New York State law enforcement was unconstitutional.

Despite the Supreme Court decision, one week later, McGohey declared that "there had been sufficient trial evidence free from wiretap taint to sustain the conviction."[41] The judge ordered the mob boss back to jail to complete his sentence. Costello took his request to remain free on bond pending his appeal to the U.S. Court of Appeals and won a 2-to-1 decision on January 8, 1958.

On June 30, the U.S. Supreme Court refused to review the lower court's decision. Despite the government's best efforts, Costello remained free on bail into the fall when the Supreme Court refused to reconsider its decision on October 13. Three days later, Costello was ordered to surrender. He was taken back to Atlanta to complete his sentence.

In February 1960, Costello was joined in Atlanta by Vito Genovese, who began serving a 15-year term for a narcotics conviction (see Chapter 6). Attorney George Wolf related the following story in his book, *Frank Costello: Prime Minister of the Underworld.* Without revealing any names or dates, Wolf claimed he was summoned to Atlanta by an anonymous phone caller who said, "Frank wants to see you." Wolf stated he went to Atlanta the next day, and, while waiting to see Costello, was called to the warden's office.

According to Wolf, the warden told him that Genovese was going to be killed. "The inmates here are angry at Genovese. They think he informed on Frank's tax stuff, and that's why Frank is in prison. We don't have enough guards in Georgia to save Genovese."[42]

When Wolf met with Costello, the jailed mob boss asked that the attorney set up a meeting with Genovese. At the meeting, a picture was to be taken of the two men shaking hands and that picture would be sent back to New York. Just how that was to quell the unrest in the prison Wolf didn't bother to explain. Wolf never revealed what happened at the meeting or if he was even in attendance, leaving the reader to reach his own conclusion.

On June 20, 1961, after serving three-and-a-half-years of a five-year sentence, Costello was released from the Atlanta Penitentiary. He was brought back to New York City to complete his 30-day contempt of court sentence at Riker's Island for refusing to answer questions about the Tropicana receipts found in his pocket the night he was shot. Released from Riker's Island on the morning of June 28, Costello went home to deal with the denaturalization fight that was still ongoing.

Denaturalization Proceedings

On June 11, 1957, the same day Frank Hogan announced that Costello's note had been tied to receipts earned at the Tropicana Hotel, government attorneys asked the U.S. Court of Appeals to reinstate its denaturalization suit against Costello. In a decision handed down on April 7, 1958, U.S. Supreme Court upheld Costello's case.

The government persisted and in January 1959, it was back in court. The case was heard without a jury by Federal Judge Archie O. Dawson. On February 20, the judge ruled that Costello should lose his citizenship for concealing his bootlegging activities at the time of his naturalization. In a 35-page decision Dawson declared:

> An application to become a United States citizen is a serious matter and is entitled to be treated with more respect than an application to join the corner pinochle club.
>
> It would be a sad day if such an oath could be taken with fingers crossed and tongue-in-cheek, as apparently was done by Costello.
>
> The willful misrepresentation and active concealment in which Costello was engaged were of a nature which would warrant an order directing his denaturalization.

With the trial over, talk quickly turned to deporting the jailed mob boss. The first response to this idea came from his native Italy. The newspaper *Il Secolo D'Italia* of Rome blasted the United States for thinking it was all right to send the hood back to the land of his birth.

An appeal to reverse the ruling made by Costello's lawyers was denied in February 1960 by the U.S. Court of Appeals. Three months later, the U.S. Supreme Court agreed to hear the case. On February 21, 1961, the Supreme Court upheld the decision to strip Costello of his citizenship. Following the decision, Attorney General Robert F. Kennedy said the government would see whether grounds existed to deport Costello.

Although still in the Atlanta Penitentiary, Costello was ordered to register as an alien and show cause at an April 10 meeting as to why he should not be deported. At an INS hearing, it was ruled that Costello's conviction on two charges of income tax evasion constituted two crimes of moral turpitude. On January 2, 1962, the Board of Immigration Appeals upheld the deportation order against Costello.

At a hearing before the U.S. Court of Appeals on June 6, Williams contended the tax crime was committed while Costello was a citizen, should be construed as a single crime, and could not be the basis for deportation as an alien. The Appeals Court upheld the deportation order of the Board of Immigration Appeals on December 4, 1962, and Costello prepared for another round before the U.S. Supreme Court.

On April 22, 1963, the Supreme Court granted a review of his deportation order. In reviewing the conviction, the high court ruled in Costello's favor, stating that the income tax evasion convictions did not fit the law under which the INS ordered his deportation. The decision ended for good the government's efforts to send Costello back to his native Italy.

AFTERMATH

After the government's failure to deport him, Costello seemed to settle into retirement. He returned to some of his old routines such as taking a steam bath at the Biltmore in the afternoon and holding court at the Waldorf. But the former mob boss kept a low profile until the afternoon of June 3, 1964, when he made front-page news again.

Costello was having lunch at Dinty Moore's on Broadway with Jeremiah "Jerry" Kelly, a bookmaker. Unknown to Costello and Kelly, IRS agents were conducting a crackdown on Broadway bookmakers who had failed to purchase federal wagering stamps. Costello found himself suddenly being served with a subpoena to appear before a federal grand jury. This was followed quickly by police officers arresting him and Kelly for vagrancy.

Costello, who was used to carrying wads of cash, had only $6 with him. The 73-year-old former mob boss was booked and taken to criminal court, where the judge dismissed the charge against him. The American Civil Liberties Union came to his defense again, deploring the manner in which Costello had been arrested. The subpoena has been issued by U.S. Attorney Robert Morgenthau's office for Costello to be questioned about gambling activities in the city. The next day, Costello appeared before the panel for five minutes before walking out of the courthouse and into a crowd of reporters and cameramen.

Costello was subpoenaed to appear before a grand jury investigating gambling in Manhattan in May 1970. When surrounded by reporters after leaving the courthouse, Costello told them, "I'm retired. I don't know any more about this than you do."

On November 21, 1970, Costello was back in the news when Nicholas Gage, an organized crime reporter for the *New York Times* wrote:

> Law enforcement officials say that a leadership vacuum in the largest organized crime family in New York has forced Frank Costello, once known as "the prime minister of the underworld," to come out of retirement and assume a role in the city's underworld hierarchy.[43]

Gage reported that police believed the "vacuum" had been created by the death of Vito Genovese in February 1969, and the recent incarceration of Gerardo Catena in New Jersey, as well as health problems suffered by Tommy Eboli. The article went on to say that Costello's role was "that of an authority figure who advises on plans and mediates in disputes and is not involved in the day-to-day operation of rackets." Some found it hard to believe that such a move could have taken place without the blessing of Carlo Gambino, by then the dominant underworld leader in New York City, but Gambino had been seen in conference with Costello at the Waldorf.

Costello was alleged to have been a frequent visitor to the Central Park South apartment of Charley "The Blade" Tourine. The illiterate mobster was said to have sought Costello's help while trying to run the Genovese Family during Eboli's absence.

Another mob leader Costello was seen in conference with was Joe Colombo. Costello reportedly warned Colombo about the unwanted publicity his picketing of FBI headquarters and his Italian-American Unity Day rallies were bringing to the underworld. Colombo didn't listen to the elder statesman's advice any more than he did to Gambino's edict to step down as president of the Italian-American Civil Rights League. On June 28, 1971, Colombo was critically wounded at the second Italian-American Unity Day rally and remained in a vegetative state until his death in May 1978.

On February 7, 1973, Costello suffered a mild heart attack in his Majestic apartment. While recuperating at Doctor's Hospital, he decided to act on an idea he had been considering for months—to have a book written about himself. He sent word to writer Peter Maas, who authored *The Valachi Papers* and *Serpico* and would later write *Underboss: The Story of Sammy Gravano,* that when he got out of the hospital, he would consent to be interviewed by the accomplished journalist.

People who knew him could only wonder what Frank Costello would have revealed; however, the opportunity to work on the book never came. At 7:30 on the morning of February 18, Costello suffered a fatal heart attack.

At Loretta's request, Costello's former underworld associates stayed away from the wake and burial. The wake was held at the Frank E. Campbell Funeral Chapel on 81st Street. On the morning of February 21, a small private service was held in the funeral home's chapel. About 50 people were in attendance. Afterwards, a hearse took Costello's body to St. Michael's Cemetery in East Elmhurst, Queens, where Costello was laid to rest in the granite mausoleum that had brought him trouble during his income tax evasion case.

The story of the Costello mausoleum was not over. On January 25, 1974, a bomb exploded, blasting the bronze doors off the mausoleum. There was speculation that it was a warning that a new "mob war" for control of the underworld was at hand. "True or not, police and criminal experts had to smile when assessing the incident, for Frank, who was the most famous and most publicized criminal of his time, could still get television and newspaper space after he died. Fame had trailed him beyond the grave."[44]

NOTES

1. Leonard Katz, *Uncle Frank* (New York: Drake Publishers, 1973), pp. 34–35.

2. This information comes from Leonard Katz's biography *Uncle Frank*. In *Frank Costello,* by Henry A. Zeiger, the author claimed Geigerman was introduced to Costello by her girlfriend. Zeiger stated that Loretta was Protestant and the two were married at Saint Michael's Roman Catholic Church. In *Frank Costello: The Gangster with a Thousand Faces,* author David Hanna stated that Geigerman was Jewish, but they got married in a Protestant church on September 22, 1914.

3. Blackwell's Island was a narrow island, less than two miles long, in the East River of New York City, between Manhattan and Queens. From 1686 to 1921, it was called Blackwell's Island. On the island were hospitals, asylums, and correctional facilities. It 1921, the name was changed to Welfare Island. The Welfare Penitentiary serviced criminals from the New York City area until Riker's Island Penitentiary opened in 1932. Today the island is mostly residential and business and is called Roosevelt Island.

4. When the government was seeking to deport Costello in the 1950s, an Immigration and Naturalization Service investigation revealed: "Costello never did serve in the military forces of the United States, although he was apparently called for induction. The exact circumstances surrounding his near-induction are still shrouded in the enigmatic cloth of the past and this investigation has been unable to pierce that veil of obscurity. It has been ascertained, however, that notwithstanding his attempt to gain exemption by virtue of his alienage, Costello was actually called for induction by his local draft board. How he avoided induction is still a mystery."

5. Katz, *Uncle Frank,* p. 54.

6. Biographies on Rothstein support this. In fact, Leo Katcher, in *The Big Bankroll,* digressed to the Costello biographers in regard to any early connections between the two men. Katcher wrote:

Frank Costello's biographers report: "As early as 1921, it was common knowledge in New York that Arnold Rothstein . . . was associated with Costello in various forms of business . . . Costello got his first instruction in the art of operating gambling rackets from the master financier of the underworld."—Leo Katcher, *The Big Bankroll* (New Rochelle: New York, Arlington House, 1958), p. 246.

In Katcher's statement, it should be noted, he was referring to gambling operations rather than bootlegging at this early stage of the 1920s, something Costello wasn't even involved with yet.

Regarding evidence of the loan Rothstein made to Costello before his death, on February 14, 1929, a complaint was filed against Costello by the estate of Arnold Rothstein. Costello did not answer and a judgment was entered in the amount of $35,000. The case dragged on for years until July 14, 1942, when Costello denied ever having been served the complaint or being notified of the judgment against him. On October 5, 1943, an attorney for the estate told a court referee that Costello had settled with them for $5,000.

7. Biographers for all of these individuals seemingly have different dates and circumstances as to how the four came together. In the *Last Testament of Lucky Luciano,* the mobster has all four of them working together as early as 1917, despite the fact that Siegel would only have been about 12 at the time.

8. Katz, *Uncle Frank,* pp. 68–69.

9. In the book *Double Cross,* a biography of Chicago mob boss Sam Giancana, author Chuck Giancana, claimed his brother once handled a dispute between Costello and Kennedy. Without putting a date to it, he claimed Costello put out a "contract" on Kennedy and that the political patriarch came to him to save his life. In the book, Chuck Giancana related how much his brother admired Costello:

Mooney [Giancana's nickname] said Costello had style like nobody else. He knew how to handle himself among the rich and famous, the politicians and kings. He called the judges "his boys," "Man oh man, I wanted to be as powerful as he was . . . I watched his every move. If there ever was a guy I wanted to be like, it was Frank Costello."

The book was panned by Sam Giancana's daughter, Antoinette, as being an untrue account of her father's life.

10. *New York Times,* December 4, 1925, "Biggest Liquor Ring Smashed by Arrests of 20 Accused Here."

11. Ibid.

12. Ibid.

13. One of the men named in the indictment was Frank Nitto of Chicago, better known as Frank Nitti. *New York Times,* January 27, 1926, "Dwyer Is Indicted With 60 Others in Wide Liquor Plot."

14. Robert H. Prall, and Norton Mockridge, *This Is Costello on the Spot* (Greenwich, CT: Fawcett Publications, 1957, third printing), p. 21.

15. Katz, *Uncle Frank*, p. 78.

16. Former judge of the New York State Court of Appeals Samuel Seabury was appointed to investigate crime and corruption in New York City's magistrates' court and the police department. The appointment came on August 26, 1930, while Seabury was vacationing in London. He quickly assembled a staff of lawyers, which became known as the Seabury Commission. The focus of the group was to investigate the purchasing of magistrates positions and accusations of police extortion through false arrests. The Seabury Committee held public hearings during the summer of 1931, at which "one Tammany figure after another was exposed in dramatic overtones."

New York County Sheriff Thomas A. Farley was one of the committee's targets. After his appearance, then-Governor Franklin D. Roosevelt removed him "because of his unfitness to hold public office and his failure to explain the source of his wealth."

The biggest name caught in the investigation was flamboyant New York City Mayor James J. "Jimmy" Walker. After a highly publicized hearing, in which Walker was questioned by Seabury, Governor Roosevelt ordered public hearings to determine the mayor's fitness to hold office. Roosevelt presided over the hearings. On August 1, 1932, while in the middle of his second term, Walker resigned his office and left for Europe.

After Walker's ouster, Seabury was offered the Republican nomination for mayor. He declined to run and instead selected Fiorella LaGuardia, who ran and won in November 1933 as the Republican/Fusion candidate.

Samuel Seabury died on May 7, 1958 at the age of 85.

17. Less than 72 hours after the execution of Louis "Lepke" Buchalter on March 3, 1944, The *New York Times* reported in a front page story that, "detectives in all police precincts of the city have been ordered to bring in Frank Costello." The reason, according to the article, was that Buchalter had allegedly told Frank Hogan during an interview just hours before his death that Costello had contributed $25,000 to the campaign of a "candidate for high public office." The newspaper could not verify who had issued the order to pick up Costello. Police Commissioner Lewis J. Valentine ignored questions from reporters, and both Hogan and Mayor LaGuardia denied any knowledge of the order. The story was never verified and quickly faded from the news.

18. Katz, *Uncle Frank,* p. 118.

19. Ibid., p. 121.

20. Thomas Kessner, *Fiorella H. LaGuardia and the Making of Modern New York* (New York: McGraw-Hill Publishing, 1989), p. 290.

21. *New York Times,* August 28, 1943, "Gangster Backed Aurelio for Bench."

22. Thomas Aurelio was still a sitting judge on the New York Supreme Court when he died on January 5, 1973, at the age of 81. He was buried in Calvary Cemetery, in Woodside, Queens. Many people agreed, including District Attorney Frank Hogan, that Aurelio was an excellent judge.

23. *New York Times,* October 28, 1944, "Costello's $27,200 Pays U.S. Tax Lien."

24. *New York Times,* February 2, 1947, "Jury Returns $27,200 to Costello, but U.S. Waits to Take It for Taxes."

25. Ibid.

26. *New York Times,* December 21, "1946, Costello Denied Underworld Links."

27. Ibid.

28. Biographer Leonard Katz puts this meeting "in early 1947." Attorney George Wolf in his biography, *Frank Costello: Prime Minister of the Underworld,* doesn't put a date to Costello's trip to Havana and never mentions that a meeting was held there.

29. The media, particularly the *New York Sun,* would question the fact that Hoffman's son was hired by the city, first as a confidential investigator in the office of Hugo E. Rogers and later as secretary to the Department of Marine and Aviation. The 27-year-old Richard W. Hoffman had been a decorated Army Air Force pilot who had flown 46 bombardier missions over Germany during the war until he was injured and disabled.

30. *New York Times,* January 26, 1949, "Costello Retires As Aide to Charity."

31. *New York Times,* October 24, 1950, "Impellitteri Links Pecora, Costello."

32. George Wolf with Joseph DiMona, *Frank Costello: Prime Minister of the Underworld* (New York: William Morrow & Company, 1974), p. 202.

33. Ibid.

34. *New York Times,* March 14, 1951, "Costello TV's First Headless Star; Only His Hands Entertain Audience."

35. During the testimony of William O'Dwyer, the former district attorney and mayor, now ambassador to Mexico, claimed he had been sent to question Costello on orders from his army superiors, to investigate a fraud involving a government clothing contract.

36. *New York Times,* January 12, 1952, "Judge Ryan Denies Costello Protest."

37. *New York Times,* August 16, 1952, "Costello Begins 18 Months' Term for Contempt of the U.S. Senate."

38. *New York Times,* September 28, 1956, "Costello Testifies In Citizenship Case."

39. The Beverly Country Club closed shortly after its ownership was exposed during the Kefauver Hearings. Michael Tanico quit his job at the Tropicana after New York authorities tied him to the note in Costello's possession the night of the shooting. Louis Lederer was the Tropicana's major shareholder. Lederer, a former Chicago bookmaker, served as a casino manager at the Tropicana. The Nevada Gambling Control Board recommended his removal after the incident.

40. Katz, *Uncle Frank,* p. 207.

41. *The New York Times,* December 17, 1957, "Costello Loses Wiretap Appeal."

42. Wolf with DiMona, *Frank Costello: Prime Minister of the Underworld,* pp. 262–263.

43. *New York Times,* November 21, 1970, "Costello Reported Back in Crime Role."

44. Wolf with DiMona, *Frank Costello: Prime Minister of the Underworld,* p. 244.

BIBLIOGRAPHY

Biographies of Costello

Brennan, Bill. *The Frank Costello Story.* Derby, CT: Monarch Books, 1962.

Hanna, David. *Frank Costello: The Gangster with a Thousand Faces.* New York: Tower Publications, 1974.

Katz, Leonard. *Uncle Frank.* New York: Drake Publishers, 1973.

Prall, Robert H., and Norton Mockridge. *This Is Costello on the Spot.* Greenwich, CT: Fawcett Publications, 1957.

Walsh, George. *Public Enemies; The Mayor, The Mob, And The Crime That Was,* New York: W. W. Norton & Company, 1980.

Wolf, George. with Joseph DiMona. *Frank Costello: Prime Minister of the Underworld.* New York: William Morrow & Company, 1974.

Zeiger, Henry A. *Frank Costello.* New York: Berkley Publishing Corporation, 1974.

Other Publications

Kessner, Thomas. *Fiorella H. LaGuardia and the Making of Modern New York.* New York: McGraw-Hill, 1989.

Mitgang, Herbert. *The Man Who Rode the Tiger: The Life and Times of Judge Samuel Seabury.* New York: J. B. Lippincott, 1963.

Peterson, Virgil W. *The Mob: 200 Years of Organized Crime in New York.* Ottawa, IL: Green Hill Publishers, 1983.

5

CARLO GAMBINO

AKA "DON CARLO"
AUGUST 24, 1902–OCTOBER 15, 1976

Carlo Gambino was the last Mafia Don who could truly be called "Boss of Bosses." Gambino was the master of intrigue. Smart and devious, he proved time and again to be the master of the double-cross as he schemed his was to the top of the New York City underworld. In doing so, he banked on his ability to keep a low profile, stay out of the lime light, and avoid public scrutiny at all times. When all else failed and the authorities attempted to put him on public display, he resorted to a tactic that served him well during the last 20 years of his life. Gambino and his lawyers used his heart ailment to continuously thwart the government's effort to question him before a grand jury and to deport him. Although many believed he faked the ailment, two things are for certain: There was absolutely no doubt that a serious heart condition existed, and Gambino embellished that condition to his own advantage.

Gambino reached the pinnacle of organized crime not by simply eliminating his enemies, but by using his manipulative powers to promote people he trusted and who would become beholden to him into positions of power atop the other New York City crime families.

Don Carlo's devotion to family was so deep that he married his own cousin. In the end, however, his decision to name Paul Castellano, his cousin and brother-in-law, as his successor would result in a bloody coup d'état and the destruction of the crime family that bears his name.

EARLY YEARS

Little is known of Carlo Gambino's early life. In fact, the first 55 years of his existence seemed to have passed with little notice. Many of the underworld figures who got their start during the Prohibition Era made a name for themselves during this lawless period, but it would not be until the late 1950s that the Gambino name would come to be recognized.

Gambino was born in Palermo, Sicily, on August 24, 1902.[1] Carlo's parents were Tommasco and Felice Gambino. Carlo's mother (nee Castellano) gave birth to three more sons, Paola (Paul) on November 20, 1904; Giuseppe (Joseph) on September 4, 1908, and Anthony in 1919. In addition, Carlo had two sisters—Josephine Giammona, born on 1901, and Frances DeMilo, born in 1915. A cousin, Thomas Masotto, was born in 1907.

Biographical references state that Carlo's "boyhood idol" was Don Vito Cascio Ferro, the "uncrowned King of Sicily."[2] Ferro carved his name in the folklore of the Sicilian Mafia when he murdered New York City Police Detective Lieutenant Joseph Petrosino. The famed detective, who led a successful attack against the Black Hand menace in the Italian ghettos of New York, knew that most of the extortionists he sought were transplanted criminals from Italy and Sicily and had records in their homeland. Petrosino traveled to Palermo seeking information on these individuals.

On the evening of March 12, 1909, Petrosino was heading back to his hotel room after finishing dinner. While he was passing near the Garibaldi statue near the Piazza Marine, two men walked up behind him. One of the men pulled a gun and fired several shots into the back and head of the unsuspecting police lieutenant, killing him instantly.

The tragic, cold-blooded murder of Joseph Petrosino made worldwide news. His funeral in New York City was a public spectacle. But in Palermo, where the murder was never solved, his killer Don Ferro was awarded hero status. An eight-year-old Carlo Gambino visited the site of the slaying with his schoolmates. Instead of mourning the loss of the decorated police officer, Gambino accorded his cowardly murderer the same reverence as many Americans gave outlaws Jesse James and John Dillinger.

One of Gambino's biographers, Paul Meskil, a New York Daily News investigative reporter, claimed in his book, Don Carlo: Boss of Bosses, that "exactly when Carlo Gambino joined the Mafia is not known to any outsiders. Investigators who have checked his background as thoroughly as possible believe he took the blood oath before he left Sicily in 1921."[3] Meskil paints a picture of Gambino as a Mafia recruit, dedicated to the sinister trade and ready to move to America where the Mafia "had established branches in New York, New Orleans, Chicago, and several other U.S. cities."[4] This was the path that Carlo Gambino had chosen.

At the age of 19, as Gambino put out to sea for the United States in the late fall of 1921, he was described as "a short, chunky man, 5 feet 7 and about 160 pounds, with brown eyes, bushy black hair brushed straight back from his forehead and a nose like an eagle's beak."[5] Gambino was the solitary passenger aboard the SS Vincenzo Floria as it sailed for America. On the night of December 23, the freighter arrived at Norfolk Harbor in Virginia.

One of the myths about Carlo Gambino is that he left Sicily because of the pressure that Italian Dictator Benito Mussolini placed on the Sicilian Mafia once he seized power. Il Duce became prime minister of Italy in late October 1922. After a trip to Sicily in 1924, he named the ruthless Cesare Mori prefect of Palermo, making him the highest ranking government official on the island. Mori began systemically jailing known members of the Mafia. Gambino had left Sicily for America in 1921, however, long before either event occurred.

There was no fanfare when Gambino disembarked the *Vincenzo Floria*. His arrival was described as "jumping ship." Gambino's first step on American soil resulted in his breaking the law; he had entered the country illegally. As so many southern Europeans were entering the country legally through Ellis Island each year, it's safe to assume that Gambino had already established a criminal record in his homeland. Why else would he have come to America as an illegal alien?

The story goes that relatives from New York or Massachusetts—he had extended family in both locations—greeted Gambino when he arrived. Blood relations would become important to Gambino over the years in both his own family and his crime family. Living in New York City already was his uncle with sons Paul and Peter Castellano, and Thomas Masotta, all first cousins on Carlo's mother's side. In the years that followed, Gambino would book passage for his two brothers, Paola and Giuseppe, to join him in America.

In addition to these relatives, the city was also home to one of Carlo's earliest childhood friends. Gaetano "Thomas" Lucchese, like Gambino, would become the godfather to a crime family that bears his name.

THE NEW WORLD

Gambino moved into a flat on Navy Street in Brooklyn. The Castellano family operated a trucking firm in the city, and some accounts had Gambino working in a position provided by family members.[6] By late 1921, at the time Carlo arrived, however, the Volstead Act had been the law of the land for nearly two years. There is no record of the kind of work Gambino became involved with once he got settled, but there's a good chance that it had something to do with illegal liquor.

Gambino soon looked up his friend "Tommy" Lucchese, who had arrived in New York with his parents in 1911. Now living in East Harlem, the two young men spent little time together, as Lucchese soon went away to prison for stealing an automobile.

As the 1920s "roared" on, Gambino became more entrenched in the bootleg business. There is no indication of who his sponsor into the trade was, but Gambino became a member of a gang led by Al Mineo, who answered to Giuseppe "Joe the Boss" Masseria's outfit:

> Carlo was assigned to the Masseria gang's bootlegging business. He learned every phase of the operation from distillery to distribution, from smuggling ship to speakeasy. He worked in the moonshine stills and on the trucks. He learned where the rum fleet anchored, how to dodge the Coast Guard and hijackers, the best spots to grab a rival mob's shipments, and how to persuade speakeasy owners to buy Masseria potables.[7]

In November 1930, Gambino was arrested on a "suspicious person" charge in Lowell, Massachusetts. The reason for the arrest and what Gambino was doing there have been lost to history, but the charge, like many of that nature, was dismissed in court. Gambino had relatives in Massachusetts, which may have been the reason for the visit.

Nearly three years passed before Gambino again found himself under arrest in the Bay State. Police apprehended Gambino in Brockton after he was accused of participating in a scam called the "handkerchief and pill game," which relieved one of the locals of nearly $1,200. After his arraignment, Gambino was released on bond and quickly fled the state.

On October 8, 1934, Gambino was arrested by New York City police and charged with possession of unpaid tax alcohol and carrying on a business of wholesale and retail liquor without a license. He posted a bond of $2,000 the next day and at his release was rearrested as a fugitive from justice for his Brockton crime. Gambino waived extradition and was released to the Brockton police on October 22. On February 28, 1935, the charges were dismissed after Gambino paid restitution of $1,000.

During the first two years of the 1930s, New York City's underworld was going through a major facelift called the Castellammarese War (see Appendix). Gambino continued to report to Al Mineo until Mineo's murder in November 1930. The gang then came under the control of Frank "Don Cheech" Scalise, who quickly changed allegiance and sided with the Maranzano faction. Scalise was later replaced as boss of the family by Vincent Mangano.

Gambino, playing no major role in the Castellammarese War, was a survivor. Joseph Valachi (see Appendix) provided the first indication that Gambino had risen through the ranks. In discussing his own role, he described the wounding of Paul Gambino in a shooting in which he was the getaway driver. Called on the carpet by an angry Salvatore Maranzano, he was told that Paul Gambino was a "nobody," so why were they shooting at him?

Valachi explained, "Well, everything turned out for the best. Paul Gambino wasn't nothing, but his brother Carlo was a big man with the Masseria group. When Carlo got word of the shooting, figuring he might be next, he brought all his people over with us."[8] It was during the Castellammarese conflict that Gambino displayed his first act in the art of deception, a trait that would become the trademark of his career. His defection to the Maranzano faction brought him back together with Tommy Lucchese, who was in high standing in the gang.

In his autobiography, Joseph Bonanno provides this picture of Gambino during the Castellammarese War. His reflection indicates one of two things—either that he wasn't aware of the friendship that Gambino and Lucchese shared before the conflict, or during the war the two men had become bitter enemies:

> Another member of the Mineo Family who was to join our side [Maranzano] was Carlo Gambino, at that time a low-ranking member. Before he defected, Gambino had drawn the ire of Tommy Lucchese—for what reason I don't know. An attempt was made on Gambino's life, but the gunman mistook Carlo's look-alike brother for his target and shot the wrong man. Carlo's brother partially lost his ear but didn't die. Ironically, after the war, Carlo Gambino and Tommy Lucchese became good friends and their children intermarried.[9]

After the murder of "Joe the Boss" Masseria, Gambino remained with the South Brooklyn gang headed by the Manganos. It was a curious setup because the underboss of the family seemed to carry more power and influence than the brothers who ruled it. Albert Anastasia, however, was calmly biding his time and all Gambino could do was watch.

FAMILY MAN AND PUBLICITY

Gambino was married on December 5, 1926, in Brooklyn to Catherine Castellano, his first cousin and the older sister of Paul.[10] Carlo was 24, Catherine 19. At the time Carlo was living in the Bronx and listed his occupation as "butcher." The Castellano family certainly appeared to be close knit. Gambino's mother was a Castellano; her sister became a Masotto. In New York City, this second generation of offspring—Castellano, Gambino, and Masotto—became a tight-knit clan. The closest friendship within the family was the one between Carlo and Paul Castellano. Cousins, the two men were also now brothers-in-law.

Carlo and Catherine became the parents of four children: three sons—Thomas Francis, Joseph Carlo, and Carl Gambino, Jr.—and one daughter—Phyllis Thomas, the oldest child, married Frances Lucchese on April 16, 1961; she was the daughter of Gambino's friend and fellow crime boss, Tommy Lucchese. Phyllis Gambino married a physician, Dr. Thomas Sinatra, no relation to the famous entertainer.

While their father was alive, the two sons were kept out of the "crime family" business. According to mob turncoat Joseph Cantalupo:

> Gambino's sons, Tommy and Joe, stayed pretty straight. They ran a trucking business in the garment center; they still do. I can remember Joe Gambino, up to his elbows in piece-work, with sweat dripping from his forehead and his shirt, busting his chops from dawn to dark at a miserable Brooklyn clothing sweatshop that he ran for his father. The Gambino boys always helped their old man—but then, that's what a son is supposed to do.[11]

The Gambino brothers controlled the garment industry through their ownership of Consolidated Carriers, which had a monopoly on the trucking in the garment center. In 1992, after an elaborate sting operation orchestrated by the Manhattan district attorney's office, the monopoly was broken when the brothers agreed to quit the garment center after pleading guilty to restraint of trade. They paid a fine of $12 million, but avoided prison time. It should be noted that the brothers were involved in a number of philanthropic efforts over the years involving New York City hospitals.

Gambino shunned publicity and advised his family and gang members to do the same. Gambino's low-key lifestyle included the homes he owned and the cars he purchased. Although it was reported that this lifestyle extended to his wardrobe, nearly all FBI records on Gambino described him as a "flashy dresser." He allowed himself one vanity. His license plate read "CG 1."

Gambino lived in a two-story dwelling at 2230 Ocean Parkway in Brooklyn. From the outside there appeared to be nothing elaborate about the home. But inside, the 13-room house was decorated with expensive Italian furniture, marble, and "antique Italian figurines, china, and glassware."[12]

In addition to the Ocean Parkway home, in May 1961, Gambino purchased a waterfront estate on Long Island at 34 Club Drive in Massapequa. The Gambinos liked to spend their summers there and their winters in Florida.

Another way Gambino eluded the publicity that was shed on his predecessors was to avoid the company of public figures—politicians, sports figures, and entertainers. The one exception seemed to be the infamous picture taken of him with singer Frank Sinatra, which included a number of organized crime figures.[13]

When Carlo's devoted wife Catherine died on August 6, 1971, Gambino notified his influential friends and associates not to come to the funeral home and to refrain from sending floral arrangements or telegrams that could be traced by law enforcement. During the wake, government agents and local police, in unmarked vehicles parked near the Cusimano & Russo Funeral Home on West Sixth Street in Brooklyn, scrutinized the crowds that came to pay their respects.

CRIMINAL ACTIVITY IN THE 1930s AND 1940s

The earliest criminal records on Gambino were kept by the Alcohol Tax Unit of the U.S. Treasury Department. A report dated November 26, 1934, stated, "Since the coming of Prohibition, there has been in the City of New York and vicinity and extending into the state of New Jersey a notorious daring group of bootleggers known as the Gambino outfit. The principal members of this outfit are: Carlo Gambino; his brother Paul Gambino; and their cousin Anthony Gambino."

One of Carlo Gambino's two financial coupes during this period came when he gained a "virtual monopoly" on illicit alcohol production in New York City and beyond. After the end of Prohibition in December 1933, he acquired whiskey stills in four states—Maryland, New Jersey, New York, and Pennsylvania—convinced that there would still be a serious demand for low-priced, untaxed liquor. With bootleggers willing to sell out cheap, he purchased additional stills and distilling equipment. This foresight resulted in the first of several "fortunes" Gambino accumulated during his lifetime.[14]

Gambino also purchased a number of commercial alcohol concerns, from which he diverted shipments of pure alcohol to his illegal stills. When the redistillation process failed to remove all the denaturants, the finished product would remain unfit for human consumption. Gambino apparently decided this was no reason not to sell the product, however, and some customers were sickened by the alcohol; others died.[15]

Because the entire operation was illegal, Gambino and his associates throughout the four states never paid taxes on their income. It was the obtaining of some 114,000 gallons of denatured alcohol from legitimate commercial companies that finally tipped off the government to the operation in 1937. On June 17, Gambino was arrested in Philadelphia for violation of Internal Revenue Service laws. The next month a federal grand jury in Brooklyn named Gambino and 35 others in an indictment containing the following counts:

- Conspiracy to redistill commercial alcohol
- Conspiracy to defraud the government of internal revenue tax
- Possession of liquor on which no federal tax was paid
- Illegal transportation of alcohol

The investigation followed the denatured alcohol from the warehouses to the illegal stills located in New York City, upstate New York, and New Jersey. The agents reported that the still operations were run in such a shoddy manner that alcohol "had been treated so inefficiently as to be poisonous."[16]

In the spring of 1939, the trial was held in federal court in Philadelphia, where Gambino was convicted of tax evasion. On May 20, he was sentenced to 22 months at the federal penitentiary in Lewisburg, Pennsylvania, and fined $2,500. Although many biographies claim that Gambino served this time, or at least a portion of it, Lewisburg prison records show Gambino was committed on May 23, 1939, but released four days later pending an appeal of the case. On January 21, 1941, the prison was advised that judgment was reversed and a new trial ordered.

It was the stiffest sentence Gambino ever faced. In early 1940, however, his conviction, along with the original indictment, was overturned when the U.S. Supreme Court ruled that the wiretap evidence that helped convict the defendants had been obtained illegally by the government.

With that ruling the case was dead in the water, but the government struck again with a new indictment issued by another federal grand jury in Brooklyn. This time, Gambino was one of 10 men charged with unpaid taxes from their illegal still operations totaling $3 million. When the case finally came to court, Gambino, his brother Paul, and four others were looking at almost $1.4 million in unpaid taxes. Despite the expensive and long, drawn-out investigation, a federal judge decided to send Gambino to jail for just 30 days. It would be the longest incarceration of Gambino's criminal career.

Government agents were angry but not deterred by this light sentence, and before the end of 1940, they were on the move again. On the day after Christmas, Gambino was arrested at his Ocean Parkway home and charged with being an illegal alien. It was the second time since his "ship jumping" arrival that Gambino faced immigration officials. Gambino was aware of the problems his illegal entry might have and decided to address the matter. During the summer of 1935, he traveled to Montreal, Canada, and tried to get a visa to enter the United States legally. The visa was refused by the U.S. Consulate in Montreal on July 29. Later that same day, he reentered the United States through Rouses Point, New York. On November 13, 1936, an arrest warrant was issued accusing him of entering the country without a visa. On January 21, 1937, without explanation, the warrant was canceled. Decades later, when efforts to deport Gambino reached their peak, the mobster claimed his trip to Canada and back, "wiped the slate clean," and it could no longer be said he had entered the United States illegally.

After this latest incident, Gambino's lawyers were able to stall the proceedings until the wartime activities in Europe made it impossible to deport Carlo back to his native land. The case would lay dormant for years, but would not disappear from the files of the Immigration and Naturalization Service (INS).

Gambino's second money-making extravaganza came during World War II after the government introduced ration stamps to the country. Believing it would help the war effort, the government announced that commodities like gasoline, meat, and certain groceries would be strictly rationed. The Office of Price Administration (OPA) was established to print and distribute the stamps, as well as administrate the program.

The American consumer needed the stamps to purchase gasoline for their automobiles and steak for the family dinner. People quickly grew tired of the restrictions and sought a way to get around the rationing limitations. The answer was to purchase the stamps on the black market, paying a premium for the opportunity.

When Gambino and others saw the profits that could be made from being the supplier of these stamps, several break-ins occurred at OPA administrative offices; safes were broken into and stamps stolen. Gambino realized that continuing this practice could be risky. Before he could contemplate his next move, OPA officials handed him the solution on a silver platter. These government jobs were mostly low-pay or no-pay positions, many staffed by volunteers. The previous theft of the stamps opened a few greedy eyes within the offices, and these unscrupulous officials quickly figured out how they could make money, too. The ration stamps were soon being sold directly to the mob.

It should be noted that Gambino's participation in the rationing stamp racket was revealed by Joe Valachi in 1963. Gambino was never arrested for these crimes, and there is no record in his FBI file of his activities in this field before Valachi's revelation.

Something that did appear in his FBI file that raised a few eyebrows was that in 1948, the Bureau of Narcotics reported that Carlo and Paul Gambino "exercised control of narcotics smuggling activities" and the smuggling of Sicilian aliens into the United States.

Ten years later, more details came to light. John T. Cusack, district supervisor of the Bureau of Narcotics, testified before the New York State Joint Legislative Committee on Government Operations on January 9, 1958. He stated that the bureau was interested in the Apalachin Summit (see Appendix) attendees because "three narcotics violators of major importance were present." In his report on Gambino he stated:

> During the spring of 1948, reliable information obtained from a Bureau of Narcotics source indicated that Carlo Gambino traveled clandestinely to Palermo, Sicily, where he joined his brother, Paul, who had fled to Italy to avoid prosecution in a Federal alcohol tax case. The Gambinos were reported to exercise control of the narcotic smuggling activities between the Mafia element in Palermo and the United States on behalf of Salvatore Lucania [Lucky Luciano] and during 1948, both Gambino brothers met with Lucania at the home of their relatives in Palermo, Sicily.
>
> Investigation conducted by the Bureau of Narcotics after 30 some odd Sicilian aliens had been smuggled into the United States aboard the S. S. *Panormus* at the Port of Philadelphia during May, 1948, disclosed that Carlo Gambino was involved in the smuggling of these aliens and that some of these aliens in turn had smuggled substantial quantities of heroin into the United States as payment for being brought into the country.

Government documents alleged that Gambino was one of the directors of the smuggling operation involving the SS *Panormus*. The report noted that an interested party in the smuggling was Santo Sorge, who ran a trading company in New York City.[17] He was reported to be an "intimate associate" of Lucky Luciano and had been observed in the company of Joseph Bonanno in Palermo during a meeting held there in October 1957.

TURMOIL IN THE 1950s

The 1950s proved to be a watermark decade for organized crime in both New York City and throughout the country. The decade began when the nefarious activities of the Mafia were brought to the public's attention by the highly publicized Kefauver Hearings. Near the end of the decade, underworld leaders from across the country were exposed after the failed Apalachin Summit.

The early 1950s also saw the removal of the leadership of one of the five crime families. The body of Philip Mangano was found near Jamaica Bay on April 19, 1951. His brother Vincent disappeared forever around the same time. Perhaps Vito Genovese saw the removal of the Mangano brothers as a way for Costello to increase his overall leadership. It was rumored that Vito's first move was to try to turn Anastasia in his favor by using Gambino as a go-between. According to *The Last Testament of Lucky Luciano* (see Appendix), Meyer Lansky apprised the deported mob boss of the situation, and Luciano advised him to notify Genovese and Gambino that he would not tolerate their attempts to "muscle in on Anastasia."

Luciano claimed he received a visit in late 1950 from Carlo Gambino in Naples. The reason for the visit was to inform Luciano about the decision to kill Willie Moretti. Luciano claimed he gave orders to Gambino that Moretti was not to be killed. Despite Luciano's attempt at intervention, Moretti was murdered while meeting with three men at a table in Joe's Elbow Room in Cliffside Park, New Jersey. One of the men asked a waitress for menus. The waitress, assuming the men were going to order lunch, went into the kitchen to retrieve silverware for them. While she was in there, one of the men pumped several slugs into Moretti, leaving his body stretched out in a pool of blood on the black and white tiled floor.

As family bosses, Anastasia and Costello would have been a formidable pair. With Costello's legal problems and prison sentences during the mid-1950s, however, Genovese was able to take advantage of the situation by plotting new moves. With Anastasia firmly entrenched as a family boss and capable of acting as Costello's strong-arm, Genovese declared the "Mad Hatter" had to go. Instead of turning the murder into an interfamily war, Genovese simply sought out the one man in Anastasia's family whose allegiance changed with the wind—Carlo Gambino.

Genovese had been able to con Gambino into coming over to his side by convincing him that Anastasia's promise to avenge the shooting of Costello would create an all-out gang war. Vito also laid out a list of grievances against Anastasia in support of his decision to have him killed. The only point that concerned Gambino, however, was that he would be promoted to boss of the family. On October 25, 1957, assassins cut down Anastasia at a barbershop in mid-town Manhattan (see Chapter 2).

ORDAINED AS BOSS

Three weeks after the sensational murder of Anastasia, Carlo Gambino's coronation as the newest of New York's five family bosses was reportedly one of several agenda items to be covered at the infamous Apalachin Summit. Gambino traveled to the upstate New York hamlet in the company of Paul Castellano, Salvatore Chiri, Carmine "the Doctor" Lombardozzi, and Joseph Riccobono. The men represented the new leadership of the family. Riccobono was consigliere, Castellano and Lombardozzi were capos, and Chiri was simply a soldier and driver.

It was never revealed how many agenda items were covered, if any, before local law enforcement showed up and the meeting's participants departed the compound like animals fleeing a burning barn. But it's safe to say the coronation ball for Gambino was not a celebration he would have cared to remember.

During the federal investigation after the Apalachin Summit, Castellano and Lombardozzi were fined and sentenced to prison terms for refusing to answer questions about what was taking place at the gathering. When questioned later by investigators, Lombardozzi claimed, "He was invited to Apalachin by Gambino when they met at a wake in a Brooklyn mortuary. He said Gambino told him he might have to undergo heart surgery, and he wanted to discuss it with Barbara, who had survived a similar operation. So Carlo decided to drive to Barbara's estate and asked Lombardozzi to go with him. Asked how come so many people made the trip with Gambino, Lombardozzi replied 'Carlo explained he was invited to bring all his friends.' "[18]

Gambino avoided the hearings by faking a heart ailment and getting a doctor's excuse. His name, however, was exposed again, the first time since the early 1940s, which caught the attention of immigration officials who recalled his 1940 arrest as an illegal alien. In October 1958, a year after the Apalachin debacle, a deportation hearing was held in federal court. When Gambino was called to take the witness stand, he collapsed and was carried out of the courtroom on a stretcher.

In *The Last Testament of Lucky Luciano,* Luciano claimed that just before the Apalachin Summit, he received a visit from Gambino, who had come to pledge his loyalty again.[19] After the meeting was raided and Genovese was humiliated among his peers, Luciano stated that Gambino came for yet a third visit in early 1958 at Santa Marinella. It was at this time that Luciano claimed that Gambino was brought into a plot with Lansky and Costello to frame Genovese on narcotics charges.

Carlo Gambino was boss of the Anastasia family for less than two years before he made his most brazen move—supplanting Vito Genovese as the "Boss of Bosses." Whereas Genovese murdered his way to the top, Gambino manipulated his way there.

> "Carlo Gambino had risen to power with the aid of Vito Genovese, but had never felt comfortable with him. Vito was ambitious and treacherous. He could not be trusted. Not long after his investiture as boss, Carlo began plotting against him."
> —Davis, *Mafia Dynasty,* 1993, p. 83

As the new family boss, Gambino had to address several organizational details by performing a little house cleaning. After returning from the Apalachin embarrassment, Gambino named Joseph "Joe Bandy" Biondo his underboss and promoted his brother Paul to capo. He then took on the task of dealing with two recalcitrant gang members, both former Anastasia loyalists. John "Johnny Roberts" Robilotto and Armand "Tommy" Rava were alleged to have made threats to avenge the murder of their former boss. Robilotto was a capo under Anastasia. A one-time mortician, he was said to have received a lot of "business" from the "Mad Hatter." Robilotto was reputedly a former associate of the Genovese family and was considered by law enforcement officials in New Jersey to be the prime suspect in the murder of Willie Moretti. He was indicted for the murder, but police dropped the charges because of lack of evidence.

Around 3:45 on the morning of September 7, 1958, Robilotto was in the East Flatbush section of Brooklyn when a gunman fired four bullets into his head. The shooter fired from such close range that powder burns were left on the dead man's face. Although his wallet was missing, his pockets turned inside out, and the labels cut from his clothing, police considered it a mob hit as opposed to a robbery. The next month Rava, a member of Robilotto's crew, simply disappeared and was never seen again.

S.G.S. ASSOCIATES: PUBLIC AND LABOR RELATIONS

From 1955 to 1965, Carlo Gambino was involved in the labor relations field as a partner in S.G.S. Associates. The firm consisted of Gambino; Henry H. Saltzstein, a burglar and bookie with a record; and George Schiller, a Russian immigrant. A labor relations partnership was formed between Saltzstein and Schiller in 1952. Two years later, a lawyer named Sylvester Garmella joined the concern and S.G.S. Associates was formed. Garmella left the firm in 1955 and was replaced by Gambino, which resulted in no change to the company masthead.

The firm operated out of a tenth-floor office at 141 East 44th Street. Most prominent among the company's list of clients was Wellington Associates, the real estate concern that owned the Chrysler Building and, at the time, was referred to as the "largest acquirer of real estate in the metropolitan area.[20] Other clients were Flower and Fifth Avenue Hospital, Bond Clothes, Howard Clothes, the Concord Hotel located in the Catskills, as well as concerns in New Jersey, Pennsylvania, and other parts of the East.

Income from the firm was reputed to be $500,000 annually. One client, who preferred to use non-union workers on his projects, paid $7,000 a month to keep labor peace. During a strike by nonmedical employees of the Flower and Fifth Avenue Hospital, S.G.S. was contacted and the strike was quickly settled.

Shortly after the Chrysler Building was sold in May 1960, maintenance and service workers went out on strike and S.G.S. was called. The strikers complained that armed "goons" driving Cadillacs showed up and took over the operation of the building's elevators. The mayor's office helped settle the strike within 24 hours. The new owners were so happy with the work of S.G.S. that they kept them on retainer until 1963 at the cost of $13,500 a year.

By April 1965, investigations of S.G.S. had been conducted by District Attorney Frank Hogan's office, the FBI, the New York–New Jersey Waterfront Commission, the McClellan Committee, the Internal Revenue Service, and the United States Attorney's office. Records of S.G.S. were subpoenaed as early as July 1956. Clients of S.G.S. that were questioned claimed they were unaware that the "G" in the firm's name stood for Gambino.

Around this time the INS was stepping up its efforts to have the aging mobster deported. After a week of observation and tests at a Staten Island government hospital, in the early spring of 1965, doctors determined that Gambino's health was "too frail" for him to be able to attend court, and the deportation hearing was again canceled. Gambino took advantage of this "health" opportunity to announce he would be retiring from S.G.S. Associates. By that time a number of clients were already disassociating themselves with the firm.[21]

On May 10, Saltzstein announced the labor-relations company was dissolved and that he would continue on his own. Gambino and Schiller moved out of the office.[22] In an interview Saltzstein stated, "We sat down with our lawyers and decided that the bad publicity wasn't good for our business. These are the facts of life. We've got to live with them."

PRELUDE TO WAR

With the conclusion of the Castellammarese War, there was no interfamily warfare for the next 30 years. There had been takeover moves within individual families, such as the killing of Philip Mangano and disappearance of his brother Vince, which elevated Albert Anastasia to the top leadership of that family. This change was short lived as Gambino arranged for the murder of Anastasia and replaced him as boss. Although there were few "house cleaning" murders beyond these, nothing could compare to the Gallo/Profaci War in the early 1960s.

Giuseppe Profaci, one of the original five family bosses, built his gang in South Brooklyn during the mid-1920s, and was an early supporter of Salvatore Maranzano. Profaci had been on the winning side of the Castellammarese War and simply continued to run his gang. Over the years he earned the nickname the "Olive Oil King," as the reputed leading importer of olive oil and tomato paste in the country. By 1960, Profaci was in his mid-sixties and gained another nickname, "the Old Man." Profaci had been a successful mob boss by isolating himself from the criminal activities he oversaw while still ruling with an iron hand.

Many of the soldiers on the street were unhappy with Profaci's way of doing business. They felt they were doing all the work, and he was collecting all the profits or directing them to his "chosen few." The crew that was most vocal about this slight was headed by Larry Gallo and included his brothers Albert "Kid Blast" and Joseph, known as "Crazy Joey."

The spark leading to the Gallo/Profaci War came in November 1959 when two masked gunmen murdered 62-year-old numbers operator Frank "Frankie Shots" Abbatemarco. At onetime an enforcer for Profaci, Abbatemarco built a $750,000-a-year racket from which he paid a high street tax to the "Old Man" to stay in business. After some unexpected losses in the fall of 1959, "Frankie Shots" fell behind in his payments to Profaci. Although Abbatemarco pleaded for more time to get caught up, his answer came in the form of five bullets to the face, throat, and stomach inside a Brooklyn bar. Profaci ordered that the killing be carried out by the Gallo crew. After the murder, the Gallos felt they were entitled to Abbatemarco's operations only to find they had been divvied up by Profaci and his selected cronies.

When the Gallos' complaints were ignored, five ranking members of the Profaci Family were kidnapped. For the release of the hostages unharmed, the Gallos wanted the Abbatemarco operations, which they felt they had earned, and amnesty for the revolt. A few weeks later the hostages were released unharmed and a sit-down was called for by the commission. The commission members felt that the Gallos had a legitimate complaint, but they were afraid to rule in their favor, concerned that "young turks" within their own families might someday revolt in the same manner. Moreover, they refused to side with Profaci. One mob writer gave the following run-down of the voting:

> The vote went against Profaci for a number of reasons. Gambino and Lucchese saw the possible fall of Profaci as a means of increasing their own power in New York. Genovese, in jail, but still wanting to be the boss of bosses in New York, was also jealous of Profaci. Magaddino in Buffalo distrusted the closeness between Profaci and Bonanno and didn't like Bonanno's recent intrusions into Canadian rackets. Magaddino considered Canada all his. Giancana and Bruno could see that a wild shooting spree was shaping up, and they elected to stay out of it.[23]

To the chagrin of Profaci, commission members decided that it was an internal family matter and the opposing parties should negotiate their own agreement. Profaci felt that Gambino and his ally Tommy Lucchese were behind the decision. Anthony "Tony Bender" Strollo, representing the Genovese Family, actually spoke for the Gallos. Profaci's only ally in the matter was Joe Bonanno. Left to handle the matter himself, Profaci negotiated the dispute by promising concessions, but never acting on them.

The war continued. On June 7, 1962, Profaci succumbed to cancer and his brother-in-law, Joseph Magliocco, took over the family. For the remainder of the year, Magliocco had his hands full trying to get approved as head of the family by the commission. Magliocco had taken control of the Profaci Family but had not been accepted by the other bosses and certainly was not being given consideration for a seat on the commission as long as the war continued. Magliocco's response was to step up hostilities and in 1963 the war heated up. He ordered his top lieutenants to kill all the Gallo crew members and associates they could hunt down. Soon a number of gang members from both sides were murdered, shot at, or vanished.

As Magliocco remained shunned by New York members of the commission, he sought the help of out-of-town commission bosses Angelo Bruno of Philadelphia, Sam Giancana of

Chicago, Stefano Magaddino of Buffalo, and Joseph Zerilli of Detroit. All stood their ground refusing to get involved. Magliocco then made his boldest move to date; he conspired with Joe Bonanno to kill Gambino and Lucchese.

Selected to carry out this double assassination was Joseph Anthony Colombo, a little known capo in the family. Colombo, however, thought the plot was ludicrous and went straight to Gambino and exposed both bosses. Bonanno and Magliocco were summoned before the commission to answer for their treachery. Bonanno, sensing he would be killed if he complied, headed west. Magliocco showed up. The bosses allowed him to live, but fined him $40,000 and let him know he wouldn't be considered as a replacement for Profaci. The disgraced Magliocco went home and soon died on December 28, 1963.[24] The Gallo-Profaci War effectively ended in December 1963 when 17 members of the Gallo gang were indicted on various criminal charges.

Joseph Colombo was rewarded for revealing the murder plot to Gambino by being confirmed by the commission as the new boss of the Profaci Family. Gambino loaned Colombo $1.2 million to get him started and help out the capos in his family. This act of generosity by Gambino purchased not only the loyalty of Colombo, but also his key people. Carlo would receive weekly interest payments until the loan was repaid. Colombo used some of the money to buy peace with the Gallos, fulfilling a promise he made to them to "spread the bread around."

The family became known to law enforcement agencies as the Colombo Crime Family and it is known by that name to this day. By awarding Colombo a seat on the commission, Gambino effectively controlled three of the five New York seats, with a fourth, the Genovese Family, already beholden to him. The only seat left that was not under Gambino's control belonged to Bonanno. With the family boss on the run, it remained empty and eventually Bonanno conceded his position in New York and retired to Tucson, Arizona.[25] There was soon a new war for leadership in the Bonanno Family. The conflict, known as the "Banana War" lasted until 1969.

THE LASTELLA POWER LUNCH

Carlo Gambino used the turmoil from the internecine warfare from the Profaci/Gallo War and the Banana War to solidify his own importance in the New York underworld. On July 13, 1967, Gambino's longtime friend and fellow crime boss Tommy Lucchese died. Lucchese had recently had brain surgery to remove a tumor, and he also suffered from heart disease. The heir apparent to the Lucchese throne, Anthony "Tony Ducks" Corallo, was serving a prison term for conspiracy to bribe a New York City commissioner. Carmine "Mr. Gribbs" Tramunti was named "acting boss" until Corallo's release.

Despite Gambino's control of the commission, there was still unrest in the New York underworld. Gambino worked hard to keep a low profile for both himself and the organization he represented. Publicity and the Mafia was a bad combination, but a series of incidents would spotlight Gambino and the organization he represented during the latter half of the 1960s.

On the afternoon of September 22, 1966, Gambino was one of 13 people arrested at the LaStella restaurant in Queens, New York. Eleven of the people were mobsters with a long criminal history, including Gambino Crime Family members Aniello DellaCroce and Joseph N. Gallo (no relation to the notorious Gallo brothers). Among the other diners were Joe Colombo and Tommy Eboli from New York and Carlos Marcello and Santo Trafficante from the New Orleans and Tampa Mafia families, respectively.

The luncheon was quickly dubbed the "Little Apalachin" meeting by law enforcement and the media. Each man was booked as a material witness for a grand jury investigation, with bonds set at $100,000 apiece. A number of reasons were given for the meeting, including the selection of a replacement for the ailing Tommy Lucchese. More than likely it was held to discuss an internal problem occurring within the New Orleans crime family of Carlos Marcello.

ARMORED CAR HEIST

On March 15, 1970, a front-page story in the Sunday *New York Times* proclaimed, "there again is a 'boss of all bosses' over the six Mafia 'families' in the New York/New Jersey metropolitan area," 67-year-old Carlo Gambino. A New York City Police Department inspector described him as "the most powerful of all the family bosses in the country." The story went on to explain the need for a new boss:

> Gambino, according to police officials, functions as overseer of the six locally based families and arbitrator of disputes within and among those groups. The long-vacant post of regional "boss of all bosses" has been reactivated because of trouble and uncertainty of command in several families caused by recent jailings of local leaders, murderous rivalries and territorial disputes.[26]

"The Gambino network includes about 1,000 men, half Mafia members and the other half associates. Gambino's rackets stretch from western Connecticut to the outskirts of Philadelphia, and he also has a highly profitable unit in New Orleans with the consent of the Mafia boss there, Carlos Marcello. The Gambino group specializes in such moneymaking rackets as gambling, loan sharking, hijacking, narcotics and labor racketeering. Gambino's power is strong in unions affiliated with night clubs, restaurants, construction and the waterfront."

—Gage, *Mafia, USA*, 1972, p. 173

Just eight days after the article appeared, Gambino was out shopping with his wife and daughter-in-law in the Burrough Park section of Brooklyn. As Gambino exited the vehicle, he was approached by two FBI agents and placed under arrest. A search of the "boss of all bosses" revealed a couple hundred dollars and a bottle of nitroglycerin pills for his heart condition.

Gambino was handcuffed and taken to the Manhattan headquarters of the FBI at 201 East 69th Street. He was charged with being involved in a scheme to heist $6 million (some reports claim $30 million) from the United States Trucking Company, an armored car provider. Gambino, along with four others, were implicated by John J. "Red" Kelly, a Boston bank and armored car robber.[27]

Kelly, allegedly at the behest of New York mobsters, cased various armored car firms in the city during 1968 and 1969 in hopes of pulling off the heist. When he was apprehended in Massachusetts for his role in a half-million dollar robbery of a Brinks armored car in

Boston, he hoped to deal his way out of a long prison term. He told authorities that Gambino was to supply "among other things, autos for the robbery and the means to dispose of the money—at 60 cents on the dollar."

As part of their investigation, in August 1969, FBI agents executed a search warrant at the Ocean Parkway home of Gambino. No one was home at the time the search was conducted. They found no incriminating evidence in the house, but they discovered four safe deposit box keys for which they obtained subsequent warrants to open. Although little of note was found in three of the boxes, in the fourth agents discovered nearly $28,000 in cash, a number of U.S. Savings Bonds, and a large quantity of jewelry valued at $109,000. The contents were confiscated by the agents. In each case the series and serial numbers of each dollar bill were recorded.

An inquiry was made into one piece of jewelry that was valued at $30,000—a white gold, diamond bracelet—and it was discovered that it was reported stolen during an armed robbery on December 6, 1967, from a Madison Avenue jeweler. During the ensuing investigation, Gambino's wife, Catherine, was subpoenaed to appear before a federal grand jury, because the safe deposit box was in her name. Catherine failed to appear. The FBI, figuring that this would happen, kept surveillance on her and observed her "free and apparently unimpaired movements" about the city. On February 2, 1971, an internal FBI report advised that the Strike Force attorney for the Eastern District of New York (EDNY), after he could "discern no federal violation in this matter, has declined prosecution on all subjects in this case, therefore, this case is being placed in a closed status." This dismissal was the result of Catherine Gambino's losing battle with cancer.

As for the contents of the safe deposit box, the diamond bracelet was claimed by the Madison Avenue jewelry store it was stolen from, and the cash and balance of the jewelry, $79,000 worth, were kept by the government after no one stepped forward to place a claim.

Meanwhile, after the March 1970 arrest for the armored car heist conspiracy, Gambino appeared in court smiling as the charges were read, but when bail was set at $75,000, the smile disappeared. "I'll stay in jail. I'm innocent from this accusation and I won't put up five cents for bail," Gambino said. Gambino's lawyer pleaded with him to sign the bail application, that he was too ill to remain in jail. After a conference with his son Thomas, Carlo agreed to post bail.

Shortly after his arrest, the FBI issued the following press release:

FBI Agents today arrested Carlo Gambino in Brooklyn, New York, on charges of conspiracy to commit an armored car robbery involving an estimated 6 million dollars, Attorney General John. N. Mitchell announced.

FBI Director J. Edgar Hoover stated that the arrest culminated an extensive investigation by the FBI. Specifically, Gambino was charged with conspiracy to violate provisions of the Interstate Transportation of Stolen Property statute by conspiring to rob the crew of an armored truck operated by the United States Trucking Company in New York City.

Mr. Hoover noted that Gambino, aged 67, a resident of Brooklyn, New York, has been publicly described as having recently taken over the gangland reins formerly held by La Cosa Nostra chieftain Vito Genovese, who died last year in a Federal prison. Gambino has also been publicly described as the most powerful member of the nine-man National Commission which controls La Cosa Nostra activities on a nationwide basis.

Mr. Hoover said that Gambino will be arraigned as soon as possible. If convicted, he faces a maximum penalty of five years' imprisonment, or a $5,000 fine, or both.

An interdepartment memo discussing the press release stated, "It is noted that Gambino has recently been described as the successor to Vito Genovese in the La Cosa Nostra organization. In view of this, it is felt that a national press release should be issued." It is interesting to note Hoover's wording about Vito Genovese. FBI correspondence, as well as the local New York newspapers, both conceded Gambino was the top man on the commission years earlier. Why would they believe that the death of Genovese, a year earlier, would have just now elevated Gambino's position in the underworld?

On April 28, a one-count secret indictment was returned against Gambino charging him with conspiracy in interstate transportation of stolen property. On May 14, he appeared in federal court and pleaded not guilty and his bond was continued. Attorneys for Gambino informed the judge that their client was too ill to be tried. The judge disagreed, but made a number of concessions. The trial, scheduled to begin on December 7, 1970, would be limited to afternoon sessions between 2:00 and 5:00 PM, with frequent 10-minute rest periods.

On the day the trial was scheduled to begin, U.S. Federal Judge Marvin Frankel of the Southern District of New York (SDNY) ruled that Gambino's life would be placed in jeopardy if he were to stand trial. He then severed Gambino's case from the other defendants. Frankel ruled that if Gambino's health improved, he could be tried at a later date. The case remained inactive, but the status was reviewed every six months by the attorney-in-charge of the Strike Force for the SDNY.

JOE COLOMBO AND THE RETURN OF "CRAZY JOE"

It was hard for Gambino to keep his customary low profile with the LaStella incident and his own arrest in the armored car case, plus the constant surveillance he was under. Still, he demanded from his subordinates, as well as the people he helped place in charge, that they stay out of the limelight. But the old adage, "blood is thicker than water," proved to be the undoing of a subservient existence by Joe Colombo, and the Mafia was given one of its more memorable exposures.

As a father, Colombo had worked hard to provide his two sons with all the material possessions they could desire, but he kept them out of the crime family business and ordered his underlings not to get them involved in any illegal activities. He also warned his shylocks never to lend his sons money. There was concern on the part of Colombo for this latter order, according to Joseph Cantalupo: "Despite what their father said and what he gave them, Anthony and Joey Junior, in particular, were always walking on the edge because they were always broke. They spent like drunken sailors on the high life, wine and women. They also loved gambling—horses, sports betting, cards, craps, the casinos."[28]

On April 30, 1970, Joseph Colombo, Jr. was arrested by the FBI and charged with melting down $500,000 worth of U.S. coins for their valuable silver content. Like a loving father who thought his kid could do no wrong, Colombo was incensed at the FBI and convinced that the whole thing was a conspiracy to get at him. At his real estate office at Cantalupo Realty, the mob boss raged:

> "It's bullshit!" he screamed. "Why would my son want to do that? If he wants money, I give him one hundred thousand dollars . . . whatever he wants! Why would my son want to do that?

"Those fuckin' feebs! They ain't satisfied with going after me, they gotta go after my kids. They're trying to get at me through my kids. They're fuckin' rotten.

"Those bastards, they got that poor kid locked up till tomorrow! For what? He ain't done nothing. This is discrimination, that's what it is. It's because the kid's named Colombo, because his name ends in a vowel. The Mafia, the Mafia . . . bullshit the Mafia. They're just trying to screw me. They just want to screw Italians. You don't see them do this to Jews or the Irish or the Polacks. Just fuckin' Italians. Well, they can't do that. I'm not gonna let them get away with it."[29]

From that famous rant the Italian-American Civil Rights League was conceived. Colombo ordered his men to take up signs and they went to Sixty-Ninth Street in Manhattan, where they picketed outside the FBI's headquarters. For the next year-and-a-half, Joe Colombo shamelessly promoted his sham Italian-American Civil Rights League, hosting dinners, giving interviews (including an appearance on the Dick Cavett show), and soliciting support from celebrities and political figures. The high point of his crusade came on June 29, 1970, when he hosted the first Italian-American Unity Day.

The highly publicized rally drew an estimated 50,000 to 70,000 people who jammed Columbus Circle in Manhattan. Colombo could not have organized the rally alone. Carlo Gambino gave his approval for waterfront longshoreman, teamsters, and warehouse workers to have the day off to attend the event. Placards were placed in storefront windows throughout the city, especially in the Little Italy neighborhood. The rally was a success and plans were made to make it an annual event.

After the rally a fundraiser was held at the Felt Forum at which entertainers Frank Sinatra, Sammy Davis, Jr., Vic Damone, Jerry Vail, and Connie Francis performed. The event raised nearly a million dollars for a Brooklyn hospital the league was to build, but never got around to. Colombo next used his newly found muscle to get the television series *The FBI* to quit using the terms "Mafia" and "La Cosa Nostra." He then took it a step further and forced the producer of *The Godfather* movie to eliminate the same words from the movie script and to use some of Colombo's people as extras in the production.

On December 1, 1970, the federal coin-melting case of Colombo's son ended in a mistrial in Brooklyn federal court. At the second trial, the next February, the government's key witness recanted his story and the judge refused to let the case go to the jury. Colombo crowed about the result declaring, "We don't fear them [the FBI] and we never will."

Colombo, meanwhile, had fallen in love with all the celebrity he had achieved. He started to believe he was invulnerable and untouchable. The publicity he was receiving was beginning to concern Gambino and the other family bosses. In mid-December 1970, FBI agents, while in search of Colombo capo Rocco Miraglia, found him and Colombo in a car at the New York State Supreme Courthouse on Centre Street in Manhattan parked illegally in the space of a Supreme Court justice. They moved in and arrested Miraglia. Beside Colombo in the vehicle was his briefcase. The agents confiscated it, claiming they believed it belonged to Miraglia. Colombo began screaming, but the FBI men carried it off. They soon returned it, but not before taking note of its contents.

Inside the briefcase was a listing of the entire membership of the Italian-American Civil Rights League, including Gambino's name. His name also appeared next to an entry marked $30,000. Gambino and a few others were called before a grand jury and questioned. Another entry on the list, Tommy Eboli, boss of the Genovese Family, was out of the country, but on his return he was detained at Kennedy Airport by customs agents.

Colombo had his day in the sun, thumbing his nose at the FBI, but his actions only caused the agency to work harder to harass him. Cantalupo revealed, "Meanwhile, things were really getting out of hand. Colombo wasn't paying attention to business, people were losing money, and associates, soldiers, capos—and worse, other bosses—were starting to feel the heat. The more Colombo mouthed off, the more he was publicized in the press, the more the Bureau turned up the heat."[30]

The FBI's investigation of Colombo revealed a falsification on his application for a real estate broker's license. He was soon indicted for lying, convicted, and given a two-and-a-half year sentence for perjury. He was then arrested and charged with illegally mediating a dispute between jewel thieves. In the spring of 1971, Colombo was arrested with 21 others, including his girlfriend, on gambling charges. Colombo's biggest problem, however, came in March when "Crazy Joe" Gallo was released from Sing Sing.

The Gallo Family was a brother short by the time Joey returned. Larry Gallo had died of cancer in 1968. It didn't take long for "Crazy Joe" to begin challenging Colombo's authority. With the second annual Italian-American Unity Day approaching, the Gallos spread out through the South Brooklyn neighborhood around President Street and began removing posters advertising the event from store windows and ordering merchants to stay open. Gallo told the store operators that, "Colombo's just using the dues from poor Italians to pay for his lousy fight with the FBI."[31]

Sometime before the second rally, Gambino called in Colombo and Joseph Cantalupo, Sr. for a conference. When they returned to the realty office, Joe Cantalupo Jr. was waiting and listened to the following conversation between the two men:

> "Joey . . . do me a favor," my father was saying. "Take Carl's advice. Step down from the league. The old man asked you to step down from the league. Jesus, Joey do it."
>
> Colombo shook his head, staring at something on the ground. My father continued, "Joey . . . put a politician in . . . an entertainer . . . a movie star, and step back. Step away. Get out of the spotlight. You know what Carl said. You can do everything you're doing now, but do it behind the scenes."
>
> Colombo shook his head vigorously. "No!" he said angrily. "This is *my* thing. I don't care what he says, what he thinks. This my thing, and I'm gonna run it."
>
> It had become an obsession with him. He couldn't let go. He loved the fame, the publicity. He was like a little Caesar, and he was ready to be crowned on Unity Day.[32]

On June 28, 1971, the second Italian-American Unity Day rally was held in Columbus Circle. The crowd was not expected to be as big as the prior year. The waterfront workers, who had been given the day off the year before and ordered to attend, were kept at work this year in defiance of Colombo's refusing to step down. Colombo arrived early at the rally. So did a young black man named Jerome Johnson, who was wearing the credentials of a newspaper photographer. The fake credentials allowed Johnson to get close to Colombo. When he did he pulled a gun and fired three shots at him, hitting the mob boss in the head.

Johnson had no time to admire his handiwork. Colombo body guards killed him instantly. At first, Johnson was believed to be a crazed lone gunman. But then authorities theorized that because Joey Gallo had such a close relationship with black criminals during the time he was in prison and was recruiting them for his own gang, he was behind the shooting. This theory melted away when Johnson was tied to the Gambino Family as a frequenter of an after-hours club run by Paul DiBella, said to be a soldier in the family.

The early money was bet that "Crazy Joe" had been behind the brazen shooting of the mob boss, but it soon became apparent that it was the sly fox Carlo Gambino who had orchestrated the plot. On July 21, Gambino was questioned by the FBI regarding the attempt on Joe Colombo's life. He told agents that he didn't attend the rally and didn't know who was responsible.

Joseph Colombo survived, but the bullets that entered his brain left him in a vegetative state for seven years. He finally died in May 1978, shortly before his 55th birthday. Joey Gallo did not live that long. After less than a year of living a celebrity lifestyle of his own, Gallo was murdered while celebrating his 43rd birthday at Umberto's Clam House in Little Italy on April 7, 1972. The killers were Colombo loyalists seeking revenge.

DEPORTATION CASE

On November 29, 1957, two weeks after the Apalachin Summit, a confidential INS memo revealed that plans were in process to apprehend Carlo Gambino on December 2. He was to be arrested and served with an "order to show cause why he should not be deported." The agents serving the warrant were instructed to "give the apprehension as much publicity as possible." The plan backfired when agents arrived at the home and were informed that Gambino was not there and his whereabouts were unknown. Agents had kept a close eye on the house and were unsure whether Gambino had slipped out undetected or was hiding in the home. His whereabouts were soon revealed; he was a patient in Flower and Fifth Hospital, reported to be seriously ill with a heart condition. The hospital was a client of his labor consulting firm, S.G.S. Associates.

Gambino was operated on for a delicate heart condition on December 9, 1957; he was scheduled to be released 10 days later. On December 12, an urgent FBI memo stated that Gambino had a "serious operation with chances of living not good."

While Gambino's deportation case dragged on, he was placed under an Order of Supervision by the INS. Anytime Gambino planned to be away from the city for more than 48 hours, he had to receive permission. Gambino had to report to INS officials every month on the first and third Wednesdays. In addition to Gambino's poor health, the INS learned that the Italian government was noncommittal about allowing the aging mob boss to return to the country of his birth.

After the December operation, Gambino received permission from the INS to leave for Florida in early February to recover. Government officials claimed if Gambino was well enough to travel, he should be well enough to appear before a grand jury. The subpoena for him to appear was not served because of his illness. Government attorneys made plans for Gambino to be interviewed at the Colonial Inn hotel, where he was staying in Miami Beach. When contacted, Gambino complained he was still ill from his recent operation.

Gambino was kept under constant watch by FBI agents. In April, 1958, a rumor was leaked to the McClellan Committee that Gambino had died. Agents in Florida were asked to check on the rumor and reported back that he "appears to be in good health."

On May 15, Gambino was back from his winter hiatus. On June 4, Gambino and his lawyer, Edward Ennis, appeared in the offices of the INS to surrender and post bond. INS officials declined serving the warrant because of Gambino's health. They contacted his doctor asking for verification of whether he could be served an arrest warrant and stand trial without fatal consequences. The doctor responded with a two-page memo claiming Gambino could be served, but he could not guarantee he would not suffer heart failure as a result. The INS notified the FBI that they would not serve an arrest warrant on Gambino until "a medical certificate could be served from the subject's physician or other responsible medical authority," who could certify that the action would not cause heart failure.

INS headquarters in Washington D.C. was concerned about Gambino's health problems. One report claimed officials were, "most anxious not to interfere with current favorable publicity received by the attorney general's office and does not wish to chance having Gambino expire while in INS custody no matter how brief that period might be."

Despite the concerns, on August 6, 1958, Gambino surrendered to the INS, where he was served with the warrant. After posting a $10,000 bond, he was released. Getting Gambino to accept the warrant was one thing; getting him into court was another. A September 3 hearing was scheduled, but on that day Gambino's lawyer and doctor appeared at INS headquarters claiming that Carlo could not attend because of his heart condition. The hearing was delayed until October 2. On September 29, Gambino was readmitted to Flower and Fifth Hospital with a cardiac condition. INS officials were notified that Gambino would be hospitalized for at least 10 days. The INS hearing was postponed indefinitely.

When a new hearing was scheduled for November 3, Gambino gave notice that he would refuse to answer any questions put to him. Officials believed that if this were the case, it would not be difficult to win a trial against him. Gambino appeared, but during the hearing he complained of chest pains. An INS nurse called for an ambulance when Gambino turned pale. Oxygen was administered as soon as the ambulance crew arrived. Gambino's brother Joseph and attorney Ennis requested that Gambino be taken to Flower and Fifth Hospital. For the remainder of 1958, Gambino was in and out of the hospital. Gambino again sought travel permission from the INS to go to Florida to convalesce. The New York INS office granted the travel request on the condition that Gambino would submit to the deportation hearing in Miami "if possible." On January 26, 1959, Gambino boarded a train of the Pennsylvania Railroad and was off on another winter sabbatical in the Sunshine State. After a five-week stopover in Fort Lauderdale, Gambino arrived in Miami Beach.

Gambino returned to New York City on March 26. On May 7, an FBI memo advised, "Because of Gambino's health and reported inactivity [in the underworld], this case is being placed in a pending inactive status. Contact is being made with INS on a continuing basis re Gambino. If in the future, information comes to the attention of the NYO [New York Office] warranting additional investigation, Gambino's case will be reopened and the Bureau will be advised."

There was a follow-up investigation every six months, but no progress was made in trying to deport the wily mob leader. The next year, after surgery on January 19, 1960, Gambino was released from Flower and Fifth Hospital on March 5, and immediately obtained permission to return to Florida. He was back in New York on April 27.

On August 16, 1960, Gambino entered the United States Public Health Service Hospital (U.S. PHSH) on Staten Island for a physical evaluation. A report prepared by the government facility showed the following diagnosis:

1. Arteriosclerotic heart disease
2. Congestive heart failure
3. Angina pectoris syndrome
4. Diabetes

The report also advised the following:

Regarding your questions about whether Mr. Gambino can take part in deportation proceedings; it is our opinion that he may be served papers and interrogated without much risk to the patient. It is possible that under the condition of emotional excitement, Mr. Gambino will have episodes of angina pectoris pain. These can be readily controlled by the patient taking nitroglycerine tablets. We suggest that the hearings be held as informally as possible and that the questioning period be no more than 20 to 30 minutes in length with a short rest interval between each questioning period. If Mr. Gambino would take a nitroglycerine prior to the questioning period he may have less difficulty with his anginal pain. A very small risk does exist that if the patient were to become severely agitated, he might have a myocardial infarction.

On January 9, 1961, Gambino was seen again by doctors, and his condition showed some improvement. He was advised to spend the winter in a warmer climate and was off again to Florida.

Despite still being under a $10,000 bond and required to inform the New York Office of the INS regarding his whereabouts, Gambino seems to have disappeared in late March 1961. Government memos sent back and forth indicated that his "present whereabouts were unknown." Apparently, Gambino had returned to New York City on March 18 and had notified his INS handler; however, a month passed before the INS acknowledged his return to the FBI. Efforts were made immediately to have Gambino enter the U.S. PHSH for reevaluation. Instead, he went to his personal physician, who advised against Gambino being recalled to the INS hearing. He stated, "It is my opinion that any such readmission for reinvestigation should be avoided if at all possible, as it would increase his anxiety and possibly cause further physical deterioration or harm."

Another year passed. In December 1961, the INS requested that Gambino return to U.S. PHSH for another evaluation. This time, Gambino checked himself into Flower and Fifth Hospital. The next month he was back in Florida for the winter. On February 11, 1962, the INS advised that the deportation hearing would be held in abeyance for another year because of Gambino's heart condition.

This time, while the mob boss vacationed in Florida, the FBI was able to get an informant close to Gambino and his wife. Despite Carlo and Catherine conversing to one another in Italian, the informant was able to advise who Gambino spoke with by telephone. Unfortunately, names and pertinent details are redacted from the Freedom of Information Act (FOIA) reports.

An FBI memo dated March 5, 1962, revealed that the "Miami office has been successful in establishing a highly confidential source covering Gambino while in Florida." The memo also stated that an agent who could speak Italian was being looked for. When an agent was found in the New York office, he was quickly sent to Florida. There was an abundance of telephone calls and conversations, but nothing criminal in nature was detected.

During this time in Florida, Gambino must have met with a fellow mobster, because shortly after his return an FBI memo discussed the clause in his bond that "stipulates he is not to consort with known criminals." In addition, the FBI was planning to bring information to the attention of the INS indicating that Gambino was physically capable of appearing at his deportation hearing. The supporting facts were that Gambino was seen in Florida at the racetrack and at parties, dancing and keeping late hours.

As 1962 moved on, more information was coming to the FBI's attention as to Gambino's role in the hierarchy of organized crime. The Bureau's "Top Hoodlum Program," established after the Apalachin Summit, was still in its early years, and field agents were working diligently to build their files. An FBI confidential memo from Hoover to the special agent-in-charge (SAC) of the New York Office, dated May 29 implored, "It is imperative that every effort be made to establish confidential coverage of Gambino in view of his position as a 'Commission' member and his obvious importance as a top leader in the criminal organization controlled by the 'Commission.' Considerable information has been developed recently indicating that Gambino is of key importance at the top level in the organized underworld in this country as an arbiter and consultant."

While Gambino was still in Florida in 1962, the FBI began microphone surveillance of his hotel room. This type of surveillance continued in New York throughout the mid-1960s. The installation of listening devices took place at both his Brooklyn and Long Island homes, as well as S.G.S. Associates. On July 16, 1964, during a conversation about a concrete business, the mild-mannered Gambino was overheard to say he was going to "break open" someone's head.

Reports from the bugs used on Gambino never produced any incriminating evidence against him. A report on one stated that because of the air-conditioning unit at S.G.S., the conversations were unintelligible. One report noted that Gambino purchased a boat in June 1964 and was now spending more time than usual at his summer residence.

By 1964, Gambino spent less and less time at S.G.S.; at one point surveillance indicated he had not been seen at the office between October 5 and December 9, 1964. In January 1965, the microphone hidden at S.G.S. was discovered. Agents made at least two "surreptitious entries" into the office thinking there was an "operational failure," but found that the device had been removed. A thorough search of the office failed to recover it. During the search for the bug, agents made note of business papers and checkbook entries.

By late spring of 1962, the FBI was urging the INS to proceed with the deportation effort. The FBI acknowledged through interoffice memos the "seeming reluctance" of the INS to move forward because of "fear" of the "adverse publicity" the agency would suffer should Gambino suffer a fatal heart attack. Based on what the FBI surveillance witnessed in Florida, the FBI determined that the mob boss "could withstand the rigors" of a hearing.

In June 1962, the FBI's New York office recommended to INS headquarters in Washington D.C. that deportation hearings against Gambino be reinstituted and that his $10,000 bond be revoked because of his "consorting with known criminals." By August, the INS was proceeding on both recommendations. A deportation hearing was scheduled for November 19. Instead of a hearing, Gambino agreed to reenter the U.S. PHSH in Staten Island for a complete physical, which was to last three to five days, after which it would be determined whether or not to proceed with the hearing.

During November, a confidential informant, someone close to Gambino who could overhear telephone conversations at the Ocean Parkway residence began forwarding information to the FBI. On November 23, Gambino was released from the hospital "certified as being fit" to participate in a deportation hearing. The hearing was scheduled for mid-January, but after a number of postponements, both sides met on February 26, 1963. The hearing lasted approximately one hour, during which Gambino took pills for his heart condition during four separate breaks. The only items covered were Gambino's first two arrests in the early 1930s. The next morning Gambino's son-in-law, Dr. Thomas Sinatra, called INS officials and said his father-in-law had spent an "uneasy night" and could not attend the hearing. A postponement until March 4 was announced.

On that date, the hearing was continued in the U.S. PHSH. One question was asked of Gambino before he complained of not feeling well and requested a doctor. He was given a sedative and the hearing was postponed until March 8, but Gambino reentered Flower and Fifth Hospital before that date, and the hearing was adjourned until his release. Months passed and on July 26, the INS reported that the hearing was again postponed indefinitely because of Gambino's poor health.

On July 29, 1963, the words, "Carlo Gambino, Boss of Gambino Family" appeared for the first time on an FBI report after an interview of the mob boss by agents at his home.

In early September, Gambino was back in U.S. PHSH for another multiple-day examination. While there, Gambino suffered a mild heart attack. He was not released until October 25, when he returned to his Brooklyn home.

On November 4, less than three weeks before the assassination of President John F. Kennedy, his brother Attorney General Robert F. Kennedy was in the New York FBI office where he expressed an interest in the intermarriages within the blood family of Carlo Gambino, "and the resulting imbeciles and morons" that these types of marriages can produce.

On March 2, 1964, the chief of medical services at the U.S. PHSH stated that, in their opinion, Gambino "cannot be subjected to stressful situations such as interrogation without danger to his health or life." The deportation hearing was adjourned, but the bond was kept intact and all requests for travel outside of New York City were denied.

Another year passed and on March 31, 1965, Gambino reentered the U.S. PHSH for yet another complete examination. Doctors reported that his heart condition had worsened since his previous examination. Gambino returned to the facility six months later for another examination, which found no change in his condition. Throughout this period, frequent reports came in about Gambino's activities from agents and confidential informants. Close attention was paid to Gambino's place of business, S.G.S. Associates, which would be dissolved in May 1965.

On December 9, 1966, a deportation official from the INS finally issued the order for Gambino to be deported. The order was based on his illegal entry into the country in 1921 at Norfolk, Virginia. It was confirmed by the INS bureau in Washington D.C. on December 30. No one expected a short appeals process.

More than two years passed. In early 1969, Gambino requested permission to return to Miami for the winter months. When he was denied by the INS, he reapplied, claiming his wife was dying of cancer, and he furnished a doctor's certificate to that effect. The second request was approved orally by officials. Unaware that permission had been granted, FBI agents became concerned when Gambino suddenly dropped out of sight. Throughout the latter half of the 1960s, FBI surveillance and investigation of Gambino was fairly constant, and good communication with the INS was maintained. A check with the INS New York office, however, now revealed that a district director had lifted all travel restrictions on Gambino, and he was free to travel anywhere at will.

After his latest return, two FBI agents paid him a visit on May 13. While he was sitting at his table eating breakfast, agents handed him an Advice of Rights form before questioning him. Gambino told them he was not interested in having his rights read to him or signing any papers; if there were any questions to be asked, he would call his lawyer. At this point he stated, "it would be better if I put a zipper on my mouth."

Gambino complained again to the agents about being a sick man. He showed them 11 pills and said he took that many every day. He then pulled another bottle from his pocket and said, "I have to take thirty" of these each day. He advised that his wife of 43 years was very sick, and he was doing everything he could to keep her alive. Gambino told the agents that his brother Joseph had suffered a recent heart attack and that Paul was also sick. His conversation with the agents ended after replying to them that it was alright to make further contact with him. "I'm always around," he said. "I never go anyplace, I'm a sick, sick, very sick man."

On August 20, 1969, Gambino was subpoenaed to appear before the Kings County grand jury to answer questions about Anthony M. Scotto, vice-president of the International Longshoreman's Association, the largest longshoreman's union local in the country, and alleged to be a capo in the Gambino Family. Scotto was married to the daughter of Anthony Anastasia. On the day Gambino was to appear, he had another sudden relapse and his attorney informed District Attorney Eugene Gold that his client was too ill to testify. A new subpoena was served and Gold announced he would "designate" a doctor to examine the aging crime boss.

On January 7, 1970, the U.S. Court of Appeals upheld the December 1966 deportation order against Gambino, ruling that his entry as a stowaway in 1921 was illegal. Gambino's only recourse was now the U.S. Supreme Court. In July 1970, the *New York Daily News* reported that a 13-year battle to deport Gambino was won, but Italy didn't want the Mafia boss back. Still the process dragged on. Gambino was subpoenaed to appear before a federal grand jury on March 10, 1971. His attorney informed the office of the Strike Force for the EDNY that his client was too ill to appear.

On August 6, 1971, Catherine Gambino succumbed to cancer. A few months later, the INS served notice on Gambino that he was to surrender himself for deportation on November 5. Gambino's lawyer and doctor offered up Carlo for examination at Victory Memorial Hospital the day before.

Attorneys for Gambino filed a temporary restraining order to prevent the INS from deporting Carlo; the action was filed in Washington D.C. A stay of deportation was filed based on ill health, and Gambino was ordered to be examined at U.S. PHSH. He had already been admitted at Victory, however; some reports claimed he was admitted after suffering another heart attack.

After Gambino was released from Victory he convalesced at home. The FBI kept a close eye on his home and his comings and goings, even stopping to visit Carlo at different times to question him. On May 12, 1972, Gambino was served with a subpoena to appear before another federal grand jury in the SDNY. On the day he was to appear, his attorney, Edward Ennis, advised that Gambino couldn't attend because of illness.

At around this same time, an informant advised that Gambino was attempting to "establish some form of peace" among feuding factions, most likely as a result of the unrest that followed the murder of "Crazy Joe" Gallo in April. As the months passed, agents continued to monitor his activities to prove that he was capable of withstanding deportation. In December 1972, during the middle of a Nassau County grand jury investigation into organized crime infiltration of legitimate businesses, Gambino was served with yet another subpoena.

Gambino was again hospitalized at Victory Memorial Hospital from May 31 to June 20, 1975. He was readmitted on July 24 and not discharged until late August.

In 1975, Gambino's orders to visit the INS every first and third Wednesday of the month were changed to one visit every three months.

NEARING THE END

Carlo Gambino's heart ailment finally took its toll. On Friday morning, October 15, 1976, he died peacefully at his Long Island home.[33] The wake, like his wife's, was held at the Cusimano & Russo funeral home. During the day, flower delivery trucks arrived constantly with elaborate arrangements. Local and government agencies were on hand in unmarked vehicles photographing the arrival of those coming to pay tribute. Mourners ignored the activity going on in the automobiles parked along the street.

On the morning of October 17, the funeral was held at Our Lady of Grace Church in Brooklyn. The doors to the church were guarded by men who allowed only relatives and known acquaintances to enter. There were only 350 people in attendance in the sanctuary that held 900. The funeral cortege, which contained less than 30 automobiles, had just one flower car. The family requested that arriving flowers be sent back to the florists. Gambino was laid to rest in a family mausoleum in St. John's Cemetery in Queens, New York.

Shortly before his death, Gambino announced that his successor would be Paul Castellano. This decision was met with anger by most members of the Gambino Crime Family, who believed the new leader should be the current underboss Aniello Dellacroce, who was well respected by the capos and soldiers. The dissention within the family ranks boiled over during the ensuing years, resulting in the public execution of Castellano and his new underboss in 1985, during a coup that put John Gotti in charge of the family.

NOTES

1. Some sources list his year of birth as 1900; an engraving on his crypt reads 1902. Other sources site the date as September 1.

2. Paul Meskil, *Don Carlo: Boss of Bosses* (Toronto: Popular Books, 1973), p. 28.

3. Ibid., p 30.

4. Ibid., p 31.

5. Ibid., p 32.

6. According to biographers David Hanna and Paul Meskil, Paul and Peter Castellano ran the trucking concern. According to former FBI agents Joseph O'Brien and Andris Kurins, however, Paul Castellano, having been born in 1915, would have been only 6 years old at the time of Gambino's arrival in America. Joseph F. O'Brien and Andris Kurins, *Boss of Bosses* (New York: Simon & Schuster, 1991), p. 29.

7. Meskil, *Don Carlo: Boss of Bosses,* p. 37.

8. Peter Maas, *The Valachi Papers* (New York: G.P. Putnam's Sons, 1968), p. 101.

9. Joseph Bonanno with Sergio Lalli, *A Man of Honor* (New York: Simon and Schuster, 1983), p. 121.

10. Catherine Castellano Gambino's first name was reported in different publications as Caterina, Katherine, and Kathryn.

11. Joseph Cantalupo and Thomas C. Renner, *Body Mike* (New York: Villard Books, 1990), pp. 236–237.

12. Ibid., p. 51.

13. The picture was taken at the Westchester Premier Theater in September 1976 while Frank Sinatra was performing there. In the picture with Gambino and Sinatra were Paul Castellano, Gregory DePalma, Tommy Marson, Salvatore Spatola, Joseph Gambino, Richard Fusco, and Aledena "Jimmy the Weasel" Fratianno.

14. John H. Davis, *Mafia Dynasty* (New York: HarperCollins Publishers, 1993), p. 49.

15. Meskil, *Don Carlo: Boss of Bosses,* p. 53.

16. Ibid.

17. Santo Sorge was described by the Bureau of Narcotics as "one of the most important Mafia leaders. Travels extensively between Italy and the U.S. in furtherance of ostensibly legitimate international ventures which probably cover for liaison duties between highest ranking Mafiosi in U.S. and Italy. Has considerable influence in Italy." Perhaps part of his influence came from the fact that he was the cousin of Giuseppe Genco Russo, known as the Mafia boss of Mussomeli, Sicily.

18. Meskil, *Don Carlo: Boss of Bosses,* p. 84.

19. Martin A. Gosch and Richard Hammer, *The Last Testament of Lucky Luciano* (Boston: Little, Brown and Company, 1974), p. 398.

20. *New York Times*, April 17, 1965, "Business Leaders Used Mafia Firms."

21. Ibid.

22. In October 1965, the *New York Times* reported that George Schiller's efforts to gain U.S. were delayed because of his association with Carlo Gambino in S.G.S. Associates. The 69-year-old Schiller had been in the country since 1905 and had no criminal record. *New York Times,* October 25, 1965, "Ex-Gambino Partner Is Facing a New Delay on His Citizenship."

23. Maclean, Don, *Pictorial History of the Mafia* (New York: Pyramid Books, 1974), pp. 328–329.

24. Joseph Magliocco died on December 28, 1963. An autopsy showed that death was due to a heart attack. During the early 1960s, the FBI bugged the telephone of New Jersey mob boss Sam "the Plumber" DeCavalcante. In one of the conversations they recorded, DeCavalcante was talking about Magliocco having been poisoned by Joe Bonanno. Magliocco's body was exhumed and a second autopsy performed. There was no evidence of poison in his body.

25. Joseph Bonanno outlived all the other original mob bosses and died in Tucson, Arizona, of heart failure on May 11, 2002, at the age of 97.

26. *New York Times,* March 15, 1970, "Gambino Is Called Heir to Genovese As 'Boss of Bosses.'"

27. The four men indicted with Carlo Gambino were Frank Miceli, of East Paterson, NJ; Louis Manocchio, of Providence, RI; Frank Venditugli of West Darrington, RI; and Maurice Lerner of Brookline, MA.

28. Cantalupo and Renner, *Body Mike,* p. 95.

29. Ibid., p. 96.

30. Ibid., p. 111.

31. Ibid., p. 112.

32. Ibid., p. 113.

33. Years later a story came out that Carlo Gambino was watching a Yankee's game at the time of his death. Gambino died during the morning hours, however, and the Yankees weren't on the field that day. The World Series began the next day, with the Bronx Bombers losing four straight to Cincinnati.

BIBLIOGRAPHY

Biographies of Gambino

Davis, John H. *Mafia Dynasty*. New York: HarperCollins Publishers, 1993.
Hanna, David. *Carlo Gambino: King of the Mafia*. New York: Belmont Tower Books, 1974.
Meskil, Paul. *Don Carlo: Boss of Bosses*. Toronto: Popular Library, 1973.

Other Publications

Bonanno, Joseph, with Lalli, Sergio. *A Man of Honor*. New York: Simon and Schuster, 1983.

Cantalupo, Joseph, and Renner Thomas C. *Body Mike*. New York: Villard Books, 1990.

Gosch, Martin, and Richard Hammer. *The Last Testament of Lucky Luciano*. Boston: Little, Brown and Company, 1974.

Maas, Peter. *The Valachi Papers*. New York: G. P. Putnam's Sons, 1968.

Maclean, Don. *Pictorial History of the Mafia*. New York: Pyramid Books, 1974.

O'Brien, Joseph F., and Andris Kurins. *Boss of Bosses*. New York: Simon & Schuster, 1991.

6

VITO GENOVESE

AKA "DON VITONE"
NOVEMBER 11, 1897–FEBRUARY 14, 1969

Vito Genovese was known as one of the most feared Mafia dons of all time, but his contemporaries should have feared more his destructive nature, which would eventually bring to an end what the "Men of Respect" referred to as *La Cosa Nostra*—Our Thing.

Despite the American Mafia being undermined by mob turncoats and government witnesses throughout the 1980s, 1990s, and beyond, no one man is more responsible for exposing the inner workings of the organization to the public eye than Genovese. His murderous rise to power, which highlighted Mafia activities in the 1950s, ended in the debacle known as the Apalachin Summit (see Appendix). The ill-fated meeting, which was allegedly called by Genovese to anoint himself as the first *Capo di tutti Capi*—Boss of all Bosses—since 1931, exposed the Mafia for the first time on a grand scale. It was this revelation that launched J. Edgar Hoover's FBI into the business of organized crime fighting. Before the Apalachin Summit, the FBI director refused to acknowledge that organized crime existed on a national level.

Genovese's destruction of the Mafia didn't end there. His lust for vengeance drove a small-time Mafia soldier named Joseph Valachi to reveal in front of a national television audience the nefarious operations of the syndicate. Valachi's testimony, before the Senate Racket's Committee in the fall of 1963, unmasked the sinister personalities that dominated the American Mafia from its heyday during the Prohibition Era through Apalachin, a period covering nearly three decades.

EARLY YEARS

Vito Genovese was born on November 21, 1897, in Risigliano, Italy, a small municipality located northeast of Naples near Cicciano and Tufino. Little is known about his early childhood. Much of the writing about his early years is based on pure speculation by his biographers. Genovese had two brothers, Carmine and Michael. Their father, Fillipo, came to the United States alone around 1912 and established a residence and employment in Queens, New York.

With the money Fillipo earned, he purchased a ticket to bring Vito to America. Arriving on the *S. S. Taormina* at the age of 15, Vito didn't remain with his father for long. He didn't take well to manual labor and his father soon lost patience with him, sending Vito to live with relatives in Manhattan's teeming Little Italy section.

Again, not much is known about his teenage years, but it was alleged that he became involved in local teenage gangs and began to build a reputation as a tough street fighter and a resourceful young hood. According to a frequently repeated story, a pushcart owner once cornered Genovese and accused him of stealing. Vito allegedly warned the peddler, "Call the cops if you want, that's okay. But I warn you, don't touch me or I'll kill you."[1]

Genovese's first serious brush with the law came on January 15, 1917, when he was arrested for carrying a concealed weapon in Manhattan. On June 4, an unsympathetic judge sentenced him to 60 days in the workhouse. Shortly after Vito's release, his mother arrived from Italy. It was one of the last times biographers mentioned his parents. According to one story, Mrs. Genovese died in 1923.

Vito spent his early twenties establishing friendships, committing crimes, and avoiding jail time for a number of arrests. Among his early companions were Michele "Michael" Miranda, Anthony "Tony Bender" Strollo, and Salvatore "Lucky Luciano" Lucania. In April 1918, Vito was arrested for felonious assault in Queens. One account claimed he shot a man four times. The police apparently couldn't find credible witnesses, as the charges were dismissed before the month was out.

Genovese's next four arrests also resulted in the charges being dismissed. On April 25, 1924, he was arrested for violating the Sullivan Law—carrying a concealed weapon—on the Lower East Side. The next day he produced a permit for the weapon and the charges were dropped. The next month he was charged with homicide for fatally injuring a man with his automobile in Brooklyn.

In January 1926, Genovese was charged as a "disorderly person" in Hoboken, New Jersey; in July he was charged with burglary after taking cigars from a Mulberry Street proprietor; and in October, he was again charged with homicide after shooting to death a "petty hood" named Gino Scioto. Early the next year, he was charged with petty larceny in Brooklyn and four years later, in January 1931, he was arrested for carrying a "dangerous weapon" in Jersey City. With the exception of the 60-day sentence in 1917, Genovese walked away scot-free from all these criminal activities.

RISING IN THE UNDERWORLD

In *The Last Testament of Lucky Luciano* (see Appendix), the fabled crime boss gave the following description of Vito Genovese:

> I never really liked him, but he did have moxie. I figured if this Vito had even part of Meyer's guts—remember, he was a little guy like Meyer—then I'd have a good man. When I first heard of him around the neighborhood, he was already makin' a rep for himself. He was livin' in a neighborhood where the Sicilians outnumbered everybody else ten to one;

to us, anybody who didn't come from Sicily was a dirty foreigner, and that made it tough, especially for a little guy like Vito, who was born in some town near Naples. But he could fight like a son of a bitch. I didn't have to love him to use him. But I thought he'd be loyal. What a mistake! But I didn't find that out until many, many years later.[2]

We will probably never know the real story of the early relationship between Genovese and Luciano. Some accounts say they were inseparable friends. If *The Last Testament of Lucky Luciano* can be relied on, Luciano's recollections are tainted by the contempt in which he held Genovese later in life. Luciano blamed Genovese for getting him involved in a narcotics deal in 1923, for which he was arrested. Once deported, Luciano would vehemently deny that he was involved in narcotics; however, he freely discussed Genovese's participation in the drug trade throughout his book, even though there was no factual evidence to support his claims.

On more than one occasion, Luciano described Genovese as a sycophant in his efforts to show loyalty and gain favor. Despite his views, in 1925, Luciano claimed he told Vito to organize the pushcart operators to help sell numbers in the "Italian lottery." Later, he says he placed Genovese in charge of liquor operations in Manhattan.

Although there's no doubt Genovese was a key member of Luciano's inner circle, he did not agree with Lucky's plan to make non-Italians part of the gang's mix, which already included Meyer Lansky and Benjamin Siegel. Luciano told about a meeting where Frank Costello suggested that the gang begin an affiliation with Dutch Schultz. Luciano related, "Vito screamed. 'What the hell is this! What're you tryin' to do, load us up with a bunch of Hebes?' Before Benny or Meyer could even open their mouths, Frank almost swung on him, and he said, very quiet, 'Take it easy, Don Vitone, you're nothin' but a fuckin' foreigner yourself.'"[3]

Genovese attended the Atlantic City Conference (see Appendix) in May 1929. The next year he was an active participant in the Castellammarese War (see Appendix). If the Luciano book is to be believed, Vito committed the war's first murder and participated in its last. Luciano claimed he ordered Genovese to eliminate Gaetano "Tommy" Reina to spite "Joe the Boss" Masseria. On the night of February 26, 1930, Reina was killed by a shotgun blast as he left the apartment of his mistress on Sheridan Avenue in the Bronx. Less than 14 months later, Genovese was alleged to have been a member of the hit team that put Masseria in his grave after shooting "Joe the Boss" inside the Nuova Villa Tammaro restaurant on Coney Island.

Shortly after the murder of Masseria, which ended the Castellammarese War, Salvatore Maranzano called a grand meeting of the Mafia to declare himself *Capo di tutti Capi*. It was during this gathering that Luciano was appointed one of the five bosses of New York City and chose Genovese as his underboss, or second-in-command. The question to this day remains why more influential men like Joe Adonis and Frank Costello were passed over for the position.

The reign of Maranzano as "Boss of all Bosses," was short-lived. Luciano had him murdered in his Park Avenue office after he learned that Maranzano was planning to have Lucky and his top associates, including Genovese, murdered. Luciano then shunned the title of "Boss of all Bosses" and the position remained vacant until a murderous coup orchestrated by Genovese in the 1950s.

MARRIAGE, POLITICS, AND A TRIP HOME

In between arrests during the Prohibition Era, Vito Genovese found time to take a bride—or two. Biographers David Hanna and Dom Frasca provide few details about the first Mrs. Vito Genovese. Hanna wrote:

> He had been married in 1924, but little is known about it except that fellow Mafiosi seldom saw the missus or thought about her. One day in 1929, Vito announced that she had died of tuberculosis. The number of top Mafiosi who showed up for her funeral paid mute testimony to the respect with which Vito was held in the organization.[4]

Frasca's tale is similar, even identifying the first Mrs. Vito Genovese as Anna Ragone.[5] He gives the year of their marriage as 1926, however, and her year of death as 1931. In between, he describes a life of abuse and despair for the young lady.

Sometime during late 1931 or early 1932, Genovese fell in love with a 22-year-old blonde beauty named Anna Vernotico, who, by some accounts, was Vito's distant cousin. How the two met and what kind of courtship they had are lost to history. There was no doubt Genovese was enamored of her, but there was one minor glitch—Anna was married.

Anna's husband, Gerard Vernotico, if the *New York Times* had its facts straight, was first arrested in 1917 at the age of 13 for vagrancy. Three years later he was charged with burglary; the charges were later dismissed. His next arrest didn't occur until April 1931, when he was arrested with Antonio Lonzo and charged with grand larceny. A year later he was facing charges of both assault and robbery.

On the afternoon of March 16, 1932, a janitor found Vernotico and his grand larceny partner, Lonzo, bound, beaten, and strangled on the rooftop of a six-story tenement building at 124 Thompson Street. Police surmised the pair had been lured to an apartment in an adjoining building on Prince Street. Inside the small flat, for which a man had put down a $15 monthly deposit the day before, police found bloodstains and a crow bar. Investigators determined the men had been beaten unconscious and then strangled with a heavy clothesline before being dragged to the roof of the Thompson Street building.

Thirty years later, during his debriefing by the FBI, Joe Valachi (see Appendix) revealed that Peter "Petey Muggins" Mione and Michael Barrese murdered Vernotico on the orders of Genovese. Valachi related that Barrese was worried about getting caught and went into hiding in Harlem. The famed informant concluded, "Well, this Barrese disappeared. I never saw him again. I don't know what happened to him, but it ain't hard to figure."[6]

Just 12 days after the murder of her husband, the former Anna Petillo Vernotico married Vito Genovese in a brief civil ceremony in which Mr. and Mrs. Anthony Strollo served as witnesses. The union of Anna and Vito produced two children: Phillip, named after Genovese's father, and a daughter, Nancy. In addition, Anna had a five-year-old daughter named Marie from her marriage to Gerard Vernotico.

It was not until the spring of 1933 that Anna and Vito boarded the SS *Conte Savoia* for a belated honeymoon to Italy. While there, Genovese wined and dined a few officials of the Fascist Party and spread money around to ingratiate himself with the local establishment. Some say it was to pave the way for future narcotics deals. The honeymoon came to an end in August, when the Genoveses sailed back to New York.

Genovese returned to an America that was in the final throes of the "Noble Experiment." With Prohibition over, the Luciano gang busied themselves with new illegal activities. Genovese focused on the Italian lottery, while Costello went big into the slot machine business. Other Luciano lieutenants became involved in gambling, unions, and labor activities on the waterfront. Meanwhile, Lucky made the unlucky decision to get involved in prostitution. He would soon pay the price.

MURDER OF FRED BOCCI

The night of September 19, 1934, was a typical one at the Gran Café, located at 553 Metropolitan Avenue in the Williamsburg section of Brooklyn. In this popular watering hole, which was part of the Christofolo Social Club, 20 men were passing the late evening playing pinochle or chatting. The cafe's proprietor, Benny Bocci, was seeing to the patron's needs when two men entered shortly after midnight.

With caps pulled down over their eyes and their hands tucked deep into coat pockets, the two strangers immediately attracted everyone's attention. Benny Bocci, sensing a robbery was about to take place, spoke up, informing the intruders, "Take everything, boys. We don't want trouble."

The two men suddenly drew revolvers from their pockets and told everyone to stand. With the help of an accomplice, unknown to the patrons, the gunmen were able to single out from the rest of the card players Fred Bocci, the 27-year-old nephew of the proprietor. Bocci, a petty gambler, had once served six years in the New Jersey State Prison at Trenton for his role in a murder in Newark. Despite his age, Bocci still lived at home with his mother and three siblings.

One of the menacing-looking gunmen called out, "We want you, Bocci. Stand over there," indicating a telephone booth in the corner of the cafe.

Bocci turned white and stumbled, nearly falling, as he followed the gunman's order. "Don't," he pleaded. "I'm a good fellow."

"You're a rat in Jersey and a rat in Brooklyn," snapped one of the gunmen. "Now if you want to pray make it snappy."

The other men in the cafe, sensing what was about to happen, began to speak.

"Keep quiet, and nobody will be hurt, except this rat," came the response.

The two gunmen moved closer to Bocci and seconds later opened fire. Six bullets ripped into his body, killing him instantly. The two killers then raced out of the cafe and got into a dark Chevrolet sedan, which sped down Metropolitan Avenue.[7]

With the investigation just a few hours old, police received a call from a taxi driver who, after hearing several gunshots, had witnessed a man's body being thrown out of an automobile onto the pavement near the corner of 66th Street and 13th Avenue in Borough Park. When police arrived, they found 26-year-old William "Willie" Gallo unconscious and rushed him to Kings County Hospital. Gallo had suffered bullet wounds in the head, back, and left leg; he also had a stab wound in his left side. Despite his wounds, the victim made a miraculous recovery.

Gallo refused to talk to detectives other than to give his name and address. It was the latter that surprised the officers—it was the same address as that of Fred Bocci's family. After continued police grilling, Gallo admitted that he had been shot by Ernest "the Hawk" Rupolo, a self-described underworld hit man.

Ernest Rupolo was a scary figure. His criminal career began at the age of 14, and by the time he was 21, he had been arrested no fewer than six times and had served two prison terms. In 1932, a fellow hoodlum who thought Rupolo was trying to kill him struck first, shooting him in the head.[8] The bullet destroyed Rupolo's left eye and for the rest of his life he wore a patch to cover the hole. A beak-shaped nose only added to his sinister look and provided his nickname, "The Hawk."

Rupolo was soon arrested for the shooting of Willie Gallo. With his past record, Rupolo was facing a stiff prison sentence. Being a good gangster, however, he kept his mouth shut, assured that his confederates would provide him with competent counsel. Rupolo was mistaken. He had been abandoned—no doubt because he had failed to carry out the murder. Not only was no counsel provided, but soon fellow gang members told Rupolo to plead guilty. Rupolo was convicted and sentenced to nine years in prison for the wounding of Gallo. The "Hawk" went off to Sing Sing a bitter man.

Nearly 13 years passed before anyone stood trial for the killing of Bocci. By that time, the newspapers had correctly identified the victim and now referred to him by a new name— Ferdinand "the Shadow" Boccia. The man accused of ordering his death, however, was an old familiar name—Vito Genovese.

THE LAND OF HIS BIRTH

The year 1936 was a watershed year for Genovese. He became acting boss of the crime family, when Luciano was convicted of compulsory prostitution and sent away to begin a 30- to 50-year prison sentence, and Vito became a U.S. citizen. He celebrated these events by fleeing the country.

One of the great mysteries of Vito Genovese's life was when and why he left America for Italy. No one source seems to be able to produce the correct date. Stories about Genovese have him fleeing the United States in 1934, 1935, 1936, and 1937. After reviewing the events that were going on in his life during this period, it's unlikely he would have left the country before November 25, 1936, the date he became a naturalized citizen.

Mob historians are divided as to why Genovese fled this country. Most claim it was to avoid prosecution for the 1934 Bocci/Boccia murder; others state it was because of Prosecutor Thomas Dewey's declaration to pursue Genovese after Luciano was sentenced in July 1936. There is little support for either of these reasons. The Boccia murder—for which Genovese was arrested on December 4, 1934, and had the charges dismissed three days later—and Genovese's role in it are discussed later. As for the second reason, one has only to look through the index of Dewey's book, *Twenty Against the Underworld*. If Dewey was about to turn the weight of his office against Genovese as he did to Irving "Waxey Gordon" Wexler, Dutch Schultz, and Lucky Luciano, one can only wonder why Vito's name appears just twice and strictly in passing.

It is more likely that Genovese feared becoming a target of Special Prosecutor Dewey and fled the United States for no other reason than what he thought might happen. In doing so, he left his wife and family, as well as his position as boss of New York City's most powerful crime family, a position it would take him the next 20 years to regain.

According to Genovese biographer Dom Frasca, Vito was not alone in Italy very long. Mike Miranda soon joined him, bringing a gift of two 1938 Packard sedans. The two men enjoyed a steady stream of prostitutes while there. Genovese had also taken $750,000 to keep him company; this tidbit of information was provided years later by Joe Valachi. Frasca claims Anna made several visits, each time arriving with at least one suitcase full of cash.

By spreading his money around, Genovese was able to gain favor with some of the leaders of Mussolini's Fascist government. At one point, he contributed $250,000 toward the construction of a new government building in Nola, a town a few miles from his birthplace Risigliano. Risigliano was rumored to have a strong presence by the Camorra, a secret crime society with its roots in Naples. He also invested in several concerns that provided electric power in and around the Nola district. After the Allied occupation, Vito used his control of these companies to force businesses dependent on his electricity "to play ball with him."

Genovese also proved his worth to the Fascist leader in another area; this time it served a dual purpose. Back in 1935, Genovese drew the ire of Carlo Tresca, the publisher of the Italian-language newspaper *Il Martello* (The Hammer). Vito was involved in developing a club on the New York docks for Italian sailors in search of gambling and women. Tresca sent word to Genovese that if he followed through with this plan, he would personally expose it in the press. Concerned with the negative print that fellow gangsters like Dutch Schultz and Luciano were currently receiving, Vito backed off, but he didn't forget Tresca's threat.

Tresca was a staunch opponent of Mussolini's Fascist regime. On the night of January 11, 1943, as he was leaving his newspaper office, Tresca was gunned down at the corner of Fifth Avenue and 15th Street in Manhattan. Although eyewitnesses were unable to positively identify the gunman, it is commonly believed that Carmine Galante was the shooter and acted at the behest of Genovese in his desire to curry favor with Mussolini.

After the Allied invasion of Italy and the occupation of the southern portion of the country, the Allied Military Government (AMG) was established to govern Italy for the duration of the war. Appointed to oversee the country's civil affairs was Colonel Charles Poletti, a former acting-governor of the state of New York. Genovese was quick to ingratiate himself with Poletti, as well with other AMG officers. He did this by presenting Poletti with one of his 1938 Packards as a gift, which the officer used as his official staff car. In addition, he supplied many of the officers with beautiful Italian prostitutes, whom he procured through a Naples madam named Innocenza Monterisi.

Soon, Genovese was serving as an interpreter for several of the high-ranking officers in the AMG. His new status helped mask his ever-widening black market activities. One of these was stealing automobiles, which had been confiscated by the AMG, and reselling them. Many of his black market activities were carried out with help from his brother-in-law, Salvatore Profeta.

ENTER AGENT ORANGE

Orange C. Dickey, a campus patrol officer at Pennsylvania State College before entering the service, was an investigator for the Criminal Intelligence Division (CID) of the United States Army. Arriving in Italy in December 1943, he was appointed criminal investigative agent on February 2, 1944. He was soon assigned to investigate black market activities involving olive oil and wheat in the region between Foggia and Naples.

As an investigator, Dickey developed relationships with a number of informants in the performance of his duty. In April 1944, one of these informants advised him of a contraband ring operated by Genovese. The informant told Dickey that "Vito Genovese was also a commendatore and had received that title from Mussolini because of large donations of money to the Fascist Party in the Nola District.[9] After receiving this title, he became good friends with Mussolini. He is known to have attended several large dinners and other fetes of honor in Naples." The next month, Dickey began a complete investigation of Genovese's activities. Also believed to be involved in the black market ring was Mike Miranda, although Dickey would later claim he was unable to find any evidence that would allow for his arrest.

In early June, Dickey located the burned-out remains of several stolen U.S. Army trucks in a vineyard outside of Nola. The trucks had been stolen from the docks in Naples, driven to a quartermaster's depot, and loaded with sugar and flour. From there they were driven to a location where the goods were transferred to a number of smaller vehicles. The trucks were then taken to the vineyard and destroyed. Two Canadian soldiers were arrested for these crimes on June 4. When questioned, they confessed their roles in driving the trucks and revealed to Dickey that when they reached their destination, they were told to say, "Genovese sent us."

After an investigation that lasted several months, Dickey received permission to apprehend Genovese. On August 27, the day after Vito moved into a newly redecorated apartment in Naples, Dickey made his move. With two British soldiers, Dickey approached Genovese outside the Nola mayor's office and requested that he accompany him to the Military Police Office in Nola. Once there, Dickey informed him that he was under arrest and placed him in a jail cell. A few hours after his arrest, a member of the Questore of Rome, an Italian police organization, arrived and stated he had been dispatched by the Public Safety Officer, Allied Control Commission, an office with which Lieutenant Colonel Poletti was connected. He demanded the release of Genovese into his custody for removal to Rome. His demand was denied.

That night, one of Dickey's informants gave the CID agent a copy of the book *Gang Rule in New York* in which a picture of Genovese appeared.[10] When Dickey showed Vito the picture the next day, Genovese responded, "Sure, that's me when I was in New York City." Suspecting some notoriety, Dickey requested, through the provost marshal general's office, Genovese's criminal record from the FBI.

In the meantime, Dickey continued his investigation. A search of Sal Profeta's apartment revealed information about "The Shed," a huge underground storeroom used to house stolen wheat. In Genovese's apartment he discovered a large amount of PX supplies, including candy, cigarettes, shaving cream, and soap, as well as a powerful radio receiver. In Genovese's wallet, Dickey found letters of recommendation from three AMG members, all officers (a captain and two majors) of the United States Army. Also found were a number of "official passes" issued by the AMG.

Dickey's investigation revealed that Genovese had been purchasing American paper currency in Italy. Dickey claimed that participating in this activity "indicates that the person may be involved in black-market activities, inasmuch as there is only one source of this money, and the original obtaining of this money is by nature illegal." Discovering that Genovese had a safe-deposit vault in a Nola bank, he tried to gain access to it, but was turned down by the local tribunal. In questioning bank officials, Dickey was told that the day after Vito's arrest, Sal Profeta had made a visit to the vault.

Despite all the evidence that Dickey uncovered in his investigation, no one in the AMG was interested in bringing Genovese to trial on black-market charges. Throughout the months that followed, Dickey was forced to accept complete responsibility for the prisoner. Seeking disposition of the matter, Dickey made several trips to see Poletti in Rome. On the first occasion, he found the colonel passed out at his desk, surrounded by several empty liquor bottles, at 10:00 in the morning. On two other occasions, he found Poletti's office full of people, "mostly girls," and liquor bottles again scattered about his desk.

On November 22, the information Dickey requested from the FBI arrived. He was shocked to see that the last entry on Genovese's record was a murder indictment on August 7, 1944, for a homicide in Kings County, New York. Three weeks later, Dickey was requested to remove Genovese from the Naples Military Jail. Contacting his superior officer, Dickey was told to "either let him go, have bond posted, or confine him in any other civilian jail." When Dickey pressed for a reason, he was informed that parties unknown "had requested Genovese's transfer, because a certain General's name had become involved." Dickey removed Genovese from the Naples facility and took him to a civilian jail in Avellino. A week later, he forwarded a request through the War Department to the FBI requesting copies of the arrest warrant from Brooklyn officials.

Some time in early January, Dickey received word that the information he requested would soon arrive. He was asked that Genovese be removed to another jail "incommunicado." Genovese was then taken to a jail in Bari and held. Dickey battled official red tape for the next few months. He determined that the army had no interest in either prosecuting Genovese for black-market crimes or in returning him to the United States. He was simply told that he was on his own, "to do anything he cared to do." Genovese had become an albatross for Dickey.

In April 1945, after the war had ended in the European theater, Dickey initiated extradition proceedings. On May 17, nearly nine months after his arrest, and some eight years after he left the United States, Vito Genovese was sailing home. On June 2, the steamship *James Lykes* docked in New York harbor. Two agents of the Security Intelligence Corps escorted Dickey and Genovese to the Kings County district attorney's office in Brooklyn. There the prisoner was turned over to Assistant District Attorney Edward A. Heffernan and the ordeal of Agent Orange C. Dickey was over. The information regarding Dickey's investigation was gathered during a question-and-answer session with interim Brooklyn District Attorney George J. Beldock on September 1, 1945. This took place before his appearance before the grand jury. During questioning in June 1945, the following exchange took place:

> *Question:* Was there any particular reason that prompted you to make these extensive efforts to get Genovese back to the United States?
>
> *Answer:* The main reason [was], I wanted to be relieved of the responsibility of his confinement.

One thing even the casual observer can't help miss in Dickey's statement to the prosecutor is that at no time does the CID investigator mention narcotics, not even as a rumor.

THE HAWK RETURNS TO ROOST

Ernest Rupolo served approximately nine years for the wounding of Willie Gallo before being released in January 1943. When he tried to return to his former gang, he found himself shunned by other members. Although he had botched the hit on Gallo, Rupolo had served his time, kept his mouth shut, and now felt he was being rebuffed by the people for whom he had gone to prison—a treatment he soon came to resent.

The near-decade spent in Sing Sing did little to deter Rupolo from continuing his life of crime. On April 17, 1944, again in the capacity of a gun-for-hire, Rupolo accepted $500 to murder Carl Sparacini, a 63-year-old Brooklyn man accused by gamblers of "fingering" a floating crap game that was later robbed at gunpoint. Rupolo shot Sparacini three times in the face but, as in the Gallo shooting 10 years earlier, the victim pulled through and identified Rupolo as his assailant.

On June 1, in the middle of his trial, Rupolo interrupted the proceedings to plead guilty. He admitted he had been hired to do the shooting, but refused to say who had hired him, claiming only that it was "the second job" he had done for the gang. Faced with a sentence of from 40 to 80 years in prison as a repeat offender, Rupolo was ready to deal. After being given a stern directive by Judge Samuel S. Leibowitz, that unless he cooperated fully he would be given the maximum sentence, Rupolo began talking. Police quickly reaped the benefits of Rupolo's betrayal. On June 29, three Brooklyn hoodlums were tossed in jail for holding up a card game three months earlier.

Rupolo soon revealed details of the 1934 killing of Fred Bocci, the murder victim who became Ferdinand "The Shadow" Boccia. Rupolo said that Boccia went to Mike Miranda and Vito Genovese with a plan to set up a wealthy businessman, who liked to gamble, in a crooked card game. By most accounts the man lost $160,000 to the conspirators. Boccia figured his take should be $35,000. It was never certain what payment he actually received, if any, but "the Shadow" was clearly upset with his cut. After reportedly badgering Genovese and Miranda for the money, he decided to take matters a step further and allegedly held up a business run by Anthony Strollo. Genovese had put up with Boccia's complaining, but after this latest incident, he decided "The Shadow" had to go.

Rupolo gave the following intimate details of the murder plot to Brooklyn Assistant District Attorney Heffernan during an interrogation on June 13, 1944:

> They [Genovese and Miranda] assigned me to kill GALLO and I said I will use 'SOLLY' Palmeri. They also assigned 'Blair' (GEO. SMURRA), GU.S. FRANSCA and another man named 'SOLLY' to kill 'SHADOW.' These orders were given to BLAIR, GU.S., SOLLY and myself at a Numbers Office in Mulberry St., PETE DEFEO gave the orders and MIKE MIRANDA was there and also 'PETE SPATZ.' SPATZ was given money to play cards with the SHADOW in his uncle's Coffee Shop on Metropolitan Ave. and the others would come in and kill him. This was about two days before the killing. The last day DEFEO sent the order out to 'cowboy' him, which meant any place you see him, shoot him.[11]

"Pete Spatz" was the nickname of ex-convict Peter LaTempa. The 35-year-old had a history of small-time criminal activity. LaTempa was the card player who "fingered" Boccia for the gunmen in the Gran Café. Although he put Boccia "on the spot," prosecutors didn't consider him an accomplice. This had more to do with New York State law than the facts of the case. Arrested shortly after Rupolo's confession, LaTempa was held as a material witness in the Brooklyn House of Detention for Men, commonly called the Raymond Street Jail. LaTempa was in fear for his life and begged to be relocated and placed in protective custody. On July 5, he was moved to a section of the jail known as the Brooklyn Civil Prison.

On Monday, August 7, Genovese, Mike Miranda, Peter DeFeo, Gus Frasca, and George Smurra were indicted by the Kings County Grand Jury for the murder of Ferdinand Boccia.[12] A sixth indictment for a "John Doe," known only as "Solly," was also returned. Two days later the New York City newspapers broke the story. Of interest, at no time does the reporting in the New York tabloids indicate that Genovese was ever a suspect in the murder before these indictments, despite being arrested and held for a few days for it in December 1934, which disproves the theory that Genovese fled New York City in 1937 because of the Boccia slaying.

The New York Times, in their reporting, stated that Rupolo's disclosures provided information on four unsolved murders, but only the Boccia killing was discussed. The newspaper also claimed that his revelations to prosecutors had leaked out resulting in the immediate indictment of the men. DeFeo, Frasca, and Smurra suddenly disappeared from their usual haunts. They would not be heard from for nearly two years. Miranda, meanwhile, was already in Italy, having joined Vito there years earlier.

The article also described Genovese and his cohorts as members of the Unione Sicilione, "self-appointed successors to the old Maffia [sic], or Black Hand Society transplanted here from Palermo, Sicily, in 1899 by an Italian murderer named Ignazio Saietta."[13] That the Unione Sicilione had replaced the Mafia was a common belief among many law enforcement officials at the time.

One week after the indictments became public, Rupolo stood in front of Judge Leibowitz for sentencing on the charge of assault in the first degree. After the Kings County district attorney's office acknowledged the receipt of "very helpful" information, the judge postponed Rupolo's sentencing indefinitely stating, "You continue to tell the truth. Tell the whole truth in every detail. If you do that, the court will consider you."[14]

As prosecutors continued to build their case against the fugitives, three prisoners from Sing Sing, named by Rupolo, were brought to the city for questioning in hopes of providing more witnesses in the case. On November 25, Acting District Attorney Thomas C. Hughes announced the apprehension of Genovese by military authorities in Rome. It would be nearly seven months before his return.

As the military red tape was being dealt with, a warrant for Genovese's arrest was issued from Brooklyn in December. That same month, perhaps because of the fear of having to testify against the underworld bigwig, Peter LaTempa attempted suicide. He was found by a guard at the prison and cut down after he had attempted to hang himself from the top bar of his cell with a towel.

On Monday, January 15, 1945, LaTempa was paid a visit by his brother Sylvester and later by two detectives from the district attorney's office. In the afternoon the detectives took him out of the prison, where he was able to get some exercise by walking. Sometime during the day he had a prescription for gallbladder medicine refilled. To all he encountered, LaTempa appeared to be in "good spirits."[15]

The next morning, LaTempa failed to rise at his usual time and a guard stepped into his cell to wake him. LaTempa was lying on his cot and was unresponsive to the guard's voice and jostling. The prison physician was called to the cell where LaTempa was pronounced dead. There was no sign of foul play. Assistant District Attorney Heffernan, after ordering the body taken to the Kings County Morgue for an immediate autopsy, announced, "We have lost one of the most important witnesses in this murder case."[16]

The next day, the assistant medical examiner's autopsy failed to reveal the cause of death. Vital organs were removed and sent to the toxicologist at Bellevue Hospital. On February 9, the city toxicologist's report was released stating that LaTempa had died from an overdose of a sedative. Where he got the drug, whether it was the so-called gallbladder medicine, and when and how he ingested it are still mysteries. Because no foul play was detected and because there had been a previous suicide attempt, Prosecutor Heffernan declared that LaTempa's death was not a murder.

On the day the report was released, a *Brooklyn Eagle* article stated that an unnamed, high police official claimed there was enough of the drug in LaTempa's stomach "to kill eight horses." Over the years this story has become part of "Mob-lore" and been twisted to make the reader believe that the Mafia somehow poisoned LaTempa and that it was the toxicologist who had issued the comment about the "eight horses." The reality was, even if he had lived to testify, LaTempa, being a participant in the murder plot, could not have been a corroborating witness. There was simply no reason for the mob to murder him.

After his ordeal in Italy with CID Agent Dickey and his subsequent extradition to the United States, Genovese was arraigned in Kings County Court on June 2, 1945, for the murder of Ferdinand Boccia. Vito pleaded not guilty through his attorney Hyman Barshay, who had once represented Lepke Buchalter. Vito languished in a jail cell waiting for the Kings County prosecutor to present a case that should never have come to trial.

It is unclear why the case took so long to see the inside of a courtroom. On May 6, 1946, the trial was scheduled to begin but, at the request of Assistant District Attorney Julius Helfand, the trial was adjourned for one month. The state claimed it needed more time to locate Mike Miranda in Italy and extradite him. Why this suddenly became an issue nearly a year later was not explained; all of the other indicted men were still at large.

On Thursday, July 6, 13 years after the murder of Ferdinand Boccia and nearly 2 years since the arrest of Genovese in Italy, the trial began in the courtroom of Judge Samuel Leibowitz. Prosecutor Helfand's first order of business was to ask the judge for another postponement, claiming he expected to hear from the FBI shortly about their effort to return Miranda to the United States.

Leibowitz would have none of it. Calling the request "too nebulous" to consider, he told Helfand that, "every defendant, whether he is good or bad, has rights under the Constitution that cannot be frittered away. This defendant has been in jail for almost a year. The trial must proceed."[17] The selection of a blue-ribbon jury to hear the case took only 80 minutes to complete. Rupolo, the state's star witness, took the stand on Friday, the second and final day of testimony. When asked by Judge Leibowitz what his occupation was, he responded, "Stabbing, killing, burglary or any other crime I got paid for." During his testimony, Rupolo related the following conversation with Miranda:

> "Frasca tells me that you are a good boy, that you could do a good job." Then he also says to me: "The Shadow and Gallo are no good. I want you to put Gallo and the Shadow on the spot, so they can be killed." I said: "No, I won't do that. I'd rather kill them myself."[18]

The prosecutor then asked Rupolo to describe his deal with Genovese and the shooting of Gallo:

> I met Genovese twice. The boys called him the big man. There was deal made for me to kill Gallo for five grand. Some other guys were to get Boccia, The Shadow.
> Gallo and I became good friends. He and I and my pal Solly Young were in Bensonhurst the night of Sept. 20, 1934 [*sic*]. I put a pistol to Gallo's head, quick-like, and fired. The gun clicked. Gallo wanted to know what I was doing. I said I was fooling around, that's all. He said I could get arrested for carrying a gun. I left him and Solly, went around the corner and oiled my gun. When I came back Solly and I let him have it. I thought we killed him. And I didn't get the five grand, either.

The day after the shooting, Rupolo claimed he was berated by Miranda for not killing Gallo and setting his body on fire afterward. He was given $135 and told to hide in Springfield, Massachusetts, until the heat was off. When Rupolo returned a week later, he was arrested.

On cross-examination by attorney Barshay, "The Hawk" stated that he was mad at Genovese "because he ruined my life." Then came the following exchange:

> Barshay: You were angry because he didn't get you a good lawyer, weren't you?
> Rupolo: I would have needed the best lawyer in the country.
> Leibowitz: You didn't need a lawyer, you needed a magician.

After 90 minutes of testimony by "The Hawk," Judge Leibowitz ruled that Rupolo had to be regarded by the jury as an accomplice in the Boccia murder. Since Rupolo was part of the conspiracy, the state would have to produce an independent witness to the crime. For this the state called on William Gallo's testimony to corroborate what Rupolo had stated. Although Gallo testified he was present when the gang discussed giving Boccia a cut of the proceeds from the rigged card game, however, he could not connect Genovese to the murder conspiracy.

After Gallo's testimony, the state rested its case. Barshay immediately asked for a directed verdict of acquittal, claiming the state had failed to prove its case beyond a reasonable doubt because Rupolo's testimony was not corroborated by an independent witness, as required by New York state law. Judge Leibowitz gave both sides until Saturday to submit briefs on whether or not the state met the burden of proof with its evidence.

On Monday, June 10, after professing that other witnesses had died or were scared off, a dejected Helfand told the court, "We are therefore constrained to advise the court we do not have the necessary evidence supporting the accomplice Rupolo. We reluctantly consent to a dismissal of this indictment."[19]

Judge Leibowitz had no choice but to agree, declaring that, "even though his [Rupolo's] testimony may be true, the defendant may not be convicted unless there is some evidence, from a non-accomplice witness" . . . and that Gallo's testimony . . . "does not fall into this category."

Leibowitz, however, was not about to let the defendant walk out of the court without giving him an earful:

> Genovese, although you have been arrested many times for crimes ranging from robbery to murder, so far as the law is concerned you have led a charmed life.
>
> You and your criminal henchmen thwarted justice time and again by devious means, among them terrorizing witnesses, kidnapping and even murdering those who would give evidence against you.
>
> I cannot speak for the jury, but I believe that if there were even a shred of corroborating evidence you would have been condemned to the chair.
>
> You have won again. Sooner or later, unless some fellow criminal rubs you out, the law will catch up with you and its heavy fist will destroy you.[20]

As the judge issued his stern rebuke to the gangster, the *New York Post* noted, "The slender little plug-ugly, didn't even bother to waste a smile of gratitude on the court. He knew nothing would be done to him."

In a final sendoff to the smug mobster, Leibowitz issued this harsh warning:

Remember that the court warns you and your agents not to attempt to harm Rupolo or Gallo because they violated the code of the underworld and dared to testify against you. If convicted of any attempt at reprisal against these state's witnesses you will be shown no mercy.

THE LONG CLIMB TO THE TOP

After the charges against Genovese in the Boccia murder case were dismissed, Vito disappeared from public scrutiny for the next five years. Many expected him to reclaim the position he had forfeited when he left for Italy a decade earlier. Whatever Genovese's plan was to return to the top of the Luciano gang, it would be a long and, at times, bloody process.

Genovese purchased a home in Atlantic Highlands, New Jersey, for $38,000, which he paid for in cash. It was reported that he spent more than $75,000 on exterior improvements, decorations, and furnishings to the English-style mansion. Described as a gracious host, Genovese entertained many of the underworld leaders from New York and New Jersey there.

Costello was keenly aware of Genovese's ambitions and did what he could to placate him without showing weakness, for example, his celebrated fundraiser for the Salvation Army in January 1949. In addition to a number of Costello's legitimate and underworld friends who attended, a few detectives from the Intelligence Division of the New York City Police Department slipped in uninvited. In the book *The Crime Confederation,* Ralph Salerno, a decorated police officer who served with the Central Intelligence Bureau of the NYPD, discussed the incident:

> Vito Genovese himself came to the affair and was met at the door by Costello who ushered him to the best seat in the house. Word of this public demonstration of "respect" traveled throughout the underworld and the New York City Police Department's intelligence accepted it as evidence that Genovese had emerged as one of the top men in organized crime.[21]

Despite a plethora of legal problems, Frank Costello was still the boss of the underworld in New York City. Costello's appearance before the Kefauver Committee in March 1951, however, signaled the start of his decline. Genovese, meanwhile, ducked the committee's subpoena and never testified. Soon thereafter, Vito began his murderous ascent to the top.

The first victim was longtime northern New Jersey mob boss Willie Moretti. The affable gangster, who had amused Kefauver and his Senate colleagues months earlier with his humorous replies, was murdered in Joe's Restaurant, located across from the Palisade Amusement Park in Cliffside Park, New Jersey. Moretti had been a close friend and confidant of Costello and other ranking underworld figures in New Jersey and New York. His alleged bout with untreated syphilis, however, raised concerns in the underworld about his ability to keep his mouth shut. Despite Costello's efforts to protect Moretti, Genovese convinced enough people that Willie had to go for the good of the others. John "Johnny Roberts" Robilotto, at the time a Genovese soldier, set up Moretti for the kill and was later indicted for the murder; the charges were dropped because of insufficient evidence.

The next murder victim was Eugene "Gene" Giannini, a member of the Gagliano/Lucchese Gang. Giannini had a long criminal record dating back to 1927. Included on his rap sheet were two homicide arrests, one for the murder of a police officer on the Lower East Side. Giannini also had two narcotics convictions under his belt for which he served

15 months apiece. By the early 1950s, he was traveling to Rome, where he purchased narcotics and dealt in black market medicine such as penicillin, which was badly needed in Italy. Some reports claimed that Giannini was working both sides of the street. Serving as an informant for the Federal Narcotics Bureau, he traded information in exchange for being able to operate with some level of impunity.

During the summer of 1951, Giannini was arrested in Rome on counterfeiting charges. The vile conditions in the jail led Giannini to seek help from Narcotics Bureau agents. What happened next is unclear, leading to several versions. In New York, instead of the Gagliano/Lucchese people taking care of one of their own bad apples, Genovese allegedly used this incident to flex his muscle and ordered the murder. Anthony Strollo relayed the order to Joe Valachi, to whom Giannini owed money. Valachi then set up the murder using brothers Joseph and Pasquale "Pat" Pagano and his own nephew Fiore "Fury" Siano. The killing took place outside a crap game Giannini was attending on Second Avenue, between 111th and 112th Streets. Giannini died from a bullet wound in the back of the head.

ANNA'S WRATH

As the old saying goes, "Hell hath no furry like a woman scorned." After a long and abusive relationship, Anna Genovese took her son Phillip and moved to a New York City apartment in March 1950. She later claimed her exodus from the Atlantic Highland's home was due to Vito's cruelty, which "endangered her health and made her life extremely wretched."[22] She soon initiated a divorce action and then dropped the suit when Vito began making $200 weekly payments to her.

In December 1952, just weeks after the government's denaturalization action against her husband, Anna filed suit for separate maintenance in Freehold, New Jersey, in the Monmouth County Clerk's office. The maintenance request asked for $350 a week and $5,000 in legal fees. Vito quickly filed a countersuit. The next month, a court ordered Genovese to pay Anna $300 a week pending disposition of the lawsuit.

The suit for separate maintenance finally came before the court on March 2, 1953. It proved to be an embarrassing moment for Genovese. Anna testified that during their nearly 22 years of marriage, Vito often beat her, once breaking her nose and blackening both eyes. On another occasion he set her hair on fire. She told the court, "I never told the doctors I was beaten, I was so ashamed of it. He threatened to put me in an insane asylum, drive me to suicide or kill me." In another statement she talked about decadent activities at the Atlantic Highland's home, "You should see the kissing parties, the games, the drunken parties."

When questioned about her husband's financial matters, Anna was quite candid about Vito's income and how he earned it, declaring that while he was in Italy she personally handled $20,000 to $30,000 each week that was brought to the home from proceeds of the Italian lottery in New York City. Anna claimed at one point, "Money was no object. I never knew the value of it." As for his illegal activities, Anna stated, "He's involved in almost all the rackets," meeting with "syndicate" members Tuesday and Thursday of each week.

The judge hearing the case barred testimony about the individuals who frequented their home as irrelevant. Later, after court had adjourned, Anna told reporters that Albert Anastasia, Frank Costello, Longy Zwillman, and the Moretti brothers Willie and Salvatore were among the regular visitors.

Anna talked about a Thomas Calandriello, a man who fronted for gambling operations at the Kearny Pier, formerly run by the navy. She said she was told by Vito and Calandriello that if she testified that Vito was earning more than $100 a week, Calandriello would "come with a shotgun and blow my head off." She later mentioned that her son Phillip, who was currently a senior at Seton Hall College, was married to Calandriello's daughter.

On the stand the next morning, Vito claimed, "I was always a devoted husband and father, and every bit of money I made went to my family. I never cursed her or got drunk or threw wild parties like she said. I never punched Anna and she never punched me. As it stands right now, the door is open to Anna and she can return." Anna actually considered Vito's offer. The judge called a recess to let her think about it, but after a hallway conversation with her lawyer she changed her mind.

After hearing final arguments, it took the judge five months to render a decision. In the meantime, on March 10, a New Jersey superior court judge found Vito in contempt of the court order to pay his wife $300 a week. Days later, it was announced that the Atlantic Highland's home was to be sold at a sheriff's sale to satisfy a construction company's claim that it was owed $32,000 for reconstruction work performed on the house in 1948 and 1949. The company's owner had testified on Vito's behalf during the maintenance suit. As an official appraiser, he claimed the home was valued at $55,000. Anna had testified during the trial that the home, overlooking Sandy Hook Bay, was worth $250,000.

Most of Genovese's underworld contemporaries were shocked when Vito did not have Anna silenced. Years later Joe Valachi would relate:

> "Nobody could understand why Vito didn't do anything about her," Valachi recalls. "The word was all around, why don't he hit her? But he must have really cared for her. She had something on him. I remember when we—Vito and me—were in Atlanta together later on, he would sometimes talk about her, and I would see the tears rolling down his cheeks. I couldn't believe it."[23]

This didn't mean Genovese stood idly by. He took out his revenge on Stephen Franse. Valachi explained that Anna "had fallen away" from Vito during his years in Italy and when Genovese returned, he blamed Franse for "not keeping a closer eye on her." There were various rumors about Anna, one that perhaps Franse had not only kept a close eye on her, but also a couple of hands. A nightclub operator, Franse was reportedly a partner with Anna in a couple of Greenwich Village operations.

In June 1953, three months after the court hearing for separate maintenance, Valachi claimed that Anthony Strollo told him that Franse was to be killed because he was a "rat." On June 18, Pat Pagano, Fiore Siano, and Franse showed up at Valachi's restaurant, the Lido, just before 5:00 AM. The two men lured Franse there under the guise of "we want Steve to see your joint."

Within minutes the two men began giving Franse a savage beating, something Valachi referred to as '"buck wheats,' meaning spite-work." They completed their mission by strangling him to death. Later that morning, Franse's body was found face-down on the rear floor of his automobile, which was then left parked in front of a liquor store on East 37th Street. The murder was made to look as if it were a mugging and a robbery. The *New York Herald-Tribune* reported:

Mr. Franse's pockets [were] turned inside out, his face swollen, his right eye badly blackened, a cut an inch and a half long under his chin, and marks around his neck. An autopsy showed that Mr. Franse had died of manual strangulation, and that he suffered fractured left ribs and contusions and abrasions of the body and face. It was learned that Mr. Franse's gold wrist watch and a sapphire and diamond ring was missing with the cash he had been carrying.[24]

On August 19, 1953, a superior court judge dismissed Anna's separate maintenance suit and Vito's counter-divorce suit. A week later the same judge agreed to allow the sheriff's sale of the Genovese home.

During an interview with the *Newark Star-Ledger* in January 1959, Anna told a reporter, "I wish I hadn't brought the case. I'm sure there was nothing between us that couldn't have been patched up."[25]

In addition to his domestic problems, Genovese was facing problems with the government. On November 21, 1953, his 55th birthday, Genovese was greeted by news that the government was moving to denaturalize and deport him for concealing his criminal record when he applied for citizenship in 1936. In a *New York Times* article announcing the action, Genovese was described as:

A short, sallow, truculent man with a weakness for flashy garb and for big mansions. He is 5 feet 7 inches tall, dark-haired and brown-eyed. He has two scars on his right check. He had a fondness for glittering limousines.[26]

When government agents tried to serve papers to Genovese at his Atlantic Highland's home, they could not find him, after which the newspapers labeled him a fugitive. A few days later, an Asbury Park attorney announced he had been hired by Genovese to represent him. The attorney issued a statement saying, "Genovese is not a fugitive from anything or anyone. He is and has been available at his home in nearby Atlantic Highlands anytime that anyone wanted to see him." A year later, in November 1953, the government officially denaturalized Genovese, opening the door for the underworld figure to be deported.

BACK TO THE MURDER SPREE

Genovese was still licking his wounds from the humiliating divorce suit and now facing deportation when he ordered the next murder. In a situation uncannily similar to the Giannini murder, Dominick "The Gap" Petrelli was gunned down in a Bronx bar and grill. Petrelli, who had been a mentor to Joe Valachi, had a rap sheet that totaled 36 arrests, including assault, robbery, policy violations, and narcotics. In 1942, he was convicted on a narcotics violation and sentenced to five years in prison. After his release he was deported to Italy on December 20, 1947.

According to Valachi, in November 1953, Anthony Strollo approached him and announced, "The Gap is back. He got picked up in Italy for something and made a deal with the junk agents. They let him come back to set us up." Strollo told Valachi that Petrelli was sure to stop in and see his old friend and when he did to give him a call.

Like Giannini, Petrelli was a member of the Gagliano/Lucchese gang and Valachi implored Strollo to "let those people handle it." Again, Genovese was determined to take the lead in administering mob justice.

Just before 4:00 AM on December 9, 1953, Petrelli was drinking at Mauriello's Bar & Grill on East 183rd Street in The Bronx. The owner, Nicholas Mauriello, was the brother of boxer Tami Mauriello, a one-time heavyweight title contender. While Petrelli talked with the owner, three men entered. Upon seeing them, Petrelli dropped his drink and ran to the rear of the restaurant. The three men, who had pulled weapons, were right on his heels and soon opened fire. Petrelli, brought down by three bullets in the back, was finished off with four in the head.

The 1950s had not been kind to Frank Costello. Nearly the entire decade was consumed with legal problems: the Kefauver hearings and contempt of Senate trial; a tax evasion trial; and finally a deportation hearing, followed by three prison stretches. With Costello's legal battles, it was impossible for him to keep a close watch on the conniving Vito Genovese, let alone try to counter his moves.

After serving 11 months of a five-year term for tax evasion, Costello won a reprieve while new evidence was being ruled on. It was during this interval that Genovese made his boldest move and sent Vincent Gigante to assassinate Costello (see Chapter 4).

After the failed assassination attempt, Genovese retreated to his Atlantic Highland's home to plot his next move. He called the gang's chief lieutenants to his residence to see who was going to follow him and who would stay loyal to Costello. In *The Valachi Papers,* Maas wrote:

> Word of what occurred at the meeting of lieutenants gradually filtered through the Family ranks. Genovese blandly declared that he had been forced to take such drastic action because Costello was actually plotting to kill *him.* He also stated that Costello could no longer be allowed to wield any influence because of his total disinterest in the welfare of Family members and from that point on, anyone caught contacting Costello would have to answer personally to him. Finally he officially confirmed himself head of the Family, in case there were any doubts, and appointed New Jersey-based Gerardo (Jerry) Catena, who had succeeded Willie Moretti, as his underboss.[27]

The only mobster of note to stay away was Anthony "Little Augie Pisano" Carfano. Many believed an all-out gang war was about to begin, but Costello refused to seek revenge. Genovese breathed a sigh of relief, knowing he had finally obtained at least part of his goal.

Costello's reaction clearly showed that he didn't have the stomach for an internecine gang war with Vito and instead was willing to step aside. That left just one obstruction in the way of Genovese—Albert Anastasia. This time, instead of ordering the hit of another family's member on his own, he conspired with Anastasia's underboss, Carlo Gambino, to have Albert murdered. On October 25, 1957, Anastasia was shot down while sitting in a barber's chair at the Park Sheraton Hotel (see Chapter 2). With Anastasia out of the way, there was no one to keep Genovese from declaring himself *Capo di tutti Capi;* all he needed was a forum in which to do it.

APALACHIN SUMMIT

On November 14, 1957, more than 60 members of organized crime in the United States met at the home of Joseph Barbara Sr. in the tiny hamlet of Apalachin, New York, described as a suburb of nearby Binghamton. All but 11 of the men were from the New Jersey–New

York–Pennsylvania area. According to one mob historian, the meeting had been called for the following reasons:

> An official justification by Genovese to his peers of his attacks on Costello and Anastasia; a demand by Genovese that he be named boss of all bosses and receive, as tribute, cash-filled envelopes from the delegates [apparently something he witnessed when Maranzano went through the same process 26 years earlier]; authorization of a massive purge to eliminate unreliable members of the Combination; the closing of books on the admittance of new members until the purge had created a tightly knit and loyal Organization; the formulation of an Organization policy on narcotics (for there was a growing belief that the massive antidrug drive by authorities was making narcotics too hot to handle).[28]

This was only one "expert's" opinion. Everyone who has written about the celebrated Apalachin Summit seems to have discovered a different agenda.

> "Gentlemen, we were trying to be considerate, Joe [Barbara] hasn't been feeling too good. His heart is on the bum. We wanted to cheer him up with a party. . . . As it turned out, it was a good thing the excitement didn't kill him."
> —Vito Genovese explaining his presence at Apalachin, New York, in November 1957 to two reporters from the *New York Journal American* during an interview at his home.
> (Frasca, *King of Crime*, 1959, p. 201)

Two alert police officers caused the meeting to breakup earlier than scheduled. Sergeant Edgar Croswell and Trooper Vincent Vasisko, of the New York State Police, became suspicious the day before when they overheard Barbara's son making reservations at a local motel for some out-of-town guests. After alerting agents from the Alcohol Tax Unit, their sleuthing continued until the next day when they drove to the Barbara home and found nearly three dozen expensive automobiles parked on the grounds.

The two officers hurriedly began writing down license plate numbers, but they were soon discovered by several of Barbara's guests, who quickly made their associates aware of the uninvited company. Croswell and Vasisko moved back down the road and set up a roadblock. Soon a local fish vendor drove out of the Barbara home and then returned, perhaps running an impromptu scouting mission for the hoods.

According to some accounts of the ensuing events, Genovese was rounded up with the others, but Croswell told a different story when interviewed for a *Parade* magazine article published on June 14, 1959. Genovese was in the first car that left the Barbara estate. With him were Russell Buffalino and three other men, not identified in the article. When the hoodlums ran into Croswell's roadblock, they were stopped and ordered out of the automobile. Each man was then searched and briefly questioned. Croswell allowed the Genovese automobile to continue on its way. Additional troopers quickly arrived as the other meeting participants attempted to leave the Barbara home. These people were ordered held for questioning before being released. By the next morning, the incident was front-page news across the nation.

The reasons for the meeting were never firmly established, but the result was that Genovese had exposed the underworld on a grand scale, leaving the obvious impression that mob bosses all over the country were working together.

APALACHIN AFTERMATH

The Apalachin disaster was the beginning of the end for Vito Genovese. His peers would blame him for the national exposure by news media across the country, for the deluge of law enforcement scrutiny, and finally for the entry of the Federal Bureau of Investigation into the war on organized crime.

Not only was Genovese plagued by law enforcement at this point, but even his family was hounded. Less than two weeks after the meeting, Mike Genovese, public relations counsel for the New York Waste Paper & Packers Association, was hauled in by police to be questioned about the murder of Anastasia, and what he knew about the meeting. He was grilled for three hours before being released. The next month, Anna Genovese was subpoenaed to appear before a Mercer County, New Jersey, grand jury. When Anna protested, saying she knew nothing about the meeting, she was told she would be held in contempt of court if she failed to appear. On December 14, Anna was questioned in Trenton, New Jersey, for 75 minutes. Her only comment to newsmen upon leaving was, "I'm exhausted."

Reacting to the meeting was Nassau County District Attorney Frank A. Gulotta, who ordered raids on the homes of 15 gangsters as part of a police harassment campaign to drive mobsters out of the county. Included in the raids were the homes of Genovese associates Mike Miranda and John "Big John" Ormento.

In January 1957, the Senate Select Committee on Improper Activities in the Labor or Management Field was established. It became known as the "Rackets Committee," because of its investigation of the country's leading labor racketeers. It was also called the "McClellan Committee," as it was headed by Arkansas Senator John L. McClellan. During the summer of 1958, the committee was holding another investigative session. In announcing this latest legal round, the *New York Times* stated, "Probably the most important of the witnesses in the opening stages will be Vito Genovese."[29] The newspaper claimed committee members would "dig deeply into Genovese's past," and one of the areas they would focus on would be Vito's employment by the United States as an interpreter in Italy during the war.

When Genovese faced his inquisitors on July 2, he surprised no one when he invoked his Fifth Amendment right and answered, "I respectfully decline to answer on grounds my answer may intend to incriminate me." By the time Genovese left the stand, he had exercised his right more than 150 times.

Before Genovese was called, a number of witnesses familiar with his past testified about his activities. One of the more interesting witnesses was Vito's old trans-Atlantic traveling companion, Orange C. Dickey. The former CID agent, now running a bakery in Altoona, Pennsylvania, told the committee about Genovese's black-market activities in Italy. The most interesting part of Dickey's testimony was that while he had Genovese in his custody, he said Vito had offered him $250,000 to release him. This was a startling revelation considering Dickey had left this out of his testimony nearly 12 years earlier when he was questioned by the acting Brooklyn district attorney.

THE TRIAL

A few days after his benign appearance before the Senate Rackets Committee, Genovese was arrested at his Atlantic Highlands home and charged with conspiring to import and sell narcotics. His arrest followed the apprehension of Vincent Gigante, two hours earlier. Paul W. Williams, the U.S. attorney for the Southern District of New York announced, "The arrest of Genovese is one of the most important arrests ever made in this field. Our investigation discloses that Genovese was the hub around which this entire conspiracy revolved, and Gigante was one of his protégés and a rising star."[30]

The next day, July 8, the two men were arraigned and the conspiracy indictment was read in court before Federal Judge William B. Herlands. The *New York Times* reported:

> The indictment named thirty-seven persons as members of a syndicate importing large quantities of heroin and other narcotics from Europe, Cuba, Puerto Rico and Mexico. The drugs were said to have been distributed in such areas as New York, Chicago, Philadelphia, Cleveland and Las Vegas.

Williams told the judge that Genovese decided in which territories narcotics would be sold and who was going to sell them. Attorney Wilfred L. Davis, representing Genovese, scoffed at Williams's portrayal of his client, calling it "grossly inaccurate." He described Genovese as a businessman who paid his income taxes and lived modestly in a "small rented house." When the judge asked about his business, Davis claimed Vito was the operator of Erb Strapping Company, a repackaging concern. By 4:00 PM, both Genovese and Gigante were free after posting bonds of $50,000 and $35,000, respectively.

With Genovese's narcotics trial pending, the Immigration & Naturalization Service announced it would await the results before making a decision on proceeding with deportation action.

The day after the indictments were announced, U.S. Attorney Williams resigned to seek the Republican nomination for governor of New York. He subsequently removed himself from the race, which was won by Nelson Rockefeller. Throughout the course of the trial, defense lawyers would claim that Williams sought the indictments for his own political gain; however, there would be more clandestine claims as to how the indictments were secured. In the book *Meyer Lansky: Mogul of the Mob,* the authors interviewed "Doc" Stacher. The aging hood claimed that in addition to Lansky arranging for Genovese's "humiliation" at Apalachin, Meyer was also responsible for Vito's narcotics indictment:

> Then Meyer trapped Genovese. The bait was set by one of Meyer's couriers, Nelson Cantellops. Meyer had been angry with Nelson because he got himself mixed up with running drugs at the same time he was working for Meyer. When Nelson was caught, Meyer refused to help him and he went to Sing Sing on a narcotics charge. Then, using his brother Jake, Meyer passed the message to Nelson that he would forgive him if he would take on a little job. Cantellops was promised a pension for life. So our friend Nelson Cantellops, despite the danger he'd be in, asked for an interview with the Narcotics Bureau in New York and

told an agent, George Gaffney, that he could provide information about how Genovese and his partners were smuggling narcotics from Europe to the United States.[31]

Nelson Silva Cantellops was described as a "sallow-faced Puerto Rican," standing five-feet, six-inches tall.[32] His knowledge of the narcotics business came from being a courier for the defendants, for whom he handled deliveries throughout the country.

In *The Last Testament of Lucky Luciano,* the deported mob boss puts a different spin on the event. He claimed it was Carlo Gambino's idea to have Cantellops set up his old friend Genovese. Cantellops was paid $100,000, of which he claims Costello would put up half as long as the plot included the arrest of Vincent Gigante, his would-be assassin.

Luciano claimed that Gambino wanted to include Thomas "Tommy Ryan" Eboli in the frame-up because he helped provide Vito's muscle, but Lucky said he vetoed the move because of his friendship with Eboli's brother Pat. Both accounts claimed that Cantellops was serving a stretch in Sing Sing for a narcotics conviction when he contacted federal narcotics agents, but the newspapers reported he had been imprisoned at Auburn State Prison for forgery.

While neither account has ever been proven, Ralph Salerno, in his book *The Crime Confederation,* weighs in with the following thought:

> Genovese's family had indeed been involved in narcotics, but Nelson Cantellops, a narcotics courier, swore in court that he had personally met and talked with Genovese about details of the business. To anyone who understands the protocol and insulation procedures of Cosa Nostra, this testimony is almost unbelievable. A top man might slip up on security precautions once in a while, but there would be no business or social reason for him to meet anyone as directly connected with the crime as a courier.

The trial began on January 5, 1959, and was held at the federal building in Foley Square before Judge Alexander Bicks. The government's case was handled by Acting U.S. Attorney Arthur H. Christy. Notable attorneys representing the defendants were Maurice Edelbaum and a young Albert Krieger, who, 32 years later, would represent John Gotti during the "Teflon Don's" final trial.

"This testimony reads like a tale from the Arabian Nights. This is all ridiculous and fantastic. It is a figment of someone's imagination. I have no worry. I'm not losing sleep over it. A clear conscience has no fear."
—Vito Genovese during an interview with *Newark Star-Ledger* reporter Tex Novellino, February 1, 1959, while on trial in federal court for narcotics conspiracy.

Most of the trial was consumed by the defense attorneys' cross-examination of the government's start witness Nelson Cantellops. Among the trial's highlights were the following:

February 3: Asked to describe defendant Joseph DiPalermo, Cantellops said he is about 6 feet tall and about 155 pounds. DiPalermo was told to stand. He was actually 5', 4" tall and weighed all of 110 pounds. When the laughter died down in the courtroom, Cantellops was asked if he expected to reap any benefits from his testimony. "I don't expect anything, but whatever the government can do for me I would be very grateful," he replied.

February 6: Judge Bicks admonished Edelbaum as the attorney berated Cantellops in his attempt to discredit him. At one point Cantellops told Edelbaum, "Okay, everything you say is correct." In a severe reprimand to the attorney, Bicks tells Edelbaum, "You have baited him, harangued him and tried to embarrass him."

February 9: By this point in the trial, defense attorneys had made 25 motions for the judge to declare a mistrial.

February 10: During a recess, U.S. Narcotics Agent John Enright was threatened by defendant Daniel Lessa. Bicks announced that he was going to revoke Lessa's bond and send him to jail, but reversed his decision after a meeting in chambers with attorneys for both sides.

February 11: As the sixth day of cross-examination by Edelbaum came to an end, Cantellop's denied that former U.S. Attorney Paul Williams had promised him a pardon if he were to be elected governor.

February 25: Cantellop's testimony, which began on January 21, ended. He was followed on the stand by Peter Contes, who identified defendants Rocco Mazzie and brothers Daniel and Nicholas Lessa as men he was involved with in numerous narcotics deals. Contes also named "Big John" Ormento, who was still a fugitive, as another participant in the deals.

February 26: Although on record as the attorney for Vincent Gigante, Maurice Edelbaum made an impassioned plea for Genovese while the jury was out of the courtroom. Claiming that Paul Williams had orchestrated the indictments for political advancement, Edelbaum stated, "Your honor, I submit this is a frame-up. This defendant, Genovese, was indicted only to serve somebody else's purpose."

Edelbaum claimed that U.S. Customs Agent Benjamin Begendorf had visited Genovese at his Atlantic Highlands home on December 6 and told him that the indictment "was a frame-up on the part of Paul Williams, who had decided to run for the governorship." The trip to the mob boss's home by Begendorf was never denied; however, in an affidavit, the agent claimed the conversation Genovese reported never took place.[33]

March 12: During the testimony of Federal Narcotics Agent Leonard Lang, defendant Louis Fiano jumped to his feet and called him a "filthy liar."

March 16: The government rested its case.

The defense did not call a single witness. Instead, they asked the judge for a directed verdict of acquittal, which Bicks refused to grant. Final arguments by defense attorneys took a week to complete. U.S. Attorney Christy gave a six-hour summation, which was delivered over two –days. This was followed by a jury charge by Judge Bicks that lasted eight hours. Finally, on April 2, the jury of five men and seven women was given the case.

Despite the length of the trial—14 weeks—and the number of defendants to make decisions on—15 in all—the jury deliberated just 12 hours before returning to the courtroom at 10:05 on the night of Friday, April 3. All of the defendants, with the exception of Louis Fiano, were found guilty.

Christy urged the judge to remand the convicted men at once. Bicks continued the bails of five and sent the rest to jail. Genovese, free on a $50,000 bond, was allowed until Monday to come up with an extra $100,000. Bicks set the date of April 17 for the sentencing.

On Friday, April 17, the 62-year-old Genovese stood before Judge Bicks and received a 15-year prison term and a $20,000 fine. His bail was revoked, and he was led off to jail as a new attorney quickly filed an appeal for him.

It would take nearly 10 months before Genovese went to prison. Two weeks after he was sentenced, and while still in a New York City jail, government attorneys got the court to freeze his assets to keep Genovese from transferring or disposing of his property. On June 5, the U.S. Court of Appeals allowed him to repost a $150,000 bond while his case was being reviewed.

Two weeks after his release, Genovese was subpoenaed to testify before the New York State Investigative Commission. After being granted immunity from prosecution by the state, Genovese took the witness stand and told the commission that he had gone to Apalachin on an invitation to attend a buffet barbecue, where he hoped to sell some steel to Joseph Barbara. Genovese claimed that because Barbara had suffered a heart attack, he was unable to conduct any business with him. He claimed that the only attendees he knew were Jerry Catena and Mike Miranda.

Genovese told his interrogators that his presence at Apalachin led to subsequent misfortunes, including being "framed" during his recent narcotics trial. Completing four hours of testimony, Genovese wrapped it up by stating, "I should have broken both my legs before accepting that invitation."

On July 2, the deal that Nelson Cantellops hoped to get from Paul Williams had he become governor was handed to him by the man who won the nomination the former U.S. attorney had been seeking. Governor Nelson Rockefeller commuted the sentence of Cantellops, stating that he hoped his decision would encourage other dope traffickers to come forward and turn against the men who reaped the greatest profits from the drug trade. In his declaration, the governor said he had been given an assurance by the federal government that Cantellops would receive "all the protection for his person that he might desire."[34]

Cantellops was given a parole date of July 16. The 24-year-old had been serving a 40-month sentence at the Auburn State Prison for "attempted felonious possession of narcotics with intent to sell." He would have been eligible for parole in February 1960. One is left to wonder why, if the allegations that Cantellops was bribed to frame Genovese weren't true, would the young man have placed his life in jeopardy just to get out of prison a mere seven months earlier in what was a relatively short prison stretch.

While Genovese sweated out the appeals process, the vindictiveness of the mob leader flared up with another brutal double-murder, this time claiming the life of an innocent woman. Ever since Anthony Carfano had failed to appear at Genovese's family unity day after the attempted assassination of Frank Costello, he had been in Vito's doghouse. Now, for whatever reason, Genovese wanted him out of the way.

Around 10:30 on the night of September 25, 1959, Carfano was found shot to death in his Cadillac on 94th Street in Jackson Heights in Queens. Beside him on the front seat was Janice Drake, a stunning blonde who had been a former Miss New Jersey and was married to comedian Alan Drake. The two, who knew each other, had a chance meeting earlier that evening at the Copacabana Nightclub. Later they dined with friends at Marino's, an Italian restaurant located at Lexington Avenue and 58th Street. From there the two left alone stating they were going to watch the Friday night televised fights, never disclosing where they were headed. Police theorized that two killers in the back seat were, either hiding or had gotten into the car because Carfano knew them. The car was found with its engine still running and the headlights on, one wheel parked on the curb.[35]

Genovese and his lawyers felt they had a pretty good case on appeal. Claiming that they were deprived of a fair trial because of the large number of defendants being tried at one time, the legal team was confident they would get the conviction reversed or, at least, be granted a new trial.

On January 12, 1960, their hopes were dashed when the U.S. Court of Appeals unanimously upheld the lower court's decision. Only one of the 15 convicted got a break and was released as a result of what the court called "insufficient evidence of his knowing participation." In regard to their ruling on Genovese, the court specifically stated:

> Although there is no proof that Vito Genovese ever himself handled narcotics or received any money, it is clear from what he said and from his presence at meetings of the conspirators and places where they met and congregated that he had a real interest and concern in the success of the conspiracy.
>
> We find upon all the evidence that there is ample proof of Genovese's participation in the conspiracy as one of its principal directing heads.[36]

On February 11, Vito Genovese surrendered himself after he was denied a bail continuation pending his appeal to the U.S. Supreme Court. Standing in a federal courtroom, Genovese was described as having "gritted his teeth and fought back tears," as the judge signed the surrender order. He was removed to the Federal House of Detention to await prison assignment by the director of federal prisons.

In April, attorneys for Genovese appealed their case to the highest court in the land. Their appeal was built around a story that Cantellops went to a Roman Catholic Church in the Bronx and, before a priest, a notary public, and three attorneys, recanted his testimony, declaring portions of it to be false. Attorneys for the government pointed out that Cantellops had since revealed that his "recantation" was the result of duress and being bribed to do so.[37] The incident was investigated by a federal grand jury in the Southern District of New York and, on May 16, the U.S. Supreme Court refused to hear the appeal.

In his absence, Genovese appointed a triumvirate to oversee the family's business: Jerry Catena, Thomas Eboli, and Mike Miranda. Anthony Strollo also played a key role until April 8, 1962. On that Sunday evening, he told his wife he was going out. She told him, "You better put on your topcoat. It's chilly." Strollo replied, "I'm only going out for a few minutes. Besides, I'm wearing thermal underwear." Anthony "Tony Bender" Strollo was never heard from again.

VALACHI

In 1959, Joseph Valachi, a longtime soldier in the family, was convicted of violating the Federal Narcotics Law and sentenced to 15 years in prison. He was sent to the Atlanta Penitentiary where he spent time as a cellmate of Genovese. In August 1961, he was returned to New York City as a defendant in another trial. Found guilty again, he received a 20-year sentence to be served concurrently with the earlier one.

Valachi returned to Atlanta, but days later was returned to New York City where agents of the Bureau of Narcotics tried to "break" him and get him to inform on other members of the Genovese family. It was while Valachi was under interrogation that Anthony Strollo disappeared.

Shortly after Valachi's return to Atlanta, Genovese began to suspect that he had "talked" to the narcotics agents. Valachi believed it was a co-defendant in the second case that lied to Vito about him to cover his own treachery. Some contend it was the Bureau of Narcotics that spread the rumor, hoping that the accusation about Valachi would create enough pressure on him to make him cooperate.

Whatever the case, in June 1962, Valachi said he was given the "kiss of death" by Genovese on the bed in Vito's prison cell. Convinced he was going to be killed any day, Valachi, scared out of his wits, grabbed a piece of pipe and bludgeoned to death an inmate named John Saupp, mistaking him for Joseph DiPalermo, a henchman of Genovese.

Now, faced with a capital murder charge and a possible death sentence, Valachi made a deal with the government to testify before the McClellan Committee. After more than a year of preparation, on September 26, 1963, Valachi began several days of testimony in the Senate Office Building in Washington D.C. By the time he was through, Valachi had become a household name and the most famous turncoat in the history of the underworld.

Valachi testified as to what he had experienced in his 30 years as a Mafia soldier. In addition, after being coached by the FBI, he released information the agency had obtained through illegal wiretaps, which it could not otherwise have made public. It was clear from Valachi's testimony, and a later book, that his vengeful act was directed at Genovese. By the time Valachi was done talking, he had exposed the inner workings of the Mafia to the entire country.

Shortly after Valachi began talking to the authorities, Genovese was transferred to the Leavenworth Penitentiary in Kansas. On October 21, 1963, his attorney Edward Bennett Williams won a legal round for his client when the U.S. Supreme Court decided that notes from an interview with a government witness taken by prosecutors should have been turned over to the defense.

The ruling was significant because many believed this was Genovese's last chance to ever leave prison alive, and that if the decision went against him, it would effectively end his rule of the crime family that bore his name. Since Genovese had been transferred to Leavenworth, it had been increasingly difficult to relay messages to the people he left in charge. As a result of this void, federal officials believed New York City was on the verge of a major mob war for leadership of the crime family.

In addition to Catena, Eboli, and Miranda as possible successors, the *Chicago American* reported, "There are at least six major aids in Genovese's 450-man crime army."[38] Commenting that the powder keg was for real, Attorney General Robert F. Kennedy stated, "Because of the power that Genovese wielded . . . and the fear in which he is held . . . no move has been made to take over the top spot while his appeal of a narcotics conviction is pending. If Genovese stays in prison . . . we anticipate a major underworld power struggle in New York."[39]

It would take the U.S. Supreme Court 16 months to decide the appeal. On March 1, 1965, the court denied a review of the appeals court decision that refused to grant Genovese, and the others convicted with him, a new trial.

Genovese had spent most of his time in Leavenworth at the prison hospital suffering from a heart ailment. On November 8, 1966, he was transferred to the U.S. Medical Center for Federal Prisoners in Springfield, Missouri. After treatment there, he was returned to the Kansas prison.

> "They gave me a bum rap in the narcotics case. I wouldn't have minded if they got me on tax evasion because that would be fair."
> —Vito Genovese commenting to a fellow Leavenworth inmate in June 1968, eight months before his death.
> (*The New York Times,* February 15, 1969)

On January 30, 1969, after his condition began to worsen, Genovese was sent back to Springfield. On February 14, the 40th anniversary of the Saint Valentine's Day Massacre, Vito Genovese died at age 71 at the Springfield medical facility surrounded by his brother Michael, his son Phillip, and his daughter Nancy.

Genovese's body was flown to the Newark Airport and from there taken to a funeral home in Red Bank, New Jersey, not far from his former home in Atlantic Highlands. FBI agents and New Jersey law enforcement officials waited outside the William S. Anderson Funeral Home, but few Mafia members were reported among the 250 viewers.

The funeral services were held on February 17 at St. Agnes Church in Atlantic Highlands. There were a reported 100 mourners in the 500-seat church, among them 42 family members and 30 fifth-grade students, pupils of Genovese's daughter who taught at the parish's school. No known "Mafia lieutenants" were reported at the church or cemetery. After the mass, the copper coffin containing Don Vitone's body was taken to St. John's Cemetery in Middle Village, Queens for burial.

Vito Genovese, the man who unwittingly had done so much to expose the Mafia in America, was laid to rest not far from Salvatore "Lucky Luciano" Lucania, the man who had done so much to build it up.

NOTES

1. David Hanna, *Vito Genovese* (New York: Belmont Tower Books, 1974), p. 18.

2. Martin Gosch and Richard Hammer, *The Last Testament of Lucky Luciano* (Boston: Little, Brown and Company, 1974), pp. 37–38.

3. Ibid., pp. 39–40.

4. Hanna, *Vito Genovese,* p. 26.

5. Another source claims that Genovese's first wife's name was Donata and that when she died in 1931, she was buried in a silver casket that was accompanied to the cemetery by a $25,000 blanket of flowers mostly paid for by Al Capone. Ted Prager and Leeds Moberley, *Hoodlums— New York* (New York: Retail Distributors, 1959).

6. Peter Maas, *The Valachi Papers* (New York, G. P. Putnam's Sons, 1968), p. 151.

7. *Brooklyn Eagle,* September 20, 1934, "Gangster Slain in Café as 20 Persons Watch."

8. Another tale had gangster Harry Green behind the shooting, allegedly after accusing Rupolo of "squealing."

9. From the files of the Brooklyn district attorney is a note, "Agent Dickey explains that Commendatore is the highest title a civilian can hold in Italy and is a position of honor granted by the King. According to Dickey, Genovese received this honor as a result of his donating $250,000 toward the erection of the Fascist Party building in Nola, Italy."—Ed Reid, *Mafia* (New York: Random House, 1952), p. 233.

10. The book *Gang Rule in New York: The Story of a Lawless Era* was written by Craig Thompson and Allen Raymond and published in 1940. Interestingly, Genovese's name appears only once in the book: "Vito Genovese, another Luciano gunman who fled to New Jersey when his boss got into trouble as the over lord of the town's commercialized prostitution."

11. This statement, taken from the papers of former New York City Prosecutor and Mayor William O'Dwyer, was reprinted in Alan Block, *East Side—West Side: Organizing Crime in New York 1930–1950* (Swansea, Wales: University College Cardiff Press, 1980), pp. 112–113.

12. Gus Frasca was described as a well-known muscleman in South Brooklyn. During Prohibition, he worked for Vannie Higgins. After the repeal of Prohibition, he and William "Wild Bill" Bailey were partners in a protection racket. In 1935, Frasca was charged with wrecking a South Brooklyn barbershop during a barber's price war. The owner refused to press charges against him.

George Smurra, known as "Blah Blah" or "Blackie," was a one-time protégé of Anthony Bonasera described as the former "chief of the Bensonhurst and Bath Beach underworld." Smurra was arrested in May 1934 with Rupolo for consorting with known criminals. At the time, Smurra had 18 previous arrests.

13. *New York Times,* August 9, 1944, "Prisoner's Story 'Breaks' 4 Murders by Brooklyn Ring."

14. *New York Times,* August 16, 1944, ' "The Hawk' Wins Lenity."

15. This in contrast to Genovese biographer Dom Frasca's claim that on that Monday LaTempa was "suffering great pain." Dom Frasca, *King of Crime* (New York: Crown Publishers Inc, 1959), p. 126.

16. *New York Post,* January 16, 1945, "Witness Found Dead in 'Shadow Murder.' "

17. *Brooklyn Eagle,* June 6, 1946, ' "Gang' Murder Jury Picked in 80 Minutes."

18. *Brooklyn Eagle,* June 7, 1946, ' "Murder's My Trade,' The Hawk Tells Court."

19. *New York Post,* June 10, 1946, "Genovese Beats Rap but Not Court's Wrath."

20. Judge Samuel S. Leibowitz's comments to Genovese were compiled from the *New York Post,* December, 10, 1946; the *New York Times,* June 11, 1946; and the *New York Herald Tribune,* June 11, 1946.

21. Compare Salerno's statement to what Costello biographer Leonard Katz writes in *Uncle Frank:*

They observed the effusive welcome Costello reserved for Vito Genovese and how he led him to the head table to sit in the place of honor.

"He practically kissed his ass in front of everyone," the detectives reported.

The significance of it all was unmistakable. In the authority conscious Mafia that could only mean one thing: Don Vitone had replaced Costello and was now the boss in the family. This was the first knowledge that police had of the changing order of things.

Salerno, as a member of that intelligence division, would certainly have a better handle on what the department believed. Few mob historians agree with Katz's view of the changing of the guard, and Genovese was a long way from being back in charge.

22. *New York Times,* December 10, 1952, "Wife Suing Genovese."

23. Maas, *The Valachi Papers,* pp. 151–152.

24. A note to movie buffs, this incident was portrayed in the movie *The Valachi Papers,* based on Peter Maas's book of the same name. The incident was the most graphic act of violence in the movie and the most talked about; however, Stephen Franse was combined with Dominick "The Gap" Petrilli as one character in the movie. It was the Petrilli character who was castrated

at the Lido restaurant, while Tony Bender and Valachi watched on the orders of Vito Genovese so that he could give Anna a present, the man's genitals, for her infidelity. The scene ended with Charles Bronson, who played Valachi, mercifully shooting Petrelli to end his suffering. This was purely Hollywood fiction. When the real Stephen Franse was discovered, no mutilation of his genitals had taken place. Valachi had not reported it in the book or in his testimony.

25. *Newark Star-Ledger,* February 1, 1959, ' "Rackets king? Phooey! . . . I work Hard,' Says Vito."

26. *The New York Times,* November 22, 1952, "U.S. Moves to Deport Genovese; Charges He Hid Criminal Record."

27. Peter Maas, *The Valachi Papers,* p. 244.

28. Richard Hammer, *The Illustrated History of Organized Crime* (Philadelphia: Courage Books, 1973), p. 273.

29. *The New York Times,* June 29, 1958, "Senate Unit Sets Inquiry on Mafia."

30. *The New York Times,* July 8, 1958, "U.S. Jury Indicts Genovese, Gigante in Narcotics Plot."

31. Dennis Eisenberg, Uri Dan, and Eli Landau, *Meyer Lansky: Mogul of the Mob* (New York: Paddington Press, 1979), p. 248.

32. Nelson Silva Cantellop's name also appeared as Nelson Silver Cantalupes and as Cantalopes.

33. The next year Agent Benjamin R. Begendorf was dismissed from the U.S. Customs Service on departmental charges, which included his disobeying a superior's directive that he not visit the Genovese home and discuss the case with him and that he had lied to obtain the home address of the mobster. Begendorf, a Civil Service employee, appealed the case for years, all the way to the United States Court of Claims. On January 23, 1965, the court upheld the dismissal.

34. *The New York Times,* July 2, 1959, "Early Parole Set."

35. *The New York Times,* January 13, 1960, "14 Convicted in Narcotics Case Lose Appeal in Federal Court."

36. During the ensuing investigation, detectives learned from interviewing eyewitnesses at Marino's that night, that Carfano spoke briefly with Anthony Strollo and Anthony Mirra. In the book *Mob Girl,* Arlyne Weiss, a girlfriend to several underworld figures, stated that Mirra called to see her the following day and alluded to the fact that he had been involved in the murder and that Drake had been killed because she was in the wrong place at the wrong time. Mirra was murdered in February 1982.

37. During the summer of 1960, Cantellops was returned to prison for a parole violation. On July 27, Cantellops was attacked and beaten by two inmates at the City Prison on White Street. He was taken to Bellevue Hospital for treatment. In 1965, Cantellops reputedly died in a barroom fight.

38. *Chicago American,* October 22, 1963, "Genovese Ruling Eases Gang War Threat in N.Y."

39. Ibid.

BIBLIOGRAPHY

Biographies of Genovese

Frasca, Dom. *King of Crime.* New York: Crown Publishers, 1959.
Hanna, David. *Vito Genovese.* New York: Belmont Tower Books, 1974.

Other Publications

Block, Alan. *East Side—West Side: Organizing Crime in New York 1930–1950.* Swansea, Wales: University College Cardiff Press, 1980.
Carpenter, Teresa. *Mob Girl.* New York: Simon & Schuster, 1992.

Eisenberg, Dennis, Uri Dan, and Eli Landau. *Meyer Lansky: Mogul of the Mob*. New York: Paddington Press, 1979.

Gosch, Martin, and Richard Hammer. *The Last Testament of Lucky Luciano*. Boston: Little, Brown and Company, 1974.

Hammer, Richard. *The Illustrated History of Organized Crime*. Philadelphia: Courage Books, 1989.

Katz, Leonard. *Uncle Frank*. New York: Drake Publishers, 1973.

Maas, Peter. *The Valachi Papers*. New York: G. P. Putnam's Sons, 1968.

Reid, Ed. *Mafia*. New York: Random House, 1952.

Salerno, Ralph, and John S. Tompkins. *The Crime Confederation*. New York: Doubleday & Company, 1969.

7

LUCKY LUCIANO (SALVATORE LUCANIA)

AKA "CHARLIE LUCKY"
NOVEMBER 24, 1897–JANUARY 26, 1962

Salvatore "Lucky Luciano" Lucania is second only to Al Capone when it comes to gangster notoriety in the United States. Considered by many to be the father of modern organized crime in New York City, Luciano had a relatively short reign. Taking charge in September 1931, he was arrested and jailed in April 1936. He issued orders from his prison cell until February 1946 when he was deported.

More mystery and fabled tales surround Luciano than any other mob leader of the 20th century. After the Castellammarese War (see Appendix), Luciano was said to have ordered the deaths of dozens of old line Mafia leaders, "Mustache Petes," across the country in what became known as the "Night of Sicilian Vespers (see Appendix)." A few years after "Americanizing" the mob, Luciano was hunted down and placed on trial for heading a prostitution ring. Sentenced to 30 to 50 years in prison, Luciano allegedly helped the United States in the war effort and was rewarded with a pardon from his prison sentence, but in turn was deported.

An ill-fated attempt to return to the United States came to an end in Havana, Cuba. After being deported back to Italy, Luciano was accused of being the world's overlord of the narcotics trade, although authorities were never able to charge him with a single narcotics offense.

Incredibly, the saga of Luciano took a turn 13 years after his death when the book *The Last Testament of Lucky Luciano* (see Appendix) was released. The semiautobiography of the mob leader was the subject of controversy before it hit the bookstands. Many believe that the book is fraudulent. Dozens of errors throughout the book are documented, both in what Luciano reportedly said, and what the authors claim they researched. Many organized crime authors, however, have used this book when writing about other subjects, not always quoting it as the source.

EARLY YEARS

Lercara Friddi was described as a "Sicilian sulphur-mining town of some thirteen thousand souls. It squats, drab and squalid, malodorous with the smell of sulphur, among the rugged bandit-infested hills southeast of Palermo."[1]

Into this "sordid poverty," Salvatore Lucania was born on November 24, 1897, the third child and second son of Rosalia and Antonio. Although just a day laborer, shoveling sulfur in the mines, Antonio was able to save enough of his meager wages to purchase steerage tickets and relocate his family to America. Arriving in the spring of 1907, the family settled on the Lower East Side, in a coldwater flat on First Avenue below 14th Street, a predominantly Jewish and Slavic neighborhood.

Two words sum up Lucania's school years, "chronic truant." A quiet kid in class, he left school for good at the age of 14. He found work at a hat factory, where he worked 10 hours a day, six days a week handling shipping and making deliveries. Most of the money was used to help his family. One night, on the way home from work, Lucania got involved in a game of craps and won more than $200. That marked the end of his legitimate career.

Lucania kept busy in his teenage years by running errands for the local hoods. In 1916, he began making heroin deliveries for a local narcotics dealer named "Cherry Nose," who some claimed worked for Giuseppe Masseria. In April, he was arrested in a bar after selling drugs to an undercover agent. Convicted of narcotics possession, on June 26, he was sentenced to one year in prison. He was placed in the Hampton Farms Reformatory and released on December 30, after serving six-months. On his return, it was said Lucania had earned some level of prestige because he hadn't "ratted" on anyone and just served his time. Partly as a result of this behavior, according to one Luciano biographer, in the fall of 1919 Lucania became an initiated member of the Mafia.

> "I never was a crumb, and if I have to be a crumb I'd rather be dead."
>
> —Lucky Luciano

WORKING FOR "THE BOSS"

One of the top leaders of the New York underworld as the 1920s and Prohibition dawned was Giuseppe Masseria, known as "Joe the Boss." During these early years of the "Noble Experiment," Lucania was involved with a number of rising gangsters in the liquor trade. Among them were Arnold Rothstein, "Legs" Diamond, Dutch Schultz, Meyer Lansky, Benjamin Siegel, and Frank Costello. Many times these men met at what was known as the "Curb Exchange," organized by Tommy "The Bull" Pennochio, where liquor deals involving stolen stocks from government bonded warehouses were consummated.

Masseria was trying to solidify his position as head of the Mafia by killing off his competition. On December 29, 1920, Salvatore Mauro was shot through the heart on Chrystie Street. Mauro's partner, Umberto Valenti, pressed the attack over the next year-and-a-half before he was murdered by Masseria bodyguards after a sham peace conference was called on August 11, 1922. Lucania was said to be one of the Masseria bodyguards involved in the slaying.

After Valenti's murder, Masseria, now truly "the Boss," began to build his organization. Some historians claim Lucania was elevated by Masseria:

> For the Manhattan district, Joe chose, as operations chief, the hard-eyed, soft-voiced young hoodlum, Salvatore Lucania. Young Lucania demonstrated such a talent for organization that the Boss made him right-hand man and personal counselor. Masseria rarely went anywhere or did anything without his able aide.[2]

Leaving his staff of lieutenants to run the show, Masseria "retired to purposeful seclusion." Lucania, on the other hand, expanded his interests in bootlegging, the Italian lottery, and narcotics. On June 2, 1923, he sold two ounces of morphine to John Lyons, who was described as an undercover Secret Service agent by one Luciano biographer and a pusher-turned-federal-informant by another. Whatever the case, when Lucania made another sale on June 5, he was placed under arrest by Federal Narcotics Bureau agents.

As a second offender, Lucania was looking at as much as 10 years in prison. During an interrogation, he refused to name his supplier or any of the people who worked for him. Instead, Lucania cut a deal with the agents, giving up his stash, which he kept in an office on Mulberry Street. The trunk, said to contain drugs valued at $150,000, was confiscated and Lucania's reward was having the charges against him dismissed.

Although the narcotics arrest did not appear on his rap sheet, during the 1920s Lucania was arrested on 17 occasions. Most of the charges were for violations of corporate ordinances (most likely traffic related), but other charges included carrying a concealed weapon (in Jersey City), assault, disorderly conduct, violation of the Volstead Act, grand larceny, and once he was held as a material witness. The corporation ordinance violations resulted in small fines, and all the other charges were dismissed.

During the mid-1920s, Arnold Rothstein became a dominant figure in the narcotics business. One of his agents was George Uffner. It was through Uffner that Lucania had dealings with Rothstein. After Rothstein's death in November 1928, police were looking to question one of his bodyguards, James "Fats" Walsh. Early on the morning of November 17, police raided an apartment on Central Park West. Police said they received a tip that there was a dice game going on there and that several of the players might know something about a recent payroll theft. Police arrested Walsh, Uffner, and Lucania.

This story has been twisted over the years, and some tales have it that the three men were arrested while rifling through Rothstein's office files on the day he died, November 6. Others claim the men were arrested for the payroll robbery when police really only wanted to question them about the Rothstein killing. At the time of his arrest, the newspapers claimed Lucania was a "waiter" in one article and a "restaurateur" in another. Lucania claimed he had gone to the apartment, Uffner's residence, "to take part in a dice game."[3] He was arraigned for the robbery the next day, but the charges were soon dismissed.

One of the mysteries that surrounded Lucania in the mid-1920s was, if he was truly Masseria's right-hand man, how he got so involved with other non-Italian underworld figures. In addition to Rothstein and the drug traffic, Lucania was said to be working with the Diamond brothers—Jack and Eddie. In 1926, Lucania was arrested in a stolen car with Eddie Diamond. More important, he built an independent bootlegging operation with Meyer Lansky and Benjamin Siegel and was a friend of Lepke Buchalter. As non-Italians, these men were considered outsiders to Masseria, who wanted nothing to do with them.

With the fortune Lucania was making, he moved into the Barbizon Plaza Hotel, taking a suite under the name of Charles Lane. Two important events occurred in 1929. First was the Atlantic City Conference (see Appendix) during May of that year, which would spotlight Luciano to mob leaders around the country as the "top man" in New York City. The second event nearly killed him.

PUTTING THE "LUCKY" IN LUCIANO

Sometime after 1:30 on the morning of December 17, 1929, a patrolman assigned to the Tottenville Precinct near Huguenot Beach in Staten Island came across a bloodied figure staggering along the road. The officer stopped his car and asked the man what happened.

"Get me a taxi," the man replied. "I'll give you fifty bucks if you do and let me go my way."

Instead the officer transported the man to Richmond Memorial Hospital, where he was identified as Charles Lucania. It was reported that, "his neck was bleeding from a deep knife thrust which had barely missed the jugular vein. His right eye was dark and nearly closed. His wrists were badly chafed."[4] Any additional injuries to Lucania were the result of embellishments by writers over the years.

Lucania told detectives that he had been standing at the corner of 50th Street and Sixth Avenue at 6:00 the prior evening. A limousine pulled to a stop and three armed men ordered him into the car. Adhesive tape was used to keep his mouth shut, and he was kicked and punched and stabbed while held captive in the car. When detectives began questioning him he concluded with, "Don't you cops lose any sleep over it. I'll attend to this thing myself later."[5]

Despite the savage beating, Lucania was well enough to stand in a police lineup in Manhattan the next day and be arraigned for grand larceny. The grand larceny charge was "technically suspicion" of stealing a car in Harlem. Lucania was placed in the Richmond County Jail on a $25,000 bond and left to lick his wounds by a less than sympathetic district attorney who explained, "we want it known that New York gunmen cannot dump their 'ride' victims on Staten Island."[6] The charges were soon dismissed and Luciano returned home.

Over the years, this episode has been embellished with each retelling. According to *The Last Testament of Lucky Luciano* Luciano met with Maranzano that night and was ordered to murder Masseria. When Luciano balked, he was hung by his thumbs, beaten, burned with cigarettes, and stabbed. The book also claims that while Luciano was recovering at home, he was paid a visit by Frank Costello and Meyer Lansky. Seeing the condition he was in, Lansky christened him with the nickname "Lucky" for surviving the beating.

All one has to do to dispel this myth is to look at the opening paragraphs of both the *New York Herald Tribune* and the *New York Times* in their coverage of the beating. The former refers to him as "Charles (Lucky) Lucania," while the *Times* came up with "Charles (Lucky) Luciania," repeating the misspelling of the last name throughout the article. A more mundane version of the nickname comes from Leonard Katz in *Uncle Frank*:

> Frank Costello added still another twist to the story of how Luciano came to be called Lucky. Luciano just gave himself the name Lucky, Costello confided to a friend, and pushed it and pushed it until everyone began to accept it. He said Luciano even made up the stories about his fabulous winnings at dice and cards because he wanted to be known as a lucky

guy. "He felt that people are attracted to a guy when he's lucky. Everyone wants to be with a winner."[7]

Over the years, Luciano was said to tell different versions of the events that night. The one that has gained the most acceptance was related by Charles Vizzini, an undercover agent for the Bureau of Narcotics, who was able to get close to Luciano a few years before his death. The story Luciano gave Vizzini was that he was grabbed by New York City police officers outside his home in the Bronx. The police were under pressure to arrest "Legs" Diamond and knew Luciano was associated with him. Luciano claims Diamond was actually in his home at the time the cops apprehended him. After giving him a vicious beating in their car, the cops drove to Staten Island. There, according to Luciano, they put a gun to his head and threatened to "blow his brains out" if he didn't tell them where Diamond was. Luciano told Vizzini:

> I got an edge on these bastards, I know they ain't about to kill me. If it's a mob hit and they got a gun against your head there ain't gonna be no more talkin'. They get that close, all you're gonna hear is a bang. And that's the last thing you'll hear.[8]

INCONSPICUOUS

The landscape of the New York underworld was about to change with the commencement of the Castellammarese War (1930–1931). Luciano turned out to be a key figure in the war and was given credit for ending it when he allegedly set up "Joe the Boss" Masseria to be assassinated in a Coney Island restaurant on April 15, 1931. This killing was followed five months later by the murder of Salvatore Maranzano. It was now that Luciano, although considered first among equals in the five-family system, seemed to fade from view. Between the Maranzano slaying, in September 1931, and the sensational murder of Dutch Schultz in October 1935, Luciano's activities were sparsely reported in the press. According to historians, however, Luciano used this period to "Americanize" the underworld. This is no doubt where the "Night of Sicilian Vespers" fable came to light. Luciano allegedly increased his influence in the "Big Seven" and stretched this group's involvement in liquor (until the repeal of Prohibition), gambling, and politics.

Luciano's participation in politics went along with his changing of the guard in the underworld. The underworld was on its way to dominating the New York City political scene. In *Gang Rule in New York* the authors wrote:

> That political overturn was merely a part of the onward march of Italian gangsters in first creating a nation-wide crime syndicate, and then coming to dominate it. But it is also an excellent illustration of the way the servant hoodlums of district politicians in the era from 1910 to 1920 were becoming their masters between 1920 and 1930.

Luciano began a friendship with Albert Marinelli during the early 1920s, when the Tammany politician served as port warden for the city. Ten years later, when Marinelli had established himself in the district, he challenged incumbent Harry Perry for the leadership of the Second Assembly District. Perry resigned after a visit by two gunmen sent by Luciano with the advice that he retire forthwith.

On April 19, 1932, Luciano and Meyer Lansky were arrested outside the Congress Hotel in Chicago with Capone gang members Paul "the Waiter" Ricca, Sylvester Agoglia, John Senna, and Harry Brown. One Lansky biographer referred to it as "probably a bootlegging trip." Held for investigation, they were charged with disorderly conduct, but the charges were dropped two days later. Although the arrest produced a classic police mug shot of the group, nothing else has ever come to light of the Windy City get together.

Two months later, Luciano was back in Chicago, this time with Frank Costello, to attend the Democratic National Convention. Luciano, also accompanied by Joseph "Socks" Lanza and Patrick J. Lupo, shared a sweet at the Drake Hotel with Albert Marinelli, who was backing former New York Governor Al Smith. Costello, in another part of the hotel, roomed with Tammany leader Jimmy Hines, who supported Franklin Delano Roosevelt. The thinking was that, by backing both candidates for the Democratic presidential nomination, they would win no matter who took office.

With the repeal of Prohibition in December 1933, two things happened. The underworld was in search of new avenues to make money, and a reform movement was underway in the city. At this time Louis Buchalter was firmly entrenched in labor racketeering and narcotics; Costello had his slot machines; Adonis was focused on politics in Brooklyn; Dutch Schultz had the Harlem policy rackets; Vito Genovese was running the Italian lottery; Benjamin Siegel was overseeing dice games and other forms for gambling in the city; and Meyer Lansky was looking to expand the gambling empire to other cities including Miami and Havana, Cuba. This left Luciano with the prostitution racket, although he would always deny this.

On April 7, 1935, Charles Lane of the Barbizon Plaza became Charles Ross of the Waldorf-Astoria Towers. During the previous three years, Luciano had gone out of his way to maintain a low profile and keep his name out of the newspapers. He had been arrested at least once a year from 1921 to 1932. While Luciano was lying low, other mob figures were under the gun from law enforcement.

The years following Repeal saw the Seabury Investigations, the election of reform Mayor Fiorella LaGuardia, and the appointment of Special Prosecutor Thomas E. Dewey. Seabury caused corrupt New York City Mayor James "Jimmy" Walker to resign in disgrace, which opened the door for LaGuardia to take his place. LaGuardia began his crusade against the underworld by going after Costello's slot machines, creating a public spectacle by smashing the machines with a sledge hammer and then having them thrown in the river.

As a member of the U.S. Attorney's office, Dewey set his sights on Irving "Waxey Gordon" Wexler in late 1933. In November, Wexler was convicted of tax evasion and sent to prison for 10 years. Next on Dewey's list was Dutch Schultz, but the beer baron went into hiding, and by the time he came out, the appointment of a new U.S. Attorney had resulted in Dewey retiring to private practice . . . for a while. In 1935, a "runaway grand jury," upset with William C. Dodge, the Tammany-backed district attorney of New York County, recommended that Governor Herbert H. Lehman name a special prosecutor. In July, Lehman responded by naming Thomas Dewey.

Dewey was hoping to begin where he left off with Schultz, but he had to wait on a pending federal income tax indictment. Before the case could come to trial, Schultz was mortally wounded in a shootout in a Newark tavern on October 23. The death of Schultz put Luciano back in the spotlight, right where he didn't want to be. Police believed that the shooting of Schultz had been on orders from a "rival gang leader." The newspaper announced detectives were looking for Charles Luciano.[9]

On October 26, in a front page article, the *New York Times* reported that former Chicago underworld leader Johnny Torrio was the new power behind the scenes, overseeing a combination of six gangs. The newspaper reported, "The new combination, according to the police, consists of gangs headed by six notorious racketeers: Charles (Lucky) Luciana, Charles (Buck) Siegel, Meyer Lansky, Louis (Lefty) Buckhouse, Jacob (Gurrah) Shapiro, and Abe (Longy) Zwillman."[10] The article also claimed that Luciano was the head of a "secret organization" known as the Unione Siciliano.

A week after the killing of Schultz and his men, Luciano was reported in Miami, having flown there the day after the shooting. Miami police offered to arrest him if there were any charges against Luciano, but the mob leader checked out of his hotel after he was made aware that his presence in Miami was known.

Details of Luciano's whereabouts over the next five months are sketchy at best. One report has him in Miami on December 28, where he registered with local police as a criminal. The next time he was heard from was in Hot Springs, Arkansas, near the end of March 1936.

Back in New York, Special Prosecutor Dewey wasted no time in determining his next target. It was Lucky Luciano. On Saturday night, February 1, Dewey's staff, assisted by New York City police officers, conducted synchronized raids on 41 houses of prostitution in Brooklyn and Manhattan, arresting 110 people, of which 100 were women. The secret raids were not announced to the press until 3:45 AM. To ensure secrecy, the women were brought to the Greenwich Street Police Station in taxicabs instead of patrol wagons.

Normally when prostitutes were arrested, a lawyer would appear at police headquarters and bail out the women. In this case the lawyers weren't allowed to see the women and were told that they were still being questioned. Instead of charging them with prostitution or running a disorderly house, the women were held as material witnesses with bonds of $10,000 each. The women were questioned in Dewey's offices, located in the Woolworth Building. Ten of the vice ring's leaders were held on a combined bail totaling $435,000. The *New York Times* reported that, "Operations of an organized vice ring said to have taken in $12,000,000 a year and to have employed between 1,000 and 2,000 women in some 200 houses in Manhattan and Brooklyn, were revealed."[11]

Throughout the first 10 days of February, Dewey's men made additional raids and arrests. In one raid, police found 200 envelopes addressed to clients that contained notification of a pending change of address. During this time, members of an extraordinary grand jury were hearing testimony from the women arrested during the big Saturday night raid. On February 6, the following men were indicted: Peter Balitzer, Meyer Bergman, David Betillo, Jack Ellenstein, James Frederico, Jesse Jacobs, Thomas Pennochio, Benjamin Spiller, Al Weiner, and Joseph Weintraub. An 11th man, David Marcus, had suffered a heart attack.

On April 1, one day before he was to be indicted in New York City, Luciano was arrested in Hot Springs. Dewey's office asked the Arkansas judge overseeing arraignment to hold him on a $200,000 bail. Instead, Luciano was released under a $5,000 bond. After pressure from New York authorities, Luciano was sent back to jail until a habeas corpus hearing could be held.

The next day, Luciano and "eleven of his alleged lieutenants" were indicted by the extraordinary grand jury in four indictments consisting of six charges each. Dewey announced that the indictments were the first ever obtained in New York City charging anyone more important than a "booker" in the vice rackets. He stated that 80 women and 30 men were being held as material witnesses and that he was ready to proceed with trial as soon as Luciano was returned. From his jail cell in Hot Springs, Luciano declared himself the victim of "the most vicious kind of politics" and vowed to fight extradition.

Governor Herbert Lehman signed extradition papers to bring Luciano back. Authorities in Arkansas were in the process of trying to move Luciano from the Garland County jail to the capital in Little Rock. Luciano's legal counsel countered this attempt by having him arrested on a warrant issued in New York back in October 1934. This move made Luciano a "local prisoner." When a fugitive warrant was issued from Little Rock by Arkansas Circuit Judge Abner McGehee, a Hot Springs jurist decided it was time to dismiss the local warrant.

The deputy sheriff of Garland County, Roy E. Ermey, refused to give up the prisoner, saying that "Luciano's status required further clarification." Edward McClean, a Dewey assistant sent to Hot Springs to bring back the prisoner, complained to Judge McGehee. During the early morning hours of April 4, McLean arrived in Hot Springs from Little Rock with 20 machinegun-armed Arkansas state rangers. Ermey was warned by the rangers that they were ready to take Luciano by force if necessary. Ermey readily gave up his infamous prisoner. Upon seeing the force that had come to retrieve him, Luciano quipped, "Is it necessary to call out the National Guard to take me to Little Rock?"[12]

Dewey took advantage of a federal law enacted in 1934, which made it a federal offense to cross state lines while fleeing a crime. Although it had already been a federal crime for years to take a stolen automobile across state lines (the Dyer Act, which tripped up bank robber John Dillinger), the new law was extended to murder, rape, arson, robbery, or extortion in which threats of violence were used. In this case, Dewey had a complaint sworn out that Luciano had extorted money by threatening Al Weiner, a booker for some of the houses.[13]

On April 6, Arkansas Attorney General Carl E. Bailey announced, during the extradition hearing before Governor J. Marion Futrell, that he had been offered a $50,000 bribe "to help effect the release" of Lucky Luciano. Addressing the court on the matter of Luciano, Bailey stated:

> Arkansas cannot be made an asylum for criminals. Officers of Hot Springs seem to have issued an invitation to criminals to come to that city where they are told not to worry, that they will be given protection and that they will not be compelled to return to answer for crimes committed elsewhere. The money these criminals pay for protection is blood money, from their murdered victims and from women. We are trying to make it impossible for that class to spend its filthy money in Arkansas.[14]

The expensive defense counsel Luciano hired called no witnesses, being content just to cross-examine. Luciano's defense was that he was in Cuba at the time Weiner had been threatened. After the hearing, Governor Futrell granted the extradition. Luciano's last gasp was a federal writ of habeas corpus. Incredibly, Luciano won a 10-day reprieve. His request for release on the habeas corpus writ was denied, but Federal Judge John E. Martineau allowed him 10 days to petition the circuit court of appeals in Kansas City as to why his appeal should be heard.

The 10-day grace period to file the appeal expired without Luciano's counsel going before the court. On April 17, the prisoner was handed over to New York City detectives to be returned. The next morning, Luciano arrived at Grand Central Station after an overnight train ride from Little Rock. Thirty detectives were on hand to escort him to police headquarters. While Luciano was being booked, he told reporters to get his name correct—it was Lucania. Arraigned before New York Supreme Court Justice Philip J. McCook, Dewey asked that Luciano be held on a bail of $350,000. Luciano's attorney, Moses Polakoff, argued for a bail of no more than $200,000, but lost. Although arraigned in Manhattan, Luciano was remanded to the Raymond Street jail in Brooklyn, instead of the Tombs because Dewey was holding several material witnesses there.

On April 23, Luciano was indicted on 90 counts of compulsory prostitution. The *New York Times* reported that, "The indictment was the first to be voted under the recently enacted statue permitting the joinder of a series of related offenses in a single true bill."[15] Judge McCook set a trial date of May 11. On April 29, Luciano and five of his co-defendants withdrew their not-guilty pleas to the charges of compulsory prostitution. Their defense counsel then filed demurrers with the court to test the validity of the new joinder law. As the trial date approached, a special panel of 200 potential jurors was drawn so that a blue ribbon jury could be selected. Just days before the trial was scheduled to begin, Judge McCook denied a motion for separate trial on the compulsory prostitution charges for the men.

THE TRIAL

By the time the trial began at 10:00 AM on May 11, there were 13 defendants, each accused in a single indictment of 90 counts covering 28 charges. Before jury selection began, three of the defendants—Peter Balitzer, David Marcus, and Al Weiner—pled guilty. Part of their plea agreement called for them to testify against the others.

July selection began that afternoon at 2:00 PM. Of the 200 potential jurors, 95 requested to be excused for various reasons; all but 20 were discharged. In addressing the group, Dewey told them that the girls worked in the houses of their own volition and that none of the defendants forced the women into them. But "the defendants gave assurance that no one working for them ever would go to jail. The case either was thrown out of court, or, if it looked too serious, the girl was ordered to 'go on the lam.' Lucania will not be shown to have placed women in houses or taken money from them. Instead, he set up his apartment at the Waldorf-Astoria and was the czar of the organized crime of this city. His word was sufficient to terminate competition."[16]

It was a slow process. Judge McCook ordered it to proceed into the evening and court continued until 11:00 PM. The next evening, just after 8:00 PM, the selection process was complete, but not without controversy. Judge McCook allowed each side 20 peremptory challenges, but "the defense lawyers, who had made futile attempts for separate trials, filed exceptions. They contended that in view of the heavy penalties to which their clients were liable if convicted they were entitled to twenty challenges per man, or a total of 200."[17]

Prominent among the defense counsel were Moses Polakoff and George Morton Levy, who represented Luciano, James D. C. Murray, Caesar B. F. Barra, and Maurice F. Cantor. It was agreed that when the defense attorneys took the floor, each would act for all the defendants. Key among those defendants were Thomas "Tommy" Pennochio, said to be the treasurer of the gang; David "Little Davie" Betillo and James "Jimmy" Fredericks, described as chief assistant and general manager; Benjamin "Benny" Spiller, a financial investor in the vice enterprises; Ralph "the Pimp" Liguori, accused by the state of having served in the capacity of a gunman to force reluctant independent houses to join the fold; Jesse Jacobs and Meyer Berkman, who provided bail bondsmen and legal aide to the girls who were arrested; Abe "Little Abie" Wahrman, a collector from bookers[18]; and Jack "Jack Eller" Ellenstein, one of the main bookers.

On May 13, both sides gave their opening statements. Dewey described for the jury how the vice industry was highly organized and run like with a business-like approach. It was estimated that the profits had soared to $12,000,000 a year, from the 200 houses that operated in Manhattan, the Bronx, Brooklyn, and Queens. He then described how the operation ran:

> The bookers were the mainsprings. They had headquarters to which inmates or house managers telephoned on Sunday nights, the women asking where they were to operate the following week, the managers reporting how many inmates they needed.[19] Each booker had two or three assistants or telephone men.
>
> A girl in the racket, usually lived with some man in a hotel. She reported for work at 1 o'clock or so in the afternoon and remained there ten to fourteen hours. Half of her gross earnings went to the woman manager of the house. Ten percent of the girl's half went to the booker. She paid $5 a week for a doctor and varying sums for "'board.'"
>
> Never did Lucania or any of the other defendants, other than the bookers, actually see or collect from the women. But Lucania always was in touch with the general details of this business.[20]

In addition, the women soon had to contribute $10 each week into a bonding fund and in case they were arrested. For this contribution the women were told they would be protected against having to go to jail.

The opening arguments by defense counsel were brief. They denied all the charges and pointed out that state's witnesses had all been granted immunity for their testimony and would say anything about the defendants to escape prison. What follows is a daily recap of the trial:

Wednesday, May 13: The first two witnesses were young prostitutes, Rose Cohn and Muriel Ryan. Both testified as to how they got into the business and which bookers they worked for, as well as the madams and houses they worked at. Cohn told the court about an arrest and what lies she was instructed to tell during the hearing, after which the charges were dismissed. The *New York Times* reported that both women testified in a demeanor that attested to "an utter disregard for the esteem with which other persons might appraise their mode of livelihood."[21]

Thursday, May 14: On the stand this morning were two women who ran "disorderly houses," Dorothy Arnold and Betty Winters. Both told how the houses operated and detailed how they interacted with the bookers. A couple more prostitutes were called. One told how she entered the business after her husband died and she was left destitute with two young children. In the afternoon, Al Weiner took the stand. A former failure at basket weaving, Weiner's father Louis was a long time booker, who was arrested a year earlier and was currently serving a five-year sentence. The younger Weiner told about a meeting held in Jesse Jacob's office where David Betillo threatened the bookers because the houses were holding out money. He repeated one of Betillo's threats to the court:

> Little Davie said, "Lots of places are holding out. I want a list of your houses from everyone. There'll be a $200 fine for holding out. You, Marcus, are a no-good rat, and if you go to the cops, we'll put the cops on you. I'm doing you guys a favor by letting you be in this here business. You're all rats. We'll run you out of town, Marcus. Harris, you're a rat. Ellenstein, I'll kick your fat stomach off."[22]

Friday, May 15: Joan Martin, one of the house madams, was on the stand for most of the day. She told of the brutality she confronted, and had the scars to prove it. She testified that as an independent operator, she was told by one of her bookers that she would have to pay $5 of her own money and $10 of the girls toward a bail fund. When she refused, Abe Wahrman and two others came to her place and began destroying the furniture in her establishment. "What was left of the furniture I put in the garbage can," she told the court. Then she was paid a visit by Jimmy Frederico, who insisted she join the "combination." This time when she refused, Frederico hit her on the head with a lead pipe and knocked her unconscious. Two of her girls took her to a doctor, who put 11 stitches in her head to close the wound. Martin got down from the witness stand to show the jury the scar.

Martin said she moved her operation. Then one day she was visited by Wahrman and Ralph Liguori. Martin was told to pick out Liguori at the defense table. At first she wasn't sure, but then pointed him out after he was told to take off his glasses. The prosecution stated that he had never worn glasses before the trial. After Martin identified him, he never put them back on. Martin then stated that Liguori returned to the house with two others and held her up. Martin fell in line for a while, but then became delinquent. Thats when Frederico returned one night and punched her in the face. When Martin's dog came to her aid, Frederico tried to shoot the dog. Martin said after that incident, she kept up her payments.

Saturday, May 17: This Saturday session lasted until 9:15 at night. The key witness was David Marcus, who used the alias of David Miller. Marcus was a booker until the takeover by the combination, who invited him to join for $10,000. When Marcus said he didn't have the money, he was threatened with death if he didn't get out of town. Before he could flee, a gunman took six shots at him one day after he got into his automobile. Marcus and his wife went out West to begin anew, but when this failed he returned to New York and suddenly fell back into the good graces of the combination. At one point Marcus testified that he asked Frederico who would take care of him if he got into trouble. Frederico answered, "Davie and Abie and Charlie." Objections from the defense prevented Marcus from testifying who he thought "Charlie" was.

Monday, May 18: Mollie Leonard, by the age of 37, had been a prostitute or house madam for 21 years. During her testimony, she said she had operated on her own until Pete Harris told her she would have to bond with the combination and begin contributing to the bail fund at $10 a girl per week. Leonard told Harris she didn't like the idea. To which Harris replied: "There are a good many people behind the combination." When she asked who, she said Harris replied "Lucky." A shower of protests rained down from the defense table. George Morton Levy had Luciano stand and asked Leonard if she had ever seen him, she replied in the negative. Other witnesses during the day included seven more prostitutes, all in their early twenties.

Tuesday, May 19: Danny Caputo, alias Danny Brooks, who was serving a term in Dannemora for operating a house in Westchester, took the stand and again injected the name of "Lucky" as one of the men he was told was behind the combination. The highlight of the day came when Caputo told of a meeting that took place that included Betillo and Frederico. Betillo jumped up, pounded on the defense table, and shouted, "You're a liar! It never happened."

Wednesday, May 20: Peter Balitzer, one of the men who pleaded guilty at the beginning of the trial, took the stand. Balitzer, who used the alias Peter Harris, was a booker who represented nearly 100 girls. He had been approached by Wahrman and nine other men on the street one day and told that he was to begin paying $250 a week. Balitzer said, no, and as the negotiations continued, he refused even when the amount was lowered to $100. At this point he was shoved into an automobile, driven to his apartment, and told to get out of town. Balitzer finally agreed to the $100 weekly payments. One day Balitzer went to see Dave Betillo with a list of the houses he represented. He said he asked Betillo who was providing the backing for the combination. Balitzer said he was told, "Don't worry about that; Charlie Lucky is behind it." Balitzer said he got in trouble later on with Jimmy Frederico because he informed several of the madams that Luciano was "behind the combination." Balitzer testified, "Jimmy told me not to use the name Charlie Lucky to them."

If the houses didn't pay the required $10 per week, per girl, they would be held up at gunpoint. One day, one of the houses Balitzer supplied, and which paid the $10 extortion, was held up. Balitzer complained to Frederico. The two of them took a ride to Brooklyn and picked up the hood who had pulled the robbery. Balitzer testified that Frederico slapped him and shouted, "Didn't I tell you to keep away from those bonded houses because they belong to Charlie Lucky?"

Thursday, May 21: Joseph Bendix, who was serving a life sentence in Sing Sing as a Baumes Law offender, was the first witness who actually testified that he spoke with Luciano and was able to tie him directly to the prostitution ring.[23] Bendix said he wanted a job as a collector and was able to get an audience with Luciano at the Villanova restaurant on West 46th Street. Although he claimed to have several conversations with Luciano about the job, he never did go to work for the ring. On cross-examination, Bendix claimed that during 1929, he "conversed frequently" with Luciano in front of a drugstore on Seventh Avenue. He stated that he and Luciano had become "quite chummy." When George Morton Levy told his client to stand up so that Bendix could identify him, Luciano half stood, glaring at Bendix the whole time.

Friday, May 22: The most memorable witness of the trial took the stand. Florence Brown used several aliases—Martin and Marsten, to name a few. But it was by her nickname that everyone remembered her—"Cokey Flo." A narcotics addict, Dewey admitted her to a treatment center before her appearance. The *New York Times* reported, "The woman was the most dramatic of the many witnesses in the trial. . . . Repeatedly and unequivocally she recited conversations at gatherings of which she was a member, in which Lucania directed the operations of the vice ring."[24]

The attractive 28-year-old testified that she had been Frederico's "sweetheart," and thus accompanied him to some of his meetings with Luciano. At one that she described, Luciano, Betillo, and Frederico were discussing how some of the bookers were holding out. Luciano told Betillo to get them all together "down on the carpet. See that it doesn't happen again." At another meeting, Betillo and Frederico talked about the recalcitrant attitude of some of the madams. Luciano had told Frederico to have a meeting with them. Frederico said he tried to talk to them separately. Brown testified that Luciano responded, "You can't talk to them. They're stubborn. Get after them! Step on them!"

While attorney Levy grilled the woman on cross-examination, Luciano sat at the trial table furiously writing notes. Levy asked Brown to identify Luciano at the defense table. Although there were several men grouped around him, Brown simply pointed and said, "the man with the yellow pencil." With that, Luciano threw down the pencil in disgust.

Saturday, May 23: The day began with "Cokey Flo" finishing her testimony. Several letters were introduced into evidence that Brown had written to Frederico after his arrest. The letters indicated the strong love Brown had for him. The defense questioned whether Brown had cut a deal with Dewey in hopes of "saving Frederico at the expense of others," an accusation she denied.

Dewey next called to the stand the manager, a maid, and a waiter from the Waldorf Astoria Towers, where Luciano lived under the name Ross from April to October 1935. The witnesses were called to identify Berkman, Betillo, Frederico, and Wahrman as visitors to Luciano's two-room suite. The maid stepped from the stand to the defense table three times and placed her hand on the shoulder of each defendant she had seen in the suite. Despite the best efforts of the defense attorneys, they could not shake her identifications.

The *New York Times* reported, "During a recess some of the defendants exchanged ties and took other seats because defense counsel, on cross examination, had suggested that witnesses had been coached to such an extent that they knew what kind of clothes the accused were wearing and where they were sitting in the courtroom."[25]

Monday, May 25: The judge ordered night sessions for the week and trial continued until 10:00 PM. Two more prostitutes took the stand—Nancy Presser and Thelma Jordan. Presser, an attractive 24-year-old blonde, stated she was Luciano's girlfriend. She testified that she was at different get-togethers where business was discussed. She claimed she frequently heard Luciano tell "the boys" to bust up the houses that weren't making payments. In discussing the ruthless Ralph Liguori, she said that she was told by him that if she didn't go to work for him "he would cut me up so that my own mother wouldn't know me."

Thelma Jordan talked about violence directed at some of the prostitutes, including Presser. Jordan said that after their arrests, they were sitting in an anteroom at Dewey's Woolworth Building headquarters. She said Liguori tried to intimidate her and Presser to prevent them from talking. She testified:

> The reason I didn't tell the truth at first was because I was afraid to talk. I knew what had happened to girls who had talked about the combination. The soles of their feet and stomachs were burned with cigar butts for talking too much. I heard Liguori say to Nancy that anyone who talked against the combination would be looked after. I heard him say that their tongues were cut when girls talked.[26]

Tuesday, May 26: Most of the day's testimony consisted of the cross-examination of Nancy Presser. George Morton Levy was able to obtain from her that she had been a narcotics addict for 18 months. She also seemed unfamiliar with a layout of the Waldorf Astoria Towers, where she said she had been a frequent visitor to Luciano's suite. Another witness on the stand was a prostitute who testified to being coached in how to lie in court by Abe Karp, a disbarred lawyer who worked for the combination.

Saul Gelb, an assistant to Dewey, told the newspapers this day that Presser had been relocated because of a number of threats that had been made against her.

Wednesday, May 27: Two bellhops from the Hotel Barbizon-Plaza were called. They identified several of the defendants as being at the hotel during the period Luciano lived there. One identified Ellenstein's attorney, Maurice Cantor as one of the visitors. In 1928, Cantor had tried to get rich from Arnold Rothstein's will,. An assistant manager at the hotel, however, was called a hostile witness by Dewey when he refused to identify any of the defendants as being guests of Luciano. During cross-examination, the man claimed he was harassed and threatened by Dewey's assistants.

The newspapers reported that a Brooklyn lawyer was arrested on Tuesday night on charges of "attempted subornation of perjury." In addition, two other men and a woman were held as material witnesses for "alleged instances of attempts to influence the case." These other attempts involved Florence Brown, Nancy Presser, and Thelma Jordan and were an effort to get them to recant their testimony. When this information came to light, Luciano's attorneys Levy and Moses Polakoff released a statement:

> Counsel for Lucania emphatically deny any improper methods in the investigation of this case. Naturally, an intensive investigation is being conducted, motivated solely by a desire to get the entire truth concerning the charges and the credibility of the witnesses against Lucania. The defense seeks only the opportunity to conduct a proper and unhandicapped investigation.[27]

Thursday, May 28: Mildred Balitzer, Peter's wife, was the state's key witness today. Balitzer was a former addict and also ran a house. She testified that Betillo told her back in 1932 that he worked for "Charlie Lucky." Once, when introducing her to the hoodlum, he stated, "I want you to meet the boss." She said she ran into Luciano a couple of times and implored him to help her husband out, that the payments the ring exacted were too high. She testified that his reply was, "I can't do anything for him. You know how the racket is."

Friday, May 29: Mildred Balitzer completed her testimony. She told of a threat being made to her while in the process of being transferred from one apartment to another for safekeeping. She said the man was Gus Franco, an old friend. "Gus told me," she stated, "if I testified against these defendants I would be killed—not only me, but also my youngster."

At 6:40 that evening, the state rested its case. On a motion requested by Dewey, 28 of the counts were dismissed, leaving 62 to be tried. Judge McCook denied a request from defense counsel to dismiss the remaining counts. The defense was given until Monday to open its case. During a recess, Luciano spoke with reporters:

> I certainly expect to be acquitted. I don't know any of the people who took the stand and said they knew me or talked with me or overheard me in conversation. I never met any of them. I never was engaged in this racket at all. Nor have I ever in my life met any of the co-defendants except Betillo before this trial.

Monday, June 1: Before the defense opened its case, defendant Jack Ellenstein pleaded guilty and was remanded for sentence until the end of the trial. Also, one of the jurors had to be replaced. Ralph Liguori was the first defendant to take the stand. He denied all the allegations made against him. He then told the court that Dewey's assistants said to him that they knew he had nothing to do with the combination, "We don't want you as a defendant. We want to get Lucania," he claimed they said. Liguori said he was threatened with 25 years in prison if he didn't cooperate.

Tuesday, June 2: The defense put a string of bookmakers and gamblers on the stand in support of their claims that Luciano made his money through games of chance.

Wednesday, June 3: Luciano took the stand. Like Liguori, under direct examination by attorney Levy, he denied all the charges and testimony against him. Dewey listened intently and was champing at the bit by the time he began his four-hour cross-examination. He went over Luciano's past criminal record and got him to admit all the lies he had told. Luciano frequently used the excuse that he would not have lied, "if anything more serious had been involved." Even on the stand this time, the hood told lie after lie, not even telling the truth about his place of birth, claiming he was born in Manhattan.

Dewey took him through a series of associates. He claimed he did not know Ciro Terranova or Al Capone. Dewey was able to trip him up with his own telephone records, however, which showed late-night calls to these individuals on their private lines. Most damaging was the list of repeated calls to Celano's Restaurant, which the ring members used as their headquarters. By the time Dewey was through with him, the outcome looked pretty bleak for the mob boss.

Thursday, June 4: Both sides closed their cases and final statements by defense counsel began.

Friday, June 5: The defense took 10 hours this day to complete their final arguments. Most of the attorneys took shots at Dewey, belittling him and his efforts before the jury. The last attorney to speak was George Morton Levy:

> I'm not accusing Tom Dewey of suborning perjury. But I say his assistants, anxious for a pat on the back or a bit of glory, have collected a group of actors who have constructed a drama which Mr. Dewey accepted as true.
>
> There is no evidence on which Tom Dewey can hope to convict Lucania. He hopes to do it by prejudice, hysteria through what you have read and by what the public has been taught to believe by the master showman. He hopes to do it by crimes Lucania committed years ago, because he was taken for a ride, because he lied to get a pistol permit. He hopes to railroad him because Lucania lied when he said he was a chauffeur in obtaining an automobile license when he was nothing but a bootlegger and gambler.[28]

Saturday, June 6: Dewey gave his closing statement, accusing Luciano of presenting on the stand under oath, "a shocking, disgusting display of sanctimonious perjury—at the end of which I'm sure not one of you had a doubt that before you stood not a gambler, not a bookmaker, but the greatest gangster in America." At the end of his statement Dewey told the jury, "Unless you're willing to convict the top man, you might as well acquit every one."[29]

Judge McCook's jury instructions lasted just short of three hours. Among his comments to the jury was that just because the witness may have been a prostitute, that alone does not make her unworthy of belief. "You must give her story the same weight as you would to that of a reputable person. If you believe what she says, then the story stands and the fact that she is a prostitute is of no moment." Judge McCook also added the following to help the jury, "If anyone received money which was the proceeds of prostitution, even though not directly received from the women, if it was in furtherance of a scheme to carry on prostitution, that person is guilty of an unlawful act."[30]

By the time the jury received the case and got back from dinner it was nearly 11:00 PM. The panel deliberated overnight and arrived at a verdict before sunrise Sunday morning. On Sunday, June 7, the *New York Times* reported:

> By 4:30 o'clock yesterday morning a decision had been reached as to each defendant, but it was 5:25 before Justice McCook, the various attorneys and the court attendants were prepared to receive the verdict. A fair-sized crowd had remained in the court room. Scores stood outside the building. A police guard of fifty men patrolled the court house and the streets, vigilant against any possible rescue effort.[31]

Luciano and his eight co-defendants were found guilty on all counts. While the men were removed to the Tombs to await a June 18 sentencing date, Dewey held a news conference in which he praised the work of his staff.

In the days that immediately followed the trial, the newspapers were full of rumors about bribery attempts and witness tampering. On June 18, a gloomy, rainy day in the city, the convicted men arrived in the courtroom to hear their sentences. The three men who pled guilty before the trial—Balitzer, Marcus, and Weiner—received terms of two to four years. Ellenstein, who pled during the trial, received a four- to eight-year sentence. Among the sentences for the men found guilty, Ralph Liguori was given 7-1/2 to 15 years; Abe Wahrman received 15 to 30 years; Jimmy Frederico and Thomas Pennochio were given 25 years apiece; and David Betillo received 25 to 40 years.

Finally, it was Luciano's turn to hear his sentence. When asked if he had anything to say, Luciano replied, "Your Honor, I have nothing to say outside of—I want to say it again—that I am innocent." With that, Judge McCook handed down a sentence of from 30 to 50 years.

Before the defendants headed back to the Tombs for transportation to their destinations, "the Court told the defendants he was convinced by the evidence at the trial and information since received that they would be responsible for any injury which the People's witnesses might thereafter suffer by reason of their testimony. He told them that if any witness for the People should be injured or harassed, the Court would request the Parole Board to keep the prisoners for their maximum sentence."[32]

POST-TRIAL BLUES

On June 30, New York State Corrections Commissioner Edward P. Mulrooney, during a visit to Sing Sing, ordered that the ring members serving their sentences there be divided among three prisons. Luciano, along with Ralph Liguori and David Betillo, were transferred to the Clinton County Prison in Dannemora, New York.

Luciano began his fight for freedom on August 11 when attorney James M. Noonan, who represented Dutch Schultz during his tax trials, filed a petition for a writ of habeas corpus to produce the prisoner at the Clinton County Courthouse in Plattsburgh, on August 24. The petition was filed to have Luciano released while the appellate court decided if the new joinder law was unconstitutional. Noonan's petition claimed that the amendment to the State Criminal Code, which allowed the combining of related acts, did not become effective until after Luciano had been indicted and was "ex post facto and unconstitutional," as to every act charged in the indictment.[33]

Concerned that a judge might actually release Luciano, Dewey had his office issue six arrest warrants—two for evading state income taxes in 1934 and 1935, and four based on indictments for compulsory prostitution, which he had not been tried for earlier. On August 24, Luciano was brought to the courthouse in Plattsburgh under heavy guard. Spectators in the courtroom were searched for weapons.

Before Clinton County Judge Thomas F. Croake, Noonan argued that his client should be released on a habeas corpus writ. Jacob J. Rosenblum, a chief aid to Dewey, declared "habeas corpus proceedings are not proper until the appellate courts have decided on the conviction."[34] Luciano, who dressed like a fashion plate during his trial, was bedecked in drab-gray prison attire for the hearing. After hearing arguments, Judge Croake gave both sides 10 days to submit briefs.

On September 14, Judge Croake dismissed Luciano's writ of habeas corpus, declaring he had found no violation of his constitutional rights. Attorney Noonan announced he would appeal the decision in what was called the Appellate Division, Third Department. In November, Noonan argued his writ of habeas corpus before the appellate court. By that time several trials had been held up while a decision on the constitutionality of the joinder law was pending. On January 14, 1937, the Appellate Court, Third Division upheld Croake's decision.

With no hope of being released under a writ of habeas corpus, and waiting for the appellate court to hear arguments on the new law, Luciano then pushed for a new trial. On March 11, affidavits were filed with Judge McCook from Mildred Balitzer, Florence Brown, and Nancy Presser. The *New York Times* reported:

> The principal point in the three affidavits was the broad suggestion that Mr. Dewey's assistants had, by providing liquor and promises of money and immunity, induced the women to give testimony they knew to be false against Lucania, resulting in his conviction.[35]

The affidavits were obtained by two former Department of Justice agents and then filed with the court by attorney Moses Polakoff. Dewey responded with a statement claiming, "I have known for some months of attempts to provide drugs for former drug addicts, and to bribe and intimidate the witnesses in the Luciano trial into giving false affidavits."

On April 20, Judge McCook began an inquiry into allegations by Dewey that the attorneys for Luciano and Ralph Liguori deliberately offered perjured evidence. The attorneys, Polakoff and Lorenzo Carlino, were ordered to appear and answer questions before McCook. In addition to the affidavits from the three women, Carlino filed another affidavit stating that juror Edward Blake claimed the "jury was in great fear because of threats made to three of its members during the trial."

Dewey claimed in his own affidavit that the defense attorneys' claims "reek with perjury and are unworthy of belief." Two of the women were receiving drug treatment in a Manhattan hospital. They were taken from the hospital to make statements recanting their testimony. Dewey produced signed statements from social workers at the Church Mission of Health, which said they were told by Presser and Thelma Jordan that they "were in fear of death and torture and that they would recant their testimony rather than suffer torture such as they had seen inflicted on other girls in the vice ring."[36]

As far as the jury members being in fear, the *New York Times* reported:

> All twelve members of the jury made affidavits which were offered by Mr. Dewey, declaring that neither they nor any member of their families had ever received any threats in connection with the trial. Mr. Blake, the juror cited by Mr. Carlino as his authority, denied that he had ever made such a statement. He said that Mr. Carlino tried to get him to sign an affidavit to this effect, but that he refused.[37]

When McCook called Polakoff to the stand to be questioned by Dewey, he admitted he had been paying money to the women. Afterwards, Polakoff accused McCook of "bias and prejudice." Carlino refused to be questioned, deciding to stand on his "constitutional rights." Three days later, a "stormy day-long" hearing took place. McCook refused to recuse himself, denying a motion by Carlino, who stated he was going to call the jurist as a witness. At the end of the day, McCook deferred his decision on the application for a new trial. While this hearing was going on, the Department of Labor in Washington D.C. ruled that Luciano would be deported to Italy at the end of his prison term.

On May 7, Judge McCook denied Luciano and Liguori's application, claiming that the affidavits of Balitzer, Brown, and Presser were "poisonously false." In his ruling, McCook claimed that statements made by the trio were, "induced by fear, financial pressure and craving for drugs." In commenting on the jailed vice king, the judge wrote, "The hypothesis of a victimized, 'framed' Luciano is utterly destroyed."[38]

On June 2, the court of appeals upheld the constitutionality of the new law in a unanimous decision. The case involved two men who worked for Dutch Schultz in the restaurant racket. With this issue already decided, on July 16, Luciano's conviction was also upheld unanimously by the same court. Although no opinion was written, one justice stated in the record that the sentence time given to Luciano was excessive. Meanwhile, at the same time, U.S. Supreme Court Judge Benjamin N. Cardoza, in a separate case, refused to permit the constitutionality of the joinder law from becoming an issue before the highest court.

On January 18, 1938, the court of appeals in Albany was the scene as new Luciano counsel, Martin Conboy, spent two hours going over alleged errors of Judge McCook. Conboy claimed the errors prejudiced the jury and kept Luciano from receiving a fair trial. Dewey, who had been sworn in as the New York County district attorney on the last day of 1937, responded to the court the next day disclaiming defense counsel's allegations and claiming, "how rigidly the prosecution was held down while to what lengths the defense was permitted to go,"[39] by Judge McCook.

In a 5-to-1 decision on April 12, the court of appeals upheld the conviction and ruled that the sentence was legally imposed. Without mentioning the joinder law, Chief Justice Frederick E. Crane wrote:

> Lucania planned with his lieutenants to place prostitution on a commercial basis and to extract whatever financial profit was possible. The actual management he may have entrusted to others, but he cannot escape his criminal responsibility as the leader and principal.[40]

Moses Polakoff filed a motion for reargument, claiming that Dewey prevented defense counsel from questioning witness Peggy Wild, thus denying Luciano his "due process of law." After hearing arguments, the court of appeals reaffirmed its decision on June 2.

The final step was the U.S. Supreme Court. On July 11, appeals were filed for Luciano and six of his former co-defendants. In the motion, the attorneys claimed that in New York City, the administration of law "is the result of a shifting set of pressures and drives, now here, now there, according to the whim or public outcry, instead of following the systematic order of prosecution."[41]

On October 10, the U.S. Supreme Court declined to review the lower court's decision. Luciano was a little over two years into his 30 to 50-year sentence and his legal avenues were exhausted.

LUCIANO THE PATRIOT

During the three months that followed the Japanese sneak bombing attack on Pearl Harbor, Germany stepped up its U-boat attacks in the North Atlantic and along the U.S. coastline. America and her allies lost more than 120 merchant vessels to the German submarines.

But the worst loss came on February 9, 1942, when the French liner *Normandie* caught fire and capsized in New York Harbor.

The immediate suspicion was that German spies on the New York docks sabotaged the former luxury liner, which was being converted into a troop carrier. Lieutenant Commander Charles Radcliffe Haffenden, in charge of U.S. Naval Intelligence, spearheaded the investigation into the *Normandie* disaster. His agents soon reported that they were getting nowhere because the longshoreman working the piers refused to talk to them.

In the spring of 1942, Haffenden sought the help of Frank S. Hogan, who had succeeded Dewey as district attorney of New York County. In turn, Hogan put him in touch with Murray I. Gurfein, another former Dewey aide, who was head of the rackets bureau. Gurfein, familiar with the racketeering that took place on the docks, recommended that Haffenden contact Joseph "Socks" Lanza, the boss of the Fulton Fish Market.

Lanza was eager to help and provided some assistance, but he soon realized the situation was a bit over his head. He suggested to Haffenden that he speak to Luciano. After a discussion between Haffenden, Hogan, and Gurfein, Gurfein contacted Moses Polakoff in April 1942. Polakoff suggested a meeting with Meyer Lansky, Luciano's longtime friend. After a sitdown, Lansky agreed to help.

One of the problems for Lansky and Polakoff in trying to meet with Luciano was that he was so far from New York City. Both men complained about the long distance to Dannemora and suggested strongly that Luciano be returned to Sing Sing. Instead, an alternative prison was selected by the commissioner of corrections, and Luciano was moved to Great Meadow Prison in Comstock just north of Albany. On May 12, Luciano left the "Siberia" of the New York State penal system behind and moved into Great Meadow.

In late May, Lansky and Polakoff arrived to speak to Luciano. The jailed mob boss, who would not be eligible for parole until April 1956, must have contemplated, "what is in this for me?" Luciano agreed to help and on June 4, Lansky and Polakoff returned in the company of "Socks" Lanza. Over the next few months, through word of Luciano's involvement, longshoremen, both Irish and Italian, helped to keep an eye out for German saboteurs. Lansky and Polakoff made numerous visits to see Luciano. There's no doubt that subjects other than the war effort were discussed between the men. On one occasion, Polakoff arrived with Frank Costello.

In early 1943, when plans were in the works for the invasion of Sicily from North Africa, Luciano, Lansky, and Joe Adonis helped provide Naval Intelligence with native Sicilians living in New York City, who shared their knowledge of the south coast of Sicily. On July 10, Allied forces landed on Licata Beach. Over the years, Luciano's war efforts have been embellished. Lansky biographer Robert Lacey wrote:

> The role of the American underworld in the Allied invasion of Sicily in July 1943 has been a fertile source of legend and exaggeration. Lucky Luciano has been pictured hitting the beaches in person, waving triumphantly from atop a tank, and there have been dark tales of planes dropping flags and handkerchiefs bearing the letter *L* behind enemy lines—signals, supposedly, from Luciano to local Mafia chieftains.[42]

On February 8, 1943, months before the invasion, attorney George Wolf, longtime counsel for Frank Costello, appeared before the New York Supreme Court on behalf of Luciano. The occasion was prompted by the plans of Judge McCook to retire from the bench to join the war effort. Wolf had petitioned the judge to suspend two sentences of 10 to 15 years for his client. This would allow him to seek parole on the sentence of 10 to 20 years that he was currently serving. Since McCook was the sentencing judge, the motion had to be made before him.

During the hearing Wolf cited Luciano's cooperation with military authorities. He told the court he was not at liberty to discuss Luciano's "military secret," but would produce two military officials to speak to the judge in private. This was the first time any hint of Luciano's activity came to the public's attention; it did not cause much of a stir in the media.

Two days later, after interviewing the officials, McCook denied Luciano's application for reduction of sentence. His ruling indicated that he may not have received much support regarding Luciano's reported efforts from the military officials:

> As a result, the court is able to conclude that the defendant probably attempted to assist them, and possibly with some success. If the defendant is assisting the authorities and he continues to do so, and remains a model prisoner, executive clemency may become appropriate at some future date.[43]

More than two years passed before Luciano made his next attempt at freedom. On May 22, 1945, Moses Polakoff made an application to Governor Thomas E. Dewey for executive clemency. He cited Luciano's service to his country from Great Meadow Prison in helping to supply military intelligence during the invasion of Sicily. His influence over the dock workers in an effort to stop sabotage had not yet been made public.

Dewey turned the matter over to the state prison parole board for a recommendation. On January 3, 1946, at the recommendation of the board, Governor Dewey commuted the sentence of Luciano, preliminary to the deportation order that went into effect back in the spring of 1937. If Luciano violated the terms of his parole and returned to the United States, he would be sent back to prison to complete the remainder of his sentence—41 years. In Dewey's statement on the commutation, the governor stated:

> Upon the entry of the United States into the war, Luciano's aid was sought by the armed services in inducing others to provide information concerning possible enemy attack. It appears that he cooperated in such effort though the actual value of the information procured is not clear. His record in prison is reported as wholly satisfactory.[44]

Luciano was transferred to Sing Sing on January 9 to await final preparation for his deportation. On February 2, Federal Immigration Bureau agents removed Luciano from the prison and drove him to Ellis Island. As the automobile passed through Manhattan, Luciano viewed the city he loved and once ruled for the last time.

On February 8, Luciano was paid a visit by Costello and Moses Polakoff at Ellis Island. Questioned about the visit, the chief detention officer stated that Luciano was given no special privileges and that his conversation with Costello was within earshot of a guard. He said, "He was locked in and guarded. Costello brought him his baggage and other personal items. His room was as plain as all the others in his wing, contained just a chair, a bed, a toilet. Costello came on one ferry and left on the next."[45]

The next day, Luciano was taken to the Bush Terminal in Brooklyn. Sitting anchored at Pier 7 was the *Laura Keene,* an ocean freighter headed for Italy with a cargo of flour and one passenger. A shipboard press conference had been arranged by the U.S. Bureau of Immigration, and all the local newspapers, wire services, and photograph organizations had been sent notice. A total of 30 to 40 members of the media were given permission to board the ship. Joachim Joesten, a veteran newspaper reporter, described what happened next:

> At the pier entrance, the newsmen ran into a solid picket line of about half a hundred stevedores. Each carried an ugly bailing hook, a long, curved, sharp-pointed, heavy metal tool used by dock workers to heave huge cases and barrels about. Lined up as an honor guard for the departing boss of the bawdyhouses, the longshoremen let no one pass but Luciano's friends.[46]

The popular belief is that Luciano's underworld friends came to see him off that Saturday night. The guest list varies depending on the writer or who is telling the story. According to *The Last Testament of Lucky Luciano,* those coming to bid farewell were Lansky, Costello, Siegel, Adonis, Anastasia, Zwillman, Willie Moretti, Joseph Bonanno, Stefano Magaddino, Tommy Lucchese, Carlo Gambino, Phil Kastel, Owney Madden, and Moe Dalitz. In addition, Luciano claims Joe Adonis had provided him with three women from the Copacabana nightclub to accompany him on the trip. As for the politicians, Luciano stated that top political leaders from around the country were present.[47]

Underworld figures identified by reporter Joachim Joesten as being there were Costello, Anastasia, Meyer Lansky, and Mike Lascari. According to Joesten, however, their presence there wasn't the reason for the bailing hook-armed guards. The reporter claims they were there to protect "certain personalities in New York politics—a former judge of the general sessions court, a Tammany district leader, and the like."[48]

Lansky biographer Robert Lacey stated that Frank Costello was the only name of consequence that boarded the ship that Saturday night. As for Lansky, attorney Polakoff claims, "He deliberately left New York," and was 200 miles away, having checked into a hotel room in Maryland at the time of the farewell party.[49]

One of the most ridiculous tales to come from *The Last Testament of Lucky Luciano* involves the sailing of the *Laura Keene,* which took off from Pier 7 around noon, February 10. A half-hour into the voyage, Luciano claimed the boat came to a stop and a fireboat came alongside. On the fireboat was William O'Dwyer who came to pay his respects, but did not want to be captured by the media.[50]

HAVANA, CUBA

The year 1946 was a busy one for Mafia chieftain Charles "Lucky" Luciano. After he was released from prison, he boarded a boat to return to his native Sicily, and within eight months, he was executing a long-range plan to return to the United States. It was Luciano's plan all along to return to America, and he carefully outlined the first steps. With an extended stopover in Havana, Cuba, his intended final destination was New York City.

When the *Laura Keene* arrived in Genoa, Italy, authorities there decided to send Luciano on to his hometown of Lercara Friddi in Sicily. Upon his arrival there, he was "treated as a local boy made good." Luciano soon received permission to move to Palermo, where he was said to have made contact with Sicilian Mafia boss Calogero Vizzini.

During October 1946, under his birth name of Salvatore Lucania, Luciano obtained two passports with the alleged help of corrupt government officials in Italy. On one of these passports, he was able to make a successful application for a six-month Cuban visa. In addition, he held passports and visas for Bolivia, Columbia, and Venezuela. According to one account, Luciano secretly boarded a freighter to take him to Caracas, Venezuela. Another tale had him flying first to Brazil and then to Venezuela. From there he flew to Mexico City and booked a private plane for a flight to Havana, Cuba. This last leg of the journey was said to be aided by corrupt Cuban officials. After arriving in Havana, Luciano was picked up by childhood friend, Meyer Lansky, and taken to the Hotel Nacional, where he registered under his real name—Salvatore Lucania—in a luxurious suite that Lansky had reserved for him. Luciano later revealed, that after checking in, it was the first time since his imprisonment in 1936 that "there was no handcuffs on me and nobody was breathin' over my shoulder."[51] The mob leader felt he had spread enough money around and had taken the necessary precautions on his sojourn so as not to arouse the suspicions of Harry Anslinger of the Bureau of Narcotics and Thomas Dewey, as to his arrival in Havana.

Between his arrival and the end of December, Luciano frequented the nightclubs, casinos, and racetracks and was often seen in the company of celebrities. After several months, Luciano was spotted by a reporter from the newspaper *Tiempo de Cuba*. "The editor, Roland Masferrer, revealed that, after exposing Lucky, both he and his staff were threatened with violence by the boys who had gathered 'round the boss.'"[52]

The following discussion deals with the alleged "Havana Conference," which was said to have been held from December 22 until at least New Years Eve. The information comes mainly from *The Last Testament of Lucky Luciano,* which in itself makes it highly suspect. There is some proof that Costello and Adonis were in Havana around this time, but there is no documentation to show that any meeting, the magnitude of which Luciano depicts, ever took place.

Lansky had scheduled a meeting at the Hotel Nacional for the week of December 22, 1946 and left to go back to Miami, Florida.[53] Luciano moved out of the hotel and into a spacious home in the Havana suburb of Miramar. Lansky shuttled back and forth between Miami and Havana, keeping Luciano informed of the upcoming meeting and making plans for Lucky to enjoy an extended stay in Cuba. He suggested that Luciano purchase an interest in the casino at the Hotel Nacional, controlled jointly by Lansky and Cuban politician Fulgencio Batista, for $150,000. Instead of paying that amount out of his own pocket, Luciano claimed that invitees to the meeting were to provide "welcome" money to him that would cover his investment. These "Christmas presents" totaled more than $200,000, which Luciano used to purchase an interest.

Luciano's long-range plan was for him and his associates to provide financial backing for Tom Dewey's presidential campaign in 1948. Once in office, Dewey would show his appreciation by rescinding the deportation action. While waiting the two years for this to happen, Lansky was negotiating six-month extensions of Luciano's visa with the Cuban minister of the interior.

One week before the meeting, Vito Genovese arrived and went to see his old friend. Luciano knew why Genovese was there. Lansky had informed him that Vito was trying to muscle in on Albert Anastasia. Genovese opened the discussion by saying that Anastasia needed to be eliminated because he was thinking about killing Harry Anslinger. Luciano rebuked Genovese and pointed out that Vito was the one interested in pushing narcotics, not Anastasia.

The next item on Genovese's agenda was to ask Luciano to retire. Things were changing in New York City and Luciano was too far away to effectively run the criminal organization. After hearing Genovese's request, Luciano advised that he was not ready to retire and that Vito wasn't to bring up the question again.

As the other "delegates" arrived for the meeting, they checked into rooms set aside for them by Lansky on the top four floors of the Hotel Nacional. The hotel's mezzanine was also reserved for meetings, banquets, and parties for the group. Luciano states that after the mobsters checked in, they would pay him a visit in Miramar to "reaffirm loyalty." The first night a dinner was hosted by Lansky, Frank Costello, and Joe Adonis as a "public showing of their private affirmations," where all the attendees came forward with envelopes filled with cash for Luciano.

Below is a recap of the Havana Conference, based on the Martin Gosch book, and written by me in June 2000:

> On the morning of December 24, 1946, the Havana Conference was underway. Luciano states that he sat at the head of a large rectangular table with Lansky, Costello, Genovese, and Adonis at his side. Other than this arrangement, there was no protocol for the seating. Luciano opened the meeting by thanking the boys for their monetary donations. He explained that the money would be invested in the hotel's casino. He then explained his need to be addressed as Salvatore Lucania so as not to draw attention to the former Charles "Lucky" Luciano now that he had left Italy.
>
> Luciano then brought up the subject of the "Boss of Bosses" title in which he "casually mentioned" that he felt it was time for him to don that designation. Anastasia stood up and, glaring over at Genovese, stated, "For me, you are the Big Boss, whether you like it or not. That's the way I look at it, and I would like to hear from anybody who don't feel the same way."
>
> There was silence in the room. Luciano claims, "That was all I was after—first, to teach Vito a lesson in public without him losin' face and also to get the title without havin' to fight for it. So I won my first point, and frankly, I didn't give a shit what happened after that."
>
> Luciano claimed that he had heard rumors of infighting between Anastasia and Genovese. He told them they needed to work out their differences in order to avoid the problems that occurred between Joe Masseria and Salvatore Maranzano, which resulted in the Castellammarese War in 1930–1931.
>
> He next spoke about his feelings regarding the narcotics trade, stating that he wanted them to get out of that business immediately; however, this argument was falling on deaf ears. As the discussion continued about the huge sums of money that could be made from drugs, Luciano could see this was a conflict he was not going to win. Soon Costello leaned over and whispered, "Charlie, don't hit your head against the wall. Vito rigged it before the meet started. Try to get out of it as soon as you can. Someday, they'll all be sorry."
>
> This discussion was followed by what Lansky introduced as "The Siegel Situation." Benjamin "Bugsy" Siegel had not been informed of, or invited to, the meeting mainly because he would be chief among the topics covered. Sent out to the West Coast in the mid-1930s to oversee the New York mob's gambling and labor racketeering interests, Siegel quickly became a Hollywood mob celebrity. He later became preoccupied with constructing a grandiose hotel and casino in the small town of Las Vegas in Nevada, a state that had legalized gambling. Working through Lansky, he got the New York mob to finance the Flamingo. The original cost had been calculated at $1.5 million. A year later, however, either through the bungling or dishonesty of Siegel, the price tag had risen to $6 million.

Although the casino was not yet completed, Siegel set a date of December 26, 1946 for its grand opening. Lansky reported he had information that Siegel's girlfriend, Virginia Hill, had been making trips abroad to deposit money in a Zurich bank account. Although Siegel and Lansky had been friends since childhood, Lansky said he believed his old partner would skim even more money and possibly flee the country if the Flamingo was a bust.

Luciano claimed that a vote was taken, minus Lansky and Phil Kastel, who were both Jewish, and it was decided that Siegel was to be killed. The contract was given to Charles Fischetti of Chicago to be carried out by Los Angeles Family boss Jack Dragna. In a possible attempt to save Siegel, Lansky suggested that they wait until after the grand opening, which was just days away.

Christmas Eve arrived and the meeting's participants took a break. The wives and girl-friends of the mobsters had arrived, and a grand party was held at the hotel in honor of sing-er Frank Sinatra, then a rising star who had traveled to Havana with the Fischetti brothers.

On the day after Christmas, the meeting reconvened in the evening as everyone was anxious to hear how the opening at the Flamingo was received. As there was a three-hour time differential between the two cities, it was well after midnight before the first reports were received. Rain and cold weather had prevented planes from bringing customers in from Los Angeles and the opening was considered a disaster.

Despite the flop, Lansky convinced the group that he could salvage the project. The Flamingo closed, work was completed, and it reopened a couple of months later. It would soon become a financial success and mobsters across the country would become rich from it and all the casinos and hotels that followed. Unfortunately for Siegel, he would not live to see his vision fulfilled. He was cut down by a hit man using a rifle on June 20, 1947, as he sat reading a newspaper on a couch in Virginia Hill's Los Angeles home.[54]

Because of the revelations made in *The Last Testament of Lucky Luciano*, many people believe that Frank Sinatra actually performed at the hotel for the mob boss on Christmas Eve. In an extensive biography about Sinatra, however, the authors revealed that the famous singer arrived in Havana on February 11, 1947, in the company of Rocco and Charles Fis-chetti. A newsreel camera caught Sinatra and the Fischettis in a crowd leaving the airplane on arrival. The suitcase Sinatra carried in the picture was believed to be loaded with cash for Luciano.

FBI and Bureau of Narcotics agents tracked the singer's activity in Havana. At the Hotel Nacional, Sinatra took a room one floor below Luciano. Over the years, Sinatra would give numerous stories about the trip and how he came to be in the company of Luciano—none of them consistent or, for that matter, believable. When tabloid stories began to appear in the *New York World Telegram* about the singer's activities there, Sinatra had his lawyers file a law suit against the newspaper. One of the stories released involved an orgy in Sinatra's hotel suite that was interrupted when a "delegation of Cuban Girl Scouts" arrived to meet the singer.

Without putting a timeframe to it, Harry Anslinger, commissioner of the U.S. Bureau of Narcotics, stated he was approached by the Cuban ambassador to the United States and asked what the presence of Luciano meant to his country. Anslinger related:

> I had received a preliminary report through a Spanish speaking agent I had sent to Havana, and I read this to the Cuban ambassador. The report stated that Luciano had already be-come friendly with a number of high Cuban officials through the lavish use of expensive gifts. Luciano had developed a full-fledged plan which envisioned the Caribbean as his

center of operations. The Isle of Pines, south of Cuba, was to become the Monte Carlo of the Western Hemisphere. Cuba was to be made the center of all international narcotic operations. We had a number of transcribed calls Lucky had made to Miami, New York, Chicago and other large American cities, and the names of hoodlums who called him. Lucky kept himself busy in Havana.[55]

Based on the "transcribed calls," it is obvious that Anslinger was aware of Luciano's presence in Cuba for nearly two months before it became public. In his book, Anslinger revealed his decision to do something about Luciano being just 90 miles from the U.S. mainland:

> I decided that our bureau was the only American agency in a position to take direct action without causing too great an international upheaval. "As long as Luciano remains in Cuba," I had our agent in Havana inform Cuban authorities, "America will not send one more grain of morphine or any other narcotics, for medicinal or any other needs. This is to go into effect immediately." Since we were the main and virtually only supplier of medicinal narcotics to Cuba, and our shipments were essential, the government was forced to capitulate, and Luciano's dream of establishing an underworld headquarters on our southern doorstep ended abruptly.[56]

According to a *New York Times* article on February 22, 1947, Luciano's presence in Cuba became public a few days earlier. The article stated that both Anslinger and Colonel Garland Williams, director of narcotic enforcement in New York for the Treasury Department, declared an embargo on narcotic shipments if the Cuban government did not move to deport Luciano. The Narcotics Bureau believed that Luciano was responsible for the increase in drug traffic into the United States. Williams said: "In the three months that Luciano has been traveling about freely we received in this country the first large shipment of European heroin—$250,000 worth."[57] Williams told the newspaper: "We believe the best for him is that place most distant from this nation. Luciano is considered to be so dangerous to narcotic law enforcement" that embargo of legitimate narcotics would remain in effect as long as the deported hood was allowed to remain.

On the day after the threat was relayed to the Cuban government, Luciano was arrested. The chief of the secret police said the arrest was made on the grounds that Luciano's presence might cause "public disorder." Police followed him from his home in Miramar to the suburb of Vedado, where he and two local bodyguards stopped at a cafe. Luciano offered no resistance. He was taken to the offices of Minister of Interior Alfredo Pequeno and questioned. Luciano was then placed in Tiscornia Camp, an immigration camp located across Havana Bay. Reports from Cuba stated that Luciano would be asked to leave the country immediately, and that if he refused the government would hold him until his six-month visa expired on April 29.[58]

Reports regarding Luciano's deportation varied. One claimed he would leave in the next 48 hours; another stated that while "officials could have forty-five days to complete deportations proceedings," it could be accomplished in a week.[59] On February 25, after the Cuban government announced that they declared Luciano an "undesirable alien due to past record," and scheduled him to sail on a steamship leaving for Europe on March 4, the U.S. government lifted its five-day embargo of narcotics shipments to Cuba.[60]

On February 28, a Cuban court rejected a writ of habeas corpus, based on lack of jurisdiction, filed by an attorney for Luciano. The writ claimed Luciano had "complied with the immigration laws, and that authorities were unable to accuse him of a crime."[61] The next day, Luciano's attorney filed another petition of habeas corpus, "on behalf of the people of Cuba," requesting that his client be released so that he could leave Cuba as a free man. In this capacity, Luciano could go to any South American country that he had a visa to enter. This time a court accepted the petition and ordered that Luciano be produced on March 3 for a hearing.[62]

Instead of appearing in court, Luciano sent word that he desired no writ and was "perfectly happy and well treated at Tiscornia Camp, although somewhat ill." The Audienca Court of Appeals, however, ordered his presence so that the case could be closed as a legal matter. Despite five separate orders to have Luciano brought to court, the mobster never appeared. Alfredo Pequeno, the interior minister, was in charge of the national police who were ordered to bring Luciano to the court. He claimed he had no right to pull Luciano out of the Tiscornia Camp. Pequeno seemed to be behind the effort to keep Luciano out of the court. While this jurisdictional battle was going on, a shipping agent said that the Cuban government obtained a reservation for Luciano aboard the Turkish steamer *Bakir,* set to sail March 12 for Genoa, Italy.[63]

On March 19, Luciano boarded the *Bakir* for his return to Italy. The ship had a scheduled stop at the Canary Islands, and the captain told Luciano he would not stop him from going ashore there. Pequeno personally escorted Luciano to the steamer, and a guard was placed aboard to make sure he didn't try to leave. The next day the *Bakir* sailed for Genoa, Italy, with Luciano. Unlike his deportation aboard the *Laura Keene* 14 months earlier, there was no gala bon voyage party for the mob boss.

Luciano's leaving did cause some excitement on the island nation. One Cuban senator accused another "of having business connections with Luciano and attempting to block the deportation order." After slugging it out in the Capitol corridor and again on the floor of the Senate, the two decided to fight a duel. On March 27, the two men engaged in a sword fight in the House of Representatives. Both men were wounded slightly before a judge suspended the duel.[64]

GETTING RESETTLED

Luciano paid $300 to travel in first class aboard the *Bakir.* During the trip he was free to go anywhere on the ship and passed the time playing cards with some of the tourist-class passengers. In Italy, plans were already being made for his return. He was to be placed in the Marassi jail until he could be transferred to Palermo, Sicily. An Italian police official in Rome stated that Luciano would be "placed under permanent police vigilance if we determine that he is a dangerous character."

On April 12, the *Bakir* entered Genoa harbor around 5:00 AM. Waiting on the dock were reporters, photographers, and a crowd of curious onlookers anxious to see the returning mob boss. Police foiled the "perp walk" by taking a launch out to the *Bakir* while it was still in the harbor and removing Luciano. Police claimed they were acting on orders from Rome to keep Luciano away from the media and the public.

Luciano remained in jail until May 1. He was then taken to Palermo under heavy guard. Upon arriving in the Sicilian capital two days later, Luciano was immediately placed in jail. A "regional commission" was requested to decide the fate of the jailed mob leader. The police wanted him to "be declared a public menace and restricted to residence." The commission members, however, "refused to do more than warn him to keep out of mischief and the public eye."[65]

On May 14, Luciano walked out of jail free to travel to any part of Italy he chose. Before leaving with his attorneys, the freed mob boss blamed the American media for maligning his reputation. "They have invented fantastic stories about my life and activities," he claimed."[66]

Luciano took up residence in the Hotel Delle Palme, said to be the "best" in Palermo. He remained out of the "public eye" for a little over a year. On May 22, 1948, he was arrested at the hotel after officials in Rome were notified that Luciano had been seen in "the company of mafia chieftains." At the Cairoli Barracks police station, Luciano was questioned for three days before being released.

While in Palermo, Luciano opened a pastry shop. The shop was in operation for about two years before it failed. He also tried to get involved in Italy's motion picture industry, but apparently he had little success.

It was believed that Luciano, once settled, moved full-time into the business of smuggling narcotics into the United States. Although Luciano vehemently denied any participation, many sources listed him as a "kingpin" of the world's narcotics traffic. Within two years of Luciano's deportation, Italian police officials began seeing increased amounts of illegal drug shipments from Italy to the United States. Their counterparts in America, the U.S. Bureau of Narcotics, confirmed this observation.

Luciano soon left Palermo and moved into a luxury hotel in Rome with his girlfriend Igea Lissoni, who was described by the authorities as a "most graceful lady." He also reconnected with former vice trial co-defendant Ralph Liguori, who had been deported by the United States in 1945. He soon became a regular companion of Luciano in Rome. They attended nightclubs together and were seen constantly at the racetrack.

The first time Luciano's name was publicly connected to the drug trade was in October 1948. Two port patrolmen with the Customs Enforcement Division uncovered 16 pounds of pure heroin aboard the Italian liner *Vulcania* during a routine search. The division chief told reporters that Luciano was "believed" to have been involved in the smuggling attempt. He also stated that five months earlier, a large shipment of cocaine had been seized on the same vessel. Luciano was "believed" to have had a hand in that, too.

Another narcotics shipment, alleged to be connected to Luciano, was seized three months later from a French vessel in the East River in New York City. This time the Customs Department released a statement declaring there is "positive information in the files of the Customs Service that Luciano is involved in all illegal transfers of narcotics from Italy and other Mediterranean countries to this country in recent years."

On June 26, 1949, Italian police officials announced they made the largest seizure of narcotics ever in Italy when they confiscated 20 pounds of raw cocaine at the Ciampino Airport in Rome. Arrested for trying to smuggle the cocaine to New York was Vincent Trupia. Police immediately tried to link him to Luciano. On July 7, Luciano and his girlfriend Igea Lissoni were picked up for questioning by police in Rome, where the mob boss was now living. Ralph Liguori was also brought in.

The police announced that Luciano had been "detained" for questioning. Italian law allowed an individual to be "detained" for up to four days without being charged with a crime. While Luciano was held in Rome, officials in Palermo raided and searched his pastry shop. After a week of detainment, Luciano was cleared of any connection to Trupia and the narcotics he was smuggling; however, he was expelled from Rome after being declared a "crime threat" and told not to return. He was ordered to return to Lercara Friddi, Sicily, and report in with the police.

Luciano was livid about his new displacement, but the citizens of Lercara Friddi were eagerly awaiting his return. Reports claimed that Luciano was being touted to run for mayor, and there were hopes that with his wealth, he would promote improved roads and a better water system for the small town.

The law banished Luciano from Rome, but it didn't force him to remain in one place. An official from the Lercara Friddi mayor's office stated, "The law is quite clear. All he has to do is write a letter to let me know where he is. Of course Rome is closed to him, but the rest of Italy is open."[67] So instead of fulfilling the townsfolk's vision of a politician and civic benefactor, Luciano stayed just long enough to obtain permission to leave.

Ironically, the next time Luciano was discussed in the newspapers was when he returned to Rome. On November 15, Luciano received a 10-day pass from the Rome police to attend to some personal affairs in the city. While there, the *Rome Daily American* newspaper reported he had married Lissoni. Both denied the unfounded story.

WARTIME BACKLASH

The release of Luciano from prison, his subsequent deportation to Italy, his return to Cuba, and the rumors of his being a worldwide drug lord would come back to haunt Thomas E. Dewey for years. No one was sure, especially the public, as to what Luciano's "patriotic efforts" were during the war. The government and the military denied everything, and it would take years before the real story came out. When the governments of two countries claimed Luciano was the world's narcotics kingpin in the 1950s, however, the notoriety reflected badly on Dewey, and his political opponents used it relentlessly to their advantage.

The first opponent to wield this club was Walter A. Lynch, the Democratic Liberal candidate for New York governor. Before the fall election of 1950, Lynch baited Governor Dewey to explain why he had pardoned Luciano. In a campaign speech on October 22, Lynch told an audience:

> I want to be sportsmanlike in giving Tom Dewey reasonable time to answer the questions. Should Tom Dewey refuse to answer the question shortly I will be forced to give the full details of the Luciano pardon to the people of the State of New York.[68]

The "question" was answered by Frederick A. Moran, the chairman of the New York State Parole Board. He claimed Dewey had commuted the sentence following an independent investigation by board members after which they made a unanimous favorable recommendation. Moran told reporters:

> During his two terms as Governor, it has been Governor Dewey's unbroken practice to refer all applications for executive action to the Board of Parole. This applies to the case of Charles Luciano as to all others. Governor Dewey has never granted an application except after independent investigation and unanimous favorable recommendation by the Board of Parole.[69]

During his final campaign speech before the election, Lynch declared that Dewey had released Luciano because of Frank Costello's influence. In addition he declared:

Our Federal Narcotics Commissioner, Harry Anslinger, has unequivocally stated that Luciano had been on the international black list as a narcotics violator. Yet Luciano was let out by Governor Dewey to prey upon the youth of America with his dope-peddling activities.[70]

Lynch then attacked Moran, calling him a liar and stating that no legitimate body had ever made a recommendation of parole for Luciano. He then added, "As a matter of record there is not one single case in the long history of the Division of Parole where a commutation had been granted for the purpose of deportation." It took state employees about a day to find 67 similar cases in the prison record books, dating back to World War I, which somewhat destroyed the candidate's credibility. In fact, Moran reported that Democratic Governors Roosevelt and Lehman had issued 43 commutations between them, but Dewey had allowed just eight. Lynch was soundly defeated in the election.

The Luciano commutation incident came up the next year when crime-crusading Democratic Senator Estes Kefauver called the commuting of the gang lord "unjustified." Later that year, the tables were turned and it was now a Republican that was lashing out at Dewey. W. Kingsland Macy was upset when Governor Dewey tried to oust him from the chairmanship of the Suffolk County Republican leadership, where he was not recognized by the Republican State Committee. By this time, embarrassed by the Luciano incident, the armed forces had denied that the crime boss had ever done anything for them. Macy challenged that allegation in light of the military's stand, how could Dewey claim Luciano was paroled because of his war effort? During a speech on July 18 on radio station WOR Macy stated:

> There is something decidedly rotten in this Dewey-Luciano business. Governor Dewey is the only man who can clear it up. The public wants to hear from him. Substitute alibis will not do.
>
> In the public interest, I now make a concrete suggestion. I suggest that the Senate Crime Investigating Committee return to New York immediately and that it demand that Governor Dewey appear before it forthwith to explain the Luciano release.[71]

The attack got uglier a couple of weeks later when Macy sent a letter to Senator Herbert R. O'Conor, chairman of the Senate Crime Investigating Committee, urging him to call Governor Dewey before the committee to be questioned about the commutation. He also suggested that an attempt be made to extradite Luciano from Italy to serve the remainder of his 30- to 50-year sentence. Referring to the fact that the committee considered Luciano the head of the international dope smuggling ring, in his scathing letter Macy stated:

> I believe you will agree that when Governor Dewey paroled Luciano he loosed upon the world a cunning, ruthless, vicious criminal through whose activities the minds and bodies of thousands of our youth have been and even at this moment are being corrupted.[72]

Even Frederick Moran came under attack by Macy, who Moran requested be called by the committee. Macy pointed out that Moran had been a Democratic appointee of Governor Lehman and remained in a day-to-day capacity for three years under Dewey until word of Luciano's release was made. At that point he suffered the brunt of the public's indignation over the incident. He was then reappointed by Dewey. Macy stated, "One wonders if the retroactive appointment was a reward for his cooperation in the Luciano release."

The Luciano release faded from the press for more than two years, then made a comeback in November 1953. This time it was Governor Dewey's attempt to oust Arthur H. Wicks from the role of majority leader and president pro tem of the New York State Senate that re-kindled the matter. The ouster followed the revelation that Wicks had paid a visit to Joseph F. Fay, a convicted labor union chief, while he was imprisoned at Sing Sing. Wicks defended himself by stating that his visit was no more improper than Dewey's commuting the sentence of Luciano.

In his accusations, Wicks claimed that Dewey was responsible for the transfer of Luciano out of the Clinton County prison in Dannemora to the less strict Great Meadows facility in 1942. Wicks's timetable was a bit off, as he failed to realize that Herbert Lehman was still governor at the time and that Dewey had nothing to do with the transfer. Despite the erroneous claims, the state Democrats seized on it to ask that the Luciano commutation be investigated. Wicks was ousted and the matter again seemed to be dropped.

The next time Dewey faced a stir from Luciano the deported gangster brought up an incident himself. While being interviewed by a correspondent for Fawcett Publications, Luciano claimed he offered to name the killers of Carlo Tresca, the murdered publisher of the Italian newspaper *Il Martello*. In exchange for naming the killers, Luciano wanted his freedom. He said Dewey turned him down.

While this interview was said to have taken placed sometime in late 1953, it did not come to the public's attention until January 1954, when Norman Thomas, chairman of the Carlo Tresca Memorial Committee, made the announcement in New York City. A spokesman for Governor Dewey told reporters:

> No offer of any information from Luciano concerning the Tresca case was ever made and there is no evidence whatever that he possessed any knowledge concerning it. If such irresponsible gossip were to be used by any investigative agency, Mr. Thomas would be among the first to protest. I am surprised he would indulge in the same practice himself.[73]

Later that month the Luciano scandal came to a head. On January 26, while both houses of the New York State government were in session to review a probe of the State Parole Board and the State Corrections Department, the question of Luciano's commutation was discussed. The Democrats demanded a list of persons who made visits to Luciano while incarcerated.

One senator suggested that if there was any evidence of illegal activities on the part of Luciano, he should be brought back to be questioned before the parole board and have his commutation revoked. Assemblyman Eugene F. Brannigan of Brooklyn claimed that the list of Luciano's visitors had been destroyed, so Democrats could not inspect it. When State Corrections Commissioner Edward J. Donovan heard this charge, he invited the Democrats to his Albany office to view the list. The next day, it was revealed by Assemblyman Brannigan that Frank Costello, Meyer Lansky, Joseph "Socks" Lanza, Willie Moretti, and Mike Miranda had all been allowed visits to Luciano. That same day, Commissioner Donovan revealed what he had found out through a conversation with Moses Polakoff. For the first time, the details of Luciano's wartime efforts were made public.

While the revelations were shocking, Republicans pointed out that all this activity took place when Democratic Governor Lehman was in office and Dewey had no part in it. Quick to respond was now-Senator Lehman from Washington D.C. He claimed, "No one visited Luciano in prison with my knowledge or consent during the time I was Governor." Attempting to deflect any responsibility, he declared, "The fact is very clear, however, that Governor Dewey commuted the thirty to fifty year sentence of this man, Luciano."

The next day, a somewhat vindicated Dewey remarked to reporters, "It blew up in their faces. They have been demanding a list of Luciano's visitors. When they got it, it turned out that the visits of underworld characters were arranged while I was a private citizen and Senator Lehman, a Democrat, was Governor."

In Naples, Italy, Luciano was following the soap opera in the newspapers. During an interview with a Reuters reporter, Luciano called the fuss about him in New York political "hot air." He said he missed the sidewalks of New York and was "getting fed up with the sun and the sea and the sky of Naples." He also made the announcement, "Lucky Luciano is dead. I'd like people to know that my name is Salvatore Lucania."[74]

With the sudden renewed interest in this activity, William B. Herlands, the New York State Commissioner of Investigations, began a probe of the whole affair. The investigation, which was held from January 28 to September 17, 1954, revealed the actions of the navy in its efforts to seek assistance from Luciano and others. It was a true vindication for Dewey, who refused to release the "Herlands Report." When asked later why he would not release the report, Dewey responded, "Since the Navy allowed the officers to testify only with the expressed wish that the report not be made public, I never released it."[75]

In 1977, *The Luciano Project* by Rodney Campbell was published. The book, subtitled "The Secret Wartime Collaboration of the Mafia and the U.S. Navy," explained the actions of Commander Haffenden in the effort to seek the underworld's help along the New York docks and later the invasion of Sicily.

NARCOTICS KINGPIN

In the early 1950s, as the Kefauver Hearings wound their way around the country, Luciano's name was prominent. From its investigation, the committee concluded that Luciano was receiving lots of cash from America and that he "still has his finger in the United States crime picture."

Banished from Rome, Luciano and Lissoni moved to Naples, where they took up residence in another hotel. In late February 1951, while Kefauver's investigators were finalizing their witness list for the New York City hearings to be held in mid-March, reporters tracked down Ralph Liguori in Rome, where he gave the following impromptu interview:

"I'm clean and so is Charlie.

"Anytime anything happens anywhere, they turn the heat on us," he said. "Why the hell don't they leave us alone?

"It's all false," he added. "Twenty years ago it might have been fun, but how can they bring it up now?

"Sure, Lucky and I played around with bootlegging and the numbers racket—who didn't? But all that stuff about narcotics and vice rings is just a crock of baloney."[76]

On June 9, Naples police arrested Luciano on charges that he had brought into the country illegally $57,000 in cash and a new American automobile. Picked up at his suite in the Hotel Turistico, Luciano was grilled for 20 straight hours before being released. He was later indicted for both crimes.[77] The incident was investigated by the Senate Crime Investigating Committee, as the committee would come to be known after Senator Estes Kefauver's departure later that month.

On June 27, Charles Siragusa, one of the top agents of the Bureau of Narcotics, appeared before the Senate Crime Investigating Committee. Siragusa was the chief of the Rome office of the U.S. Bureau of Narcotics. In his book *The Murderers: The Shocking Story of the Narcotic Gangs,* U.S. Commissioner of Narcotics, Harry J. Anslinger stated:

> Charles Siragusa, on my instructions, launched an investigation into what was happening in the matter of diversion of heroin from legal medical uses (Italy is one of the few countries where heroin is used as a medicinal narcotic under medical prescription). Our findings indicated that hundreds of pounds of heroin were being diverted by men acting in close association with Luciano.[78]

While testifying before the committee, Siragusa was asked whether Luciano was the kingpin of the Mafia. The agent responded that if "Lucky" isn't the kingpin, "he is one of the royal family."[79] Siragusa claimed that Luciano received large sums of money from American mobsters and that he "certainly wields influence in Mafia policy matters." To the question, "Is Lucky Luciano the kingpin of the narcotics traffic in the United States?" Siragusa answered, "The United States and Italy." The agent stated that, "in Mafia circles, Luciano enjoys the honorable title 'Don,' a symbol of the respect and esteem the membership holds for him."[80]

> "Someone once asked Lucky Luciano, Mafia millionaire, vice and dope-smuggling King, what present he would like Santa to bring him. Through clenched teeth Luciano spat back, 'Siragusa in a ton of cement.'"
> —Siragusa (Siragusa, *The Trail of the Poppy: Behind the Mask of the Mafia,* 1966, p. ix)

Luciano read about Siragusa's testimony in the newspapers and complained immediately that he was being persecuted. He was not alone in that conclusion. Eugenio Testa, head of the Naples Surveillance Squad assigned to keep an eye on Luciano, spoke out. Testa declared, "There is nothing at all in Luciano's activities which can back up the charges of Siragusa. It is ridiculous to say that Luciano is the brains behind a large narcotics distribution outfit as Siragusa said. He may be a prominent federal narcotics agent, but I think he's wrong this time."[81]

Over the next year it seems that narcotics peddling and the name of Luciano became synonymous. In late July, the U.S. Attorney's office in New York City announced that a "World Crime Ring" had been cracked by agents of the Bureau of Narcotics and the Secret Service. Ten members of the ring were in custody and another 10 were being sought. The men and women were accused of trafficking in narcotics and counterfeit money. Assistant U.S. Attorney Louis I. Kaplan claimed that Luciano was the head of the Italian link of this French-Italian smuggling cartel.

A few days later, Irving "Waxey Gordon" Wexler and three of his associates were arrested for trying to sell heroin to an undercover agent of the Bureau of Narcotics. The federal agency claimed Wexler was competing with narcotics rings "controlled" by Luciano.

Two days after Wexler's arrest, five men were apprehended by the Royal Canadian Mounted Police as part of an international gang of narcotics couriers. The arrests were made in Montreal, Canada, with the assistance of the Bureau of Narcotics. The chief of the Royal

Canadian Mounted Police advised the *Associated Press* that the ring was linked to an international narcotics cartel run by Luciano.

All of these accusations against Luciano caused him to speak out publicly:

> The name of Lucky Luciano has been associated for some time with all the criminal acts of American gangsters, and I was said to be the mastermind of them all. I feel indignant about that. They are defaming me and my reputation.

In a surprising statement, he claimed that the charges of his running an international narcotics ring were being bantered about in the hearings before the Senate Crime Committee for political purposes to embarrass Governor Thomas Dewey. Luciano declared, "I got my pardon because of the great services I rendered the United States, and because, after all, they reckoned I was innocent."

Luciano finished his railing by promising to "put an end to all the dirty speculation about me" and divulge, "certain stories which will make everybody in the United States take notice." These stories, he said, would not be revealed until after the 1952 presidential elections.[82] As it turned out, Luciano's revelations were never revealed.

The outburst by Luciano had no effect on what the federal government believed. Before the month was out, the Senate Crime Investigating Committee in a formal report, stated:

> Experienced enforcement officers believe that the present influx of heroin from abroad is managed by the Mafia with Charles "Lucky" Luciano, notorious gangster, vice king, and racketeer deported convict, now resident in Italy, as the operating head. His chief lieutenant is believed to be an Italian resident named Joseph Pici.[83]

In March 1952, after the indictment in San Francisco of 23 members of a coast-to-coast narcotics ring, a Bureau of Narcotics official announced that Luciano was "definitely" behind the ring. The indictment contained the names of alleged drug dealers in nine states. An assistant U.S. attorney claimed that the indicted men were freely talking. The "boys are singing all over the place now," he declared, and what they were revealing was "so hush, hush, I'm even afraid to talk about it." One of the indicted was Irving Wexler, who was serving a long term in Attica from his August 1951 arrest.[84]

Luciano's "definite" participation caused little stir in Italy, but a few months later his name appeared in a report of the United Nations Committee on Narcotic Drugs. At a meeting on April 30, the Italian representative to the commission reported that local authorities had no evidence connecting Luciano to any drug smuggling activities since his arrival. This statement was in stark contrast to one made by Harry J. Anslinger four months later when he revealed in a speech that top police authorities in Italy confirmed that Luciano was overseeing the narcotics rackets between Italy and the United States.

In September 1952, Luciano's name surfaced after the murder of Eugene Giannini in East Harlem (see Chapter 6). A government informant, Giannini told authorities he had met with Luciano in Palermo. He claimed the exiled mob boss told him that he and Joe Pici were partners in the narcotics rackets in Italy.

During the next few years, Luciano's name appeared in the newspapers after drug arrests and investigations of his former associates. The accusations by American law enforcement officials continued. On October 26, 1954, Luciano received a summons to appear before a Naples admonition board. The board was described as a "warning body," dealing with "idlers, habitual vagrants who are able to work but have no means of subsistence or who are suspected of criminal activities, and with persons designated by public opinion as socially dangerous." Weeks later, on November 19, after hearing testimony from government officials, law enforcement officers, and attorneys for Luciano, the six-man board issued its edict. Claiming to have "reason" to believe he was involved in drug trafficking, the white-slave trade, and fixing horse races, Luciano was declared a danger to society. He was given a dusk-to-dawn curfew and was ordered to stay at home every night for the next two years. He was placed under constant police surveillance and was restricted in travel to a 16-mile radius of Naples. Travel outside this perimeter was by police permission only.

In addition, Luciano was forbidden from attending racetracks and other areas of public amusement, banned from wine shops, and ordered not to consort with "shady" characters. During Luciano's entire exile from America, he was constantly receiving visits from fellow deportees, as well as crime figures from the United States. Luciano was ordered to report to the Naples police every Sunday.[85] He was also ordered to "get a job." When asked by a reporter what he was going to do, Luciano gave thought to becoming a bookkeeper. "You know I can count money," he laughed. "I'm pretty good at spending it, too."

Four days before Christmas, Luciano traveled to Rome to appeal the crackdown order before an interior ministry commission. After waiting for five hours, his appeal before the commission lasted 10 minutes. A dejected Luciano told waiting reporters, "They didn't let me say a single word. They just looked at me. Then my lawyers said a few words about me not having done anything in Italy, and then they told me to go."[86] The decision of the Naples admonition board was upheld. Luciano went to police headquarters, where they reviewed his papers and ordered him out of Rome. He traveled back to Naples on a special police pass that allowed him to be out that night.

In August 1955, after a major heroin-ring bust by the Bureau of Narcotics, Luciano was again linked to the operators. Informed by reporters of these allegations in Naples, Luciano complained, "I'm innocent. Why do they keep trying to accuse me?"

Luciano was one of a dozen deported racketeers who asked for reentry to the United States in November 1956, after the reelection of President Dwight D. Eisenhower. A lawyer presenting the petition to the president claimed the exiled men were tired of being under constant police protection. To no one's surprise, the petition was denied.

After another major narcotics ring was broken in January 1958, Luciano earned a reprieve. U.S. Attorney Paul W. Williams, who indicted Genovese on the narcotics charges that would send him away for the rest of his life, denied that Luciano had any role in this latest operation. "We have absolutely no information at this time that Luciano is involved in the case," Williams stated in a news conference.

In March 1958, Naples police sought to retain restrictions on Luciano's movements, claiming he was seen in the company of "dubious characters" again and living beyond his visible means. After a hearing before a judiciary commission, Luciano was declared to be "leading a perfectly regular life that does not call for censure." The commission deemed him, "a free citizen."[87]

Police continued their efforts to conduct surveillance. On July 23, 1958, at the public prosecutor's request, Luciano came in for a hearing. One of the topics he was asked about was the ill-fated Apalachin Summit (see Appendix) in November 1957. Luciano replied, "They're still trying to frame me. Until I read all that trash in the papers, I never even heard of Apalachin. I still don't know where it is and don't care. I'm clean. I even pay my income tax. They got nothing on me and never will have."[88] When asked about his employment, Luciano said he was a sales representative for a pharmaceutical house. He told his inquisitors, "All this publicity is hurting my business."[89]

After the hearing, the Naples city court ruled that because the police had not been able to connect Luciano to any postwar drug activity or any other serious wrong-doing, the order of surveillance should not be reinstated. If the courts upheld this ruling, Luciano would be eligible for a passport to leave the country, and for applying for a drivers' license.

> "I don't want to stay in this country [Italy] any more. I don't feel like an Italian. I want to go somewhere where I'd be left in peace—even in Soviet Russia if they want me. I don't care about politics or anything else. I just want peace."
> —*New York Herald-Tribune*, December 21, 1954, "Unlucky Luciano Wants to Quit Italy, Eyes Russia"

THE AUTUMN OF HIS LIFE

The late 1950s would prove to be a dark time for Luciano. He had turned 60 and was in deteriorating health. The ousting of Frank Costello from power by Vito Genovese and the ensuing murder of Albert Anastasia were highlighted by the debacle of the Apalachin Summit. None of this would prove to be good for Luciano's health or his wallet. The turmoil in the United States surely meant less money coming into the exiled boss, and, with Costello out of the picture and heading back to prison, Luciano was not going to see any tribute from Genovese, who was now said to be his sworn enemy.

The year 1958 brought some highs and lows for Luciano. On July 7, Genovese and Vincent Gigante headed a group of 37 people who were indicted for conspiring to import and sell narcotics. The belief to this day is that Luciano conspired with Costello and Carlo Gambino to frame Genovese. The plot worked and the next year Genovese was convicted and sentenced to 15 years in prison, where he died. The low point came during late September when Luciano lost the one true love of his life. Igea Lissoni lost a bout to cancer and died at the age of 37.

Early the next year, Luciano had a mild heart attack. After failing to heed his doctor's advice, he suffered a major coronary attack in the spring of 1959. During his recovery, Luciano decided to act on something he had considered for some time. He looked into having a movie made about his life. After meeting film producer Barnett Glassman, Luciano got more serious about the project. Glassman, who was busy with other projects, eventually introduced Luciano to Martin A. Gosch.

What happened next depends on whose version you believe. Gosch claimed he developed a friendship with Luciano, who soon began dictating his memoirs to him. The book was not published until 1974, because, according to Gosch, Luciano didn't want the book to be released until 10 years after his death. In the book, Gosch claimed that Luciano's plans for a movie were nixed by the New York underworld, the edict delivered by Tommy Eboli. Luciano blamed Meyer Lansky for pulling the strings. Incensed at this betrayal, Luciano was going to get even by giving Gosch the material for a tell-all biography, *The Last Testament of Lucky Luciano*.[90]

On January 26, 1962, Luciano drove to Capodichino Airport in Naples to meet Gosch. According to Gosch, he was delivering the movie script, every page of which Luciano had initialed. The Italian authorities, who had Luciano's phone tapped, had raided his apartment after hearing a phone conversation between him and Gosch on January 24. Not finding anything, they followed Luciano to the airport. Cesare Resta of the Naples police was there when Luciano arrived to greet Gosch. As the three made their way toward the parking lot, Gosch describes what happened next:

> Suddenly Lucky put his arms around me. His eyes began to roll. "Charlie," I asked him, "what's wrong with you?" He fell forward in my arms and died without uttering a word.[91]

A lot of controversy followed Luciano's death. The United Press International reported on the day he died that U.S. and Italian authorities were about to arrest Luciano as part of a crackdown on yet another international drug ring. There was much speculation that Luciano was murdered—poison being substituted for his heart medication by a Mafia hit team. An autopsy later revealed he died of a coronary attack; no traces of toxic agents were found.

Luciano's 72-year-old brother, Bartolo Lucania, arrived in Naples two days later. A funeral service was held on January 29 at the Holy Trinity Church in Naples. Included among the 300 mourners were said to be Joe Adonis and the Fischetti brothers, as well as U.S. and Italian narcotics agents who took movies of everyone present. Afterwards, the body was taken to Poggio-Reale's English Cemetery to await permission for return to the family mausoleum in New York City.

On February 7, a casket with the name Salvatore Lucania arrived at New York International Airport. There to greet it were Bartolo and Joseph Lucania and 50 law enforcement officers from the FBI, Bureau of Narcotics, New York State Police, and local police. A hearse and simple mourner's car drove to St. John's Cemetery in Middle Village, Queens, followed by a dozen vehicles containing the officers, reporters, and photographers.

Luciano's casket was quickly placed in a vault in the mausoleum, which also contained the remains of his parents and an aunt and uncle. There was no graveside ceremony. The two brothers left without fanfare. It was nearly 16 years to the day that Luciano had left New York. He was now back in the city he loved.

NOTES

1. Sid Feder and Joachim Joesten, *The Luciano Story* (New York: David McKay Company, 1954), p. 39

2. Ibid., pp. 54–55.

3. *New York Evening Post,* November 17, 1928, "M'Cabe Gives Up to Banton to Bare Rothstein's Debts."

4. *New York Herald Tribune,* December 18, 1929, "Racketeer Saved by Patrolman Refuses to Talk."

5. *New York Times,* December 18, 1929, '"Ride' Victim Wakes on Staten Island."

6. *New York Herald Tribune,* December 18, 1929, "Racketeer Saved by Patrolman Refuses to Talk."

7. Leonard Katz, *Uncle Frank* (New York: Drake Publishers Inc., 1973), p. 89.

8. Sal Vizzini with Oscar Fraley and Marshall Smith, *Vizzini* (New York: Arbor House, 1972), pp. 168–169. In this book, Sal Vizzini talks about his career as an undercover agent with the Fed-

eral Bureau of Narcotics. In the disguise of a U.S. Air Force Major, he befriends Luciano in the latter years of the mobster's life. He relates some entertaining stories about Luciano while in his company. He also states, however, that he is present and overhears Luciano talking to a courier regarding conversations with both Frank Costello and Vito Genovese regarding money coming to him. During the time frame in which these conversations took place, "the spring of 1961" according to Vizzini, both Costello and Genovese were in the Atlanta Penitentiary.

9. The *New York Times* had referred to the gang leader as "Charles (Lucky) Luciania" in their December 18, 1929 article reporting his beating. The article dispelled the rumor that the nickname "Lucky" was born of that event. Now, six years later, the *Times,* calling him Charles Luciania, reported:

> Luciana is called "Lucky" Luciana because he is one of the few persons who ever came back alive after being "taken for a ride" by gangland enemies.

10. *New York Times,* October 26, 1935, "7 Gangsters Seize Schultz Rackets; Fourth Aide Dies."

11. *New York Times,* February 3, 1936, "Vice Raids Smash '$12,000,000 Ring': Leaders In Jail."

12. *New York Times,* April 5, 1936, "Arkansas Rangers and Machine Guns Upset Luciana Luck."

13. *New York Times,* April 6, 1936, "New Law Invoked to Thwart Luciana."

14. *New York Times,* April 7, 1936, "$50,000 Bribe Offer for Luciana Fails; Extradition Fixed."

15. *New York Times,* April 24, 1936, "Lucania Is Accused in New Indictment."

16. *New York Times,* May 12, 1936, "Three Admit Guilt As Vice Trial Opens."

17. *New York Times,* May 13, 1936, "Jury Is Completed in Lucania Trial."

18. Bookers were the people who informed the prostitutes each week of the houses they were to report to for work.

19. The term *inmates* was a name Dewey and the newspapers used in place of "prostitutes" in referring to the women who worked the various houses.

20. *New York Times,* May 14, 1936, "Vice Ring 'Seizure' Is Laid to Lucania."

21. Ibid.

22. *New York Times,* May 15, 1936, "Vice 'Booker' Tells of Payments."

23. The Baumes Law, enacted in 1926, called for a sentence of life imprisonment for a person convicted of three or more felonies in New York State.

24. *New York Times,* May 23, 1936, "Lucania Is Named Again As Vice Chief."

25. New York Times, May 24, 1936, "Big Hotel Suite Lucania's 'Office'."

26. *New York Times,* May 26, 1936, "'Friend' of Lucania Acts As Accuser."

27. *New York Times,* May 28, 1936, "Vice Case Threats Bring Arrest of 4."

28. *New York Times,* June 6, 1936, "Dewey Assailed at Lucania Trail."

29. *New York Times,* June 7, 1936, "Fate of Lucania Weighed by Jury Throughout Night."

30. Ibid.

31. *New York Times,* June 8, 1936, "Lucania Convicted with 8 in Vice Ring on 62 Counts Each."

32. Hickman Powell, *Lucky Luciano: His Amazing Trial and Wild Witnesses* (Secaucus, NJ: Citadel Press, 1975), p. 303.

33. *New York Times,* August 12, 1936, "Fight for Freedom Begun by Lucania."

34. *New York Times,* August 25, 1936, "Lucania in Court with Heavy Guard."

35. *New York Times,* March 12, 1937, "3 Women Recant Lucania Testimony."

36. *New York Times,* April, 21, 1937, "Perjury Is Charged to Lucania Counsel."

37. Ibid.

38. *New York Times,* May 8, 1937, "Luciano Plea Denied."

39. *New York Times,* January 20, 1938, "Dewey Attacks Lucania Appeal."

40. *New York Times,* April 13, 1938, "Luciano Plea Lost in Appeals Court."

41. *New York Times,* July 12, 1938, "High Court Review Asked by Vice Chief."

42. Robert Lacey, *Little Man: Meyer Lansky and the Gangster Life* (London: Little, Brown and Company, 1991), pp. 124–125.

43. *New York Times,* February 11, 1943, "Lucania Loses Plea to Get Out of Prison."

44. *New York Times,* January 4, 1946, "Dewey Commutes Luciano Sentence."

45. *New York Times,* February 2, 1946, "Deportation Set for Luciano Today."

46. Feder and Joesten, *The Luciano Story,* pp. 224–225.

47. Martin Gosch and Richard Hammer, *The Last Testament of Lucky Luciano* (Boston: Little, Brown and Company, 1974), pp. 286–287.

48. Feder and Joesten, *The Luciano Story,* p. 227.

49. Lacey, *Little Man: Meyer Lansky and the Gangster Life,* p. 128.

50. Gosch and Hammer, p. 287.

51. Ibid., p. 305.

52. Feder and Joesten, *The Luciano Story,* p. 235.

53. In *Lansky,* by investigative journalist Hank Messick, the author claimed Meyer Lansky was in the midst of his divorce at the time and "couldn't be at Lucky's elbow all the time." Messick claimed the Federal Bureau of Narcotics was tracking Luciano's telephone calls and that among the dates he called and spoke to Lansky was December 24, 1946, a date on which he would have been at the meeting.

54. Allan R. May, *Havana Conference—1946 (Part 2),* AmericanMafia.com, June 6, 2000.

55. Harry J. Anslinger and Will Oursler, *The Murderers* (New York: Farrar, Straus and Company, 1961), p. 106.

56. Ibid. In *Lansky,* author Hank Messick claimed that Meyer Lansky supplied the "preliminary report" that Harry Anslinger refers to. Messick stated, "He [Lansky] sent an informer to have a quiet talk with a Federal Narcotics Bureau agent in Havana."—Hank Messick, *Lansky* (New York, G. P. Putnam's Sons, 1971), p. 136.

57. *New York Times,* February 22, 1947, "U.S. Ends Narcotic Sales to Cuba While Luciano Is Resident There."

58. *New York Times,* February 23, 1947, "Cuba Puts Luciano in Detention; Seeks End of U.S. Narcotics Ban."

59. *New York Times,* February 26, 1947, "Cuba Will Deport Luciano to Italy."

60. *New York Times,* February 26, 1947, "U.S. Narcotic Ban on Cuba Is Lifted."

61. *New York Times,* March 1, 1947, "Luciano Denied Freedom Writ."

62. *New York Times,* March 2, 1947, "Luciano Gets Writ for Review in Cuba."

63. *New York Times,* March 4, 1947, "Court Calls Luciano."

64. *New York Times,* March 28, 1947, "Cuban Senators in Duel."

65. *New York Times,* May 15, 1947, "Luciano Released From Palermo Jail."

66. Ibid.

67. UPI article carried in the *Youngstown Vindicator,* July 23, 1949, "Luciano Arrives in 'Exile,' Stays Less Than 1 Day."

68. *New York Times,* October 23, 1950, "Lynch Asks Why Luciano Is Free."

69. *New York Times,* October 25, 1950, "State Parole Chief Denies Politics Entered into Luciano Commutation."

70. *New York Times,* November 4, 1950, "Favor to Costello in Freeing Luciano Charged to Dewey."

71. *New York Times,* July 18, 1951, "Dewey Is Assailed on Luciano Parole."

72. *New York Times,* July 30, 1951, "Macy Renews Fire on Luciano Parole."

73. *New York Times,* January 6, 1954, "Tresca Case Failure Is Charged to Dewey."

74. *New York Times* (through the Reuters News Agency), February 1, 1954, "Luciano Calls Ado Over Visits 'Hot Air.'" This was the second time Luciano made a public statement regarding his name. The first time came after he was returned to New York from Arkansas following his extradition from that state in 1936.

75. Rodney Campbell, *The Luciano Project* (New York: McGraw-Hill Book Company, 1977), p. 16.

76. *New York Times,* March 1, 1951, "'It's Bunk! They Always Turn the Heat on Us,' Luciano Aide in Rome Says of Crime Report."

77. In March 1952, the Italian Treasury Ministry fined Luciano $4,000 for "illegally importing" the $57,000. Joseph Pici was fined $2,400 for the same transaction. Luciano had to be threatened with jail time before he made good on the fine.

78. In 1966, Charles Siragusa's book, *The Trail of the Poppy: Behind the Mask of the Mafia,* was published. The retired law enforcement officer had spent nearly 25 years as a member of the Federal Bureau of Narcotics. Although he continually identified Luciano as the head of the narcotics ring in Italy, he never provided any evidence or information to show that these accusations were anything more than speculation.

79. Anslinger and Oursler, *The Murderers: The Shocking Story of the Narcotics Gangs,* p. 107.

80. Organized Crime in Interstate Commerce: Final Report of the Special Committee to Investigate Organized Crime in Interstate Commerce, August 31, 1951.

81. Ibid.

82. *New York Times,* August 5, 1951, "Luciano Says He'll Talk."

83. Organized Crime in Interstate Commerce: Final Report of the Special Committee to Investigate Organized Crime in Interstate Commerce, August 31, 1951.

Joseph Pici was a convicted white slaver from Pittsburgh. According to Charles Siragusa, Pici was deported with Luciano aboard the *Laura Keene.* At one time Pici reentered the United States, delivering 15 kilos of heroin to the Kansas City underworld. Near the end of 1950, Pici was arrested in Milan, Italy, with several pounds of cocaine in his possession and was sent away to prison.

In the late-1950s, Anslinger believed that Luciano and Pici were involved in an illegal alien ring, using the aliens to transport narcotics as the price for being relocated to the United States. Anslinger stated, "Our reports indicated that the aliens being used for this purpose might number in the hundreds, but the Luciano-Pici operations was so smooth that neither we nor Immigration had been able to uncover a single tangible piece of evidence during months of investigation."—Anslinger and Oursler, *The Murderers: The Shocking Story of the Narcotics Gangs,* p. 110.

84. *New York Times,* March 9, 1952, "Luciano Is Linked to Heroin Arrests."

85. *New York Times,* November 21, 1954, "Luciano 'Danger to Society,' Is Ordered to Stay Home Nights in Naples for 2 Years."

86. *New York Herald-Tribune,* December 21, 1954, "Unlucky Luciano Wants to Quit Italy, Eyes Russia."

87. *New York Times,* March 21, 1958, "Inquiry Clears Luciano."

88. *New York Times,* July 25, 1958, "Luciano Disclaims Link to Apalachin."

89. Ibid.

90. Martin Gosch's book *The Last Testament of Lucky Luciano* was under attack before it hit the bookstores. Nicholas Gage was the first to question the legitimacy of the book. In 1975, Tony Scaduto, a former features writer for the *New York Post* penned *Lucky Luciano: The Man Who Modernised the Mafia.* The book, oddly enough dedicated to Ernest "The Hawk" Rupolo, was not without its own numerous mistakes; however, Scaduto took liberty in blasting Gosch as a fraud and bald faced liar.

91. *New York Times,* January 28, 1962, "Luciano's Links to Underworld Investigated by Italian Agents."

BIBLIOGRAPHY

Biographies of Luciano

Campbell, Rodney. *The Luciano Project*. New York: McGraw-Hill Book Company, 1977.

Feder, Sid, and Joachim Joesten. *The Luciano Story*. New York: David McKay Company, 1954.

Gosch, Martin, and Richard Hammer. *The Last Testament of Lucky Luciano*. Boston: Little, Brown and Company, 1974.

Poulson, Ellen. *The Case Against Lucky Luciano*. Little Neck, NY: Clinton Cook Publishing, 2007.

Powell, Hickman. *Lucky Luciano: His Amazing Trial and Wild Witnesses*. Reprint ed. Secaucus, NJ: Citadel Press, 1975. (This book was originally published as *Ninety Times Guilty* in 1939.)

Other Publications

Anslinger, Harry J., and Will Oursler. *The Murderers*. New York: Farrar, Straus and Cudahy, 1961.

Dewey, Thomas E. *Twenty Against the Underworld*. Garden City, NY: Doubleday & Company, 1974.

Katz, Leonard. *Uncle Frank*. New York: Drake Publishers, 1973.

Lacey, Robert. *Little Man: Meyer Lansky and the Gangster Life*. Toronto: Little, Brown and Company, 1991.

Messick, Hank. *Lansky*. New York: G. P. Putnam's Sons, 1971.

Peterson, Virgil W. *The Mob: 200 Years of Organized Crime in New York*. Ottawa, IL: Green Hill Publishers, 1983.

Siragusa, Charles, as told to Robert Wiedrich. *The Trail of the Poppy*. Englewood Cliffs, NJ: Prentice-Hall,1966.

Summers, Anthony, and Robbyn Swan. *Sinatra: The Life*. New York: Alfred A. Knopf, 2005.

Turkus, Burton, and Sid Feder. *Murder, Inc*. New York: Farrar, Straus and Young, 1951.

Vizzini, Sal, with Oscar Fraley and Marshall Smith. *Vizzini*. New York: Arbor House, 1972.

8

ARNOLD ROTHSTEIN

AKA "THE BIG BANKROLL"
JANUARY 17, 1882-NOVEMBER 6, 1928

Known by many names—A. R., Mr. Big, The Fixer, The Big Bankroll, The Man Uptown, and The Brain—Arnold Rothstein seemed more myth than man. He was the inspiration for Meyer Wolfsheim in "The Great Gatsby," and Nathan Detroit in "Guys and Dolls." He was rumored to be the mastermind of the "Black Sox" scandal, the fixing of the 1919 World Series. Arnold Rothstein was money, and he was considered by many to be the "father of organized crime. He was Mr. Broadway and had his own booth at Lindy's restaurant in Manhattan where he held court.

Part of Rothstein's mystique was his legendary prowess as a gambler. Author David Pietrusza, however, in the most recent biography of Rothstein, wrote:

> A. R. pretended to be almost everything he was not, including a gambler. He hated real gambling, because real gambling involved real risk. And Arnold was too smart to take risks.[1]

Still, there are the fictionalized accounts of Rothstein betting thousands of dollars on a simple cutting of the deck. The appeal of the dice or card game was believed to be fueled by his rebellious attitude toward his pious father. His early success at it led to the building of his "roll," his money, which he was soon lending out in a loan shark capacity, constantly increasing it and moving on to the next phase in his criminal career.

Donald Henderson Clarke was one of a few newspapermen that Rothstein was friends with. Within months of Rothstein's death, Clarke wrote *In the Reign of Rothstein,* a memoir of the reporter's friendship with such luminaries of the day as William J. Fallon, Nicky Arnstein, Fanny Brice, Gertrude Vanderbilt, Peggy Hopkins Joyce, and Rothstein himself. Here are some of the personal observations Clarke revealed about Rothstein:

- He never smoked tobacco or drank alcohol.
- His voice was mild and pleasing; his mannerisms graceful; his grammar was not perfect . . . And his wit was amazing.

- When he first appeared in the news, Rothstein was a slim, young man of 26, with dark hair, a complexion remarkable for its smooth pallor—as if it never had to worry about razors—white, skillful hands, and amazingly vital, sparkling, dark brown eyes.
- The Rothstein eyes were features above all others that those who met him recalled most faithfully—those laughing, brilliant, restless eyes glowing in the pale but expressive face.
- He prided himself inordinately on his ability to read character.
- In gambling, those who lost to him insisted that it was not skill, but good luck that won for Arnold Rothstein.

Clarke went on to say:

And contrary to common belief, the underworld is inhabited exclusively by human beings. My picture of Rothstein physically is simply of a quiet, medium-sized man, inconspicuously dressed, in this restaurant or that, in this courtroom or that, or strolling on a sidewalk with a friend, frequently reaching down to snap the garter on his sock, his ready laughter revealing those white, even, artificial teeth, hardly whiter than his pallid skin, which was like a woman's.[2]

IN HIS BROTHER'S SHADOW

Arnold Rothstein, unlike most of the underworld figures in this book, was actually born in the United States. On January 17, 1882, Arnold was born in a brownstone on East 47th Street in Manhattan, the second of five children.[3] Shortly after his birth, the family moved to a larger home on East 79th Street.

Arnold, whose parents Abraham and Esther were brought together in an arranged marriage, was considered different from his siblings at an early age. He was not a happy child or outgoing like the others. Arnold spent many hours alone in cellars and closets, choosing dark places in which to play. At the age of three he had already taken a disliking to his older brother Harry. One night Abraham entered the boy's bedroom to find Arnold standing over Harry with a knife in his hand. When the father pleaded for an explanation, Arnold simply replied, "I hate Harry."

Years later, Rothstein told a psychologist that when he was six years old, his mother took Harry and his younger sister, Ethel, on an extended trip to San Francisco to visit relatives. The first night she was gone Abraham found Arnold hidden away in a closet weeping uncontrollably. "You hate me," cried Arnold. "She hates me and you hate me, but you all love Harry. Nobody loves me." It was the only time Rothstein had shown any deep emotion during his childhood.

Arnold continued to live in Harry's shadow, lacking an identity of his own. He fell two years behind in grade school and found himself a classmate of his younger brother Edgar. This didn't seem to bother Arnold, who from this point forward kept up with his classes. Edgar would later recall, "I'd do all the homework and Arnold would copy it and remember it. Except in arithmetic. Arnold did all the arithmetic. He loved to play with numbers."[4]

When Harry Rothstein was 13, he informed his parents that he wanted to study to become a rabbi. This decision delighted Abraham. Arnold, who had shunned his religious studies even more than his regular schooling, was chided by his father, "You should be proud of being a Jew." A defiant Arnold responded, "Who cares about that stuff? This is America, not Jerusalem. I'm an American. Let Harry be a Jew."

After completing two years at Boy's High School, Arnold quit school for good in 1898 at the age of 16. He had found his calling in the streets. He began shooting dice for nickels and pennies and kept a record of his winnings. Arnold frequented pool halls, which in the early days of their existence were places where betting was transacted and lotteries played. While gamblers waited around for game or race results, there was usually a billiards table to occupy their time. Rothstein earned a reputation at the billiards table and his pocket money began to grow.

Rothstein became a regular at Hammerstein's Victoria Theatre where a craps game was in action every Monday. The popular game drew the likes of Monk Eastman and Herman "Beansy" Rosenthal.[5] Rothstein's success at the dice table made him a popular figure at the game and at other gambling spots. He soon began loaning money to the players. For every four dollars he loaned, he collected five in return. If any problems arose in collecting the loans, Rothstein would turn to his newly found friend Monk Eastman. The bullet-headed thug, with a broken nose and cauliflower ears, met little resistance when trying to retrieve payments due Rothstein.

> "I wasn't fifteen years old before I had learned my limitations. I never played with a man I wasn't sure I could beat. I knew how to size them up. I still do. That's all there is to making money."
> —Arnold Rothstein (Pietrusza, *Rothstein*, 2003, p. 5)

While building a reputation as a gambler and money loaner, while still only 16, Rothstein began to cultivate a friendship with Timothy D. Sullivan, Tammany Hall's East Side political boss. Sullivan, known as "Big Tim," gained his powerful political standing by delivering the democratic vote on Election Day. In return, Sullivan looked out for the people in his district, delivering coal and food for the needy and helping others get jobs or legal assistance when necessary.

Rothstein became a regular at Sullivan's headquarters. He ran errands for "Big Tim" and served as a translator for Sullivan's Jewish constituents. Sullivan soon realized that Rothstein was a young man with a future. Meanwhile, Rothstein found in Sullivan the father figure he desperately wanted.

As conflict continued in the Rothstein household, Arnold, now 17, took a job as a traveling salesman peddling headwear. He informed his not-too-disappointed father that he would be moving out. Rothstein's work took him to upstate New York, Pennsylvania, and West Virginia. Two years into the job he received a telegram while he was in Erie, Pennsylvania, informing him that Harry had died of pneumonia.

Years later Rothstein would tell his wife Carolyn, "Somehow, I had the feeling that I was responsible for Harry being dead. I remembered all the times that I wished he were dead, all the times I had dreamed of killing him. I got to thinking that maybe my wishing had finally killed him."[6]

CAREER AND MARRIAGE

After the death of his brother Harry, Arnold made a serious attempt at mending his relationship with his father. He moved back home, worked at his father's factory, stayed away from the poolrooms, and even attended synagogue. Arnold's efforts failed. After an argument, he left home again feeling that he was unloved and unwanted. He would never spend another night in his parents' house.

Rothstein's new home was the Broadway Central Hotel and his new profession was that of a cigar salesman, which kept him in close contact with gambling houses, hotels, and saloons. His favorite hangout became a poolroom owned by John J. McGraw, the manager of the New York Giants baseball team. Here Rothstein honed his talents as a pool player and gained the reputation of being one of the best on Broadway.

During this period, the first decade of the twentieth century, Rothstein began working on his bankroll. He believed that carrying a large sum of money and flashing it helped gauge his prominence. "Money talks," Rothstein once told a reporter. "The more money the louder it talks."

In Leo Katcher's biography of Rothstein, *The Big Bank Roll,* the author discussed Rothstein's work philosophy:

> The cigar salesman made a good living. He lived frugally, did not dissipate. Each week the roll in his pocket grew a little thicker. He knew he could never attain his ultimate aim by simple economies, but these could start him on his way. He didn't like long range projects. He was essentially a short-term, quick-turnover man.
>
> Rothstein pursued a fixed course. He worked at selling cigars until he accumulated $2,000. He decided that this was sufficient to base an entry into gambling as a profession. He quit his salesman's job. He would never again work for anyone else. All the rest of his life, no matter what else he might be, he would always be a professional gambler.[7]

With "Big Tim" Sullivan's backing, in 1902 Rothstein began working on his own. He booked bets on baseball games, elections, horse races, and prizefights. In addition, he gambled on his own—shooting craps, playing pool, and participating in poker games. Rothstein had a simple philosophy, "Look out for Number One. If you don't, no one else will. If a man is dumb, someone is going to get the best of him, so why not you? If you don't, you're as dumb as he is."[8]

Rothstein was cautious never to overexpose himself in bets. He found that the secret of winning was simply to "have a large enough bank roll to be able to lose one more bet than anyone else could afford to lose." Rothstein continued to prosper from his gambling endeavors, and he was still loaning money at exorbitant interest rates. He began to invest his income in legitimate businesses as a silent partner. He became part-owner of an automobile dealership and several drugstores.

By 1906, his bankroll had grown from $2,000 to $12,000. Flashing his roll served as a sign of his ability and success and earned him respect in his chosen field. In 1907, he met his future wife Carolyn Greene, a 19-year-old actress. He once took her to dinner and spread his money out over the table. "This is going to make me important," he told her. "I know how much money means. I'm going to have more and more of it. Nothing is going to stop me."[9]

Rothstein had selected his wife very carefully. Not a womanizer, he had Carolyn checked out thoroughly before presenting her to his family. At an uncomfortable meeting in his parent's home, Abraham questioned his daughter-in-law to be:

"Are you Jewish, Miss Greene?" he inquired.

"My father is Jewish and my mother is Catholic. I have been brought up as a Catholic," Carolyn replied.

"But you will change your religion if you and Arnold should marry, will you not?" Abraham asked.

"No, Mr. Rothstein," came Carolyn's response.

"If he marries outside his faith, he will be lost to me," said Abraham.

Rothstein left his parents' house for yet another time with a feeling of being unloved. His father's wishes had no effect on his plans to wed Carolyn. On August 12, 1909, Rothstein and Greene were married in Saratoga, New York, during the heart of horse racing season. Newspaperman Herbert Bayard Swope was Rothstein's best man.[10] Rothstein's parents did not attend. When word of the wedding reached Abraham, he reacted by donning a prayer shawl and reciting the *Kaddish,* the Jewish prayer of mourning.

POOL GAMES AND MARKS

Rothstein had promised Carolyn that after he made $100,000, he would retire from being a gambler. Rothstein was comfortable discussing his philosophy of gambling with his wife, but never the actual mechanics, and certainly not the people with whom he interacted. During their honeymoon, spent at Saratoga, he pawned all of the expensive jewelry he had given Carolyn, including her engagement ring, to obtain cash. This was more lucrative than borrowing the money at a higher interest rate. By the end of the honeymoon, which coincidentally coincided with the end of race season at Saratoga, Rothstein had won $12,000, but it took him six months to get Carolyn's ring out of hock.

Returning to New York, Rothstein decided to open his own gambling house. He rented two brownstones on West 46th Street. He and Carolyn took up residence in one, and the other was outfitted with roulette wheels, faro, and poker tables. Rothstein then went to "Big Tim" Sullivan to discuss "protection." Sullivan, an Irishman who believed in marriage and large families, was delighted that his protégé had wed. His wedding gift to Rothstein was protection, but with a string attached; Rothstein had to take on William Shea, a deposed building inspector, as his partner.

Shea, a self-proclaimed anti-Semite, distrusted Rothstein from the beginning of their relationship and felt that his partner was always cheating him. Rothstein, who "made a lot of acquaintances, but few friends," did not mix well with others and was constantly in the habit of referring to people as "chumps." When a group of Rothstein's detractors got together to take advantage of his pool-playing vanity, a Broadway legend was created.

The group brought Jack Conway to town. A Philadelphia sportsman and accomplished jockey, Conway just happened to be an expert pool player. One night at Jack's, a popular Manhattan hangout, Rothstein walked in and was invited to sit down with the group as they discussed baseball and prizefights. During this talk it came out that Conway was "probably" the best amateur pool player in the country. Rothstein, unaware of Conway's background or that he was being set up, sensed a challenge.

The two men agreed to play to 100 points for $500 at John McGraw's Billiard Parlor. The game began on a Thursday night at 8:00 PM. By the time it ended, at 4:00 AM. Saturday morning, Rothstein was rumored to have won more than $10,000. The match received so much publicity that it was reported on in two of the New York City newspapers. In one account Rothstein was referred to as "a well-known sportsman."

To increase the winnings at his gambling house, Rothstein was in constant search for what the gamblers called "marks." A mark was a wealthy individual who enjoyed gambling and believed he could "beat the house." One of the first "marks" that Rothstein was able to land was Charles Gates, whose father had become wealthy from the invention of barbed wire. Gates came in one night and dropped $40,000 at the roulette wheel and faro games.

Gates wrote a check for the amount and accompanied William Shea to the bank the next morning to cash it. By evening Shea had not returned with the money. Soon Shea sent word that he was keeping the entire $40,000 because he felt he had been cheated by Rothstein in the past. After consulting with Sullivan, Rothstein told "Big Tim" that he was going to let Shea keep the money, of which he was entitled to one-third anyway, but that he had to sign a contract releasing him from the partnership. When Rothstein caught up with him, Shea was drunk and readily signed the papers, thinking he had pulled a fast one on his "sheenie" partner. After Shea sobered up and realized the blunder he had made, he went crawling to Sullivan for help. "Nothing doing," Sullivan told him.

Rothstein realized that using attractive women could be a great help in bringing in the marks. One of the women Rothstein used was Peggy Hopkins, a beautiful ex-show girl. One night, Hopkins brought in Stanley Joyce, a man she would later wed, and Percival H. Hill, of the American Tobacco Company. While Joyce dropped $17,000, the unlucky Hill ended his night of gambling by signing over an IOU to Rothstein good for $250,000. Rothstein suffered through a restless night wondering if he would have any trouble collecting the money. Carolyn urged that if he did collect, he should keep his promise to her and retire from gambling. When morning arrived, Rothstein took a cab to the offices of the American Tobacco Company and collected a certified check for a quarter of a million dollars. Carolyn, however, never would collect on the promise made to her.

"BEANSY" AND BECKER

By 1910, the unholy alliance of police, politicians, and the underworld had been going on in New York City for half a century—at least. The Democratic political leaders were supplied by Tammany Hall. The underworld leadership had passed from Monk Eastman, who was imprisoned in 1904, to William Alberts, better known as "Big Jack" Zelig. The main figure in the police corruption was Captain Charles Becker.

This combination began to self-destruct around 1912 based on two factors—the deteriorating mental state of "Big Tim" Sullivan and the greedy single-mindedness of Becker. Sullivan had been institutionalized before being placed in a home in Williamsburg. On occasion Sullivan would slip past his attendants and return to his old stomping grounds in the

Bowery or along Broadway. In September 1913, Sullivan disappeared after an all-night card game with his guards. A few days later his body was found on the railroad tracks near the Westchester freight yards. An engineer stated that Sullivan was dead before the train ran over his body. "Big Tim's" funeral was attended by more than 25,000 mourners.

Long before Sullivan met his maker, two men were trying to muscle in on his control of local gambling. One was Tammany Hall politician Thomas Foley; the other was Captain Becker. The rise and fall of Charles Becker would be short but spectacular. His brief time in the limelight, however, would be the subject matter of no less than five books.

Herman "Beansy" Rosenthal got involved in gambling around the same time as Rothstein. Despite the backing of Sullivan, Rosenthal's operations were always a failure. He was not a particularly bright individual. With "Big Tim" in fading health, Becker decided to make his move on Rosenthal's latest operation—the Hesper Club. Becker ordered Jack Zelig to collect protection payments. Rosenthal refused to pay and went to Florrie Sullivan, Tim's brother, for advice. When Florrie suggested that Rosenthal hire some muscle of his own, "Beansy" sought out an ex-lieutenant of Monk Eastman, Bridgie Webber. No sooner had the alliance formed than word got back to Becker. Zelig and his gang invaded Webber's clubhouse and destroyed it, nearly beating Bridgie to death in the process.

Florrie Sullivan's next piece of advice was for Rosenthal to give in, which he did by making Becker a partner in the Hesper Club. The partnership was not amicable and Rosenthal let it be known—to almost everyone—that when "Big Tim" regained his health, the matter would be straightened out. When Becker's order for Rosenthal to keep his mouth shut went unheeded, the captain had the Hesper Club raided and "Beansy" was arrested and fined.

Shortly thereafter a Becker associate was charged with murder. Becker sent word to all the gamblers under his protection to fork over $500 for the defense fund. When Rosenthal refused, Becker ordered his thugs to administer a vicious beating to him. Rosenthal went to Tom Foley for help, only to be rebuffed. Turning to Rothstein, Rosenthal was advised that he was fighting a losing battle. Rosenthal then turned to alcohol. With his tongue loosened by the liquor, he told his story to Rothstein's friend, newspaper reporter Herbert Bayard Swope.

This information soon got to the district attorney and eventually back to Becker. It was Rosenthal's plan to just scare Becker; he didn't plan to testify against him. He told Rothstein, "They can't make me say what I don't want to say."

Rothstein responded by offering Rosenthal $500 to get out of town. The stubborn gambler refused. Becker then got word to Zelig, who at the time was in jail, to put together a hit squad to kill Rosenthal. Zelig got out of jail and was given $2,000 to hire a team of killers to silence "Beansy." After being threatened in a restaurant in front of his wife, Rosenthal finally realized the grave situation he was in. He went back to Rothstein to take him up on his offer.

"You waited too long," Rothstein informed him. "You're not worth $500 to anyone anymore, Beansy."

On July 15, 1912, the four assassins hired by Zelig shot Rosenthal to death outside the Metropole Hotel. In just two weeks, all four gunmen were behind bars. They quickly ratted out Zelig as the man who hired them. Zelig was apprehended and turned government witness implicating Captain Becker, who was arrested on July 29. The trial of the four assassins was scheduled to begin on October 6, 1912. The day before, Zelig was murdered as he boarded a streetcar. Despite the loss of the state's star witness, the men were convicted of first-degree murder and all four died in the Sing Sing electric chair on April 13, 1914.

Becker was then tried in a highly publicized trial, found guilty, and sentenced to die in the electric chair. While his appeals were pending, Becker was desperately seeking help from Tammany Hall. Katcher wrote:

> Other forces, even more powerful, and other men, however, were no longer interested in Becker. His usefulness to them was over. They knew that changing times had caught up with The System, that it was now necessary to divorce the police department from direct control of vice and graft.
>
> It was not that The System was obsolete, but that this one part of it was. It was an essential part, so a substitute had to be found for it. A new kind of bag man, a new "man between," was necessary.[11]

Following Rosenthal's murder and the aftermath of the trials, the police issued a "legendary" edict—"No permanent gambling establishments!" The police remained adamant in their enforcement. This led to the "floating games" that soon became an institution in the city.

NEW "MAN BETWEEN"

With Sullivan in the grave and Becker soon to be executed, Rothstein's new protection came from an even higher source—Tammany Hall Boss Charles F. Murphy and his closest advisor, Tom Foley. The year 1913 was a watershed year for Rothstein—the year he would move to the top. This all came about as a result of his relationship with Murphy. The politician used Rothstein as the "man between" Tammany Hall and the underworld.

In 1910, as a favor to Foley, Rothstein bailed a confidence man out of jail. In doing so, he realized the high premiums that could be charged for this service, and he went into the bonding business for himself. Rothstein began to work with reputable bonding and surety companies, paying them a lower interest rate for the money he borrowed than he charged for his own services. The risk he faced was potentially larger if a client decided to skip bond, but when jailed men were asked to give their word to appear at trial and were told, "God help you if you don't," Rothstein had few problems.

With everything Rothstein was involved in, he handled himself with the air of a successful businessman. Murphy, Foley, and James J. "Jimmy" Hines, a future Tammany stalwart, relied on Rothstein and his services, which included anything from posting a bond to having a ballot box stuffed. Rothstein became the conduit between Tammany Hall and the underworld and he was getting richer because of it. Leo Katcher wrote:

> Lawyers, fixers, people in trouble, sought him out. He was a pipeline to "Fourteenth Street" (location of Tammany Hall). If you wanted a favor from the Hall, Arnold Rothstein could expedite it, assure it, for you. And so you paid him.[12]

Rothstein took cash for everything he did. Soon he and Carolyn moved to an apartment at the corner of Broadway and 52nd Street. Their new home had eight rooms and two baths, as well as separate quarters for a butler and a maid.

WAS ARNOLD THE SHOOTER?

During the early morning hours of May 16, 1917, Rothstein was enjoying one of his favorite pastimes—rolling dice in a floating crap game. The game was being held in a second-floor suite at the Hotel St. Francis on West 47th Street. Rothstein, who was sponsoring the game, made sure all the proper hotel employees were tipped handsomely to ensure that the game was not bothered. Around 3:00 AM, five gunmen entered the hotel lobby after being notified by an accomplice who was participating at the dice tables that the game was in progress and there were a number of wealthy players there with cash,. While two of the men stayed downstairs, the other three went up to the room and used the elevator boy, who doubled as an errand runner for the gambler, to get inside.

Rothstein knew most of the players in the room. In addition to professional gamblers, the group included stockbrokers, doctors, actors, attorneys, and businessmen. One man that stood out to Rothstein was a two-bit gambler, who had the distinction of being present at several games that had recently been held up. When the masked gunmen entered the room, Rothstein's first reaction was to drop his bankroll, estimated to be $60,000, to the floor and kick it under a rug. His next response was to keep his eyes on the man he suspected as the inside accomplice, who had seen Rothstein drop the money, throughout the whole ordeal.

When the robbers searched Rothstein and found just $2,600 in his watch pocket, they angrily removed a diamond stickpin he was wearing.

"I'll send you the pawn ticket, AR," the gunman said.

"Don't bother," Rothstein replied. "I'll have it back before the mail carriers arrive tomorrow morning."

Rothstein never took his eyes off the man he suspected of being the finger man for the robbers. When the gunmen left, he bent down and picked up the hidden wad of cash. As Rothstein had vowed, he had his stickpin back the next morning. As he discussed the robbery with his friend Swope, the newspaperman poked fun at the gambler and told him the police were already aware of what took place and that they considered Rothstein "too yellow" to talk to them. Telling Rothstein, "They're laughing at you, Arnold. The word is out that you're buffaloed," Swope finally got the gambler's goat. Rothstein went to the police station and identified two of the robbers from mug shots.

On August 22, 1917, Rothstein appeared in court and testified against the two gunmen. Based on his testimony the two men were convicted and sentenced to Sing Sing. One of the men, Albert Johnson, cursed Rothstein and vowed to get him. On August 26, 1919, Johnson was being transferred from Sing Sing to Dannemora Prison. On the train ride he escaped from his guards and leapt off the moving locomotive. The police notified Rothstein of the escape. Although his friends advised him to leave town until Johnson was captured, Rothstein refused, claiming it would make him look scared and that it would tarnish his fearless reputation. Despite the iron façade, Carolyn later revealed that he was afraid.[13]

Less than two years later, on January 19, 1919, Rothstein was operating a floating crap game in a fourth-floor apartment on West 57th Street. The police were tipped off to his participation and a raiding party showed up. One of the officers pounded on the door and shouted, "Open up, before we bust in." The raiding party was dispersed by a volley of bullets that crashed through the door. Miraculously the gunfire caused only two minor flesh wounds.

The officers cried out, "This isn't a stickup, it's the police." The door was quickly un-locked and the angry raiders, led by Police Inspector Dominic Henry, entered and arrested 19 men including Abe Attell, a Rothstein bodyguard and former featherweight boxing champion. The men were searched, but no guns were found. One of the raiders demanded to know where Rothstein was, a clear indication that the police were aware it was one of his operations. The gamblers replied that he had not been there. A patrol wagon was sum-moned and the men were escorted to it. As the gamblers were being loaded on, a bystander watching the procession pointed out to one of the officers a figure hiding on the second floor fire escape.

After the wagon took off, two officers reentered the building and climbed out on the fire escape, where they discovered Rothstein hiding with a revolver. Rothstein then offered to drive the wounded officers to the hospital, where their wounds were attended to, and then back to the station house where he was booked on an assault charge. Rothstein then provided bail money for all the gamblers who had been arrested.

Although the police officers admitted they had made a mistake by not properly iden-tifying themselves, the overzealous Inspector Henry, with the help of an assistant United States attorney, pushed for an indictment against Rothstein and received two—one for each wounded officer. There were no charges for possession of a weapon, as Rothstein had a pistol permit. District Attorney Edward Swann assigned Assistant District Attorney James E. Smith to investigate the case. Because the police were outside the door and didn't know who fired the shots, all Smith could do was question the gamblers inside the suite. Not a single gambler could recall anything about a shooting or Rothstein even being there that night. When the case came to trial, on June 5, 1919, Rothstein's attorney requested a dismissal. As the prosecution could not produce a single witness against him, the judge readily agreed, calling the indictment "incomprehensible." Later, the *New York American,* owned by William Randolph Hearst, hinted that Rothstein had paid $32,000 to get the case quashed.

Because of the accusations by the newspaper, Swann ordered two grand jury investiga-tions. The first one, which investigated Rothstein, was soon dismissed. The second looked into allegations that Inspector Henry had accepted money to allow disorderly houses to flourish in his precinct. Henry was indicted and charged with of neglect of duty. The police inspector was tried and acquitted on May 15, 1920. Ten days later, he was indicted by the extraordinary grand jury, this time for perjury.

The charges grew out of a series of six affidavits made out by Henry, charging Assistant District Attorney Smith with seeking protection "for disorderly resorts conducted by friends of his and with having offered through intermediaries to enter a partnership with the inspec-tor in the sale of public protection to gambling places."[14] After these affidavits were made public, Henry was called before the grand jury and repeated the substance of the documents. When Smith and others mentioned in the affidavits were called to testify before the same grand jury, they denied the allegations and Henry was indicted.

In late May 1920, the case came to trial and Henry was found guilty. The New York State Appellate Court later reversed the verdict, but it would take the maligned police official until 1924 to get his life, finances, and career with the police department straightened out. Although the incident showed the power of Rothstein's influence, the publicity, which he always sought to avoid, troubled him.

BOOKMAKING AND CASINOS

By 1914, Rothstein was already on his way to becoming the go-to guy for lay-off betting in the bookmaking business. Since its early years, America has had a love affair with horse racing and betting on horses. As placing wagers on the sport became more popular, especially in the country's larger cities, the art of bookmaking, also known then as pool operating, became popular, too. It was not until Rothstein came along to organize the various bookmakers, however, that it became a huge money-making venture. By the mid-teens Rothstein's ever-growing bankroll allowed him to set the terms for what became known as the lay-off bet, the process of evening out a bookie's slate when one horse has so much money riding on it that the results can break the bookie's bank. He simply bets the other way with someone with enough money to handle the bet, and the two split the winning percentage from the bets placed.

Rothstein was soon known from coast to coast as the man who could handle any lay-off bet. By assembling a loyal group of men who worked around the clock for their master, Rothstein was able to take care of this type of betting for the rest of his life.

Meanwhile, as the country moved through the 1910s, Rothstein's gambling contemporaries in New York fell by the wayside. Having one of the few reputable gambling houses in the city, Rothstein decided to close his West 46th Street location because it had become too well known. In 1916, he opened a new casino in Hewlett, Long Island, where the cost of "protection" was not nearly as high as in Manhattan. Both the building and the land the gambling house occupied were owned by a state senator who was recognized as a major political figure in the area. The casino was lavishly furnished and provided the gamblers, who arrived by invitation only, with the best in food and drink. All of the casino's employees were required to dress in appropriate eveningwear.

Rothstein took advantage of what he termed "snob appeal" for his gambling den. "People like to think they're better than other people," Rothstein once told Damon Runyon. "As long as they're willing to pay to prove it, I'm willing to let them." For three years he allowed them to "pay," to the tune of $500,000 in profits, before he closed the club in 1919 after the local authorities became greedy.

Rothstein did not remain out of the casino business for long. In 1917, he bankrolled a gambling house at Saratoga until closing his Long Island operation. Rothstein then opened his own place in Saratoga, which he named "The Brook." The combination cabaret, gambling casino, nightclub, and restaurant was described as one of the grandest of its kind. The Brook drew the wealthiest gamblers in the country. Katcher claimed, "Rothstein wanted only the best people as customers. To him 'best' and 'wealthiest' were synonymous. He had no other gauge than money by which to judge."

After the 1922 racing season was completed, a reform mayor was elected in Saratoga. The new mayor ran on a platform to rid the area of bookmakers and gamblers. Shortly after the election, an "emissary" of the mayor-elect contacted Rothstein to let him know the new city leader was "willing to forget some of the promises he made."

"How much?" barked Rothstein.

"You can take care of it for $60,000," came the reply.

Rothstein shot back, "You go back and tell him to go to hell. Anyone who'd sell out a whole town wouldn't hesitate to double-cross one man."

By the mid-1920s, Rothstein grew tired of Saratoga and The Brook. He sold his shares to his partner, Nat Evans, in 1925. Although Rothstein stayed clear of owning anymore casinos at Saratoga, he continued to bankroll various operations until he died. Rothstein allegedly hired Meyer Lansky and Lucky Luciano to operate roulette wheels and *chemin-de-fer* tables at The Brook. Soon they opened a place of their own, the Chicago Club, with Rothstein's backing. As for The Brook, on New Years Eve 1934, two months after Nat Evans insured the place for $117,000, the casino burned to the ground.

LEGENDARY FEATS

Three events took place in Rothstein's life that became legendary and created a reputation for the gambler that certainly preceded him and made him the talk of New York. The first incident occurred in 1917. August Belmont owned a horse named Hourless, whose trainer, Sam Hildreth, was considered one of the best in the country. During the 1917 racing season, Hourless lost in a three-horse race to that year's Kentucky Derby winner, Omar Khayyam. Hildreth knew he had been outsmarted by Hourless's rider, a dishonest jockey who dropped his whip during the race. When the New York season was over, an enterprising track owner agreed to put up a purse for a grudge match between the two horses.

On October 17, the day before the race, Rothstein decided to bet $240,000 on Hourless but could not find anyone willing to handle a wager that large. Later that day, Rothstein received a telephone call and was informed that whatever bet he was willing to place, there was a man who would accept it—no limit. Rothstein knew immediately that there must be a fix. He called Hildreth and voiced his concern regarding the bookmakers' sudden change of heart to take his bet. If there was going to be a sucker in this race, it was not going to be Arnold Rothstein. At the last minute, Hildreth changed jockeys and Hourless won convincingly. Rothstein pocketed a cool $300,000.

This bet was the largest Rothstein had won up until this time, and he would exceed it twice in 1921. The first time was on July 4. Independence Day was the second of the three big racing days that took place at the New York horse racing tracks (the other two being Memorial Day and Labor Day). On this holiday Rothstein was betting on his own horse, Sidereal.

Sidereal's entrance in the day's third race was a last-minute decision by Rothstein. In fact, the horse was stabled at Belmont Park while the race was being run at Aqueduct. Rothstein sent Carolyn to fetch the horse while he maneuvered around the busy track drumming up business and, at the same time, trying to be as inconspicuous as possible so as not to tip his hand. Rothstein "borrowed" as many as 40 trackmen to do his bidding in placing bets on Sidereal. By the time the horse arrived at the track, the paddock judge told the trainer he had beaten the deadline by a mere six seconds. Sidereal won the race and Rothstein earned an incredible $850,000.

Weeks later, on August 20, Rothstein won $500,000 by betting on another of his horses, Sporting Blood, in the Travers Stakes. Rothstein had received some quality information about problems the favored horse was experiencing. He was quick to take advantage of the information, for which he always rewarded the provider well.

Despite the rumors that swirled about Rothstein's horses, both Herbert Bayard Swope and Carolyn Rothstein insisted that he ran an honest stable. "Arnold was never mixed up in a crooked race," Carolyn maintained. "He made his big winnings on races where he had superior information. He used every possible trick to find out more than anyone else and get the best odds."[15]

One of those who believed the rumors was August Belmont. Leo Katcher described Belmont's confrontation with Rothstein in his effort to keep him away from his racetrack:

> "You know your reputation," Belmont said. "It hurts racing to have you such a conspicuous figure."
>
> "What are you trying to say?" Rothstein demanded.
>
> "You know what people are saying, Arnold," Belmont replied. "And what they're thinking. Half the country believes you were the man who fixed the World Series."[16]

Next to the "Night of Sicilian Vespers," Arnold Rothstein's "fixing" of the 1919 World Series is the underworld's most popular myth. The reality, however, is as Leo Katcher claimed, "He did not fix the Series. Rothstein's name, his reputation, and his reputed wealth were all used to influence the crooked baseball players. But Rothstein, knowing this, kept apart from the actual fix. He just let it happen."

The series between the Chicago White Sox and the Cincinnati Reds was won by the underdog Cincinnati team, five games to three (at the time the series was best of nine). Eight players from the Chicago team conspired to throw the games because of their intense dislike of owner Charles Comiskey, who they considered a cheapskate. The American League, however, did not respond until more than a year later after the completion of the 1920 season. At that time, all eight players involved were banned from playing baseball for life. Ban Johnson, the president of the American League, was certain of Rothstein's participation in the fix and openly said so. Rothstein responded, "My only connection was to refuse to do business with some men who said they could fix it . . . I intend to sue Ban Johnson for libel."

Rothstein traveled to Chicago to testify before a grand jury investigating the fixed games. Part of his testimony follows:

> The whole thing started when (Abe) Attell and some other cheap gamblers decided to frame the Series and make a killing. The world knows I was asked in on the deal and my friends know how I turned it down flat. I don't doubt that Attell used my name to put it over. That's been done by smarter men than Abe. But I wasn't in on it, wouldn't have gone into it under any circumstances and didn't bet a cent on the Series after I found out what was underway. My idea was that whatever way things turned out, it would be a crooked Series anyhow and that only a sucker would bet on it.

An attorney representing Comiskey and the White Sox believed Rothstein, as did the members of the grand jury. Although Rothstein was cleared and never charged, his name will forever be linked to Major League Baseball's darkest hour.

NICKY ARNSTEIN

Charming, aristocratic, and worldly were all words used to describe Jules W. Arnstein. In the 1890s, when bicycle racing was popular, Arnstein picked up the nickname "Nicky," which was bestowed on him because of the nickel-plated bicycle he rode. His father was a German Jew and his mother was Dutch. They raised Nicky as an Episcopalian. Although he had a refined upbringing, his passion for gambling caused a split from his family.

In 1912, he met two people who would have the most influence on his life—Arnold Rothstein and Fanny Brice, the star of the Ziegfeld Follies. Both Arnstein and Brice were married to other people at the time. Brice fell for Nicky, however, and spent the next six years supporting him through legal problems, gambling, and confidence scams. After both divorced, they married each other in October 1918.

Beginning in 1918, a series of robberies occurred involving Wall Street security houses. There was a basic pattern to the robberies. A messenger on his way to a bank or brokerage house, carrying as much as several thousand dollars in securities, mostly Liberty Bonds, would be stopped, sometimes beaten, and relieved of the negotiables. The Liberty Bonds, which helped finance America's participation in World War I, were bearer bonds, redeemable by the individual who had possession. Despite the frequency of the crimes, the security houses made no precautions to provide protection to the messengers. The losers were not the security houses that deployed the messengers, but rather the bonding companies that provided insurance to the brokers. While police seemed helpless in rounding up the thieves, the monetary value of the stolen securities by early 1920 was estimated at $5 million dollars. The police determined that a "mastermind" was at work.

In early February 1920, the police broke the gang when they apprehended seven men after $2,500 was stolen from another messenger. One of the men arrested, Joseph Gluck, after spending 10 days in jail, felt he had been double-crossed, having been led to believe his bail money and lawyer would be provided by his "employer." Angered by this turn of events, Gluck spilled out the details of the robberies to the authorities. The information revealed that many of the victimized messenger boys were actually involved in the robberies.

Gluck insisted that he knew his employer only as "Mr. Arnold." Detectives flew into a frenzy, surmising they had finally obtained information to put away the nefarious Arnold Rothstein. Their excitement was short-lived when Gluck could not identify Rothstein from a photograph. After giving a physical description of Mr. Arnold, detectives provided Gluck with a number of pictures from which he picked out Nicky Arnstein, who had often used the name "Jules Arnold" as an alias.

Detectives friendly to Rothstein informed the gambler of Gluck's cooperation. Rothstein contacted Arnstein and advised him to leave town immediately. Arnstein fled to Ohio to hide out. A nationwide manhunt was begun for Arnstein, which, spurred by his marriage to Brice, filled the front pages of newspapers across the country. Meanwhile, as details of Gluck's confession leaked out regarding Arnstein's role as the "mastermind" of the robberies, Fannie Brice quipped, "Mastermind! Nicky couldn't mastermind an electric bulb into a socket."

While Arnstein was in hiding, Rothstein was preparing for his defense and fending off allegations that he was behind the robberies. Rothstein hired the legal team of William J. Fallon and Eugene McGee to handle the case. In a move that was indicative of Rothstein's influence, he was able to establish a bail amount before he negotiated Arnstein's surrender. Arnstein returned on May 15, 1920, surrendering on his own terms, amusing himself by riding with Brice and Fallon down Fifth Avenue in New York's annual police parade.

Rothstein's generosity was not solely out of friendship. Carolyn later revealed that her husband told her, "They're not after Nicky, they're after me. A lot of people would like to tie me into this and some of them think they can get Arnstein to say something that would lead them to me." Rothstein was correct in his thinking; however, Arnstein never revealed a thing. Despite promises of leniency, Arnstein always maintained his innocence.

Fallon successfully argued for the case to be tried in Washington D.C., as a federal crime punishable with a two-year sentence, as opposed to a New York State offense in which Arnstein could face up to 25 years. The first trial resulted in a hung jury in which Arnstein did not testify. Before the second trial, Fallon ran off with a woman, leaving McGee to handle the defense. McGee failed and Arnstein was convicted and sent to Leavenworth.

Throughout the remainder of Arnstein's life, he maintained he never knew the reason why Rothstein had helped him. There is some doubt that Arnstein was truly guilty and that Rothstein was involved in the actual thefts; however, no one doubted that Rothstein was the only man in New York who could have fenced the stolen bonds.

BUCKET SHOPS AND LAWYERS

In *The Big Bankroll,* Leo Katcher gave the following description/definition of the "bucket shop," an operation that began shortly after the Civil War when railroad stocks flooded the market and were purchased by thousands of investors:

> The bucket shop was a cut rate, bargain basement securities supermarket. It operated on the layaway, or installment, plan, with very little down. Purchasers of stocks could buy on a margin as low as one point.
>
> The bucket shop was a brokerage house. It had the normal complement of tickers and a board on which prices were posted and they came over the tickers. In their early days the bucket shops were straight gambling houses.[17]

The bucket shops enjoyed their initial popularity from 1900 until the "financial panic" of 1907. A decade after the booming economy, brought on by World War I, began a second round of activity, this one lasting until the market crash in 1929. The operations were not exclusive to New York City. Several successful operations had branch offices in other cities in the country. No dollar figures from the bucket shop operations were ever tallied, but New York State bankruptcy courts did report that during one five-year period, customers were bilked to the tune of more than $212 million.

Rothstein did not have a direct hand in the ownership of these bucket shops. He backed some of the major operations such as Dillon & Company and E.M. Fuller & Company. These operations, although large and profitable, required less startup money. What they did require, however, was protection. This is where Rothstein prospered. With Rothstein's influence with the police, the prosecutor's office, and Tammany Hall, he helped protect the bucket shop operators from legal harassment and from regulatory laws that might be initiated in the state capital.

When a bucket shop operator was arrested, Rothstein would post bail and provide legal counsel. However, when E.M. Fuller & Company, an operation run by Edward Fuller and William McGee, went under, costing investors $5 million, a newspaper journalist, Nat J. Ferber of the *American,* investigated the losses, which resulted in sensational trials and media coverage—and Rothstein's presence in front of a grand jury.

When E.M. Fuller & Company filed bankruptcy, all of the assets, as well as the two principals, disappeared. The two stayed in hiding in the Rothstein home until the law firm of Fallon and McGee (no relationship) was hired to represent them. This would begin a five-year saga involving trials and grand jury hearings, with the case never really being resolved.

In the ensuing investigation prosecutors found checks totaling $353,000 made out to Rothstein, who was then called before the grand jury to testify. Allegations were made that the payments were either gambling losses Fuller was repaying to Rothstein, including supposed bets made on the 1919 World Series, or that Rothstein was laundering the stolen Liberty Bonds through the company. This latter belief arose after it was revealed the same type of bond laundering occurred with Dillon & Company, a bucket shop run by Rothstein intimate Philip "Dandy Phil" Kastel, in which $407,000 had been loaned to Rothstein with Liberty Bonds put up as collateral.

During the inquiries Rothstein seemed nervous at first, but then began to enjoy matching wits with the prosecutors. As the inquests dragged on for years, he became a formidable foe. Perhaps the highlight of Rothstein's testimony came during an exchange regarding how the gambler had obtained the Liberty Bonds. After much bantering among the prosecutor, judge, and Rothstein, the judge suggested the question put to Rothstein be rephrased.

"Where did you buy the Liberty Bonds, or, if you did not buy them, where did you procure them," asked the prosecutor.

"Now, that's a question I can answer," replied Rothstein. "I can't remember."

In the meantime, Fallon and McGee were busy defending Fuller and McGee, each time the trial ending in a hung jury. After the second trial, a juror admitted he had been bribed by Fallon, not only in the Fuller trial, but also in an earlier one in which he had sat on the jury. When a second person came forward to corroborate the allegations, Fallon found himself on trial. In what was considered his greatest courtroom performance, Fallon ably defended himself and was acquitted by an awestruck jury. As Fallon made his way out of the courtroom, he stopped in front of Nat Ferber, the journalist whose investigation had initiated the bucket shop trials. In a voice loud enough for the entire courtroom to hear, Fallon told him, "I promise you I'll never bribe another juror."

Fallon's trial brought to an end the sensationalism that surrounded the bucket shop investigations. It also was the last hurrah for Fallon. The "Great Mouth Piece" died not long afterward, and one of the shooting stars of the 1920s Broadway scene was extinguished.

ORGANIZING CRIME

The *Mafia Encyclopedia* defines Prohibition as "the greatest day for organized crime in America." Little did Rothstein know at the advent of the "Noble Experiment" that he would become one of the founding fathers of organized crime in the United States. In fact, Rothstein actually believed the new law would be effective.

When Prohibition began on January 16, 1920, Rothstein had many of the component parts of organized crime in place. Leo Katcher explained:

Rothstein was one of the first rumrunners. He made the smuggling of uncut diamonds and narcotics a side enterprise.

He operated one of the largest bail bond businesses in New York. Each man for whom he provided bail had to give Rothstein his insurance business.

Rothstein had "pieces" of many night clubs and cabarets. This was a bonus he took for financing them, at his usual rate of interest. His "partners" found that they had to purchase or rent such equipment as silver and linens from firms that Rothstein owned. They also had to place all their insurance with Rothstein's firm.

Rothstein financed many retail outlets for bootleggers. His realty firms negotiated rentals and leases.

"He bankrolled many bootleggers and provided them with trucks and drivers to transport their illegal cargo.

Rothstein's main function though was organization. He provided money and manpower and protection. He arranged corruption—for a price. And, if things went wrong, Rothstein was ready to provide bail and attorneys. He put crime on a corporate basis when the proceeds of crime became large enough to warrant it.[18]

One of Rothstein's first ventures into rum running came after a meeting with Irving "Waxey Gordon" Wexler and Detroit bootlegger Maxie Greenberg. While in Detroit, Greenberg began smuggling in whiskey from Canada. Realizing how profitable this venture was, he wanted to expand but needed $175,000. He traveled to New York in hopes that through Wexler, he could obtain financing from Rothstein. Wexler knew Rothstein from having worked for him in the garment district as a labor enforcer.

Rothstein met the two in Central Park. Sitting on a park bench, he listened to their plan to smuggle in Canadian whiskey. The next day, the three men met again, this time in Rothstein's office where he made a counterproposal. Rothstein would finance the venture, but the liquor would be purchased and brought in from Great Britain. Wexler, who was acting as a middleman, asked to be included in the deal and was cut in for a small "piece." From this "piece," Wexler launched a successful rum-running empire and became a wealthy man. After Rothstein ended his partnership with the two in 1921, he continued to help finance them. Wexler took over two large warehouses when they split, one in the city and the other on Long Island. Rothstein would later use Wexler's speedboats to smuggle in diamonds and dope.

Rothstein got out of the rum-running business for one reason—he couldn't control it. Although he continued to bankroll rum-running operations throughout the 1920s, Rothstein would focus on letting other individuals take the risks while he collected the profits.

OVERLORD OF NARCOTICS

Opium-based narcotics and cocaine flowed freely into this country until the first two decades of the 20th century. The first attempt to regulate drugs came with the Pure Food & Drug Law of 1906, but few restraints were imposed. In 1916, the Harrison Act was passed and although it was enacted to control the narcotics traffic, it was mainly a revenue measure. It was effective enough, however, that by 1921 there was for the first time a demand for illegal drugs.

Rothstein was not a pioneer in the field of dope peddling; instead he was introduced to the big money potential by both Lucky Luciano and Irving Wexler. By the mid-1920s, many of Rothstein's income producers had gone by the wayside. The bucket shops were gone, the stolen bond market had ceased, he no longer owned gambling houses, and he had retired from rum running. Rothstein was still collecting money from all the people he had bankrolled in illegal activities. His bail bonding and insurance companies were still thriving, as were all of his legal enterprises. Several individuals who had entered the rum-running and bootlegging market after him were becoming millionaires many times over. Rothstein's only influence over them was with his connections to Tammany Hall.

"I don't believe that Rothstein ever laid out the plans for any individual rackets. This wasn't his reputation, even among those who hated him. But he backed the racketeers with his resources, and he knew what they were doing."
—Henderson, *In the Reign of Rothstein*, 1929, p. 304

It was during this time that Rothstein decided to devote his efforts to organizing the drug trafficking in this country. His interest was in wholesaling, not the street pushing of narcotics. Entering at this level, his only competition came from unscrupulous members of the medical profession. Rothstein's goal was higher as he set out to regulate supply and demand and organize the drug trade on an international basis.

Rothstein employed several men to do his overseas bidding. Among them were Harry Mather, "Dapper Dan" Collins, Sid Stager, George Uffner, and Jacob "Yasha" Katzenberg. Rothstein then purchased the well-known importing house, Vantines. The establishment had a legitimate reputation, and shipments arriving from China and the Orient received only a cursory inspection. Rothstein made sure that, when he got word someone was furnishing a home, Vantines received part of that business. It was reported that Fanny Brice "was made" to purchase thousands of dollars of furnishings and bric-a-brac from Vantines to adorn a new apartment. In addition to Vantines, Rothstein purchased several antique shops and art galleries to serve as legitimate fronts for his drug business.

As waves of narcotics began to permeate the city and create a new generation of drug pushers and addicts, Rothstein's bail bond business kicked into high gear following increased arrests. Nat Ferber, the American journalist who had earlier exposed the bucket shop rackets, was instrumental in revealing the narcotics epidemic. Ferber wrote, "Rothstein established himself as the financial clearing house for the foreign dope traffic. . . . He was the only man in the United States who could, and did, establish a credit standing with the foreign interests sending drugs into this country."[19]

According to Leo Katcher, "Of all Rothstein's enterprises, this had been the most carefully developed. He had given it time, effort and all his intelligence. Yet, it was the most costly business that ever occupied his time, his interest and his money."[20] Ironically, Rothstein never made a cent from his narcotics ventures. Every dollar he received was put back into the operation and he died while the business was moving forward—at full steam.

A COLLECTION OF PUPILS

Rothstein reached his pinnacle during the wild days of the Roaring Twenties. Despite his wealth, power, and influence—outside of his fictionalized participation in the 1919 World Series fixing—Rothstein will be remembered most for the future underworld leaders he allegedly tutored. In addition to the aforementioned Irving Wexler, other major underworld upstarts who came under Rothstein's wing were Jack "Legs" Diamond, Charles "Lucky" Luciano, Meyer Lansky, Frank Costello, and Lepke Buchalter.

Jack "Legs" Diamond

Among the men that served as bodyguards for Arnold Rothstein over the years was Jack "Legs" Diamond. When Rothstein began bankrolling bootleggers in the early 1920s, he helped provide them with trucks, drivers, and protection. He hired Diamond and his brother Eddie to oversee this part of the operation. Diamond began hijacking some of the shipments he was hired to safeguard. Rothstein soon wearied of Diamond and his antics.

In *Anatomy of a Gangster,* author Gary Levine provided this inflated image of Diamond's association with Rothstein:

> Legs Diamond became Rothstein's official bodyguard, consultant on drugs and whiskey, and hit man. Rothstein, in turn, protected Diamond from the authorities and financed many of his gang's operations. As Rothstein's power and operations grew in scope he came to rely more on Legs who, in turn, grabbed a bigger share of Rothstein's profits for himself. Legs guaranteed the security of Rothstein's fifty and one-hundred-thousand-dollar card games and when a gambler was found floating in the Hudson River, it was a good guess that Diamond had escorted him home.[21]

Whomever Rothstein had Diamond "hit" is still a mystery. Rothstein wasn't the only crime figure who tired of Legs. There were several attempts to murder Diamond throughout the 1920s and early 1930s. Legs was wounded so many times that he earned the nickname the "Clay Pigeon of the Underworld." On December 18, 1931, Diamond was murdered in upstate New York.

> "It was not until Arnold became associated with the Diamonds, and ceased for the most part mingling with men of good reputation in sports and betting, that he lost his perspective, and started to drift downwards."
> —Rothstein, *Now I'll Tell,* 1934, p. 231

Charles "Lucky" Luciano

Luciano always credited Rothstein with teaching him the finer things in life.

> He taught me how to dress, how not to wear loud things but to have good taste; he taught me how to use knives and forks, and things like that at the dinner table, about holding a door open for a girl, or helping her sit down by holding the chair. If Arnold had lived a little longer, he could've made me pretty elegant; he was the best etiquette teacher a guy could ever have—real smooth.[22]

Rothstein once took Luciano to Wanamaker's, an expensive clothing store, where the young future crime boss purchased "two or three of everything." When the question of whether to buy suits ready made or made to order came up, Rothstein insisted Luciano have his suits made by a gentile tailor. Luciano gave credit to Rothstein for creating a whole new image for him. "By watching, practicing, imitating, listening to the lessons of Rothstein, [Luciano] had learned the ways of the rich and had acquired the veneer of a gentleman."[23]

Meyer Lansky

Rothstein introduced Lansky to the modern business practices used by large corporate firms. He showed Lansky how to turn bootlegging into a formal business operation. Through Rothstein, Lansky met Waxey Gordon. Although the two men would later become personal enemies, during the Prohibition years they were bootlegging partners after Gordon relocated to Philadelphia.

Rothstein introduced both Lansky and Luciano to affluent society people who saw a certain excitement attached to bootleggers. Lansky shied away though, preferring to remain anonymous and work behind the scenes.

Lansky told a biographer, "Rothstein invited me to dinner at the Park Central Hotel, and we sat talking for six hours. It was a big surprise to me. Rothstein told me quite frankly that he had picked me because I was ambitious and 'hungry.'"[24] It is no wonder who his mentor was when Lansky, who would outlive most of his contemporaries, remembered this dinner with Rothstein 50 years later.

Frank Costello

In the early 1920s, Frank Costello and his brother Eddie started out as small-time rum-runners. They allegedly worked briefly for Rothstein before using his financing to go big time. By the mid-1920s, the Costello/"Big Bill" Dwyer combine was one of the biggest rum-running operations on the East Coast.

With the money Costello made, he and Rothstein were frequently involved in business deals together and borrowed from each other. After Rothstein's death investigators found an IOU for $40,000 from Costello in Rothstein's papers.

Costello's biographer, Leonard Katz, wrote in *Uncle Frank* that "There's no question that the younger, less sophisticated Costello admired Rothstein's shrewdness and learned from him many things not taught in Harvard's School of Business."[25] Whether the finer points of organized crime were taught to Costello or whether he stole them is questionable. Costello once told a reporter that the things he admired in other people he stole for himself.

After Rothstein's death Costello became the new "man between" with Tammany Hall. No other underworld figure would ever have more political influence with the corrupt New York political machine.

Louis "Lepke" Buchalter

The relationship between Rothstein and Buchalter, if there ever indeed was one, was questionable at best. Both Rothstein and Buchalter biographers claim the two interacted and that Lepke learned from the master; however, there isn't any proof that the two men had any association together.

That being said, what follows is compiled from the writers who claim that a relationship existed. Leo Katcher tells us that of all Rothstein's disciples, only one, Louis "Lepke" Buchalter, came from a similar background. Katcher stated, "Lepke came from a good family, his antecedents much like Rothstein's. His people were honest, in comfortable financial condition, pious and educated. Of their children they had trouble only with one, Louis."[26]

Rothstein had held a grip in labor racketeering, but did not get involved in a big way. Buchalter's entrance in the field came in the mid-1920s when Rothstein gave him the opportunity to move into the garment rackets. Buchalter, described as a dreamer with imagination, saw the potential for wealth and power in this area at a time when his contemporaries continued to get rich from Prohibition.

In addition to becoming the number 1 labor racketeer in America after Rothstein's death, Buchalter took over his mentor's drug trade. In 1939, Buchalter was convicted of federal narcotics charges and sentenced to 14 years in Leavenworth. During the Murder, Inc. (see Appendix) trials of the early 1940s, Buchalter was found guilty of murder and was executed at Sing Sing in 1944.

LAST HOURS OF MR. BIG

"Man reported shot in Park Central Hotel, Seventh Avenue and 56th Street. Ambulance dispatched." That was the message recorded at 10:53 on Sunday night, November 4, 1928, by a desk sergeant in Manhattan's West 47th Street Police Station. By midnight, the information had been updated to show that Arnold Rothstein, 46 years old of 912 Fifth Avenue, had been shot in the abdomen and found near the employee's entrance of the Park Central Hotel.

Earlier that evening, Rothstein arrived at Lindy's restaurant on Seventh Avenue and went to his private booth. Lindy's was Rothstein's office. He kept a regular schedule there, and several men were already waiting to see him when he walked in that night. One of the men, Jimmy Meehan, ran the Park City Club, one of the city's biggest gambling dens during the 1920s. Meehan operated the plush club with a bankroll supplied by Rothstein.

About 10:15, Rothstein received a telephone call. After a short conversation, he hung up and motioned for Meehan to walk outside with him. "McManus wants to see me at the Park Central," Rothstein said. He then pulled a gun out of his pocket and handed it to Meehan saying, "Keep this for me, I will be right back." Meehan then watched Rothstein walk up Seventh Avenue.

The man who had requested Rothstein's presence at the hotel was George "Hump" Mc-Manus. A bookmaker and gambler, McManus was well connected in the city, with one brother serving on the police force and another serving as a priest. Several weeks earlier, McManus hosted a high-stakes poker game in which Rothstein had participated. The game began on September 8 and continued nonstop into the morning of September 10, a full 36 hours. Other players participating in the game were West Coast gambler Nathan "Nigger Nate" Raymond, Alvin "Titanic" Thompson, and Joe Bernstein. By the end of the marathon card game, Rothstein was a big loser. He owed Raymond $219,000, Bernstein $73,000, and Thompson $30,000. When Rothstein walked out, without so much as signing an IOU, a couple of the players became irritated. McManus assured them, "That's A. R. Hell, he's good for it. He'll be calling you in a couple of days."

A week passed and Rothstein had still not made good. Rumors began to circulate that the game was crooked. Rothstein confided to Nicky Arnstein, who by know was out of prison and back in New York, "A couple of people told me that the game was rigged." Arnstein's advice to Rothstein was to pay the players off, "no point to your advertising you were a sucker."

Rothstein held off paying his debt, however, hoping to make the gamblers sweat and maybe take a lesser payoff. The players were beginning to pressure McManus, as he was the host and had promised them that Rothstein would make good. McManus sought help from his friend Jimmy Hines of Tammany Hall. Hines, who was also a friend of Rothstein, began to pressure him to clear up the matter.

As the weeks passed, the pressure began to get to McManus, who began drinking and threatened Rothstein for not making good on the debts. On Sunday night, November 4, McManus called Rothstein from Room 349 in the Park Central Hotel where he was registered as George Richards. He requested that Rothstein come over right away.

Still a mystery to this day was who was in the room when Rothstein arrived and what conversation and events took place. Shortly after Rothstein entered Room 349, he was shot once in the lower abdomen. The revolver was then tossed out the window where it bounced off the hood of a parked taxi and landed in the street. Employees later found Rothstein walking down the service stairs, holding his stomach and asking for a cab to take him home.

A police officer arrived, summoned an ambulance, and Rothstein was taken to New York's Polyclinic Hospital, where doctors immediately operated. The bullet, which was removed, had entered just above the groin and traveled downward severing an artery. Rothstein had sustained tremendous internal bleeding. He left the operating room in a coma and was placed in an expensive suite of three rooms on the eighth floor of the hospital.

Rothstein's brothers, Jack and Edgar, were summoned to the hospital along with Carolyn. Rothstein was given a blood transfusion and morphine for his pain. He regained consciousness Monday morning and told his wife he wanted to go home. During the day, Rothstein signed a will prepared by his attorney and talked with several friends. When questioned by police as to who shot him, he replied, "I'll take care of it myself."

Late on Monday afternoon, Carolyn was permitted to see him again. He repeated his request to go home and told her, "Don't go away. I don't want to be alone. I can't stand being alone." As he tried to raise himself he fell back and into unconsciousness. By 7:00 AM, Tuesday morning, Election Day, it was apparent that Rothstein was not going to live. At 9:55, the hospital superintendent issued a bulletin that, "The patient is sinking rapidly." The *New York Evening Post* reported:

> His wife, Mrs. Caroline [*sic*], Rothstein, who had remained in the suite all night, knelt by the bed. Standing at his side were his mother and father, Mr. and Mrs. A. E. Rothstein and his brother. Suddenly the patient's face twitched and his eyes closed. It was 10:17 AM.
>
> Dr. Alexander O'Hare, house surgeon, put a stethoscope to the body.
>
> "He has just passed away," Dr. O'Hare said.
>
> Rothstein's mother now wept loudly and broke down. Her husband led her away. The gambler's wife cried bitterly. They left hurriedly through a side door of the hospital.[27]

From the day of the shooting until weeks afterwards, the New York newspapers were full of stories and speculation about the motive. Many believed an all-out gang war was imminent. On the morning of November 7, the *New York American* reported:

> Arnold Rothstein, arch gambler, has died without mentioning the name of his assailant.
>
> He counted upon the law above law, the law of the private gunmen's feud, to avenge him.
>
> The city is now threatened with a revival, in more terrible form, of private vengeance as a substitute for the orderly processes of public justice.
>
> We are threatened with the finding of more bodies of gangsters "taken for a ride" and thrown into ditches from fleeing automobiles.
>
> We are threatened with more street duels, with flying bullets of machine guns and revolvers endangering the lives of citizens who stray about under the delusion that the streets are intended for men and women peaceably going about their business.

Arnold Rothstein was murdered. The public interests require that his murderer should be apprehended and punished. If Arnold Rothstein considered this the surest way of dealing with him, Rothstein would have disclosed his name to the police.

Rothstein's silence is an eloquent commentary upon the power of the super-state of professional wrong-doers which has grown up in America, more particularly in New York and Chicago.

The ominous circumstances of Rothstein's death serve notice upon the police to prepare for a grapple with the most desperate forces of lawlessness.[28]

Rothstein had bet heavily on the election that year. Had he lived, it was said he would have collected $570,000. His death negated the wagers. In the Jewish tradition, Rothstein was buried the next day. Laid out in a bronze casket, he was dressed in a white skullcap with a purple-striped prayer shawl over a muslin shroud. The family requested that no flowers be sent. Several police officers guarded the outside of the Riverside Memorial Chapel, at 180 West 76th Street. After a brief service there, the police accompanied the cortege to Union Field Cemetery in Queens, where the body was laid to rest.

AUTOPSY AND WILL

The events that happened in Room 349 of the Park Central Hotel that night will always be shrouded in mystery. After performing the autopsy at Bellevue Hospital, Medical Examiner Charles Norris stated:

The man who fired the shot might have been standing on his right side or even partly behind him. It is impossible to be sure that Rothstein was sitting, but this seems to have been the case. The reason is that the skin is marked above and to the right of the wound in a way that indicates the victim was seated while the assailant was standing. Rothstein was certainly not facing the man who shot him. It seems probable he was not expecting the shot at all, and possibly that he did not know who shot him.

It is not surprising that he got out of the hotel. A man might recover quickly from the shock and might walk a half-mile with such a wound. There was hardly any bleeding. Even his shirt was only slightly stained. What killed him was infection caused by the bullet tearing through his intestines.[29]

While the battle of the "who" and "how" was going on, there was another subplot—that of Rothstein's will. One of the people Rothstein asked to see when he was brought into the hospital was his attorney, Maurice Cantor, a Democratic assemblyman from West Harlem's 11th District. Rothstein wanted to see his will. In a bizarre sequence that reeked of deceit, Cantor rushed to the hospital, but neglected to bring the will, which was the only reason he was summoned. Rothstein had revised it back on March 1. Supposedly a new will had been executed without Rothstein's signature.

Cantor went back to his office, retrieved the will, and returned to the hospital. He was not allowed to see Rothstein until 4:00 AM on November 5. Cantor spoke to the dying man, telling him that he had brought the will. Rothstein was too weak to respond, so Cantor put a pen in his hand and made the sign of an "X" on the document. He then got two reluctant nurses to sign as witnesses. According to the new will, Cantor and two co-executors, William Wellman and Samuel Brown, became the major beneficiaries of Rothstein's estate.

The new will was written to the effect that after all funeral and legal expenses were satisfied, payments were to be made to his brothers Jack and Edgar and his black servant. In addition, trust funds were to be established for the two brothers. A third of the balance was to be set up in a trust fund for Carolyn, of which she was entitled only to the interest. The principal, upon her death, would go to charity. Another third was designated similarly for his latest girlfriend, Inez Norton. After 10 years, however, the principal would go to Cantor, Wellman, and Brown. A $75,000 trust fund was established for Sidney Stajer, with its principal also reverting back to Cantor et al. Any balance left after these transactions would go to the three executors. Nothing had been designated for Rothstein's parents or his sister Edith.

On the night of November 16, federal and state officials working with detectives opened a safe deposit box at the American Exchange-Irving Trust Company on Seventh Avenue. Inside they found 10 pieces of jewelry that had been pledged as collateral for loans made by Rothstein. In addition, two life insurance policies were discovered. One was for $25,000 and named Carolyn as the beneficiary. The other had originally been payable to his estate, but had been changed to reflect Inez Norton as the beneficiary.

In the meantime, lawyers hired by Carolyn were fighting the latest will, charging Cantor with "virtually forcing the famous gambler to sign a will he had not the mental power to understand as he lay on his death bed." On December 3, Carolyn and Rothstein's family, after reaching an agreement, "issued an ultimatum to the other contestants." The ultimatum was ignored and a long legal battle was predicted.

In mid-December, the trial began in surrogate court. On December 17, one of the nurses who witnessed the signing of the will testified. Elizabeth Love told the court that Cantor held the pen in Rothstein's hand and made the "X" with it. She stated that Rothstein was on the verge of delirium and that she allowed Cantor to approach him "more to get rid of him and let the patient sleep that anything else." In describing the scene she recalled, "Mr. Cantor said: 'Arnold, this is your will. You know the will we talked over yesterday. Rothstein's eyes were closed, but he said, in a very weak voice, 'Will.' Then Cantor said: This is your will, Arnold. I made it this morning, just as you told me to.' Mr. Rothstein didn't know what was happening."[30]

Love related that Rothstein never opened his eyes, and that the paper the will was made out on was folded in such a way that only a few lines could be read. She then said that she and the other nurse were told by Cantor "not to tell anything that went on in the sick room."

Surrogate Judge John P. O'Brien tried to bring about an amicable settlement. On April 9, 1929, a decision was reached to have the "X"-marked will withdrawn. The decision meant that Inez Norton was cut off from receiving any portion of the estate. On June 28, O'Brien approved a compromise in which the three executors received a $175,000 settlement, with the balance going to the family. In May 1931, Norton won a long court case and received the $20,000 life insurance policy settlement in which Rothstein had made her the beneficiary.

BIG GEORGE

George McManus was clearly the leading suspect in the shooting. His Chesterfield coat, with his name labeled on the inside, was left behind in Room 349. The details of the 36-hour card game had been publicized. The other players had all been brought in and questioned. But McManus had disappeared the night of the shooting and police couldn't find him. In addition, police were looking for "Tough" Willie McCabe, a Rothstein bodyguard, and James

"Fats" Walsh, a former bodyguard. Another person the police looked into was Chicago's "Machinegun Jack" McGurn, who was three months away from masterminding the St. Valentine's Day Massacre. Police claimed McGurn made frequent visits to New York.

The police were under tremendous pressure to resolve the murder, and Mayor James J. "Jimmy" Walker, unhappy with the progress being made, was putting the heat on them. On November 18, a *New York Evening Post* article stated: "Reports from City Hall were that the Mayor is about convinced that the present responsible officials of the department—the professional policemen—operate on methods that are too obsolete to cope with the modern criminal."[31] It was reported that Walker issued an ultimatum to Police Commissioner Joseph Warren, "Clean up the Rothstein case in four days or I'll put somebody in there who can."

McCabe surrendered to police at the West 47th Street Police Station. Walsh was arrested at the apartment of George Uffner at 225 Central Park West. With him at the time was Lucky Luciano. The police claimed they had a "tip" the men were involved in a payroll robbery back on October 5. The three were arraigned the next day and charged with suspicion of robbery. The police, however, used that excuse as a way to hold the men and question them about the Rothstein murder.

At 11:00 on the morning of November 26, the grand jury inquiry began. Claiming that documents and witnesses had already been tampered with, District Attorney Joab H. Banton requested that five of the key people called to testify—Nate Raymond, "Titanic" Thompson, Sid Stajer, Jimmy Meehan, and Norton Bowe—be held as material witnesses. When asked why by reporters, Banton replied, "They refused to testify. They have been threatened by friends of the murderer and so I asked the Court to protect them in the only way possible, that is, to lock them up where they'll be guarded."

The next day, the man the police had been looking for since the November 4 shooting turned himself over to authorities. Accompanied by attorney James D. C. Murray, two detectives arrived at a barbershop on 242nd Street and Broadway around 7:00 AM. There, relaxing in the middle of a shave, was George McManus. Taken to the district attorney's office, McManus, on the advice of Murray, refused to answer questions. He was then taken to the general sessions courtroom of Judge Francis X. Mancuso. The judge was in the middle of a trial. The case was stopped, the jury removed, and the jury box taken over by photographers for the brief hearing.

McManus was being charged with first-degree murder and Banton asked that Mancuso hold him without bail. The judge agreed and McManus was on his way to the Tombs. Murray gathered reporters together an issued the following statement:

> McManus was in no sense a fugitive after the discovery of Rothstein's pistol shot wound. He would have appeared at once had he not, conscious of his innocence in the act, believed that Rothstein would divulge the circumstance of the shooting to at least someone who had visited him at the hospital.
>
> We still hope Rothstein has done so. If he has, and if Rothstein's statement was communicated to the authorities, McManus knew that there would have been no necessity for his return at once, because he thought Rothstein would have exonerated him of any complicity.
>
> McManus's appearance before the District Attorney this morning was on his own initiative. He requires no lawyer and my only function in this case is to see that an innocent man has his rights safeguarded. McManus today and any time in the future is ready to face any accusation of any accuser if such there be.[32]

On December 5, the grand jury indicted McManus and three others for the murder of Arnold Rothstein. Named in the indictment were Hyman "Gillie" Biller and two "John Does." At arraignment, McManus's attorney pled his client not guilty and asked for 15 days to review all the evidence from the grand jury hearings. McManus remained in jail through Christmas and New Years. The weeks that went by were now turning into months. In March 1929, attorney Murray was finally able to get McManus released on a $50,000 bail.

After a long run, the Rothstein murder and botched investigation disappeared from the newspapers. It was revived briefly in July 1929 when "Fats" Walsh was murdered in Florida. Police determined that Walsh's death had nothing to do with the Rothstein killing.

In November 1929, a year after the killing, Banton finally went to trial. The case was weak and there were no witnesses who could place McManus in Room 349 the night Rothstein was shot. After the prosecution presented its case, the defense asked for an immediate directed verdict of acquittal and received it. McManus walked out of court a free man, wearing the Chesterfield coat the police had held for over a year as evidence.

Rothstein's murder remains officially unsolved. There has been some speculation over the years that there was more to the murder plot than just the unpaid gambling debts, that other organized crime members wanted to take over Rothstein's lucrative rackets and political connections. If this were the case, it's unlikely that Rothstein would have been shot the way he was, taking just one bullet in the abdomen instead of a more traditional two in the head. It is entirely possible that when Rothstein arrived in Room 349, he was confronted by a drunken, angry McManus who may have threatened him. When police searched the room they found several empty whiskey bottles. Rothstein may even have been shot accidentally during a struggle with McManus.

The organizer of organized crime was gone. In the end Lucky Luciano, Meyer Lansky, Frank Costello, and Lepke Buchalter took over the Rothstein empire . . . and the legend.

NOTES

1. David Pietrusza, *Rothstein* (New York: Carroll & Graf Publishers, 2003), p. 5.

2. Donald Clarke Henderson, *In The Reign of Rothstein* (New York: The Vanguard Press, 1929), p. 82

3. Abraham and Esther Rothstein were the parents of six children. Bertram, called Harry, was born July 1880; Arnold was born in 1882; Edgar, September 1883; Edith, August 1886; Sarah, March 1888; and Jacob, called Jack, March 1891.

4. Leo Katcher, *The Big Bankroll* (New Rochelle, NY: Arlington House, 1958), p. 19.

5. Herman Rosenthal's nickname was often spelled "Beansie."

6. Katcher, *The Big Bankroll,* p. 31.

7. Ibid., pp. 33–34.

8. Ibid., p. 38.

9. Ibid., p. 43.

10. Herbert Bayard Swope was the first journalist to win the Pulitzer Prize for reporting. He was best noted for serving as the executive editor of the *New York World*.

11. Katcher, *The Big Bankroll,* p. 97.

12. Ibid, p. 99.

13. Albert "Killer" Johnson was a member of a bank robbery team that struck the Cleveland Trust bank branch in Bedford, Ohio, on October 21, 1920. The leader of the gang was George

"Jiggs" Losteiner, known as "Cleveland's Baddest Man." Citizens of Bedford, alerted to the robbery, took up arms and began shooting at the robbers. Johnson, who was waiting with the getaway car, was struck in the neck. He died hours later on a hospital operating table.—John Stark Bellamy, *They Died Crawling* (Cleveland, OH: Gray & Company Publishers, 1995), pp. 214–216.

14. *New York Times,* May 26, 1920, "Henry Is Indicted on Perjury Charge."

15. Katcher, *The Big Bankroll,* p. 137.

16. Ibid.

17. Ibid., pp. 182–183.

18. Ibis., p. 232.

19. Ibid., p. 293.

20. Ibid., p. 299.

21. Gary Levine, *Anatomy of a Gangster* (Cranbury, NJ: A.S. Barnes and Company, 1979), p. 44.

22. Martin A. Gosch and Richard Hammer, *The Last Testament of Lucky Luciano* (Boston: Little, Brown and Company, 1974), p. 41.

23. Ibid., p. 69.

24. Robert Lacey, *Little Man: Meyer Lansky and the Gangster Life* (London: Little, Brown and Company, 1991), p. 49.

25. Leonard Katz, *Uncle Frank* (New York: Drake Publishers, 1973), p. 68.

26. Katcher, *The Big Bankroll,* p. 283.

27. *New York Evening Post,* November 6, 1928, "Rothstein Dies with Lips Sealed; Gun War Feared."

28. *New York American,* November 7, 1928, "Police Watch Group at Grave for Slayer."

29. *New York Evening Post,* November 7, 1928, "Arnold Rothstein Buried with Simple Ceremony at Cypress Hills Cemetery."

30. *New York Evening Post,* December 17, 1928, "Rothstein Signing of Will Described."

31. *New York Evening Post,* November 18, 1928, "Warren Wins Day in Rothstein Hunt."

32. *New York Evening Post,* November 27, 1928, "McManus Surrenders and Is Put in Tombs As Rothstein's Murderer."

BIBLIOGRAPHY

Biographies of Arnold Rothstein

Clarke, Donald Henderson. *In the Reign of Rothstein.* New York: The Vanguard Press, 1929.

Katcher, Leo. *The Big Bankroll: The Life and Times of Arnold Rothstein.* New Rochelle, NY: Arlington House, 1959.

Pietrusza, David. *Rothstein.* New York: Carroll & Graf Publishers, 2003.

Rothstein, Carolyn. *Now I'll Tell.* New York: The Vanguard Press, 1934.

Tosches, Nick. *King of the Jews.* New York: HarperCollins Publishers, 2005.

Other Publications

Anslinger, Harry, and Will Oursler. *The Murderers: The Story of the Narcotics Gangs.* New York: Farrar, Straus & Cudahy, 1961.

Conable, Alfred, and Edward Silberfarb. *Tigers of Tammany.* New York: Holt, Rinehart & Winston, 1967.

Dan, Uri, Dennis Eisenberg, and Eli Landau. *Meyer Lansky: Mogul of the Mob.* New York: Paddington Press, 1979.

Dimona, Joseph, and George Wolf. *Frank Costello: Prime Minister of the Underworld.* New York: William Morrow Company, 1974.

Fowler, Gene. *The Great Mouth Piece: A Life Story of William J. Fallon*. New York: Grosset & Dunlap, 1931.

Fried, Albert. *The Rise and Fall of the Jewish Gangster in America*. New York: Holt, Rinehart and Winston, 1980.

Gosch, Martin A., and Richard Hammer. *The Last Testament of Lucky Luciano*. Boston: Little, Brown & Company, 1974.

Joselit, Jenna Weissman. *Our Gang: Jewish Crime and the New York Jewish Community (1900–1940)*. Bloomington: Indiana University Press, 1983.

Katz, Leonard. *Uncle Frank: The Biography of Frank Costello*. New York: Drake Publishers, 1973.

Lacey, Robert. *Little Man: Meyer Lansky and the Gangster Life*. Toronto: Little, Brown & Company, 1991.

Levine, Gary. *Anatomy of a Gangster: Jack "Legs" Diamond*. New York: A. S. Barnes, 1979.

Logan, Andy. *Against the Evidence: The Becker-Rosenthal Affair*. New York: McCall Publishing, 1970.

Marx, Samuel. *Broadway Gangsters and Their Rackets*. Girard, KS: Haldeman-Julius Publications, 1929.

Peterson, Virgil W. *The Mob: 200 Years of Organized Crime in New York*. Ottawa, IL: Green Hill Publishers, 1983.

Raymond, Allen, and Craig Thompson. *Gang Rule in New York*. New York: Dial Press, 1940.

Sifakis, Carl. *The Mafia Encyclopedia*. New York: Facts on File Publications, 1987.

Walker, Stanley. *The Night Club Era*. New York: Frederick A. Stokes Company, 1931.

9

DUTCH SCHULTZ (ARTHUR FLEGENHEIMER)

AKA "THE BEER BARON OF THE BRONX"
AUGUST 6, 1902–OCTOBER 24, 1935

Arthur Flegenheimer was not the kind of name that was going to instill fear into the heart of an enemy. So when friends nicknamed him "Dutch Schultz," after a legendary member of a Bronx gang, Flegenheimer gladly accepted the new "rough and tumble" sobriquet. Today, more than 70 years after the demise of Dutch Schultz, his name is synonymous with the image of the ruthless, fearless gangster. During the late 1920s and first half of the 1930s, Schultz held sway in New York City despite the presence of the much-ballyhooed Italian underworld.

Tales of the "Dutchman's" viciousness are legendary, from blinding a man by placing infected bandages over his eyes to shoving a .45 into a subordinate's mouth and pulling the trigger during a drunken rage. Schultz backed down from no man until he ran into Thomas E. Dewey. Then Schultz pulled a disappearing act to keep out of the crosshairs of the famous New York prosecutor.

During the early 1930s, Schultz fought one of the most celebrated mob wars against a former associate, Vincent "Mad Dog" Coll. The war raged on for 10 months until Coll was machine-gunned to death in a classic telephone booth murder. One of the tragic victims of their famous war was a five-year-old youth.

Before Prohibition came to an end in 1933, the forward-thinking Schultz made a move to take over the Harlem numbers rackets. The move earned him millions, but made his underworld peers jealous. When Schultz was tried on charges of evading federal income taxes, his enemies were sure he was not coming back. No one ever beat the government. But Schultz did.

Popular legend has it that when Thomas Dewey decided to take a second shot at Schultz, the Dutchman responded by plotting to assassinate the special prosecutor and future governor of the State of New York. Whether it was this rumor or just the greed of his contemporaries will never be known, but they planned to remove the Dutchman and his top aides in one fell swoop.

The infamous shooting of Schultz and three of his men at the Palace Chop House in Newark, New Jersey, in October 1935, was second only to the St. Valentine's Day Massacre in pure carnage. Before dying, Schultz's last words, uttered in delirium and recorded by a police stenographer, became famous as a death-bed gangster discourse. But that was not enough. Five years after the slaughter, the event became even more sensationalized when it was retold by members of the infamous Murder, Inc. gang of Brooklyn. The question to this day is, did it really happen the way they claimed? And for the reason they provided?

EARLY YEARS

Arthur Simon Flegenheimer was born on August 6, 1902, in the Bronx. His parents were both German Jews. His mother, Emma, tried to raise little Arthur in the Orthodox faith. Her efforts were not entirely in vain; in later years Schultz would develop respect for his religious upbringing. At different stages of his life he claimed to be Jewish, Protestant, and Catholic. It was not uncommon for him to turn to religion at times of crisis during his career.

Growing up in the tough Bergen and Webster Avenues section of the Bronx, Flegenheimer joined a street gang for protection and to be part of a cohesive group in which he could make a name for himself. He attended Public School #12, where the principal, Dr. J. H. Condon, would one day gain notoriety by delivering the Lindbergh baby ransom money to Bruno Richard Hauptmann.

When Flegenheimer was 14 his father left home. What effect this had on the young man is hard to determine. Shortly after this desertion though, Flegenheimer quit school. Schultz never admitted that his father abandoned the family. He preferred to tell people that his father was a fine person who died during Schultz's teenage years. Working a variety of odd jobs, Flegenheimer soon realized that an honest day's work was not going to make him happy—or rich. He began hanging out at the Criterion Club where he was befriended by Marcel Poffo, a local hoodlum whose police record included bank robberies and extortion. Hoping to impress his mentor, Flegenheimer began his criminal career by holding up crap games that refused to pay a percentage to Poffo.

At the age of 17, Flegenheimer received his first and only prison sentence. Arrested for burglarizing a Bronx apartment, Flegenheimer said his name was Charles Harmon (an alias he would continue to use). He was sent to Blackwell's Island, a brutal prison located in the middle of the East River. It later became Welfare Island and today is known as Roosevelt Island. Flegenheimer was not an ideal prisoner, and the experience certainly did nothing to rehabilitate him. In fact, he was so unruly that he was transferred to a tougher prison, Westhampton Farms, from where he once escaped for a few hours. He was returned and an additional two months were added to his sentence. On his return to the Bronx, his old Bergen Gang buddies anointed him "Dutch Schultz," much to the chagrin of his loving mother.

By the mid-1920s, Schultz realized that bootlegging was the way to make serious money. He got involved in the beer trade, working as a strong arm goon for some of the bigger operators. At one time he and Charles "Lucky" Luciano were members of the Jack "Legs" Diamond gang.

In early 1928, Schultz was bartending in a speakeasy owned by childhood friend, Joey Noe.[1] While working there Schultz gained a reputation for brutality when someone triggered his temper. It was perhaps this ruthlessness that made Noe admire him and take him on as a partner. The two men were soon on their way to building a beer empire in the Bronx and beyond.

With the profits from their speakeasy, they opened more operations. They began to purchase their own trucks to avoid the delivery cost of wholesale beer. The beer for their operations was obtained from Frankie Dunn, a Union City, New Jersey, brewery owner. Schultz would ride shotgun to protect his trucks from being hijacked.

The two partners realized they could increase their profits by supplying beer to their rivals. If speakeasy owners turned down overtures to purchase beer from the Schultz/Noe combine, they were soon warned to buy it, or else. Joe and John Rock were brothers who decided to play hardball with Schultz. John quickly stepped aside, but his stubborn Irish brother refused to give in. One night Joe Rock was kidnapped by members of the Schultz/ Noe gang, who brutalized him. Rock was beaten and hung by his thumbs on a meat hook. The gang allegedly wrapped a gauze bandage over his eyes that had been smeared with the discharge from a gonorrhea infection. His family reportedly paid $35,000 for his release. Shortly afterwards Joe Rock went blind.

These tactics, real or embellished, instilled fear among Schultz's competitors and heightened his reputation for utter ruthlessness. It also made it easy for the partners to muscle in on the beer trade in the Bronx. As the operation grew, new beer suppliers were needed to fill the orders the gang was receiving. In addition, they began to attract a group of enforcers who would soon make names for themselves. Among this group of toughs were Abe "Bo" Weinberg and his brother George, Vincent Coll and his brother Peter, Larry Carney, "Fatty" Walsh, Joey Rao, and Edward "Fats" McCarthy.

The operation, which began modestly in the Bronx, was now expanding to Manhattan's upper West Side into the neighborhoods of Washington Heights, Yorkville, and Harlem. Schultz and Noe moved their headquarters out of the Bronx and onto East 149th Street in Manhattan, a move that brought them into direct competition with Jack "Legs" Diamond.

The response from the Diamond gang came quickly. At 7 o'clock on the morning of October 15, 1928, Diamond's men ambushed Joey Noe outside the Chateau Madrid nightclub on West 54th Street near Sixth Avenue, while Schultz was rumored to be meeting with rumrunner William V. "Big Bill" Dwyer. Although Noe was wearing a bulletproof vest, slugs ripped through his chest and lower spine. Noe apparently got off a number of shots in return. Witnesses reported seeing a blue Cadillac bounce off a parked car and lose one of its doors before speeding away. When police found the car an hour later, they discovered the body of Diamond gunman Louis Weinberg (no relation to Bo and George) dead in the back seat.

Noe was rushed to Roosevelt Hospital. Despite a valiant effort by the hospital's staff, Noe slowly faded away. By the time he died, three weeks later on November 21, he weighed a mere 90 pounds. In Paul Sann's biography, *To Kill the Dutchman,* Schultz's feelings about Noe's death are described:

> There is no question that Schultz was crushed. Noe was the closest intimate of all his days. He might have drawn some inspiration from a hoodlum like Marcel Poffo, but Noe, who always called him Arthur, as when they were kids on the street corner without a care in the world, put him on the golden highway. When Noe was with him, he could give the armed guard a night off, and Noe for that matter, was the only one he ever took along when he went to see his mother.[2]

In the wake of the shooting of Joey Noe, Schultz was bent on revenge. On November 4, 1928, the financier of the New York underworld, Arnold Rothstein, was shot in the Park Central Hotel and died two days later. The common theory for the murder was that Rothstein welshed on a gambling debt, but another prevalent rumor was that Schultz was involved because of Rothstein's friendship with Diamond. Perhaps supporting this theory was the fact that the first person McManus called after the shooting was Tammany big wig James J. "Jimmy" Hines, who in turn contacted Schultz's top lieutenant, Bo Weinberg, to pick up McManus and spirit him away. McManus was later cleared of the killing.

Another theory involved Diamond because he felt Rothstein had double-crossed him in a recent narcotics deal. Whatever the case, when Diamond, the so-called clay pigeon of the underworld because of the number of times he was shot, met his demise on December 18, 1931, Bo Weinberg's name was connected to the murder.

Schultz was now on his own. He would never again have a partner, and he moved freely in the New York underworld as an independent operator. By the late 1920s, his influence had become so great that he was invited to meetings called by Lucky Luciano and his associates as they began to build a national organized crime structure.

In *The Last Testament of Lucky Luciano* (see Appendix), a story is told about one of Luciano's meetings at which the importance of police and political payoffs was being discussed. A vote was taken and everyone agreed with Luciano that more money should be expended for protection, except for Joe Adonis. Schultz, suffering from the flu, sat alone in a corner of the room so as not to spread his germs. Adonis stood looking at himself in the mirror and combing his hair. He then wheeled around and, referring to himself, said, "The star says yes." With that, Schultz darted across the room, grabbed Adonis in a headlock, and breathed heavily into his face.

> "Now, you fuckin' star, you have my goims," roared Schultz.
> The others howled in laughter. Adonis, however, did get the flu and was grounded for a week.[3]

In May 1929, Schultz participated in the Atlantic City Conference (see Appendix). The meeting was attended by dozens of mobsters of various ethnic and religious backgrounds from around the country. The main topics of the conference were cooperation between the gangs and the cities they represented and plans for the day Prohibition was repealed.

As a result of his working relationship with Luciano, when the Castellammarese War (see Appendix) began in February 1930, Schultz was aligned with the forces of Giuseppe "Joe the Boss" Masseria. Opposed to the Masseria faction was Salvatore Maranzano who was actively seeking to become the *Capo–di–tutti Capi,* Boss of all Bosses. The war raged on for 14 months until Luciano set up Masseria to be murdered in a Coney Island restaurant. Not satisfied with the spoils of war, Maranzano put together a hit list of people he wanted out of the way. On the list were Luciano, Adonis, Costello, Genovese, and Schultz himself. Hired to carry out these murders was Vincent "the Mad Mick" Coll, who at the time was in the middle of a gang war with Schultz.

When Luciano was informed of the hit list from traitors inside the Maranzano organization, an assassination team was put together to murder the treacherous newly crowned Boss of Bosses. The hit squad murdered Maranzano in his Park Avenue office on September 10,

1931. Rushing out of the building, one of Maranzano's employees ran into Coll and warned him to leave. The "Mad Mick" was on his way to a meeting with Maranzano. Reported to be part of the hit squad was Schultz's man Bo Weinberg.

THE SCHULTZ/COLL WAR

On January 24, 1931, Schultz got into a fight at Club Abbey with Charles "Chink" Sherman, an associate of rival bootlegger Irving "Waxey Gordon" Wexler. During the donnybrook, Sherman was beaten with a chair and stabbed seven times with the shards from a broken peanut bowl. Schultz was identified as the man wielding the chair, while his sidekick, Marty Krompier, performed the stabbing. The Dutchman did not walk away from the fray unscathed. Schultz took a bullet in the shoulder, but quickly recovered. It was later revealed that the fight broke out over a joke about a girl one of them was seeing.

Shortly after this fracas, Schultz gunman Vincent Coll decided he wanted a more important role in the gang and told the Dutchman he wanted to be taken on as a full partner. Schultz rebuffed him. Coll split from the gang and branched out on his own, taking some of Dutch's underlings with him. It was reported that Schultz was only too glad to see him go.

Described as tall, handsome, and egotistical, Coll had very little business savvy, but made up for it with an almost impulsive fearlessness. Coll's first move on his own was a plot to kidnap a local radio and nightclub personality. He was then going to use the ransom money to finance his new gang. The kidnapping plot was revealed to the police, however, and eight members of Coll's gang were arrested. The police confiscated the "Mad Mick's" arsenal, as well as several automobiles.

Before the split, Schultz had provided $10,000 to bail Coll out of prison on a Sullivan Law violation (carrying a concealed weapon). When the trial date arrived in the spring of 1931, Coll was a no-show, forcing Schultz to forfeit the 10 grand. Schultz responded by having Coll's older brother Peter murdered on a Harlem street corner on May 30. Incensed by the killing of his sibling, Coll went on a rampage, hijacking the Dutchman's beer trucks and declaring open season on Schultz gang members. Within weeks, four of the Dutchman's associates were killed at the hands of Coll and his men.

The war was costly for Schultz. He lost gunmen, had numerous beer shipments hijacked, and had several of his speakeasies shot up. His greatest loss was Danny Iamascia, a friend and bodyguard. Schultz had moved into a Fifth Avenue apartment that overlooked Central Park. An anonymous caller, a woman, notified police that a resident on the ninth floor of the building, Russell Jones, was none other than Dutch Schultz.

On June 18, 1931, New York City Detectives Stephen DiRosa and Julius Salke staked out the apartment from a park bench across the street. The detectives caught the attention of Schultz as they stared at one another through binoculars. Around 6:00 AM, four men, including Schultz and Iamascia, left the apartment and walked over to find out what the two men in plainclothes were up to. As the four gang members approached the bench, one of them barked, "Who are you guys and whaddya doin' here?"

DiRosa replied, "We are the law, put up your hands." With that DiRosa drew his revolver. Iamascia may have thought the pair were Coll's gunmen. Whatever the case, he responded by pulling his own gun. DiRosa opened fire hitting Iamascia in the abdomen and left wrist. Schultz took off running toward 101st Street, with Detective Salke in pursuit. The other two men hopped over a stone wall and disappeared into Central Park. Schultz quickly discarded his own revolver and, after Salke sent a bullet past the Dutchman's ear, came to a stop and put his hands up.

According to Salke, Schultz told him, "Listen, I've got a large sum of money. Take it and let me run. I'm having a lot of trouble. I'm on the edge. I'm being followed by mobsters. They want to give me the works. I don't fight cops."[4] Salke arrested Schultz. The four men rode to Mount Sinai Hospital in a taxicab, Iamascia lying on the floor bleeding profusely. On the way Schultz offered the officers $50,000 apiece and each a house in Westchester, New York.

Iamascia was dropped off at the hospital and Schultz was taken to the 104th Street stationhouse where he was booked for felonious assault and carrying a concealed weapon. He asked if he could have a sedative to calm his "frayed" nerves.

The next day Iamascia died from his wounds. Iamascia's funeral was a gangland extravaganza. Both Schultz and Ciro Terranova, Iamascia's former employer, tried to outdo one another for the gaudiest floral tribute. The funeral service, held at Our Lady of Carmel Church, drew thousands. The funeral procession to St. Raymond's Cemetery consisted of 125 cars, 35 of which carried flowers.

Schultz's trial for the felonious assault charge ended with the jury deciding there was not enough evidence to show he had pulled his gun on the detectives. As far as possession of the gun itself, Schultz had a permit from a Suffolk County judge to carry it. Over the years Schultz had gone to great lengths to be able to carry a concealed weapon, including being made a deputy sheriff in the Bronx.

On July 15, desperate for money, Coll and his cronies drove to Club Argonaut on Seventh Avenue and kidnapped George Jean "Big Frenchy" DeMange, an intimate of Owney "Killer" Madden, owner of Harlem's Cotton Club. Madden paid $35,000 for the safe release of his friend and then patiently plotted his revenge.

On July 28, 1931, in the middle of a heat wave that had already taken 80 lives in the Northeast, New York City witnessed one of its most notorious gang war killings. Instead of lawless gunmen falling to the wayside, five innocent children were senselessly shot down in a botched murder attempt on Schultz associate Joey Rao. On this steamy hot evening as children played on the sidewalk along East 107th Street and adults leaned out open windows in hopes of catching a slight breeze, an open touring car containing five men slowly made its way down the block. As it passed the Helmar Social Club, the men spotted Joey Rao lounging out front. With one gunman blasting away with a shotgun and another with a .45, gang warfare reached an all-time low. Five-year-old Michael Vengali was hit and died the next day. His seven-year-old brother was wounded five times, and a three-year-old, sleeping in a stroller, was hit twice in the back. Two other children, 5 and 14 years old, received slight wounds.

Despite the angry public outcry, police were hard pressed to find anyone in the neighborhood who would talk to them. Rao had spotted his assailants and ducked for cover. When the shooting stopped, he calmly stood up and walked away. Five days later an eyewitness to the shooting, George Brecht, came forward claiming he had been standing across the street as the touring car drove by. Brecht identified Coll and Frank Giordano, a former Schultz gunman, as the two shooters.

When Coll's name was released to the newspapers as the main suspect in the shootings, the press dubbed him, "the Baby Killer." As a nationwide manhunt was on for him, Coll dyed his blond hair black and grew a mustache. On October 4, he was arrested at the Cornish

Arms Hotel on 23rd Street, near Eighth Avenue. In late December 1931, Coll and Giordano were tried for the murder of Michael Vengali. Coll was ably defended by Samuel S. Leibowitz, one of the city's high-profile defense attorneys.

Leibowitz tore apart prosecution witness George Brecht during cross-examination. He told the jury that Brecht had fabricated the story in hopes of collecting the $30,000 reward being offered for the killers. Leibowitz claimed that Brecht had acted in a similar capacity in another case in which his testimony could not be substantiated. By the end of the trial, the jury found Brecht to be "absolutely unreliable." He was committed to the psychopathic ward at Bellevue Hospital for observation. Coll and Giordano were acquitted.

Giordano would not be as fortunate the next time he faced a jury. On October 2, two days before Coll's arrest, Joseph Mullen, a Schultz employee, was murdered in front of a Bronx beer drop off by Giordano and Dominic Odierno. This time, reliable eyewitnesses identified the two killers. A rarity in gangland history, the two men were tried, convicted, and executed for the murder.

Coll celebrated his acquittal and release from jail by marrying his girlfriend, Lottie Kriesberger. Part of their honeymoon was spent at police headquarters, as they were arrested on a conspiracy charge.

On February 1, 1932, another sensational killing in the war made headlines. Again, another innocent victim was shot down. This time it was Schultz's gunmen pulling the triggers. The gang received word that Coll would be attending a card party at a small home on Commonwealth Avenue in the North Bronx. Four gunmen entered and began blasting. Killed were Coll triggermen Patsy Del Greco and Fiorio Basile, as well as Emily Torrizello, who was playing cards. Wounded were Basile's brother Louis and another woman. Miraculously, four children, two of whom were in cribs, avoided injury. Thirty minutes after the shooting, Coll arrived.

Coll's reprieve from gunfire lasted a scant eight days. On February 9, Coll entered the London Chemist, a drugstore, with his bodyguard at 23rd Street near Eighth Avenue. He stepped into a phone booth where it was alleged he called Owney Madden. Things had been tough for the baby-faced Irishman since his acquittal a month-and-a-half earlier. Down to his last $200, he was living in a hotel room with his new bride and was said by one reporter to have "been reduced to the lowly job of guard for a craps game."

The rumor regarding the telephone conversation was that Madden kept Coll on the line long enough for a trio of killers to arrive. When the car pulled up, three men got out. While two stood watch outside, the third walked into the drugstore with a Thompson submachine gun telling several customers to "Keep cool now." Coll's bodyguard, who was believed to have helped set him up, got off his seat at the soda fountain and walked out past the two lookouts on the street, one of whom was rumored to be the seemingly omnipresent Bo Weinberg.

Depending on the particular account of the murder, the machine gunner fired anywhere from 10 to 50 rounds at Coll. The coroner's report stated 15 bullets had hit the "Mad Mick," mostly in vital places. Whatever the number, Coll was dead before he hit the floor.

The gunman ran out and jumped into the automobile, where Weinberg was already at the wheel, and took off. The ordeal for the killers was not over yet. Two police detectives, ironically, assigned to tail Coll, came running at the sound of gunfire. One jumped on the running board of a taxicab and ordered the driver to pursue the speeding getaway car. With the detective firing from the running board, the taxi driver chased the gunmen 27 blocks down Eighth Avenue at speeds of up to 65 miles per hour before the get-away car pulled away.

Back at the drugstore a crowd gathered to see the fallen "Baby Killer." Soon Coll's wife, possibly alerted to the shooting by the turncoat bodyguard, came on the run from her hotel room across the street, screaming as she forced her way through the swelling crowd of on-lookers. Later at police headquarters, she played the gangster moll/wife role to a tee, refusing to answer questions, and when she did, giving half-truths. Lottie Kriesberger Coll would later serve time for violation of the Sullivan Law. She would also get slapped with a 12-year sentence in a woman's reformatory after two companions killed a young lady during an armed robbery in the Bronx.

Less than 100 people attended Coll's wake at the Walter B. Cooke Funeral Home in the Bronx. Only family members were present at his burial at St. Raymond's Cemetery. In ret-rospect, a quote Coll made to reporters after Legs Diamond's murder may have come back to haunt him. The "Mad Mick" stated, "I feel sorry for anyone who is bumped off, especially when a guy is lucky enough to beat a trial—and so soon after acquittal." Diamond had been celebrating his acquittal the night he was murdered. The 23-year-old Coll at least had the luxury of enjoying his acquittal for six weeks.

THE HARLEM POLICY RACKETS

With the Schultz/Coll War over, the Dutchman had more pressing matters to attend to in Harlem. There seems to be several versions of Schultz's involvement in the Harlem policy rackets, or numbers as it was often called. Much of the information came from his attorney and partner in the operations, Richard J. "Dixie" Davis. In his book, *Twenty Against the Un-derworld,* Dewey provided this description of Davis:

> Dixie Davis was an improbable figure to be a top commander of a New York racket. He . . . worked his way through Syracuse Law School and was admitted to the Bar in 1927. This made him the professional contemporary of many of the men on our staff. Davis was given a clerkship in an honored law firm, but he soon went into business for himself.
>
> Soon he became known around the mob as "the Boy Mouthpiece." His work pleased his ignorant clients. In court he talked loudly and waved his arms, putting on a good show. He shouted in the courtroom, but in the back rooms he whispered. And his clients seemed to go free with increasing regularity. The usual fee for a lawyer in numbers cases in those days was $25. Dixie Davis cut the fee to $15 and did a wholesale business.[5]

A Harlem newspaper reported in the early 1920s that 30 policy banks were operating in Harlem. Each operation employed 20 to 30 "runners." These were the people who collected the daily bets and made the payoffs. Although there were several big-time operators such as Marcellina Cardena, Joseph Mathias Ison, and Stephanie St. Clair, a black woman known as the "Policy Queen of Harlem," they were not an organized syndicate and were basically operating as independent bankers.

Policy in 1920s Harlem was seen as a harmless vice. Many reputable citizens played pol-icy and/or operated numbers' banks. Rufus Schatzberg, a former New York City detective-turned-writer stated, "the policy operators employed reputable people to work in their banks. They reasoned that reputable people would take precautions against being arrested. If the workers were discreet and protective of their jobs, it follows that they would, in return, pro-tect the policy operation. Teachers and unemployed wives of prominent community leaders, people who would feel a lasting shame to be arrested, worked in policy banks."[6]

The policy game, which collected as little as a penny per bet, looked like small beans during the Prohibition years when money flowed as easily as the illegal liquor that created it. With the "Noble Experiment" in its death throes in the early 1930s, however, mobsters were looking at other sources of income and the Harlem numbers/policy rackets drew the attention of the Dutch Schultz gang.

As Schultz made his move on the policy operators, he realized that more than muscle alone was needed to achieve his goal. It was the political clout from James J. "Jimmy" Hines, the Tammany Hall West Side leader, and the Dutchman's protection payoffs to the police that would make this takeover successful. The other factor was that black policy operators were not career criminals, and violence had not been a part of their trade.

As told by Dewey, Schultz's lawyer, "Dixie" Davis, represented many of Harlem's black policy operators and had a strong influence over them. It was this influence, combined with Hines's political protection and the Dutchman's guns and muscle, that made Schultz's newly organized policy combination a money-making force to be reckoned with.

The Schultz gang began their takeover by inviting Alexander Pompez, one of Harlem's more successful policy bankers, to a meeting at the Oswasco Democratic Club, a Tammany Hall affiliate, on West 118th Street. George Weinberg and Solly Girsch told Pompez that he would need to pay them $600 a week for protection. Girsch then brought in Joseph Matthias "Spasm" Ison and told him the same thing. Ison immediately sought out his lawyer, "Dixie" Davis, who advised him that the Schultz forces were too powerful to buck.

Acting as an advisor to Ison, the two men met with George Weinberg and his brother Bo and worked out an agreement whereby Ison would pay them $500 a week for protection. As part of the protection, Ison wanted Jose Enrique "Henry" Miro to stop infringing on his territory. The gang responded quickly. Davis summoned Miro to a meeting with the Dutchman. The policy banker was so shaken when he received the request that he went to the meeting still wearing his pajamas. Schultz laid a .45 automatic on the table and told Miro that he was to begin paying $500 a week for protection and was to stay out of Ison's territory. Miro assured Schultz that the protection he was being offered was "just what he needed."

Between Pompez, Ison, and Miro, Schultz had the three largest policy operators under his control. His next target was Stephanie St. Clair. "Madame Queen" proved to be a tougher prospect. She balked at Schultz's overtures and went to the Harlem newspapers where she bought advertising space to reveal how the Dutchman's politically backed combination was trying to steal her business. She then went to the mayor and district attorney and demanded that the gunmen who were harassing her be prosecuted. That she was a woman meant nothing to Schultz. After her failed attempt to get other black policy operators to form a coalition against Schultz, the Dutchman simply forced her out of business. A few years later, when Schultz lay dying in a Newark hospital, a telegram arrived from St. Clair stating, "As ye sow, so shall you reap."

The profits from Schultz's policy operation were tremendous. The odds of winning were 999 to 1, but the house only paid off at 600 to 1. It was estimated that the average daily take was $35,000, of which only 25 percent was being disbursed to the winners. Of course, out of this balance came the payoff to the police and politicians for protection, but that still left Schultz with an impressive profit margin.

The Dutchman improved his earnings when he brought Otto Berman into the fold. Known as "Abbadabba" because he possessed a gifted mathematical mind, Berman approached Schultz in 1932 with a $10,000 proposition. The winning policy numbers were derived from horse race tracks from the betting results on the pari-mutuel Schultz turned him down because he wanted to keep the game honest. The next year, however, when Schultz was embroiled in expensive tax matters, he hired Berman.

Berman would go to the designated track where the winning policy numbers would be established, usually Cincinnati (where Schultz had hidden ownership in River Downs Race Track), New Orleans, or Florida. After the races that produced the first two numbers were concluded, he would call George Weinberg in New York, who would tell him which numbers would cost them the most money for that day. Berman would then go to the pari-mutuel windows and place a bet that would influence the third digit in the gang's favor. Once when asked about the success of Berman's efforts, George Weinberg replied, "pretty near everyday was a winning day." Estimates of Schultz's income from the policy rackets were from $12 to $14 million annually.

JULES MARTIN AND THE RESTAURANT RACKETS

While Schultz was making a fortune in the policy rackets, he conceived another money-making venture involving union racketeering in the restaurant industry. In 1932, a Schultz lieutenant, Julius Modgilewsky, called "Modgilewsky the Commissar" but better known as Jules Martin, opened a small "greasy spoon" diner as a front for gaining access to Local 16 of the Hotel & Restaurant Employees International Alliance. Local 16 handled the waiters in Manhattan north of Fourteenth Street. With Schultz's, backing, Martin's employees ran for union offices, stuffing the ballot boxes to obtain the positions of president and secretary-treasurer. Their efforts were so effective that they received 38 more votes than the entire membership of the union.

The next move was to take over Local 302. This time instead of supplying his own candidates, Martin and another Schultz associate, Sam Krantz, simply advised the union's leadership to join them—or else. The final step was to establish the Metropolitan Restaurant & Cafeteria Owners Association to sign restaurant and cafeteria owners and collect tribute from them. Martin handled this task himself, forcing the owners into signing certificates of membership stating that they were doing so of their own free will. Jack Dempsey, the former boxing champion and owner of the well-known "Dempsey's" restaurant, then located across the street from Madison Square Garden, was even photographed signing the agreement. Martin was so successful that he was able to move into the background of the association and let Krantz and another Schultz gang member, Louis Beitcher, run the operation.

No one realized that it was Schultz who was behind the scenes working through Martin to build the illegal enterprise. Restaurant owners were told that the waiters' union was demanding a doubling of the wages, but this could be avoided if they joined and paid tribute to the association. One small cafeteria operator said he was forced to pay a $250 initiation fee and $30 annually in dues. In addition, he was told to pay $1,500 for "association fees" to avoid a threatened strike. Larger establishments were required to shell out initiation fees from $5,000 to $25,000 in addition to substantial annual dues.

One owner who refused to pay tribute to the association was Hyman Gross. Having already invested $100,000 in his new restaurant, Gross refused to give in to the Schultz mobsters. One night a stink bomb was dropped down the restaurant's chimney, and Gross was forced out of business, losing his entire investment. The stink bombs the gangsters used were made of valerian or butyric acid. Once detonated, they created an offensive odor that permeated carpets, draperies, wood, even concrete and plumbing. The acid would ruin all the tables and fixtures, requiring furniture to be replaced and leaving the restaurant closed for months, if not permanently.

One of the key men in the association was Paul Coulcher, who had ballot-box stuffed his way to secretary-treasurer of Local 16. He later became a recognized name in the labor movement.

In March 1935, while absorbed in a government tax case and forced to remain in the Albany area, Schultz called Martin and ordered him to bring $21,000 from the coffers of the association to him at once. Martin was accompanied on the train ride by Bo Weinberg and Dixie Davis. The men met Schultz at the Harmony Hotel in Cohoes, New York. Schultz grilled Martin about $70,000 that was missing from the restaurant association's bank accounts. Schultz suspected Martin of investing the money in a factory he owned in Elkhart, Indiana, that rebuilt taxicabs. With both men drinking heavily, Schultz emphasized his point by slugging Martin in the eye, after which the commissar admitted to having removed "only" $20,000 from the accounts.

Davis was not accustomed to the physical violence that was part of the underworld. He could hardly have anticipated what happened next, which he revealed years later:

> Dutch Schultz was ugly; he had been drinking and suddenly he had his gun out. The Dutchman wore his pistol under his vest, tucked inside his pants, right against his belly. One jerk at his vest and he had it in his hand. All in the same quick motion he swung it up, stuck it in Jules Martin's mouth and pulled the trigger.
>
> It was as simple and undramatic as that—just one quick motion of the hand. The Dutchman did that murder just as casually as if he were picking his teeth.[7]

Schultz apologized to Davis for his having to witness the brutal murder. Davis was further shocked when he read that Martin's body was found in a snowdrift with 12 stab wounds in the chest. When questioned by Davis about this Schultz replied, "I cut his heart out."

Although there was another version of events that night of the murder, author Paul Sann concluded, "the Martin slaying was one of the very few that Dixie Davis did not charge up to Bo Weinberg. That had to count for something."[8] Ironically, the other version had Bo Weinberg doing the killing.

Although Martin was in the grave and Schultz would join him before the year was out, the restaurant racket was so successful that it continued to thrive until an investigation by Special Prosecutor Thomas E. Dewey resulted in the indictments of 10 men. The trial, which began on January 18, 1937, lasted two-and-a-half months, with 40 prosecution witnesses and 60 defense witnesses taking the stand. The jury took just six hours to return a verdict of guilty on all counts. Among those handed jail sentences was Paul Coulcher who received from 15 to 20 years.

DEWEY AND THE DUTCHMAN'S LEGAL WOES

Thomas E. Dewey was born in Michigan in 1902. He attended the University of Michigan and graduated in 1923. He then enrolled at Columbia University Law School. After graduation he joined a law firm where he met George Z. Medalie, a prominent attorney. Medalie was so impressed with Dewey's legal skills that when he was named U.S. attorney for the Southern District of New York, he appointed the young Dewey to the position of chief assistant.

Dewey gained valuable experience in trial preparation and in the administration of the prosecutor's office. He learned about the city's underworld structure and the relationship between gangsters and politicians. In the early 1930s, as chief assistant U.S. attorney, Dewey took part in several income tax prosecution cases against policy racketeers including Henry Miro and Wilfred Brunder. Here he received his first exposure to Dixie Davis, the lawyer who later represented Schultz.

In 1931, the U.S. attorney's office began a tedious investigation into the bootlegging operations of both Schultz and Irving "Waxey Gordon" Wexler. The case against Gordon went to trial in November 1933. With Dewey personally handling the prosecution, Gordon was convicted in December and received a 10-year prison sentence and a $50,000 fine.

On November 1, 1933, Medalie resigned as U.S. attorney and returned to private law practice. Dewey, a Republican, was appointed to fill the vacancy until a replacement was named by President Franklin D. Roosevelt, a Democrat. The president named Martin T. Conboy to the position on November 25, and Dewey returned to private practice by year's end.

Meanwhile, Schultz, who had been indicted on January 25, 1933, decided that instead of going to trial like Gordon and losing, it was better to go on the lam. Schultz had not filed tax returns for 1929, 1930, and 1931, and the government claimed he owed them $92,000. In addition, he was facing up to 43 years in prison and a fine of more than $100,000.

Schultz needed time and money. Prohibition was in its last year and all his income from the "Noble Experiment" would soon dry up. The money was needed not just for his defense fund, but also to help Jimmy Hines make sure their man got into office in the upcoming election for Manhattan district attorney. Schultz would remain in hiding for the next 22 months. The New York City Police Department distributed 50,000 wanted posters worldwide for him; however, Schultz never left the greater New York area. During his months in hiding, in broad daylight Schultz visited his wife Frances, had dinner and attended nightclubs with Jimmy Hines and Dixie Davis, and was a frequent quest at Polly Adler's midtown house of sin.

All of 1933 passed without law enforcement finding Schultz, who was operating freely right under their noses. Paul Sann attributes this to the fact that the mayor's office was still in control of Tammany Hall. Things were about to change. New Yorkers elected reform candidate Fiorello LaGuardia mayor in 1934. The "Little Flower" was soon putting the squeeze on the city's underworld.

On November 1, 1934, LaGuardia received a telephone call from Henry Morgenthau, Jr., Roosevelt's secretary of the treasury. Through this conversation Morgenthau teamed LaGuardia with FBI Director J. Edgar Hoover to put pressure on finding Schultz. Hoover made the Dutchman his "undercover" Public Enemy No. 1. Schultz's first reaction was to send his legal team to Washington D.C. to negotiate a settlement. Morgenthau's reply was a flat, "We don't do business with criminals."

On November 28, 1934, Schultz appeared before the U.S. Commissioner in Albany, New York, saying, "I'm Arthur Flegenheimer. I am under indictment in the Southern District of New York. I wish to surrender." With that short statement, 22 months as a fugitive came to an end as the Dutchman gave himself up.

Bail was set at $50,000 and then doubled. This would be the longest period of time Schultz spent behind bars since his teenage years. Dixie Davis got the bail reduced to $75,000, but it took several weeks before the Dutchman was released. It was at this point, while Schultz awaited trial, that he murdered Julie Martin. Despite that incident, Schultz kept himself busy by trying to improve his public image. Just before the trial got underway, the Dutchman held a press conference. With Davis at his side, he answered many questions about his life and business activities. One of the questions regarded his wardrobe. The underworld leader's appearance was sometimes ridiculed in the press. One reporter referred to him as "an ill-dressed vagrant" and stated that Schultz had "a special talent for looking like a perfect example of the unsuccessful man." Paul Sann wrote the following:

> Schultz, for that matter, made no secret of the frugality that governed his wardrobe. He said he never spent more than $35 or so for a suit or more than $2 for a shirt. "You take silk shirts now," he told the assembled press in the big Syracuse session, "I think only queers wear silk shirts. I never bought one in my life. Only a sucker will pay $15 or $20 for a silk shirt."[9]

Schultz's "frugality" was also apparent to Lucky Luciano who declared:

> Schultz was one of the cheapest guys I ever knew, practically a miser. Here was a guy with a couple of million bucks and he dressed like a pig. He used to brag that he never spent more than thirty-five bucks for a suit, and it hadda have two pairs of pants. His big deal was buyin' a newspaper for two cents so he could read all about himself.[10]

Before leaving the press conference, Schultz received a set of rosary beads from one citizen and another wished him "Good Luck," in Yiddish. The tax trial began on April 16, 1935. The prosecution was handled by John H. McEvers, a member of the team that successfully convicted Al Capone. Many of the early witnesses McEvers put on the stand were bankers who were used to detail the Dutchman's bootlegging income. The government also had subpoenaed 20 witnesses, many of whom were reluctant to speak. Some of the witnesses that were subpoenaed went into hiding. One witness, scheduled to testify during an afternoon session, went for a morning walk and kept on walking. Bo Weinberg and several other Schultz associates developed amnesia on the stand or pleaded the Fifth Amendment, even while being threatened with contempt charges by Federal Judge Frederick H. Bryant. New York Police Detectives Salke and DiRosa, who had arrested Schultz the morning Danny Iamascia was shot, were asked to testify. The government's thinking was that if Schultz had $100,000 to bribe the two officers, surely he had money to pay his taxes.

Schultz's defense lasted three hours. Calling just three witnesses, the Dutchman's defense was that he had been given "expert" legal advice that he did not need to pay taxes on his illegal income. When this advice turned out to be erroneous, Schultz made a concerted effort to pay his debt, only to be rebuffed by the government. Outside the courtroom Schultz complained to reporters that the government had turned down his offer to pay them $100,000. Crying that he was being "persecuted" and wanting to pay, he claimed the government was accepting deals "from everybody else, but they wouldn't take it from me. I tried to do my duty as a citizen."[11]

On April 27, the case went to the jury. For a day-and-a-half Schultz walked the court's corridors nervously chain-smoking cigarettes. Perhaps it was nervousness, but while Schultz waited, he spent much of his time making statements to the press on a variety of topics from his own life to Al Capone and Alcatraz. He had become a media celebrity and was seemingly enjoying the publicity he was receiving.

Despite all of the government's evidence, the jury was hopelessly deadlocked. After the first day the vote stood at six to six. On the second day it was seven to five for conviction. The judge discharged the jury at 3 o'clock on the afternoon of April 29.

A second trial was scheduled for Malone, New York, a tiny community located 10 miles south of the Canadian border. In what Paul Sann called a "social rampage," Schultz arrived in town a week ahead of the trial to show the townsfolk that he was a regular guy. He picked up tabs in bars and restaurants, and attended a local baseball game with the mayor and two of Malone's prominent businessmen, all in the hopes of softening up the town. After one of Malone's clergymen rebuked his congregation for "fawning" over the gangster, Judge Bryant revoked Schultz's bail.

The prosecution's case was basically the same—the bankers, the reluctant subpoenaed witnesses, and Bo Weinberg with his faulty memory. In an effort to make Schultz seem more like one of them, the defense hired a local lawyer as lead attorney. The trial, which began in mid-July, went to the jury on August 1. After a nine to three vote for acquittal on the first ballot, the jury came back on August 2, with a verdict of not guilty. Judge Bryant was furious and he banged his gavel to quiet the joyous outburst in the courtroom. He then admonished the jurors:

> You have labored long and no doubt have given careful consideration to this case. Before I discharge you I will have to say that your verdict is such that it shakes the confidence of law-abiding people in integrity and truth. It will be apparent to all who have followed the evidence in this case that you have reached a verdict based not on the evidence but on some other reason. You will have to go home with the satisfaction, if it is a satisfaction, that you have rendered a blow against law enforcement and given aid and encouragement to the people who would flout the law. In all probability, they will commend you. I cannot.[12]

Also disappointed at the trial's outcome was Mayor LaGuardia who told reporters, "He won't be a resident of New York City. There is no place for him here." To which Schultz replied to the press, "Tell LaGuardia I will be home tomorrow."

In reality, the acquittal was a surprise to Schultz and his defense team, not to mention his gangland peers in New York City. Law enforcement was not giving up on Dutch Schultz, however, and his time was running out.

BEGINNING OF THE END

Schultz did not return to New York City, nor to Queens where his wife Frances had given birth to a son. Instead he took up residence at the Stratfield Hotel in Bridgeport, Connecticut, and later at the Barnum Hotel there. Schultz was still considered a fugitive because of an outstanding federal warrant for him on tax counts that were separate from the ones he was tried on in Syracuse and Malone. In Connecticut, Schultz and his bodyguard, Bernard "Lulu" Rosenkrantz,[13] found themselves the darlings of the social set and were invited to several activities. One socialite reported to a *New York Sun* reporter:

> My dear Arthur was the answer to a hostess's prayer. When it became known that he had been invited to your party, you had nothing to worry about. Everyone came. . . . And, really, he was charming. It was hard to believe all those horrid stories.

While hobnobbing in Connecticut, Schultz held meetings with his lawyers and Jimmy Hines. Schultz told Hines that as a result of his legal expenses, the Tammany boss would have to take a 50 percent wage cut until the Dutchman's problems were cleared up. Soon Schultz realized he was fighting a war on two fronts. A bloody policy war was going on in New York City, undoubtedly begun when his enemies wrongly predicted that Schultz wouldn't be coming home from Malone. It wouldn't take Schultz long to figure out that it was Bo Weinberg, looking out for his own interests, who instigated the trouble.

Schultz knew it would only be a matter of time before he was arrested on the second charge. Around mid-August, Schultz's attorneys made a $75,000 offer to the IRS to resolve the matter. IRS officials said they were not interested. On September 6, Schultz was served notice by the New York State Tax Commission that the amount of taxes they claimed he owed from 1929 and 1930 had nearly doubled—from $36,000 to $70,280. The notice was served on him at the Bridgeport hotel.

During the summer while Schultz was battling the federal tax indictments, Thomas Dewey was appointed to the position of special prosecutor by New York Governor Herbert H. Lehman. Following this appointment, the district attorney of New York County, Tammany man William Copeland Dodge, held a news conference to announce Dewey's return. (The appointment of a special prosecutor had been the demand of the grand jury, which was disgusted with, and refused to work with, Dodge and his staff.) At the press conference, Dodge stated that Dewey had the complete support of his office. Dewey later claimed this was an outright lie, that he had no support at all, and that he was given the title of deputy assistant district attorney by Dodge—the lowest title in the prosecutor's office. Dewey joked that he was appointed to "clean up New York—with no staff, no office, no police, no budget appropriation and, . . . no sense whatever."[14]

Meanwhile, Schultz was back on Dewey's radar. While Dewey was in the U.S. attorney's office, he was responsible for obtaining the federal income tax indictments against Schultz. He was ably assisted by Jacob J. Rosenblum. When Dewey offered him a position as an assistant on September 12, Rosenblum resigned his government job the same day. Although Dewey didn't come out and say so, the newspapers intimated that Dewey was going to go after Schultz now as special prosecutor.

> "His personal brutality and his reputation as a mad dog killer concealed, in my opinion, what must have been a brilliantly inventive mind."
>
> —Dewey, *Twenty Against the Underworld,*
> 1974, p. 271

On September 24, 1935, Schultz checked out of Bridgeport and headed to New Jersey. Schultz was shopping around to find out where it would be best for him to be arrested. Where did he stand to have the best chance of a lower bail? It was believed Schultz's attorney made a deal with New Jersey officials. On September 26, Schultz registered at a hotel in Perth Amboy and then "tipped" officials to his whereabouts. Within minutes Schultz was arrested.

He was taken before a federal commissioner in New Brunswick and released after posting a $10,000 bail.

The government, however, had been made aware of Schultz's plan. Before he could leave the commission's courtroom, he was served with a bench warrant for his arrest. He was then taken to Newark, where he was brought before Federal Judge William Clark. A no-nonsense jurist, Clark had been made aware of Schultz's plan and was ready with one of his own. He set bail at $75,000 and Schultz was remanded to the Hudson County jail.

When Judge Clark refused to reduce the bail and declined to accept $97,600 in Newark real estate, Schultz's attorneys went to another federal judge, asking for a writ of habeas corpus, based on the claim that Schultz was "being compelled to associate with common crooks," who were keeping him awake at night.[15] The judge proved unsympathetic, but told the attorneys they could make a plea before the circuit court of appeals in Philadelphia.

After four days in the Hudson County jail, Schultz was released when a circuit court judge in Philadelphia approved a $50,000 bail. The court approved as bond the Newark real estate offered a few days earlier. Reporters gathered outside the jail as the Dutchman was released. Schultz was not in a talkative mood, but he did tell reporters the government was "hounding" him. "They've tried me on the same charge in New York," he complained. "They've dug up a new legal trick to repeat that maneuver."[16]

Schultz went to Newark where he took a suite at the Robert Treat Hotel and began working on his public relations image again. Schultz held court at the Palace Chop House, located around the corner from the hotel. Rosenkrantz and Abe Landau were present to keep "undesirables" away. The following is a sampling of comments Schultz made to one reporter who interviewed him from the Newark *Star Ledger*:

Q. What about the government's latest charges?

A. They're after me now because some puny individuals in the government can't stand up and take a licking like a man. By licking I mean they can't swallow that I was acquitted once and another jury disagreed on exactly the same charges they've got against me now. The only difference between the charges now and then is that they slapped a different name on them. . . . Now right here I'm going to tell you something, and I wouldn't give you a bum steer. Perjured witnesses were used against me in both trials and the government knew it.

Q. What about the Public Enemy No. 1 label?

A. I never did anything to deserve that reputation, unless it was to supply good beer to people who wanted it—and a lot of them did.

Q. What about the future?

A. I want to settle down and be a plain citizen and be given a chance to earn a living. I want to be plain Arthur Flegenheimer and forget there ever was a Dutch Schultz. That bird has had too much trouble.

On October 9, the government issued a new indictment with 10 separate counts against Schultz charging him with failure to pay $200,727 in federal income taxes for the years 1929, 1930, and 1931. The next day a bench warrant was issued in Judge William Bondy's court in New York City after Schultz failed to appear. When Schultz appeared in a federal court in Newark on October 17, he was represented by four lawyers including J. Richard "Dixie' Davis and a former governor of New Jersey and a former state senator, who asked Judge Clark to disqualify himself. The request was based on Clark being quoted in "a newspaper article three years ago as disapproving the granting of a 3.2 beer permit to [Schultz], and inferring he was linked to a double slaying among beer bootleggers."[17] On October 22, Judge Clark, in a 20-page ruling, declared he had no "disqualifying prejudice." Schultz's counsel announced they would immediately appeal the ruling.

In addition to the ruling, an incensed Judge Clark filed an affidavit with the Federal Bar Association, where "he accused the attorneys of unethical conduct, of attempting to select the trial judge before whom their client should be heard and attempting to postpone their client's day in court."[18] In the meanwhile, Schultz remained free on bail as the hearing on application to remove him to New York on the income tax evasion charges was postponed.

It's easy to recognize that the pressure being exerted on Schultz regarding his income taxes was coming from the federal government, not from Special Prosecutor Tom Dewey. Despite the federal indictment, it was Dewey who had incurred Schultz's wrath . . . at least according to the popular tale. Dewey's wife, Frances, began receiving threatening phone calls. One instructed her to go down to the morgue and identify her husband's body. Frances Dewey was almost nine months pregnant at the time; she gave birth to a son on October 18. Dewey heard from street sources that there was a $25,000 price tag on his head. J. Edgar Hoover heard the same rumors and wrote Dewey a letter warning him to be careful.

The plot to assassinate Dewey was revealed to law enforcement by Abe "Kid Twist" Reles in 1940, five years after Schultz's death. Burton Turkus discussed the plot in detail in *Murder, Inc.* (see Appendix). Dewey's morning ritual was to leave home accompanied by two bodyguards (these assigned after the threatening phone calls). He would enter a drugstore just a few blocks from his home, and while his bodyguards waited outside, he would call his office from a phone booth inside the store. The plan called for a gunman with a silencer to be in the drugstore waiting until Dewey was in the booth. The assassin would then kill the prosecutor and the store's proprietor.

There are different versions of what happened next. According to Luciano, he called a meeting, which lasted almost six hours, to discuss the plot and its ramifications. He claimed a vote of the "Sicilian" participants was taken, and it was decided that Schultz had to be hit immediately.

What Turkus reported in *Murder, Inc.* was quite different. He claimed that a meeting was called, separate from Schultz's problems with Dewey, and a discussion was held about what to do with the prosecutor. Turkus wrote, "Following protocol and procedure very carefully, the new democratic order limited discussion to the question of whether Dewey should be stopped and if so, the extent of the stopping." The group decided that "murdering a prosecutor was not just any mob job . . . to allow for profound thought," a one-week moratorium was agreed upon.[19]

Schultz, according to the Turkus version, urged the group to be proactive and have a plan in the works if the decision came through to kill Dewey. It was at this point, according to this scenario, that Anastasia was dispatched to stake out Dewey and propose a plan of action. When the group reconvened, Anastasia presented his plan. After a long discussion, the group, spurred on by "Lepke's sage and forceful persuasion, backed by Lucky . . . decided to permit Dewey to live."[20] Schultz was incensed at the group's decision and decided he was going to execute the murder plan himself. Turkus claimed, "He boasted that he was going to get the big racket-buster in forty-eight hours!"

One is left to wonder why Schultz would want Dewey dead. As the story of this plot to murder Dewey came from Abe Reles, is there really any truth to it? One can only consider the old adage, "There's no honor among thieves." The plot to murder Schultz to take over his policy rackets and other operations simply out of greed is certainly more plausible than killing the Dutchman because he wanted Dewey dead. It's more likely this latter myth came up as a justification for their treachery.

PALACE CHOP HOUSE

There was much unrest in the policy rackets after Schultz's acquittal of the tax charges during the Malone trail. The popular belief is that Bo Weinberg sold out Schultz to Luciano in exchange for 15 percent of the business, thereby providing Luciano with a monetary incentive to now eliminate Schultz. The wave of violence began on August 19, when Batiste Salvo the "Westchester policy king," was kidnapped and released after a $9,000 ransom was paid. Police believed an ex-member of the Amberg brothers' gang, Al Stern, was behind the kidnapping. Stern was then believed to have murdered Benjamin Holinsky and Frank Dolak, who aided him in the kidnapping-shooting, both at Third Avenue and 174th Street in the Bronx.

By early September, Schultz realized who had betrayed him. Schultz had his men stake out the palatial estate of Longy Zwillman in East Orange, New Jersey. Allegedly, on September 9, Weinberg was spotted at the home. Schultz was notified and arrived outside of Zwillman's to confront Weinberg as he left. Luciano claims that one of Schultz's men on the stakeout revealed that he watched the Dutchman kill Weinberg with his bare hands. Another rumor had it that Schultz's men kidnapped Weinberg and encased his feet in cement before dumping him still breathing into the East River. Despite a variety of rumors, Bo Weinberg was never seen again. On September 24, the *New York Post* reported that Weinberg was either dead or in hiding. Also missing, according to the newspaper, was Weinberg's wife and "moll."

Abe Meer and Irving Amron were murdered in Brownsville on September 16. The newspapers speculated that the two Bronx men were sent to Brooklyn by Schultz to "study the racket situation for him."

On September 30, Joe Amberg and Morris Kessler were slaughtered in a garage at Blake Avenue and Christopher Street in Brooklyn. Shortly thereafter, the body of Frankie Teitelbaum was thrown from a speeding automobile on the Lower East Side. On October 15, Harold "Shake" Cooper, a Schultz gang associate, was gunned down at Madison Avenue and 120th Street.[21] That night Irving "Red" Blauner, another man with a connection to Schultz, was found shot and dumped in Central Park near 79th Street. Cooper's murder was called "the seventh death in the Schultz and Abe Reles gangs in recent weeks."[22]

Around 1:30 AM on October 23, police were called to 131 North Elliott Street where a man reported an automobile on fire with a man inside. After the fire was extinguished, police found the body of Louis "Pretty" Amberg, the second of three brothers to meet a violent death. An autopsy revealed Amberg had been beaten about the face and head with nine blows from an axe or hammer. Blankets were then wired around his nude body and doused in gasoline, before being set ablaze.

Two nights later, Albert "The Plug" Schuman was shot and wounded on East Houston Street on Manhattan's Lower East Side. Police claim Schuman was shot in retaliation for the wounding of Blauner, who was shot to avenge the kidnapping of Salvo.

The police and newspapers could only speculate about what was going on. Was it a gang war? Did it involve the policy rackets? Was it a war over loan sharking as some theorized? Were all the murders connected? These were questions that there didn't seem to be answers for. The most sensational murder, however, was yet to come, and in the history of gang murders, it was second only to the St. Valentine's Day Massacre.

While Schultz was waiting on his tax case in Newark, he was staying at the Robert Treat Hotel. Around the corner from the hotel was the Palace Chop House. Schultz was using the restaurant as a headquarters and meeting place. On the night of October 23, less than a day after the brutal murder of Louis Amberg, Schultz was in a small private dining room in the back, which could be accessed only by way of a narrow hallway. The room had eight small booths and several tables in the middle of the floor. On the green painted walls of the dining room were a number of mirrors. Schultz used a table on the right-hand side of the secluded dining room, from where he had a view through the doorway and down the hall, off of which was a door on the right that led into the kitchen. A doorway to the left in the hallway led back into the bar area and main dining room.

That evening he was visited by his wife Frances. In the first reports of the shooting, it was not known that the woman visiting Schultz was his wife, so it was suspected that the woman was used to "put the finger" on him. After Frances left, Schultz sat with his bodyguards Abe Landau, alias Leo Frank, and Lulu Rosenkrantz. Joining them was Otto Berman, known as "Abbadabba," who had arrived earlier from Cincinnati. The men were most likely discussing business, as an adding machine tape and account ledger books and papers were found at their table.

Around 10:20 the restaurant was nearly deserted. The *New York Times* reported, "On the second floor of the building, in a night club conducted by the management of the tavern, were three musicians, two couples seated at a table and a check-room girl."[23] Most accounts claim the bar/dining room area was empty, except for the bartender Jack Friedman, who was described as either "polishing glasses" or "was leaning lazily on the bar."[24] To show a disparity in the reporting, however, the *New York Herald Tribune* wrote that Schultz and his men "were the only persons in the back room, but in front a dozen persons, including three women, sat at tables before the sixty-foot bar, at which Jack Friedman presided."[25]

It's safe to say that on the main floor, except for the four men in the back room, the only men present were Friedman; the bartender; King Lou, a Chinese chef; and Benjamin Berkenfeld, a waiter—the last two were in the kitchen at this time. Schultz rose from the table in the back room to use the men's room. This room was off the main dining room and at the end of the bar. Friedman (or Freedman) described what happened next after the door closed behind the Dutchman:

A big fellow came in. He was about 44 and weighed more than 200 pounds. He had his top coat collar up. He reached inside his coat and I thought he was the law, a detective, and was going to show me his badge.

He had a gun in a shoulder holster under his left armpit and he showed me the butt of it. "Get down and keep quiet," he said, and I flopped on the floor behind the bar.

A few seconds later all hell broke loose in the back room. I was in the army during the war and the noise sounded like the rat-tat-tat of a machine gun. The firing moved from the back room through the barroom and out in front. I didn't see anybody except the man who told me to get down. I kept out of sight.[26]

A second man had entered the barroom/dining room seconds after the first, described as about 35, 5-foot, 10-inches and of stocky build. He was said to be wearing a pea green suit and green hat. The two men moved toward the back dining room, seemingly assured of where they were heading. Anyone stepping into the hallway could immediately be seen by Schultz's men at the table, so as soon as the men walked from the bar area into the hallway, they opened fire. Because of Friedman's recollections that the gunfire sounded like the chatter from a machinegun, several news agencies reported that a machinegun was the weapon used; however, ballistics would prove otherwise. The first man was firing away with a .38 revolver, while the second man unleashed three blasts from a shotgun.

According to a diagram in the *New York Post*, Berman was sitting with his back to the door. His wounds, as reported in the *New York Times,* however, don't support that position. Berman was shot twice in the chest and once in the left arm, cheek, and abdomen, which is more indicative of his sitting to the left of where Schultz had been, with his back to the wall on the right. Berman hit the floor and remained there until ambulances arrived.

Landau was wounded in the neck and both arms, while Rosenkrantz was hit six times, suffering wounds in the face, neck, torso, and hands. Both Landau and Rosenkrantz immediately pulled .45 revolvers and began firing back. At the sound of the gunfire, Schultz came out of the men's room. Unfortunately for him, this put him right in the line of fire from his own men firing from the dining room. The *New York Post* reported:

> [Landau] was still shooting when Dutch came out of the washroom. He got a single .45 bullet through the abdomen, a clean wound. The bullet was found on the floor. The visiting gunmen apparently turned just about that time and fled. Whether they saw Schultz and were afraid to stop to give him a blast with [Landau's] gun barking behind them, or simply failed to notice that they hadn't gotten the right man, is only guesswork.[27]

As the gunmen retreated into the dining room, Landau charged after them. The men stood shooting at each other in the barroom/dining room. The first gunman in was also the first gunman out. He jumped into a parked sedan and was driven away. The other gunman took off in a different direction, toward Military Park, located at the corner. Landau continued to chase after the two, running out of the restaurant still firing; several windows on East Park Street had bullet holes in them. Out in front of the Palace Chop House, he fell in a sitting position into a trash can.[28]

Back inside the bar, the mortally wounded, but still thrifty Schultz, "reached in his pocket, slung a dime on the bar and got nickels in change. Holding his stomach, he walked the length of the bar to a telephone.[29] He called the Newark police headquarters and told the radio dispatcher, "I've been shot. Get me an ambulance."[30]

Schultz staggered back to the dining room and was found there when police arrived. A famous photograph shows Schultz in a chair wearing his topcoat, his legs spread wide, his head down on the table between outstretched arms. Newark's Deputy Director of Public Service, A. J. Dougherty, was at headquarters when the calls of the shooting came in. He rushed over to the restaurant. While in the backroom, he overheard Schultz ask the dying Berman if he recognized the shooters. Dougherty watched as Berman shrugged his shoulder and answered "no" to Schultz. If the Dutchman knew who his assailants were, he would have had no need to ask Berman. Still the newspapers wrote about the gangster's code of silence, omerta, in covering up who the shooters were.

All four men were transported to Newark City Hospital and were surrounded there by police officers asking questions.

"Who shot you?" asked Newark Police Chief John Harris.

"Let me alone," replied Schultz. "You're killing me. I'm getting weaker."

Rosenkrantz was even less cooperative. "Get the hell away from me," he hollered. "Go out and get me an ice cream soda."

Berman was the first to die, passing away in the operating room at 2:55 AM, about four-and-a-half hours after the shooting. Landau, who was photographed in a hospital bed smoking a cigarette, followed him at 6:30 AM. Surgeons had Landau in the operating room and were considering amputating his left arm when he died. The loss of too much blood from a severed artery in his neck was listed as the cause of death. Rosenkrantz held out the longest of the four victims. He passed away at 3:20 AM on October 25.

The men shot with the Dutchman in the Palace Chop House were not the only Schultz associates under the gun that night. Apparently somebody was going for a clean sweep. Marty Krompier, Schultz's accomplice in the "Chink" Sherman beating, had been assigned to keep an eye on the Dutchman's Manhattan interests while the boss was in self-imposed exile across the Hudson River. Krompier was Schultz's chief enforcer of the Harlem numbers rackets and kept the policy bankers in line.

As was his custom, Krompier stopped at the Hollywood Barber Shop at Seventh Avenue and 47th Street around midnight with his brother Jules and bookmaker, Sammy Gold. The three men occupied barber chairs, with Marty in the middle. His shave completed, Krompier stood looking at himself in the mirror, while a black porter was poised behind him waiting to help him on with his coat.

At that moment, a gunman, described as a short, dark man wearing a dark hat, brown overcoat, and dark suit, entered the shop. Waiting for the porter to clear his line of fire, the gunman grew impatient and sent a bullet crashing into the ceiling. Bullets from at least two guns were flying, with four slugs hitting Marty Krompier and two catching Gold. Jules Krompier escaped harm. Another gunman had fired from the doorway because at least seven bullets were spent, and witnesses saw four men hurry away. The first shooter sped out the door and fled through a nearby subway, discarding a .38 Smith & Wesson revolver on the steps. The gun still had two live rounds in the cylinder.

Marty Krompier was critically wounded. He was hit in the chest, stomach, and both arms. Gold was hit in his left side and arm. When police arrived, they asked Krompier if he saw the gunman.

"Sure," replied Krompier. "I'd know him if I saw him again."

Had he ever seen the man before, questioned one officer.

"No, I don't know him. I'd know him if I ever saw him again," repeated Krompier.

The wounded men were taken to New York's Polyclinic Hospital, where Arnold Rothstein had succumbed to a gunshot seven years earlier. Krompier received blood transfusions from Jules and another brother, Milton. Doctors could not remove the bullet in

Krompier's abdomen, which had lodged itself deep in his intestines. The prognosis was not good.

Back at Newark City Hospital, Schultz was still languishing. The bullet that went through him was a rusty steel-jacketed .45 that entered just below his chest on the left side. The slug ripped through his abdomen, passing through his large intestines, gallbladder, and liver before exiting his body. His spleen and stomach were also perforated. There was tremendous internal damage and bleeding. In addition, peritonitis, an inflammation of the abdominal wall, had set in. Schultz was on the operating table for 90 minutes.

The Dutchman was placed in a vacant four-bed ward on the hospital's second floor. He was surrounded by police officials still trying to question the dying mobster. While still coherent, he asked for a priest, and Father Cornelius McInerney was summoned. Schultz wanted to die a Catholic. Father McInerney baptized him and gave Schultz the last rites of the Catholic Church. He then stayed and comforted the three women in the Dutchman's life—his mother, sister, and wife.

Schultz showed some signs of rallying, but by 2:00 PM on October 24, he began to fade. As he lay dying, he began to ramble incoherently. Police officials in the room began to write down what the Dutchman was saying. By 4 o'clock, Police Chief Harris assigned a stenographer to record the statements of Schultz who was passing in and out of consciousness with a 106° fever. His last words were spoken at 6:00 PM, and then Schultz fell into a deep coma. At 8:20 PM, the Dutchman's young wife was allowed to enter the room and say her farewell. She was soon taken to the police station and was not made aware of her husband's death until hours later. At 8:35 Schultz passed into eternity.

Schultz's deathbed statements were a cryptic, yet poetic, rambling in gangster jargon. It was reported that the text of his statements was practically a glossary of mobster lingo, so rich in form that they would later be studied by scholars as a piece of American folk literature. Priceless among his incoherent uttering was the comment, "Mother is the best bet and don't let Satan draw you too fast." In 1969, writer William S. Burroughs, author of *Naked Lunch,* wrote *The Last Words of Dutch Schultz: A Fiction in the Form of a Film Script,* based on the Dutchman's last hours.

In life, Schultz had been able to avoid a fate that happened to many of his bootlegging colleagues—being taken for a "one way ride." Ironically, in death, that's exactly what happened, and it took place under the noses of police guards assigned to watch his body. On October 28, employees of Daniel F. Coughlin & Brothers, an undertaking establishment, were able to sneak Schultz's coffin out of the funeral parlor and into a hearse. From 4:30 to 10:00 AM they drove the body around the city making frequent stops for coffee. At 10:00 AM they met Richard Coughlin at the Yonkers city limits and he accompanied the hearse to the Gate of Heaven Cemetery for burial.

The hearse was met at the cemetery by just three mourners—Mrs. Emma Flegenheimer, Mrs. Helen Ursprung, and Mrs. Frances Flegenheimer—Schultz's mother, sister, and wife. The three were accompanied by two state troopers and Father McInerney, who had baptized Schultz just before he died. At his mother's request, the traditional Jewish *talis,* or praying shawl, was draped over his shoulders. Because of his deathbed conversion to the Catholic faith, Schultz was buried in consecrated ground. The gravesite was located less than 100 yards from slain bootlegger and Broadway personality Larry Fay. An apparent gangland snub, only four floral tributes arrived at the grave.

VERSIONS

Perhaps because of the lack of witnesses the night of the shooting at the Palace Chop House, different versions of the shooting came to light as years passed. In 1939, former Schultz attorney "Dixie" Davis wrote "Things I Couldn't Tell till Now," for *Collier's Magazine*. It was through this article that the first telling of the "Night of Sicilian Vespers" (see Appendix) came out, Davis claiming he heard the story from Bo Weinberg.

Davis claimed that three gunmen entered the Palace Chop House that night and opened fire in the back room, while Schultz was in the men's room. According to Davis, after Landau chased the men out:

> Cowering in the lavatory stood the Dutchman, safe. All this banging and shooting was for him, and it never touched him. Trust him, old experienced fighter, to hold his cover. Now all was quiet, the executioners were gone, and Schultz came out.
>
> There on the floor lay the trusted Lulu, mortally wounded, filled with slugs, his .45 clutched in his hand. As the Dutchman stepped toward him, Lulu, in one last convulsive effort, fired at the moving form. One slug tore through Dutch Schultz's abdomen.
>
> Vengeance for Bo Weinberg's murder, as well as greed, had sent the executioners there that night. But the Dutchman actually died at the hand of his own bodyguard, the same man who had gone out for him and slain Bo. To this day, no living man knows why Lulu shot Schultz. Some like to believe that he knew he was done for and, blaming Schultz for his plight, decided to take him with him. Others think he fired convulsively, taking Schultz for another enemy shooter.[31]

Davis obviously wasn't at the restaurant that night and never explained how he knew that the shooting could have happened that way. Still, it beats the fairy tale that came from the lips of Abe Reles when the Murder, Inc. investigations began less than eight months later. Incredibly, all the facts that were known about the case went out the window when Reles let go with his mythological retelling of the shooting. Sadly enough, it's still the version most historians talk about to this day.

In Burton Turkus's book *Murder, Inc.*, he initiates the story that Schultz wanted Dewey murdered and calls a meeting before "the board of governors" of the Syndicate to get their permission. The only names mentioned as being part of this meeting are Lucky, Lepke, and Gurrah. Obviously Turkus never spoke to anyone that attended this alleged meeting, yet he used quotes from it as if this were all somehow documented. He claimed Albert Anastasia was given the assignment to track Dewey's movements to see if an assassination was possible. He came back with a plan, but it was supposedly vetoed by Lepke and Lucky. Schultz decided he's going to carry out the plan and being a "blowhard," he tells an associate he is going to have Dewey murdered in the next "forty-eight hours."

This unknown "associate" reported back to Lepke about the Dutchman's plan. Turkus wrote, "The directors discussed it—and ruled that the Dutchman himself must die to guarantee Dewey's life. The mob actually ordained that it would rub out a mobster—to save a prosecutor."[32]

Selected to carry out the hit were Murder, Inc. stalwarts Charles "Charley the Bug" Workman, Emanuel "Mendy" Weiss, and the driver, an individual who will be remembered throughout the ages only as "Piggy." On the night of the murders we have one version of what happened from second-hand knowledge of the killings. Workman and Weiss never confessed to law enforcement the events of that evening, but they allegedly had conversations with other members of Murder, Inc. who later ratted out their compatriots—Reles and Albert Tannenbaum—to the authorities.

According to the Turkus version, Reles claims that Workman "strolled" into the Palace Chop House while Weiss provided cover, and "Piggy" sat poised behind the wheel outside on East Park Street. Workman walked the length of the bar and then "flipped" open the door to the men's room. Inside was a man washing his hands who Workman thought was a Schultz bodyguard. He shot the man who immediately dropped to the floor.

Workman "now advanced on the boys in the back room" and opened up on the Schultz men—Rosenkrantz, Landau, and Berman—killing, not wounding, all three. Not seeing Dutch among the dead, Workman realized Schultz must have been the man washing his hands. Turkus wrote, "Back into the gents' room barged the Bug, and he gave Dutch's pockets a thorough and total frisk."[33]

Paul Sann provided a different description of the shooting. He stated that both Weiss and Workman blasted away at the three men in the dining room first. Then, after not spotting Schultz, Workman went into the men's room and found Dutch relieving himself at the urinal. Workman fired twice and one bullet hit Schultz, causing a mortal wound. Again, Workman was said to have searched Schultz for money.

If Turkus's tale is true, it seems amazing that two armed bodyguards would have just sat and done nothing at the sound of gunfire in the men's room. All the crime scene information indicates that the three men were seated when they were initially fired upon. If Sann's account is true, why didn't Schultz react by trying to hide or escape when he heard all the shooting start? Sann stated that after Workman emptied his .38, he looked in the men's room and found Schultz still relieving himself. Certainly the cautious 35-year-old Schultz would have heard the shots and have been on the move.

The most incredulous part of the story is of Workman taking the time to "rifle" Schultz's pockets after the shooting. From all credible accounts, Landau and Rosenkrantz immediately returned fire when the shooting started, and Landau chased the gunmen out of the restaurant. How could Workman have had the time, not only to shoot Schultz, but to go through his pockets? Helping to dispel this ludicrous story was the fact that the *Newark Star Eagle* reported that an intern at the hospital attending to Schultz was handed $725 by the gangster and told, "Here's something for you, pal; take good care of me, will you?" The intern handed the money to Dr. Earl H. Snavely, hospital superintendent, who turned it over to police. In addition, Schultz had another $335 in his possession.[34]

AFTERMATH

After a series of operations, and a nine-week hospital stay with around-the-clock security, Marty Krompier was released on New Year's Day 1936. Sammy Gold had recovered from his wounds and was released not long after the shooting.

On July 14, 1937, a grand jury handed down a dozen policy racket indictments. Heading the list was former Schultz attorney, Dixie Davis, who, for all intents and purposes, had taken over the Harlem numbers operations. Also indicted were George Weinberg and Harry Schoenhaus who oversaw the Harlem bankers. Davis and Weinberg fled to Philadelphia where they were later arrested and extradited back to New York. Schoenhaus turned himself in.

Despite the trio's years of illegal activity in the numbers rackets, Thomas Dewey was willing to make a deal with them because he wanted to put the corrupt Tammany leader Jimmy Hines away. The three men agreed to plea bargain for reduced sentences and testify against Hines. On May 25, 1938, Hines, the most powerful Democrat in New York State, was arrested for his role in the numbers operation. His trial began on August 15, 1938. The key witnesses testified against Hines: first Weinberg, then Davis, and finally Schoenhaus. Other witnesses were called to prove that Hines was the money conduit between the Schultz organization and the election of William C. Dodge as district attorney in 1934. Nevertheless, in September, the judge declared a mistrial after Dewey made a comment about Hines's one-time participation in a poultry racket.

On January 26, 1939, Jimmy Hines's second trial got underway. A new judge was assigned to hear the case. The three witnesses were held in protective custody and moved around to avoid detection. Weinberg grew increasingly fearful that he would be murdered for turning state's evidence. On Sunday January 29, three days after the second trial began, Weinberg went to a closet in the safe house where he was being kept and lifted a gun from the jacket pocket of one of his guards. He took it into a bathroom and committed suicide.

Weinberg's previous testimony was read back to the jury and when the case concluded, Hines was found guilty on 13 counts on February 25, 1939. Hines was sentenced to four to eight years in prison. After his appeals were exhausted, he entered Sing Sing Prison on October 14, 1940. He was released in August 1944 and returned to New York City where he died in 1957.

As a result of his cooperation, Dixie Davis received a one-year prison sentence. Upon his release he moved to California. On December 31, 1969, Davis raced home after learning that his Bel Air home had been the site of an armed robbery. Thieves had entered the house, tied up his wife, grandson, and a maid, and then ransacked the home. Davis entered the house, sat down in the living room, and suffered a massive heart attack that took his life.

Frances Flegenheimer, the young cigarette girl who had bore Schultz two children (it was never really clear if the couple had married), moved West to raise her family out of the New York City limelight.

In March 1940, when Abe Reles became a government witness and began to rat out the Murder, Inc. gang, the trial of Charles Workman for the murder of Schultz and his henchmen was one of the first to get underway. A report in the hands of Essex County Prosecutor William A. Wachenfeld clearly stated, "It was not Workman who killed Schultz . . . that beyond a shadow of a doubt that Schultz had been killed by a bullet from the revolver belonging to Rosenkrantz." During the trial, however, Workman suddenly changed his not guilty plea to no contest and the judge sentenced him to life in prison. Before leaving the courtroom, he turned to his younger brother, Abe Workman, and said, "Whatever you do, live honestly. If you make 20 cents, make it do you. Keep away from the gangs. Don't be a wiseguy." In December 1941, after the Japanese sneak attack on Pearl Harbor, Workman volunteered for a suicide mission to retaliate. The mission never materialized.

In March 1959, a bizarre tale came out about Workman's arrest and trial. Wachenfeld, the former prosecutor, had a long and distinguished career in the New Jersey State Supreme Court. While a prosecutor, in 1940 he received a call from Brooklyn Prosecutor William O'Dwyer, who asked Wachenfeld to come to Brooklyn so he could speak with him. O'Dwyer said he had been holding Workman for several months as a suspect in the Murder, Inc. investigation. Recently Workman had retained a lawyer and O'Dwyer would soon have to charge him or release him.

O'Dwyer suggested to Wachenfeld that he take Workman to New Jersey and "try to convict him" in the Palace Chop House killings. Wachenfeld recalled:

> I asked O'Dwyer what evidence there was and he said he had a witness (Abe Reles) who would testify that Workman had confided in him that he had shot Schultz.
>
> I said that wasn't enough evidence and I'd look foolish if I had to turn him loose in New Jersey for lack of evidence.
>
> Some time later O'Dwyer asked me to come see him again. I went over to New York and he said he had another witness (Albert Tannenbaum) to whom Workman had admitted killing Schultz.
>
> On the strength of that I had Workman indicted for murder. When he went on trial, O'Dwyer attended every session.

Both Reles and Tannenbaum testified that Workman confided to them that he had shot Schultz and his men on the orders of Louis Buchalter. Workman was represented at trial by Samuel I. Kessler. At one point in the trial, Kessler called a Brooklyn undertaker who testified Workman was employed by him at the time of the shooting. Wachenfeld cross-examined the witness but couldn't shake his testimony. Wachenfeld then continued:

> That night, O'Dwyer had his funeral establishment raided and the undertaker arrested. O'Dwyer sweated the man and told him the New Jersey prosecutor knew he was lying and he'd better change his story and tell the truth if he wanted to save himself a lot of trouble.
>
> The next morning O'Dwyer told me he thought the undertaker would change his story. He didn't want me to tip off Kessler as to what had happened. But I said Kessler was a reputable lawyer and should know. So we all went into the judge's office and I told Kessler about it and said I thought the undertaker would recant.
>
> That's exactly what happened. Then Kessler asked for an hour's recess. At the end of it, Kessler said Workman wanted to plead non vult (no defense).
>
> I didn't want the plea accepted because I felt I could now get the jury to send Workman to the electric chair. But O'Dwyer argued the jury might disagree or even acquit Workman.
>
> I told the court that after all it was O'Dwyer's case and that was what O'Dwyer wanted. So the plea was accepted and Workman was sentenced to life imprisonment.[35]

Wachenfeld pointed out that on a plea of *non vult,* the death sentence is not permitted. When interviewed about Wachenfeld's comments, Samuel Kessler said, "I have always taken the position that Workman did not kill Schultz. He insisted on pleading non vult against my advice because, he said, he wanted to save his wife and child from embarrassment."[36]

After 24 years in prison, Workman was released in 1964. He spent a grand total of six years in jail for each man that was killed in the Palace Chop House that night.

Although not tried for the Schultz murder, Emmanuel "Mendy" Weiss suffered a worst fate. He was found guilty of the murder of a storeowner along with Lepke Buchalter and Louis Capone. After final pleas to then Governor Dewey were declined, the three men were put to death in Sing Sing's electric chair on March 4, 1944.

In 1937, Dewey was elected district attorney of New York County. He was sworn in on December 31. In 1943, Dewey became governor of New York and served three terms. While governor, Dewey was the Republican candidate for president twice. He lost in 1944 to Franklin D. Roosevelt and in 1948 to Harry S. Truman. Thomas Dewey died on March 16, 1971, in Bal Harbour, Florida, at the age of 69.

Adding to the Schultz legend was a story that before his death, the Dutchman had driven to the village of Phoenicia in the Catskill Mountains. There he was said to have buried a metal box containing diamonds, gold, and an untold number of $1,000 bills. To this day, treasure hunters have searched the area looking for the hidden treasure.

NOTES

1. Pronounced Noy or Noey, depending on which source you read.

2. Paul Sann, *Kill The Dutchman* (New Rochelle, NY: Arlington House, 1971), p. 118.

3. Martin Gosch and Richard Hammer, *The Last Testament of Lucky Luciano* (Boston: Little, Brown and Company, 1974), pp. 79–80.

4. Sann, *Kill The Dutchman,* p. 128.

5. Thomas E. Dewey, *Twenty Against the Underworld* (Garden City, NY: Doubleday & Company, 1974), p. 320.

6. Rufus Schatzberg, *Black Organized Crime in Harlem: 1920–1930* (New York, Garland Publishing, 1993), p. 11.

7. Paul Sann, *Kill The Dutchman,* p. 235.

8. Ibid., p. 237.

9. Ibid., p. 238.

10. Gosch and Hammer, *The Last Testament of Lucky Luciano,* p. 176.

11. Sann, *Kill The Dutchman,* p. 248.

12. Ibid., p. 254.

13. The last name of Bernard Rosenkrantz was also spelled Rosencrantz in some stories and articles.

14. Dewey, *Twenty Against the Underworld,* p. 152.

15. *New York Post,* September 28, 1935, "Schultz Beaten in 2 Court Moves."

16. *New York Post,* October 1, 1935, "Schultz Runs Out on Public Again."

17. *New York Post,* October 22, 1935, "Schultz Loses Fight to Show Bias of Judge."

18. *New York Post,* October 23, 1935, "U.S. Bar Probes Schultz Lawyers."

19. Burton Turkus and Sid Feder, *Murder, Inc.* (New York: Farrar, Straus and Young, 1951), p. 135.

20. Ibid., p. 139.

21. Some articles list his name as Harold Cohen.

22. *New York Post,* October 16, 1935, "Schultz Pal Dies from Gang Guns."

23. *New York Times,* October 24, 1935, "Schultz Is Shot, One Aide Killed and 3 Wounded."

24. The *Newark Star-Eagle* gave his name as Jack Freeman and stated he was one of the owners along with Louis Rosenthal.

25. *New York Herald Tribune,* October 24, 1935, "Schultz and 3 Aids Shot in Newark, 2 More Fall on Broadway in Racket War."

26. *Newark Star-Eagle,* October 24, 1935, "Schultz Dying of Gun Wound; Two Aides Slain in Gang War."

27. *New York Post,* October 24, 1935, "Racketeer Shot Accidentally by Own Lieutenant."

28. Another account claims he ran down the street firing before he collapsed in front of a diner 20 feet from the Chop House entrance.

29. *New York Post,* October 24, 1935, "Racketeer Shot Accidentally by Own Lieutenant."

30. *Newark Star-Eagle,* October 24, 1935, "Schultz Dying of Gun Wound; Two Aides Slain in Gang War."

31. J. Richard "Dixie" Davis, *Collier's,* "Things I Couldn't Tell till Now," August 19, 1939,

32. Turkus and Feder, *Murder, Inc.,* p. 140.

33. Ibid., p. 142.

34. *Newark Star-Eagle,* October 24, 1935, "Interne Spurns $725 from Schultz."

35. *The Sunday Star-Ledger,* March 15, 1959, "Who Really Held the Gun That Killed Dutch Schultz?"

36. Ibid.

BIBLIOGRAPHY

Biographies of Schultz

Addy, Ted. *Dutch Schultz*. New York: Belmont Tower Books, 1973.

Burroughs, William S. *The Last Words of Dutch Schultz*. New York: The Viking Press, 1975.

Sann, Paul. *Kill the Dutchman*. New Rochelle, NY: Arlington House, 1971.

Other Publications

Dewey, Thomas E. *Twenty Against the Underworld*. Garden City, NY: Doubleday & Company, 1974.

Gosch, Martin, and Richard Hammer. *The Last Testament of Lucky Luciano*. Boston: Little, Brown and Company, 1974.

Levine, Gary. *Anatomy of a Gangster*. Cranbury, NJ: A. S. Barnes and Co., 1979.

Peterson, Virgil. *The Mob: 200 Years of Organized Crime in New York*. Ottawa, IL: Green Hill Publishers, 1993.

Schatzberg, Rufus. *Black Organized Crime in Harlem: 1920–1930*. New York: Garland Publishing, 1993.

Thompson, Craig, and Allen Raymond. *Gang Rule in New York*. New York: The Dial Press, 1940.

Turkus, Burton B., and Sid Feder. *Murder, Inc.* New York: Farrar, Straus and Young, 1951.

10

ABNER ZWILLMAN

AKA "LONGY"
JULY 27, 1904–FEBRUARY 26, 1959

Dubbed the "Al Capone of Newark," Abner "Longy" Zwillman was the leading rackets figure in northern New Jersey from the Prohibition years until his death from suicide in 1959. A suave and sophisticated underworld personality, Zwillman was introduced to crime as a result of his family's financial destitution during his adolescent years, when he and his siblings were forced to go to bed hungry because their father was unable to earn enough money to put food on the table.

In later years, Zwillman reflected to a childhood friend, "I still remember what it felt like to skip meals, to go to sleep early because there wasn't enough in the house to feed all of us any supper. I'd swore I'd never let that happen to me, or any of mine, ever again." These bitter memories remained with Zwillman throughout his life. As he became more successful in his criminal endeavors, he branched out into legitimate operations, often providing employment for family members.

Zwillman's membership in the "Big 6," the unofficial syndicate also referred to as the Group of Six or Group of Seven (see Appendix) that was responsible for running organized crime in the eastern seaboard cities, enhanced his underworld status. From rumrunner to businessman to political leader, Zwillman ran the gamut of the underworld boss, building relationships at every turn. His legitimate efforts included ownership of a successful vending business, investments in railroads, real estate and steel companies, and as a Hollywood film producer.

Zwillman, in his post-bootlegging days, always maintained that he was a legitimate businessman. As late as January 1954, law enforcement had information to support this assertion. In a memo that month to FBI Director J. Edgar Hoover from the special agent-in-charge of the Newark field office was the statement, "Allegations are often made in the local press that ZWILLMAN is connected with criminal and illegal enterprises. However, no specific is known to have been revealed definitely tying him to any such operations."

Zwillman met actress Jean Harlow in 1930 while she was engaged in a promotional tour for the film *Hell's Angels,* produced and directed by Howard Hughes. Zwillman fell in love
with the platinum blonde beauty and accompanied her on the
remainder of her six-week tour. Zwillman secretly sent money
to Hughes to make it look like he got Harlow a salary increase
and purchased her a red Cadillac and a jeweled charm bracelet,
and provided her with a full-time hairdresser. He later secured
a two-picture deal for Harlow with Harry Cohn of Columbia
Pictures by loaning Cohn $500,000.

DIRT POOR IN NEWARK

Abner Zwillman was born on July 27, 1904 in one of Newark, New Jersey's poorest Jewish
ghettos.[1] He was third of six children born to immigrant parents, Rubin and Ella Zwillman,
who arrived in the United States from Russia before 1900.[2] Rubin operated a public market
stall on Prince Street from where he sold live chickens. Despite his efforts, the meager income he earned seldom provided adequate food for his young family.

Harsh memories of he and his siblings going to bed hungry during these early years were
etched in Zwillman's mind and would shape his future, creating a burning desire to never
have to do without again. By the age of 12, Zwillman was running errands for a local alderman, using his meager earnings to help support his family.

Although growing up in an environment where education was not paramount on a young
man's mind, Zwillman had a report card that showed surprisingly few absences and tardy
marks. Abner had an athletic build and, from an early age, was always one of the tallest
and strongest in his age group. His height, close to 6-feet, 2-inches, led to a lifelong nickname, "Longy."[3] One story has it that the moniker came from the Yiddish term *Der Langer,*
which meant "The Tall One." Many of the residents in Newark's Third Ward looked up to
Zwillman—both literally and figuratively. As a young man he developed a reputation "for
toughness and reliability."[4]

During the summer of 1918, Zwillman's life, and any early course he had been contem-
plating, changed completely with the death of his father. Longy took it upon himself to become the provider for his family, which meant having to leave school at the age of 14. He
realized that performing errands for the alderman was not going to put food on the table
for his family. Nor did he have the desire to take over his father's chicken stall. A forward
thinker, he decided not to waste his time selling produce in his impoverished neighborhood.
Instead, he rented a horse and wagon and set out to peddle fruits and vegetables in the Clinton Hill section of Newark and other well-to-do neighborhoods.

In Newark, as in most ethnic neighborhoods around New York City, many pushcart operators and produce peddlers paid protection money to remain out of the clutches of local
teenage gangs. Zwillman's size and reputation prevented the area toughs from making him a

target, allowing Longy to focus on his customers and their needs. A childhood acquaintance later remarked of his abilities:

> He was a handsome kid. He looked older than 14. The housewives would come out to his wagon, or greet him at the door, and he would kid with them, you know, make joking remarks about their good looks, pay them compliments about the way they dressed. He was smart as a whip. He could sell those women anything.[5]

During the late 1910s, Zwillman found another product to sell his growing clientele of housewives—lottery numbers. With America's involvement in World War I, many of the young men who manned northern factories were sent packing for Europe or military training facilities. The manpower shortage was filled by black men streaming in from the southern states looking for work and to escape the oppressive conditions of the South. With them they brought a new form of gambling known as policy—a.k.a. numbers, lottery, and clearinghouse.

Anyone could play and everyone did. All that was needed to place a bet on a three-digit number was a penny. Payoffs were as high as 500 and 600 to 1, provided you were dealing with an ethical "banker." Realizing the profits that could be made as a number's "runner," Zwillman quickly got involved. He had a ready customer base—the housewives he peddled produce to on a daily basis. Instead of the women having to seek out the local bookie and take their money to him, they could deal discreetly with their produce man, who showed up on their doorstep daily. Zwillman's lottery earnings gave him more income in a day than his produce selling provided in a week. In addition, in these well-to-do surroundings, the players usually bet nickels, dimes, and quarters as opposed to the pennies that were bet in the ghetto.

It didn't take long for Zwillman to realize even more money could be gained by serving as his own bank, as opposed to working as a collector for the hoods operating in the city. Longy soon organized many of his friends into a gang he called "The Happy Ramblers." Members spread out all over Newark, except the Italian First Ward, to peddle numbers. By 1920, Zwillman had built one of the largest policy banks in the city. Part of Zwillman's success came from paying his runners and collectors a flat weekly salary instead of a percentage. In addition, he paid for lawyer's fees, court costs, and fines if the men were arrested. In an effort to prevent the latter, he built clout by paying off the police and local politicians. In doing so he helped pave the way for his next business venture, a money-making bonanza brought about by the passing of the 18th Amendment—Prohibition.

NEWARK'S PROHIBITION YEARS

In no other state in the union was Prohibition more unpopular than New Jersey. State political figures fought for years to get changes accepted into law that would allow some form of beer manufacturing and consumption. The law was so despised that many of the larger metropolitan areas of the state simply refused to waste their time enforcing it. This included police, prosecutors, and judges, all of whom could make easy money simply by looking the other way.

Zwillman's mentor in the bootlegging and rum-running field was Joseph H. Reinfeld, one of two brothers who operated a saloon at the corner of Eighth Avenue and High Street in

Newark's First Ward. It didn't take long for Longy to give up his produce wagon and horse and get into the business of bootlegging fulltime.

Reinfeld cut a deal with the Bronfman brothers of Montreal, Canada, and began receiving whiskey from their Seagram's distillery stowed in vessels that would dock just outside the three-mile limit along the New Jersey coastline. The "Reinfeld Syndicate" purchased speedboats to pick up the liquor and transported it in through the Port of Newark. From there a fleet of trucks, said to number as many as 50, distributed the liquor around the state and into New York City.

Getting the product to shore, past the Coast Guard and local police, was only half the battle. Once landed, liquor shipments were often the target of hijackers, who thought little of shooting it out to get their hands on a contraband that was sure to turn a large profit. Zwillman was soon providing protection for Reinfeld's liquor, and the saloon operator placed him in charge of transportation.

Through Reinfeld, Zwillman was taught a valuable lesson in providing his customers with the best product. Many unscrupulous rumrunners would take a shipment of liquor and cut it by unsealing the original product and diluting it with water or, worse yet, industrial alcohol, which could lead to poisoning or even death. The product was then rebottled and sold for additional profits. In Zwillman's operation, "His customers learned that a deal with Longy was honest and safe."[6]

In addition, Zwillman was involved with another group of bootleggers who distilled raw alcohol. Included in this gang were James "Niggy" Rutkin and Philip Kull, a former sergeant on the Newark police force. Kull was soon brought up on departmental charges after being found AWOL from his post. At a subsequent hearing, it was revealed that Kull used his squad car to ride shotgun on Zwillman's liquor shipments.

In 1923, Longy's reputation for dispensing muscle was enhanced after an incident with a Newark tough named Leo Kaplas (sometimes listed as Kapaus). There are conflicting stories about Kaplas's activities. An FBI report claimed he controlled what was known as "Bootlegger's Row" in Newark. Biographer Stuart described him as a freelance hood, who made money by "extorting numbers men and shopkeepers." When this happened to a few associated with Longy, Kaplas was told to back off. Instead of heeding this advice, Kaplas responded with threats. One night Kaplas was spotted by a Zwillman associate in a saloon. Longy was notified and arrived minutes later. Zwillman wasted no time in meting out punishment. He simply walked up to Kaplas's table, pulled a gun, and shot him in the leg. He then sent an associate to the hospital to retrieve the bullet. Kaplas didn't press charges and, having learned his lesson, was later put on Zwillman's payroll.

During this period, Zwillman's chief underworld associates were Joseph "Doc" Stacher, Gerry Catena, Willy Tiplitz, Charles Haber, James "Niggy" Rutkin, and Daniel Zwillman, Longy's cousin. Although only 19 years old, Zwillman was seen as a born leader and he had the confidence to strike out on his own, just like he had in the policy racket. On Thanksgiving Day 1923, he met with Abe and Joe Reinfeld to inform them of his decision. The brothers countered with an offer of 20 percent of the gross profits. Zwillman was ready with his own counteroffer—a 50/50 split. Realizing the growing empire that Longy was building, his ability to secure necessary muscle, and his own growing underworld connections, the Reinfeld brothers reluctantly accepted the deal.

During the second half of the 1920s, Zwillman was arrested on five occasions. On December 1, 1926, he was charged with disorderly conduct and received a suspended sentence.

When he was being booked, Zwillman gave his name as "George Long." Some believe this is where the nickname "Longy" actually came from, as opposed to the childhood Yiddish version.

The next four arrests showed that Zwillman truly possessed a violent streak, which helped build a ruthless reputation early in his career. On March 8, 1927, he was arrested, again as "George Long," and charged with atrocious assault and battery with intent to kill. The next month the complaint was dismissed. On June 6, 1927, he was arrested under the name "Longy" Zwillman, charged again for atrocious assault and battery; the charge was dismissed when the victim withdrew the complaint. The next year, on March 6, as Abe Zwillman, he was charged with atrocious assault and battery and again the complainant withdrew and the charge was dismissed on March 16.

Two days later, on March 18, 1928, a black pimp with the unusual name of Preston Buzzard swore out a warrant for Longy's arrest. Buzzard, who worked as one of Zwillman's numbers runners, claimed he was blackjacked several times by his boss. It took police a week to find the highly visible Zwillman, who was charged with assault and released on a $1,000 bond. It was later revealed that Buzzard owed Zwillman a lot of money and was not paying it back at an acceptable rate. Zwillman told friends he didn't kill the pimp because he felt sorry that he was black.

Between his arrest and the trial date, several men confessed to the beating of Buzzard; however, Daniel Brennan, a headstrong jurist, refused to accept the pleas and pushed ahead with the case. On February 11, 1929, Zwillman was found guilty. After a long appeals process, his sentencing date was scheduled for December 2, 1930, but Zwillman missed the appearance because he was on a business trip in Montreal visiting the Bronfmans. Ten days later, after a deal was worked out between Zwillman's lawyer and the judge, Brennan sentenced Longy to six months in the Essex County Prison. While there, Zwillman was allowed weekend furloughs provided he spent them at the home of an associate in nearby Caldwell, from where he could quickly make his way back to the jail if needed. On March 31, 1931, after serving a little over three months, Zwillman received an early release for good behavior.

As the Prohibition years were giving birth to organized crime in this country, new bonds of friendships were being forged nationwide. Zwillman was introduced to underworld stalwarts Albert Anastasia and his brother Anthony, Willie and Salvatore Moretti, and Joe Adonis. It was through Willie Moretti that Zwillman was introduced to other rising underworld leaders, including Frank Costello, Lucky Luciano, Meyer Lansky, and Benjamin Siegel. In May 1929, Zwillman was one of the many mobsters who attended the Atlantic City Conference (see Appendix). He joined mob bosses from around the country strolling through the sand barefoot and making decisions that would govern the underworld for years to come.

During the fall of 1930, Zwillman became a key participant in a short-lived bootlegging war in the city. The conflict began when Ruggiero "Richie the Boot" Boiardo, jealous of the power and influence that Zwillman had acquired, decided to challenge Longy's rule. A note in Zwillman's FBI file stated:

> It has been alleged that when RUGGERIO [sic] BOIARDO alias "Ritchie" [sic], was confined to the New Jersey State Penitentiary in the 1930s, many members of the so-called BOIARDO Mob went over to the ZWILLMAN Mob. As a result of this, AL CAPONE reportedly came to Newark to straighten out the differences between BOIARDO and ZWILLMAN.

If this were true, Capone would have had to have made the trip in 1930 or early 1931; otherwise, he was indisposed with his tax evasion trial or in prison. Why would Capone have been called in from Chicago when there were plenty of New York City mobsters—both Italian and Jewish—who could have arbitrated the dispute?

Boiardo was the crime boss of the First Ward, known as Newark's Little Italy. His first move on Zwillman's territory was to order a Third Ward speakeasy operator to stop purchasing his beer from Longy. The proprietor met with Zwillman and his top aide, Gerry Catena, to inform them of the muscling-in attempt.

Zwillman first confirmed that it was Boiardo and his gang who were starting trouble. This was accomplished when "Richie the Boot" came to the speakeasy and left his calling card before being ordered out by one of Longy's thugs. The next day, when the speakeasy proprietor arrived at his place of business, he found the place had been broken into and the back bar sprayed with machinegun fire.

A short while later, one of Zwillman's truck drivers was making a delivery. After stopping inside a Third Ward saloon, he heard a single gunshot, then the sound of breaking glass. Returning to the truck, he found the young man who had accompanied him dead with a bullet hole through his eye. The gunman had then blasted away at the load of bootleg hooch with a machinegun.

Bioardo's next move was to send several of his hoods to the Third Ward Political Club where they robbed a number of members. Zwillman's response to this incident was quick. Three of his top gunmen met Bioardo and his bodyguards at the corner of Broad and Market Streets in Newark. According to biographer Stuart, Bioardo's men took off, leaving their boss the recipient of eight near-fatal bullets fired by Longy's men. Incredibly, Bioardo survived and tried to wage the war from his hospital bed.

Longy's men struck again, capturing three of Bioardo's toughs in a Bloomfield Avenue eatery. Instead of killing the trio, they took them to an industrial section of the city and gave them such a severe beating with baseball bats that they were crippled for life.[7]

Bioardo's attempt at retaliation was novel. He sent two teenage gang members, disguised as call girls, to Zwillman's Riviera Hotel suite. The young men made lousy hookers and were revealed before they reached Zwillman's room. Facing two armed men, the teenagers trembled in fear. Zwillman sent the two boys back to Bioardo with a message that he wanted a meeting. Members from the two warring sides met and a truce was agreed to, bringing the brief mob war to an end.

After the March 1932 kidnapping of the son of Charles A. Lindbergh, Jr. from his Hopewell, New Jersey home, the heat was suddenly turned up on the state's bootleggers. Booze trucks were being stopped and searched by law enforcement people all over the state. Zwillman put up a $50,000 reward for information leading to the location of the baby. Other than a scam perpetrated in New York City to collect the reward, the offer was to no avail. Zwillman later told FBI agents he would have offered $100,000, which would have been raised from local bootleggers. The reward, he claimed, would have been worth it, because of the profits they were making from their illicit liquor business.

Another incident that proved Zwillman's ruthlessness during this period occurred on April 12, 1933, when Max Greenberg and Max Hassel were murdered in the Elizabeth Carteret Hotel in Elizabeth, New Jersey. The "two Maxes" were rumored to have been associates of Irving "Waxey Gordon" Wexler. Zwillman was able to develop friendships and working relationships with most of his Prohibition contemporaries, but he developed disdain for

Wexler, a South Jersey mobster. Wexler was also staying in the same hotel. Longy found out that the two were planning to kill him so he struck first. After the double-murder, Zwillman and his associates took control of their victims' liquor interests. Zwillman's participation in the murders was never proven. It was reported, however, that he had once supplied the gunmen who guarded Gordon's beer shipments.

Zwillman has been linked to Verne Miller, the infamous Midwest Crime Wave figure whose ill-fated attempt to rescue fellow bank robber, Frank "Jelly" Nash, resulted in the Kansas City Massacre. Zwillman's only connection to the outlaw, however, was through Albert Silverman, who worked for Lepke Buchalter. Silverman was said to be a "lieutenant" of Zwillman's for a short while in Newark. Zwillman's connection to this famous crime may be the reason the FBI kept records on him dating back to the mid-1930s.

When Prohibition came to an end, in December 1933, Zwillman was not only a survivor, he was a wealthy man. In 1951, Edwin A. Baldwin, a retired Treasury Department intelligence agent, testified before the Kefauver Committee regarding his investigative work of Zwillman during the Prohibition years. The agent declared that the Zwillman-Reinfeld combine took in $50 million between 1926 and 1933, describing both Waxey Gordon and Dutch Schultz as "pikers" in comparison. By the former treasury agent's estimate, the Zwillman-Reinfeld combine provided 40 percent of the uncut liquor to the United States. The money the two collected was deposited in banks throughout New Jersey and New York on accounts set up under phony names. Baldwin stated at one point they ran out of made-up names and began to take them from the telephone book. In one instance they used a Chinese name.

In reporting the agent's testimony the *New York Times* wrote:

Mr. Baldwin testified that Zwillman made frequent trips to Europe during prohibition to tap new liquor sources in Germany and in Belgium; that the stuff was landed at St. Pierre and Miquelon, a French colony off Nova Scotia, and then run to New York and New Jersey for distribution. At the same time, he said, the syndicate members were converting some of their liquor profits into gold and shipping it out of the country against the day when they might have to flee the United States.[8]

Baldwin testified that in 1931, Zwillman filed three years of delinquent tax returns. When the agent asked him why, he said Longy replied, "I saw what happened to Al Capone, and I said to myself, 'Who am I? If they can put Al Capone in jail, these fellows, they can also put me in.'"

The agent also disclosed during his 1951 testimony that after he returned to his Bureau of Internal Revenue position following military service in World War II, he learned that copies of his reports on Zwillman had been stolen. When asked by Senator Herbert R. O'Conor, "Do you think that he continued in business?" referring to Zwillman's criminal activities after Prohibition, Baldwin replied, "I don't know what he's been doing. I did hear he was trying to get away from his associates, but I've always heard, once in the mob you can't get out, because you know too much."

POLITICS

As Zwillman's underworld power grew, so did his political clout. The Third Ward Political Club in Newark served as a "hangout" for Democrats and Republicans from Essex County. Here's how Zwillman biographer Mark A. Stuart described Zwillman's role:

> Longy's reputation as the political "czar" of Newark fed off his bootlegging business. He was an easy touch for campaign funds. The state Democratic leadership grew into the habit of turning to Longy whenever it came up short. His money helped to finance statewide political campaigns from the late Twenties through the Forties.

During the 1932 election, the count in the Third Ward was 587 for Roosevelt, and every Democrat on the ballot, to 9 for Herbert Hoover and 8 for every Republican. The Republicans were used to losing in the Third Ward, but they found this lopsided margin astonishing and asked that the ballot boxes be impounded.

On November 15, 1932, the polling books from four of Newark's wards, along with the ballot boxes from three wards, were stolen. A confidential informant later told FBI agents that three city officials had met with Zwillman at the Riviera Hotel and planned the theft. Zwillman supplied the men for the job. Newark's director of public safety, William J. Egan, was responsible for the custody of the ballot boxes. The newspapers were quick to take note that Egan and Zwillman were friends. An investigation ensued and a few men were indicted, but no one was ever convicted. Egan was forced out of office in the next election, however, only to become one-third of the triumvirate to run the Essex County Democratic Party.

Egan and Zwillman were connected again in 1951. While running for a second term, Republican State Senator Alfred C. Clapp, dean of the Rutgers University School of Law, charged in his campaign speeches that Egan was linked to Zwillman. Egan responded by swearing out a complaint and having Clapp arrested on a charge of criminal libel. When the case went to the Essex County Grand Jury in November, Zwillman was called to testify. After hearing testimony for two days, including two hours from Zwillman, the panel dismissed the complaint.

In the spring of 1935, a public enemies list was complied by the Justice Department and the New York Police Department, listing the top hoodlums in the New York/New Jersey area. Zwillman was number 23. The information released with the listing stated that Zwillman was connected with the Salinsky brothers—Abe, Frank, and Ike—in the operation of a bucket shop and alcohol.[9]

Zwillman was not seen in public after the report was released, and it was alleged that he had made himself "scarce." On May 20, he sat down to answer a *Newark News* reporter's questions regarding the story. Eating breakfast at one of his favorite downtown haunts, Longy told the newspaperman that the accusations were "all wet" and compiled "using plenty of misinformation." Of the other men listed on the public enemies list, Zwillman admitted to knowing a few of them, "But I don't believe they are mixed up in any such rackets charged against them any more that I am."

The reporter asked Zwillman about his business activities in the wake of the repeal of Prohibition. Longy, in a reflective mood, responded:

Things have been somewhat upset for me in the past several years as they have been with thousands of others. I have been negotiating with several business houses and expect to make a decision on one of them soon. Things like this public enemy list and the charges that went with it don't help a fellow.[10]

The mobster denied knowing the Salinsky brothers and said he had never stepped foot inside a bucket shop. When asked about the alcohol, he claimed he had not been involved with any since the repeal of Prohibition. "So far as the bucket shopping and the like are concerned, those charges against me are almost too ridiculous to answer. But there are hundreds of men and women in Newark and vicinity who respect me, and I owe it to them, as well as myself, to say emphatically that there is not a shred of truth to any of the charges," Zwillman declared.

During the interview, Zwillman particularly wanted to address a reference to himself as the leader of the Third Ward gang:

I suppose the Third Ward gang refers to the Third Ward Political Club. In the first place, the club disbanded over two years ago. While it was going the club membership included a lot of fellows who were not exactly Sunday school boys, and it was true that some of them went haywire once in a while and got into trouble. But there was never any serious crime rightfully brought to the door of that club.

At the same time there are thousands of poor persons who have reason to remember the club, especially during the Depression winters. The good which the club did was plenty and its members never went around town carrying banners or shouting about it.[11]

Zwillman was referred to in numerous newspaper articles as a "political string puller." This power was seen by a number of political office seekers. One of the powerful people Zwillman supported was Democratic Jersey City Mayor John V. Kenny, who came to power in 1949, ending the 32-year reign of Democrat Frank Hague. Kenny was elected city commissioner, defeating Mayor Frank Hague Eggers, Hague's nephew. The Jersey City mayor was selected by a majority vote of the five city commissioners. During the election it was alleged that Zwillman contributed $100,000 to the "Freedom Ticket" campaign, which Kenny ran under.

During the gubernatorial race in the fall of 1953, Eggers lashed out at Zwillman and Kenny. In a letter to the Hudson County voters, he urged all Democrats to support the Republican candidate for governor to prevent the "Kenny Machine" from seizing control of the governor's office with the election of the Kenny-Zwillman-backed candidate. He impelled voters to support the entire Republican ticket, declaring it was "the only way to destroy the cancerous growth of the Kenny-Zwillman corrupt-gangster government and to rescue the Democratic Party from its gangster leadership."[12]

FAMILY

During the 1920s, Zwillman made his home at the Riviera, a residential hotel in downtown Newark. He provided for his widowed mother and several siblings by moving them to a new home at 120 Hansbury Avenue in the Weequahic section, a predominantly Jewish neighborhood southwest of downtown Newark.

Despite his increasing wealth, Zwillman was never flashy when it came to spending his money. He dressed conservatively, provided for family members, spoke quietly, and didn't drive new or expensive automobiles.

In June 1937, Zwillman met and fell in love with Mary DeGroot Mendels Steinbach, a 23-year-old divorcee with a young son. Longy doted on the young lady and, despite close friends trying to discourage her from continuing the relationship, Mary was completely devoted to her new love. Shortly after they announced their engagement, Mary was forced to quit her job at a women's shoe store in East Orange because too many curiosity seekers were coming in just to see the young lady who had stolen Zwillman's heart.

The two were married on July 7, 1939. The marriage was performed by the Recorder of Caldwell, New Jersey, at the Chanticler restaurant in Millburn. The guest list included a former New Jersey governor, as well as politicians and city officials from Newark and Jersey City. Although the *Newark News* reported that most of the 300 guests in attendance were "notorious racket men throughout the East," not a single name was mentioned.

Longy and Mary spent three weeks out West during a honeymoon that was said to have lasted 40 days, which included some Hollywood arrangements allegedly made by "Bugsy" Siegel. A confidential informant told FBI agents that Zwillman set up a million-dollar trust for his wife.

Their marriage would not be an easy one. In the years to come Zwillman's well-publicized involvement in the underworld and his legal problems would hurt their children. From all accounts Longy, had a warm relationship with his stepson, John. Zwillman never adopted the boy as his own, explaining to him, "If I adopt you, you'll carry my name. You'll be marked for life."[13] In 1944, Mary gave birth to a daughter they named Lynn. Her relationship with Longy was not described in glowing terms, although there is no doubt they loved each other.

During Longy's appearance before the Kefauver Committee, one panel member inquired about his children asking, "What are you raising them to be?"

Zwillman shot back, "They will never be like this!"

> "To understand me, you have to understand my past. Sure, I was a bootlegger. I didn't consider that a sin in the old days. I'd be one again, given the same setup. My father was dead. My kid brothers and sisters were hungry. There was no food in the house. We had bills to meet. In the same circumstances today, I might even do worse than sell bootleg whiskey."
> —Longy Zwillman during an interview with Helen Worden
> of the *New York World-Telegram*.
> (Mark Stuart, *Gangster #2: Longy Zwillman:
> The Man Who Invented Organized Crime*, 1985)

In the summer of 1946, the Zwillmans moved to a large estate at 50 Beverly Road in West Orange, which was said to have a purchase price of $50,000. Zwillman also maintained a summer residence in Deal, New Jersey, and at one time kept a suite at the Park Lane Hotel on Park Avenue in Manhattan. In the winter months, Longy and Mary would head for Miami for several weeks, where Zwillman was said to have an interest in a popular gambling den there called the Green Acres. It was not unusual for him to be seen in the company of other known gangsters from around the country in South Florida; they all came for the warmth and entertainment the area had to offer during the winter.

In the 1950s, as Zwillman's legal problems mounted and his face appeared on television and front-page newspaper stories, Mary stayed at home. One article claimed, "She was content to confine her social life to entertaining friends in her living room. She never went to parties and was rarely seen in public."[14] Although she longed for a European vacation, Mary conceded, "I don't want them to think Abe's running away, that's why we never leave the country." Instead, the former member of the Junior League busied herself volunteering in the "Fight for Sight League," a medical research society for the blind.

LEGITIMATE BUSINESSMAN

After the repeal of Prohibition, the former members of the Reinfeld Syndicate reformed as Browne-Vintners. The stock was listed under one nominee to avoid public disclosure of the owners. In 1940, Seagram's purchased Browne-Vintners for $7.5 million. In a court settlement two years later, Reinfeld paid the following amounts: Zwillman, $308,000; Rutkin, $250,000; and Stacher, $250,000.

In 1935, Zwillman purchased a 40 percent interest in the United States Yeast Company. According to Zwillman, the company manufactured yeast for baking only, not for producing beer. Despite pouring money into the concern, the business operated at a loss before being sold in 1947. The same was true for the United States Brewing Company. One investment, the Harr-Keg Tap beer cooler, showed early promise, but then it was revealed that the inventor of the device had infringed on another patent. Zwillman failed to show up at the hearing and lost his entire investment.

The most successful venture Zwillman muscled into was the Public Service Tobacco Company (PSTC). Al and William Lillian founded the concern when both were bootleggers along the Jersey Shore, much of their product being supplied by Zwillman. Al Lillian was killed during Prohibition and William decided to pursue a less dangerous profession. He went into the cigarette-vending machine business and founded PSTC, setting up headquarters at 1464 North Broad Street in Hillside, New Jersey.

In 1936, Zwillman decided to muscle in on the lucrative trade and held a number of discussions with Lillian. When the owner refused to sell, he was given a severe beating. He recovered and signed over ownership. Zwillman stated before the Kefauver Committee that he purchased his share from Jerry Catena and Doc Stacher; Mike Lascari, a close friend of Lucky Luciano, owned the remainder. Longy then claimed that he and Lascari were only "employees" of the firm, that actual ownership was in the names of their wives and families. Zwillman said he received one-and-a-half cents for every pack of cigarettes sold.

Under Zwillman's direction, the company was soon selling 650,000 packs of cigarettes each month from the 1,000 machines it serviced. As a businessman, Zwillman spent most of his time at PSTC, and it was the only place he could be generally contacted.

Another successful business venture began in the fall of 1949 when Zwillman acquired a General Motors franchise in Newark to sell GMC trucks. Longy's nominee in this concern was I. George Goldstein, an accountant with an alleged client list that included several gamblers. When questioned by Senate investigators, Goldstein admitted he represented Zwillman because Longy feared he wouldn't get the approval from General Motors if it knew he was involved. The city of Newark purchased more than $375,000 worth of trucks from

Zwillman, despite bids from competitors that were reported to be substantially lower. Perhaps the fact that one of Zwillman's attorneys, Charles Handler, served as corporate counsel for the city helped grease the way. Handler was the registered agent for Longy's GMC concern and resigned after the connection came to light. When made aware of Zwillman's role, Newark Mayor Ralph Villano declared the city would no longer do business with the company.

Zwillman and Mike Lascari also operated the Federal Automatic Company, which leased and installed washing machines and dryers in apartment houses for tenant use. One of the firm's largest customers was the Dryden Gardens development in East Orange, which was owned by the Prudential Insurance Company of America.

Other companies Zwillman owned an interest in included E&S Trading Company, a scrap iron and steel concern; A&S Trading Company, which purchased and resold used machinery; and the Diamond T. Parsons Service Company, an auto-collision repair business.

In October 1946, Zwillman bought 1,000 shares of common stock of the A.M. Byers Company, a Pittsburgh steel concern. Although it was reported that Longy was one of the largest individual shareholders, company officials claimed he held less than 1 percent of the outstanding stock.

The next year, Zwillman purchased bonds of the Hudson & Manhattan Railroad Company, which carried thousands of Newark commuters to and from work daily under the Hudson River. Zwillman claimed he only purchased the bonds thinking they would lead to an opportunity to place vending machines in the depots. He reported it turned out to be a "bum" investment, even though he walked away with a $1,500 profit after just 90 days of ownership.

Zwillman invested his money in other enterprises as well, including the motion picture industry[15] and hotels and real estate. He once invested $400,000 in the purchase of a U.S. Post Office site in Louisville, Kentucky. Although he later sold it at a profit, he reported it as a loss on his tax returns. One of his more notable investments was with his wife in purchasing 2 percent of the stock of Barium Steel Company, controlled by J.A. Sisto, Zwillman's longtime friend.

Most of Zwillman's investments were transacted in the names of friends and associates as nominees or "fronts," as they were known in the underworld. Many of these were under the name of attorney Arthur Garfield Hays. Another "front" was Jules Endler, a friend and business associate of Zwillman. Endler, the wealthy owner of the Novelty Bar & Grill in Newark, dabbled in motion pictures and real estate. Endler testified favorably about Longy during the Kefauver Hearings. During his testimony the committee asked him why Zwillman needed to use "fronts." Endler explained that Longy was afraid that if his participation were known, it "might injure" other investors.

From the repeal of Prohibition until the day he died, Zwillman insisted that he was a legitimate businessman. In 1939, Zwillman was subpoenaed to appear before a federal grand jury to answer questions about gambling on the East Coast and the allegations that the "Big 6" combine was harboring fugitives seeking to avoid interrogation into gambling activities. Mathias F. Correa was one of three federal prosecutors directing the inquiry. On August 14, Longy appeared with his attorney, Arthur Garfield Hays, described as the William Kunstler of his day, as a prominent civil rights advocate. The next day Zwillman kept his mouth shut and let his lawyer plead the Fifth Amendment. After a meeting in chambers with the judge, Zwillman was able to duck all the questions referring to the harboring of fugitives.

On August 21, Correa switched tactics and grilled Zwillman strictly about who his "business associates" were during his bootlegging days when he serviced northern New Jersey with illicit liquor. Attorney Hays refused to let his client answer the questions on the grounds of self-incrimination, claiming government attorneys were trying to get Longy to "talk himself into trouble."[16] This time, however, the judge ordered Zwillman to answer or face contempt charges. When Zwillman refused, the judge sentenced him to serve six months in a federal penitentiary; Correa asked for a $10,000 bond pending appeal. The ruling was eventually heard before the U.S. Circuit Court of Appeals and the sentence was reversed on January 15, 1940.

The same day that Zwillman was cited for contempt of court, Essex County Prosecutor William A. Wachenfeld spoke with FBI agents and assistant U.S. attorneys in New York City about information he had that would be of interest to the government in connection with union activities. In exchange, he said he would appreciate any information uncovered by the federal grand jury on Zwillman and Willie Moretti.

Later that year, when an Essex County grand jury was conducting an investigation into gambling, vice, and racket conditions in Newark, Prosecutor Wachenfeld, who was directing the grand jury, advised the FBI that the panel members had requested any and all information the bureau might have that could be instrumental to their investigation. In a memo from Hoover, the FBI director told the special agent-in-charge of the Trenton office to inform Wachenfeld that the only information the bureau possessed was subject matter in a current investigation and could not be turned over.

Although Hoover was notorious for squirreling away information and refusing to share it with other law enforcement agencies, there was also the belief that there was too much corruption in city and county government in Newark and Essex County to risk revealing what information the bureau had acquired. Also, Wachenfeld was once an attorney for Zwillman before his appointment as county prosecutor, a decision that no doubt met with Longy's approval.

ON THE KEFAUVER HOT SEAT

In early March 1951, the crime crusade of Senator Estes Kefauver came knocking on Zwillman's door only to find him not home. Kefauver told reporters that they had been searching for Longy "day and night," and that he had successfully ducked Senate subpoena servers.

On March 22, he allowed himself to be served in the office of Arthur Garfield Hays on Broadway in Manhattan. His late acceptance of the subpoena may have coincided with the fact that the committee's investigation was winding down and would have limited time for a thorough examination. But what also may have drawn Zwillman out were accusations, made during the recent testimony of Ambassador and former New York City Mayor William O'Dwyer and former New York City Deputy Police Commissioner Frank Bals, that Zwillman was one of the "king pins" of Murder, Inc. (see Appendix). When Zwillman was questioned in Hays' office, he said he wanted to deny "the stinking story."

While being interviewed, Zwillman was asked about Kefauver's statement about his "ducking" the senators. Longy answered that he had been led to believe the government probers were not interested in questioning him. He refused to say where he had been for the past few weeks, but stated, "My family's had enough publicity in the past."

The subpoena called for him to testify on Saturday morning, March 23, in Washington D.C. On Friday, Zwillman checked himself into the emergency ward at Beth Israel Hospital in Newark, suffering from a kidney ailment. There was a rumor that Longy had "spurned" advice to have kidney surgery to alleviate the problem.

Angered by the sudden hospitalization, Senator Charles Tobey lashed out at Zwillman through the press:

> I find it difficult to understand why a man who claims he is so honest, clean and above-board took a couple of weeks to find.
>
> I have heard that Zwillman has constantly complained that he has been wronged by this committee. When he had his chance to step forward and say something in his defense, he was nowhere to be found. Is that the way to prove your innocence? Is that the way to defend your good name?
>
> If someone said anything against me, I'm sure I'd find the simplest way to clear myself—a straightforward desire to have myself heard. This person has had his chance all along—and when we needed him, we couldn't even find him.[17]

Kefauver sidestepped the issue of the hospitalized witness by stating they were postponing his testimony because of the absence of Chief Counsel Rudolph Halley, who had returned to New York to draft the "voluminous report" on the committee's year-to-date findings. In the meantime, Zwillman's appearance was rescheduled.

On the night of Monday, March 26—a dubious date in the history of the proceedings—Zwillman appeared before the committee on national television. It was on this night that Cleveland Syndicate stalwarts Morris Kleinman and Louis Rothkopf, following Zwillman to the stand, showed their disdain of the publicity and responded in a novel way. After reading a statement that the presence of cameras in the courtroom violated their constitutional rights, both men clammed up and "refused even to refuse" to answer questions from committee members. Disgusted at the turn of events, Kefauver had the two arrested and escorted out of the courtroom by the sergeant-at-arms of the Senate.

Zwillman's answers to the Senate investigators were not much better. Time and again, he contended he would be risking prosecution by the Internal Revenue Service if he discussed matters regarding the money he made and the people he made it with. All of the committee's questions about his financial matters were parried with, "I decline to answer that on the ground that it would incriminate me."

The most intriguing exchange came when Longy was asked about "frequent telephone calls" made from his vending machine business office to former New Jersey Governor Harold G. Hoffman. Zwillman claimed the calls were made by Joseph Rosenbaum, a lawyer who handled his business affairs. When told that some of the calls had originated from his home, Zwillman insisted that they regarded "Social Security matters." The political connection, Zwillman insisted, emanated from his 10-year leadership of the Third Ward Political Club of Newark.

One of the most memorable points of the questioning came when Senator Tobey asked Zwillman, "Is it true that you have been known in New Jersey as the 'Al Capone' of New Jersey? You needn't be modest about that."

Zwillman responded:

> That is a matter that has been developing, Mr. Senator, for a good many years and during the time I should have had sense enough to stop it and get out of the state. I didn't have the

sense until it blossomed until I am here today. In my opinion I don't belong here today. I am trying to make a living for my family and myself. Those rumors get around. I walk into a restaurant and I own the restaurant; I walk into a hotel and I own the hotel; I take a shoe shine and I own the bootblack.

Zwillman received a chuckle from panel members when asked if he knew Virginia Hill, the former paramour of Bugsy Siegel. Longy said he didn't realize that he knew her until she admitted to knowing him during her televised testimony. "From seeing her on television, she didn't look too hard to know," he quipped.

When given the "who do you know" routine by the panel, Zwillman acknowledged being acquainted with Joe Adonis, Meyer Lansky, and Willie Moretti—but he never had any business dealings with them. He admitted to having lunch "occasionally" at Duke's Restaurant in Cliffside Park, New Jersey. As for gambling in Essex County, Longy had not been involved in anything in the past 20 years.

Many believed that Zwillman ruled the northern New Jersey underworld during the two decades since Prohibition ended. He therefore must have had substantial involvement in the area's gambling activities. Zwillman did his best to answer honestly many of the questions put to him by committee members, even admitting to being a major bootlegger, as well as being acquainted with many of the top underworld figures of that era. So it is interesting to note the following exchange:

Q: Have you any interest whatever in any gambling establishments?

A: Under oath I am saying no.

Q: Have you had any?

A: In twenty years: no!

The fireworks that the media promised would happen regarding his political connections during his testimony never transpired. One unnamed investigator had predicted that there would be "red faces from Sussex County to Atlantic City" by the time the committee was through with Zwillman. As far as the allegations of Zwillman's role in Murder, Inc., the issue was never discussed during questioning.

Zwillman's testimony drew an immediate response from former Governor Hoffman. Now executive director of the New Jersey State Unemployment Compensation Committee, he issued a statement in an effort to show distance from the gangster during his years as the state's chief executive, 1935 through 1938. Hoffman said he asked for Zwillman's support from the Third Ward Political Club in 1946 while seeking the Republican nomination for a second term as governor. He concluded that Zwillman's influence was ineffective, as he lost the election after an unimpressive showing in Newark.

A key part of Zwillman's testimony came when he denied he was involved in New Jersey state politics and that he had never made any large campaign contributions. Longy told the Senate panel, "Between you and me, if I support somebody they lose." These statements would lead to a recalling of Zwillman for further questioning.

With the Kefauver Committee investigation scheduled to close on March 31, the members had little time to scour Zwillman's testimony to determine if a contempt of Senate citation should be issued to him. This alone was believed to be the reason Zwillman was off the hook for too many recitings of his Fifth Amendment rights. Although Zwillman was not charged, the government was not through with him.

THE SENATE CALLS AGAIN

During the spring of 1951, Senator Kefauver withdrew as chairman of the crime investigating body and was replaced by Democratic Maryland Senator Herbert O'Conor. Now known simply as the Senate Crime Committee, the new panel was holding its last public hearing on August 16, 1951, in Washington D.C. The Senators wanted to question Zwillman more and his lawyers were advised in July that he was to be present. When he suddenly disappeared, the conclusion drawn by committee members was that Zwillman had reason to hide.

The newspapers claimed Zwillman was ducking the Senate probe by disguising himself as a fisherman, adopting an alias, and sailing with a New England fishing fleet outside territorial waters off Boston to avoid being served with another subpoena. Morris Shilensky, one of Zwillman's high-priced mouthpieces, called the allegations outrageous and claimed that Longy had simply gone on a fishing trip. "He just doesn't know anything about the hunt for him," Shilensky stated. "If they know where Zwillman is and can communicate with him, it would not be necessary to serve him with a subpoena because he is not dodging anything."

Joining Justice Department officials in the hunt for Zwillman was the FBI, which wanted to keeps its efforts undercover. An interoffice memo dated August 10 stated, "The Newark Division is continuing to make very discreet inquiries as to Zwillman's whereabouts, but is being careful not to give anyone the impression that an FBI investigation is being conducted." The reason for the cloak and dagger approach was never revealed.

As the time drew closer to the Washington hearings, the search for Zwillman intensified. Richard G. Moser, the new chief counsel for the Senate Crime Committee, urged that a nationwide crime alert be issued for Zwillman. In his statement, Moser declared, "This former big-time bootlegger is believed to be bigger than Costello, but so far has been more successful in avoiding the public spotlight." Chairman O'Conor released a statement that he would seek a senatorial warrant for the arrest of Zwillman, Jerry Catena, and Doc Stacher, the latter two also avoiding being served with subpoenas.

The Coast Guard was tracking a yacht named *Howdy Podner*. The boat was registered out of Fort Lauderdale in the name of M. B. D'Alitz of Detroit. Authorities quickly assumed it belonged to former Cleveland Syndicate leader Morris B. "Moe" Dalitz. The yacht was discovered docked at Block Island, Rhode Island. When questioned, those on board readily admitted that Zwillman had been a passenger when the craft left Boston on Thursday, August 9, but he was dropped off at Marblehead on Friday evening. Two Marblehead harbor patrolmen claimed Zwillman was there Saturday night. They saw and recognized him from newspaper photographs. They didn't say why they had failed to seize him or at least notify authorities. Another report claimed he had been spotted in Chelsea, outside of Boston the next day. On Monday it was reported Zwillman boarded a new yacht, the *Duke,* in Sea Bright, New Jersey, and that the Coast Guard was involved in a search for the craft from the south New Jersey coast up to the Canadian border.

When a *Newark Star-Ledger* reporter contacted Willie Moretti for a comment about his old friend's flight, the mobster replied that Zwillman went on a fishing trip to Canada. Taking full credit for Zwillman's absence, Moretti disclosed, "Longy called me three weeks ago and told me he was going on vacation, and I said, 'Why don't you go on a fishing trip without a radio?'" When asked about the statement that Zwillman was bigger than Frank Costello, the diplomatic Moretti responded, "None of them are bigger than anyone else. We're all equal."[18]

On the eve of the new chapter of the Senate Crime Committee hearings, Zwillman still was nowhere to be found. Chief Counsel Moser said the first day of testimony would focus on underworld ties to politicians in New York City. The millions who had enjoyed the popular airing of the Kefauver hearings were disappointed to find out the new sessions would not be televised. No explanation was given for this decision.

Senator O'Conor had not gone before the Senate to request warrants for Zwillman and his missing associates. Speculation was that he would step out of the committee hearings to take the Senate floor and make the request. If granted, which required unanimous consent of the Senate, the FBI would be called in on the manhunt. In the end, the committee decided not to seek a warrant vote, Moser stating, "The warrant papers are prepared, but the Senate's calendar is so heavy we don't know if the matter even will come up."

The committee called James A. Bishop, a onetime employee of the *Newark Star Ledger*. Bishop related an incident involving George Kesselhaut, the assistant to the Essex County Democratic Chairman, in which Zwillman offered to make a political donation of $300,000 to the party's candidate for governor in 1949, New Jersey State Senator Elmer H. Wene, a former congressman, in exchange for being allowed to select the state's new attorney general. Bishop, who at the time was handling Wene's political campaign, said he was asked by Kesselhaut to take the offer to the candidate. Bishop told the committee he met with Wene over breakfast one morning in Newark's Essex House. After telling him Zwillman wanted to contribute $300,000 to his campaign, Wene interrupted to reply, "I don't want to have anything to do with it. Let's get out of this county. I don't want to hear the rest of it."

By this late stage of the committee hearings, with the leadership mantel having passed from Kefauver to O'Conor, key staff members, such as Rudolph Halley and Joseph Nellis, had resigned and been replaced by younger less experienced investigators. This led to a number of mistakes, causing the senators some embarrassment. Author William H. Moore, in his recap of the famous hearings, *The Kefauver Committee and the Politics of Crime 1950–1952*, related, "In its final stages the Committee failed to develop sufficient background information prior to hearings and therefore suffered further humiliation."[19]

One of the most glaring examples of this failure occurred on August 17, when Hugh J. Strong was questioned. Strong was a former Newark police officer, who at the time of the hearings was the mayor of Kennilow Borough, a suburb of Newark. Strong expressed a dislike of Zwillman and claimed that the mobster's alleged influence over the Third Ward voting bloc was simply a reflection of his Jewish heritage, not his personal influence.

It was when Strong denied a personal relationship with Zwillman that Chief Counsel Moser was ready to strike. Moser produced telephone company records showing several calls between the Zwillman and Strong residences. "You say you haven't talked to Zwillman in years," Moser inquired. "Telephone company records show calls from the Zwillman home to your home on May 5, May 12, May 15, and June 8, 1946. Can you explain those?"

Moser seemed pleased with himself, sporting the expression of a man who just caught another in an obvious lie. The courtroom grew tense as Moser awaited the reply.

"I was in the dog business," Strong shot back. "I had a kennel, Mary Mendels [Longy's wife] had asked me to sell her a dog. I'd known her ten years before I knew Zwillman. She asked me by telephone how she could housebreak the dog."[20]

After the laughter in the courtroom subsided, Strong received permission to read a prepared statement. He asked the committee "to give him a clean bill of health so that neighbors would understand he was in no way involved with the underworld figures mentioned in the hearing."[21] The committee complied.

On September 8, after nearly a 60-day period when he was not heard from, Zwillman telephoned the *Newark Star-Ledger* to announce his return. During the brief conversation, he was asked about the $300,000 campaign offer to Wene. Zwillman denied the accusation by stating he would not dignify the question with an answer. He ended his conversation by telling the reporter he was leaving town on a 10-day business trip.

Just three days after Zwillman's return, Frank Hague, who had recently been deposed as the state boss of the Democratic Party, claimed Longy was the "czar" of Democratic politics in New Jersey:

> It is regrettable that the Democratic party has come under the control of gangster and rack-eteer leadership and that several of our city governments in New Jersey are completely under [Longy's] domination.[22]

In a rambling four-page statement, the 75-year-old former mayor of Jersey City, who left a legacy of corrupt machine politics, declared Zwillman "is the boss, the king." In response to the self-serving statement, many prominent Democrats around the state denounced Hague.

TAX TRIAL

Twenty years after the conviction of Al Capone, the government's best weapon against organized crime figures was still going after them for income tax evasion. In the wake of the Kefauver investigation, IRS agents were said to have targeted 400 underworld figures in the New York/New Jersey area to investigate their past due income taxes.

Zwillman's "ducking" of the August 1951 session of the Senate Crime Committee hearings may have saved him some embarrassment, but it didn't keep him out of the government's crosshairs for long. On June 25, 1952, the largest tax lien ever filed against an individual in New Jersey, $728,956, was lodged against Longy. The filing followed a federal grand jury investigation and covered the years 1943 to 1946. The amount included penalties and interest, which accounted for nearly 50 percent of the total. Additional liens were filed for securities transferred by Zwillman to the tune of $210,515. These transfers included assets to Zwillman's wife, daughter, stepson, and father-in-law. The liens were filed to freeze Zwillman's assets until tax claims could be fully investigated. Levies for overdue assessments were filed with banks, brokerage firms, and corporations in which Zwillman had funds or an interest.[23]

On September 12, Zwillman delivered a check for $118,000 to lift liens against his wife and children. Two months later, after the IRS determined that Zwillman owed $276,280 in back taxes for the years 1933 to 1939 and 1942 to 1946, an appeal was filed by attorney Samuel I. Kessler. It would take months for the government to complete its investigation.

On June 18, 1953, a criminal complaint against Zwillman was filed, charging him with evading $55,114 in income taxes for a single year, 1946. The paperwork was completed just hours before the six-year statute of limitations was due to expire on the matter. The complaint charged that Zwillman should have paid taxes of $74,782 on income of $114,306 that year, but instead paid $19,668. Four days later, Zwillman surrendered to government agents and was arraigned and released on a $3,000 bond with a vow from his attorney that the complaint would be dismissed by the grand jury. It was—23 days later.

In March 1954, Zwillman received considerable publicity after it was announced he was heading a group of local businessmen in putting up $250,000 for redevelopment in Newark's slum section. Within weeks, another federal grand jury was investigating him for income tax fraud.

On April 1, 1954, a federal grand jury in Newark began hearing testimony from 30 witnesses as the government began to build a tax case against Longy. Many of the witnesses, officials called from churches, hospitals, and schools concerning tax-deductible donations, were questioned about Zwillman's "charitable contributions."

One result of the grand jury investigation was a federal inquiry into the election of Jersey City "Freedom Ticket" candidate John V. Kenny in 1949. It was alleged that a $100,000 contribution made by Zwillman led to Kenny's selection.

On May 26, after nine weeks of hearing testimony from 325 witnesses, including a number of politicians, the grand jury charged Zwillman in a two-count indictment with income tax evasion for the years 1947 and 1948, stating he had "willfully evaded" $46,100 in taxes. A federal judge issued a bench warrant for his arrest, after which his attorney, Samuel I. Kessler, announced he would surrender his client the next day. Two days later Zwillman pleaded not guilty and, after posting a $5,000 bond, was released.

Zwillman's longtime friend and business associate Jules Endler, who had given supportive testimony about Zwillman during the Kefauver Hearings, was to be a key defense witness in Zwillman's trial. In September 1954, Endler gave a deposition to Zwillman's attorneys. Government investigators, sensing that it conflicted with statements he made during prior testimony, served him with a subpoena on September 22, ordering him to produce records related to the deposition. He was told he could face a federal perjury indictment if he didn't cooperate. Later that day, Endler suffered a stroke and died at Doctor's Hospital in Manhattan at the age of 59.

The federal tax evasion trial of Zwillman was scheduled to begin on February 15, 1955. The date was pushed back, however, because Albert Anastasia's November 1954 federal tax trial ended in a hung jury and was rescheduled for the spring. Additional delays ensued and Zwillman's trial did not commence until January 1956; by this time the tax burden has been reduced to $38,911. On February 27, the prosecution rested its case and the defense asked the judge for a directed verdict of acquittal. The judge denied the request, stating that the government, which sought to prove that Longy had spent in excess of $90,000 for the two years without showing income, had presented sufficient evidence.

After hearing closing statements, the jury of six men and six women received the case on February 29. The panel deliberated 26 hours straight without meals or sleep before informing the judge that they could not reach a decision on either count. Zwillman was released on a $5,000 bond while the government considered whether or not to retry the case. Following an FBI inquiry on December 20, 1957, almost two years after the mistrial, a U.S. attorney advised the bureau that a decision had yet to be made.

SUICIDE AT 50 BEVERLY ROAD

The hung jury that ended Zwillman's tax trial would have been a blessing to the North Jersey mobster if he hadn't made the mistake of trying to buy off a couple of the jurors. The government refused to drop its case against Zwillman, and soon details came out about jury tampering. Still, nearly three years would pass before anyone was indicted.

In early 1958, another government crime committee was making news in America. This time it was the Select Committee on Improper Activities in the Labor or Management Field, known as the both the McClellan Committee and the "Rackets" Committee. One of the areas the committee was investigating was the vending machine industry, and investigators were interested in discussing the Public Service Tobacco Company with Zwillman. Whereas the Kefauver Committee's bulldog counsel was Rudolph Halley, Zwillman would now have to face an even more aggressive attorney this time in Robert F. Kennedy.

The government's investigators had been looking into Zwillman's holdings and activities for nearly a year-and-a-half. The entire year of 1958 went by without Zwillman being called to appear. As 1959 began, word came down that Zwillman would have to come to Washington D.C. to testify sometime during the late spring.

By mid-February, Zwillman was faced with both the McClellan Committee hearings and a new grand jury investigation into the bribing of jurors during his tax trial. Moreover, he was still under indictment on the tax evasion charges. In addition to his legal dilemmas, Zwillman was having health problems and was seeing a heart specialist.

Depressed and despondent, the 54-year-old Zwillman was in a desperate state on Wednesday night, February 25, 1959. While dining out that night, Zwillman was described as "unusually quiet" by his dinner companions, which consisted of his wife Mary, sister Ethel, and a married couple who were close friends of the family. Zwillman and Mary arrived home around 10:00 PM. After Mary mentioned that she had not been sleeping well, her husband suggested that she take a sedative.

Around 3:00 the next morning, Mary awoke to find her husband pacing about in the bedroom, complaining of chest pains. After assuring her it was nothing serious, she went back to sleep. Mary awoke again at 7:00 AM to find Zwillman gone. She assumed he had gone to his office at the Public Service Tobacco Company. Later that morning, she descended the cellar stairs to retrieve tissues from a storeroom. In the game room she spotted a bottle of whiskey and a glass. After opening the door to the storeroom, Mary was confronted with the horrific sight of her dead husband, in a kneeling position, hanging from a makeshift noose. Mary's screams of anguish brought her elder father and the family chauffeur on the run.

A doctor was summoned, who quickly pronounced Zwillman dead. An ensuing autopsy revealed Zwillman suffered from high blood pressure, heart trouble, and kidney disease. The medical report indicated that Zwillman's heart was more than a third its normal size. Dr. Edwin H. Albano, the Essex County medical examiner, ruled that Zwillman's death was a suicide brought on by "temporary insanity." Family members claimed that he did it to shield his wife and family from the pending embarrassment of his legal problems.

On Thursday night, a service was held for Zwillman at the funeral chapel of Philip Apter & Sons. The 350-seat chapel was filled to capacity, as an estimated 2,000 to 2,500 mourners passed by the casket despite pleas from the family for privacy. The next day a simple 15-minute service was conducted by a rabbi from Temple B'nai Abraham of Newark. The service was attended by Zwillman's 80-year-old mother, as well as his brothers and sisters. If any of his old underworld associates were in attendance, the newspapers didn't mention them. After the short service a funeral cortege consisting of 75 automobiles, including three limousines carrying family members, made its way to B'nai Abraham Memorial Cemetery in Union, New Jersey, for the burial.

To this day rumors persist alleging that Zwillman's death was not a suicide, but a well-orchestrated Mafia execution. Reasons given for the killing were that Zwillman had not supported Vito Genovese with his coup d'état to remove Frank Costello and Albert Anastasia. Another rumor held that Zwillman was too old to take the pressure of another investigation and would turn informer to avoid prison. This latter theory didn't hold much weight considering that underworld leaders older than Zwillman were also being investigated. Part of the theory was that his killers allowed him to dull his senses with his favorite whiskey before helping him to his death. This rumor was quashed by the toxicologist's report, which revealed that in addition to no sedatives being found in Zwillman's system, there was "just a trace of alcohol."

It's ridiculous to think that Mafia hitmen would enter the Zwillman home after 3:00 o'clock in the morning to hold a discussion with the distressed mob boss about how better off everyone would be if he let them make his murder appear to be a suicide. If Genovese had wanted Zwillman dead, he would have had him shot in the head just as he did with Anastasia and as he tried to do with Costello.

One Mafia historian wrote, "Zwillman was killed, but with a measure of respect," they allowed it to look as if he took his own life. This same historian claimed of the murder of Willie Moretti, "Willie had been shot up front [in the face], supposedly a mark of 'respect' accorded to bosses. They had a right to see what was happening."

So much for respect—Mafia style!

NOTES

1. Some sources list Zwillman's year of birth as 1899.

2. Zwillman's brothers were Lawrence, Irving, and Barney; his sisters were Ethel, Phoebe, and Bessie. According to biographer Mark A. Stuart, his parent's names were Avraham and Anna, but FBI files list his parents as Rubin and Ella.

3. Zwillman's nickname was often spelled "Longie."

4. Mark A. Stuart, *Gangster #2: Longy Zwillman, The Man Who Invented Organized Crime* (Secaucus, NJ: Lyle Stuart, 1985), p. 22.

5. Ibid., p. 23.

6. Ibid., p. 41.

7. *New York Times*, August 17, 1951, "Zwillman Sought to Buy Prosecutor, Witness Declares."

8. Stuart, *Gangster #2: Longy Zwillman, The Man Who Invented Organized Crime*, p. 62.

9. Bucket shops were fraudulent brokerage firms, also known as boiler rooms. At a time before instant price quotes, an unscrupulous broker would make trades, offering the client a certain price. The broker would then place the ticket in a bucket. If a better price came along before the end of the trading day, the broker would make the trade and pocket the difference.

10. *Newark News*, May 21, 1935, "Charges Held False by Longie."

11. *Newark News*, May 21, 1935, "Charges Held False by Longie."

12. *New York Times*, October 22, 1953 "Eggers for Troast in Jersey Party Bolt."

13. Stuart, *Gangster #2: Longy Zwillman, The Man Who Invented Organized Crime*, p. 122.

14. *Newark Star-Ledger*, February 27, 1959, "Roses for Abe . . . with love, Mary."

15. Zwillman's involvement in Hollywood included an interest in the following film production companies:

- **Manhattan Productions, Inc.,** which produced *It's in the Bag!* (1945) starring Fred Allen, Jack Benny, William Bendix, John Carradine, and Jerry Colonna with cameo appearances by Don Ameche and Rudy Vallee.

- **Greentree Productions,** which produced *Guest Wife* (1945) starring Claudette Colbert and Don Ameche. The film was nominated for an Academy Award for Best Music Scoring of a Dramatic or Comedy Picture.

It was reported during the Kefauver Hearings that none of the actors knew the identities of the investors.

In addition, Zwillman's name came up during the infamous "Hollywood Extortion" case in which several Chicago mobsters, including Paul "the waiter: Ricca, Louis "Little New York" Campagna, and Charles "Cheery Nose" Gioe, were convicted of shaking down Hollywood film moguls. Louis Kaufman, a New Jersey business agent of the International Alliance of Theatrical Stage Employees (IATSE) one of seven convicted, was alleged to be under the control of Zwillman. Despite the allegations that Zwillman was never charged with any wrongdoing. Zwillman's brothers, Lawrence and Irving, were operators and members of Local 244 of IATSE.

16. *New York Times,* August 22, 1939, "Guilty of Contempt of Crime Inquiry."

17. *Newark Star-Ledger,* March 24, 1951, "Zwillman Reported Ill, Had Hospital Checkup; He'll Testify Next Week."

18. *Newark Star-Ledger,* August 14, 1951, "Longie Hunt Shifts Back to N.J. Coast."

19. William H. Moore, *The Kefauver Committee and the Politics of Crime 1950–1952* (Columbia, MO: University of Missouri Press, 1974), p. 221.

20. *New York Times,* August 18, 1951, "Senate Crime Body Ends Its Hearings."

21. Ibid.

22. *New York Times,* September 12, 1951, "Hague Denounces Zwillman As Czar."

23. *New York Times,* June 26, 1952, "$728,956 Lien Filed Against Zwillman."

BIBLIOGRAPHY

Biography of Zwillman

Stuart, Mark A. *Gangster #2: Longy Zwillman: The Man Who Invented Organized Crime*. Secaucus, NJ: Lyle Stuart, 1985.

Other Publications

Katz, Leonard. *Uncle Frank*. New York: Drake Publishers, 1973.

Lacey, Robert. *Little Man: Meyer Lansky and the Gangster Life*. London: Little, Brown and Company, 1991.

Moore, William Howard. *The Kefauver Committee and the Politics of Crime 1950–1952*. Columbia: University of Missouri Press, 1974.

Peterson, Virgil W. *The Mob: 200 Years of Organized Crime in New York*. Ottawa, IL: Green Hill Publishers, 1983.

BIOGRAPHIES OF OTHER PROMINENT FIGURES MENTIONED IN THE TEXT

JOHN HARLAN AMEN (1898–1960)

One of America's forgotten racket busters, Amen was born in Exeter, New Hampshire, and attended Phillips Exeter Academy, where his father was once the headmaster. After graduating from Princeton in 1919, he enrolled at Harvard Law School, where he earned his law degree in 1922.

Amen was part of a private practice for five years. In 1928, he was appointed special assistant to U.S. Attorney General Homer S. Cummings to handle antitrust violations. Amen began to specialize in using the antitrust statutes against industrial racketeers. At one point, he had successfully prosecuted 13 of 14 cases in such diverse fields as artichokes, furs, fish, and trucking. Between 1935 and 1938, Amen won nearly 200 convictions. The only reversal of these convictions was Louis Buchalter, whose conviction was overturned by U.S. Judge Martin Manton. The justice was later indicted for accepting bribes while on the bench. He became the first federal judge convicted of accepting bribes and was sent to prison.

In 1938, New York Governor Herbert H. Lehman named Amen to supersede Brooklyn District Attorney William F. X. Geoghan to investigate official corruption in that borough. The probe lasted four years, during which time Amen was appointed in 1940 to special assistant state attorney general to increase the scope of his investigation.

When Amen's final report was filed in December 1942, his work was called the "country's longest and most sweeping study of municipal misconduct." Incredibly, the lengthy probe made money. The cost of the investigation, which ran from October 30, 1938, through November 30, 1942, was $1,147,000. In the end, federal, state, and city fines, penalties, and restitution recovered $2,077,000.

A trademark of Amen's court appearances was a white carnation that he wore as a good luck charm. A neighborhood florist delivered the flower to his home every morning. Amen never explained the significance of this practice.

During World War I, Amen served as a second lieutenant in the U.S. Marine Corps. He was a full colonel in the army during World War II. After the war, he served as associate trial counsel for the United States during the Nuremberg Trials.

From 1946 to 1953, Amen served as a member of the Federal Loyalty Review Board under the Truman Administration. Amen then returned to private law practice. He never ran for public office.

Amen was married to Marion Cleveland, the daughter of President Grover Cleveland. He died on March 10, 1960, at the age of 61. Attending the funeral were former judges John McCrate and John C. Knox.

WILLIAM V. DWYER (1883-1946)

Dwyer was born in the Hell's Kitchen section of New York City on February 23, 1883. Little is known of Dwyer's life before he amassed his rum-running empire beginning in 1922. Before going to prison in 1927, Dwyer cried poverty, claiming he was broke and more than $150,000 in debt, but Dwyer had made some wise sports investments.

In the early 1920s, the popularity of professional ice hockey in Canada began to spill over into the United States. In 1923, Thomas Duggan, a sports promoter, had options on three National Hockey League franchises. One was sold to Charles Adams, a Boston grocery store magnate; a second franchise was made available to Tex Rickard to play in "the third edition" of Madison Square Garden, when it was completed in 1925 (the last franchise ended up in Philadelphia).

Duggan and Dwyer began their ownership of the New York Americans, which began play during the 1925–1926 season. The team began with former players from the Hamilton (Ontario) Tigers when that franchise was suspended from the league after a player strike. Although the Americans were a mediocre team for the most part (they made the playoffs only twice during Dwyer's 11-year ownership), Dwyer retained the team through the 1935–1936 season.

In 1931, Dwyer and fellow Manhattan "sportsman" William Gallagher opened Tropical Park, a horseracing track, in Dade County, Florida. The new facility would be in direct competition with the nearby Hialeah track. Dwyer also served as head of the Gables Racing Association.

In 1934, the federal government claimed that Dwyer owed more than $4.3 million in back taxes dating back to 1922. The government's case wallowed in the courts until 1939. On May 25, the government presented its case during a 10-minute trial, which Dwyer did not attend and his attorney offered no defense. The prosecution claimed Dwyer had banked more than $6.5 million and had never "paid a penny of income tax." A federal judge, hearing the case without a jury in Brooklyn federal court, awarded a judgment of $3.7 million to the government.

Dwyer was said to be "penniless" when he died on December 10, 1946, at the age of 63, at his Belle Harbor, Queens, home.

GIUSEPPE "JOSEPH" FLORINO (1895-1964)

Florino was a gunman connected to the Brooklyn underworld and a close friend and associate of Albert Anastasia. He earned the reputation of being an expert with a rifle, not the first weapon of choice for a gangster. Florino and Anastasia spent several months together on Sing Sing's death row during 1921–1922 for the murder of George Terillo. The murder conviction was reversed and the charges dismissed at a second trial in 1922.

Florino's police record shows four arrests for assault and robbery from 1918 to 1921, all of which were discharged by the court. Just a few months after Florino and Anastasia's release from the Terillo murder, they were arrested again for the murder of a Red Hook grocer, only to have the charges dismissed. Florino was arrested twice in 1923. The first time was for assault and the second time was for possession of a concealed weapon. The charges for the first crime were dismissed, but Florino served a prison term on the weapons charge.

In early 1928, Florino was arrested for felonious assault after trying to kill a woman. The victim in this attack was Margaret Farrara Vicce, now Margaret Melichi, whose testimony almost landed Florino and Anastasia in the electric chair. Florino had allegedly found out that she was living in New Haven, Connecticut, and went there and slashed her throat. She survived the attack, but the charges against Florino were dismissed on March 23.

After the murder of Frankie Yale on July 1, 1928, two suspects the police wanted to question were Giuseppe "The Clutching Hand" Piraino (not to be confused with Giuseppe "The Clutching Hand" Morello) and Florino, both said to be associates of the Brooklyn mob boss. Piraino was found, questioned, and released. On July 11, Florino was arrested while in a taxicab in Brooklyn and charged with violation of the Sullivan Law, carrying a concealed weapon, his second violation. In the courtroom of New York Supreme Court Justice Selah Strong on August 5, attorney Samuel Leibowitz produced a gun permit signed by Columbia County Judge William Tracey. An infuriated Judge Strong had no choice but to release the defendant.

During the late 1920s and early 1930s, Florino was closely associated with Brooklyn crime bosses Joe Adonis, Albert Anastasia, Anthony Carfano, and the Mangano brothers. In early March 1930, the group found itself dealing with the "poaching" of Giuseppe Piraino, who was allegedly trying to sell his alcohol in the territory of the South Brooklyn gang. On March 27, Piraino attended a "conference" at which he agreed not to go out of his territory again, but he refused to surrender any of the profits he had made during his encroachment.

A short time after the meeting, Piraino was gunned down on Sackett Street by a sniper who put three bullets into his heart "within a space that could be covered by a half-dollar." While police were combing the street for evidence, Florino showed up and was questioned. They decided to search his apartment at 151 Sackett Street and discovered two shotguns and a quantity of ammunition. Florino produced a hunting license, but police took him to the Butler Street Station and arrested him for murder. Charges against Florino were soon dropped for lack of evidence. Piraino was buried "with the gaudy pomp which has become traditional for gang chieftains." On October 6, 1930, less than seven months after his father's murder, 23-year-old Carmine Piraino was gunned down on 85th Street, in the Bath Beach section of Brooklyn.

When Anastasia was arrested for the murder of John Bazzano in August 1932, his address was also given as 151 Sackett Street. It was unclear if the men were roommates or just happened to live in the same apartment building.

In 1940, Florino went into hiding after Abe Reles began talking to the Brooklyn district attorney's office. One story had him going with Murder, Inc. gunman Vito Gurino to Arizona for treatment of a lung ailment. Whatever the case, he was not a factor in the Brooklyn underworld again. Florino died in New Jersey in November 1964 at age 69.

HARRY "BIG GREENIE" GREENBERG (1891–1939)

Harry Greenberg was the alias of Harry Gottesman. The story goes that Gottesman jumped a Polish freighter and entered the United States illegally during the first decade of the 20th century. He changed his name to Harry Greenberg, from which associates arrived at the nickname "Big Greenie," taking Gottesman's size into consideration. Greenberg didn't become a model U.S. citizen. Instead, his record of 12 arrests, which began in 1911, included three terms in Sing Sing for burglary and arrests ranging from grand larceny to disorderly conduct, one of which netted him a stretch in Elmira. Along the way immigration officials caught up with him and on May 29, 1926, he was deported back to Poland, only to return a short while later to resume his criminal career.

By the late 1920s, he had become one of the chief lieutenants of Louis Buchalter and Jacob Shapiro, specializing in applying muscle where needed. His most famous exploit was organizing the brazen daylight attack on the Needle Trades Workers' Industrial Union headquarters in April 1933 (see Chapter 3). Later that year he was indicted in a massive federal indictment of the rabbit fur industry along with Buchalter and Shapiro.

Sometime during the early 1930s, Greenberg met Ida Schacter. The two were married in Paris, France; it was her second marriage. In addition to his employment with the "Gorilla Boys," Lepke and Gurrah, Greenberg operated a trucking business in New York City and ran a dress manufacturing concern, where he employed Allie Tannenbaum as a security guard. One could question whether Greenberg had the mental capacity to operate these on his own, as opposed to serving as a front Buchalter and Shapiro. Greenberg never had the reputation of being more than just muscle for hire, this being apparent when he was arrested during a fur manufacturers' strike in 1935. Greenberg was turned back over to immigration officials and redeported to Poland.

While Greenberg was plotting his return to the United States, Ida was left to run his business interests in New York. From this point, the timeframe of Greenberg's movements are unclear. It is believed he took the name of Ida's ex-husband, George Schacter, and, using the passport of the man's deceased father, entered Canada, settling in Montreal. He sold his trucking concern to a business partner and during the spring of 1939, Greenberg was beginning to run low on funds. It was during this time that Thomas E. Dewey and Buchalter found themselves at opposite ends of the witness search. Dewey was trying to secure witnesses to testify against the infamous fugitive labor racketeer, while Lepke was busy trying to scare away or kill all those who could help the prosecutor make a case against him.

Greenberg certainly knew enough that he could hurt Buchalter, and he figured that was worth something. Greenberg soon got word to Buchalter's chief lieutenant, Mendy Weiss, and let him know that he wanted $5,000, or else. After a meeting between Buchalter and Weiss, at which Abe Reles was in attendance, it was decided that instead of sending money, they would send Allie Tannenbaum to kill him. Tannenbaum knew Greenberg and could probably get close to him. He went to Montreal but found Greenberg had already left.

From Montreal it was believed Greenberg spent a short time in Detroit before heading to Los Angeles in June 1939. There he and Ida took up residence as Mr. and Mrs. George Schacter at 1804 North Vista Del Mar Avenue in the heart of Hollywood, just a few blocks away from the famous intersection of Hollywood and Vine.

A few days before Thanksgiving, a man known to Greenberg became a houseguest at their home. Greenberg told Ida that the man worked for the studios and might consider renting a room from them. While the man was never identified publicly, he may have been Benjamin "Whitey" Krakower, a person Greenberg would most likely be familiar with from New York. It's unlikely that Ida would not have known this man, especially after he had been there several days, but she never admitted it to police. Around this time Greenberg was earning a small income by acting as a chauffeur to an official in the movie industry. Again, Ida claimed never to have been told the name of the man who employed her husband.

It was Greenberg's habit to leave his home every night around 11:00, many times accompanied by Ida, and drive his 10-year-old automobile to Hollywood and Vine to purchase a newspaper. On the night of Wednesday, November 22, the eve of Thanksgiving, Greenberg made his last newspaper run. Ida would later recall the events of that night:

> We were going out together, but the man who was going to rent a room from us telephoned and asked me to wait for a lady friend of his who was supposed to be coming to the apartment. I waited, but no one came.
>
> Harry had been gone about a half hour and I was reading in bed when I heard what I thought was the backfire of an automobile. Then I heard an automobile roar away.
>
> In a little while I realized that there was still an automobile in the street, for I could hear the motor running. I looked out and then went down, and found out it was our car.
>
> When I opened the door, I saw my husband there, dead. The car began to roll and I screamed for help.[1]

It had been a perfect setup. Five bullets had been fired through the driver's side window just as Greenberg had returned from buying the newspaper. He never even had a chance to turn the ignition off. One newspaper reported, "One bullet entered his left cheek, another penetrated the left side of his neck and the third struck him at the base of his throat."[2] Police arrived quickly and tried to piece together what happened. The early lack of correct information provided by Ida Schacter certainly delayed things. Police knew from their very first interview with the widow that she was holding something back. After identifying the dead man as her husband, *George* Schacter, she related how she ran to the car after hearing the shots and upon finding the body, screamed out, "Harry, Harry, open your eyes."

Many of the questions asked by the police regarding George Schacter's background were answered with, "My husband never told me." Ida proved to be the perfect mob –wife; she was even slow to admit that her husband's real name was Harry Gottesman. Working with this piece of information, Los Angeles police contacted New York City authorities and discovered that George Schacter, Harry Gottesman, and Harry "Big Greenie" Greenberg were all the same person. From here, it wasn't long before the connection to Louis Buchalter was made. The newspapers speculated that the murder was ordered to prevent Greenberg from testifying at Lepke's upcoming federal narcotics trial, scheduled to begin November 30.[3]

Two days after the murder, police discovered the getaway car a few blocks from where Greenberg's body was found. Inside were a .38 revolver, with five spent shells, and a cocked .45 automatic. The two weapons, as well as the car itself, had been wiped clean of prints. The serial numbers on the handguns had been removed.

After the connection to Buchalter was made, it didn't take long to link Greenberg to Benjamin "Bugsy" Siegel, who by now was living in Los Angeles and representing the East Coast mob's interests. Just three days after the murder, Los Angeles police considered that Greenberg had been killed because he was trying to "shake down" Lepke with the threat of talking to authorities.

On November 26, funeral services were held for Greenberg at the Glasband Mortuary in Los Angeles. He was then laid to rest in Mount Carmel Cemetery.

In August 1940, Buchalter, Benjamin Siegel, Emmanuel "Mendy" Weiss, Frankie Carbo, and Harry "Champ" Segal were indicted for the murder of Greenberg based on information provided by Albert "Allie" Tannenbaum and Abe Reles. After meeting with Brooklyn District Attorney William O'Dwyer in December, the Los Angeles district attorney asked that the charges be dismissed.

In September 1941, Siegel and Carbo were reindicted for the murder. After the death of Reles that November, the case against Siegel was weak. The trial began in January 1942. On February 5, the charges against Siegel were dismissed. Jurors then deadlocked on Carbo's guilt. On March 24, the murder charges against Carbo were dismissed.

RUDOLPH HALLEY (1913–1956)

Halley, who was the chief counsel for most of the Kefauver Hearings, resigned the position to run for New York City Council president in the fall of 1951, as the candidate of the Liberal-Independent-City Fusion Party. He explained his party affiliation by stating that before the hearings he was "proud to be a Democrat." After hearing testimony for nearly two years, he claimed both the Democrats and the Republican parties were shown to be full of corruption and connected to the underworld. During a bitter, mud-slinging campaign, Halley was accused of having connections to Abner Zwillman because he once served as counsel to the Hudson & Manhattan Company, of which Longy held an interest.

He also had to defend himself over a chance encounter with Frank Costello outside a Manhattan restaurant. Halley was entering as Costello was leaving. Halley claimed they were both equally surprised to see each other. "Costello stuck his paw out and grabbed my hand," Halley said. "Then he ran away. There was no conversation."

Halley won the council president election by a wide margin over both his Democrat and Republican opponents. In 1953, Halley ran for mayor as the Liberal candidate, finishing third. On November 19, 1956, Halley died of acute pancreatitis at the age of 43.

ARTHUR GARFIELD HAYS (1881–1954)

Hays was a prominent attorney who specialized in cases involving civil liberties. Born in Rochester, New York, he was named after three U.S. presidents. Known as a man of "genuine sympathy and understanding," he was said to be drawn to cases involving "society's underdogs."

After graduation from Columbia Law School in 1905, Hays started his own law firm. He soon became involved in cases involving civil liberties. The firm drew attention and criticism for representing German interests during the World War I. In 1920, Hays became general counsel for the American Civil Liberties Union.

Hays earned his money by representing businessmen, authors, and gamblers. Then he took cases without pay for those he considered "downtrodden." Among the famous cases Hays worked were the Scopes Trial in Tennessee in 1925, which became famous as "The Monkey Trial." He was part of a defense team headed by the famous Clarence Darrow. He also served on the defense counsel of Sacco and Vanzetti, one of the most famous murder trials of the 20th century. The two Italian anarchists were executed in 1927 for murders committed during a robbery; later information seemed to point to a Mafia gang in Boston as the actual culprits.

In 1931, Hays served as counsel in the Scottsboro Case in which eight black men from Alabama were accused of raping two white women. During the three trials, Clarence Darrow and Samuel Leibowitz were also a part of the defense counsel. In 1933, Hays defended a Bulgarian Communist accused of taking part in the burning of the Reichstag in Berlin.

In addition to being a noted attorney, Hays was an accomplished author of many articles, book reviews, and several books. Among his writings was *City Lawyer: The Autobiography of a Law Practice*. Hays died on December 14, 1954, of a heart attack at the age of 73.

HAROLD GILES HOFFMAN (1896–1954)

Hoffman served as the 41st governor of New Jersey from 1935 to 1938. The Republican politician earned a reputation as the most corrupt governor to serve the state. A feisty politician, Hoffman was twice involved in fistfights with reporters while governor. There were two notable incidents in his career. The first was a visit to the cell of condemned Lindbergh baby kidnapper Bruno Hauptman. Hoffman doubted Hauptman's guilt but was unable to convince others to reexamine the case. The second was in February 1950. Hoffman was one of four panelists on the television game show *What's My Line?* during its debut presentation.

In March 1954, Hoffman was suspended from his position at the State Unemployment Compensation Commission after an embezzlement scheme was uncovered. He died three months later of a heart attack in a New York City hotel room after confessing to embezzling more than $300,000 from the state.

SALVATORE MARANZANO (1886–1931)

Maranzano was one of the principals in the Castellammarese War of 1930–1931. A mysterious figure in organized crime history, he was the only person to take on the title of *Capo di tutti Capi,* "Boss of all Bosses," after the murder of his rival Giuseppe "Joe the Boss" Masseria in April 1931.

As with the Castellammarese War, practically all of the information about Maranzano comes from three books—*The Valachi Papers, The Last Testament of Lucky Luciano,* and *A Man of Honor,* the autobiography of Joseph Bonanno. In comparing the descriptions of Maranzano given by Bonanno and Luciano, it's hard to believe that they are discussing the same man. Bonanno pinpoints Maranzano's arrival in America with the following statement: "My life took a decisive turn at the end of 1925 when Salvatore Maranzano, a hero of mine in Sicily, immigrated to the United States."[4] Luciano and Joseph Valachi put Maranzano in the United States after World War I in 1918; however, Valachi has no reference in his book to any activities of Maranzano before 1930.

An article in the *New York Sun* reporting Maranzano's murder in September 1931 stated, "Maranzano migrated from Sicily only four years ago and accumulated wealth quickly. He bought a $30,000 house at 2706 Avenue J in Brooklyn, where he lived with his wife and four children; Dominic, 20, Antoinette, 16, Angelo, 10, and Mario, 9, and operated two expensive automobiles."[5]

Bonanno paints a picture of Maranzano as the daring and romantic "chief warrior" from his homeland in Castellammare del Golfo, Sicily. Maranzano's date of birth is listed in a few places as 1868, which would have made him 57 in 1925, but at that time Bonanno claimed he was about 40. It's hard to believe that Bonanno could be 17 years off in assessing his age. When Maranzano was murdered, both the *New York Times* and the *New York Herald*

Tribune gave his age as 47. A picture of Maranzano's headstone at Find-A-Grave.com clearly shows his year of birth as 1886, making him 45 at the time of his death.

The following physical description of Maranzano is offered by Bonanno, "He was a fine example of a Sicilian male: robust, about five feet nine inches tall, full bodied but with no excess flaccid flesh on him, deep chested, with sturdy muscular arms and legs. He was said to be able to snap a man's neck with his thumbs and to leap amazing distances."[6] Bonanno goes on to describe Maranzano as handsome and having all the skills of a charismatic politician:

> Within a short time after his arrival to America, Maranzano established himself as an expert entrepreneur. In his own way his was a classic American success story. He built up an important export business, had real estate holdings and had considerable interests in the bootlegging industry. He recirculated his profits, becoming a financier. He made connections and soon had well-placed friends in all circles of life.[7]

Maranzano was given a welcome banquet in America, thus again indicating his arrival is no earlier than late 1925. Bonanno claims he shared an apartment with Maranzano in Manhattan while he waited for his wife and children to join him from Sicily.

One of the Maranzano characteristics that Bonanno described—one of the few Luciano agreed with—was that "in business matters, Maranzano loved perfection. He took great pride in his ledgers, his account books, his records and files. All his books had to be in order, each entry had to be immaculate—an exquisite tapestry of numbers."[8]

In the late 1920s, Maranzano foresaw that a war was coming. It would involve the Castellammarese and the gang of Giuseppe Masseria and would be fought in New York City. Yet the Castellammarese in the city were doing nothing to prepare themselves. Maranzano went to Buffalo to meet with Stefano Magaddino, Bonanno's cousin and a strong underworld leader in that area, taking Bonanno and Gaspar DiGregorio with him. Bonanno wrote:

> As a result of this meeting, it was understood that Maranzano would spearhead the campaign against Masseria in New York. In essence, that made Maranzano the supreme commander in the New York theatre of war. Since the Castellammarese in New York would do most of the fighting, it was also agreed that Detroit and Buffalo would supply Maranzano with money, arms, ammunition and manpower.[9]

In a nutshell, according to Bonanno, Maranzano didn't arrive until late 1925, and didn't become the leader of the Castellammarese faction in New York City until sometime between May 30 and July 15, 1930.

Compare Bonanno's description of Maranzano and his rise with Luciano's description. Luciano claims that in 1923 the "major figures in the Italian underworld" were Giuseppe "Joe the Boss" Masseria, Ciro Terranova, and Salvatore Maranzano. Luciano claims to have had contact with Maranzano before 1920:

> I always knew, I felt it in my bones, that someday this old bastard was gonna get in touch with me. But I always knew that no matter what that guy would offer me, I was gonna turn it down. When he first come to this country, right after the war, and I was just startin' out, that old shitheel would come around the neighborhood once in a while and hold up his hands, spread out like he was a Pope givin' the people on the street a blessin'.[10]

Without giving a timeframe, but it must be assumed it's 1923 or earlier, Luciano said that Maranzano wanted to have a meeting. During their talk he claimed Maranzano asked him to join his organization. Luciano figured that by joining Maranzano, it would mean breaking ties with his closest friends Meyer Lansky, Benjamin Siegel, Louis Buchalter, and Arnold Rothstein. Luciano sent his driver to deliver a message: "To thank Don Salvatore for his very nice offer and just to say that this wasn't the right time and we should sorta leave the door open."[11]

The next encounter between Luciano and Maranzano came on the night of September 14, 1923, during the Dempsey/Firpo heavyweight championship fight at the Polo grounds. Luciano boasted that he spent $25,000 to purchase choice seats to impress his gangster friends and politicians from New York and around the country. He claimed, "Boss Jim Pendergast came all the way from Kansas City in a private railroad car."[12] It must have been a funeral car because Jim Pendergast died in 1910.

Luciano claimed that right before the main bout, Maranzano walked over and they greeted each other "cordially, like equals, and chatted for a few minutes." At this time Maranzano asked for another meeting. When the two men met again Luciano said that Maranzano told him, "As things now stand we are interfering with each other. We are competing for the same whiskey markets, and, unfortunately, killing each other's people. This is foolish and it costs us both too much money and too many good men. This should come to a stop."[13] Maranzano made an offer to Luciano:

Charles Lucania would become chief lieutenant in the Maranzano family, and Maranzano would turn over to him the family's entire liquor territory, abandoning the business himself and giving Charlie and his friends a free hand. With this one move, Maranzano said, Charlie Lucania would become the whiskey czar of New York.[14]

Luciano claimed that he discussed the offer with his inner circle and then sent a polite message to Maranzano declining the offer. He claimed this "rejection of the second Maranzano offer without any serious consequences spread quickly through the underworld and won Luciano increased respect from his elders and peers."[15] One of the people he supposedly won the "respect" of was "Johnny Scalise," one of the "bootleg powers in Cleveland." We can only assume he is referring to John Scalish, who was the recognized leader of the Cleveland Mafia from 1944 to 1976. Luciano refers to "Scalise" a couple of times. In 1923, however, John Scalish was only 11 years old.

Luciano claimed his rejection of the offer also caused "Joe the Boss" Masseria to notice him. Now, before 1924, Luciano stated both sides were wooing him. Sometime in 1926 or 1927, Luciano finally joined forces with Masseria. At this point in the book, either Luciano or the authors seemed to lose track of events chronologically, as the Milazzo murder is discussed as if it happened in 1928 or 1929 (instead of 1930). Luciano talked about Gaetano "Tommy" Reina, the leader of a Bronx Family, switching sides from Masseria to Maranzano. Both Luciano and Valachi indicate that the first blow of the Castellammarese War was the murder of Reina in February 1930. Bonanno claimed that Maranzano didn't become a power until sometime after the death of Milazzo, which occurs more than three months after Reina's murder.

Tommy Lucchese, the underboss to Reina, met with Luciano to inform him of Reina's defection. Luciano told Lucchese to set up a meeting between him and Maranzano. At this meeting on October 17, 1929, Maranzano's men allegedly gave Luciano a savage beating because he refused to "personally" murder Masseria. Luciano claimed that while hanging by his thumbs, he kicked Maranzano in the groin. When Maranzano recovered, he took a knife to Luciano's face and permanently caused the disfigurement to his eye.

It was after this brutal beating, which Bonanno never discusses in his book even though it was released nine years after Luciano's, that Luciano claimed Meyer Lansky gave him the nickname "Lucky." Luciano claimed that during his early days of recovery, Joe Adonis would stop by twice a day and inject narcotics into him. Luciano recalled, "Whenever I got one of them shots, I'd figure out a new way to bump off Don Salvatore Maranzano."

Luciano finally found a way to "bump off" Maranzano. Killers entered his Park Avenue office on the afternoon of September 10, 1931, and murdered him (See Castellammarese War appendix). Ironically, Maranzano and Luciano are both buried in Saint John's Cemetery in Middle Village, Queens.

GIUSEPPE "JOE THE BOSS" MASSERIA
(CA. 1887–1931)

Masseria was born around 1887 in Sicily, where he began his criminal career. He arrived in the United States in 1903, reportedly after committing a murder in his hometown. Taking up residence in New York's Mulberry Bend district, Masseria soon became involved in the activities of the city's Italian underworld. Between 1907 and 1920, he was arrested for various offenses including murder, burglary, and extortion. In June 1913, he was given a prison term of four-and-a-half years in Sing Sing for attempting to "plunder" a pawnshop in the Bowery. He became associated with a gang run by Giuseppe "The Clutching Hand" Morello, Ciro Terranova, and Ignacio "Lupo the Wolf" Saietta, all of whom were related. Known as the first family of Italian crime in the city, the gang controlled activities in uptown Manhattan and in the Bronx. Ciro Terranova would later become infamous as "The Artichoke King" by cornering the market on artichokes, said to be an Italian delicacy in New York City.

An ambitious man, Masseria began his ascent to the top of the New York underworld in the early 1920s. That both Morello and Saietta were serving long prison terms for counterfeiting during the 1910s helped clear the path for Masseria's rise. According to one police official, Masseria gained control over, "every kind of racket in existence." Included in these activities was murder. On December 29, 1920, the body of Salvatore Mauro was found on Chrystie Street, a few doors from his cheese shop. Masseria was a prime suspect in his murder, but was soon cleared.

As with any aspiring mob boss, there was sure to be competition for the position. Early in Masseria's career, that competition came from Umberto Valenti. On his way up the ladder, two incidents involving Valenti helped to ensure Masseria of legendary status among his followers. The first took place on May 8, 1922, after Valenti's men ambushed and killed Vincent Terranova, an ally of Masseria, on 116th Street near Second Avenue. Seeking revenge, Masseria and several gunmen set up an ambush of their own on Grand Street, between Mulberry and Mott Streets, just a block from Police Headquarters. It was shortly before 6:00 PM and the street was full of pedestrian traffic, consisting mostly of workmen heading home after a busy day, with their wives and children awaiting them. As Valenti and an associate, Silvio Tagliagamba, drew near, Masseria and his men opened fire.

Nearly 60 bullets were fired in the fusillade, none of them hitting Valenti. Instead, five innocent people were hit as they ran for cover. Police raced out of the headquarters and were at the scene in seconds. Two plainclothes detectives, who were within 75 feet of Masseria and his men when they began shooting, began a foot chase. One of the gunmen escaped by running up the stairs of an apartment building and escaping across the roof. The second detective, however, soon overtook the heavier Masseria and arrested the porky gangster.

Masseria was taken to police headquarters where he refused to talk. A search of his person revealed a pistol permit, signed by a New York Supreme Court justice, marked "unlimited," meaning the bearer had permission to carry the weapon in any part of the state. Before 8:00 PM that night, Tagliagamba arrived at Bellevue Hospital in an ambulance. He refused to tell police how he had ended up with a bullet in his back. Tagliagamba's condition worsened and within a few weeks he died. Masseria was then charged with murder and released on a $15,000 bond. The charges were later dropped because of lack of evidence and witnesses.

Three months to the day after the Grand Street shooting, Valenti struck back. Around 1:00 PM on August 8, a blue Hudson touring car arrived at Second Avenue and Fifth Street. Two men got out while the driver and a fourth man in the backseat remained. The two men entered a restaurant directly across from Masseria's three-story brownstone residence at 80 Second Avenue. They ordered coffee and cake while they sat waiting, keeping a constant eye on the building across the street. At 2:00 PM, Masseria left his home and walked north along Second Avenue. Both men rushed out of the restaurant and crossed the street toward Masseria. As one man pulled an automatic, Masseria suddenly realized his predicament. He turned and tried to enter a millinery shop, but decided to get back to his home. He made it as far as Heiney Brothers at 82 Second Avenue, a woman's clothing store. One of the Heiney brothers described what happened next:

> The man with the revolver came close to the other fellow [Masseria] and aimed. Just as he fired the men jumped to one side. The bullet smashed into the window of my store. Then the man fired again and this time the man being shot at ducked his head forward. Again the man fired and again his target ducked his head down. The third shot made a second hole in my window.[16]

Masseria had miraculously escaped three bullets fired at near pointblank range, suffering just two bullet holes in his straw hat. At the first sound of gunfire, "From all directions came women, children and men." This undoubtedly resulted in the hasty retreat of the gunmen without completing their task. As the men in the Hudson drove toward their companions, a crowd began to surge closer. The two gunmen ran to the automobile and jumped inside. One of the men then climbed back out, stood on the running board, and with a revolver in each hand unleashed a barrage of bullets at the pavement in front of the pursuers.

At the same time, a group of strikers, cloak makers from the International Ladies Garment Workers' Union, who had gathered at Beethoven Hall, were just leaving the building when the first shots were fired. Seeing the Hudson heading toward them, they strikers raced to the street in an attempt to block their escape. Three of the car's occupants opened fired, unleashing at least 25 bullets directly into the strikers. Six of the men fell, and two others were trampled by the retreating workers. In addition a small pony, hauling a vendor's lemonade equipment, was hit by two stray bullets. One of the strikers died the next day in Bellevue Hospital from a wound below the heart.

Masseria enjoyed his new folk status as the man who was quicker than bullets, but he was determined not to test his invincibility again. Three days after having his hat ruined, Masseria orchestrated yet another shootout in which innocent victims were critically wounded, including an eight-year-old girl. This time Masseria gunmen, one of whom was believed to be Salvatore "Lucky Luciano" Lucania, got their prey and Valenti was finally out of the way.

New York Police Captain Arthur Carey, head of the homicide squad, was in charge of investigating these last three shootings. After questioning a number of witnesses, Carey concluded that Valenti had been lured to Twelfth Street and Second Avenue under the guise of a peace treaty that would divide the profits from bootlegging and gambling in the neighborhood with an even split and end the recent bloodshed. Valenti was not about to be tricked into meeting his rival in a secluded area. To bring Valenti out in the open, the scheduled peace conference was to take place right on the street at 11:45 in the morning. Valenti was accompanied by two of his men.

According to witnesses, at some point during the meeting, Valenti must have realized he had been drawn into a trap. He suddenly turned and began running down the street. Whether the men he had with him had betrayed him will never be known, but they took off in another direction apparently without drawing weapons. Valenti made it to a taxi parked at Twelfth Street and Second Avenue, jumped on the running board, and drew his revolver. Turning to face his assailants, he was hit in the solar plexus and crumbled to the pavement. The *New York Times* described the action and gave the account of an excited young man who witnesses the shooting:

> Some of the assassins were nervous and fired wildly, but one of them planted himself in the street and fired shot after shot, taking careful aim each time until his revolver was empty.
>
> "It was the coolest thing I ever saw," said Jack Kahane, 19 years old . . . of the Bronx. "People were shrieking and running in all directions, and this fellow calmly fired shot after shot. He did not move until he had emptied his weapon."[17]

A detective, who sprinted two blocks to the scene, escorted Valenti to St. Mark's Hospital hoping to get a dying declaration. It was to no avail as Valenti expired an hour after the shooting. In addition to the eight-year-old who was hit in the chest, a city street cleaner was severely wounded in the neck. Both were rushed to Bellevue Hospital, where they recovered.

With his immediate enemies out of the way, Masseria basically let his lieutenants do the work over the next eight years, collecting tribute from them and others who wanted to operate illegal activities in the city. In July 1928, he was questioned about the machinegun slaying of Frank "Frankie Yale" Uale, and the next summer the police brought him in for interrogation when the body of Galfono "Frank Marlow" Curto turned up in Flushing, New York.

See the Appendix for the Castellammarese War for Masseria's activities during that conflict. This story picks up with the aftermath of his murder on April 15, 1931.

The *Daily News* claimed Masseria was the father of six children; the *New York Evening Post* stated he lived with his wife and "tubercular" son. The newspaper went on to say that "The gangster was devoted to his ailing son, who had been expensively educated, and was careful to keep the underworld from encroaching upon the private lives of his family."[18]

The funeral of Giuseppe Masseria turned out to be a saga of its own. The body was laid out at his West 81st Street home in a $15,000 silver-plated, bronze coffin, engraved with his name. On the days leading up to the funeral, dozens of floral arrangements arrived at the apartment. The funeral, scheduled for Saturday, April, 18, was delayed for a few days as the family sought permission for a church funeral. Masseria was "refused a church funeral in accordance with a diocesan rule that notorious characters such as he shall be denied Christian burial unless there are extenuating circumstances."[19]

Masseria's family had been insistent upon a church funeral. A secretary to Cardinal Hayes explained there was "no general rule to the burial of men of the general reputation of Masseria. Each case is considered by the bishop of the diocese when it is reported to him that a request has been made for a church funeral for one who has died by violence."[20] Still, Masseria's family made several requests, pointing out that Brooklyn's most notorious gangster, Frankie Yale, was permitted a church funeral, including a high mass.

On April 20, the funeral for Masseria was held at his penthouse apartment. The funeral cortege consisted of 32 automobiles, half of which contained floral tributes. The number of mourners was estimated at 50, causing the *New York Evening Post* to comment, "Gangland, which raised 'Joe the Boss' to wealth and power and then murdered him, deserted him in death today and left him to be mourned at his bier only by relatives and unsympathetic detectives."[21]

There was a strong police presence, including detectives from "every part of the five boroughs." The morbid curious crowd began to arrive at 8:00 that morning. They gathered along Central Park West, into Colonial Park and along West 81st and 82nd Streets. Police kept the crowd away from the East 82nd Street service entrance to the building. Among the gawkers were:

> women for the most part, maids, delivery boys and loafing taxi drivers. The next hour brought the police—detectives from the gangster squad, the bomb squad, radical squad. By 9 o'clock every window was full. The stoops of the brownstone houses on the north side of Eighty-Second Street were packed, with photographers at every vantage point. Household duties went unattended, groceries undelivered all for a momentary glimpse of a silvery casket as it was carried from beneath the canopied rear entrance to a waiting black hearse.[22]

The floral tributes came out first. Some of the crosses were six and ten feet high. One was marked "Sympathy," and took four men to carry. These were loaded into the 16 flower cars and sent on their way to Calvary Cemetery. Neither police nor reporters were told where the procession was headed until the flower cars were on their way.

One of the undertaker's assistants told reporters that the cost of the funeral was $75,000. Another assistant distributed black-bordered memorial cards with the picture of "The Mother of Sorrows," on one side and a message on the other that stated:

> Blessed are they that mourn, for they shall be comforted.
>
> Of your charity, pray for the repose of the soul of Joseph Masseria, 45 years old, who died April 14, 1931.
>
> Let us pray: O Divine, eternal Father, I offer Thee the Precious Blood of Jesus Christ in reparation for my sins, for the wants of Holy Church, for the wants of the land, for the conversion of poor sinners and for the release of the suffering souls in Purgatory.[23]

A half-hour later, six professional pallbearers appeared, "panting and grunting beneath the weight of the casket." A dozen cars were required for family members; women and children were numerous among the mourners. The cortege then took off, as far as the police and bystanders could tell, for Calvary Cemetery.

The next day, the *New York Sun* revealed that the family and friends of Masseria had found a priest, who had never heard of "Joe the Boss," and did not know the background of his life or death. The secret plans were not finalized until Sunday night and only certain family members were aware of the arrangements.

When the cortege left the apartment, it headed across Central Park with instructions to funeral director Anthony Provenzano to head toward Calvary Cemetery by way of the Queensboro Bridge. Once across Central Park, the cortege moved south on Fifth Avenue. At 62nd Street, a family member instructed Provenzano to head downtown by way of Madison and Fourth Avenues. Provenzano was not made aware of the destination until the cortege reached the parish of Mary Help of Christians at East 12th Street.

At the Italian congregation church, Reverend Paul J. Zolin conducted a 45-minute funeral mass. On completion, the funeral cortege headed to Calvary Cemetery, where the body of "Joe the Boss" was placed in a receiving vault.

VERNE MILLER (1896–1933)

In early 1933, Meyer Lansky and Ben Siegel became involved in a bootleg war with members of the Irving "Waxey Gordon" Wexler gang. Joseph Valachi would later refer this to as the "Jew War." On February 19, 1933, Buchalter began a two-week vacation in Hot Springs, Arkansas. He checked in with New Jersey mob leader Abner "Longy" Zwillman. While there, Buchalter met Verne C. Miller, a decorated war soldier and former county sheriff from South Dakota, turned outlaw. During this meeting it is believed that Buchalter and Zwillman talked Miller into coming east as a hired gun to help out in the war against Wexler.

Between April 12 and June 8, 1933, five members of Wexler's gang were killed, including Max Greenberg and Max Hassel during a sensational double murder at the Elizabeth-Carteret Hotel in New Jersey. It's quite possible Miller may have been involved in the slaying. If he was, he would have been better off staying in the Garden State rather than returning to Kansas City.

Back in the Midwest, Frank Nash, an outlaw and friend of Miller who had escaped from Leavenworth Penitentiary in October 1930, was arrested by FBI agents in Hot Springs, Arkansas. The group boarded a train in Fort Smith headed for Kansas City's Union Station. Miller had been alerted to the plight of his friend by Nash's desperate wife, who pleaded with him to "spring" her husband. This ill-fated rescue attempt resulted in the infamous Union Station or Kansas City Massacre on June 17, 1933, in which five people—four law enforcement officers and Nash—were slaughtered.

A few days after the massacre, Miller headed east looking for protection from his new friends, Buchalter and Zwillman. During the weeks that followed, Buchalter and his wife Betty were reported at different times to be in the company of Miller's paramour, Vivian Mathias. When Miller's participation in the shootout was confirmed by the FBI, he became the most sought after fugitive in America. The pressure to capture him drew unwanted attention to both Buchalter and Zwillman and resulted in these two Prohibition Era big shots having early FBI files.

During the fall of 1933, Al Silvers, a close associate of both Buchalter and Zwillman, helped Miller by purchasing him an automobile in New York. Abandoned in Chicago, the car was traced back to Silvers, and, on November 6, he was charged in a federal complaint with conspiracy to conceal and harbor a federal fugitive. Two weeks later, Silvers's naked body was found outside Somers, Connecticut. He had been strangled, stabbed seven times in the head and once in the heart, and left draped over a barbed wire fence covered with a bloody blanket.

On November 28, Buchalter was questioned by the FBI about the murder. He admitted to knowing Silvers and revealed that he had actually been in Connecticut on the weekend of the murder. When agents inquired about Miller, Buchalter simply said, "No one will have anything to do with him now. If Miller shows up in New York you'll know about it."

The next day Miller showed up, but not in New York—and not alive. His battered and naked body was found curled under a blanket in a ditch in northwest Detroit. Miller was tied up with a clothesline in such a way that any effort to struggle would result in strangulation. In addition, he had been clubbed about the head 11 times with a hammer or pistol butt.

WILLIE MORETTI (1894–1951)

Moretti was New Jersey's most colorful underworld figure. A friend and confidante to New York mob bosses, Moretti played a pivotal role in the life of entertainer Frank Sinatra. In the aftermath of his sensational murder in October 1951, a photograph of his lifeless bloody body sprawled on the floor of restaurant appeared in newspapers across the country and served as a testament to the brutality of the underworld.

Born on East 109th Street in New York City in 1894, Guarino Moretti was one of two sons; the other was Salvatore. Early in grade school, a teacher was said to have changed his name to William. According to the story, "Nobody knows why, not even William," but the name stuck.

Moretti went to work at a young age to help his family. He once stated, "I started at 25 cents a week working for a milkman when I was five years old." As a teenager Moretti served as an altar boy and had aspirations of becoming a priest one day. That ended when his father got sick and Willie had to earn more money. He soon went to work as a pin setter in a bowling alley. For a short time Moretti was a pugilist.

In 1913, the first entry on Moretti's rap sheet was recorded when he assaulted a barber. The arresting officers wrote down his name as "John" according to Moretti, because neither could spell Guarino. Moretti moved to Philadelphia in 1915, where he "gambled and shot craps," before returning to New York three years later.

During the mid 1910s, Moretti and Frank Costello began a long friendship. Some sources state that the two men were cousins. Costello remembered that he used to call him "Chief Meyers" as a kid. In *Uncle Frank,* Leonard Katz discussed the relationship:

> One of Frank's good friends in those years was a small, thin, neighborhood youth who seemed to always be around. Sometimes he would act as a lookout during a stickup or keep a storekeeper busy while his merchandise was being looted. He was three years younger than Frank and only about five-foot-four. He had all the guts in the world, though, and wouldn't hesitate to take on someone twice his size.
>
> Frank liked Willie Moretti, liked his good humored, wise-cracking personality. It was a relationship that lasted throughout their lives. As Frank rose in the world, so did Willie until he was recognized as Frank's top lieutenant in New Jersey, the man who ruled the Mafia in the Garden State.[24]

During the Atlantic City Conference (see Appendix) in May 1929, according to *The Last Testament of Lucky Luciano* (see Appendix), Moretti and "Longy" Zwillman were there representing "Nassau County and Northern New Jersey." During the Castellammarese War (see Appendix), Moretti, being a friend of Costello, was obviously in the group backing "Joe the Boss" Masseria. There is no information about any role Moretti played in that conflict.

After Prohibition ended, Moretti was involved in gambling in various sections of northern New Jersey. Moretti was one of the regulars at Duke's restaurant in Cliffside Park, where Costello, Adonis, and others met on Tuesdays. In 1946, according to *The Last Testament of Lucky Luciano,* Moretti was one of the many friends to see him off to Italy during his going-away party aboard the *Laura Keene*. Before the year was out, Moretti was said to be a participant in the alleged Havana Conference.

When Frank Sinatra's singing career began in the mid-1930s, he became a favorite of a number of New Jersey underworld members—Moretti, Joe Adonis, and Angelo "Gyp" DeCarlo, among them. Although he would deny it his whole life, Sinatra liked the company of underworld figures. He became particularly close with Moretti. In the mid-1940s, Sinatra lived in a house in Hasbrouck Heights just around the corner from the Moretti home; their backyards "just about touched." Although Sinatra would always downplay their friendship, Sinatra's daughter Tina claimed her father knew Moretti "all his life." Frank claimed to know him "very faintly."[25]

In January 1940, Sinatra signed with Tommy Dorsey. Although the combination of Sinatra's voice and Dorsey's band were an instant hit, the personalities of the two men clashed. Within a couple of years, Sinatra wanted out. During the late summer of 1942, Sinatra signed a severance agreement without reading the fine print. He was able to begin his solo career but, "You're not gonna leave this band as easy as you think you are," Dorsey told him.

> Frank had ignored the stern clauses in the document that set him free. Under the terms of the release, Frank agreed to pay a third of all future earnings over $100 a week to Dorsey for the next ten years. Another 10 percent "off the top" was to go to Dorsey's manager. These deductions were to be made before expenses and taxes.[26]

Sinatra desperately wanted out of the contract. There are a number of stories surrounding how the contract issue was finally resolved; one of them involves Moretti. This incident was the influence for the famous tale related in the *Godfather* movie, where Don Corleone meets with the "bandleader" regarding the career of his godson, Johnny Fontaine, and "makes him an offer he can't refuse." Sinatra biographer Anthony Summers wrote in *Sinatra: The Life*:

> Before his death in 1956, Dorsey told Lloyd Shearer, then the West Coast correspondent for *Parade* magazine, "I was visited by Willie Moretti and a couple of his boys. Willie fingered a gun and told me he was glad to hear that I was letting Frank out of our deal. I took the hint."[27]

Moretti was said to be a "real homebody" and doted on his three daughters, Marie, Rose, and Angelina (Angela). Frank Costello, who was best man at Willie's wedding, was Marie's godfather. Moretti was the best man of Joe Adonis, who was Rose's godfather. Although Moretti told the Kefauver Committee he earned $200 a week from his job as "boss" of the U.S. Linen Supply Company, the family lived in a "palatial" home in Hasbrouck Heights, New

Jersey, reputed to be worth $100,000, and owned a "baronial" home in Deal said to be valued at $400,000. Moretti claimed he supplemented his income by winning at the racetrack.

In 1943, after the murder of Carlo Tresca (see Chapter 6), District Attorney Frank Hogan received permission to put a wiretap on Costello's telephone. Hogan didn't believe Costello was behind the murder but thought he might be able to pick up a clue through one of his conversations. Hogan never did get anything on the Tresca killing; however, he did pick up the infamous call of Thomas Aurelio thanking Costello for the judgeship nomination. He also picked up a number of telephone calls between Costello and Moretti, who at the time was on "a long vacation out West."

The story goes that Moretti, like Al Capone before him, had untreated syphilis and "began to act strangely." He began spouting off about betting, and allegedly Costello responded by sending him out West with a male nurse to take care of him. There's no record of how long he was out there, or if he received any treatment, but the telephone calls indicated that he wanted to come home. Biographer Leonard Katz claimed Costello "was protecting Willie from himself" so that a "mercy killing" wouldn't be ordered.

Despite this alleged condition, when Moretti was called to testify before the Kefauver Committee, he was a comedic hit. After being questioned about all the people he knew, Moretti was then asked by Rudolph Halley, "Well, aren't these people we have been talking about what you would call racket boys?" To which Moretti replied, "Jeez, everything is a racket today."

Moretti told Halley that he had met most of the people he was questioned about at the track. Halley suggested that wouldn't he consider them part of the "mob." Moretti shot back, "They call anybody a mob who makes six percent more on money."

When Moretti's testimony was completed, committee members thanked him for his "forthrightness," "frankness", and for a "rather refreshing" session with the senators. Moretti quipped as he left the stand, "Thank you very much. Don't forget my house in Deal if you are down on the shore. You're invited."[28]

According to the popular belief, Vito Genovese used Moretti's alleged illness and open testimony before the Kefauver Committee to convince others that he had become a loose cannon and had to be silenced. This also was part of his plan to reduce Costello's allies in his quest to take back leadership of the gang he abandoned in 1937. On October 4, 1951, Moretti was murdered in Joe's Elbow Room restaurant in Cliffside Park, New Jersey, while seated and talking with four men. Johnny Robilotto, who, according to Valachi was involved in the murder, was eventually charged with the killing. He was acquitted because of lack of evidence and was eventually murdered himself.

In investigating the murder for his book, *The Secret Rulers,* Fred J. Cook questioned the motives for the Moretti killing. In reviewing his testimony before the committee, Cook concluded, "Anyone, however, who has read Willie's words in the Kefauver transcript quickly discovers that all the evidence there points, not to a softening brain, but to a quick and agile one."[29]

Cook is critical of the murder investigation and the people running it, mainly Deputy Attorney General Harry L. Towe, who clashed with Co-Deputy Attorney General Nelson Stamler. The Bergen County medical examiner announced that during his autopsy, he found no "softening of the brain" and "no evidence whatsoever of any disease." The next day Towe released a statement claiming his office was not interested in knowing if Moretti was a victim of this malady, that the autopsy was performed only to determine the cause of death. Cook suggests that the killing was a result of a gambling investigation by Nelson Stamler, which was currently underway in Bergen County. Harold Adonis was alleged to have accepted $228,000 from gamblers to help cripple Stamler's gambling probe. Two days after Moretti's murder, Fred Stengle, the police chief of Fort Lee, New Jersey, was found dead from an apparent suicide. He had been scheduled to appear before a Bergen County grand jury that Stamler was conducting.

Moretti's funeral took place on October 8. The newspaper described the rite as "riotous." The *Newark Star-Ledger* wrote: "So insistent and unruly were the nearly 10,000 persons in all who pushed, shoved and shouted for a look at the Moretti procession that the funeral was delayed an hour." Moretti's body was taken to the family mausoleum in St. Michael's Cemetery in South Hackensack. After his casket was placed in the family vault, his distraught wife screamed, "You're in a new home now honey. You're with your mother and father. How happy they must be. They have you. I have lost you and my heart aches."[30]

JAMES "NIGGY" RUTKIN (1899–1956)

Rutkin was a business and gang associate of Abner "Longy" Zwillman. In the late 1940s, he was reportedly $22 million in debt and filed a lawsuit against Joseph Reinfeld, claiming he had been defrauded of profits from Browne-Vintners. In court, it was revealed that Rutkin had received $250,000 from the sale of Brown-Vintners to Seagrams, an amount he hadn't paid taxes on. Rutkin was indicted for tax evasion. At trial in 1950, attorneys for Rutkin introduced confidential information about the operations that could only have come from the reports stolen from the files of IRS Agent Edwin Baldwin. Zwillman was questioned by government investigators but was never called to testify. The government's key witness was Reinfeld, whose testimony was crucial. Later, Reinfeld admitted that he had been questioned about Zwillman's proceeds, but no action was ever taken against Longy.

Rutkin was convicted and sentenced to four years in federal prison. He was placed in the Hudson County Jail to await a decision on his appeal for a new trial. Rutkin spent two years in the county jail while his case was being reviewed. During this time Rutkin was treated for ulcers and at one time underwent emergency surgery.

Rutkin was released on a $250,000 bond in June 1954. He remained free until April 13, 1956, when his appeal was finally denied. He reentered the Hudson County Jail to await transfer to the federal penitentiary in Danbury, Connecticut. The denial of his application caused Rutkin's ulcers to flare up and he was removed to the prison's hospital. On April 20, just hours before he was scheduled to be moved, Rutkin asked for a razor "to prepare" himself for the trip. Rutkin walked into the washroom of the hospital wing and slashed his throat. Rushed to the Jersey City Medical Center, he died an hour later. Rutkin was 57 years old.

FRANK SCALISE (1894–1957)

Scalise had always been kind of a shadowy figure in the New York underworld. He began his criminal career with a burglary arrest on December 18, 1920, in New Rochelle, New York. He was bailed out and was arrested for another burglary two days later. He was paroled for both crimes. Another burglary in Manhattan, on December 15, 1923, resulted in charges being dismissed.

After the Castellammarese War in 1931, Scalise was named one of the bosses of the five families by Maranzano. Scalise, who originally worked for Giuseppe Masseria, was one of the defectors from that gang. He and Maranzano became close. During the banquet that followed the death of "Joe the Boss," Scalise was said to have sat at the table where all the "tribute" money was dropped off for Maranzano.

After Maranzano's murder, Joseph Bonanno claimed, "Scalise's star fell. Scalise had been too close a supporter of Maranzano. With Lucky's rise to power, Scalise became a liability to his Family, which didn't want to antagonize the powerful Luciano and his cohorts. Scalise was replaced as Father by Vincent Mangano."[31]

There is little information on Scalise's activities during the 1930s and 1940s. According to his tax returns, he was the vice president of the Mario & DiBono Plastering Company, Inc. in Corona, Queens. In addition to housing projects, the firm held the contract on the construction of the international arrivals and departures building at New York International Airport in Idlewild, Queens.

After the murder of Anastasia bodyguard Vincent Macri in the Bronx in April, 1954, followed by the disappearance of his brother Benny a few days later, police wanted to question Scalise; however, they never seemed to be able to locate him. Another murder the police wanted to question him about was Dominick "The Gap" Petrilli (see Chapter 6), in December 1953.

According to law enforcement, some sources say Scalise became the mob boss of the Bronx; others claim he became heavily involved in the narcotics trade. In June 1955, he was subpoenaed to appear before a U.S. Senate subcommittee that was conducting an inquiry into federal narcotics laws. Scalise did not appear, claiming he was recovering from surgery.

Based on this scant information, it's hard to tell how close he became with Anastasia or why he would be considered for the underboss position with Anastasia's takeover of the Mangano Family in 1951. After Anastasia became boss, it was reported that his family became one of the strongest. Joseph Valachi would testify in 1963 that between 1954 and 1958, some 200 new members were initiated into the family. At this point the story gets cloudy. According to Peter Maas in *The Valachi Papers,* Scalise "had actually been selling memberships for amounts up to $50,000, and Anastasia ordered his death forthwith."

Virgil W. Peterson, however, related in *The Mob: 200 Years of Organized Crime in New York,* that, according to Valachi, "It was learned that Anastasia and Scalise had 'commercialized' memberships by charging some men as much as $40,000." When the other families became aware of this, Anastasia made Scalise the fall guy and had him killed.

Still there are some who believe that the killing of Frank Scalise was just another murder ordered by Vito Genovese to weaken the competition on his way to the top of the New York underworld. At any rate, the murder was carried out on June 17, 1957, in broad daylight, while New York was in the midst of an insufferable heat wave.

The 64-year-old Scalise was purchasing fruit at an Arthur Avenue produce stand in the Bronx. He was approached by two gunmen who fired four bullets into his head and neck. He died instantly. The killers escaped in a black sedan that was double-parked in front of the produce shop. The attempted assassination of fictional mob boss Vito Corleone in the movie *The Godfather* takes its inspiration from the murder of Frank Scalise.

A strong police presence, along with federal agents, was on hand the day of the Scalise funeral from the Scocozza Funeral Home on Crescent Avenue in the Bronx. After the burial in Woodlawn Cemetery, an announcement was made by the Bronx district attorney's office that "it had subpoenaed the record of all visitors to the bier and all senders of flowers and cards."[32]

No one was ever arrested for the murder of Frank Scalise. Some sources say New York City waste cartage racketeer Vincent Squillante was one of the gunmen; however, his size (5-foot, 1-inch) would have excluded him, as witnesses would have likely remembered someone of that stature. Squillante did play another role. After the murder, Scalise's brother, Joseph made a vow to avenge the killing. When he found that Anastasia remained silent and unsupportive, he realized his mistake and went into hiding. A few weeks later, he was assured that all had been forgiven by Squillante.

Joseph Scalise was reported missing by his son on September 7, 1957. It was reported that Scalise had been invited to a party at the home of Vincent Squillante, who cut his throat. His body was then believed to have been cut into pieces and taken away in one of Squillante's garbage trucks.

JACOB "GURRAH" SHAPIRO (1897–1947)

Shapiro was born in Minsk, Russia, on May 5, 1897, one of nine siblings.[33] He arrived in the United States in 1907 with his family and settled on the Lower East Side. According to one report, Shapiro "was unschooled and even in later years could barely read and write. The criminal bent in his makeup developed early in his East Side childhood. Before he was 18, he was a pushcart thief, bully, and East Side hoodlum."[34]

Shapiro was a scary-looking figure compared to Buchalter. A *New York Times* article gave this description of Shapiro:

> Gurrah Jake was loud-mouthed, hoarsely guttural, thick-lipped, given to exaggerated gesticulation. He was the Donald Duck of the New York underworld, constantly out of temper. He was short—only five feet, five inches in height—squat, a 200-pounder with flattened nose, ugly, fat fingers, brown hair strong as curled wire, large eared.[35]

There is more than one story as to how he got his famous nickname, "Gurrah," but the one most quoted is based on his way of yelling in his thick Yiddish accent at some timid individual to "get out of here," which came out "Gurrah da here." Whatever the origin of the tale, the nickname stuck from an early age.

The first entry on Shapiro's rap sheet appeared seven months before Buchalter's. Twelve of his arrests, between February 1915 and April 1933, resulted in the charges being dismissed. In between, he served prison sentences in Elmira and Sing Sing for burglary, grand larceny, assault, and gun possession.

After Buchalter's release from prison in 1922, the two men became part of the labor racketeering gang headed by Jacob "Little Augie" Orgen. After a shootout with members of the Nathan "Kid Dropper" Kaplan gang in early August 1921, Shapiro was wounded and named Kaplan as one of his assailants. During a courtroom appearance at the end of the month, Shapiro refused to identify Kaplan. As Kaplan left the courthouse for another arraignment, he was murdered by Louis Kushner.

Over the next four years, Shapiro and Buchalter worked under Orgen, but at the same time continued with their own petty crimes, suggesting that they weren't becoming wealthy.

After a dispute with Orgen during a painter's strike in 1927, Shapiro and Buchalter found out that Orgen had walked away with $50,000, which he kept to himself. On the night of October 15, the duo ambushed Orgen on the Lower East Side, killing "Little Augie" and wounding "Legs" Diamond.

After Orgen's murder, Shapiro and Buchalter became the leading labor racketeers in the United States and earned a reputation for their ruthlessness. The main industries they targeted were the garment, fur trade, flour, trucking, and bakery.

The first law enforcement efforts to go after Shapiro and Buchalter came in 1933. Needle Trade Workers' President Morris Langer was killed by a car bomb in New Jersey in March of that year, and the Fur Workers' Union headquarters in Manhattan was attacked the following month. In November, a massive federal indictment was issued charging 80 individuals for violating the Sherman Antitrust Act in the fur industry. Shapiro and Buchalter were arrested, arraigned, and released on bail.

By early 1936, Shapiro, who had previously tried to keep a low profile, was recognized by all members of law enforcement. Shapiro had recently been named to the Number 6 spot on Police Commissioner Lewis J. Valentine's Public Enemies list. On February 16, Shapiro was arrested with Albert "Allie, Tick-Tock" Tannenbaum at Madison Square Garden, while the two men watched a hockey game. The newspapers described Tannenbaum as Shapiro's "bodyguard," although both men told police they had never seen each other before. The pair was charged with vagrancy and released after posting a $500 bail the next day. Charges were dismissed after a hearing later that month.

The fur industry trial would not take place until almost three years later. On November 8, 1936, Shapiro and Buchalter were found guilty of violating the Sherman Antitrust laws after a two-week trial. They were each sentenced to two years in prison and a $10,000 fine. In March 1937, with the help of corrupt Federal Appeals Judge Martin Manton, Buchalter's conviction was overturned, but Shapiro's was affirmed.

On June 1, Shapiro's conviction was upheld by the Second Circuit Court of Appeals. Shapiro was ordered to surrender on June 21 in federal court. When he failed to appear, his $10,000 bond was forfeited. Shapiro and Buchalter were due back in federal court on July 6, as their second trial involving violations of the Sherman Antitrust Act in the fur trades was scheduled to begin. On that date neither man appeared. Federal Judge Sidney C. Mize ordered their $3,000 bonds forfeited and issued a warrant for their arrests (see Chapter 3 for his movements from this point).

On August 9, Shapiro and Buchalter were 2 of 16 men named in an indictment for conspiracy to extort money from clothing manufacturers. The indictments followed a year-and-a-half investigation by Thomas Dewey and his assistants and was presented to an extraordinary grand jury. At the time of the announcement, the *New York Times* stated that because of the low bail sent by Judge Manton after their conviction in the first fur trades trial, the two decided "to disappear when they learned that Mr. Dewey was on their trail."[36] On August 20, the Board of Estimate posted a $5,000 reward for the capture of either fugitive; in November, the federal government posted their own $5,000 reward.

Rumors were reported from all over the world about the whereabouts of the two. In February 1938, a report out of Warsaw, Poland, claimed Shapiro and Buchalter had sent a letter to the fiancée of a Polish prince threatening to kidnap her unless a sum of money was paid.

Authorities determined that as the two men were used to living a life of luxury, the route to take was to shut off as many of their sources of income as possible. Anybody thought to have any contact with the men were investigated. Firms that had any association with the pair were also investigated. Little by little the money passing into their hands while on the lam was being shut off.

At 3:30 on the afternoon of April 14, 1938, a man walked into the Federal House of Detention at Eleventh and West Streets and calmly announced, "I'm Jacob Shapiro. I want to give up." The warden called Reed Vetterli, the special agent in charge of the New York FBI office, who drove to the prison to pick up Shapiro.[37] Taken to FBI headquarters for questioning, Vetterli later reported, "Gurrah said he was getting tired of the government's being so close behind him and thought it best to surrender."[38] After 17 months on the run, it was reported that Shapiro had never left the city.

As to where Shapiro had been, "For three weeks immediately following his disappearance last summer he had worked as a laborer in the Berkshires, near Pittsfield, Mass.—long enough to map out his plans and throw off immediate pursuit—but beyond that his movements were not definitely known."[39]

Shapiro was arraigned before Judge John C. Knox, who had sentenced him in the Fur Trades trial. He pleaded not guilty, and because he was already under a two-year sentence, no bail was allowed. A trial date for the second indictment in the fur trades case was scheduled for May 16. While being questioned by Special Deputy Attorney General John Harlan Amen, Shapiro claimed he was tired of seeing his wife and children harassed by investigators.

To show how low the plight of Shapiro had gone, his scheduled arraignment before New York Supreme Court Judge Ferdinand Pecora on April 18 was postponed because the racketeer had no suit to wear to court. The suit he had worn when he surrendered was being fumigated at the Federal House of Detention. Shapiro appeared before Pecora a week later and pled not guilty to charges of conspiracy in garment racket and extortion in the bakery racket without counsel present.

Shapiro's second federal trail began on June 12. Defense counsel was Vincent R. Impellitteri, who would replace William O'Dwyer as mayor of New York City when the latter was appointed ambassador to Mexico in 1950. One of the key witnesses was Abraham Beckerman, who hired Shapiro and Buchalter for the Fur Dressers Factor Corporation "to keep the members in line." During the trial, Prosecutor Amen brought out that fur prices across the country had risen as much as 70 percent because of the activities of Shapiro and Buchalter. The defendant did not take the stand and Impellitteri did not call a single defense witness. On June 17, the jury received the case for deliberation. After four hours, the jury had its verdict. Sitting in the courtroom at 7:45 that evening were Shapiro's mother, two sisters, his wife, and three children. The defendant was found guilty of violating the Sherman Antitrust Act.

As Shapiro stood weeping, Federal Judge Grover M. Moscowitz immediately sentenced him to three years in federal prison and fined him $15,000. The sentence was to be served consecutive to his 1936 conviction. As Judge Knox had complained at the earlier trial in which Shapiro was found guilty, Judge Moscowitz stated, "My only regret is that under the Sherman Antitrust Law I am prevented from imposing a heavier sentence."[40]

Shapiro shouted, "I am getting railroaded for my name. I have paid for everything I did and I don't have to commit any crimes. I pay income taxes on $30,000 a year." The *New York Herald Tribune* reported, "With tears streaming down his heavy jowls, he hardly looked the part of the 'most vicious killer in New York,' a description given him in a Department of Justice report which had been handed to the judge just before sentence was pronounced."[41] Within days, Shapiro was headed to the federal penitentiary in Lewisburg, Pennsylvania.

Shapiro's name remained out of the news for more than a year. After the murder of Irving Penn, when the search for Buchalter reached its peak, Thomas Dewey announced that Shapiro was one of Lepke's former associates who was "marked for slaughter." At this point, a day and night police guard was placed on Shapiro's family. Within weeks, Buchalter turned himself over to authorities.

In the wake of Buchalter's surrender, the federal government sought to prosecute those responsible for harboring him and Shapiro. The government contended that the five indicted defendants, including Shapiro's brother Carl, had provided $250 a week to Shapiro and Buchalter while they were fugitives, the money coming from two legitimate clothing concerns. The defense claimed the payments had been made to the men's wives, which was perfectly legal. Carl Shapiro and the others were found guilty of conspiracy to harbor on November 4. The convictions were reversed on July 29, 1940.

During Buchalter's trial for the murder of Joe Rosen, Shapiro was brought in from the federal penitentiary in Atlanta, where he had been transferred. It was reported that he was being called to refute testimony given by Rosen's daughter; however, he never took the stand. He was returned to prison and at some point transferred to the federal facility at Milan, Michigan. The *New York Times* reported: "Overindulgence at the table, fright and self-pity had begun to work on him by this time. His weight fell off, stomach disorders became chronic and his heart was weakened. He was in and out of the prison hospital."[42]

On December 10, 1942, Shapiro completed his federal prison sentence at the penitentiary in Milan, Michigan. By now he was a broken man dealing with numerous health-related issues. He was arrested immediately and brought back to New York City the next day. At Grand Central Station, Shapiro was met by 15 detectives and 15 uniformed officers and taken to the East 51st Street Police Station. There he was booked on 36 charges of conspiracy and extortion in the baking and garment industry. He was then taken to the Tombs.

Shapiro was arraigned on the extortion conspiracy in the garment district charges on December 17. His attorney, Millard Ellison, a former member of Dewey's staff, said his client could produce a $50,000 bail, but Assistant District Attorney Sol Gelb requested $200,000. The Judge did Gelb one better and remanded Shapiro without bail to the Tombs. As Gelb was leaving the courtroom, he got a swift kick in the leg from Shapiro's wife, Ann, who then got into a foot race with photographers as she scrambled to flee the Criminal Courts Building.

The next day a New York Supreme Court justice set bond at $100,000 to the delight of Shapiro, who told his jailers he would be freed by friends before midnight. At this point District Attorney Frank Hogan got an appellate judge to stay the order. The bail battle continued into February 1943, when the Appellate Division, First Department decided by 4 to 1 vote that Shapiro's criminal record was sufficient to refuse bail. On April 22, the court of appeals affirmed the decision, and Shapiro would never again be a free man.

On June 15, jury selection began in general sessions court in Shapiro's extortion trial. If convicted, Shapiro faced a life sentence as a fourth offender in the state. During the trial, witnesses told of payments to Shapiro and Buchalter and of threats if payment demands were not met. One of the key witnesses was Philip Orlovsky, the actual target when Irving Penn was murdered. He testified to being a collector for the duo and paying tribute himself out of fear. Max Blauner, a dress manufacturer, told of making payments to Lepke-Gurrah gang collectors Abraham "Whitey" Friedman and Herman "Hyman" Yuram, both of whom were ordered killed by Buchalter.

On July 9, after deciding his chances for acquittal were futile, Shapiro pled guilty to one count of the 36-count indictment. It was his last effort to avoid being convicted as a fourth offender. Shapiro was scheduled to be sentenced on September 10, but he fell ill. He was held in the prison hospital at Riker's Island and was not formally sentenced until May 5, 1944. On that day, Judge John A. Mullen sentenced him to 15 years to life. Before the judge, Shapiro "trembled and blubbered" then collapsed. A few days later he was transferred to Sing Sing prison to begin his term.

In Sing Sing, Shapiro continued to suffer from health problems. He was in and out of the prison hospital. In October 1946, he reentered the hospital and stayed there until his death from a coronary thrombosis on June 9, 1947. He was 50 years old. Shapiro was buried in Montefiore Cemetery in St. Albans, New York.

IRVING "WAXEY GORDON" WEXLER (1888–1952)

Wexler was born into a large, wretchedly poor Polish-Jewish immigrant family on Manhattan's Lower East Side. According to the popular story, he got his nickname "Waxey" from friends who said that as a pickpocket, he was able to remove a victim's wallet "as though it were coated with wax." Family members claim "Waxey" was just a play on the shortened last name of "Wexey." The name Gordon was from one of several aliases he used.

Wexler's police record began in 1905, when he was arrested for pick pocketing and sent to the Elmira Reformatory in October of that year. He was returned there for a short while after a parole violation in 1908. Later that year, he was arrested in Boston and served four months in the workhouse. Wexler was then arrested in Philadelphia where he did a 19-month stretch. Both arrests were for picking pockets. This last stint must have convinced him there was no future for him in this field because he returned to Manhattan and became a strong-arm goon in the labor gang of "Dopey Benny" Fein.

Wexler was described as a "gruff, powerful, thickset man," with a particular talent for what the Jews called *schlamming*, which translates to roughing up or beating a person. In 1914, during a gang street fight, a municipal court clerk was killed by a "stray" bullet. Wexler was one of 13 hoods arrested for the shooting. He and another gang member were the only ones tried for the murder, and after a lengthy trial they were acquitted. That same year, Wexler was sent to Sing Sing for two years for beating a man and robbing him of $465. He was released in 1916. It would be his last prison term until Thomas Dewey prosecuted him for income tax evasion in the 1930s.

By the time Wexler was released from prison and returned to Manhattan, "Dopey Benny" had left the labor rackets. Wexler hired himself out to other gangs as a labor goon, strike breaker, dope peddler, and robber until Prohibition came along. In the fall of 1920, Wexler met Max "Big Maxey" Greenberg, who had recently left St. Louis for Detroit after double-crossing members of the St. Louis Egan's Rats Gang by taking sides with another gang. While in Detroit, Greenberg began smuggling whiskey from Canada. Quickly realizing how profitable this venture was, he wanted to expand and needed $175,000 to do so. He traveled to New York in hopes that through Wexler he could obtain financing from Arnold Rothstein. Wexler knew Rothstein from having worked for him in the garment district as a labor enforcer.

Rothstein met the two in Central Park. Sitting on a park bench, he listened to their plan to smuggle Canadian whiskey. The next day, the three men met again, this time in Rothstein's office, where a counterproposal was made. Rothstein would finance the venture, but the liquor would be purchased and brought in from Great Britain. Wexler, who was acting as a middleman, asked to be included in the deal and was cut in for a small "piece." From this piece, Wexler would launch a successful rum-running empire and become a wealthy man. After Rothstein ended his partnership with the two in 1921, he continued to help finance them. Wexler took over two large warehouses when they split, one in the city and the other on Long Island. Rothstein would later use Wexler's speedboats to smuggle in diamonds and narcotics. As with rum running, according to rumor, it was Wexler who saw the large profit potential in narcotics and later introduced it to Rothstein. And, just as with the run running, Wexler lacked the finances to enter the racket on a large scale.

Wexler put together a gang of hoods from the old neighborhood to help him with the rum-running business. From his headquarters in the Knickerbocker Hotel on 42nd Street and Broadway, Wexler operated an efficient operation, which he modeled after his mentor, Rothstein. The liquor would be retrieved from "Rum Row," the fleet of ships anchored off the coast of New York and New Jersey, just outside the three mile limit (later extended to 12 miles). It would then be brought ashore and taken to the warehouses where it would be cut and stored and then sold to restaurants, clubs, and bootleggers in the New York metropolitan area. The best clientele always received the uncut merchandise.

Wexler lived in a lavishly decorated, 10-room apartment on Manhattan's Upper West Side and owned a large home on the Jersey Shore. In his book, *The Rise and Fall of the Jewish Gangster in America,* Albert Fried described Wexler's transformation from street thug to "a captain of the bootleg industry":

> Gone was the schlammer and gunsel of yore. He was reborn Irving Wexler, free-spending New York businessman, owner of real estate and stocks and other properties of a vaguer nature, . . . a gentleman about town conspicuous by his fancy dress and limousine and companions. He too cultivated a persona. And while he could not yet be a Rothstein—he was still too grubby and coarse and arriviste-looking—he was definitely cutting his own swath of respectability.[43]

In 1925, government agents, who had been watching Wexler's operation, got lucky when one of his ship captains, Hans Furhman, became disgruntled with the amount of money he was receiving from a shipment. Furhman decided to get even by going to the authorities and telling them about a Canadian steamer that was on its way to Queens with a hidden cargo of liquor consigned to Wexler. On September 23, agents raided Wexler's headquarters, arresting everyone there, including Maxey Greenberg, and seized maps, charts, and radio codes. Wexler, who was en route to Europe for a family vacation, was arrested when he returned. Before Wexler's trial was to begin, Furhman mysteriously died in a guarded New York hotel room. The police ruled it a suicide and the case against Wexler went down the drain.

With his operation exposed and his boats seized, however, Wexler abandoned the rum-running business and relocated to Hudson County, New Jersey. Along with Maxey Greenberg and Max Hassel, Wexler muscled his way into the bootlegging business and opened several breweries that were licensed to produce near-beer. Wexler rigged the breweries to produce the "real stuff." By 1930, he was the main supplier of bootleg beer to northern New Jersey and eastern Pennsylvania. He paid Jersey City Mayor Frank Hague and his political machine handsomely for protection. To throw off law enforcement, Wexler operated legal near-beer breweries in Paterson, Newark, Union City, and Elizabeth. From these breweries, trucks left daily with legal near-beer shipments. Meanwhile, the genuine beer was produced in the same vats, but before it went through the denaturing process, it was pumped by underground pipes to bottling plants, sometimes miles away. The gang of triggermen Wexler hired to make sure both his near- and real beer reached their destinations was said to be headed by Abner "Longy" Zwillman.

By the late 1920s, some of the younger men whose names would become synonymous with organized crime began to emerge on the East Coast: Charles Luciano, Meyer Lansky, Benjamin Siegel, Frank Costello, and Joe Adonis. They, along with Wexler, became part of what was termed the "Group of Seven" (see Appendix) or the "Big Seven." After the 1925 raid on Wexler's office, crime writers have always attached him with Philadelphia mobsters Max "Boo Boo" Hoff and Harry "Nig Rosen" Stromberg. How much influence and how many operations Wexler had going in Philadelphia was never quite clear.

In the *Last Testament of Lucky Luciano* (see Appendix), Luciano talked about a trip he made with Joe Adonis to Atlantic City sometime around 1927–1928. Luciano was badly in need of imported liquor to supply his customers and went to see Enoch "Nucky" Johnson. According to Luciano, he was willing to make Johnson a partner in his gambling enterprise, but "Nucky" had to come up with some much needed Scotch for him. Luciano demanded, "I need Scotch now . . . So, who's making the next shipment?" Depending on which book you read, the shipment was coming in for either Masseria or Maranzano, and it was going to Wexler, either for his customers or to be "cut" by him, in Philadelphia. For whomever it was intended, it never got to them. The shipment was hijacked by a gang that Luciano claimed to be a part of, which included Lansky, Siegel, and Adonis.

There have been different accounts of the hijacking. Some claim that as many as three or four of the men were murdered in a gunfight and that one of the survivors recognized Lansky and told Wexler. From that point on, Wexler and Lansky were bitter enemies. It started what Joseph Valachi (see Appendix) referred to as the "Jew War."

In addition to his feud with Lansky, Wexler was facing an investigation of his income tax returns by the Internal Revenue Service (IRS). According to Luciano, he and Lansky formulated a plan to feed the IRS incriminating evidence to help them put Wexler away. The plan was allegedly carried out by Lansky's brother, Jake, who was said to have several friends who were IRS agents. Jake traveled to Philadelphia and supplied the agents with financial information that led to Wexler's indictment. Thomas Dewey represented the government at the Wexler tax trial. If there was any truth to Luciano's statement, Dewey never acknowledged it. In Dewey's book *Twenty Against the Underworld,* neither Jake nor Meyer Lansky is mentioned.

With the spectacular conviction in Chicago against Al Capone, the special agents of the Intelligence Unit of the IRS were reassigned to New York to begin the same process on East Coast bootleggers Irving Wexler and Dutch Schultz. For two years, six investigators worked full time collecting evidence on Wexler that would stand up in court.

While Wexler prepared himself for the tax case, he was fighting another battle. The newspapers claimed that the trio of Wexler, Greenberg, and Hassel had killed those who got in the way of establishing their lucrative bootleg business. Local bootleggers James "Bugs" Donovan and Frank Dunn were part of this slaughter. With Wexler now entrenched in his legal problems, his enemies struck back. *The New York Times* stated that it was a north Jersey gang, made up of the "remnants of the one deposed" by the Wexler gang, that made its move.

Wexler later testified, in April 1933, that while he, Greenberg, and Hassel were meeting at the Elizabeth Carteret Hotel in Elizabeth, New Jersey, he heard "sort of like a rattle of dishes out in the hall." When he went to investigate, he saw "some of the men that worked for Mr. Hassel and Mr. Greenberg running along the hall." He claims the men told him "they just shot Max and Jimmy." Wexler, however, said he was unable to identify any of the men in the hallway that day. In Mark Stuart's biography of "Longy" Zwillman, *Gangster #2*, Stuart claimed gunmen sent by Dutch Schultz did the shooting and that Wexler escaped by jumping out a window.

After the shooting, Wexler hid at a hunting lodge he owned in Sullivan County, New York. Wexler kept two bodyguards on hand, a speedboat docked by the lakeside, and a pistol under his pillow. He stayed there until May 1933 when government agents tracked him down and brought him back to be charged with income tax evasion.

In his book, Dewey described some of the tasks the agents had to perform to prepare the indictment against Wexler:

> Agents needed to find out, for example, who sold the beer barrels to the Gordon breweries? Who sold the malt? Who sold the fleet of trucks the Gordon organization used for distribution? Who sold the oil, the gasoline, the tires, the brewing machinery, the cooperage coating, the air compressors, the cleaning compounds, the kettles and pipes, the hops, the yeast, the repair parts for the trucks, and the materials for repairing beer barrels, the heads, shooks, and rivets? Who installed the piping and the electrical equipment?
>
> How were all these goods and services paid for, and in whose names had delivery been taken? What did the sellers' books show about the checks and who had signed them? On what banks had the checks been drawn?[44]

Dewey claimed that in several instances, the agents were in a foot race to get to the company records and banks before Wexler's men. They often lost. The agents investigated companies and found that accounting entries had been rewritten where they involved Wexler. There were times when agents went into New Jersey banks and were told to sit and wait. Soon Wexler's men would show up and withdraw all of the money from his account and remove any evidence of ownership of the account. One time agents were arrested in a Hoboken bank by the local police. They were held until Wexler's men arrived and carried off the records.

Although Wexler never opened a bank account in his own name, he was careless at times and endorsed checks with his name or the name on the dummy account that had been set up. Dewey would claim that the handwriting expert assigned to the case "did more than any other single factor to tie the whole case together."

As the Dewey investigation ground on, Wexler battled back. Perhaps the most intriguing part of his fight involved New York's corrupt Democratic machine, Tammany Hall. The district attorney of New York County, "the perennially inactive" Thomas C. T. Crain, announced that he was initiating an investigation of Wexler. After a few weeks he gave up, stating publicly there were no witnesses brave enough to testify against Wexler. Dewey stated that this incident created one of the darkest days of the investigation, as a number of witnesses the prosecution had lined up suddenly forgot everything they had to say.

Dewey's men persevered. By the end of the two-year investigation, they had interviewed more than 1,000 witnesses, reviewed 200 bank accounts, traced the toll slips of more than 100,000 phone calls, and sat through several thousand hours of grand jury examination.

Wexler was indicted for attempting to evade payment of federal income taxes. The indictment at trial time claimed he had an unreported net income of $1,338,000 for 1930 and $1,026,000 for 1931.

The trial was set to begin on November 20, 1933, but Dewey had one more hurdle to clear. U.S. Attorney George Z. Medalie, Dewey's boss , resigned on November 21 and returned to private practice. The next day Dewey was sworn in. At the age of 31 he became the youngest man ever to hold the office of U.S. district attorney.

When the trial opened, Dewey introduced the Wexler empire to the jury. He presented information on the breweries, washhouses for the barrels, drops for the delivery, and concealment of the beer, the barrels, a vehicle repair garage, five offices, two houses, several hotel suites, and 60 Mack trucks. After nine days, 131 witnesses, and more than 900 exhibits, Dewey rested his case. It was now up to Wexler to prove how he acquired these assets with a net income of $8,100 that he claimed for 1930.

Wexler's attorney tried to convince the jury that the business had been owned and operated by the now deceased Greenberg and Hassel. Any wealth his client had accumulated had been given to him by the two men. When the defense called on an insurance man to prove that Wexler was actually a poor man, Dewey demolished his credibility by producing several memos sent to the insurance company that showed Wexler's heavy investments in several hotels.

The final defense witness was Wexler himself. His testimony proved pathetic. He claimed to be "lured" into the beer business and "lured" into investing in the hotels by Greenberg and Hassel. When presented with the paperwork for a building loan where he had signed one personal guarantee for $1 million and another for $795,000, his answer was simply that it was "just a favor" for Max Greenberg. Wexler testified that none of the brewery employees worked for him; instead they worked for "Max and Jimmy."

Wexler tried to convince the jury that what he did he did for his family, but he floundered terribly under the young prosecutor's acute cross-examination. At one point, Dewey's assistants suggested he close his examination because Wexler, "looking physically sick," would gain sympathy from the jury while under this much pressure.

The case went to the jury on the afternoon of December 1, 1933. A verdict was reached in just 5l minutes. Back in the courtroom, the jury foreman announced, "We find the defendant guilty on the first count, the second count, the third count and the fourth count." The newspapers reported Wexler's "jaw sagged and his dark eyes (were) fixed in hatred on the men in the jury box as their verdict was pronounced." Seated behind Wexler was his wife Leah, who cried openly as the verdict was read. The judge fined Wexler a total of $80,000 and sentenced him to 10 years in the federal penitentiary in Atlanta.

In addition to his conviction and jail sentence, Wexler suffered a personal tragedy as well. Over the years Wexler tried to shield his family from his criminal activities. The veil of middle-class respectability that his wife and children lived under was shattered by Wexler's high-profile trial and conviction. His wife, Leah, the daughter of a rabbi, endured much shame. Wexler's oldest son, Theodore, was in his first year of premed at the University of North Carolina. Wexler was proud of his son and often boasted about him. His son remained in New York with his mother throughout the trial, but returned to school after the verdict was announced. Wexler's brother, Nathan, called Theodore and urged him to return to New York a few days later to plead to the judge and Dewey for a reduction in sentence for his father, and for Wexler to be freed on bail while an appeal was pending. On his way back to New York, Theodore was killed in a car accident on snow- and sleet-covered roads.

In 1940, Wexler was released from Leavenworth Penitentiary after serving seven years. Upon leaving he declared, "Waxey Gordon is dead. From now on it's Irving Wexler salesman." He traveled to San Francisco during the summer of 1941. At the time it was reported that he still owed the government $2.5 million in back taxes. When San Francisco police officers found him registered at an expensive hotel, he told them that he had come west to begin anew and was selling a "revolutionary type of cleaning fluid." Although he had more than $400 in cash on him, the police arrested him for vagrancy. He posted $10 bail and left town.

If Wexler became a salesman, he wasn't an honest one. When America began sugar rationing during World War II, Wexler was caught selling 10,000 pounds of it to an illegal distillery. He was convicted and served another year in jail.

Wexler got involved in the drug trade and, by 1950, the Federal Narcotics Bureau had a large file on him. In December 1950, the bureau used an ex-convict to befriend Wexler and set him up for what would be his final arrest. After two successful drug transactions, Wexler was apprehended on August 2, 1951, by federal agents for selling heroin. Wexler was not just facing a sentence for heading a narcotics ring that was believed to have international connections; it was his fourth felony offense, which meant under New York's "Baumes Law" that he was subject to a sentence of life in prison if convicted. New York General Sessions Judge Francis L. Valente found Wexler guilty and sentenced him on December 13 to 25 years to life.

Wexler was sent to Sing Sing; on March 8, 1952, he was transferred to Attica. On April 10, he was charged in another federal indictment for participating in a coast-to-coast heroin racket. A warrant for his arrest was issued in San Francisco and he was transferred to California on May 21 to be arraigned. Wexler pled not guilty to two counts of narcotics trafficking. He was one of 23 people indicted in the nationwide narcotics case. Ten had pleaded guilty, and two were still fugitives. The trial with the remaining 10 people was set to begin August 18. Wexler was being held in the San Francisco County jail but was soon transferred to the federal facility on Alcatraz. Wexler, who had been ill for some time, was confined to the prison hospital. On the afternoon of June 24, 1952, Wexler was sitting in a chair speaking to a physician when he suffered a massive heart attack and died. Wexler's body was taken back to New York, where he was buried in Mount Hebron Cemetery in Flushing Queens.

An assistant U.S. attorney, who announced Wexler's death, surprised many by stating that Wexler was expected to be a government witness against the other defendants. Whether Wexler had worked out a deal to reduce his own sentence by this action, the government wasn't saying.

NOTES

1. *Los Angeles Examiner,* November 27, 1942, "Heavily Guarded Tannenbaum Takes Stand in Siegel, Carbo Slaying Trial."

2. *Los Angeles Examiner,* November 23, 1939, "Hoodlum Revenge Is Believed Motive for Brutal Killing."

3. Prosecutor Thomas E. Dewey denied that Greenberg had been slated to testify at Buchalter's upcoming narcotics trial, even though the case was being prosecuted by the federal government.

4. Joseph Bonanno with Sergio Lalli, *A Man of Honor* (New York: Simon and Schuster, 1983), p. 70.

5. *New York Sun,* September 11, 1931, "Link Midtown Murder Victim to Smugglers."

6. Bonanno with Lalli, *A Man of Honor,* pp. 70–71.

7. Ibid., p. 74.

8. Ibid., p. 75.

9. Ibid., pp. 96–97.

10. Martin Gosch and Richard Hammer, *The Last Testament of Lucky Luciano* (Boston: Little, Brown and Company, 1974), p. 46.

11. Ibid., pp. 47–48.

12. Ibid., p. 58.

13. Ibid., p. 59.

14. Ibid., p. 60.

15. Ibid., p. 63.

16. *New York Times,* August 8, 1922, "Gunmen Shoot Six in East Side Swarm."

17. *New York Times,* August 12, 1922, "Gang Kills Gunman; 2 Bystanders Hit."

18. *New York Evening Post,* April 16, 1931, "Hint 'Joe the Boss' Own Gang Victim."

19. *New York Sun,* April 20, 1931, "Joe the Boss Is Buried at Last."

20. Ibid.

21. *New York Evening Post,* April 20, 1931, '"Joe the Boss' Goes to Grave Without Benefit of Gangland."

22. Ibid.

23. Ibid.

24. Leonard Katz, *Uncle Frank* (New York: Drake Publishers, 1973), p. 43.

25. Anthony Summers and Robbyn Swan, *Sinatra: The Life* (New York: Alfred A. Knopf, 2005), pp. 46–47.

26. Ibid., p. 74.

27. Ibid., p. 75.

28. Katz, *Uncle Frank,* pp. 183–184.

29. Fred J. Cook, *The Secret Rulers* (New York: Duell, Sloan and Pearce, 1966), p. 294.

30. *Newark Star-Ledger,* October 9, 1951, "Moretti's Rites Riotous, Widow Faints Twice; Probe's End Seen Near."

31. Bonanno with Lalli, *A Man of Honor,* p. 141.

32. *New York Times,* June 23, 1957, "Police Photograph Funeral of Scalise."

33. This according to his obituary in the *New York Times* on June 10, 1947. Other sources indicate the year of birth as both 1895 and 1899.

34. *New York Times,* June 10, 1947, "Gurrah Jake Dies in Prison Hospital."

35. Ibid.

36. *New York Times,* August 10, 1937, "16 in 'Ring' Indicted in Garment Racket."

37. Reed Vetterli was the special agent in charge of the Kansas City FBI office in June 1933 and was present when the Union Station Massacre took place. He survived the notorious attack that killed four law enforcement agents and escaped bank robber Frank "Jelly" Nash. Vetterli left the FBI in August 1938.

38. *New York Herald Tribune,* April 15, 1938, '"Gurrah,' Hunted for 17 Months, Hiding in City, Gives Himself Up."

39. *New York Times,* April 16, 1938, "Taste for Luxury Cornered Gurrah."

40. *New York Times,* June 18, 1938, "Gurrah Convicted, Gets 3-Year Term As Fur Racketeer."

41. *New York Herald Tribune,* June 18, 1938, "Gurrah Gets 3 Years, Weeps, Protests That He Was 'Framed.'"

42. *New York Times,* June 10, 1947, "Gurrah Jake Dies in Prison Hospital."

43. Albert Fried, *The Rise and Fall of the Jewish Gangster in America* (New York: Holt, Rinehart and Winston, 1980), p. 98.

44. Thomas E. Dewey, *Twenty Against the Underworld* (Garden City, NY: Doubleday & Company, 1974), p. 118.

BIBLIOGRAPHY

Bonanno, Joseph, with Sergio Lalli. *A Man of Honor*. New York: Simon and Schuster, 1983.

Cook, Fred J. *The Secret Rulers*. New York: Duell, Sloan and Pearce, 1966.

Dewey, Thomas E. *Twenty Against the Underworld*. Garden City, NY: Doubleday & Company, 1974.

Fried, Albert. *The Rise and Fall of the Jewish Gangster in America*. New York: Holt, Rinehart and Winston, 1980.

Gosch, Martin, and Richard Hammer. *The Last Testament of Lucky Luciano*. Boston: Little, Brown and Company, 1974.

Katz, Leonard. *Uncle Frank*. New York: Drake Publishers, 1973.

Summers, Anthony, and Robbyn Swan. *Sinatra: The Life*. New York: Alfred A. Knopf, 2005.

APPENDIX

APALACHIN SUMMIT (1957)

The purpose for the underworld's most famous barbeque held at Joseph Barbara's home in a little hamlet called Apalachin in upstate New York on November 14, 1957, has been the subject of speculation for more than 50 years. There is the belief among many organized crime historians that police were tipped off to the meeting in Apalachin to discredit and embarrass Vito Genovese, who it was believed had arranged the sit-down. Some believe that the people behind this meeting were Lucky Luciano, Frank Costello, Meyer Lansky, and Carlos Marcello—none of whom were there. Some Carlo Gambino biographers, John H. Davis in particular, claim that Gambino was part of the plot even though it was to be his coronation and that he knew he would be arrested. Davis's explanation for Gambino putting himself in this situation was, "It was worth the risk to ensure the undermining of Genovese. Almost anything was worth the risk if it would diminish Genovese's power and curb his ambitions."[1]

Although one can certainly understand the intense dislike generated by the greedy and power-hungry Vito Genovese and the desire to knock him down a notch, was it worth it for the plotters to expose all the other mob bosses at the meeting, many of whom they had known and been friends with for years? In addition, the testimony of New York State Trooper Edgar G. Croswell, the officer credited with breaking up the meeting, would have to be considered perjured if he had indeed been notified of the meeting from an outside source.

The "summit," which took place while the McClellan Committee Hearings were in session, caused Senator John L. McClellan to proclaim:

> The meeting gave to millions of Americans their first clear knowledge that we have in this country a criminal syndicate that is obviously tightly organized into a secret brotherhood which none of its members dare betray, and which has insinuated its tentacles into business and labor and public life at high levels.[2]

Dwight C. Smith, Jr. was the director of institutional research at the State University of New York (Albany) and a visiting professor of police science at John Jay College when he wrote *The Mafia Mystique*. In it, he accurately depicted, "that law enforcement officers speak knowingly of the event and its significance in the development of organized crime. Virtually every book from the sixties concerning organized crime refers to it in a way that implies extensive knowledge of what transpired. The public is thus 'told' about an event by people who were not there."[3]

Despite the best guesses of organized crime historians, the reason for the gathering has never been clearly defined. First among the arguments has always been how many people were present. Below is a sampling of the numbers claimed:

- 58—Senator John McClellan in his book *Crime Without Punishment*.
- 60-plus—Frederic Sondern, Jr., in *Brotherhood of Evil: The Mafia*.
- 62 or more—*Report on the Activities and Associations of Persons Identified As Present at the Residence of Joseph Barbara, Sr., at Apalachin, New York, on November 14, 1957, and the Reasons for Their Presence.*
- 65—*The Report of the State of NY Joint Legislative Committee on Government Operations.*
- 75—The 1967 *Task Force Report on Organized Crime*.
- 100-plus—U.S. Attorney General Robert F. Kennedy.

There have even been discrepancies in the weather reported that day. Frederic Sondern related, "The weather was unusually mild for November." Renee Buse in *The Deadly Silence* gives us, "The sky was gray. The November temperature hovered just above freezing. Cold, damp rain-winds swirled through the barren trees." The actual forecast for the day, according to the local newspaper, was a high of 60 degrees with a light rain.

Attendance figures and weather conditions aside, the nature of the meeting is still the question that counts. What follows is a sampling of what crime experts and writers have stated were the reasons for the mid-November get-together:

- **John T. Cusack,** the district supervisor of the Federal Bureau of Narcotics, told the New York State Legislative Committee that the summit, "should be considered a meeting of the Grand Council" of the Mafia.

- **Robert F. Kennedy,** lead counsel for the McClellan Committee, told the committee that the summit was a meeting of the "commission" that runs Cosa Nostra and "makes policy decisions for the organization." Kennedy told the committee that the commission consists of "between 9 and 12 members."

- **Frederic Sondern, Jr.,** the first writer to author a book on the incident, *The Brotherhood of Evil: The Mafia,* related, "The business of the meeting at Barbara's—according to well placed informers who pieced the picture together for the Treasury Department's agents—concentrated on two questions crucial to the future of big organized rackets, narcotics and gambling."

- **Renee Buse,** author of *The Deadly Silence,* weighed in with the story that the meeting was "an appeal to 'the Bosses' by Carmine Lombardozzi against conviction by 'a kangaroo court of his peers . . . for having tried to muscle into another man's exclusive juke box territory." Lombardozzi was reportedly a capo in the gang formerly headed by Albert Anastasia.

- **Joseph Valachi,** the underworld's most famous informant, told the McClellan Committee, "The meeting was held for two main reasons that I know of. One was to talk about the justifying of the shooting of Albert Anastasia. The other one was that they were going to talk about eliminating some couple hundred new members."
- **Michael D. Lyman and Gary W. Potter,** educators and co-authors of *Organized Crime,* suggest that, "by most accounts it was an assembly of top Mafia dons in the country who had gathered to anoint Vito Genovese as their new boss of bosses and to cover an agenda of mob business, most notably whether to go into the drug trafficking trade in a major way."[4]

There were secondary theories as well. One was that the men were there to discuss the garbage-hauling business. It just so happened that this was the topic the McClellan Committee was discussing in their Washington hearings. Another was labor issues in the garment industry in New York and northeastern Pennsylvania. Both of these issues were supported by the geography from which the participants arrived. Lyman and Potter discount these theories by stating, "Reasonable suggestions about the garment industry or the garbage-hauling investigation being topics of discussion were simply dismissed as not being sufficiently sinister."[5]

Of course the analysis wouldn't be complete unless some of the attendees weighed in also. When they were asked during the interrogations, the most repeated tale was that they had all arrived, coincidentally on the same day, to visit Joseph Barbara, Sr., who had recently suffered a heart attack.

One of the immediate results of the gathering was to launch the FBI into the organized crime-fighting arena. For years, J. Edgar Hoover had declared there was no "organized" crime in America. Now he and his bureau had to scramble to put together files on the individuals who had attended the Apalachin Summit. When Robert Kennedy requested any criminal files the various crime fighting agencies had on the individuals who attended the meeting for the McClellan Hearings, the only agency to report was the Federal Bureau of Narcotics, who had been tracking the activities of alleged Mafia members for decades.

Some reports claim Hoover was jealous of his counterpart at the Bureau of Narcotics, Harry J. Anslinger. One account presented the hypothesis, "Since Mr. Anslinger insisted the Mafia existed, the idea goes, Hoover denied its existence."[6]

Hoover demanded action from his agents who responded to the call. But the report they turned in proved to be an embarrassment to the director, as it showed that the Mafia/Organized Crime had been in operation for the entire time he denied its existence. Hoover initiated his "Top Hoodlum Program" at this point, which required bureau chiefs across the country to identify the top organized crime figures within their jurisdictions and get a handle on their activities. This meant the use of what was then illegal wiretaps. The mystery conclave generated four separate investigations. The first was ordered by New York Governor W. Averell Harriman, who selected Arthur L. Reuter, the acting commissioner of investigation, to "make a complete investigation of the activities and associations of those present at Barbara's house, as well as the reasons for their presence." Reuter's work was completed and published in a report released on May 2, 1958.

The second was conducted by William F. Horan, chairman of the New York State Joint Legislative Committee on Government Operations, during December 1957 and January 1958. Run by the Republican state legislative leaders, the investigation proved to be more of a political move against the Democratic governor to keep the incident in the public spotlight, eventually resulting in the election of a Republican governor during the fall of 1958.

The third investigative body was the McClellan Committee. The inquiry phase was conducted in Washington D.C. from June 30 to July 3, 1958. Dwight C. Smith, Jr., summed up the government's session as follows:

> What the evidence showed was that a group of men who were related by marriage and of Italian heritage, who had close relationships with each other, and who could be shown to have criminal records and business or labor associations had been observed together at a single location in upstate New York. From that limited evidence the committee had to build hypotheses. The assemblage at Apalachin was obviously a "meeting," for purposes that must equally obviously have been nefarious—especially since none of them would tell what those purposes were. Even if the purpose had been benign, silence before the committee demonstrated contempt for the government, and that was a clear sign of evil intent.[7]

Finally, the fourth investigation began in August 1958 and was conducted by the New York State Investigations Commission (SIC). Many of the New York attendees to the summit were subpoenaed to appear. They were granted immunity and those who didn't answer questions were jailed. Although several of the men spent months in jail (Costenze Valenti spent nearly two years behind bars), none was willing to discuss the events of that November day. The commission filed its final report in February 1963, revealing no clearer evidence than the Horan investigation, which was completed more than five years earlier.

Two important points of interest about the notorious meeting should be mentioned. Despite the lack of hard evidence, the Apalachin Summit created a perception about organized crime in the public's mind that Italian criminals, under the banner of the Mafia, were organized and functioning on a national level. Second, it set a benchmark in the history of organized crime in America, because it marked the entrance of Hoover's FBI on to the scene.

ATLANTIC CITY CONFERENCE (1929)

The Atlantic City Conference was held in Atlantic City, New Jersey, from May 13 to May 16, 1929. Unlike the preempted meeting at the Statler Hotel in Cleveland, Ohio, five months earlier, which consisted of approximately 23 attendees, all of Sicilian background, the Garden State meeting was reportedly composed of gang leaders of various nationalities and religions.

Atlantic City was chosen because of the control and protection that allegedly could be provided by Enoch "Nucky" Johnson. Known as the "Boss of Atlantic City," Johnson at one time or another served as sheriff, county treasurer, and clerk of the supreme court. He was reputed to be one of the most influential Republicans in the state. Most of the illegal activities in the area were under his control.

One of the reasons for the meeting, which most historians agree on, was to reign in Chicago boss Al Capone. In February, the slaughter of seven men in a North Side Chicago garage, which became known internationally as The St. Valentine's Day Massacre, aroused public indignation against underworld activities. Capone topped this off by allegedly beating to death with a baseball bat, three men who he accused of plotting his assassination a week before the meeting. Depending on who is telling the story, either Costello or Johnny Torrio talked Capone into getting himself arrested on weapon possession charges in Philadelphia after the meeting. Supposedly, with Capone in jail there would be a "cooling off" period for the gangs with the public.

As with the Apalachin Summit, the purpose for the Atlantic City Conference is based on who is telling the story. In addition to the senseless killings, the other topic believed to be addressed was cooperation between the gangs and a suggestion that they begin to look toward the end of Prohibition.

Another point of contention has been who called the meeting. According to Frank Costello biographer Leonard Katz, "Costello often discussed this visionary concept . . . with his closest mob confederates." Important underworld leaders from across the country attended. "In this company, Costello was relatively a lower echelon man. Yet according to FBI informants, he was the 'maitre d' of the convention,' putting people together, laying out the agenda, influencing the decisions that were reached with his persuasive powers and good sense."[8]

In *Lansky,* by Hank Messick, the author claimed, "Various writers over the years have credited the inspiration for the gangland convention held in Atlantic City to Costello, Lucania, or Al Capone—depending on whom they were attempting to portray as the boss of all bosses. Lansky was no boss, but the inspiration for the gathering was his. As Lansky explained it to Lucania, the meeting on its surface would be designed to create a national combination, outside the Mafia, to facilitate distribution of booze and eliminate some of the expensive competition that drove up the wholesale price in Canada, the Bahamas, and England. If it also developed a power base which Lucania could later use to challenge the authority of the Mustache Petes, especially Joe the Boss, so much the better."[9]

In *The Last Testament of Lucky Luciano,* the authors gave Luciano credit for organizing the meeting, but added a twist to the timing. They claimed that the meeting followed the wedding of Meyer Lansky in May 1929, and was scheduled to be held in Atlantic City where the Lanskys happened to be honeymooning.[10]

Contradicting Messick's and *The Last Testament of Lucky Luciano* authors' descriptions of Lansky's role is biographer Robert Lacey. In *Little Man: Meyer Lansky and the Gangster Life,* Lacey claimed Lansky and his new bride spent their honeymoon in Canada. In fact, he failed to even mention the Atlantic City Conference in his book.

Another biographer, Mark Stuart, in his work on Abner "Longy" Zwillman, claimed that, "In 1929, it was pure nonsense to speak of organized crime in terms of the Mafia . . . they weren't organized into anything like a national 'trust' until Longy Zwillman arranged the 1929 convention in Atlantic City."[11]

It is interesting to note the comments from the earliest books that discuss the Atlantic City meeting. In a Luciano biography by Hickman Powell, written in 1939, 10 years after the meeting, the author claimed "Frankie Costello, the slot machine man" spent $25,000 of his own money to arrange the conference. Then, without listing a single name, he wrote: "The aim of the Atlantic City conference was to establish peaceful co-operation in the underworld instead of warfare. One disturbing element had been a group commonly called 'greasers' who were very influential in the Unione Siciliana—old-line, unassimilated Italian leaders and recent immigrants. Out of that conference grew the movement to modernize the underworld or, as some expressed the idea, to Americanize the mobs."[12]

In *Gang Rule in New York,* published the next year, the authors added to this theme about the Unione Siciliana. Citing that the "Yale-Lombardo killings had every appearance of internal conflict in the Unione" They wrote the meeting "was attended by most of the leaders in the national Unione Sicilane (sic)"[13] The authors seemingly had this meeting mixed up with the Cleveland meeting in December 1928, where all the participants were Sicilian.

THE CASTELLAMMARESE WAR (1930–1931)

During the first two years of the 1930s, what is considered by many to be the most significant "mob war" in the history of the underworld in the United States was fought between two Sicilian-born Mafia bosses operating in New York City. The two principals in the war were Giuseppe "Joe the Boss" Masseria and Salvatore Maranzano; however, there is little verifiable information about the war and the body count. Although some accounts claim the death count was as high as 60, a closer look at history reveals the number to be in the range of 9 to 12.

Other than the murder victims, police had no idea that these killings were all part of the same conflict. The name "Castellammarese War" wasn't even introduced to law enforcement until Joe Valachi began talking to the government in 1962. It was not made public until the next year. With the murder of Giuseppe "Joe the Boss" Masseria on April 15, 1931, many police officials and members of the press believed his death was the opening volley of a new mob war, not the final act in an old one.

Nearly all the information about the Castellammarese conflict comes from three sources: *The Valachi Papers*; the autobiography of Joseph Bonanno, *A Man of Honor*; and the questionable biography of Luciano, *The Last Testament of Lucky Luciano*. The real foundation of this information is Joseph Valachi's 1963 testimony before the McClellan Committee and Peter Maas's book *The Valachi Papers*. Much of what Valachi tells us, however, is questionable because of what he reveals, or doesn't reveal, about his personal role, and the fact that it seems incredible that a person of his rank would have been exposed to such high level "insider" information.

In the autobiography of Joseph Bonanno, *A Man of Honor,* the mob boss stated:

> I must digress briefly here to say a few words about Valachi, because in the public mind he has assumed a role way out of proportion to the actual part he played in the war. The American public first heard of Valachi in the early 1960s when he appeared before the McClellan Committee of the U.S. Senate. What the public and the police know about the Castellammarese War is still largely based on what Valachi told them. This has resulted in a great deal of distortion. Valachi did not see the entire picture and he was an unreliable interpreter of events.[14]

During the McClellan hearings, while discussing the war, committee members wanted to find out the causes of the conflict. Valachi offered up "Masseria's alleged intention to kill persons who came from the Sicilian town of Castellammare del Golfo."[15] But Valachi never understood why he was out hunting and killing rival gang members, telling the senators, "I never found out the reason. I never asked for the reason. All I understand is that all the Castellammarese were sentenced to death."

According to Valachi, the Castellammarese War would take the lives of "some sixty" men. When one examines the murders discussed by the three principals in their books, where the victims are actually named, a different picture emerges. The casualty list is significantly low—only 12 names. Bonanno's book, *A Man of Honor,* lists 10, and *The Last Testament of Lucky Luciano* and *The Valachi Papers* reveal 9 apiece. Seven of those killings are consistent throughout the three books, including Joseph Pinzolo, but whether or not his death pertained to the war is questionable.

There is some argument as to which murder actually began the Castellammarese War in 1930—the killing of Gaetano Reina on February 26 or the slaying of Gaspar Milazzo in Detroit on May 30. What follows is a chronological listing of the murders. In discussing the disparity in the details, we begin with *The Valachi Papers,* which was the first of the three books to be published, followed by *The Last Testament of Lucky Luciano,* and Bonanno's *A Man of Honor.* In addition, several newspaper accounts of the murders also add to the disparity.

February 26, 1930—Gaetano "Tommy" Reina
The Valachi Papers

Valachi stated that as 1930 began, Masseria was "bidding for absolute supremacy in the Italian underworld." In his bidding Masseria set out to eliminate Maranzano and all the Castellammarese powers in New York City and other parts of the country. In addition, Masseria also muscled in on one of his allies, Gaetano "Tommy" Reina, who controlled most of the city's ice distribution in a period before electric refrigeration. Valachi stated that when Reina resisted Masseria's attempts, "Joe the Boss" ordered him killed.

The Last Testament of Lucky Luciano

Luciano claimed that Reina was in the process of changing allegiance from Masseria to Maranzano. This would break up a monopoly Luciano was working on in the garment industry with Reina's underboss Tommy Lucchese and Louis "Lepke" Buchalter. When Masseria got word of Reina's treachery, he ordered Luciano to make sure Reina didn't change sides. But Luciano decided Reina had to go. He stated he ordered Genovese to kill Reina "face-to-face accordin' to the rules." According to the book, Luciano discovered that Reina spent Wednesday evening with an aunt who lived on Sheridan Avenue. Genovese went to the Bronx location on February 26, 1930, and when Reina came out, "Vito blew his head off with a shotgun."

A Man of Honor

Bonanno doesn't discuss the murder in his book other than to say that Reina was murdered in the Bronx. This would seem to indicate that Bonanno didn't consider this killing to be an integral part of the war, let alone the opening volley.

Newspapers

Newspapers described a more lurid ending. Reina had spent the evening with Mrs. Maria Ennis, a widow, whom Reina was obviously having an affair with. Reina had rented the Sheridan Avenue apartment where the couple was known as Mr. and Mrs. James Ennis. Reina also maintained a home on Rochambeau Avenue in the Bronx where the 40-year-old's wife and nine children lived.

When Reina and Ennis left the apartment together that night, two men confronted them, one armed with a sawed-off shotgun. Reina took the force of the blast in the chest. The Bronx medical examiner "found ten slugs in the right side of Reina's chest. The buttons of his shirt were ripped off and embedded in the skin." The police and newspapers said the killing was for revenge. Reina had turned state's evidence in the November 1914 murder of Barnett Baff, a poultry dealer, and informed on several men who received long prison sentences.

May 30, 1930—Gaspar Milazzo and Sasa Parrino (Murdered in Detroit)

The Valachi Papers

Valachi did not discuss the murders at all; in fact, Milazzo's name doesn't appear in the index.

The Last Testament of Lucky Luciano

Luciano stated that Masseria sent gunmen to kill Milazzo, never mentioning Parrino in his book. Luciano claims the murder solidified the Castellammarese countrymen under Maranzano and was the event that started the war. Luciano mentioned the Castellammarese War only twice in his book.

A Man of Honor

Bonanno is the only participant who mentioned both Milazzo and Parrino and claimed that, after these murders, the Castellammarese clans of New York City united under Maranzano, who for the first time took on a leadership role. Bonanno claimed that after Cola Schiro, the previous leader of the family, fled in fear of his life, Masseria supported Sasa Parrino's brother, Joseph, to "become the new father of the Castellammarese clan" in the New York City. He then simply stated, "Joe Parrino was shot to death in a restaurant."[16]

August 15, 1930—Pietro "Peter the Clutching Hand" Morello and Giuseppe Pariano

The Valachi Papers

Valachi credited the legendary "Buster from Chicago" with these murders. He claimed Buster described the shootings to him. "He said [Morello] kept running around the office, and Buster had to give him a couple of more shots before he went down. He said there was some other guy in the office, so he took him, too." Valachi's only reference to Morello was to say he was a vicious enforcer for Masseria.

The Last Testament of Lucky Luciano

Luciano described Morello as Masseria's "constant bodyguard and shadow." He stated that he was told by Albert Anastasia that Morello had to be killed. Luciano claimed he ordered Anastasia and Frank Scalise to make the hit, and the two trapped Morello in his loansharking office in East Harlem and gunned him down. According to Luciano's account, another man named Pariano was in the office at the time and was also killed. The men had been counting money at the time, and the two shooters made off with more than $30,000.

A Man of Honor

Bonanno wrote that Morello was the true mastermind of the Masseria forces:

Maranzano used to say that if we hoped to win the war we should get at Morello before the old fox stopped following his daily routines, as Maranzano had already stopped doing. Once Morello went undercover, Maranzano would say, the old man could exist forever on a diet of hard bread, cheeses and onions. We would never find him. Morello never got a chance to go on such a severe diet. He went to his Harlem office as usual one morning, along with two of his men. All three were shot to death.

Bonanno never offered an opinion as to who killed them.

Bonanno was the only one to catch the fact that three men were actually murdered in the shooting. Gaspar Pollaro, the uncle of Pariano, was shot and later died in the hospital. It was reported that Morello was the stepbrother of Ciro Terranova, although the "Artichoke King" would deny this relationship vehemently after the murder. The building the men were murdered in on East 116th Street was owned by Morello. He kept an office on the second floor and living quarters on the fourth.

September 5, 1930—Joseph Pinzolo

The Valachi Papers

Valachi stated that Girolamo "Bobby Doyle" Santucci was the triggerman in this killing. Valachi quoted Santucci, "I got the break of my life. I caught him alone in the office."

The Last Testament of Lucky Luciano

Luciano claimed Dominic "The Gap" Petrilli shot Pinzolo twice in the face "according to the rules."

A Man of Honor

Bonanno didn't name a shooter. He wrote:

> After the death of Peter Morello, Masseria went into hiding. He had lost Morello, and this was followed by the loss of Joe Pinzolo, the man Masseria had supported to head the Reina Family after the slaying of Tom Reina. People within the Reina Family eliminated Pinzolo. The Reina Family could no longer be counted on to aid Masseria.

It's questionable whether this murder can be tied to the war itself. It was more or less the result of an internecine struggle for the leadership of the Reina Family that would have occurred whether or not there was a war. Pinzolo had been handpicked to lead the family by Masseria. Gaetano Gagliano and Tommy Lucchese, however, plotted his death and the takeover of the family.

The newspapers reported that Pinzolo was found in an office of the California Dry Fruit Importers on the tenth floor of the Brokaw Building on Broadway by a "scrubwoman." He had been shot twice in the back, twice in the chest, and once in the side. Thomas Lucchese was indicted for the murder, but the charges were later dropped.[17]

October 23, 1930—Joseph Aiello (Murdered in Chicago)

The Valachi Papers

Valachi confirmed only that Aiello was cut down by machinegun fire.

The Last Testament of Lucky Luciano

Luciano's spin on the murder was that Al Mineo was sent to Chicago by Masseria to "handle things."

A Man of Honor

Bonanno wrote: "The Castellammarese side lost Joe Aiello of Chicago. Earlier in the year, to escape harm from Al Capone, Aiello had sought and had been given refuge in Buffalo by Stefano Magaddino. Against the advice of Magaddino and Maranzano, however, Aiello didn't remain in Buffalo but returned to Chicago. Shortly after he returned there, Aiello was shot to death." Aiello was murdered in a machinegun ambush on the night of October 23, 1930, as he was leaving from a safe house to go to the train station for which he had a ticket to Mexico. The coroner removed 59 slugs from his body.

November 5, 1930—Steven Ferrigno and Al Mineo

The Valachi Papers

Valachi claimed the killers were Buster from Chicago, Girolamo "Bobby Doyle" Santucci, and Nicholas "Nick the Thief" Capuzzi. In the book, Valachi claimed that Ferrigno and Mineo "were finally slain without his knowledge and while he was away from the scene of the shootings." Valachi put the killings at about 2:45 PM.

The Last Testament of Lucky Luciano

Luciano gave very few details in his book other than to say three killers ambushed the men. What is questionable in Luciano's telling is that he was supposed to be Masseria's second in command, which would mean both Ferrigno and Mineo were subordinates to him. Yet he offered no description of the men or any other information.

A Man of Honor

Bonanno claimed that Mineo headed what became the Gambino Family and had become Masseria's chief strategist after the murder of Morello. Bonanno stated the men were killed as they came out of the building "shortly after daybreak."

Newspapers

Despite the relative importance of the two men, and the fact that it was a double murder carried out in broad daylight, neither the *New York Times* nor the *Herald Tribune* ran the story on page one. Both papers did confirm that the murders took place around mid-afternoon as the Valachi book has stated.

February 3, 1931—Joseph "Joe the Baker" Catania

The Valachi Papers

Valachi is the only one who discussed this murder. His description seems laughable compared to the newspaper reports of the day. Valachi claimed they began stalking Catania in late January, taking an empty apartment in the Fordham section of the Bronx. Although Catania kept to the same daily routine, the apartment didn't offer them a good vantage point. On the day of the shooting, Valachi, "Buster from Chicago," and two other gunmen forced their way into a ground-floor apartment in the building just before Catania was due to arrive across the street. On entering the apartment, Valachi claimed they encountered three painters "hard at work." The two gunmen lined the painters up against the wall and held them at gunpoint while Valachi and Buster went to the widow to wait. Valachi claimed Catania appeared with his wife.

At this point Valachi claimed he left the apartment to make sure their car "was ready to go." Afterward Valachi described his conversation with Buster:

"How did it go?" Valachi asked.

"He came out of the office with his wife," Buster replied. "He kissed her in front of the office, and I was worried I wouldn't get a shot. But he turned and went for the corner. She was just standing there watching when I got him. I don't think I missed once. You could see the dust coming off his coat when the bullets hit."

"It's too bad the wife had to see him go," Valachi said."

Newspapers

The newspapers reported that Catania had been entering the tobacco and candy store of Mrs. Emma Petrella, not an office. He was not in the company of his wife, but arrived there alone. Petrella had stepped into the kitchen area of the store to tend to her children when Catania walked back out to the sidewalk where he was shot.

Meanwhile, the three "hard at work" painters, turned out to be just two painters who were "sitting down to their noonday lunch." The painters told police that (instead of four men descending upon them and holding then at gunpoint) two masked men with sawed-off shotguns entered. "Get out, you," one of the gunmen snapped. With that both painters raced from the apartment. They were hardly outside the building when the shooting took place. Catania was rushed to Fordham Hospital where he died the next day.

Another possible angle regarding this murder that would explain why Bonanno and Luciano did not include it in their accounts was that Catania was the nephew of Ciro Terranova, a man who Valachi despised. In the mid-1920s, Terranova had brokered a peace between two rival gangs, one of which Valachi was a member. Unbeknownst to Valachi was that his death was one of the conditions of the treaty, and an attempt was made to kill him while he was serving a prison stretch. The would-be assassin was Peter LaTempa (see Chapter 6) who managed to leave a gash in Valachi's side that would take 38 stitches to close. Catania's murder clearly would have meant revenge for Valachi.

April 15, 1931—Giuseppe "Joe the Boss" Masseria

The Valachi Papers

By the early spring of 1931, the tide of war was turning against Joe the Boss and "two of Masseria's most trusted sidekicks, Charley Lucky Luciano and Vito Genovese, secretly turned against him." Luciano invited Masseria to lunch at a Coney Island restaurant. "From all accounts," said Valachi, "Joe the Boss, surrounded by trusted aides, had a fine time during the meal—the last one he ever ate." According to Valachi, the "others in attendance" at Masseria's killing were Vito Genovese, Frank Livorsi, and Joseph Stracci.

Newspapers

While omitted from Valachi's book, the *New York Times* printed the following statements about Ciro Terranova that Valachi made before the government committee:

Terranova, once a feared figure, did not behave well immediately after the slaying, according to Valachi. "Terranova was supposed to drive the getaway car," Valachi said, but he "was so shaking in putting the key in the ignition, they had to remove him."

"After that, he got 'the buckwheats' [loss of prestige] and his power was taken away from him," Valachi continued. "He died of a broken heart."

One has to wonder if, because of Valachi's total disdain for Terranova, he didn't make up this tale as a final slur to the reputation of the old mob boss who died in 1938. It is clear that Terranova was still active in East Harlem, including being a partner of Dutch Schultz in the policy rackets until his death.

The Last Testament of Lucky Luciano

Luciano claimed he spent the morning at Masseria's Second Avenue office in Manhattan outlining his "blueprint" for the slaughter of Maranzano's men. Around noon Luciano called the Nuova Villa Tammaro restaurant, owned by Gerardo Scarpato, and "ordered enough food to stuff a horse." Luciano claimed that just the two of them entered the restaurant to have lunch and that it took Masseria three hours to get his fill. Around 3:30 PM Luciano pulled out a deck of cards and, after playing one hand, excused himself to go use the men's room.

According to Luciano, a hit team consisting of Vito Genovese, Joe Adonis, Albert Anastasia, and Bugsy Siegel entered the restaurant and shot "Joe the Boss" to death. Masseria was clutching the ace of diamonds as he lay dead.

In a statement of arrogance, Luciano claimed that when interviewed by the police afterward, "They asked me where I was when it happened—and every newspaper printed that I said, 'As soon as I finished dryin' my hands, I walked out to see what it was all about.' That's an absolute lie. I said to them, 'I was in the can takin' a leak. I always take a long leak.'"

Luciano's book also contains the tale of Ciro Terranova being behind the wheel of the getaway car. In Luciano's version, the car was actually running, but Terranova was unable to get it in gear. Siegel, according to Luciano, shoved Terranova out of the way and commandeered the car. Just why a crack team of killers would use an old man (Terranova was 50 years old at the time) to drive a getaway car from a murder scene was never explained. This story is also not supported by eyewitnesses who saw the killers enter and leave the restaurant.

A Man of Honor

Bonanno wrote very little about Masseria's death. "He died on a full stomach, and that leads me to believe he died happy."

Newspapers and Other Sources

The newspapers painted a much different tale from the ones we have heard for years. Interesting though, is that neither newspaper mentions Luciano being there; for that matter, neither did the *Brooklyn Eagle,* the *New York Daily News,* the *New York Evening Post,* the *New York Sun,* or the *New York World-Telegram,* all having missed that tidbit. The footnotes from Robert Lacey's *Little Man: Meyer Lansky and the Gangster Life* reveal that Luciano's name never appeared in the police reports from the incident.

The newspapers had Masseria arriving at the restaurant at 2715 West 15th Street in Coney Island in his "armored steel car" in the company of three other men shortly before 3:00 PM. The *New York Daily News* accurately stated, "The restaurant was miles away from the domain of Joe the Boss." Scarpato's mother-in-law, Mrs. Anna Tammaro, waited on them while they played cards. According to two eyewitnesses, "two well dressed young men drove up and parked their car at the curb. They strolled leisurely into the place and the shooting began immediately. Some twenty shots were fired. Then the two gunmen came out without any visible signs of haste, entered their automobile and drove away." Masseria was hit with four bullets in the back and one in the back of the head. The bullets were identified as .32 and .38 caliber. In an alley next to the restaurant police recovered two guns matching those caliber bullets.[18]

The shooting brought 50 police officers and detectives, as well as a crowd of onlookers estimated at 1,000. Inside the restaurant the hats and coats of Masseria's fellow card players were left behind. Interviewed by police, Anna Tammaro said, "The four men ordered coffee when they arrived, and after they started to play cards asked her to cook them some fish." When she left to purchase the fish the shooting occurred. Masseria may not have entered the hereafter on a full stomach after all. As for the infamous Ace of Diamonds stuck in the hand of the dead mob boss, a newspaper reporter placed it there "for effect." A photograph of the dead man's hand clearly shows it was the Ace of Spades, not Diamonds.[19]

In leaving the restaurant, the bodyguards left behind their hats and coats, as well as $40 scattered among the cards on the floor. Police soon found a Buick coupe abandoned on West First Street in Coney Island. Bloodstains found in the vehicle led police to believe that at least one of the assassins had been wounded. The automobile had been reported stolen in Manhattan on November 30. The brand new license plates on the car had never been issued and were believed stolen from the Bureau of Motor Vehicles.

There was much speculation in the press as to what would happen next. The *New York Sun* reported, "Detectives considered it certain today that Masseria's death would not go unavenged for long. Some considered it the opening blast of an outbreak of gang warfare that will exceed anything the city has yet seen."[20]

Jersey City police arrested Anthony Devere, who was driving an automobile owned by Gerardo Scarpato, the owner of the restaurant. When Devere gave a phony address, police held him "for investigation and driving without a license." Devere was released after he was able to prove he was a cook at the Nuova Villa Tammaro and had taken the car at Scarpato's request to have some repairs made.

Scarpato was described as a "wealthy inn owner," who was married to the former Alvera Tammaro. There are conflicting stories as to whether Scarpato owned the Nuova Villa Tammaro, or just managed it for his mother-in-law, for whom the restaurant was named. Whatever the case, Scarpato left the restaurant to go for a walk that afternoon and was joined by a friend, thereby establishing a firm alibi for himself during the time "Joe the Boss" was murdered. When questioned at the police station, however, he implored, "Take my finger prints. Take them for your records. I think you may need them. I may be next." Scarpato was scared that friends of Masseria might think he had helped put "Joe the Boss" on the spot, not that the killers might have considered him a witness.

The *New York Daily News* provided this colorful account of events after Masseria's assassination:

A few hours after the head of the Unione Siciliana was put on the spot in a Coney Island restaurant, more than a score of his racketeering minions attended an all-night council of war in Joe's $15,000 duplex apartment at 15 West 81st St.

When this meeting broke up, a cordon of torpedoes was strung around the building, in which the widow of Joe the Boss . . . and her children reside amid the gaudy luxuries provided by his racket revenues.[21]

The newspapers depicted Masseria as an enemy, a "sworn foe of Al Capone," whereas Bonanno, Luciano, and Valachi described "Big Al" as his ally. When Masseria's 21-year-old son, James, returned from a meeting at Brooklyn police headquarters, the day after the murder, he told reporters he did not know that his father was an enemy of Capone. James Masseria and a relative were questioned for several hours by the police. The only information contributed by them was that Masseria was in a partnership with Anthony Carfano in a horseracing stable.

The following night, April 17, the murder of Ernest "Hoppy" Rossi, a Brooklyn bootlegger, was called the "opening salvo in a gang war to avenge the betrayal of Joe the Boss." Rossi's killer fired a machinegun from a sniper's position, down through the roof of the car hitting him twice in the head and once in the neck, killing him instantly. Ironically, the automobile careened to a stop in front of the 68th Street Brooklyn home of then-Police Captain Lewis J. Valentine.

Another victim in the wake of the murder was Sam Polaccio, who according to some sources was Masseria's underboss. Polaccio disappeared sometime after the killing and was never seen again. It was rumored he was "taken for a ride and buried upstate." By some accounts, Polaccio was with Masseria at the restaurant when he was murdered.

Two men believed to be suspects, if not the shooters, were John "Johnny Silk Stockings" Giustra and Carmelo Liconti. The two were partners in an undertaking business and were labor organizers among barbers and longshoremen. During the late 1920s, Giustra muscled his way into the leadership of six chapters of the International Longshoremen's Association, which came to be known as the Camarda locals (see Chapter 2). In addition, the two were also involved in bootlegging and the policy rackets.

A *New York Herald Tribune* article claimed the men were enemies of Masseria and stated, "Underworld gossip accused Leconti [*sic*] and his partner Giustra of killing Masseria."[22] The newspaper reported that on May 10, the men received a telephone call at their place of business on Henry Street in Brooklyn. The caller, according to the *Herald Tribune,* asked them to come to an apartment at 75 Monroe Street in Manhattan "to make peace with Masseria's friends."

On the way to Monroe Street, their car got a flat tire. Liconti stopped the vehicle to change the tire at Carroll and Lafayette Streets. It was decided that Giustra should go on ahead by cab to make sure one of them was at the meeting on time. The cab dropped off Giustra at a tenement building under the Manhattan Bridge just after nightfall. Around this time, residents of the building "heard shouts and sounds of a struggle in the rear of the hallway on the ground floor. A volley of pistol shots followed and several men ran out and disappeared."[23] When police arrived, they found Giustra's body at the bottom of a stairway in a rear hallway. In addition to being shot, his throat was cut. Scattered around his body were several empty shell casings from a .45 automatic. A .38 revolver found at the scene was believed to belong to the dead man. Liconti arrived at the tenement just in time to see the body of his friend and partner being carried out.

Ten days later, another associate of Giustra and Liconti was attacked. Vincent Gisino was shot and critically wounded by gunmen in Brooklyn. Liconti was not around when the murder attempt took place. The *Herald Tribune* reported, "The shock of Giustra's murder crazed Leconti and he was confined to the observation ward of Kings County Hospital for three weeks. A hunted man since his release, he had been hiding out at various mid-town hotels."[24]

On July 8, the 45-year-old Liconti left his Clara Street home in Brooklyn in "good spirits," telling his wife Anna he would be home in time for dinner. Sometime around 3:00 that afternoon, Liconti arrived at the Paramount Hotel with a man, who had checked in as "Mr. Grossman," less than an hour earlier. Grossman had come in with a "Mr. Harris," and the two had registered in side-by-side rooms on the eighth floor. Grossman accompanied Liconti to the eighth floor to Room 814. Police speculated the meeting was to resolve differences. The result was far from that:

> As if negotiating a peace treaty to end the underworld strife, the men sat on the bed in 814, smoking one cigarette after another. They never entered 815.
> The conference in Room 814 broke up with a bang that stunned Leconti, who must have supposed up until then that he must be among friends. A rope was twisted around his neck, his throat was slashed from ear to ear and a knife was plunged deep five times in an attempt to cut out his heart. In a final gesture of contempt his upper lip was split, the Sicilian mark for "squealer."[25]

Liconti, who was said to be fond of eating, didn't make it home for dinner that night, nor breakfast the following morning. At 8:40 on the morning of July 9, a chambermaid at the Paramount Hotel entered Room 814 and encountered a ghastly scene. Liconti's body was sprawled on the bathroom floor. After being mutilated, his body had been hanged from a water pipe with a rope and later cut down.

The last known murder associated with the killing of "Joe the Boss" Masseria was that of Gerardo Scarpato. After the murder of Masseria in the Nuova Villa Tammaro, Scarpato had police fingerprint him. What scared him the most was that he would be murdered and his body never identified. Apparently, Scarpato did not have a police record. Then to play it safe, Scarpato and his wife were said to have booked passage to Italy.

At some point, Scarpato felt it was safe to return. He went back to work at the Nuova Villa Tammaro and soon opened a new restaurant, the Seaside Inn at 1306 Surf Avenue. He suddenly became a "sportsman," getting involved in boxing in Coney Island and seeking a partnership in the bicycle races held at the Velodrome. Scarpato also became involved in local politics, becoming an executive member of the Surf Democratic Club. The 42-year-old now lived with his wife in a luxurious apartment above his new restaurant.

Scarpato may have had a dark side also. In *East Side West Side: Organizing Crime in New York 1930–1950,* author Alan Block, an assistant professor in criminal justice at Delaware University, revealed some startling information about Scarpato from an obscure note found in the Municipal Archives. The note's author was not revealed, but he claimed to be an undertaker by trade and an extortion victim by chance.

The undertaker claimed he was approached by Giuseppe "The Clutching Hand" Piraino about becoming involved in the "policy business," because of his wealth and popularity in the city. When the undertaker refused, he said he and his family were threatened by Piraino and Anthony "Little Augie Pisano" Carfano. The undertaker went along, but his only participation seemed to be paying out money to people who claimed they had won on a policy number.

When Piraino was murdered on March 27, 1930, allegedly by Albert Anastasia associate Giuseppe "Joseph" Florino, the undertaker thought he would be left alone. But he was soon contacted by Gerardo Scarpato, who declared he was taking over for the late Piraino.

On April 15, 1931, the undertaker claimed he was told to meet Scarpato at the Nuova Villa Tammaro. Just as he arrived there, an automobile containing Anthony Carfano pulled behind him. Scarpato and Carfano wanted to know why he was there since Scarpato had telephoned him at his home earlier and left word for him not to come. The undertaker was ordered to leave immediately and later that day he heard about the murder of Joe Masseria at the restaurant.

By the summer of 1932, the undertaker said he was begging Scarpato to allow him to get out of the business. Scarpato claimed it would be easy because "New York people were involved in the game." The people he referred to were "Santoro" and "Tony Benda." In September, Scarpato said he thought he could get the undertaker out, but it would cost him $1,000.

There was an arrangement to meet that night at Fourth Avenue and Union Street in Brooklyn. The undertaker arrived and gave the money to a "nervous and very excited" Scarpato, who said he was to be called to a meeting. While the undertaker waited, he saw Scarpato meet with a man named James Demino, and the two left. The undertaker wrote, "I waited and in about an hour the same man who had left with Scarpato returned and was accompanied by Little Augie [Carfano]. They came over to me. Augie said to me 'listen, no matter what happens, you never knew Scarpato. Get the hell out of here and keep your mouth shut.'"

The undertaker soon read about the finding of Scarpato's body. A week later James Demino contacted him and told the undertaker that he (Demino) would now be Little Augie's representative replacing Scarpato.

The extortion scheme continued until October 1941, by which time the undertaker had lost $40,000. At that point he refused to have anything more to do with these men and declared himself "not only a financial wreck, but a physical and moral one as well." In closing his note the undertaker declared: "All the information I give is the truth and I make this statement knowing full well that I am on my way to certain death."[26]

The undertaker's statement, if true, indicates that Scarpato may have had some involvement in Masseria's death, and that Anthony Carfano may have been one of the other men in the restaurant that afternoon.

Police reports claim that Scarpato was last seen at the Seaside Inn on early Saturday morning, September 10, 1932. On Sunday morning, two neighbors on Windsor Place, in the Prospect Park South section of Brooklyn, became curious after noting an automobile parked outside their homes. When they went together to investigate, they saw "a bulky knobby bundle behind the front seat, wrapped in burlap bags." Both men knew police detectives who lived on the street and went to get them. After looking at the car, one of the detectives smashed a rear window. He then cut the burlap sack with a pocket knife, exposing the face of Gerardo Scarpato.

The body was easily identifiable. Although Scarpato felt it was all right to come home, he wasn't sure he was completely safe. Shortly before his body was found, Scarpato had his full name tattooed on his left arm. Scarpato was beaten and strangled, then "trussed like a roasting fowl," before being stuffed in the burlap sacks. A sash cord was believed to be the murder weapon. It was used to bind his knees together under his chin, tie his wrists together and then looped around his neck.

The car in which Scarpato's body was found, a black sedan, was reported stolen on June 5. Ironically, it was stolen from the corner of Fifth Avenue and 46th Street, two blocks from the Paramount Hotel, where Carmelo Liconti was butchered. The license plates were unregistered. Police believed they may have been included with a shipment of plates stolen while being transferred from Auburn prison to the Motor Vehicle Bureau in Brooklyn during the spring of 1932.

September 10, 1931—Murder of Salvatore Maranzano
The Valachi Papers

After the murder of Masseria on April 15, Maranzano called a meeting. According to Valachi it was held in the Bronx "in a big hall around Washington Avenue." Valachi claimed there were "four or five hundred of us jammed in." At this meeting Maranzano declared himself the Capo di tutti Capi, Boss of all Bosses. He announced the new organizational structure of "Cosa Nostra," introduced the new five-family bosses, who will report to him, and named their underbosses.

In addressing the group about the recently ended war, Maranzano stated:

Whatever happened in the past is over. There will be no more ill feelings among us. If you lost someone in this past war of ours, you must forgive and forget. If your own brother was killed, don't try to find out who did it to get even. If you do, you pay with your life.[27]

According to Valachi, there was a second get together that summer:

A huge banquet held in Brooklyn to honor Maranzano—in spirit and in cash. As a sign of their obeisance Cosa Nostra bosses throughout the United States purchased tickets to the affair. Even Al Capone sent $6,000. In all, according to Valachi, about $115,000 was collected. As representatives of various Families arrived at the banquet, each threw his contribution on a table. "I never saw such a pile of money in my life."[28]

After this second banquet, Valachi began working directly for Maranzano as a bodyguard and chauffeur. On the afternoon of September 9, 1931, Maranzano told Valachi he wanted him to come to his Brooklyn home on Avenue J that night. There he told Valachi, "we have to go to the mattresses again," meaning they have to go back to war. Valachi stated:

I'm listening as he explains why. He said, "I can't get along with those two guys"—he was talking about Charley Lucky and Vito Genovese—"and we got to get rid of them before we can control anything." He talked about some others who had to go too—like Al Capone, Frank Costello, Willie Moretti from Fort Lee, New Jersey, Joe Adonis, and Charley Lucky's friend from outside the Cosa Nostra, Dutch Schultz.[29]

Valachi said that Maranzano told him he was "having one last meeting the next day at two o'clock," with Luciano and Genovese. He told Valachi, "All right, call the office at a quarter to two to see if I need you." Valachi stated, "That afternoon I called the office and this guy Charlie Buffalo, who is one of the members with us, answered the phone and said that everything was fine and that I don't have to go down there."[30] That afternoon was spent by Valachi with Dominick "The Gap" Petrilli with "a couple of new girls" in Brooklyn, while Maranzano was slaughtered in his Park Avenue office.

The Last Testament of Lucky Luciano

Luciano stated that, "In a few weeks after Masseria stopped bein' a pig and become a corpse," Maranzano was planning his coronation. Invitations were sent to underworld leaders around the country, and more than 500 attended a banquet held in the Bronx at the grand Concourse. Invitees were assigned seats according to ranking.[31]

Although this version is similar to the Valachi story, one big difference is in the disbursement of cash tribute to the new leader. Luciano claimed, "At the banquet that followed, every invited guest—even those who had not been able to come but had sent surrogates instead—was required to demonstrate his fealty to Maranzano and the New Order. At a nod from Maranzano, the guests approached one at a time and laid cash-filled envelopes on the table."[32] Luciano claimed it came to more than "a million bucks," quite a difference from Valachi's tally.

During the summer of 1931, Luciano plotted to take over Maranzano's throne. The book claimed that in August, Meyer Lansky "imported, from Baltimore, Philadelphia and Boston, three Jewish gunmen, all with stereotype Semitic features. Then Red Levine, Luciano's longtime aide, was named to head the four-man murder squad." In late August, Luciano claimed that Frank Costello was informed by Harry "Nig Rosen" Stromberg in Philadelphia about the alleged plot of Maranzano to murder Luciano et al. The killer was to be Vincent "Mad Dog" Coll and the murder was to take place in Maranzano's office.

Luciano said he received a call from Maranzano requesting his and Genovese's presence in his office for a meeting on September 10, at 2:00 PM. The next day, Maranzano waited for Coll to arrive. With him were five bodyguards, but aside from his secretary, Grace Samuels, he had no other visitors. At that moment Tommy Lucchese arrived, who supposedly needed to see Maranzano on a "vital matter." Just as quickly four men entered and identified themselves as "federal agents."

After lining everyone up, two of the men ushered Maranzano into his office where they first tried to stab him to death. But Maranzano put up a fight and "the battle became almost desperate and the two killers finally pulled out their guns and began to pump bullets into him. He collapsed across his desk, dead—stabbed six times in the chest and body, his throat cut, and with four bullets wounds in his head and body."[33]

According to Luciano, the escaping bodyguards ran into Coll, who was on his way up the stairs, and told him what happened. He claimed Girolamo Santucci (see entry in *The Last Testament of Lucky Luciano* section) ran down the steps and was stopped on the street by arriving police officers. Luciano then claimed he received word of Maranzano's murder "just before three [o'clock]."

A Man of Honor

Most of Bonanno's previous recounting of events had been rather low key, but his account of events taking place after the death of Masseria was quite dramatic. He wrote, "After Masseria's demise, the Castellammarese hailed Maranzano as their hero. Maranzano was the victor of the most cataclysmic conflict ever to disrupt our world in America."[34]

Bonanno claimed that the "view" by "unreliable sources" of Maranzano proclaiming himself as Boss of all Bosses, was "vulgar and superficial." He actually stated that Maranzano simply accepted himself as one of the five-family leaders, naming Angelo Caruso as his underboss. As far as the "huge banquet," Bonanno stated that it was held in Wappingers Falls, New York, and that while the meeting was in progress, an airplane "armed with machine guns and bombs" circled the site overhead looking for police cars. Here is his first-hand account of that event:

Into a large room sallied perhaps three hundred men from all over the country. At the front door stood four of Maranzano's musketeers, each carrying arms. Everyone entering the room was frisked for guns and checked to see what Family they represented. All exits in the room, except for the front door, were either boarded or blocked. The guests were told that once the meeting began no one could leave the room for any reason. If someone had to go to the toilet, one of the musketeers had to escort him. The most important guests, the Fathers, sat randomly at a very long table; the rest of their entourage stood.[35]

The timing for the meeting was shortly after the death of Masseria, because Bonanno claimed that it was only a "prelude to a national convention in late May of 1931 in Chicago—our first national conference."[36] At this meeting, held at the Hotel Congress, Capone played the "extravagant host," picking up the tab for everyone's accommodations.[37] Bonanno wrote:

> Once all the major leaders had been recognized and confirmed by the congregation, the gathered leaders had their turn to show their respect for Maranzano. Capone gave a speech praising Maranzano. We all applauded, acclaiming as much the man as what he stood for. Here was the man who, because of his preeminence, once again made it feasible for all of us to return to normal activity. We hailed Maranzano.[38]

Bonanno never mentioned any tribute being paid to Maranzano at any of these meetings. He did say, however, that a banquet took place in June in Brooklyn to honor Maranzano and his "war staff" that was "a fund-raiser of sorts." Shortly afterwards, Bonanno says Maranzano asked him to hold on to $80,000 for him. Bonanno claims he refused to, worried about how the others might perceive this.

Bonanno wrote, "Maranzano seemed to be more comfortable as a warrior than he was as a statesman. Leadership during peacetime, however, demands different talents, which I think Maranzano possessed to a lesser degree."[39] Bonanno claimed he saw Maranzano less frequently as that summer was nearing its end. When he got the word that his beloved leader had been murdered, he went into hiding, staying there and not even attending Maranzano's funeral. Bonanno added nothing to the details of the murder. What he does repeat was written about before he penned his autobiography

Newspapers

There was as much mystery surrounding the murder of Maranzano as there was Masseria. It would be years before most people had any understanding about the murder that took place in the Park Avenue office. What follows is gleaned from the newspaper reports of the day. There are many discrepancies between what the newspapers reported and what appeared in the three books, and much additional information

Maranzano operated Eagle Building Corporation, with offices on the ninth floor of the New York Central Building, located at 230 Park Avenue. What Maranzano was "building" is unclear, but the government had him under investigation for several months as a suspected leader of a major alien-smuggling operation. U.S. Attorney George Medalie was overseeing the extensive investigation, which stretched all the way to Chicago and smuggled aliens in from Canada and Mexico. Shortly before Maranzano's murder, 19 arrests had been made.

In announcing the arrests of the men, the secretary of labor said the ring was responsible for smuggling in an estimated 8,000 aliens over the past few years.

Around 3:45 on the afternoon of September 10, four men entered Maranzano's ninth floor office. Although one of the men announced, "We're the police," there was no report of any of the men wearing uniforms. In fact, left behind by the men were two "expensive" hats with Chicago labels inside. Police, even fake ones, would have worn the department standard issue hats. Inside the office were nine men, in an anteroom waiting to see Maranzano, and Miss Grace Samuels, described as a secretary/receptionist.

The four men drew weapons and one covered Miss Samuels and the men in the waiting room, while the other three "burst" into Maranzano's private office. The *New York Sun* reported, "A quarrel was heard, then the sound of blows. Five shots rang out, and the gunmen came running from the office and vanished down the stairs."[40] The *New York Daily News* reported, "Two of the men pinned Maranzano against the wall while the third thug put the "traitor sign" across his face with a stiletto."[41]

Samuels rushed to Maranzano's aid when the men ran out. It was reported she "found him slumped in a chair dead." This is unlikely, however, as the only picture of the dead man shows him lying on the floor.

The men waiting to see Maranzano also scattered. All raced down stairways and hallways except one. James Santuccio decided to take the ninth floor elevator. He was stopped by a special policeman of the New York Central Railroad and detained until police arrived. Santuccio was an ex-boxer, who fought under the name "Bobby Doyle." Under questioning, Santuccio said he had gone to the ninth floor to visit John F. Alicia, who had an office there. Under questioning from two assistant district attorneys and Police Commissioner Edward Mulrooney, Santuccio claimed:

> I was visiting Maranzano with several men, including Johnny Alicia, who leased the office. We were talking about alcohol purchases when the four men came in. One said, "Come on, get in there," and I put my face toward the wall. Then I heard the shots and I was the last to run out. I saw Maranzano in his shirt sleeves lying on the floor with his head toward the door. I didn't know whether he was dead or not.[42]

Santuccio claimed he was on his way to "find a doctor" when he was stopped by the railroad policeman. The police and prosecutors were sure Santuccio was not telling them the complete story. An order was obtained to remand him as a material witness and a judge ordered him held in bail of $2,500. As for Alicia, he had completely disappeared.

Inside Maranzano's office, police recovered two revolvers and the stiletto knife. A search of the building the next day uncovered two more revolvers on different floors. Police were focused on the fact that Maranzano's killing had something to do with the alien smuggling, but they were also aware that he had his hands in other illegal activities.

The government's investigation of the smuggling ring had taken them to Capone territory in Chicago. Because the two hats had Chicago labels, there was immediate speculation that gunmen from the Windy City were involved. One theory was that Chicago racketeers "killed Maranzano because they feared he was under suspicion and might squeal on them."[43] Fueling this theory was the fact that an elevator operator in the building had told police a week earlier that he was sure he took Al Capone to the ninth floor. Police doubted that Capone would be so far from home without his contingent of bodyguards. Another report stated the gunmen actually went to the building Wednesday afternoon, but Maranzano had already left.

In Maranzano's office, police found files with paperwork describing various methods of evading immigration laws, as well as printed forms from the immigration bureau and circulars from the U.S. Department of Labor. When Miss Samuels was questioned about these, she claimed that any letters she had written for Maranzano to immigration officials in Washington, D.C. were all in regard to legitimate matters. When asked about the frequent visitors and telephone calls to the office, Samuels said that, invariably, all the conversations took place in Italian.

Adding to the alien smuggling mystery, a book containing 36 names, addresses, and telephone numbers, as well as other information, was tossed out a window and found on the sidewalk outside the building. A reporter picked it up and turned it over to a detective. A review of the book at the police station sent detectives scurrying to Buffalo, Chicago, and other cities.

Police questioned Maranzano's 20-year-old son Dominic about his father's business. The young man stated his father owned a fishing fleet, based at Sea Isle, New Jersey.

The *New York Sun,* in its reporting of Maranzano's murder, released these interesting tidbits of information about Maranzano and what took place after Masseria's murder:

> The Brooklyn detectives said that they were convinced that Maranzano had instigated the shooting of Joe the Boss last April, and that if he was not actually elected Joe's successor . . . he was at least the runner up against "Lucky" Lucciano [sic].
>
> The police said there is a difference of opinion in the Italian sections as to whether Maranzano or Lucky Lucciana [sic] took up the leadership that Joe the Boss surrendered by dying last spring.
>
> During the first three days of August several thousand Italians held a three-day feast and religious festival at Coney Island, in the same restaurant, the [Nuova Villa Tammaro], in which Joe the Boss was killed. Ostensibly it was a festival to raise money for the Maritime Society of Sciacca, but it was rumored at the time that the real purpose was to elect someone strong enough to take over Joe the Boss's interest and keep things straight in the underworld.
>
> Although the police supervised the feast and "frisked" every man who attended, they found only four or five guns, made no arrests, and everything seemed to be peaceful.[44]

GROUP OF SEVEN

Also known as the "Big Seven" and even the "Big Six," the group was initially referred to as the combination of rumrunners who ran activities in the eastern seaboard cities from Boston to Baltimore. According to the authors of *Gang Rule in New York,* the "old Big Seven" lineup was composed of the following:[45]

1. The Unione Siciliano
2. Irving "Waxey Gordon" Wexler, Owney Madden, and William Dwyer
3. Benjamin Siegel and Meyer Lansky
4. Louis "Lepke" Buchalter and Jacob "Gurrah" Shapiro
5. Frank Costello and Phil Kastel

6. Abner "Longy" Zwillman (Newark)

7. Charles "King" Solomon (Boston)

The authors claim this lineup changed in 1932 to the following:[46]

1. Lucky Luciano, Johnny Torrio, and Joe Adonis

2. Irving Bitz and Salvatore Spitale

3. Benjamin Siegel and Meyer Lansky

4. Abner "Longy" Zwillman (Newark)

5. Charles "King" Solomon (Boston)

6. Danny Walsh (Providence)

7. Cy Nathanson (Atlantic City)

This same lineup is cited in *The Luciano Story* by Sid Feder and Joachim Joesten.[47] In their description, they add that Luciano, Torrio, and Adonis represented the Mafia; the Siegel-Lansky partnership represented Philadelphia; and that Bitz and Spitale were New York "independents."

In *The Last Testament of Lucky Luciano,* the authors claimed the "Seven Group" was born out of discussions with Johnny Torrio for the most powerful bootleggers on the East Coast to combine. In this lineup, the seven are listed as follows:[48]

1. Lucky Luciano and Johnny Torrio

2. Benjamin Siegel and Meyer Lansky (New York, New Jersey, and surrounding area)

3. Joe Adonis (Brooklyn)

4. Abner "Longy" Zwillman and Willie Moretti (Nassau County, northern New Jersey, and Newark)

5. Irving Bitz and Irving "Waxey Gordon" Wexler and Harry "Nig Rosen" Stromberg (Philadelphia)

6. Charles "King" Solomon (Boston)

7. Enoch "Nucky" Johnson (Atlantic City and south Jersey)

Mark A. Stuart weighed in with his biography on Abner Zwillman, claiming that the idea to set up a "federation" to "monopolize" bootlegging and gambling on the East Coast came from "Longy." He wrote that Zwillman revealed it to kindred spirits at the Atlantic City Conference, which Stuart also claims was "arranged" by "Longy." Calling this group the "Big Six," the lineup consisted of the following: Abner "Longy" Zwillman, Lucky Luciano, Meyer Lansky, Frank Costello, Joe Adonis, and Benjamin Siegel.[49]

After the death of Dutch Schultz in October 1935, New York City Police Commissioner Lewis J. Valentine informed the *New York Times* that there was a "new combination" in town. This new lineup "consists of gangs headed by the following six notorious racketeers: Charles (Lucky) Luciana, Charles (Buck) Siegel, Meyer Lansky, Louis (Lefty) Buckhouse, Jacob (Gurrah) Shapiro, and Abe (Longy) Zwillman.

It was obvious by the names, as given by Valentine, that the New York City Police Department did not have a complete picture of who the enemy was.

THE LAST TESTAMENT OF LUCKY LUCIANO

The Last Testament of Lucky Luciano is the most controversial book ever written on the history of organized crime in this country. Written by Martin A. Gosch and Richard Hammer, the book was shrouded in controversy before it was ever published. Was this really dictated by Luciano himself? Or, was it a fraud perpetrated by Gosch?

On December 17, 1974, reporter Nicholas Gage's front page story in the *New York Times* raised questions about a soon-to-be released book titled, *The Last Testament of Lucky Luciano*. In the 1970s, Gage was the *New York Times* organized crime expert. During that decade he wrote the book *The Mafia Is Not an Equal Opportunity Employer* (1971) and edited and contributed to *Mafia USA* (1972), a compilation of stories by the era's most celebrated organized crime writers.

Gage revealed that controversy over the book, published by Little, Brown and Company, started when a full-page advertisement appeared in the November 18, 1974, issue of *Publisher's Weekly* claiming that Luciano had dictated the book to Gosch 10 years before he died. His reason was revenge for the New York mob bosses taking away the payments he had been receiving. The article claimed that Luciano had been recorded on tapes, which had been locked safely away in a vault.

Richard Hammer and Roger Donald, who edited the book for Little, Brown and Company, were quick to acknowledge that no "tapes" ever existed and that all the information had come from 30-plus interviews between Gosch and Luciano. They explained that the advertisement was a misunderstanding, stating that the sensationalized copy was written by *Penthouse Magazine* when it printed a "serialized" portion of the book. Hammer acknowledged that he was suing *Penthouse* for misrepresentation. An executive at *Penthouse Magazine* claimed that no papers had been served at the time Nicholas Gage contacted him for the article.

William Guthrie, who produced the advertisement for Little, Brown and Company, admitted he was "influenced" by the *Penthouse* ad. He explained he had received incorrect information to write the advertisement. Gosch can hardly be blamed for this faux pas; he died of a heart attack on October 20, 1973, 15 months before the book was released.

Gosch met with Richard Hammer in 1972, approximately a year before he died. Hammer, on one of his jacket covers, is described as "an award-winning reporter for the *New York Times*." Hammer's mob book credits include *The Illustrated History of Organized Crime* (1974), *Gangland USA* (1975), *Hoodlum Empire* (1975), and *Hoffa's Man*, with Joseph Franco (1987). Hammer also wrote about civil rights, law, Vietnam, and politics. Two of Hammer's books, *One Morning in the War*, which dealt with the My Lai massacre during the Vietnam War, and *The Court-Martial of Lt. Calley*, were nominated for the National Book Award. Another book, *The Vatican Connection*, won an Edgar Award.

Gage inquired into Hammer's decision to assist Gosch. Hammer claimed he checked with some Hollywood "people" about Gosch before proceeding. Hammer added, "that he did not like Mr. Gosch personally, but became convinced that the producer had genuine notes that were based on conversations with Mr. Luciano and decided to collaborate with him on the book.

"He and Mr. Gosch stopped speaking following differences about how the book should be written. 'He started thinking he was a writer,' he said of Mr. Gosch."[50]

Roger Donald told Gage that he "has two sworn affidavits and three signed letters from friends and relatives who were close to Mr. Luciano and knew he was telling his life story to

Mr. Gosch." Of these people, some were sharing in the book's royalties. Donald said, "But just because a person receives money doesn't mean he's not telling the truth."[51]

Of the five people who were sharing in the royalties, Donald identified four of them—Rosario "Chinky" Vitaliti, a close friend of Luciano; Adriana Rizzo, Lucky's last lover; and Luciano's two sisters, Concetta and Francesca. Vitaliti was the only one Gage interviewed for his article. He told Gage that he was in Italy when Luciano had his interviews with Gosch. Gage asked if Luciano "had specifically told him [Vitaliti] that he was recounting his life story to Mr. Gosch." Vitaliti said he was "positively sure." Vitaliti revealed that he and Luciano's two sisters and two sisters-in-law would receive a share of the book's royalties, as well as a share of any movie rights.

Hammer told Gage that he was, "persuaded that the Gosch notes were genuine 'by the fact that Gosch had been meeting Luciano . . . the fact Adriana Rizzo said she was aware of these meetings . . . and little anecdotal kind of things that Gosch just didn't have the imagination to have invented.' "[52] Hammer also informed Gage that the original notes were in the possession of Gosch's widow, Lucille. When Gage contacted Lucille Gosch in Las Vegas, however, she informed him that she had destroyed them.

Gage reported, "She said her husband made tapes for Mr. Hammer in which he discussed the material in the notes and that she didn't think it was necessary to keep the notes themselves. 'I'm not a lawyer,' she said." Lucille Gosch told Gage she was present during several of the interviews between her husband and Luciano. She claimed the two had at least 30 meetings.[53]

Upon finding out that the notes had been destroyed, Hammer expressed his disappointment to Gage. He stated that he never made copies for himself because, "at first it just didn't occur to me . . . and later when it did, Mr. Gosch and I were not speaking. I never thought anyone would destroy the notes. I've learned a bitter lesson."[54]

When contacted for comment by Gage, author Peter Maas, who had read an advance copy of the book, stated the information in the book had already appeared in other publications. Maas claimed that it paralleled the historical account given by Joseph Valachi. Maas wrote *The Valachi Papers*, which was published in 1968.

This is a curious statement by Maas, given the fact that, number one, Valachi and Luciano's description of many key events have major disparities, and number two, Luciano, according to Gosch, discussed things that were never brought to light and today are being questioned as to their veracity. Examples of this are the Havana conference, which Gosch claims took place in late December 1946, and Luciano's role in and description of the murder of Joe Masseria. One key incident in particular is Valachi's retelling of "The Night of Sicilian Vespers." The Gosch book may have been the first to publicly deny that it ever took place. The first two major researchers to question Bo Weinberg's "Vespers" fairytale were Humbert Nelli in 1976 and Alan Block in 1980, both released after Gosch's revelations.

Peter Maas pointed out that in *The Valachi Papers*, Maas misspelled the name of Girolamo Santuccio—writing Santucci. The same incorrect spelling appeared in the Gosch/Hammer book. Hammer claims the mistake was his fault, as he used the index of Maas's book to check his names. Again Hammer's statement clears Gosch of any intentional wrongdoing.

Gage also contacted Hank Messick, the dean of mob authors of that period. Messick, who also read an advance copy, claimed that he found "information from several of my books in it. Errors from other books, including some of my own, are repeated here and put in Lucky's mouth. Things attributed to Lucky that he could not have said."[55] Gage, however, never reveals any of the "errors" that Messick refers to in the article.

In 2002, I interviewed Richard Hammer for an article for AmericanMafia.com. Nearly 30 years after the release of *The Last Testament of Lucky Luciano,* Hammer still stands by his comments that the book is correct, even to the extent that when questioned about the glaring discrepancies in the description of the murder of Tommy Reina (presented earlier in this appendix) he stated he would "go with" what Luciano said.

Hammer related that, in 1972, Gosch contacted him and the two came to an agreement to co-author *The Last Testament of Lucky Luciano.* When Hammer met with Gosch, the "movie producer" had notebooks filled with his 30-plus interviews with Luciano. With notes Gosch provided from his interviews with Luciano, Hammer wrote the entire book. The two men became at odds, according to Hammer, when Gosch tried to "rewrite my writing."

Hammer said that one of the problems was that there were so-called Mafia experts of the day who didn't take lightly to their ground being tread upon by new organized crime writers. Nicholas Gage was one of these people. Hammer claimed he discussed the book with Gage before its release and was disappointed that Gage had come out arguing against its authenticity the way he did.

When asked about Gosch's career in California, Hammer replied:

"Well, he produced a couple of Abbott and Costello movies (actually only one). He was mainly a 'go-for' for Louis B. Mayer, and a couple of other studios." Although the Internet Movie Database listed him as a writer, Hammer declared, "He never wrote a word. He couldn't. He could hardly write his own name!"[56]

Hammer said that while writing the story he had access to all of the notes, which Gosch demanded be returned to him. When asked about the story that Gosch's wife destroyed the notes, Hammer remarked, "I knew her very well. When he died she had the apartment on Crescent Drive, in Beverly Hills, and she couldn't stay there so she was going to live with her niece in Las Vegas. She had an apartment full of stuff that she didn't know what to do with. I knew her well enough to know, and my wife knew her well enough to know, that indeed, she never discussed it with anyone, she just told the superintendent, 'I'm moving. Take all the stuff and throw it in the incinerator.' She didn't think it was worth anything."[57]

When asked if other than doing those initial interviews did Gosch do anything else as far as research, Hammer replied:

> As far as I know, he wrote a screenplay with somebody—I don't know who—based on his conversation with Luciano. That was the Genesis of the whole thing. He had met Luciano and here he was a Hollywood guy living in Spain and Luciano asked him to do this so he worked with Luciano on developing a screenplay and then the boys from New York came in and said "there's not going to be a movie about you Charlie." So the screenplay, which I'll tell you I saw it, it never could have been made into a movie, it was so bad, but when he [Luciano] was told he couldn't make it that's when he came to this agreement with Gosch. There was a piece of paper, a signed piece of paper, about what would be covered (personal comments, recollections and editorializations) and Gosch would do his biography and nothing would be done with it until 10 years after Luciano's death, because he was going to say things about people who were his friends.[58]

Among the people Gage interviewed for his December 1974 attack on the book was Moses Polakoff, one of Luciano's attorneys at his 1936 trial for compulsory prostitution. Gage wrote that the aging attorney "read the 65-page section of the book describing events in which he was directly involved and said that 'not 5 per cent of the accounts bear any resemblance to reality.'"[59]

One of the errors Polakoff pointed out was that the book described attorney Francis W. H. Adams as participating in Luciano's defense. Richard Hammer claimed his own research showed that Adams did participate as one of Luciano's attorneys. When Gage interviewed Adams, who at one time served as New York City police commissioner, he claimed he was not at the trial, he was only involved in the appeal and that he had never met Luciano.

Another error Polakoff discovered was that the book stated that after Luciano's arraignment in New York in April 1936, he "quickly posted" bail and returned to his Waldorf Towers apartment where he met with Polakoff and several key New York underworld figures. Polakoff told Gage that Luciano had never posted bond, that no meeting ever took place, and that he had never been in the mob boss's Waldorf suite.

In response to Polakoff's remarks, Hammer gave Gage two statements. First, "if he didn't make bail, it raises a major question about this section of the book."[60] Later, Hammer said, "Luciano was very insistent [to Gosch] that he got out. Maybe he got out secretly at night. He was a powerful man and anything was possible in those days."[61]

Despite Gage's hoopla over the book, he never really implies in the article where the fault lies. Did Gosch make the whole thing up, or did Luciano lie and embellish his story? Hammer and Roger Donald had agreed that "confused recollections are inevitable when a man looks back on his life in his old age as Mr. Luciano did."[62]

Gage places full responsibility on Gosch for one discrepancy—Luciano's comments about a casino in the Bahamas that Meyer Lansky had an interest in. The casino in question didn't open until January 1964, two years after Luciano's death. Of this last revelation regarding the casino, Hammer's response was, "If Gosch made that bit up, I don't think there's much else that he did. I think the rest of the book hangs. It may be self-serving and it may be inaccurate in parts, but it's Luciano's story as he told it." In retrospect, Hammer now states that gambling in the Caribbean had been going on for years and perhaps Luciano was referring to a different casino.[63]

The immediate fallout from the Nicholas Gage article was that the New American Library, which agreed to pay $800,000 to publish the paperback edition of the book, suspended its printing plans. The article also caused embarrassment for the Book-of-the-Month Club and the Playboy Book Club, both of which had made *The Last Testament of Lucky Luciano* one of its "main selections."[64]

On December 26, 1974, Little, Brown and Company announced that they were going ahead with their plans to publish the book, claiming it had "received all the available data on which the manuscript was based." Simultaneously with this decision, the Book-of-the-Month Club made *The Last Testament of Lucky Luciano* its February 1975 selection, even though the judges who made it their choice "were now embarrassed by their vote."[65]

Edward E. Fitzgerald, president of the club, stated in a *New York Times* article, "There was . . . never any question as to the manuscript's authenticity. There may be inaccuracies in the book, but there has been no challenge to the basic fact that it is indeed based on meetings and conversations with Luciano."[66]

Capitalizing on the new interest in Lucky Luciano, the Citadel Press in 1975 re-released Hickman Powell's *Ninety Times Guilty*. First published in 1939, the book, now called *Lucky Luciano: His Amazing Trial and Wild Witnesses,* focused on the 1936 court case. The next year Sphere Books Ltd. of Great Britain released *Lucky Luciano: The Man Who Modernised the Mafia.* The author, Tony Scaduto, was a former features writer for the *New York Post.* He had written biographies on the Beatles, Mick Jagger, Bob Dylan, and Frank Sinatra. Although Scaduto claimed, "most of my adult life has been devoted to an investigation and exploration of the Honored Society, the Mafia," the Luciano piece seems to be his only book on the subject of organized crime.

Scaduto was not as diplomatic as Gage in his assessment of *The Last Testament of Lucky Luciano,* or of Martin Gosch for that matter. Referring to Gosch's effort as a "piece of humbug," he claimed the entire book was "fraudulent." While attacking one point, Scaduto calls Gosch's statements, "Balderdash, bullshit and garbage."[67] It should be noted that Scaduto does not acknowledge Gosch's co-author, Richard Hammer, once throughout his diatribe. There is no reason given for this omission.

In dedicating a 12-page appendix to deride the book's authenticity, Scaduto wrote:

> Now that Gosch has been dead for almost two years it may seem rather unfair and callous to attack his integrity since he can no longer defend himself. But the fact is that Gosch's book is such a complete fantasy that it would have come under attack were he still alive.[68]

Scaduto claims, "I have found, without exaggeration, at least fifty major errors in Gosch's book."[69] After expounding on just a few of them—some hypothetical—he boasts, "I could go on for another fifty pages or more, but space does not permit (nor does the queasy feeling the stench of this book leaves in my stomach)."[70] He then "ticks off" several other errors, five to be precise, some of which were already questioned by Gage.

One of the "errors" pointed out by Scaduto, which was mentioned earlier by Gage and Moses Polakoff, was Luciano's claims, through Gosch, that he had meetings at his Waldorf Towers apartment after his arraignment in April 1936. He even claims to have had "sexual intercourse" with his then girlfriend, Gay Orlova. They point out Luciano never posted bond and remained in jail the whole time. It should be noted that this is not unique. In the mid-1920s, Chicago's Terry Druggan and Frankie Lake, as federal prisoners, were said to have "spent about as much time outside the Cook County jail as they did inside," and Mahoning Valley mobster S. Joseph "Sandy" Naples also accomplished the same feat in 1958. Naples was actually photographed arriving back at the jail after a weekend sexual tryst with his girlfriend. Luciano was far wealthier and influential than these men.

Despite all of Scaduto's allegations against Gosch, and after trashing him on numerous occasions for his lack of journalistic intelligence and research skills (none of which Gosch claimed to have), Scaduto practically destroys his own credibility by making the colossal blunder of acknowledging the "Night of Sicilian Vespers:"

> Throughout the remainder of that day [September 10, 1931] and over the next day, approximately forty Maranzano men in the New York area and in several other cities were murdered in what has come to be known in Mafia circles as The Night of the Sicilian Vespers.[71]

Since Scaduto makes himself out to be "devoted to investigation and exploration of the Honored Society," perhaps forced by his own pride, he was compelled to admit the "Night of Sicilian Vespers" really took place for the sole reason that Gosch/Luciano denied it!

Scaduto, after claiming to "know Luciano well" and without offering any information to back up his claims, wrote, "during his teens and his twenties, when he was hustling on New

York streets, and after his formal induction into the Mafia at the start of Prohibition, Luciano killed at least 20 men"

Gosch isn't the only Luciano biographer Scaduto attacked. In his criticism of Hickman Powell's book, he stated *Ninety Times Guilty* was one of "Dewey's approved books," meaning that Powell placated Dewey by writing the book. Yet Scaduto took large portions of Powell's work—word for word—and includes it in his book without crediting Powell.

Scaduto made numerous errors when discussing peripheral people and events—not an uncommon error for mob writers when they leave their area of focus. But to believe Scaduto's account, one has to believe that Dewey and all his people were part of a massive conspiracy to frame Luciano and put him away unjustly for 30 to 50 years. None of the information from Hickman Powell's book that would exonerate Dewey from Scaduto's allegations was presented. But then, of course, Powell was on the "Dewey approved" list.

In his book, Scaduto discussed Barnett Glassman, "a Hollywood film producer," although neither his name nor work appears in the Internet Movie Data Base.[72] Glassman met Luciano in Italy and the two talked about making a movie based on the mob boss's life. Glassman, however, was tied up with a movie project in Spain, where he met Martin Gosch. Glassman said Gosch became interested in the Luciano film and offered to "help" and was hired as an assistant and introduced to "Charlie."

Scaduto claimed he was told by Glassman that Gosch "never produced a film on his own. Gosch was just a hustler in the film business, conning guys all over the place." Scaduto wrote:

> When Gosch came up with his idea for a book, long after Luciano was dead, he began to negotiate with Glassman since Glassman was his employer and holds the original film contract signed by Luciano. In the midst of those negotiations, Glassman says, Gosch took an advance from Little, Brown "and then told me our whole deal was off."
>
> Glassman promptly sued Gosch and the publisher. The case dragged on and the book was published—but not until Little, Brown paid Glassman to drop his suit. In the settlement both Glassman and his attorney "got a substantial amount of money," Glassman says. As part of the settlement Glassman also received from Gosch's literary agent "a large percentage" of receipts from any film which may be made of *The Last Testament*. Glassman is still suing Gosch's estate.[73]

Hammer claimed otherwise. He stated that in the Supreme Court of New York County, "In the only one of the many cases between the two enemies ever decided—and decided in Gosch's favor—Justice Jacob Markowitz, for the court, stated, 'I accept the testimony of Gosch . . . as wholly credible.' There are several noteworthy inconsistencies in the statements of Glassman which cast serious doubt as to the accuracy and veracity of his testimony."[74]

Scaduto repeatedly denies that Luciano and Gosch ever collaborated on anything. He jumped on the bandwagon with Glassman condemning Gosch, claiming that he "never got close enough to Luciano to have received the benefit of his reminiscences," and that Luciano didn't trust him enough to discuss "mob business" with him. Yet in one of the lawsuits against Gosch, Glassman's basic contention was, "Gosch did interview on many occasions Salvatore Lucania and . . . obtained considerable information not in the public domain."[75]

Produced in paperback, Scaduto's *Lucky Luciano: The Man Who Modernised The Mafia,* was not a commercial success. It was reviewed in the *New York Times Book Review* on April 27, 1975. At that time Richard Hammer responded to the book's "scurrilous assaults" on *The Last Testament of Lucky Luciano,* claiming "Since my collaborator, Martin A. Gosch, died in October 1973 and cannot defend himself, I feel that I, too, must come to the book's defense and respond for both of us with the truth."[76]

In a six-page letter to John Leonard, editor of the *New York Times* Book Review, on April 28, 1975, Hammer outlined the long, bitter battle between Gosch and Glassman. But he also added a story Scaduto curiously left out of his book. Hammer wrote:

> It is equally appalling and incredible that neither The Times nor Scaduto felt it necessary to inform readers of Scaduto's deep personal interest and motives in attempting to discredit "The Last Testament of Lucky Luciano." Scaduto is not merely, as he says, a mafia expert and a Sicilian-American with a curiosity about "the more bizarre aspects of my heritage." He has been as well, as he informed me during a telephone conversation on May 23, 1973, a paid employe [*sic*] of one Barnett Glassman, whom he cites as an unimpeachable source throughout his diatribe.
>
> Scaduto told me that he had been hired by Glassman to write a book on Lucky Luciano and was only reluctantly putting it to one side when he learned the status of the book on which Gosch and I were collaborating. However, I have since been told by a major paperback publisher that Scaduto was only one of a number of so-called "mafiologists" approached by Glassman during 1972 and 1973 to write a supposed "authorized" biography of Luciano; all were told they would have to do most of the research on their own since Glassman's information was, at best, sketchy and incomplete, and then write as though Luciano were the source. All save Scaduto, rejected the Glassman proposal. Perhaps Scaduto imagines that if he helps destroy "The Last Testament of Lucky Luciano," his Glassman-sponsored "authorized" biography can be resurrected.[77]

In the end, Scaduto, Gage, as well as many others have brought up legitimate points to challenge *The Last Testament of Lucky Luciano.* Jerry Capeci, the current dean of organized crime writers, had identified at least 50 mistakes in the book. The question remains, did Luciano provide Gosch with a story to inflate his own ego and embellish his image for decades to come? Or did Gosch produce a completely fraudulent story on his own?

One must consider this. Gosch said he waited 10 years to publish the book because of his agreement with Luciano. If this is false, and Luciano never dictated the notes to him, then it must have taken Gosch 10 years to write the notes that Richard Hammer claims to have used himself. If Gosch did write this himself, then why did he need Richard Hammer? Why would he share the profits of his book with anyone if he had written it himself? And in the end, Gosch received no profits, except from an advance. He died well before the book was released.

In Hickman Powell's book, he details how Tom Dewey ripped Luciano apart when the mobster decided to take the witness stand in his own defense. Dewey pointed out lies, time and again, that Luciano had told over the years. Couple this with the fact that Luciano was incensed because "the boys" from New York had nixed his movie deal right at the time he was communicating with Gosch. One wonders how anyone could be surprised that Luciano told the tale to Gosch the way that he did.

Although the book has a great many mistakes and embellished stories to feed Luciano's well-known ego, did Gosch fabricate the tale or is it based on what Luciano told him? In short, it's a search for the truth. Errors have been documented and more will eventually become known, but what's left is a unique story of one of America's most notorious crime bosses—and liars.

MURDER, INC.

Murder, Inc. was not the creation of the New York underworld, but rather the name invented by an overzealous newspaper reporter, Harry Feeney of the *New York World-Telegram,* to describe two groups of killers that operated in a freelance fashion during the mid- to late 1930s. Popularized in books, movies and songs, the activities of these individuals have been highly fictionalized.

There is no denying that the killers were as callous a murdering crew that has ever existed in the underworld, or that they were responsible for dozens of murders, some even committed outside of New York City. But the stories that these murderers operated like a fine-tuned Fortune 500 business and was run by a board of directors made up of mob kingpins is pure exaggeration. So, too, is the number of deaths attributed to Murder, Inc., which was said, "coast to coast to have taken a thousand lives." The New York newspapers, which kept track of the body count as Reles made his revelations, never seemed to top 63.

The young hoods that came together to form what became known as Murder, Inc. were the products of two Brooklyn neighborhoods—Brownsville and Ocean Hill. Although these hoodlums were more than a ragtag band of sociopathic killers and gang member wannabes, the question remains: Were they the precision-drill team and murder machine that has been written about by Burton Turkus, the Brooklyn assistant district attorney who prosecuted them, and the writers who have romanticized them since their uncovering in 1940?

The story of Murder, Inc. came to light when Abe Reles began talking to authorities on Saturday, March 23, Easter Eve 1940. The newspapers covered every news bite released by O'Dwyer's office. Despite the top news story of the day being the escalating war activities of Germany and Japan, the daily Murder, Inc. reports held the attention of many New Yorkers.

It was years after the murder trials were history and the key participants were either executed or murdered that Burton Turkus's book, *Murder, Inc.* was published, followed by a movie several years later. The book has stirred up more controversy in recent years than it did when it was released in 1951, as mob historians tear away at the story written by the prosecutor and his coauthor Sid Feder.

In *Little Man: Meyer Lansky and the Gangster Life,* biographer Robert Lacey, while debunking some of the myths of organized crime, discusses how a number of these tales began:

> *Murder, Inc.,* a book published in 1951, set the style. Ostensibly a work of reportage, it told the story of the 1940–41 organized crime prosecution which could claim to be the most successful ever, in that the boss who ordered the hits, Lepke Buchalter, and some of his most important accomplices actually went to the electric chair. *Murder, Inc.,* the book, however, did not stop with the facts. It mixed solid, court-proven evidence with speculative dramatization, without distinguishing the two. It interspersed real testimony with invented dialogue, again without distinction—and at crucial points in the story, the reader is treated to the "thoughts," literally rendered, that were going through the protagonists' minds.
>
> Coauthored by Burton Turkus, the assistant DA who tried the cases, and Sid Feder, a New York crime reporter, *Murder, Inc.* was a runaway success, its exaggerations perfectly suiting the tenor of the Kefauver years. The book went through three printings in three months, and its mixture of fact and imagination came to be widely imitated by a series of organized crime books in a hybrid formula that was half documentary and half soap opera. They could only be described as pulp fiction.[78]

Burton Turkus described how the Murder, Inc. gang came together. It was actually the combination of two ruthless gangs that formed after the last of a gang led by the three Shapiro brothers was slaughtered:

> Reles and his pal, Buggsy, and the kill-crazy Pittsburgh Phil ruled Brownsville and East New York—the rackets, the homicide, the protection. Maione and Abbandando and Vito Gurino conducted identical operations in Ocean Hill. It was all one combination, with, of course, the supervising and executive guidance of Albert Anastasia. This was Brooklyn, Inc., at its formal unveiling.[79]

Reles and Maione didn't always get along and Anastasia felt if they weren't held in check, open warfare between them would start. Reles said Louis Capone was brought in by Anastasia because he was respected by members of both gangs. Capone simply served as Anastasia's front man in the gang.

Based on a set of popular theories as to how the gang operated, here is a listing of the key participants:

- *Leaders*: Albert Anastasia and Louis "Lepke" Buchalter. Some accounts claim that Anastasia was the real leader and Buchalter the gang's best customer, but testimony seems to bear out a larger role for Buchalter. Also, some claim that as a result of his partnership with Buchalter, Jacob "Gurrah" Shapiro was also a leader, but again this is not confirmed by testimony.
- *Top Lieutenants*: Louis Capone and Emmanuel "Mendy" Weiss
- *Top Killers*:

  Frank "The Dasher" Abbandando—executed February 19, 1942 in Sing Sing
  Frankie Carbo—died of natural causes
  James "Dirty Jimmy" Feracco—unknown
  Martin "Buggsy" Goldstein—executed June 12, 1941 in Sing Sing
  Vito "Chicken Head" Gurino—sentenced to 90 years in prison
  Harry "Happy Maione—executed February 19, 1942 in Sing Sing
  Abraham "Kid Twist" Reles—found dead on November 12, 1941
  Harry "Pittsburgh Phil" Strauss—executed June 12, 1941 in Sing Sing
  Charles "The Bug" Workman—died of natural causes
- *Gang Members Turned Informants*: Sholem Bernstein, Angelo "Julie" Catalano, Abraham "Pretty" Levine, Anthony "Dukey" Maffetore, Seymour "Blue Jaw" Magoon, Abraham "Kid Twist" Reles, Meyer "Mikey" Syckoff, Albert "Allie, Tick-Tock" Tannenbaum.

Murder, Inc. is a biased look at the whole prosecution process, simply focusing on the work of Turkus. Several important trials of gang members are not included. Although Abe Reles is the most prominent figure in the book, little is discussed about the investigation into his unusual death while under police protection. Another important missing piece is the inquiry into Brooklyn District Attorney William O'Dwyer's failure to prosecute Albert Anastasia, after claiming his "perfect case" went out the window with Abe Reles.

The death of Abe Reles is still a mystery. The popular belief is that Frank Costello fronted the money to make sure Reles would not be around to testify against Anastasia. In charge of protecting the most important mob informant of his time was Frank Bals, who would ride O'Dwyer's coattails when he was elected mayor of New York City in 1944.

During an inquiry into Reles's death, Bals offered up that "Kid Twist" was attempting to play a trick on his guards. He was going to use a sheet to climb out the sixth floor window and enter through a window directly below before coming up and surprising the men assigned to protect him. During this attempt, a wire attaching the sheet to a radiator broke and Reles fell to his death. In support of this theory was a report that a check of the window on the fifth floor, which happened to be locked from the inside, showed not only that a screen had been pushed up on the outside, but that there were shoe prints and paint chipped off the outside window sill.

A story soon circulated, however, that Reles's body had been found 23 feet away from the building. This story is still believed today. A look at any of the pictures of the crime scene shows one important clue to refute this claim. If Reles's body were 23 feet out, it would have dropped him down to the next level of the hotel. Just thinking of the physics of this rumor, how could these alleged assailants have thrown a heavy man like Reles through a relatively small window so that he would land 23 feet out? The running long jump record could not have been much more than that in 1941. In addition, a hotel official related in a report to a member of the Brooklyn district attorney's office that when he spotted Reles's body from his office window, which was on the same level as the roof extension, it was only six feet away.

Still, there are several motives to lead one to believe that something more sinister than Reles playing a practical joke on his guards occurred that fateful morning. In addition to the possibility that a trial involving Anastasia could have taken place—Albert was still a fugitive at this time—was the fact that Reles was only days away from being called as a witness in the trial of Lepke Buchalter, Louis Capone, and Mendy Weiss.

Another important reason for "Kid Twist" to take a dive happened an unlucky 13 days before his death. Special Sessions Judge Matthew F. Troy "challenged" District Attorney O'Dwyer to turn over Reles to Special Prosecutor John Harlan Amen in order to "bring to justice those who made it possible for the slayers of Murder, Inc., to operate, by the acceptance of protection money." Troy declared, "I charge that District Attorney O'Dwyer has failed to prosecute politicians and political fixers who have remained immune from prosecution under" his administration. If Reles was in the know about this area, it would have been easy to connect O'Dwyer to Joe Adonis and the politicians he supported that patronized his restaurant. This alone provides a motive for O'Dwyer to want to see Reles out of the way.

NIGHT OF SICILIAN VESPERS

The Night of Sicilian Vespers is without a doubt the most famous myth in the history of the Mafia in America. According to the tale, it occurred on the evening of September 10, 1931, after the murder of Salvatore Maranzano, the first and only true *Capo di tutti Capi,* Boss of all Bosses. The massacre of 30 to 90 underworld leaders (depending on who is telling the story) was said to have been ordered by Lucky Luciano in his effort to "Americanize the mob."

Over the years organized crime experts have become curious as to the identity of the 30 to 90 individuals who perished in one night of butchery. After all, look at the attention the St. Valentine's Day Massacre generated, and that was only seven people.

According to *The Last Testament of Lucky Luciano,* the man who allegedly ordered the murders:

All that stuff them writers always printed about what they called the "Night of Sicilian Vespers" was mostly imagination. Every time somebody else writes about that day, the list of guys who was supposed to have got bumped off gets bigger and bigger. The last count I read was somewhere around fifty. But the funny thing is, nobody could ever tell the names of the guys who got knocked off the night Maranzano got his. I, personally, don't know the name of one top guy in the Maranzano group in New York or Chicago or Detroit or Cleveland or nowhere who got rubbed out to clear the decks.[80]

The book claims that the only person who was murdered that night was Gerardo Scarpato, the owner of the Nuova Villa Tammaro restaurant in Coney Island. It was in his restaurant that Luciano had allegedly set up Joe "The Boss" Masseria to be murdered on April 15, 1931. Scarpato was found strangled in a burlap sack that was tossed into a stolen automobile and abandoned in Brooklyn, but that murder actually took place a year later in September 1932.

Below is a look at what some of the earlier writers had to say about this event:

- 1940—*Gang Rule in New York*. Authors Craig Thompson and Allen Raymond wrote the first, or at least one of the first, books that discusses the murders. The authors stated, "That was the day on which the principal greasers were liquidated. The Americanization campaign bumped into an important snag, for in the Unione there were many old-line leaders or men of importance who, clannish and illiterate, had no sympathy for the ideas of cooperation that the younger and far-sighted members of the Unione were advocating. These old fogies were called the 'greasers' by the younger generation."

- 1951—*Murder, Inc*. Burton Turkus, the assistant district Attorney of Kings County who helped prosecute the Murder, Inc. gang members, stated, "The day Maranzano got his, it was the end of the line for the Greaser Crowd in the Italian Society—the finish of 'The Moustache Petes'—and a definite windup to the Mafia as an entity and a power in national crime. For in line with Lucky's edict—some thirty to forty leaders of the Mafia's older group, all over the United States, were murdered that day and in the next 48 hours!"

- 1968—*The Valachi Papers*. In 1963, mob turncoat Joseph Valachi, a Genovese Crime Family member, testified before the McClellan Committee about his life in organized crime. Five years later, Peter Maas wrote *The Valachi Papers*, reporting Valachi's testimony, "The murder of Maranzano was part of an intricate, painstakingly-executed mass extermination engineered by the dapper, soft-spoken, cold-eyed Charlie "Lucky" Luciano. On the day Maranzano died, some forty Cosa Nostra leaders allied with him were slain across the country, practically all of them were Italian-born old-timers eliminated by a younger generation making its bid for power."

- 1969—*Theft of the Nation*. Donald R. Cressey, a professor of sociology at the University of California, Santa Barbara, and a consultant to the President's Commission on Law Enforcement and Administration, wrote *Theft of a Nation: The Structure and Operations of Organized Crime in America*. Cressey stated: "The Maranzano slaying was not an isolated incident. It was part of the last major battle of a war. The day Maranzano was killed has long been known as 'purge day' in Cosa Nostra. On that day and the two days immediately following, some forty Italian-Sicilian gang leaders across the country lost their lives in battle. Most, if not all, of those killed on the infamous day occupied positions we would now characterize as 'boss,' 'underboss,' or 'lieutenant.'"

Each new book seemed to reveal new information about the mass murders except who got killed and where. As late as 1975, the story was still making the rounds.

- 1975—*Brothers in Blood: The Rise of the Criminal Brotherhoods*. David Chandler, who won a Pulitzer Prize in 1962 for investigative reporting, puts a bizarre spin on the episode. Chandler stated that there were 60 victims. He wrote:

  Each of the sixty victims must have been kept under surveillance to establish his daily pattern. For each of the sixty, a hit team had to be organized and gunmen chosen who wouldn't betray the plan. When Purge Day arrived, the hit teams had to be delivered to their target's area. A communications liaison must have been worked out to relay the go-ahead message from New York—that Maranzano had been killed—to each of the teams. At least 300 men must have been in on the plot. Yet it went off without a hitch, so smoothly that it took more than a year before the first hint of a brotherhood purge filtered out to police. One reason the shake-up went off so quietly was that in many cases it took days, even months, before the bodies were discovered. Some of the bodies have never been found.

The mystery was finally solved in 1976 by a history professor from the University of Kentucky. Humbert S. Nelli, working on a grant from the National Endowment for the Humanities and the Kentucky Research Foundation, traveled to 14 cities and performed an extensive examination of Italian criminal activity. His work culminated in the book, *The Business of Crime: Italians and Syndicate Crime in the United States*.

In Nelli's research he tracked down the origin of the tale. In 1939, J. Richard "Dixie" Davis, the former attorney for Dutch Schultz, told *Collier's* magazine that former Schultz gunman Abe "Bo" Weinberg revealed the killings to him. According to Davis, Weinberg, who allegedly participated in the Maranzano murder, stated that the killing "began a nationwide attack on the old-timers. In fact, 'at the very same hour' as Maranzano's death, 'there was about 90 guineas knocked off' all over the country."

Now that we have the origin of the story, who were the murder victims, of which there are now 90? Nelli's research revealed that three men in the New York area, in addition to Maranzano, were murdered on September 10. Samuel Monaco and Louis Russo's bound bodies were found in the Hackensack River, and James La Pore was murdered on a Bronx street. In addition to Maranzano, that was New York's portion of the purge. This appears to have been the extent of the great massacre.

Part of Nelli's research was an extensive review of newspapers in the following cities; Baltimore, Boston, Chicago, Cleveland, Denver, Detroit, Kansas City, Los Angeles, New Orleans, Philadelphia, Pittsburgh, and San Francisco. This review of newspapers covered the months of September, October, and November 1931. His findings showed that only one murder occurred during this period that could even remotely be tied to the purge, and that was in Denver.[81]

We'll never know the motivation behind the fairy tale Bo Weinberg presumably started. A few years after the fictional purge, Bo himself was purged by his boss Dutch Schultz. Many believe he was given a "cement foot bath" and tossed into the East River. Whatever the disposal method may have been, Weinberg was never around to tell mob bedtime stories again.

JOSEPH VALACHI

Valachi was the Mafia's first significant informant. A soldier in the Genovese Family, Valachi was serving a 15-year prison term in the federal penitentiary in Atlanta in the early 1960s. Incarcerated there at the same time was Vito Genovese. It is the popular belief that Genovese was told that Valachi was an informant for the Bureau of Narcotics. Valachi was then given the "kiss of death" by Genovese and knew it was only a matter of time before one or more of the other inmates, under orders from Genovese, would try to kill him. Valachi struck first, killing an innocent man whom he thought was his would-be assassin. Facing a possible death sentence, Valachi "flipped," became a government informant, and testified before the McClellan Committee, revealing his life and all he knew about the Mafia . . . and then some.

It must be understood that Valachi did not testify as a disinterested party. When asked why he was cooperating with the Department of Justice, Valachi answered, "The main reason to that is very simple. Number one: It is to destroy them."

By the time Valachi was brought before the McClellan Committee, he had been debriefed by the FBI for nearly a year. He appeared during public sessions held in late September and early October 1963. He became the first person to discuss the inner workings of the Mafia, or as he termed it Cosa Nostra—"Our Thing." Valachi talked about the organizational structure, syndicate rules, and the illegal activities such as loan sharking, labor racketeering, extortion, and infiltration of legitimate businesses. Incredibly, Valachi also described Mafia business that a person in his position within the organization, meaning basically a small fry, would have no way of knowing.

Unlike Abe Reles in 1940 and 1941, and later Salvatore "Sammy the Bull" Gravano during the 1990s, Valachi was never used as a witness during criminal trials, save one involving Carmine "The Snake" Persico. Despite appearances before grand juries in the Bronx and Manhattan, no criminal prosecutions followed. One crime expert commented, "Sometimes, as in the case of Joseph Valachi, they are only lowly members of the organization and their observation point is limited. And often, they are reporting hearsay and depending upon fuzzy recollections of people and events that are far in the past."[82]

In August 1963, more than a month before he testified, stories of his revelations were being reported by the *Washington Star* and the *Saturday Evening Post*. Dwight C. Smith, Jr. wrote, "Once the fact of Valachi's confessions was known publicly, Justice Department sources were happy to cooperate with the media. By the time Valachi appeared in public, there was little he could add to what was already known."[83] Another source states that the "law enforcement value of his information had already been pretty much maximized."[84] Smith continued, "Valachi had failed to catch public attention as a fully credible witness. The press had focused in advance on the dramatic nature of his forthcoming testimony, and the anticlimactic results of his appearance took the steam out of an organized-crime-control drive."[85]

Valachi was not even a hit back in his home town. One attorney commenting on his testimony for the *New York Times* assessed, "The most disgusting thing I've ever seen is a Senator asking this killer, this bum, what the United States should do."[86] His credibility was berated by the New York Police Department, who considered Valachi "a small, publicity-loving bum," who was only repeating "stale rumors and underworld gossip," not producing any information that wasn't already known.

In 1966, FBI Director Hoover claimed that, "all the Valachi information . . . had been obtained from informants of the Bureau," before being testified to before the McClellan Committee.[87] When asked if there had been a criminal conviction based on anything Valachi had said, Hoover replied, "There has been no person convicted as a direct result of any information furnished by Valachi."[88]

Even Valachi biographer Peter Maas conceded, "Valachi's televised appearance before the subcommittee was a disaster." Maas "placed the blame on Valachi's inability, after years of avoiding publicity, to cope with the circus-like atmosphere of the hearing room and on the subcommittee's essentially undisciplined—and thus disordered—approach to his appearance."[89]

After five days of testimony, "The subcommittee also concluded that Valachi lacked any redeeming social value other than his testimonial accuracy, and that he was motivated solely by desires of revenge and self-preservation." "His role as an informer," read the final report, "was not dictated by conscience, nor was it a result of remorse for his crimes."

One part of Valachi's testimony that baffled the committee was the recollection of his initiation ceremony. Even a casual review of everything we've been led to believe over the years, combined with Valachi's own testimony, leads us to question whether he was ever an actual initiated member of the Mafia—or rather, Cosa Nostra, as he claimed it was called. Let's look at the following points:

- It is alleged that, at this time only Sicilians were given the blood oath to join this secret society. Valachi was born in East Harlem; his parents were both Neapolitan, just like Al Capone, who couldn't become an initiated member for the same reason.

- A proposed member had to "make his bones" commit a murder for the gang or family. Valachi claimed he was initiated after the murders of Al Mineo and Steven Ferrigno in November 1930, during the Castellammarese War. Valachi claimed these murders were carried out by a sinister character he calls "Buster from Chicago." This multimurderer, however, seems to exist only in Valachi's mind. Although Valachi claimed not to have been involved in the murders, he said it was then that he became an initiated member.

- Valachi described an initiation rite that nobody has ever talked about again, with members throwing fingers out to determine who Valachi would report to. According to Valachi, Joseph Bonanno became his godfather and was responsible for him. In Bonanno's autobiography, A Man of Honor, however, Bonanno fails to acknowledge any association with Valachi, never states that he was initiated, and mentioned him only in demeaning terms. Bonanno wrote: "Valachi also identified me as being his 'godfather.' I never met or talked to this guy, either. How could I be his 'godfather?' "[90]

- Although Valachi claimed the initiation was witnessed by some 40 people, as it was a custom for made members to attend, he said over the next 30 years he never attended another initiation, even though he claimed to have proposed several people for membership.

- As a made member of the Mafia, one of the benefits was "a share in its illicit gains." Valachi was asked about his "cut," to which he replied, "You get nothing, only what you can earn yourself."

- Then there is the question of "protection from prosecution and the penalties of the law" as a benefit of membership in which "the family will help with lawyers, bail bondsmen, et cetera, if anything goes wrong." Here is an exchange between Valachi and Senator Jacob Javits:

Javits:	How did you seek the help of your family when you were picked up?
Valachi:	I used to get my own help. What family do you mean?
Javits:	The family to which you belonged, the Genovese family.
Valachi:	I never bothered them. If I got picked up, I got myself out, I got my own lawyers.
Javits:	Did they ever give you any protection in the 35 years?
Valachi:	No.
Javits:	They did not furnish lawyers?
Valachi:	Never.
Javits:	Or bondsmen?
Valachi:	Never, I got my own bondsmen, my own lawyers.
Javits:	So your membership in the family had nothing to do, in your opinion
Valachi:	I was never in a position where the family helped me.

It takes quite a leap of the imagination to believe that Valachi was a made member of the Mafia as he claimed. A further explanation of his role comes from Joseph Bonanno, who held Valachi in complete disdain. Bonanno wrote: "Often [Valachi] described historical events in which he never participated but nonetheless inserted himself to make himself seem important to his gullible audience. Valachi gave an interpretation to my Tradition that made it look cheap and totally criminal in operation. Because he never rose very high himself, Valachi mainly came in contact with the dregs of our society, our lowlife. In his unsophisticated mind, he probably thought everyone in our Tradition was like that."

Another part of Valachi's testimony that drew the attention of law enforcement officials was insistence that the organization he belonged to was called Cosa Nostra. When asked by a committee member if it was "anything like the Mafia, or is it part of the Mafia, or is the Mafia?" Valachi answered:

> Senator, as long as I belong to this Cosa Nostra, all I can tell you is that they never express it as a Mafia. When I was speaking, I just spoke what I knew. . . . I know this thing existed a long time, but in my time I have been with this Cosa Nostra and that is the way it was called.[91]

Long-time Mafia historian Fred J. Cook was astonished by this statement. He related, "There is a consensus among the nation's best investigators, men with the most intimate knowledge of the underworld and its rackets that they had never heard the name before Valachi used it. . . . This has cast some doubt upon the validity of Valachi's story."[92]

Other organized crime experts claim that, in lieu of 25 investigative agencies of the federal and local governments pooling information, "It seems a little surprising that out of all those who appeared before the committee not one person was found to confirm Valachi's evidence on this matter."[93]

Valachi's testimony is also of interest when he gave information that was outside his narrow area of expertise. This included talk about the "Commission," the underworld supreme council, the hierarchical structure, and the geographical distribution of families throughout the United States. The man whose own crime family shunned him continuously when it came to participating in new induction ceremonies and made him provide for his own bail money and lawyers somehow was able to get a handle on the size and locations of other organized crime families across the United States. These cities included Boston, Buffalo, Chicago, Cleveland, Los Angeles, Newark, New Orleans, Philadelphia,

Tampa, and Utica. He estimated the number of initiated men in each city and specifically named 289 members.

How could Valachi, as a "small fry" in the organization have such vast knowledge? The common belief is that after the Apalachin Summit and the FBI's frenzy to learn as much as possible about organized crime, the bureau initiated a number of illegal wiretaps. Information gained from these wiretaps could not be exposed because they were illegal, but the FBI could use Valachi as a conduit to make it public. In short, the information was fed to Valachi during his year of debriefing, and committee members just assumed it was information he or any other member of organized crime would know. Because of what law enforcement gained after his testimony, they figured the ends justified the means.

Despite all the inconsistencies and shortcomings of the Valachi testimony, law enforcement prevailed. "Unlike the Kefauver hearings and the Apalachin incident, it resulted in far-reaching new laws designed to combat organized crime more effectively. His accounts became part of the rationale for legislation permitting widespread use of wiretaps, special grand juries, witness immunity, and other prosecution tools."[94]

According to one of Valachi's colleagues, Vincent Teresa, who was allegedly a high-ranking member of the Mafia, "Valachi's story was an exaggeration, a dim memory of the past. How much of Valachi's stories were true, partially true, or created out of whole cloth? It is impossible to say. But we do know they contained the stuff of myth, in this case, the Mafia myth. For many, these insider stories confirmed their preconceived notions about the Mafia. *The Valachi Papers* movie starring Charles Bronson as Valachi simply added to the aura and mystique."[95]

NOTES

1. John H. Davis, *Mafia Dynasty: The Rise and Fall of the Gambino Crime Family* (New York: HarperCollins, 1993), p. 83.

2. Norval Morris and Gordon Hawkins, *The Honest Politician's Guide to Crime Control* (Chicago: University of Chicago Press, 1969), p. 226.

3. Dwight C. Smith, Jr., *The Mafia Mystique* (New York: Basic Books, 1975), p. 10.

4. Michael D. Lyman and Gary W. Potter, *Organized Crime* (Upper Saddle River, NJ: Prentice Hall, 1997), p. 28.

5. Ibid., p. 30.

6. Donald R. Cressey, *Theft of the Nation* (New York: Harper & Row, 1969), p. 22.

7. Smith, Jr., *The Mafia Mystique,* p. 178.

8. Leonard Katz, *Uncle Frank* (New York: Drake Publishers, 1973), p. 80.

9. Hank Messick, *Lansky* (New York, G. P. Putnam's Sons, 1971), pp. 36–37.

10. Martin Gosch and Richard Hammer, *The Last Testament of Lucky Luciano* (Boston: Little, Brown and Company, 1974), p. 103.

11. Mark A. Stuart, *Gangster #2: Longy Zwillman* (Secaucus, NJ: Lyle Stuart, 1985), p. 71.

12. Hickman Powell, *Lucky Luciano: His Amazing Trial and Wild Witnesses* (Secaucus, NJ: The Citadel Press, 1939), p. 65.

13. Craig Thompson and Allen Raymond, *Gang Rule in New York* (New York: The Dial Press, 1940), p. 357.

14. Joseph Bonanno with Sergio Lalli, *A Man of Honor* (New York: Simon and Schuster, 1983), p. 118.

15. Castellammare del Golfo is an agricultural and trading center on the northern coast of Sicily, in the far western province of Trapani. The name is of Latin origin meaning "castle by the sea." Some sources state that the name translates to "Sea Fortress of the Golf."

16. In *Gangster City*, author Patrick Downey states that Giuseppe "Joseph" Parrino was murdered for much the same reason as Joseph Pinzola—he had been placed in a leadership position by Joe Masseria and his men resented it and murdered him. Parrino was killed in the Del Pezzo restaurant at 100 West 40th Street on January 31, 1931.

17. An interesting side note: both the *New York Times* and the *Herald Tribune* reported the office was leased to a Thomas Luckese. This is the same spelling that appears on his grave in Calvary Cemetery in Queens. For almost 60 years writers have used the Lucchese spelling, which is how the crime family name is spelled, although recently it has been appearing as Luchese.

18. Several newspaper accounts claim the guns were left behind in the restaurant.

19. The first edition of the *New York Daily News* reported that the card "clutched in a bejeweled paw," was the Ace of Spades, which a picture of the corpse clearly indicates is stuck between his fingers, not in a way a playing card would normally be held. Later editions of the *Daily News*, as well as most of the other newspapers, however, state it was the Ace of Diamonds. This adds to the Mafia mythology in portraying the Ace of Diamonds as the death card.

20. *New York Sun*, April 16, 1931, "One Gang Killing Is Solved."

21. *New York Daily News*, April 17, 1931, "'Joe the Boss' Mob Guards Kin."

22. *New York Herald Tribune*, July 10, 1931, "Coney Island Feud Leader Slain in W. 46th St. Hotel."

23. *New York Herald Tribune*, May 11, 1931, "Lured to Tenement, Shot Dead by Gang."

24. *New York Herald Tribune*, July 10, 1931, Coney Island Feud Leader Slain in W. 46th St. Hotel."

25. Ibid.

26. Alan Block, *East Side—West Side: Organizing Crime in New York 1930–1950* (Swansea, Wales: University College Cardiff Press, 1980), pp. 249–252.

27. Peter Maas, *The Valachi Papers* (New York, G. P. Putnam's Sons, 1968), p. 107.

28. Ibid., pp. 108–109.

29. Ibid., p. 110.

30. Ibid., p. 111.

31. Gosch and Hammer, *The Last Testament of Lucky Luciano*, p. 133.

32. Ibid., p. 135.

33. Ibid., p. 142.

34. Bonanno with Lalli, *A Man of Honor*, p. 124.

35. Ibid., p. 125.

36. Ibid., p. 126.

37. Of the seven biographies on Capone, the only one that acknowledges this meeting is Laurence Bergreen's *Capone: The Man and the Era*. Published in 1994, well after Joseph Bonanno's *A Man of Honor*, Bergreen merely repeats the same comments made by Bonanno, offering no proof to substantiate them.

38. Bonanno with Lalli, *A Man of Honor*, p. 129.

39. Ibid., p. 131.

40. *New York Sun*, September 11, 1931, "Link Midtown Murder Victim to Smugglers."

41. *New York Daily News*, September 11, 1931, "Gang Kills 4, 1 in Offices on Park Ave."

42. *New York Sun*, September 11, 1931, "Link Midtown Murder Victim to Smugglers."

43. Ibid.

44. Ibid.

45. Thompson and Raymond, *Gang Rule in New York* , p. 358.

46. Ibid., p. 375.

47. Sid Feder and Joachim Joesten, *The Luciano Story* (New York: David McKay Company, 1954), p. 63.

48. Gosch and Hammer, *The Last Testament of Lucky Luciano*, p. 94.

49. Stuart, *Gangster #2: Longy Zwillman* , p. 76.

50. *New York Times,* December 17, 1974, "Questions Are Raised on Lucky Luciano Book."

51. Ibid.

52. Ibid.

53. Ibid.

54. Ibid.

55. Ibid.

56. Author interview with Richard Hammer for AmericanMafia.com September 2, 2002.

57. Ibid.

58. Ibid.

59. *New York Times,* December 17, 1974, "Questions Are Raised on Lucky Luciano Book."

60. Ibid.

61. Author interview with Richard Hammer for AmericanMafia.com September 2, 2002.

62. *New York Times,* December 17, 1974, "Questions Are Raised on Lucky Luciano Book."

63. Author interview with Richard Hammer for AmericanMafia.com September 2, 2002.

64. *New York Times,* December 20, 1974, "Publisher Suspends Luciano Paperback."

65. *New York Times,* December 27, 1974, "Publisher to Go Ahead with Luciano Book."

66. Ibid.

67. Tony Scaduto, *Lucky Luciano: The Man Who Modernised the Mafia* (London, Sphere Books, 1976), p. 197.

68. Ibid., p. 199.

69. Ibid., p. 206.

70. Ibid., p. 206.

71. Ibid., p. 94.

72. Some sources list Barnett Glassman as the associate producer of the film *John Paul Jones* starring Robert Stack. The film was released in 1959 and produced by Samuel Bronston. Bronston and Glassman, however, fought a bitter battle in the "press and in court over ownership of the production company and Glassman's credit for the film."—American Film Institute Catalog cited in Alan Gevinson, *Within Our Gates: Ethnicity in American Feature Films, 1911–1960* (Berkeley: University of California Press, 1997), p. 531.

73. Scaduto, *Lucky Luciano: The Man Who Modernised the Mafia,* p. 198.

74. Letter from Richard Hammer to John Leonard, editor, *New York Times Book Review,* April 28, 1975.

75. Ibid.

76. Ibid.

77. Ibid.

78. Robert Lacey, *Little Man: Meyer Lansky and the Gangster Life* (Boston: Little, Brown & Company, 1991), pp. 313–314.

79. Burton B. Turkus, and Sid Feder, *Murder, Inc.* (New York: Farrar, Straus and Young, 1951), p. 463.

80. Gosch and Hammer, *The Last Testament of Lucky Luciano,* pp. 143–144.

81. Similar researched was also performed, with the same results, by Alan Block in *East Side—West Side: Organizing Crime in New York 1930–1950,* pp. 3–8.

82. James O. Finckenauer and Dennis J. Kenney, *Organized Crime in America* (Belmont, CA: Wadsworth Publishing, 1995), p. 50.

83. Smith, Jr., *The Mafia Mystique,* p. 223.

84. Finckenauer and Kenney, *Organized Crime in America,* p. 237.

85. Smith, Jr., *The Mafia Mystique,* p. 220.

86. Ibid., p. 225.

87. Morris and Hawkins, *The Honest Politician's Guide to Crime Control*, p. 224.

88. Ibid., p. 226.

89. Ibid., p. 224.

90. Bonanno with Lalli, *A Man of Honor,* p. 119.

91. Morris and Hawkins, *The Honest Politician's Guide To Crime Control,* p. 213.

92. Fred C. Cook, *The Secret Rulers* (New York: Duell, Sloan and Pearce, 1966), p. 12.

93. Morris and Hawkins, *The Honest Politician's Guide to Crime Control,* p. 214.

It has been rumored by some of J. Edgar Hoover's detractors that the director or his agents pushed this term to explain the fact that they hadn't pursued it as organized crime in the past because they didn't know what it was until now.

94. Jay S. Albanese, *Organized Crime in America,* third edition (Cincinnati, OH: Anderson Publishing Co., 1996), p. 107.

95. Finckenauer and Kenney, *Organized Crime in America,* p. 249.

BIBLIOGRAPHY

Albanese, Jay S. *Organized Crime in America.* 3rd ed. Cincinnati: Anderson Publishing, 1996.

Block, Alan. *East Side—West Side: Organizing Crime in New York 1930-1950.* Swansea, Wales: University College Cardiff Press, 1980.

Bonanno, Joseph, with Sergio Lalli. *A Man of Honor.* New York: Simon and Schuster, 1983.

Cook, Fred C. *The Secret Rulers.* New York: Duell, Sloan and Pearce, 1966.

Cressey, Donald R. *Theft of the Nation.* New York: Harper & Row, 1969.

Davis, John H. *Mafia Dynasty: The Rise and Fall of the Gambino Crime Family.* New York: HarperCollins, 1993.

Downey, Patrick. *Gangster City: The History of the New York Underworld 1900-1935.* Fort Lee, NJ: Barricade Books, 2004.

Feder, Sid, and Joachim Joesten. *The Luciano Story.* New York: David McKay Company, 1954.

Finckenauer, James O., and Dennis J. Kenney. *Organized Crime in America.* Belmont, CA: Wadsworth Publishing, 1995.

Gevinson, Alan. *Within Our Gates: Ethnicity in American Feature Films, 1911–1960.* Berkeley: University of California Press, 1997.

Gosch, Martin, and Richard Hammer. *The Last Testament of Lucky Luciano.* Boston: Little, Brown and Company, 1974.

Katz, Leonard. *Uncle Frank.* New York: Drake Publishers, 1973.

Lacey, Robert. *Little Man: Meyer Lansky and the Gangster Life.* Boston: Little Brown & Company, 1991.

Lyman, Michael D., and Gary W. Potter. *Organized Crime.* Upper Saddle River, NJ: Prentice Hall, 1997.

Maas, Peter. *The Valachi Papers.* New York: G. P. Putnam's Sons, 1968.

Messick, Hank. *Lansky.* New York: G. P. Putnam's Sons, 1971.

Morris, Norval, and Gordon Hawkins. *The Honest Politician's Guide to Crime Control.* Chicago: University of Chicago, 1969.

Peterson, Virgil W. *The Mob: 200 Years of Organized Crime in New York.* Ottawa, IL: Green Hill Publishers, 1983.

Powell, Hickman. *Lucky Luciano: His Amazing Trial and Wild Witnesses.* Secaucus, NJ: Citadel Press, 1939.

Scaduto, Tony. *Lucky Luciano: The Man Who Modernised The Mafia.* London: Sphere Books, 1976.

Smith, Jr., Dwight C. *The Mafia Mystique.* New York: Basic Books, 1975.

Sondern, Jr., Frederic. *Brotherhood of Evil: The Mafia.* New York: Farrar, Straus and Cudahy, 1959.

Stuart, Mark A. *Gangster #2: Longy Zwillman.* Secaucus, NJ: Lyle Stuart, 1985.

Thompson, Craig, and Allen Raymond. *Gang Rule In New York.* New York: The Dial Press, 1940.

Turkus, Burton B., and Sid Feder. *Murder, Inc.* New York: Farrar, Straus and Young, 1951.

BIBLIOGRAPHY

Albanese, Jay S. *Organized Crime in America*. 3rd ed. Cincinnati: Anderson Publishing, 1996.

Block, Alan. *East Side—West Side: Organizing Crime in New York 1930–1950*. Swansea, Wales: University College Cardiff Press, 1980.

Bonanno, Joseph, with Sergio Lalli. *A Man of Honor*. New York: Simon and Schuster, 1983.

Cook, Fred C. *The Secret Rulers*. New York: Duell, Sloan and Pearce, 1966.

Cressey, Donald R. *Theft of the Nation*. New York: Harper & Row, 1969.

Davis, John H. *Mafia Dynasty: The Rise and Fall of the Gambino Crime Family*. New York: HarperCollins Publishers, 1993.

Dewey, Thomas E. *Twenty Against the Underworld*. Garden City, NY: Doubleday & Company, 1974.

Downey, Patrick. *Gangster City: The History of the New York Underworld 1900–1935*. Fort Lee, NJ: Barricade Books, 2004.

Feder, Sid, and Joachim Joesten. *The Luciano Story*. New York: David McKay Company, 1954.

Finckenauer, James O., and Dennis J. Kenney. *Organized Crime in America*. Belmont, CA: Wadsworth Publishing, 1995.

Frasca, Dom. *King of Crime*. New York: Crown Publishers, 1959.

Fried, Albert. *The Rise and Fall of the Jewish Gangster in America*. New York: Holt, Rinehart and Winston, 1980.

Gage, Nicholas. *Mafia, USA*. New York: Playboy Press, 1972.

Gevinson, Alan. *Within Our Gates: Ethnicity in American Feature Films, 1911–1960*. Berkeley: University of California Press, 1997.

Gosch, Martin, and Richard Hammer. *The Last Testament of Lucky Luciano*. Boston: Little, Brown and Company, 1974.

Henderson, Donald Clarke. *In the Reign of Rothstein*. New York: The Vanguard Press, 1929.

Katz, Leonard. *Uncle Frank*. New York: Drake Publishers, 1973.

Kefauver, Estes. *Crime in America*. Garden City, NY: Doubleday & Company, 1951.

Lacey, Robert. *Little Man: Meyer Lansky and the Gangster Life*. Toronto: Little Brown & Company, 1991.

Lyman, Michael D., and Gary W. Potter. *Organized Crime*. Upper Saddle River, NJ: Prentice Hall, 1997.

Maas, Peter. *The Valachi Papers*. New York: G. P. Putnam's Sons, 1968.

Messick, Hank. *Lansky*. New York: G. P. Putnam's Sons, 1971.

Morris, Norval, and Gordon Hawkins. *The Honest Politician's Guide to Crime Control*. Chicago: University of Chicago, 1969.

Peterson, Virgil W. *The Mob: 200 Years of Organized Crime in New York* Ottawa, IL: Green Hill Publishers, 1983.

Pietrusza, David. *Rothstein*. New York: Carroll & Graf Publishers, 2003.

Powell, Hickman. *Lucky Luciano: His Amazing Trial and Wild Witnesses*. Secaucus, NJ: The Citadel Press, 1939.

Raymond, Allen. *Waterfront Priest*. New York: Henry Holt and Company, 1955.

Rothstein, Carolyn. *Now I'll Tell*. New York: The Vanguard Press, 1934.

Scaduto, Tony. *Lucky Luciano: The Man Who Modernised The Mafia*. London: Sphere Books LTD, 1976.

Siragusa, Charles. *The Trial of the Poppy: Behind the Mask of the Mafia*. Englewood Cliffs, NJ: Prentice Hall, 1966.

Smith, Jr., Dwight C. *The Mafia Mystique*. New York: Basic Books, 1975.

Sondern, Frederic, Jr. *Brotherhood of Evil: The Mafia*. New York: Farrar, Straus and Cudahy, 1959.

Stuart, Mark A. *Gangster #2: Longy Zwillman*. Secaucus, NJ: Lyle Stuart, 1985.

Summers, Anthony, and Robbyn Swan. *Sinatra: The Life*. New York: Alfred A. Knopf, 2005.

Thompson, Craig, and Allen Raymond. *Gang Rule in New York*. New York: The Dial Press, 1940.

Turkus, Burton B., and Sid Feder. *Murder, Inc.* New York: Farrar, Straus and Young, 1951.

Valentine, Lewis J. *Night Stick: The Autobiography of Lewis J. Valentine*. New York: The Dial Press, 1947.

INDEX

Abbandando, Frank "The Dasher," 99, 110, 393

Abbatemarco, Frank "Frankie Shots," 166

Accardo, Anthony J., 19

Adler, J. Arthur, 85, 87, 88

Adler, Polly, 292

Adonis, Harold J., 25, 26, 28

Adonis, Joe (Giuseppe Antonio Doto), 32 n.1, 38, 40, 42, 50–51, 231, 284, 323, 346
  arrests, 2–3, 4
    involved in cigarette hijackings, 4
  assault and kidnapping indictment, 9–13
    Adonis surrenders, 11
    Gasberg arrest and trial, 11–13
    treatment in Raymond Street Jail, 12
  Bergen County gambling, 19–22
  birth 1, 2
  Brooklyn politics, 5–7, 8, 14, 134, 218
    O'Dwyer, 7, 14–15, 48, 394 (*see also* Joe's Italian Kitchen)
  Brooklyn underworld leadership, 3
    Yale, Frank, 3, 4 (*see also* Carfano, Anthony [Little Augie Pisano] as Brooklyn underworld boss)
  Castellammarese War, 3, 374, 379
  Costello as gambling partner, 14, 132–33, 135
  death and funeral of, 31–32, 36 n.86
  deportation of, 26–30, 57, 141, 143
  description and personal traits, 2, 5
    origin of nickname, 2
    vanity, 2, 284
  family and home, 1–2, 5, 7, 13, 27, 29, 31, 32 n.6, 49

  Havana meeting, 35 n. 71, 234, 235
  Kefauver Committee, 15, 17–19, 24, 134–35, 139
    questioned about Virginia Hill, 18
  legitimate business interests, 4, 8–9, 33 n.18, 34 n.42
    problems after not supporting LaGuardia, 8–9
  Luciano, 233, 248, 340
    banished to Ancona, 31
    dispute over money deposited in Zurich, 30
    funeral 31
    Milan, life in, 30
  move to Fort Lee, New Jersey, 13 (*see also* Duke's Restaurant)
  New Jersey gambling indictment, 16–17
  New Jersey politics and corruption, 22–26
  underworld leadership role, 3–4, 41, 67, 80, 92, 185, 313, 333, 346, 356, 384

Agoglia, Sylvester, 217

Albano, Dr. Edwin H., 328

Alberts, William "Big Jack Zelig," 76, 258, 259

Allied Military Government (AMG), 127, 189, 190

Alo, Vincent, 14, 16, 53

Aloise, Maria Saveria, 118

Amalgamated Clothing Workers of America, 79–80, 102, 111, 114 n.15

Amberg, Joe, 298

Amberg, Louis "Pretty," 298, 299

Ambro, Jerome G., 5–6, 7, 32 n.12

Amen, John Harlan, 33 n.22, 45, 331–32, 352, 394; Buchalter fur trade indictment and

trial, 83, 86–88; indictment of Adonis and Gasberg, 10–13
American Civil Liberties Union, 142, 145, 149, 336
Amorusa, Joseph, "Strawberry Joe," 91
Amron, Irving, 298
Anastasia, Albert (Umberto Anastasio), 3, 10, 14, 80, 164, 197, 233, 313, 349, 377
Apalachin Summit, 61, 364–65
assassination of, 58–60, 146, 163, 200, 202, 247, 329
Coppola, Anthony arrested, 60–62
Cuban gambling connection, 64
Gallo gang's alleged involvement, 64
revelation by Father Salvatore Anastasia, 62–63
Squillante, Vincent involvement, 62, 70–71 n.54
Brooklyn waterfront, 40, 41, 48–49, 50, 67 n.10 (*see also* Anastasia, Anthony "Tough Tony" [Antonio], Romeo, Anthony "Tony Spring")
Buchalter association, 40–41, 44, 80, 89, 92, 93, 100, 115 n.31
Castellammarese War, 40, 370, 374
denaturalization effort, 54–55
early years
arrests, 39–40; birth, 38
Bazzano murder, 41, 333
illegal entry into the United States, 38
Santora murder, 41
family and home, 38, 40, 49, 54–55, 59, 60, 61–62
House auction, 61–62 (*see also* Anastasio, Jerry [Gerardo], Anastasio, Joseph [Giuseppe])
Florino, Joseph, 43, 45, 332–33
involved in Terillo murder, 38
sentenced to death, 39, 333
Genovese, 57, 162, 163, 201, 234, 235, 328
Kefauver Committee, 37, 48, 49–50, 55, 56
Luciano, 40–41, 67 n.8, 68 n.19
Macri brothers, 48–49, 50, 51–52, 69 n.35
Mafia membership selling, alleged, 349–50
Mangano Family boss, 51, 166, 349
Murder, Inc., 44–45, 99, 297, 303, 393, 394
becomes a fugitive, 45, 47
failure of O'Dwyer to indict Anastasia, 46, 47–48
murders
Diamond, Morris, 44–45
Ferri, Charles, 56, 57
Mangano, Phil, 50–51, 69 n.33
Panto, Peter, 42–43, 45–46, 48

Schuster, Arnold L., 54, 70 n.41
tax trial, 55–57, 327
underboss of Mangano Family, 3–4, 40–41, 158
United States army, 47, 68 n.22
Waterfront probe, 43, 52–54
Anastasia, Anthony "Tough Tony" (Antonio), 38, 40, 42, 45, 48, 49–50, 59, 60, 63, 64, 66 n.1, 67 n.10, 69 n.32, 178
Anastasia, Elsa, 49, 56, 59, 60, 61
Anastasio, Albert, 63
Anastasio, Father Salvatore, 60, 62
Anastasio, Gloriana, 59
Anastasio, Jerry (Gerardo), 40, 53, 60, 63, 66 n.1, 69 n.32
Anastasio, Joseph (Giuseppe), 38, 40, 63, 66 n.1, 69 n.32
Anastasio, Joyanna, 59
Anastasio, Jr., Umberto, 54, 59, 60, 61
Anastasio, Richard, 59
Ancona (Italy), 31
Andrews, Lincoln C., 121
Anslinger, Harry J., 365, Luciano in Cuba, 234, 236–37, 250 n.56, 251 n.83, Luciano in Italy, 241, 244, 245
Apalachin Summit, 61, 65, 163, 164, 173, 247, 364–66, 367, 400; Genovese role, 146, 184, 199–202, 203, 206; investigation of, 62, 162, 163, 176, 202–3, 206, 246, 364–66
Arbeiter, Beatrice. *See* Buchalter, Beatrice "Betty"
Aristocrat Baby Carriage Factory, 22–23
Arlington Hotel, 83, 87
Armone, Stephen, 66
Arnold, Dorothy, 222
Arnstein, Nicky, 253, 265–67, 273
Arrowhead Inn, 17
Askenas, Irv, 89
Atlanta Penitentiary, 353, 358; Costello at, 140, 141, 143, 147–48, 249; Genovese at, 147–48, 198, 207–8, 249, 397
Atlantic City Conference, 3, 40, 80, 123, 185, 216, 284, 313, 346, 366–68, 384
Attell, Abe, 262, 265
Aurelio, Thomas A., 133, 152 n.22, Costello telephone call, 128–29, 137, 138, 347
Auteri, Antonio, 40
Automotive Conveying Company, 8, 23, 34 n.42

Bailey, Carl E., 220
Bakir, 238
Baldwin, Alexander R., 33 n.22
Baldwin, Edwin A., 315, 348

Balitzer, Mildred, 226, 229
Balitzer, Peter "Pete Harris," 219, 221, 223–24, 228, 230
Bals, Frank, 45, 321; Reles death, 47, 393–94
Banana War, 167
Banton, Joab H., 277, 278
Barbara, Sr., Joseph, 65, Apalachin Summit, 163, 201–1, 206, 363, 364, 365
Barkley, Alben W., 134
Baron, Robert F. (Patrolman), 2–3, 32 n.3
Barra, Caesar B. F., 68, 221
Barrera, Frank, 68
Barrese, Michael, 186
Barshay, Hyman, 194, 195; Buchalter murder trial, 100, 102–5
Basile, Fiorio, 287
Basile, Louis, 287
Bastian, Walter M., 29
Batista, Fulgencio, 294
Baumes Law, 224, 249 n.23, 359
Bazzano, John, 41, 333
Beatty, Warren, 18
Becker, Charles, 76, 258–60
Beckerman, Abraham, 82, 352
Begendorf, Benjamin R., 205, 211 n.33
Beitcher, Louis, 290
Beldock, George J., 48, 191
Bellevue Hospital, 59, 113–14, 193, 211 n.37, 275, 287, 341, 342
Belmont, August, 264, 265
Bender, Tony. See Strollo, Anthony,
Bendix, Joseph, 224
Bennett, Edward J., 24
Bennett, John J., 5
Berger, Paul, 103, 105
Bergman, Meyer, 219
Berkenfeld, Benjamin, 299
Berman, Otto "Abbadabba," 289–90; murder of, 299–301, 304
Bernfeld, Julius, 87
Bernstein, Joe, 273
Bernstein, Sholem, 101–2, 393
Betillo, David "Little Davie," 219, 221–26, 228
Beverly Hills Club (New Orleans), 125, 136, 146, 153
Bicks, Alexander, 204–6
Biddle, Francis, 107–8
Biller, Hyman "Gillie," 278
Binion, Benny, 143
Biondo, Joseph "Joe Bandy, Jose the Blonde," 66, 164
Bishop, James A., 325
Black, Hugo, 142
"Black Sox" scandal, 253
Blackwell's Island, 40, 119, 150 n.3, 282

Blake, Edward, 229
Blauner, Irving "Red," 298, 299
Blauner, Max, 353
Bloom, Anna, 10, 11
B'nai Abraham Memorial Cemetery, 328
Bocchino, Joseph, 58
Bocci, Benny, 187
Bocci, Fred. See Boccia, Ferdinand "The Shadow"
Boccia, Ferdinand "The Shadow," 132, 187, 188, 196; Boccia murder trial 192–95
Boiardo, Ruggiero "Richie the Boot," 313, 314
Bonadio, Joseph, 8
Bonadio, Paul, 8, 32–33 n.17
Bonanno, Joseph, 40, 51, 180 n.25, 233, 349, 398–99, 401 n.37; Banana War, 167; Castellammarese War, 368–75, 380–81; Commission takeover attempt, 167, 180 n.24, Gambino relationship, 158, 168; Maranzano, 337–38, 339, 340; Profaci/Gallo War, 166
Bonasera, Anthony "The Chief," 41, 210
Bondy, William, 296
Boran, Wayne G., 125
Bourke, Matthew, 9
Bowe, Norton, 277
Bozza, Joseph, 25
Brannigan, Eugene F., 242
Brecht, George, 286, 287
Brennan, Daniel, 313
Brice, Fanny, 253, 266, 270
Brickner, Frank, 87
Bronfmans, 312, 313
Bronson, Charles, 211 n.24, 400
Brook, The (Saratoga gambling den), 263, 264
Brooklyn City Prison. See Raymond Street Jail,
Brooklyn House of Detention. See Raymond Street Jail
Brown, Florence "Cokey Flo," 224–25, 226, 229, 230
Brown, Harry, 218
Brown, Samuel, 275, 276
Browne, Martin J., 23
Brownell, Herbert, Jr., 28
Browne-Vintners, 319, 348
Brunder, Wilfred, 292
Bruno, Angelo, 166
Bryant, Frederick H., 293, 294
Buchalter, Barnett, 74
Buchalter, Beatrice "Betty," 81, 111
Buchalter, Emanuel, 113
Buchalter, Harold, 81,
Buchalter, Joseph, 100
Buchalter, Louis "Lepke," 11, 194, 383

Amorusa, Joseph, 91–92
Anastasia, relationship with, 37, 40, 41, 44, 80
    harboring, 44, 92–93, 100
Atlantic City Conference, 80
bakery and flower trucking industry, 83–85
    murder of Snyder, 84
    trial, 96–98, 115 n.38 (*see also* Goldis, Morris and William, and Silverman, Harold and Max)
Costello, 80, 152 n.17
description and personal traits, 75, 80
Dewey, 85–86, 91, 92, 93, 96, 98, 126, 303, 334
    garment industry extortion, 88–89
early years, 74, 75, 350
    arrests, 75, 76, 77, 80, 81, 113 n.6
    birth, 74, 113 n.3 (*see also* Holtz, Hyman "Curly")
execution, 306
    appeals process, 105–110
    last days, 110–112
fugitive, as a, 89–91, 126, 351, 353
fur trades racket, 81, 332, 334, 351, 352
    attack on union headquarters, 83
    murder of Langer, 82–83
    trial, 85–88
    verdict overturned, 88, 351
Group of Seven, 80, 383
home and family, 74, 75, 100, 111, 113 n.2, n.5, 344
    marriage, 81
Hotel Franconia raid, 80–81
labor racketeering, 77, 79–80, 218
    previous gang leaders, 76 (*see also*, Hillman, Sidney; Orlovsky, Philip)
Lansky, 80
Luciano, 80, 215, 339, 369
Miller, Verne, 344–45
Murder, Inc., 44, 73, 393
murders 89–90, 126
    Diamond, 44
    Greenberg, 81, 83, 94, 99, 334–36, 359 n.3
    Penn, 45, 90–91, 126, 352
    Rosen, 85–86, 306, 353, 394
    Salles, 100
    wounding of Max Rubin, 89, 102, 103–4
narcotics, 91, 273
    trial, 93–96, 115 n.33, 335 (*see also* Katzenberg, Jacob "Yasha")
Orgen, Jacob, 76, 77–78, 79, 351
origin of nickname, 74, 113 n.4
Rosen murder trial, 99–105
    verdict and death sentence, 105
Rothstein, relationship with, 77, 78, 79, 270, 272–73, 278

Schultz, 297, 303, 306
Siegel, 80, 81, 99, 335
surrender, 45, 126, 92–93, 115n. 30, 353 (*see also* Wolensky, Morris "Moey Dimples")
Zwillman, relationship with, 80, 91, 114 n.28, 344
Buchalter, Rose, 74–75, 112
"Bucket shop," 267–68, 269, 270, 316, 317, 329
Buckner, Emory R., 121
Bugas, John S., 17
Bugsy (movie), 18
Burroughs, William S., 302
Burt, Samuel, 83, 87
Buzzard, Preston, 313

Cahill, John T., 11, 125; Buchalter narcotics trial, 93–96
Calandra, Anthony, 56, 57
Calandriello, Thomas, 198
Callahan, Joseph, 131
Camarda, Emil, 42, 43, 45, 67–68 n.12
"Camarda Locals," 42, 45, 376
Cammerone, Sonny, 64
Cantalupo, Sr., Joseph, 172
Cantellops, Nelson Silva, 203–5, 206, 207, 211 n.32, n.37
Cantor, Maurice F., 221, 225, 275–76
Capeci, Jerry, 66, 391
Capone syndicate, 24, 217
Capone, Al, 24, 125, 209 n.5, 214, 227, 293, 309, 313–14, 315, 322, 326, 347, 355, 366–67, 371, 375–76, 379, 381, 382, 398, 401 n.37
Capone, Louis, 7, 42, 92, 100, 306; death sentence and execution, 105, 107, 108–9, 110–12; funeral of, 112; member of Murder, Inc., 44, 393, 394; Rosen murder trial, 99, 101–2, 104, 105
Caputo, Danny "Danny Brooks," 223
Carbo, Frankie, 99, 336, 393
Cardena, Marcellina, 288
Cardoza, Benjamin N., 230
Carfano, Anthony (Little Augie Pisano), 53, 67 n.10, 333; as Brooklyn underworld boss, 3, 4, 5, 40, 41; Genovese defiance, 200, 206; Masseria murder, 376, 377–78; murder of, 206–7, 211 n.36
Carney, Larry, 283
Castellammarese War, 40, 123, 158, 165, 185, 213, 217, 235, 284, 346, 349, 380, 398; detailed activities of, 368–79; Maranzano and Masseria participation, 337–40, 342
Castellano, Catherine. *See* Gambino, Catherine

Castellano, Louis J., 11, 12

Castellano, Paul, 155, 179 n.6, 180; at Apalachin, 163, as Gambino successor, 179; family, 156, 157, 158; murder of 179

Castellano, Peter, 157, 179 n.6

Castiglia, Luigi, 118, 119, 133

Catalano, Angelo "Julie," 44, 393

Catena, Gerardo "Jerry," 14, 149, 200, 206, 207, 208, 312, 314, 319, 324

Cestari, Dr. Robert, 59

Chapey, Frederick, 130

Chatham Cadillac Rental Service LTD, 20

Chicago White Sox, 265

Chiri, Salvatore, 163

Christy, Arthur H., 71, 204, 205, 206

Cincinnati Reds, 265

City Democrat Club (Brooklyn), 41–42

Clapp, Alfred C., 316

Clark, William, 295, 297

Clarke, Donald Henderson, 253–54

Cliffside Park (New Jersey), 8, 32; Duke's Restaurant, 1, 13, 323, 346; Willie Moretti murder, 22, 51, 52, 162, 196, 347

Club Bali, 23

Club Boheme, 17

Cohen, Edward, 52

Cohen, Louis, 77, 90, 113 n.9

Cohen, Mickey, 62

Cohen, Philip "Little Farvel," 100, 104, 115 n.42

Cohn, Rose, 222

Coll, Peter, 283, 285

Coll, Vincent "Mad Dog," "The Mad Mick," 281, 283; hired by Maranzano, 284–85, 380; murder of, 287–88; war with Schultz, 285–88

Collins, "Dapper Dan," 270

Collins, William, 28, 29

Colombo, Anthony, 170

Colombo, Jr., Joseph A., 170–71

Colombo, Sr., Joseph A., 149, 167, 170–73; death of, 173; shooting of, 149, 172

Colombo Crime Family, 167, 173

Colonial Inn, 16, 17, 173

Comiskey, Charles, 265

Conboy, Martin T., 230, 292

Condon, Dr. J. H., 282

Conger, Edward, A., 100

Coniff, Frank, 112

Conte Biancamano (ship), 29

Contes, Peter, 205

Conway, Jack, 258–59

Cook, Fred J. (author), 2, 27, 347, 399

Cooper, Harold "Shake," 298

Copacabana nightclub, 126, 133, 144, 206, 233

Copeland, Royal S., 8

Coppola, Anthony, 58, 60–61, 62

Coppola, Mike "Trigger Mike," 81

Corallo, Anthony "Tony Ducks," 167

Corbin, Harold H., 17, 18, 24, 28

Coronato, Jerry, 45–46

Correa, Mathias F., 320–21

Corridan, John Michael, 53

Corsi, Edward, 15, 134

Costa, Leonard, 20, 22, 23, 35 n.61

Costa's Barn, 20, 22, 23, 26

Costello, Frank (Francesco Castiglia), 5, 41, 80, 197, 231, 284

Adonis, relationship with, 4, 14, 23, 24, 132

Anastasia, relationship with, 37, 40, 41, 51, 163, 393

questioned about murder of, 60–61

Apalachin Summit, 61, 201, 363

assassination attempt, 57, 64, 65, 143–145, 200, 206

imprisoned for refusing to answer questions, 145

Tropicana receipts, 143, 145, 146, 153 n.39

Vincent Gigante arrested, 146

Atlantic City Conference, 123, 366, 367

Aurelio affair, 128–29, 152 n.22

bootlegging, 120–21

Buchalter, relationship with, 45, 92, 115 n.30, 126, 152 n.17

Castellammarese War, 123, 379, 380

death and funeral, 150

description and personal traits, 117, 124–25, 126

Dwyer, "Big Bill," 121–22

early years

arrests, 118, 119

birth, 117

Horowitz Novelty Co., 119–20

gambling associates, 14, 23, 24, 64

Genovese, narcotics plot against, 164, 204, 247

in Atlanta prison with, 147

Genovese, plot to remove by, 57, 132, 163, 185, 196, 200, 210 n.21, 247

Group of Seven, 356, 383–84

Havana meeting, 132, 152 n.28, 234, 235

home and family, 118, 125

Eduardo (Eddie), 118–19, 120, 122

marriage, 119, 150 n.2

Kefauver Committee, 134–39

chance meeting with Halley, 336

the "hand ballet," 137

walks out on committee, 138

Kennedy, Joseph, 121, 151 n.9

Lansky, 120, 125, 132

Luciano, relationship with, 120, 124, 132, 214, 215, 216–17, 231, 232, 233, 240, 242, 248–49 n.8

Mangano murder, 51, 162
money left in cab, 129–131
Moretti, relationship with, 51, 119, 196, 324, 345–46, 347
politics, 15, 127, 134
  Democratic National Convention (1932), 124, 218
  O'Dwyer, 14, 47, 48, 127, 138, 153 n.35
  Tammany Hall, 127, 129
psychiatrist, sees, 133
Rothstein, relationship with, 120, 123, 150–51 n.6, 270, 272, 278
Salvation Army dinner, 133–34, 196, 210 n.21
slot machines, 123, 124, 136, 187, 218
  LaGuardia attack, 8, 124
  move to Louisiana, 125, 136 (see also Kastel, Phillip "Dandy Phil")
trials, 200
  contempt of Senate, 24, 139–41
  deportation, 54, 141–42, 148, 149, 150 n.4
  federal income tax evasion, 57, 142–43, 147–48, 200
Zwillman, relationship with, 313, 324, 328, 329
Costello, Loretta, 119, 140, 142, 144, 150, 150 n.2
Coulcher, Paul, 291
Crain, Thomas C. T., 357
Crane, Frederick E., 230
Creegan, John B., 130–31
Crime in America (book), 18
Croake, Thomas F., 228–29
Croswell, Edgar, 61, 65, 201, 363
Cummings, Homer S., 83, 331
"Curb Exchange," 120, 214
Cusack, John T., 162, 364
"Cyclone Louie," 73

Dalitz, Moe, 233, 324
Damone, Vic, 171
Dannemora Prison, 95, 115, 223, 228, 231, 242, 261
Davis, Jr., Sammy, 171
Davis, Richard J. "Dixie," 291, 292–93, 297, 303, 304–5, "Night of Sicilian Vespers" tale, 396; Schultz policy rackets, 288–89
Davis, Wilfred L., 203
Dawson, Archie O., 148
DeCarlo, Angelo "Gyp," 346
DeCavalcante, Samuel "Sam the Plumber," 180 n.24
DeFeo, Peter, 192–93
Delaney, Joseph L., 142, 143
Dellacroce, Aniello, 167

Del Greco, Patsy, 287
Del Tufo, Raymond, 57
DeMange, George Jean "Big Frenchy," 286
DeMilo, Frances, 156
DeNoia, John "Duke," 34 n.32
DeQuatro, Dominick, 146
DeVito, Ferdinand, 27
Dewey, Frances, 297
Dewey, Thomas E., 13, 48, 68, 124, 125, 188, 291; alleged assassination plot, 297–98, 303; as federal prosecutor, 218, 291–92, 356, 358; as New York County district attorney, 306; as special prosecutor, 44, 85, 89, 103, 104, 218, 295, 351; bid for presidency, 306; Buchalter investigation and indictment, 44, 85–86, 88–89, 90–93, 94, 96–98, 99, 115 n.30, 126, 334, 353, 359 n.3; Buchalter execution, 106–9, 111–12, 306; death of, 306; on "Dixie" Davis, 289, 289; elected governor, 53, 306; on Hines, 305; Luciano: aftermath of trial, 132, 228–30, 231, 232, 234, 245, investigation and indictment, 219, 220–21, pardon by Dewey, 232, 240–43; prostitution trail, 221–28, 249 n.19, 390, 391; Schultz investigation, 218, 281, 295, 297–98, 303; Wexler prosecution, 218, 292, 354, 356–58
Diamond, Eddie, 77, 215, 271
Diamond, Jack "Legs," 5, 282, 288; and Luciano, 214, 215, 217; Orgen murder, 77, 78, 113–114 n.11, 351; Rothstein bodyguard, 77, 78, 270–71, 284; Schultz competitor, 283
Diamond, Morris "Moishe," 44, 45, 46, 90
Diamond, Patrick J. "Paddy," 6–7
DiBella, Paul, 172
DiCarlo, Joe "The Wolf," 41
DiCarlo, Sam, 41
Dick Cavett show, 171
Dickerson, John, 25
Dickey, Orange C., 189–91, 194, 202–3, 210 n.9
DiGregorio, Gaspar, 338
DiPalermo, Joseph, 205, 208
DiRosa, Stephen, 285, 293
Dishbach, David, 94
Dishbach, Emma, 95
Dodge, William C., 218, 295, 305
Dolak, Frank, 298
Donovan, Edward J., 242
Donovan, James "Bugs," 356
Dorsey, Tommy, 346
Doto, Ann Marie, 29
Doto, Antonio (Anthony), 2, 5, 7, 9, 27

Doto, Elizabeth 29

Doto, Ettore (Albert), 2, 5, 27

Doto, Genesio, 2, 5

Doto, Jean (Mrs. Jean Adonis), 9, 10, 12, 16, 28, 29, 31

Doto, Jr., Joseph A., 16

Doto, Maria Dolores, 29, 31

Doto, Mary (Mother Elk), 2, 5, 26, 27, 32 n.6

Doto, Michele, 2, 27, 28

Dougherty, A. J., 300–301

Dragna, Jack, 19, 236

Drake, Alan, 206

Drake, Janice, 206, 211 n.36

Drake Hotel (Chicago), 124, 218

Driscoll, Alfred E., 25, 53

Duke's Restaurant, 323, 346; Adonis headquarters, 1, 13, 14, 34 n.32, 34 n.33

Dunn, Frank, 283, 356

Dwyer, William V. "Big Bill," 121, 272, 283, 332, 383; indictment and trial, 121–22

Eastman, Monk. See Osterman, Edward "Monk Eastman,"

Eboli, Pat, 204

Eboli, Thomas "Tommy Ryan," 14, 146, 149, 167, 171, 204, 207, 208, 248

Edelbaum, Maurice, 146, 204–5

Egan, William J., 316

Eggers, Frank Hague, 317

Eisenhower, Dwight D., 55, 246

Ellerstein, Jack "Jack Eller," 219, 221, 222, 225, 226, 228

Ellison, Millard, 253

Endler, Jules, 320, 327

Ennis, Edward, 173, 174, 178

Erickson, Frank, 14, 16, 23, 123, 135; Kefauver Committee Hearings, 15, 134, 135, 139

Ermey, Roy E., 220

Evans, Nat, 264

Fabrizio, Louis "Louis the Wop," 79

Fallon, William J. "The Great Mouthpiece," 253, 266, 267, 268

Farley, Thomas A., 152 n.16

Fay, Joseph F., 242

Fay, Larry, 302

Federal Narcotics Bureau, 32, 52, 132, 161, 162, 180 n.17, 197, 203, 208, 215, 217, 359; Apalachin Summit, 162, 364, 365; forcing Luciano out of Cuba, 234, 236, 237, 239; investigation of Luciano in Italy, 243–44, 245, 246, 248, 248 n.8, 250 n.53, n56, 251 n.78; Valachi arrest, 208, 397

Fein, Benjamin "Dopey Benny," 76, 354

Ferber, Nat J., 267, 268, 270

Feracco, James "Dirt Neck Jimmy," "Dirty Face" and "Dirty Jimmy," 43, 45–46, 101, 393

Feracco, Rose, 45–46

Ferri, Charles, 56, 57

Ferrigno, Steven, 123, 372, 398

Ferro, Vito Cascio, 156

Fiano, Louis, 205

Fischetti, Charles, 236, 248

Fischetti, Rocco, 236, 248

Flamingo, The (Las Vegas), 133, 235–36

Flegenheimer, Arthur Simon. See Schultz, Dutch

Flegenheimer, Emma, 282, 302

Flegenheimer, Frances, 302, 305

Florino, Giuseppe "Joseph," 3, 42, 332–333; Murder, Inc. probe, 45, 67 n.10; Panto murder, 43; Terillo murder, 38–39

Flour Truckmen's Association, 83–84

Flour, Furniture, Grocery & Bakers' Supply Drivers Union, 83

Flower and Fifth Avenue Hospital, 165, 173, 174, 175, 177

Foley, Samuel E., 90–91

Foley, Tom, 159, 260

Folliard, Edward T., 124

Ford Motor Company, 8, 17, 34 n.42

Fort Lee (New Jersey), 16, 348, 379; Adonis home, 1, 13, 29, 33; Adonis burial, 32; Anastasia home, 49, 50, 51, 52, 55, 56, 58, 61, 62; gambling dens, 20, 21, 23, 34 n.54

Francis, Connie, 171

Frankel, Marvin, 170

Franse, Stephen, 198–99, 210–11 n.24

Frasca, Dom, 186, 188, 210 n.15

Frasca, Gus, 192–93, 194, 210 n.12

Frederico, Jimmy (James Fredericks), 219, 221, 223–25, 228

Freschi, John J., 96, 97, 98, 115 n.38

Friedman, Abraham "Whitey," 90, 353

Friedman, Irving "Danny Fields," 90

Friedman, Jack, 299–300

Fuller, Edward, 267, 268

Fulton Fish Market, 231

Fur Dressers Factor Corporation, 82, 88, 352

Furhman, Hans, 355

Futrell, J. Marion, 220

Gaffney, George, 204

Gage, Nicholas, 251; on Last Testament of Lucky Luciano book, 251, 385–89, 391

Gagliano/Lucchese Gang, 196–97, 199

Galante, Carmine, 189

Gallo Brothers Gang, 64, 166, 167, 172

Gallo, Albert "Kid Blast," 166
Gallo, Joe "Crazy Joe," 64, 172–73, 178
Gallo, Joseph N., 167
Gallo, Larry, 166, 172
Gallo, Orlanda, 27
Gallo, William "Willie," 187, 188, 191, 192, 194–96
Gallo/Profaci War, 165, 166, 167
Galston, Clarence, 110
Gambino Crime Family, 167, 172, 177, 178, 372
Gambino, Anthony, 156
Gambino, Anthony (cousin), 160
Gambino, Carlo, 66, 149, 158
  Anastasia murder, 64, 163, 200
  Apalachin Summit, 61, 162, 163, 363
  arrests, 157–58, 160, 161
    armored car heist, 168–70, 180 n.27
    as illegal alien, 161
    deportation efforts, 165, 173–79
    post-Prohibition bootlegging operation, 160
  death and funeral, 179, 180 n.33
  description and personal traits, 156, 163
    shunning publicity, 159, 170
  early years, 155
    "boyhood idol," 156
    illegal entry in United States, 156–57
      (*see also* Lucchese, Gaetano "Tommy; Gambino, relationship with)
  family and home, 156, 157, 177
    children, 159
    death of wife, 159, 178
    marriage, 158
    son's control of garment industry, 159 (*see also* Castellano, Paul)
  Gambino Family boss, as, 166, 177, 178
    assisting Joe Colombo, 167
    control of Commission, 166–67
    LaStella restaurant meeting, 167–68
    murder of Joe Colombo, 172 (*see also* Gallo/Profaci War; Colombo, Joseph A.; Italian-American Civil Rights League)
  Genovese, plot to remove, 164, 204, 247
  health problems, real and alleged, 163, 170, 173–78, 179 (*see also* Flower and Fifth Hospital; United States Public Health Service Hospital [U.S. PHSH])
  Luciano, alleged visits to, 162, 164, 233
  member of Mangano Family, 158
    brothers eliminated, 162, 165
  murders ordered by, alleged, 164, 173
  narcotics involvement, 161–62
  photograph with Sinatra, 180 n.13
  smuggling involvement, 162, 180 n.17

Gambino, Catherine, 158–59, 169, 175, 179 n.10; death of, 159, 178
Gambino, Felice, 156
Gambino, Joseph (Giuseppe), 156, 157, 178
Gambino, Joseph Carlo, 159
Gambino, Jr., Carl, 159
Gambino, Paul (Paulo), 156, 157, 158, 160, 161, 178
Gambino, Phyllis, 159
Gambino, Thomas Francis, 159
Gambino, Tommasco, 156
Garfein's Restaurant, 84
Garmella, Sylvester, 164
Garrantano, Giovanni (John Hayes), 20
Gasberg, Samuel, 10–11, 12, 13
Gates, Charles, 258
Geigerman, Dudley, 125, 131
Geigerman, Loretta "Bobbie," *See* Costello, Loretta,
Gelb, Saul, 225, 353
Genoa (Italy), 29, 30, 233, 238
Genovese, Anna, 186, 188, 197–99, 202, 210–11 n.24
Genovese, Carmine, 184
Genovese, Fillipo, 184
Genovese, Michael, 184
Genovese, Nancy, 186, 209
Genovese, Phillip, 197, 198, 209
Genovese, Vito, 15, 31, 40, 53, 133, 134, 143, 166, 169, 170, 210, n.10, 218, 246, 248–49 n.8, 284
  Anastasia murder, behind, 37, 64, 163, 200, 235
  Apalachin Summit, 61, 164, 200–202, 363–66
    called before McClellan Committee, 202
    turmoil caused by, 202–3
  Boccia murder and trial, 132
    murder, 187–88, 192–93
    suicide of Peter LaTempa, 193
    trial, 194–96 (*see also* Gallo, William "Willie," Rupolo, Ernest "The Hawk")
  Castellammarese War, 185, 369, 373, 374, 379, 380
  Costello, behind assassination attempt, 57, 145, 146, 147, 200
  death of, 149, 209
  deportation effort, 55, 199, 203
  description and personal traits, 184, 185
  early years
    arrests, 184
    arrival in America, 184
    birth 183
    exodus to Italy, 125, 188–89

arrested by Dickey, 190
black-market activities, 190
murder of Carlo Tresca, 189
return to United States under arrest, 191
serving Allied Military Government, 189
(*see also*, Dickey, Orange C.)
family and home, 184, 196
children, 186
first marriage, 186, 209 n.5
Kefauver Committee
avoiding, 50, 54
Luciano, 184, 185, 247
Havana Meeting, 234, 235
narcotics, 164, 185, 234, 247
arrest, 203
Cantellops conspiracy, 204–6, 211 n.37
trial and prison sentence, 204–7, 208–9,
211 n.33
plot to take over crime family, 57, 117, 162,
163, 196, 210n. 21
Carfano/Drake murders, 206–7, 211 n.36
Giannini murder, 196–97
Moretti murder, 196, 347
Petrelli murder, 199–200
Scalise murder, 58, 349
Valachi, 186, 188, 197, 198, 207–8, 397–400
Vernotico, Anna
divorce, 197–99
Franse murder, 198–99, 210–11 n.24
honeymoon to Italy, 186
marriage to, 186
murder of first husband, 186
Zwillman, 328–29
Geoghan, William F. X., 7, 33 n.22, 103–4,
331
Gerhardt, Fred, 97
Giammona, Josephine, 156
Giancana, Antoinette, 151 n.9
Giancana, Chuck, 151 n.9
Giancana, Sam, 151 n.9, 166
Giannini, Eugene "Gene," 196–97, 199, 245
Gigante, Vincent "The Chin," 146, 200, 203,
204, 205, 247
Gioe, Charles "Cheery Nose," 329–30 n.15
Giordano, Frank, 286–87
Girsch, Solly, 289
Gitlin, Samuel, 51
Giustra, Anthony, 53, 69 n.35
Giustra, John "Johnny Silk Stockings," 42,
376
Glassman, Barnett, 247, 390–91, 402 n.72
Gluck, Joseph, 266
Goddard, Henry, 122
Gold, Ben, 83, 85, 87

Gold, Eugene, 178
Gold, Sammy, 301, 304
Goldis, Morris, 84, 94, 115 n.38
Goldis, William, 84–85, 94, 97, 115 n.38
Goldstein, I. George, 319
Goldstein, Jonah J., 14–15, 34 n.35, 48
Goldstein, Martin "Buggsy," 45, 90, 99, 109,
393
Goldstein, Nathan L., 108
Gordon, Waxey. *See* Wexler, Irving
Gosch, Martin A., 235, 247–48, 251 n.90,
386–91
Gottesman, George. *See* Greenberg, Harry
"Big Greenie"
Gottfried Baking Company, 97, 98
Gotti, John, 179, 204
Grammauta, Stephen "Stevie Coogan," 66
Grasso, Arthur, 58, 61, 70 n.50
Grasso's barbershop, 58, 59, 61, 62, 66
Great Meadow Prison, 76, 231, 232, 242
Green Acres, 16, 17, 318
Greenberg, Harry "Big Greenie," 81, 83, 87,
90, 94, 99, 103, 334–336, 359 n.3
Greenberg, Max, 269, 314, 344, 354, 355,
356–57, 358
Greene, Carolyn. *See* Rothstein, Carolyn,
Gross, Hyman, 290
Gross, Nate, 94–95
Group of Seven, 80, 310, 356, 383–84
Grumet, Jacob, 68, 98, 115
Guarini, Anthony, 16, 20
Gulotta, Frank A., 202
Gurfein, Murray I., 85, 88, 231
Gurino, Vito "Chicken Head," 45, 333, 393

Haber, Charles, 312
Hackett, Buddy, 62
Haffenden, Charles Radcliffe, 231, 343
Hague, Frank, 317, 326, 355
Half Moon Hotel, 47, 103
Hallendale (Florida), 16
Halley, Rudolph, 56, 325, 328, 336; death
of 336; Kefauver hearings questioning
of: Adonis, 17, 18, Costello, 134,
135–36, 137–38, 139, 140; Moretti, 347,
Zwillman 322
Handler, Charles, 320
Hanley, Joseph, 48
Hanna, David, 150 n.2, 179 n.6, 186
Harriman, William Averill, 62, 365
Harris, John, 301, 302
Harrison Act, 269
Hasenflug, Henry, 6
Hassel, Max, 314, 344, 355, 356–57, 358

Havana (Cuba), Adonis trip, 18, 27, 35 n.71; Anastasia interest, 62, 64–65; Costello trip, 132, 133, 152 n28; Luciana visit, 214, 218, 233–38, 250n. 56
Havana Conference, 132, 235–36, 346, 386
Haye's Garage (Lodi, NJ), 20
Hayes, Johnson J., 114 n.28
Hays, Arthur Garfield, 106, 108, 109, 320–21, 336–37
Healy, Joseph, 13
Healy, Leo J., 68
Hearst, William Randolph, 262
Heffernan, Edward A., 43, 48, 191, 192, 193
Held, Aaron, 84, 97
Held, Isidore, 84
Helfand, Julius, 194, 195
Helmar Social Club, 286
Henry, Dominic, 262
Herlands, William B., 203, 243
"Herlands' Report," 243
Hildreth Sam, 264
Hill, Percival H., 258
Hill, Virginia, 18, 236, 323,
Hillman, Sidney, 79–80, 81, 111, 114 n.15
Hines, James J. "Jimmy," 124, 218, 260, 273, 284, 289, 292, 295, 305
Hoff, Max "Boo Boo," 356
Hoffa, James R. "Jimmy," 147
Hoffman, Dr. Richard H., 133
Hoffman, Richard W., 152 n.29
Hoffman, Harold Giles, 322, 323, 337
Hogan, Frank S., 14, 16, 19–20, 64, 65, 89, 98, 148, 231, 353; Aurelio affair, 128–29, 152 n.22, 347; Buchalter execution, 110–11, 152 n.17
Holinsky, Benjamin, 298
Holtz, Hyman "Curly," 77, 78, 81, 114 n.14
Holy Cross Cemetery, 5, 32 n.8, 60, 68, 112
Hoover, Herbert, 316
Hoover, J. Edgar, 169, 176, 292, 297, 309, 321, 365, 398; Buchalter arrest, 45, 91, 92, 93, 115 n.30, 126
Horan, Frank, 131, 132
Horowitz, Harry, 119
Hot Springs (Arkansas), 15, 219–20, 344
Hotel & Restaurant Employees International Alliance, 290
Hotel Franconia, 81, 114 n.15
Hotel Nacional, 234, 235, 236
Hourless (horse), 264
Howdy Podner, 324
Hughes, Thomas Craddock, 46, 107, 116 n.49, 193
Hutchinson, John, 79, 81, 82

Iamascia, Danny, 285–86, 293
Illiano, "Punchy," 64
Immigration and Naturalization Service (INS), case against: Adonis, 26, 27, 28, 29, Anastasia, 54, Costello, 141, 150n. 4, 148, Gambino, 161, 165, 173, 174–75, 176–77, 178, 179, Genovese, 203
Impellitteri, Vincent, 127–28, 134, 352
Inch, Robert, 69 n.32
Irish, Ned S., 14
Ison, Joseph Mathias "Spasm," 288, 289
Italian-American Civil Rights League, 149, 171

"Jew War," 344, 356
Joe's Elbow Room, 162, 347
Joe's Italian Kitchen, 1 3, 4, 6, 7, 8
Johnson, Albert "Killer," 261, 278–79 n.13
Johnson, Ban, 265
Johnson, Enoch "Nucky," 356, 366, 384
Johnson, Jerome, 172
Jordan, Thelma, 225–26, 229
Joseph, Joseph E., 87
Joyce, Peggy Hopkins, 253, 258
Joyce, Stanley, 258
Juffe, Isidore, 10, 12, 13, 33 n.22

Kaplan, Louis I., 244
Kaplan, Nathan "Kid Dropper," 76–77, 78, 90, 350
Kaplas, Leo, 312
Kardonick, David, 94, 96
Karp, Abe, 225
Kastel, Philip "Dandy Phil," 123, 125, 130, 131, 136, 137, 146, 233, 236, 268, 383
Katz, Jacob, 112
Katz, Leonard, 120, 123, 126, 127, 146, 152 n.28, 210 n.21, 216, 272, 345, 347, 367
Katzenberg, Jacob "Yasha," 91, 93, 95, 270
Kaufman, Irving R., 70–71 n.54
Kaufman, Louis, 330
Kauver, Rose. *See* Buchalter, Rose
Kauver, Solomon, 74
Kavolick, Philip "Little Farvel," 81
Kefauver, Estes, 137, 196, 241, 321, 324, 325
Kefauver Committee Hearings 1, 30, 31, 34 n.33, 50, 51, 53, 54, 55–56, 63, 65, 134, 153 n.39, 162, 243, 326, 328, 330–31 n.15, 337, 392, 400; Adonis as witness, 7, 15–19; Adonis contempt charges, 23–24, 27, 28; Anastasia brothers as witnesses, 48, 49–50, 56, 63, 69 n.32; Costello as witness, 135–39, 196, 200; Costello contempt charges, 139–41; Moretti as

witness, 346, 347; Zwillman as witness, 315, 318, 319, 320, 321–23, 327
Keith, Norval, 146
Kelly, Frank V., 6, 7
Kelly, Jeremiah "Jerry," 149
Kelly, John J. "Red," 168
Kelly, Paul. *See* Vaccarelli, Paulo
Kennedy, John F., 177
Kennedy, Joseph, 121, 151 n.9
Kennedy, Michael, 127, 129, 138
Kennedy, Phil 144
Kennedy, Robert F., 148, 177, 208, 328, 364, 365
Kenny, John V., 317, 327
Kerwin, John, 8,
Kesselhaut, George, 325
Kessler, Morris, 298
Kessler, Samuel I., 306, 326, 327
Kiendl, Theodore, 53
King Lou, 299
Kirby, Robert, 106
Klein, Solomon, 106, 109
Kleinman, Morris, 322
Kleinman, William W., 94, 95, 98, 104
Knox, John C., 87–88, 94–96, 98, 115 n.33, 332, 352
Krakower, Benjamin "Whitey," 335
Kramer, T. B., 8
Krantz, Sam, 290
Kravitz, Louis, 81, 95
Krieger, Albert, 204
Kriesberger, Lottie, 287, 288
Krompier, Jules, 301
Krompier, Marty, 286, 301–2, 344
Kull, Philip, 312
Kushner, Louis. *See* Cohen, Louis

Lacey, Robert, 65, 231, 233, 367, 392
LaGuardia, Fiorello H. "The Little Flower," 1, 6, 8–9, 10, 11, 13, 47, 48, 89, 124, 126, 127, 128, 129, 130, 151–52 n.16, n.17, 218, 292, 294
Landau, Abe "Leo Frank," 296, 299, 300, 301, 303, 304
Lang, Leonard, 205
Langer, Morris, 82–83, 87, 351
Lansky, Jake, 16, 125, 203, 356
Lansky, Meyer (Suchowljansky), 125, 218, 363, 388, Adonis relationship, 16, 30; Anastasia murder, 62, 64, 65; as an organized crime leader, 4, 53, 80, 214, 219, 313, 356, 383–84; Atlantic City Conference, 367; Buchalter relationship, 80, 115 n.30, n.31; Costello relationship,

125, 132–33; Genovese narcotics arrest, 203; Luciano relationship, 30, 162, 164, 215, 216, 217–18, 231, 233, 242, 247, 339, 340, 356, 374, 380; Luciano stay in Havana; 234, 235–36, 250 n.53, n.56; Rothstein relationship, 264, 270, 272, 278; Siegel relationship, 120, 121, 185, 215, 236, 344, 356, 383–84; Zwillman relationship, 323
Lanza, Joseph "Socks," 218, 231, 242
Lascari, Mike, 233, 319, 320
Last Testament of Lucky Luciano, The, 213, 247, 251 n.90, 337, 368; analysis of book, 385–91; Castellammarese War references, 368–83; controversies cited, 68 n.19, 80, 115 n.30, 151 n.7, 204, 216, 233, 236, 367; references from, 3, 30, 31, 40–41, 132, 162, 164, 184–85, 233, 284, 346, 356, 384, 394–95
LaStella Restaurant, 167, 170
LaTempa, Peter "Pete Spatz," 192, 193–94, 210 n.15, 373
Laura Keene, 18, 132, 232, 233, 238, 251 n.83, 346
Leavenworth Penitentiary, 95, 99, 208, 267, 273, 344, 359
Lederer, Louis, 153 n.39
Lefkowitz, Joseph P. 35 n.78
Leggett, James B., 60
Lehman, Herbert H., 5, 6, 241; appoints Amen special prosecutor, 33, 331; appoints Dewey special prosecutor, 85, 218, 295; Luciano: extradition from Little Rock, 220; pardon of 241–43
Leibowitz, Samuel S., 5, 7, 336; attorney, 41, 287, 333; Boccia murder trial; 192–95; judge, 14, 109
Leonard, Mollie, 223
Lessa, Daniel, 205
Lessa, Nicholas, 205
Levine, Abe "Pretty," 90, 393
Levine, Gary, 271
Levine, Red, 380
Levy, George Morton, 135, 136; Luciano trial, 221, 223–27
Lewisburg Federal Prison (Pennsylvania), 62, 140, 160, 352
Leyden, J. Wallace, 16, 21
Liebmann, Harry, 87
Liguori, Ralph "The Pimp," 221, 223, 225, 226, 228, 229, 230, 239, 243
Lillian, Al, 319
Lillian, William, 319
Lindy's, 253, 273

Lissoni, Igea, 239, 240, 243, 247
"Little Apalachin," 168
Litwace, Julius, 87
Lodi (New Jersey), 20, 21, 22, 23, 34 n.52
Loma Dress Company, 85
Lombardozzi, Carmine "The Doctor," 163, 364
Long Island College Hospital, 63
Long, Huey P. "The Kingfish," 125, 136
Longano, Arthur, 16, 16, 20
Lonzo, Antonio, 186
Love, Elizabeth, 276
Lubetkin, Abraham, 97
Lucania, Antonio, 214
Lucania, Bartolo, 248
Lucania, Joseph, 248
Lucania, Rosalia, 214
Lucchese, Frances, 159
Lucchese, Gaetano "Tommy," 14, 53, 54, 115, 128, 134, 168, 233, 401; Castellammarese War, 158, 339, 369, 371, 380; death of, 167; Gambino, relationship with, 157, 158, 159, 166, 167
Luciano, Lucky (Salvatore Lucania), 34, 73, 124, 126, 189, 210 n.10, 319, 356, 363
  Adonis, relationship with, 2, 3, 4, 18, 30–31, 35 n.71, 231, 233, 248, 340, 356
  Anastasia, relationship with, 37, 40–41, 67 n.8, 68 n.19, 162, 233, 234
  Atlantic City Conference, 367
  attack on, 216–17
  Buchalter, relationship with, 80, 89, 93, 115 n.30, n.31, 215
  Castellammarese War, 185, 217, 339, 369–74
  Costello, relationship with, 120, 124, 132, 214, 216, 232, 233
  death and funeral, 248
  deportation, 132, 232–33 (*see also* Laura Keene)
  Dewey, 218, 219–228, 229, 234
    pardon, 132, 232, 240–43, 245
  Diamond, "Legs," 215
  early years, 214
    arrests, 215
    education, 214
  Gambino, relationship with, 233
  Genovese, relationship with, 184, 185, 209, 234–35
    narcotics plot against, 204, 247
  Group of Seven, 384, 217
  Havana, Cuba, 233–34
    meeting, 132, 235–36
    thrown out by Anslinger, 236–38
  health problems, 247–48

  home and family, 214, 248, 386
  Lansky, 214, 215, 216, 217–18, 231, 233, 234, 250 n.53, n. 56, 340, 356
  Last Testament of Lucky Luciano (book), 213, 385–91
  Maranzano, 216, 217, 337, 338–39, 340, 379–80
    on hit list, 284, 380
  Masseria, 214–15, 216, 217, 284, 339, 342, 374, 375 (*see also* Valenti, Umberto, 214, 215, 340, 341–42)
  Moretti murder, 162, 233
  narcotics, 93, 162, 185, 214, 215, 239–40, 243–44, 245–47, 251 n.78, n.83, 269
    "declared danger to society," 246
  "Night of Sicilian Vespers," 213, 217, 386, 394–95
  origin of nickname, 216–17
  politics, 217
    Democratic National Convention (1932), 124, 218
  prison term, 228
    motions for release, 228–29, 230
  prostitution ring, 125, 187, 188, 218, 219
    arrested in Hot Springs, 219–221
    indicted, 219, 221
    trial, 221–228
    verdict and sentence, 228
  return to Italy, 233–34, 238–39
    life in Palermo, 239
    Naples, 243, 248
    Rome, 239, 240, 246 (*see also* Lissoni, Igea)
  Rothstein, relationship with, 214, 215, 264, 270, 271–72, 277, 278
  Schultz, relationship with, 214, 282, 284, 293
    plot to kill, 297, 298
    Weinberg, Bo, 298
  Siegel, Benjamin, 214, 215, 218, 218, 233, 235–36
  Sinatra, Frank, 236
  war effort, involvement in, 231–32, 242, 243, 245
  Zwillman, relationship with, 219, 233
Lupo, Patrick, J., 218
Lurye, William, 51–52, 71 n.35
Lvovsky, Jake, 95
Lynch, James P. "Pinkie," 16, 19, 20
Lynch, Walter A., 240–41

Maas, Peter, 121, 150, 200, 210 n.24, 349, 368, 386, 395, 398
Macri, Benedetto "Benny," 48, 50, 51–52, 69 n.35
Macri, Betty, 52

Macri, Nicholas, 52

Macri, Vincent, 49, 52, 349

Macy, W. Kingsland, 241

Madden, Owney "Killer," 119, 233, 286, 287, 383

Madden, Thomas M., 57

Madison Dress Company, 49, 50

Maffia, Alice, 42

Mafrici, Ralph, 64

Magaddino, Stefano, 166, 167, 233, 338, 372

Magliocco, Joseph, 166–67, 180 n.24

Magoon, Seymour "Blue Jaw," 45, 90, 104, 393

Maione, Harry "Happy," 4; alleged role in Rosen murder, 108–9, 110; member of Murder, Inc., 44, 99, 393

Malbin, David I., 6

Malone (New York), 294, 295, 298

Mancuso, Francis X., 277

Mangano Family, 40, 41, 50, 158, 333; Anastasia takeover, 50, 349

Mangano, Gerolimo, 67 n.10

Mangano, James V., 5, 6

Mangano, Philip, 5, 40, 42, 67 n.10; murder of, 50, 51, 162, 165

Mangano, Vincent (Philip's son), 51

Mangano, Vincent, 5, 40, 42, 51, 53, 67 n.10; family boss, 3, 158, 349; missing, 50, 51, 69 n.33, 162,165

Manton, Martin T., 88, 331, 351

Maranzano, Salvatore, 124, 165, 201, 235, 337, 356, 389; Bonanno relationship, 337–38; Castellammarese War, 158, 284, 368–74; establishing the five families, 3, 41, 185, 349; Luciano, 216, 217, 339–40; murder of, 165, 284–85, 340, 379–383, "Night of Sicilian Vespers," 394–96

Marcantonio, Vito, 128

Marcelle, Joseph P., 7

Marcello, Carlos, 125, 136, 167–68, 363

Marcus, David, 219, 221, 222, 223, 228

Marden, Ben, 81, 91

Marinelli, Albert, 124, 217, 218

Marlow, Frank (Galfano Curto), 342

Martin, Rev. Bernard, 111

Martin, George W., 100

Martin, Joan, 223

Martin, Joseph P., 94

Martin, Jules, 290, 291, 293

Martineau, John E., 220

Masferrer, Roland, 234

Masotto, Thomas, 156, 157, 158

Masseria, Giuseppe "Joe the Boss," 3, 123, 157, 158, 214, 216, 235, 284, 337, 338, 346, 349, 356, 380, 381, 383, 395, 401 n.16; Castellammarese War, 158, 185, 368–72; early years, 340–42; funeral of, 342–44; Luciano relationship, 120, 214–15, 217, 339, 340; murder of, 40, 373–78, 379, 386

Massie, Peter, 46

Mather, Harry, 270

Mathias, Vivian, 288, 344

Mattuck, Maxwell, 87

Mauriello, Nicholas, 200

Mauriello, Tami, 200

Mauro, Salvatore, 214, 340

Mauro, Vincent, 143–44, 146

Mazzie, Rocco, 205

Mazziotta, John "Chappie," 70 n.41

McCabe, William "Tough Willie," 276, 277

McCarran Act, 26, 35 n.70

McCarran, Pat, 18–19

McCarthy, Edward "Fats," 283

McCarthy, Joseph R., 141,

McCarthy, William, 103–4

McCarty, William H., 22

McClean, Edward, 220

McClellan Committee, 57, 165, 173, 202, 327–28, 363, 364, 366; Valachi testimony before, 208, 365, 368, 395, 397–400

McClellan, John L., 202, 363, 364

McCooey, John H. ("Tammany's Uncle John"), 5–6, 32 n.8

McCook, Philip J., 85, Luciano trial, 220–21, 226, 227, 228, 229–30, 231–32

McCrate, John, 10, 12–13, 332

McEvers, John H., 293

McFarland, Ernest W., 15

McGee, Eugene, 266–67, 268

McGee, William, 267, 268

McGehee, Abner, 220

McGohey, John F. X., 23, 24, 141, 142, 143, 147

McGraw, John J., 256, 258

McGurn, "Machinegun Jack," 277

McInerney, Father Cornelius, 302

McLaughlin, James, 137, 138

McManus, George "Hump," 273–74, 276, 277–78, 284

Medalie, George Z., 291, 292, 358, 382

Meehan, Jimmy, 273, 277

Meer, Abe, 298

Men of Respect (book), 31

Mendoza, Roberto "Chiri," 65

Meskil, Paul, 156, 179 n.6

Metropolitan Restaurant & Cafeteria Owners Association, 290

Miami (Florida), 10, 16, 24, 26, 27, 35 n.61, 56, 62, 133, 134, 234, 237, 318; trips by Gambino, 174, 175, 177; Luciano hiding, 218, 218

Miami Beach (Florida), 6, 173, 174

Milan (Italy), 30, 31, 36 n.86, 251 n.83

Milan Federal Correctional Institution (Michigan), 57, 140, 353

Miller, Cindy, 144

Miller, John, 121, 144

Miller, Joseph, 88, 90

Miller, Samuel, 97–98

Miller, Verne, 344–45

Mills Novelty Company, 123

Mineo, Alfred, 123, 157, 158, 371, 372, 398

Mione, Peter "Petey Muggins," 186

Miraglia, Rocco, 171

Miranda, Michele "Mike," 184, 194, 242; at Apalachin, 202, 205; Boccia murder, 192, 194, 195; in Italy, 188, 190, 193; triumvirate, 208

Miro, Jose Enrique "Henry," 289, 292

Mirra, Anthony, 211 n.36

Mitchell, John N., 169

Mittelman, Samuel, 82, 83

Mize, Sidney C., 88, 351

Modarelli, Alfred E., 56

Modgilewsky, Julius "Modgilewsky the Commissar," See Martin, Jules

Montefiore Cemetery, 354

Montemarano (Italy), 1, 27

Montgomery, Robert, 134, 136

Moore, William H., 325

Moran, Frederick A., 240, 241

Moran, James J., 46, 48

Morello, Giuseppe "The Clutching Hand," 333, 340, 370, 371, 372

Moretti, Angelina "Angela," 346

Moretti, Guarino "Willie," 22, 23, 25, 40, 51, 52, 197, 233, 242, 313, 321, 345–48, 379; Adonis association, 14, 346; Costello association, 51, 119, 196, 345, 346, 347; Genovese plot to kill, 57, 162, 196, 200; murder of, 162–63, 164, 196, 329, 347–48; Zwillman association, 323, 324, 384

Moretti, Marie, 346

Moretti, Rose, 346

Moretti, Salvatore "Sollie," 19, 23, 25, 197, 313; arrest with Adonis, 16, 20, 21, 22; death of, 23

Morgenthau, Jr., Henry, 292

Morgenthau, Robert, 149

Morris, Newbold, 127

Morton, Robert, 24

Moscowitz, Grover M., 352

Moser, Richard G., 324, 325

Mount Hebron Cemetery, 112, 359

Mullen, John A. 68, 354

Mullen, Joseph, 287

Mulrooney, Edward P., 228, 382

Murphy, Charles F., 260

Murphy, Frank, 96

Murray, James D.C., 68, 221, 277, 278

Naples (Italy), 30, 162; Genovese at 183, 185, 189–90, 190, 191; Luciano exile, 243, 244, 245, 246, 247, 248

Nash, Frank "Jelly," 344, 360 n.37

Needle Trades Workers' Industrial Union, 82, 83, 334, 351

Nellis, Joseph, 326

New Jersey Joint Legislative Committee, 25

New Orleans, 40, 125, 130, 133, 136, 146, 156, 290, 396, 399

New Orleans Crime Family, 167, 168

New York City Anti Crime Committee, 51–52

New York State Crime Commission, 42, 43, 53

New York State Joint Legislative Committee, 162, 364, 365

New York Waterfront Crime Commission, 54

New York Yankees, 180

"Night of Sicilian Vespers," 213, 217, 265, 303, 386, 389, 394–96

Nissenbaum, Samuel, 83, 87

Noe, Joey, 282–84

Noonan, James M., 228–29

Normandie, 68, 231

Norris, Charles, 275

Norton, Inez, 276

O'Brien, John P., 276

O'Connor, Vincent A. G., 26

O'Conor, Herbert R., 34 n.42, 50, 135, 136, 241, 315, 324, 325

Oddo, John "Johnny Bath Beach," 41, 53

Odierno, Dominic, 287

O'Dwyer, William, 63, 134, 210 n.11, 233, 352; Brooklyn politics, 7, 33; Brooklyn district attorney, 11, 107, 336; Buchalter murder trial, 99, 100, 104, 105, 109; Kefauver Committee, 135, 138, 153 n.35; mayor, 14–15, 47–48, 100, 127; Murder Inc., 43, 44, 45–46, 99, 305–6, 321, 392–94; U.S. army, 47–48

Office of Price Administration (OPA), 287

O'Hare, Dr. Alexander, 274

Omar Khayyam (horse), 264

Orecchio, Michael, 22, 23, 26, 35 n.63

Orgen, Jacob "Little Augie," 76–79, 113 n.9, n.10, n.11, 350–51

Orlovsky, Philip, 45, 79, 80, 90–91, 353

Ormento, John "Big John," 202, 205

Osterman, Edward "Monk Eastman," 76, 255, 258, 259

Pagano, Joseph, 197

Pagano, Pasquale "Pat," 197, 198

Paige, Samuel, 27

Palace Chop House, 282, 296, 298–301, 303, 304, 306

Palermo (Sicily), 31, 66, 156, 162, 193, 214, 233, 238, 239, 245

Palisades Amusement Park, 13, 51

Palmieri, Edmund I., 141–42

Palmieri, Paul, 41

Panormus, 162

Panto, Peter, 42–43, 45, 46, 48, 99

Parisi, "Dandy Jack," 42, 44, 45, 67 n.10

Park Central Hotel, 58, 272, 273, 274, 275, 284

Park Sheraton Hotel, 58, 66, 146, 200

Parsons, Theodore D., 21–22, 24, 25

Pecora, Ferdinand, 15, 85, 88, 89, 130, 134, 352

Pelican Novelty Company, 125

Penn, Irving, 45, 90, 92, 126, 353

Pennochio, Thomas "Tommy the Bull," 70 n.41, 214, 219, 221, 228

Pequeno, Alfredo, 237, 238

Perfection Coat Front Manufacturing Company, 85, 90

Perry, Harry, 217

Peterson, Virgil W., 52, 349

Petrelli, Dominick "The Gap," 199, 200, 210–11 n.24

Petrosino, Joseph, 156

Philadelphia Phillies, 144

Pici, Joseph, 245, 251 n.77, n.83

Pietrusza, David, 113–14 n.11, 253

"Piggy," 303, 304

Piping Rock Casino, 14, 17

Piraino, Carmine, 333

Piraino, Giuseppe "The Clutching Hand," 333, 377

Pisano, Little Augie. *See* Carfano, Anthony,

Plantation (Hollywood, FL gambling den), 7

Poffo, Marcel, 282

Polakoff, Moses, 221, *Last Testament of Lucky Luciano* book comments, 387–88, 389; Luciano trial, 226, 229, 230; Luciano war efforts, 231, 232, 233, 242

Poletti, Charles, 106, 189, 190

Polyclinic Hospital, 274, 301

Pompez, Alexander, 289

Pope, Jr., Generosa, 144

Potash, Irving, 83, 87

Presser, Nancy, 225, 226, 229, 230

Profaci Family, 166, 167

Profaci, Joseph, 53, 165–66, 167

Profeta, Sal, 189, 190

Proskauer, Joseph M., 53

Protective Fur Dressers' Corporation, 82, 86

Protter, Marcy, 42–43

Provenzano, Anthony, 344

Quayle, Francis J., 6–7

Rackets Committee. *See* McClellan Committee

Rager, Edward, 134

Ragone, Anna, 186

Rao, Joey, 283, 286

Rao, Vincent, 120

Raum, Arnold, 35 n.78

Rava, Armand "Tommy," 164

Raymond, Nathan "Nigger Nate," 273, 277

Raymond Street Jail (Brooklyn City Prison and Brooklyn House of Detention), 6, 12, 13, 39, 192, 221

Regional General Hospital (Italy), 31

Reilly, Michael J., 6

Reina, Gaetano, "Tommy," 185, 339, 369, 371, 387

Reinfeld Syndicate, 312, 315, 319

Reinfeld, Abe, 312

Reinfeld, Joseph H., 311, 312, 319, 348

Reles, Abe "Kid Twist," 4, 67 n.10, 99, 298, 305, 334, 397; aiding fugitive Buchalter, 89; confessions of, 45, 333, 392; death of, 46, 47, 103, 303, 393–94; Dewey, plot to murder, 297–98, 303; member of Murder, Inc., 44, 393; murders described by, 43, 44, 89, 336; Schultz murder, 304, 306; trials testified at, 102, 103, 104, 306

Renay, Liz, 62

Resta, Cesare, 248

Ricca, Paul "The Waiter," 217, 329–30 n.15

Riccobono, Joseph, 163

Richter, Daniel, 84

Riker's Island, 145, 148, 150 n.3, 354

Robert Treat Hotel, 296, 299

Roberts, Owen J., 106

Robilotto, John "Johnny Roberts," 164, 196, 347

Rock, Joe, 283

Rock, John, 283

Rockefeller, Nelson, 203, 206

Rogers, Hugo E., 133, 152 n.29

Romeo, Anthony "Tony Spring," 41, 42, 43, 45, 46, 67 n.10
Romeo, Josephine, 46–47
Roosevelt, Franklin D., 47, 105, 106, 107, 108, 110, 111, 151–52 n.16, 218, 241, 292, 306, 316
Rosen, Estelle, 101, 104, 105
Rosen, Harold, 101
Rosen, Harold "Nig." *See* Stromberg, Harry
Rosen, Joseph (Murder victim), 86, 89, 97; murder trial, 99–110, 353
Rosen, Joseph (Hotel Franconia), 81, 114 n.14
Rosen, Sylvia, 101, 104
Rosenbaum, Joseph, 322
Rosenblum, Jacob J., 228, 295
Rosenkrantz, Bernard "Lulu," 294, 296, 299, 300, 301, 304, 305, 307 n.13
Rosenthal, Herman "Beansy," 76, 255, 258–60, 278 n.5
Rosenthal, Sydney, 101, 109
Rothkopf, Louis, 322
Rothstein, Abraham, 253, 254–55, 256, 257, 276, 278 n.3
Rothstein, Arnold, 58, 124, 146, 214, 225, 301
  Arnstein, 265–67
  Becker, Charles, 258–60
  Buchalter, 78, 93, 272–73, 278
  bucket shops
    Fuller and McGee, 267–68 (*see also* Fallon, William "The Great Mouthpiece")
  Costello, 120, 150–51 n.6, 278
  description and personal traits, 253–54, 256, 263
  Diamond, "Legs," 77, 270–71, 284
  early years, 254, 255
  Erickson, 123
  family and home, 254, 256, 260, 278 n.3
    brother Harry, 254–55, 256
    education, 255
    marriage to Carolyn Greene, 256–57
  financing bootlegging operations, 120, 268–69, 354–55
    casinos, 263–64
    lay-off bet handler, 263
  gambling raid shooting, 261–62
  labor racketeering, 79, 354
    Orgen, with, 77, 78, 114–15 n.11
  Lansky, 272, 278
  legendary feats, 253, 257, 264–65
  Luciano, 215, 271, 278, 339
  McManus, arrest and trial of, 276–78
  nicknames, 253
  narcotics, involvement in, 93, 215, 269–70, 273

  shooting, death and funeral, 120, 123, 284, 273–75
    dispute regarding will, 275–76
  Sullivan, relationship with, 255, 256, 258, 259
  Tammany leaders, relationship with, 260
  Wexler, 269, 354–55
  World Series, "Black-Sox" scandal, 265
Rothstein, Bertram "Harry," 254–55, 256, 278 n.3
Rothstein, Carolyn, 255, 256–57, 258, 260, 261, 264, 266, 274, 276
Rothstein, Edgar, 254, 274, 276, 278 n.3
Rothstein, Edith, 278, 278 n.3
Rothstein, Esther, 254, 276, 278n.3
Rothstein, Jacob "Jack," 274, 276, 278 n.3
Rothstein, Sarah, 278 n.3
Rubin, Max, 85, 89; Rosen murder trial, 97–98, 102–5
Rudnick, George "Whitey," 90
Runyon, Damon, 263
Rupolo, Ernest "The Hawk," 187–88, 209 n.8, 210 n.12, 251 n.90; Genovese indictment and trial, 191–96
Russo, Gaetano, 66
Russo, Giuseppe Genco, 66, 180 n.17
Ruthberg, Max, 82
Rutkin, James "Niggy," 14, 312, 319, 348
Ryan, Joe, 45
Ryan, Muriel, 222
Ryan, Sylvester, 139, 140

Sabatino, Salvatore, 68 n.12
Sabatino, Sylvester, 7, 68 n.12
Saffer, Oscar, 85
Saietta, Ignacio "Lupo the Wolf," 193, 340
Salerno, Ralph, 196, 204, 210 n.21
Salinsky, Abe, 316
Salinsky, Frank, 316
Salinsky, Ike, 316
Salke, Julius, 285–86, 293
Salles, Sidney, 100
Saltzstein, Henry H., 164–65
Salvation Army, 133, 196
Salvo, Batiste, 298, 299
San Vittore Jail (Milan), 31
Sancor Marine Corporation, 49
Sands Point, 138–39, 145
Sann, Paul, 283, 291, 292, 293, 294, 304
Santora, Joseph, 41
Saratoga (New York), 14, 133, 257, 263–64
Saratoga Springs (New York), 17
Saupp, John, 208
Scaduto, Tony, 251 n.90, 389–91
Scaglione, Pietro, 31

Scalise, Frank "Don Cheech," 37, 58, 158, 348–50, 370
Scalise, Joseph, 339
Scalish, John, 339
Scannavino, Constantino "Gus," 43, 53
Schacter, George. *See* Greenberg, Harry "Big Greenie"
Scharf, Leon, 90
Schiller, George, 164, 165, 180 n.22
Schmukler, Max, 94, 95, 96
Schneider, Charles A., 84
Schoenbaum, Joseph, 135
Schoenhaus, Harry, 304, 305
Schornstein, Abraham, 97
Schorr, Samuel, 84, 85, 94, 115 n.38, 97
Schultz, Dutch (Arthur Flegenheimer), 89, 99, 126, 185, 188, 189, 214, 218, 219, 228, 230, 315, 357, 384
  bootlegging operations, 283
    Rock brothers, 283
  controversy about murder, 303–304
  description and personal traits, 281
    viciousness of, 283, 284, 293
  Dewey, 218, 291, 306, 356
    alleged plot to kill, 297–98
    indictment for federal tax evasion, 292
  Diamond, "Legs," 282, 283, 284, 288
  early years
    birth, 282
    first crimes, 282
    sent to Blackwell's Island, 282
  family and home, 282, 302
    wife Frances, 292, 294, 299, 302, 305
  fugitive, 292
  Krompier, Marty, 285
    shooting of, 301, 304
  Luciano, 284, 293
  Maranzano hit list, on, 284, 379
  murder of, 217, 299–302
    deathbed statement, 302
    funeral of, 302 (*see also* Palace Chop House)
  Noe, Joey, 282–83, 284
  origin of nickname, 281, 282
  policy rackets, 288, 304, 374
    "Abbadabba" Berman, 289–90
    policy war murders, 295, 298–99
    profits from, 289
    suicide of George Weinberg, 305
    takeover efforts, 289 (*see also*, Davis, Richard J. "Dixie," Hines, James J. "Jimmy")
  restaurant rackets, 290–91 (*see also*, Martin, Jules)
  Schultz/Coll War, 285–88
    kidnapping of "Frenchy" DeMange, 286
    killing of Danny Iamascia, 285–86
    murders of Basile, Del Greco and Torrizello, 287; Peter Coll, Vincent Coll, 287, 285; Joseph Mullen, 287; Michael Vengali, 286
  tax trials, 292
    first tax trial, 293–94
    Malone trial, 294
    new indictment, 295, 296
    settlement offered, 292
    Weinberg, 283, 287, 290, 295, 396
    murder of, 298
  Workman, Charles
    released from prison, 306
    trial, 305–6
Schultz/Coll War, 285–88
Schuman, Albert "The Plug," 299
Schuster, Arnold L., 54, 69 n.34, 70 n.41
Schuster, Max, 70 n.41
Scioto, Gino, 184
Scotto, Anthony M., 64, 178
Seabury, Samuel, 124, 151–52 n.16, 218
Sears, Charles B., 129
Sedway, Moe, 98
Segal, Harry "Champ," 99, 336
Selser, John E., 16, 21, 22, 25
Senate Permanent Investigations Subcommittee, 57
Senate Select Committee on Improper Activities in the Labor or Management Field. *See* McClellan Committee,
Senna, John, 217
Serra de' Conti (Italy), 31
S.G.S. Associates, 164–65, 173, 176, 177, 180 n.22
Shapiro, Ann, 91, 353
Shapiro, Carl, 94, 104, 353
Shapiro, Jacob "Gurrah," 40, 104, 113 n.7, n.9, 219, 334; and Buchalter, 73, 101, 102, 104, 350; crimes with Buchalter, 81–85, 89, 94, 96, 351; death of 354; fugitive, 88, 89, 91, 92, 351–52; fur trades trail, 85–88, 351; early years, 75, 75–81, 350; trials and punishment, 352–354
Shea, William, 257, 258
Sherman Antitrust Act, 83, 88, 351, 352
Sherman, Charles "Chink," 285, 301
Sherman, Irving, 14, 15, 48
Shilensky, Morris, 324
Siano, Fiore "Fury," 197, 198
Sidereal (horse), 264
Siegel, Benjamin "Bugsy," 46, 48, 81, 120, 132–33, 151 n.7, 185, 214, 218, 233, 313, 318, 339, 374; Greenberg murder, 90, 99, 335, 336; Lansky relationship, 121, 215,

236, 344, 356, 383–84; Las Vegas, 235–36; Virginia Hill relationship, 18, 236, 323

Silesi, Joseph, 65

Silverman, Harold, 94, 97, 98, 115 n.38

Silverman, Max, 84, 85, 86, 89, 94, 97, 98, 101, 115 n.38

Silvers, Al, 344–45

Simmons, Maurice, 130

Sinatra, Dr. Thomas, 159, 176

Sinatra, Frank, 159, 171, 180 n.13, 236, 345, 346, 389

Sinatra, Tina, 346

Sinnott, Francis, 6

Siragusa, Charles, 243–44, 251 n.78, n.83

Sisto, J. A., 320

Slater, Sidney, 64

Smith, Al, 218

Smith, James E., 262

Smith, Stephen, 121

Smith, William F., 55, 56

Smurra, George, 192–93, 210 n.12

Snavely, Dr. Earl H., 304

Snyder, William, 44, 84, 94, 98, 115 n.38

Snyder, William E., 110–11

Solomon, William, 97–98

Solomon, William Roderick, 66

Soprano, Tony, 117, 133

Sopranos, The (television series), 34 n.52

Sorge, Santo, 66, 162, 180 n.17

Sparacini, Carl, 191–92

Spence, Kenneth M., 140

Spiller, Benjamin "Benny," 219, 220

Sprizza, Ralph, 3

Squillante, Nunzio, 70–71 n.54

Squillante, Vincent J., 62, 70–71 n.54, 350

S.S. Conte Savoia, 186

S.S. Taormina, 184

Stager, Sid, 270

Stamler, Nelson F., 16, 21, 24–25, 35 n.68, n.69, 347–48

Statcher, Joseph "Doc," 81, 203, 312, 319, 324

St. Clair, Stephanie "Madame Queen," 288, 289

Stein, Solomon, 95

Steinbach, Jr., John, 318

Steinbach, Mary DeGroot Mendels, 318

Stevens, Harold A., 20, 21

St. John's Cemetery, 179, 209, 248

St. Michael's Cemetery (Queens), 142, 150

Strauss, Harry, "Pittsburgh Phil, Pep," 44, 99, 101, 109, 393

Strollo, Anthony "Tony Bender," 14, 60, 143–44, 166, 184, 186, 192, 197, 198, 200, 207, 208, 211 n.36

Stromberg, Harry "Nig Rosen," 71, 312, 356, 380, 384

Strong, Hugh J., 325

Strong, Selah, 124, 333

Stuart, Mark A., 312, 314, 316, 329 n.2, 357, 367, 385

Studio, The, 20, 23, 34 n.54

Sullivan Law, 76, 184, 285, 288, 333

Sullivan, Florrie, 259

Sullivan, Timothy D. "Big Tim," 255, 257, 258–59, 260

Sutton, Willie, 37, 54, 70 n.41

Swann, Edward, 119, 262

Sweder, Morris, 94, 95

Swope, Herbert Bayard, 257, 259, 261, 264, 278 n.10

Tagliagamba, Silvio, 340, 341

Talley, Alfred, 101, 104, 105

Tamm, Edward A., 28

Tammaro, Anna, 374, 375

Tanico, Michael, 146, 163 n.39

Tannenbaum, Albert "Allie Tick-Tock," 43, 99, 103, 104, 105, 304, 306, 334, 336, 351, 393

Tannenbaum, Benjamin, 99

Taylor, Franklin, 100, 101, 102, 103, 105, 109, 110

Teitelbaum, Harry, 81

Teitelbaum, Frankie, 298

Tenuto, Frederick J., 54, 70 n.41

Terranova, Ciro "The Artichoke King," 227, 286, 338, 340, 371, 373–74

Testa, Eugenio, 244

Third Ward Political Club (Newark), 310, 314, 316, 317, 322, 323, 325

Thomas, Norman, 242

Thompson, Alvin "Titanic," 273, 277

Tiplitz, Willy, 312

Tiscornia Camp, 237, 238

Tobey, Charles W., 19, 134, 135–36, 322

Tompkins, William F., 55, 56

Torrio, Johnny, 218, 366, 384

Torrizello, Emily, 287

Tourine, Charley "The Blade," 149

Towe, Harry L., 347

Trafficante, Jr., Santo, 64, 65, 167

Traina, Joseph, 41

Tramunti, Carmine "Mr. Gribbs," 167

Tratner, Samuel, 84

Tresca, Carlo, 128, 189, 242, 347

Tropicana Night Club, 143, 145, 146, 148, 153 n.39

Truman, Harry, 127, 306

Trupia, Vincent, 239–40

Turkus, Burton, 43, 44; Buchalter, 88, 92, 111, 112–13; Dewey murder plot, 109, 297–

98; Murder Inc., 392–94; Rosen trial, 99, 102–5, 109, Schultz murder, 303, 304

Uffner, George, 216, 270
Umberto's Clam House, 173
Union Field Cemetery, 275
Union Station Massacre, 344, 360 n.37
Unione Siciliana, 18, 92, 193, 219, 367–68, 375, 383, 395
Unites States Medical Center for Federal Prisoners, 208
Unites States Public Health Service Hospital (U.S. PHSH), 174, 175, 176, 177, 178
Unites States Senate Interstate & Foreign Commerce Committee, 15, 53
Ursprung, Helen, 302

Vaccarelli, Paulo (Paul Kelly), 76
Vail, Jerry, 171
Valachi Papers, The (movie), 150, 200, 211 n.24, 337, 349, 386, 395, 400; Castellammarese War, 368–79
Valente, Francis L., 359
Valenti, Umberto, 214, 215, 340, 341–42
Valentine, Lewis J., 14, 91, 104, 152 n.17, 376, 384
Vanderbilt, Gertrude, 353
Vanderwart, Herman, 34 n.54
Vandeweghe, Charles, 87
Van Siclen, James C., 38–39
Vasisko, Vincent, 201
Vengali, Michael, 286–87
Vernotico, Anna Petillo. See Genovese, Anna
Vernotico, Gerard, 186
Vetterli, Reed, 352, 360 n.37
Vicce, Margaret Farrara, 38–39, 333
Victory Memorial Hospital, 178
Villa Nuova Tammaro (restaurant), 3, 40, 185, 374, 375, 377, 383, 395
Villano, Ralph, 320
Vincenzo Floria, 156, 157
Vizzini, Calogero, 233
Vizzini, Charles, 217
Vizzini, Sal, 248–49 n.8
Volpe, Arthur, 41
Volpe, James, 41
Volpe, John, 41

Wachenfeld, William A., 305–6, 321
Wahrman, Abe "Little Abie," 221, 223, 225, 228
Walker, James J. "Jimmy," 77, 80, 114 n.15, 124, 128, 151–52 n.16, 218, 277
Walsh, George, 14, 20
Walsh, James "Fat," 215, 277, 278, 283

Walters, Carroll, 130
Wapinsky, Isidore, 9, 10, 11, 12, 13
Warren, Joseph, 277
Wasserman, Beatrice. See Buchalter, Beatrice "Betty"
Wasserman, Jacob, 81
Waterfront Commission Act, 53, 55, 165
Waters, Edward, 129, 130
Wegman, Bertram, 106, 109, 110, 111
Weiler, John "Johnny Spanish," 76
Weinberg, Abe "Bo," 283, 284, 285, 287, 291, 293, 294, 295, 298, 303, 386, 396
Weinberg, George, 283, 289, 290, 304–5
Weinberg, Louis, 283
Weiner, Al, 219, 220, 221, 222, 228
Weintraub, Joseph, 219
Weiss, Arlyne, 211 n.36
Weiss, Blanche, 104
Weiss, Emmanuel "Mendy," 100, 393; Diamond murder, 44; execution of, 107–108, 109, 110–12, 306; Greenberg murder, 99, 334, 336; Panto murder, 43, 46, 99; Rosen murder and trial, 99, 101, 103–5, 394; Schultz murder, 99, 303–4
Weiss, Sidney, 105
Wellman, William, 275–76
Wene, Elmer H., 325, 326
Wexler, Irving (Waxey Gordon), 3, 126, 188, 285, 314–15, 344, 356, 383–84; Dewey tax trial, 218, 292, 356–58; early years, 354–55; narcotics involvement, 244–45, 359; Rothstein relationship, 269, 270, 272, 354–55
Wexler, Leah, 358
Wexler, Nathan, 358
Wexler, Theodore, 358–59
White Auto Sales Company, 4, 8–9, 33 n.18
Wicks, Arthur, H., 241–42
Wild, Peggy, 230
Willemse, Cornelius, 77, 113 n.9
William J. Mahoney, 122
Williams, Edward Bennett, 141, 143, 144, 147, 148, 208
Williams, Garland H., 132, 237
Williams, Paul W., 143, 203, 205, 206, 246
Winchell, Walter, 45, 69 n.35, 92–93, 126
Winne, Walter G., 15, 22–23, 25–26
Winters, Betty, 222
Wittenberg, Arnold "Witty," 66
Wogan, Thomas F., 6
Wolensky, Morris "Moey Dimples," 81, 92, 115
Wolf, George, 130, 131, 132, 133,147, 152 n.28, 231–32; Kefauver hearings, 134–40
Woolworth Building, 85, 219, 225
Workman, Abe, 305

Workman, Charles "Charlie the Bug," 44, 100, 303–4, 305, 306, 393

Yale, Frankie (Frank Uale), 3, 343; murder of, 3, 4, 333, 342, 367
Yanow, Benjamin, 62
Yeager, Oscar, 82
Yuram, Herman "Hyman," 90, 353

Zerilli, Joseph, 167
Zink, Homer, 26
Zolin, Rev. Paul J., 344
Zurich (Switzerland), 30, 236
Zwacker, Joseph, 97
Zwiebach, Maxwell "Kid Twist," 76
Zwillman, Abner "Longy," 14, 53, 55, 80, 197, 219, 233, 337, 357
  Alleged crimes
    bucket shops, 316–17, 329 n.9
    contempt of court, 320–21
    "Hollywood Extortion" case, 329–30 n.15
    jury bribing, 328
  Atlantic City Conference, 313, 346, 367
  Buchalter, pursuit of, 91, 114–15 n.28
  crime investigation committee
    appearance before committee, 322
    "Capone" comment, 322–23
    "ducking" subpoena, 321–22
    Kefauver Committee, 319, 320
    McClellan Committee, 328
    Moretti questioned, 324
    political donations, 325
    questioned about Virginia Hill, 323
    search for by FBI, 324
    Senate Crime Committee, "ducking" the crime probe, 324
    Strong questioned, 325
  early years
    birth, 310
    childhood, 309, 310
    education, 310
    lottery, 311
  family and home
    early concerns, 310
    homes 317
    marriage, 318, 319
    siblings, 329 n.2

  gambling: 323
    interest in gambling joints, 318
  Group of Seven (Six), 309, 320, 383–84
  health problems, 328
  "Jew War," (Verne Miller), 344–45
  legitimate businessman, 309, 319–21
    Browne-Vintners, 319
    General Motors franchise, 319–20
    involvement in movies, 329 n.15
    Public Service Tobacco Co., 319, 328
  origin of nickname, 310, 313
  personal traits, 310, 311, 312, 317
  politics, 317
    "czar" of Democratic politics, 326
    theft of ballot boxes in 1932, 316 (*see also* Third Ward Political Club [Newark])
  prohibition years
    arrest, 312–13
    bootlegging, 312
    conflict with Boiardo, 313–14
    Lindbergh kidnapping, 314
    partner of Reinfelds, 311–12
    profits from bootlegging, 315
    reputation for ruthlessness, 312, 313, 314
  suicide and funeral, 328
    rumors about death, 328–29
  tax trial
    charged with tax evasion, 327
    criminal complaint filed, 326
    investigated by federal grand jury, 327
    tax lien filed, 326
    trial ends in hung jury, 327
  underworld associates, 313, 323 (*see also* Rutkin, James "Niggy")
  Wexler, 356
    Hassel and Greenberg murders, 314–15
Zwillman, Barney, 329
Zwillman, Bessie, 329
Zwillman, Daniel, 312
Zwillman, Ella, 310, 317, 328
Zwillman, Ethel, 329
Zwillman, Irving, 329
Zwillman, Lawrence, 329
Zwillman, Lynn, 318
Zwillman, Phoebe, 329
Zwillman, Rubin, 310

ABOUT THE AUTHOR

ALLAN R. MAY has had an interest in organized crime since he saw his first episode of *The Untouchables* in the early 1960s. Today, May's library contains more than 750 books on organized crime. May's writing first appeared on the Internet Web site Jerry Capeci's *Gang Land News* in the weekly column titled "This Week in Gang Land." At *AmericanMafia.com,* May wrote a weekly historical column called "A Look Back," and later "Allan May's Current Mob Report." May's articles also appear on *CrimeMagazine.com*, and he has contributed nine short stories to Court TV's *CrimeLibrary.com*. May resides in Cleveland, Ohio, with his wife Connie.

Lightning Source UK Ltd.
Milton Keynes UK
UKOW07n1925070517

300614UK00013B/136/P